The History of Hylomorphism

The History of Hylomorphism

From Aristotle to Descartes

Edited by
DAVID CHARLES

OXFORD
UNIVERSITY PRESS

Great Clarendon Street, Oxford, OX2 6DP,
United Kingdom

Oxford University Press is a department of the University of Oxford.
It furthers the University's objective of excellence in research, scholarship,
and education by publishing worldwide. Oxford is a registered trade mark of
Oxford University Press in the UK and in certain other countries

© The several contributors 2023

The moral rights of the authors have been asserted

All rights reserved. No part of this publication may be reproduced, stored in
a retrieval system, or transmitted, in any form or by any means, without the
prior permission in writing of Oxford University Press, or as expressly permitted
by law, by licence or under terms agreed with the appropriate reprographics
rights organization. Enquiries concerning reproduction outside the scope of the
above should be sent to the Rights Department, Oxford University Press, at the
address above

You must not circulate this work in any other form
and you must impose this same condition on any acquirer

Published in the United States of America by Oxford University Press
198 Madison Avenue, New York, NY 10016, United States of America

British Library Cataloguing in Publication Data
Data available

Library of Congress Control Number: 2023936101

ISBN 978–0–19–289766–4

DOI: 10.1093/oso/9780192897664.001.0001

Printed and bound by
CPI Group (UK) Ltd, Croydon, CR0 4YY

Links to third party websites are provided by Oxford in good faith and
for information only. Oxford disclaims any responsibility for the materials
contained in any third party website referenced in this work.

Contents

Preface   vii
List of Contributors   ix

   An Introduction to the History of Hylomorphism:
   From Aristotle to Descartes   1
   David Charles

1. Epicurean Materialism   44
   Alexander Bown

2. Stoics and Hylomorphism   68
   Brad Inwood

3. The Octopoid Soul: Stoic Responses to Aristotle's
   Soul-Body Hylomorphism   83
   Christof Rapp

4. Alexander of Aphrodisias and the Stoics: Blending, Forms,
   and the Upwards Story   106
   Reier Helle

5. Galen on the Form and Substance of the Soul   133
   Patricia Marechal

6. Alexander of Aphrodisias' Emergentism: Hylomorphism
   Perfected   154
   Victor Caston

7. Alexander of Aphrodisias on the Ancient Debate on
   Hylomorphism and the Development of Intellect   174
   Frans A.J. de Haas

8. Plotinus on Hylomorphic Forms   197
   Riccardo Chiaradonna

9. Strengths of Embodiment in Neoplatonism   221
   Pauliina Remes

10. Philoponus and Alexander in Historical Context on Relations
    between Matter and Form Inside and Outside Philosophy
    of Mind   245
    Richard Sorabji

11. Hylomorphism in Neoplatonic Commentaries on Aristotle?
    Perception in Philoponus and Pseudo-Simplicius   255
    Miira Tuominen

12. Natural, Artificial, and Organic Forms in Avicenna   280
    Peter Adamson

13. Averroes, Intellect, and Liberal Hylomorphism   303
    Stephen R. Ogden

14. *Hoc Aliquid*: Aquinas' Soul Is This Something   330
    Christopher Shields

15. Suárez' Compositional Account of Substance   351
    Dominik Perler

16. Descartes' Mind-Body Holism and the Primacy of Experience   376
    Lilli Alanen

General Index   405
Index Nominum   408

Preface

The initial idea for this collection emerged several years ago in discussions in Helsinki where, under the gentle but firm guidance of Lilli Alanen and Simo Knuuttila, several of us came to appreciate the value of collaborative diachronic study of philosophical issues, examining the ways in which central ideas were formed, reformed, and transformed by different philosophers over a long period. Their work, and that of their colleagues in the Finnish Center of Excellence, showed the importance of constructing a narrative which includes and builds on detailed studies of individual authors. It is a matter of great regret that neither lived to see the completion of a project to which both had contributed so much.

Diachronic studies enable us to see more clearly how our own philosophical tradition has developed, how certain questions came to be the ones which preoccupy us today. They can also point to major assumptions and mistakes, or mis-steps, that were made along the way. Perhaps our current problems could have been better formulated or more easily addressed. It is wildly optimistic to assume that all of them are ideally set up when we first encounter them! A longer view of the history of a subject may lead to a better understanding of some philosophical issues than can be obtained from a narrower focus on individual past authors, let alone individual chapters or paragraphs of their writings. While studies of the latter kind have great value, diachronic investigations have a distinctive role in our attempt to understand the past and how it has formed the present.

Diachronic work of this type is best done when people with specialist expertise in different areas work together. There will be very few, if any, who can by themselves cover in appropriate depth the range of philosophers discussed in this volume, Hellenistic, Roman, Arabic, medieval, and early modern alike. Indeed, it has become increasingly difficult for any one individual to do so as the standard of detailed work on individual writers has improved. A collaborative approach offers the best way to bring together high grade work on a wide range of differing authors with the aim of building a shared narrative. Contributors to the present volume have read and commented on each other's essays in an attempt to situate the philosophers they know best in a wider context and, where possible, on a common conceptual map. I have tried, in consultation with contributors, to capture in the Introduction some of their suggestions in a brief and partial overview of the period studied.

The present volume has been made possible by a number of recent major scholarly initiatives. The explosion of outstanding studies on Hellenistic, Roman,

Arabic, and medieval philosophy has changed our understanding of important authors in the centuries between Aristotle and the development of early modern philosophy. The work of Richard Sorabji and the 'Ancient Commentators on Aristotle' series has put us in a position to begin to assess the philosophical contribution of the (so-called) commentators who were, as is now clear, frequently independent thinkers willing to modify Aristotle's own views when they found them inadequate or incomplete. There is also a growing body of work on the complex interactions between early modern philosophers and their immediate predecessors in the Aristotelian tradition.

The present volume builds on this work in discussing and seeking to understand the first 2,000 years of the history of hylomorphism. But much remains to be done. Some highly significant authors and issues are not examined here. There are other commentators to discuss. Several Arabic and major late medieval philosophers, particularly William of Ockham and Scotus, need to be considered. The discussion of individual forms is seriously incomplete. There is much more to say about the suggestion that matter and form are in some way 'parts' of a natural substance. It is left to others to fill these and many other gaps, and to improve or modify the story sketched in this collection. There will be, it is to be hoped, further diachronic studies of this and other topics in the future.

I am greatly indebted to the enthusiasm and commitment of the contributors who have made the preparation of this volume an exciting cooperative adventure. It is to be hoped that readers will experience something of the same excitement in thinking through the issues it raises.

David Charles

20th July 2022

List of Contributors

Peter Adamson is Professor of Late Ancient and Arabic Philosophy at Ludwig-Maximilians-Universität in Munich. He is the author of *Al-Kindi* and *Al-Razi* in the series 'Great Medieval Thinkers', and is the host of the *History of Philosophy* podcast, which appears as a series of books with Oxford University Press.

Lilli Alanen was Emeritus Professor of History of Philosophy at Uppsala University, the first woman to be appointed as a professor in philosophy in Sweden. She was the author of *Descartes Concept of Mind* (2003) and co-edited with Charlotte Witt *Feminist Reflections on the History of Philosophy* (2004). She held visiting positions at Pittsburgh, Chicago, and University College Berkeley.

Alexander Bown is a Fellow and Tutor in Ancient Philosophy at Balliol College, Oxford, and an Associate Professor in the Faculty of Philosophy, University of Oxford. He has published articles on Epicurus' views on truth, and is currently writing a monograph on Epicurean theories of inference.

Victor Caston is Professor of Philosophy and Classical Studies at Michigan University and was the editor of *Oxford Studies in Ancient Philosophy* (2015–22). Recent publications include *Aristotle and the Cartesian Theatre* (2021); *Aristotle on the Transmission of Information: Receiving Form without the Matter* (2020); and *The Stoics on Mental Representation* (2023). He is currently working on a book entitled, *The Stoics on Content and Mental Representation*.

David Charles is Howard H. Newman Professor of Philosophy at Yale University and Emeritus Professor of Philosophy at Oriel College, Oxford. He is the author of *The Undivided Self: Aristotle and the 'Mind-Body Problem'* (2021) and edited *Definition in Greek Philosophy* (2010). He is currently working with Michail Peramatzis on a book entitled, *Aristotle's Metaphysics: The Philosophical Project of the Central Books*.

Riccardo Chiaradonna (1970) is Professor of Ancient Philosophy at Roma Tre University. His books include *Sostanza movimento analogia. Plotino critico di Aristotele* (2002); *Plotino* (2009); and *Boēthos de Sidon. Exégète d'Aristote et philosophe* (2020, with Marwan Rashed). He has published articles on various aspects of ancient Greek philosophy including on Galen, Plotinus, and the Platonic and Aristotelian traditions.

Frans A.J. de Haas is Professor of Ancient and Medieval Philosophy at Leiden University. He has published widely on Aristotle, the late ancient commentary tradition, and the connections between philosophy and the mathematical sciences. His current research interest is Alexander of Aphrodisias' philosophy of mind and logic. Recent publications include *Aristotle and Alexander on Active Intellectual Cognition* (2020); and *Deduction and Common Notions in Alexander's Commentary on Aristotle's Metaphysics A 1–2* (2021).

Reier Helle is Assistant Professor of Philosophy at Ludwig-Maximilians-Universität in Munich. His recent publications include *Self-Causation and Unity in Stoicism* (2021); and *Hierocles and the Stoic Theory of Blending* (2018). He is currently working on a book on corporeal unity in Stoic philosophy.

Brad Inwood is William Lampson Professor of Philosophy and Classics at Yale University and Professor Emeritus, University of Toronto. He is, most recently, the author of *Later Stoicism: 155 BC to 200 AD: An Introduction and Collection of Sources in Translation* (2022); and of *Stoicism: A Very Short Introduction* (2018). He continues to work on various aspects of Stoicism and on Plato's *Crito*.

Patricia Marechal is Assistant Professor of Philosophy at the University of California, San Diego. Her research focuses on ancient theories of the soul in Classical Greek and Hellenistic philosophy and medicine. She has published articles on Plato's and Aristotle's moral psychology and ethics; Porphyry on non-human animals; and Galen's psychological writings.

Stephen R. Ogden is Assistant Professor of Philosophy at the University of Notre Dame. He is the author of *Averroes on Intellect: From Aristotelian Origins to Aquinas's Critique* (2022). His recent essays include, 'Avicenna and Spinoza on Essence and Existence' (2021); 'Averroes's Unity Argument against Multiple Intellects' (2021); and 'Avicenna's Emanated Abstraction' (2020).

Dominik Perler is Professor of Philosophy at Humboldt-Universität, Berlin, and Member of the Berlin-Brandenburg Academy of Science. His research focuses on medieval and early modern philosophy. His books include *The Faculties: A History* (editor, 2015); *Feelings Transformed: Philosophical Theories of the Emotions, 1270–1670* (2018); and *Causation and Cognition in Early Modern Philosophy* (co-editor, 2020).

Christof Rapp is Professor of Philosophy at at Ludwig-Maximilians-Universität in Munich. He has published on many aspects of Aristotle's practical and theoretical work; and on ancient philosophy more generally. He is the author of *Vorsokratiker* (2008); *Metaphysik* (2016); *Aristoteles zur Einführung* (2020); and co-editor of *Aristotle, De Motu Animalium* (2020). He was the editor of *Phronesis* from 2009 to 2015.

Pauliina Remes is a Professor of Theoretical Philosophy at Uppsala University. She is the author of *Plotinus and the Self* (2011); and *Neoplatonism* (2014). Her recent essays include 'Plotinus and Augustine on Self-Constitution' (2021); 'From Natural Tendencies to Perceptual Interests and Motivation in Plato's *Timaeus*' (2021); and 'Self-Knowledge and Self-Reflexivity' (2022).

Christopher Shields is UC Distinguished Professor Henry E. Allison Endowed Chair in the History of Philosophy at University of California at San Diego. His recent books include *Ancient Philosophy: A Contemporary Introduction* (2011); *The Philosophy of Thomas Aquinas* (co-authored with Robert Pasnau, 2015); and *Aristotle's De Anima: Translated with Introduction and Commentary* (2016). He has edited the *Oxford Handbook of Aristotle* (2012); and, with Rebecca Copenhaver, *History of the Philosophy of Mind* (2019).

Richard Sorabji is an Honorary Fellow of Wolfson College, Oxford, and Emeritus Professor of Philosophy, King's College, London. He has written very extensively on Aristotle and the commentators, and is the founding editor of the 'Ancient Commentators on Aristotle' series, which currently contains over 115 volumes. His recent publications include *Self: Ancient and Modern Insights About Individuality, Life and Death* (2006); and 'Intentional Objects in Conscious Activity and Other Contexts: An Inter-cultural History' (2021).

Miira Tuominen is University Lecturer of Theoretical Philosophy at Stockholm University. She has written on the Platonic-Aristotelian tradition in antiquity (*Commentators on Plato and Aristotle*; 2009), especially on questions related to knowledge and philosophical psychology (*Apprehension and Argument*; 2007). She is currently completing a book on Porphyry's *On Abstinence*, a topic on which she has also recently published several essays.

An Introduction to the History of Hylomorphism
From Aristotle to Descartes

David Charles

1. The First Steps

Although Aristotle was not the first to understand objects in terms of their matter and their form, the account he developed has exercised a major influence on western philosophy to this day. In the intervening two and a half millennia, it has been widely used to address issues in metaphysics, aesthetics, ethics, political philosophy, and the philosophy of mind, including the problematic relation between the mind, or psychological states more generally, and the body.

Aristotle proposed that natural substances, including humans, and artefacts, such as bronze spheres, are best seen as made up of their matter (*hulē*) and their form (*eidos*) or shape (*morphē*). His approach, which built on some of Plato's earlier suggestions, came to be described as 'hylomorphism' because it sought to account for certain features of these objects in terms of their matter (*hulē*) and their form (*morphē*).

The present collection of essays considers aspects of the first 2,000 years of the history of hylomorphism, starting with Aristotle's immediate successors and ending with Descartes. Some of the writers to be studied saw themselves as following Aristotle's own account, others as challenging it and articulating alternatives, still others as modifying it to accommodate his later critics. However, all were engaged, whether as opponents or defenders, with his viewpoint as they conceived it. Hylomorphism, as we understand it today, owes a great deal to the way in which it was interpreted, and reinterpreted, during this period.

To make Aristotle's original suggestion more determinate, consider one of his examples: that of a sphere or ball made of bronze. In his view, the bronze in question is its matter, its distinctive round shape its form. Its being circular is what makes this object a sphere. The bronze could have been moulded to make different objects, such as a bronze cube or triangle. Or it could have been left as a lump of bronze without any of these shapes being imposed on it. Were it to be melted down or cut in two, it would cease to be a sphere.

The bronze so shaped is, in his example, a unified object: this bronze ball. It is not a collection of different objects, still less a heap of distinct bits of matter. Were it to disintegrate into bronze fragments, it would cease to be one unified object. Its shape, being circular, makes the object, made up of bronze, a ball and a unified object.[1]

The shape of the ball plays a further role. It is because it is round that the ball rolls in the way it does. Its shape, being round, explains, or at least is part of the explanation of, why the ball moves in this way. Its form, in Aristotle's terminology, causes round objects to act as they do.

So much for a simple example: Aristotle attempted to understand natural substances, such as particular horses or particular humans, in similar terms. They too are made up, in some way, of their matter and their form. In the case of humans, other animals, and plants, he identified their form with their soul, what makes them living beings, their matter with their bodies (or its ingredients).

What, in more detail, was Aristotle's hylomorphic account for natural substances and artefacts? How was it understood by later writers? The present volume addresses these two questions, focusing especially on the case of natural substances. It does not consider Aristotle's attempt to extend his account to a wider range of entities, including mathematical and geometrical objects.

2. Aristotle's Theory: What Is Clear and What Is Unclear

Aristotle, it would be generally agreed, aimed to say what makes a particular object, such as the particular human or bronze ball before us, the object it is. His answer involves, in his terminology, its 'formal cause': its form (or shape). It would further be generally agreed that, unlike Plato, he thought that such forms have to be instantiated in matter to exist as the forms they are. Plato, by contrast, held that the relevant forms could exist without being instantiated in matter.[2]

Most would also accept that, in Aristotle's view, the forms of natural substances are the starting points (or 'efficient' causes) of various material processes. They differ from mathematical or geometrical forms which do not have the causal power to move material objects. As Aristotle put it: 'mathematical triangles do not cut'.[3] He also clearly thought of forms and matter as, in some way 'parts' of the composite object.[4] In addition, he called his forms *energeiai*, variously translated as activities or actualities.[5]

---

[1] See *Meta.* H.6, 1045b19ff; it is similar to search for the cause of its being one thing of a certain type and its being one thing.
[2] For Aristotle's perspective on Plato's and Socrates' account of forms, see *Meta.* M.9, 1086b1–13.
[3] *De Caelo* Γ.8, 307a17ff.   [4] *Meta.* Δ.25, 1023b17–22.
[5] See, for example, *Meta.* Θ.8, 1050b2. For discussion of the best translation of 'energeia', see Beere (2009).

It would be widely, although not universally, agreed that Aristotle used talk of 'form' (or 'form and matter') in seeking to *explain* the existence and nature of natural substances and artefacts. He did not, that is, take particular composite objects as explanatorily basic and use talk of 'matter and form' to elucidate a prior and more basic item: the particular ball or human in question. Form and matter were, in his metaphysical picture, explanatorily more basic than the objects of which they are, in some way, 'parts'.

So far, perhaps, so good. But many questions remain. What exactly was Aristotle looking for when asking what makes this particular human the object it is? Was it

(a) What makes this object *a human* (as distinct from a horse)? What is essential to its being a human?
(b) What makes this object a *unity*? What makes this particular human one unified object as opposed to a particular collection of distinct body parts? [Unity] or
(c) What makes this human the *particular* human it is as opposed to any other human? [Particularity]

Was he trying to answer all or only some of these questions? Was his focus, perhaps, confined to (a) and (b)? Or did he also consider (c)? Were all his answers expressed in terms of form alone? Or did he also refer to matter, either in addition to form or by itself, in addressing some or all of them?

When we begin to raise questions, others flood in. Some concern the nature of the forms themselves, others matter, still others the ways in which matter and form combine to make a particular natural substance or artefact. Here are a few:

(i) What type of entity is a form? To what ontological category does it belong? Is it, for example, an object or a feature of an object? Or the member of an irreducibly distinct, *sui generis*, category? How are we to understand Aristotle's talk of 'activity' or 'actuality'? Do these terms refer, for example, to a ball's shape or structure or capacity? Or to its rolling? Or its being capable of rolling? Is one of these referred to when talking of the form of a human being?
(ii) Can the same form be shared by distinct objects? Or is every form unique to the particular object that possesses it? If it is unique, how is it individuated? Can the very same object have both a unique and a shared form? If so, is one of these types of form more basic than the other?
(iii) Even if forms cannot exist without matter, are the forms of natural substances and artefacts to be defined in ways which explicitly refer in

their definition to matter? Or can they be defined without any reference of this type to matter, even though they cannot exist unless instantiated in it?
(iv) Can the matter in question exist without this form? Can it be defined without reference to the form in question?
(v) To what ontological category does the matter in question belong? Is it also an object? Or a quantity of stuff? Or a feature of an object? What is intended by Aristotle's association of matter with 'capacity' or 'potentiality' (*dunamis*)? Is matter itself to be understood as a capacity of some kind or as what is capable in this way?
(vi) How are the form and the matter combined in composite objects? In what way are they both 'parts' of the whole? Does the form, for example, 'supervene' (or in some way 'rest') on the matter in question? Does the form make the matter the type of matter it is? Or both?

While there is ongoing scholarly discussion about Aristotle's answers to these questions, most interpreters agree that he aimed to address all or most of them using his hylomorphic theory.

It is clear, at the outset, that he faced serious problems in doing so. This is, in no small measure, because he was, or so it seems, committed to several claims which are difficult to hold together. He held that:

[A] the form, in question, is prior in definition to the composite object and to its matter [PRIORITY],[6]
[B] forms (or possibly forms and matter) underwrite the unity of the composite as a human being or as a bronze ball as one unified object [UNITY],[7]
[C] the matter in some way 'underlies' the form. There is, it might appear, a true upwards story which begins with matter at some level and ends with a type of matter which (in some way) 'underlies' form. [UPWARDS STORY],[8] and
[D] forms are the basic efficient and teleological causes of material changes [CAUSE].[9]

I shall concentrate on two difficulties that arose, focusing on a subclass of natural substances, living beings, and leaving aside others such as fire or water.

---

[6] *Meta.* Z.3, 1029a5–7.   [7] *Meta.* H.6, 1045b19ff.

[8] For matter as that which 'underlies' form, see, for example, *Phys.* 191a9ff. For Aristotle's views on matter at varying stages of development, see *Meta.* Θ.7, 1049a24–8. He discusses these issues in more detail in his biological writings and in his work on generation and corruption. On these texts and related issues, see Furth (1988); and Charles (1988).

[9] See *Meta.* Z.17, 1041a29f, and *De An.* Γ. 4, 415b10–12, on the soul. They are, in Aristotle's terminology, *per se* causes.

3. Two Difficulties

(1) Aristotle's commitment to PRIORITY might seem to require him to define the forms in question without explicit reference in their definition to matter. His forms—like Plato's—will then be what I shall call *pure*.[10] However, if this was his view, he would need to show how such forms can be the basic efficient causes of material changes. Can they be the starting points and controllers of material processes?[11] Or are they—like mathematical forms—causally inert? However, if under the pressure of CAUSE, Aristotle must define forms, like other efficient causes, as in their nature enmattered, it is difficult to understand how they can be definitionally prior to matter, as PRIORITY requires. They might seem to be properties of matter or to depend for their identity on relations between bits of matter. How then can they be definitionally prior to matter?

There is, it seems, a dilemma: *either* the forms of living beings are definitionally prior to matter and causally inert *or* they are efficient causes of material changes but not definitionally prior to matter. However, Aristotle seems to have thought of them *both* as definitionally prior to matter *and* as efficient causes of material change. Did he find a way to do so?

(2) Aristotle, it appears, sought to maintain the definitional priority of the form of a living being by defining its relevant matter (at some level) in terms of that form. Indeed, this may have been part of his attempt to underwrite the unity of the resulting material body. Its matter will be defined as what is arranged so as to underlie the relevant form. However, if this how Aristotle spelled out his claims concerning PRIORITY and UNITY, what kind of upwards story could he tell? How did he develop [C]? If matter itself is to be defined at some level in terms of its capacity to underlie the form of the living animal, how is matter, so defined, connected to any lower level of matter, not defined in terms of this capacity?

There seem to be two answers to the last question. *Either* matter at the lower level is defined independently of the form of the living animal *or* it is not. If it is, at some lower level (wherever that is) the higher level forms (such as being alive as a human) and matter defined as thus enformed will in some way rest on matter defined independently of them.[12] However, if this was Aristotle's view, he was, it seems, committed to the presence—at some level—of two distinct, independently defined, types of material components in one unified object. But how then is the resulting object itself a unified object, not a collection of two or more distinct entities, each with its own distinct causal capacities? How can he maintain UNITY, if he is willing to define matter (at some level) independently of form?

---

[10] A form is pure if and only if it is defined without explicit reference in its definition to matter or material bodies.

[11] In Aristotle's terminology: they are starting points (*archai*) of processes (*kineseis*); *Phys.* B.1, 192b28.

[12] See, for example, Whiting (1995: 75–92).

What is more: how could he defend his claim that the forms of living animals are the basic efficient causes of their material changes? Why aren't there other, possibly equally basic, causes at work?

Nor are these the only problems for this alternative. It also needs to spell out its central idea of forms—such as souls—and the matter defined in terms of them—as at some level 'emerging' from, matter defined independently of such forms. To some, however, this suggestion may seem, to use Thomas Huxley's striking phrase, as mysterious as Aladdin's Djinn emerging out of his bottle![13] Could Aristotle rest content, at a central point in his theory, with a brute, unexplained, claim: form just arises out of matter? If form, as some suggest, 'supervenes' on matter, shouldn't he have sought to explain why this is so?[14] Lacking that his account may seem to resemble what he himself described as a badly constructed tragedy: one in which no one can see how one scene follows from the previous one. Surely, he was aiming at a unified metaphysical picture in which different levels fit together in an intelligible account?

What of the other alternative: to define matter at all levels—even down to the most basic one—in terms of its being able to underlie the form, or soul, of a living being? If one adopts this option, matter at the lowest level will be defined in terms of its potentiality for life. The relevant supervenience conditionals will be grounded in the presence of matter, so defined. However, if this was Aristotle's view, he would have been committed to some version of what we call 'panpsychism': matter will be, to echo Myles Burnyeat's striking phrase, 'pregnant with consciousness' from the bottom up.[15] If matter is defined 'all the way down' as what is capable of underlying the form of the resultant living composite, the basic material components will—in our case—defined in terms of our capacity for experience and thought. Was this really Aristotle's view? If it is, shouldn't it, as Burnyeat suggested, simply be 'junked'?

---

[13] Huxley (1886: 193).
[14] By 'supervenience' I understand the following claim:

[S] [Necessarily] Indiscernibility with regard to subvening, lower level, features entails indiscernibility with regard to supervening, higher level features

[S], so understood, is non-symmetric. It does not preclude the possibility that indiscernibility with regard to supervening features entails indiscernibility with regard to subvening features but nor does it require it. There is a large family of supervenience claims, depending on (i) whether the relevant domain is, for example, specified in terms of this world, all worlds or all accessible worlds, all or some substances, all or some times, etc.; and (ii) whether the types of features referred to are properties or predicates.

'Emergence', as I shall use this term, involves in addition to [S], the further claim that:

[E] There is no adequate (or appropriately intelligible) explanation of why the relevant supervenience claim is true.

There are distinct types of emergentist views depending on, for example, whether (i) [E] is taken to mean that there is not now or could not be an adequate explanation of the type required; and (ii) how strict the demands on 'adequate explanation' are (how much linking theory is required...?). Some philosophers attracted to [E] also hold that there are irreducible causal powers among the supervening features.

[15] Burnyeat (1992: 422–43).

There is, it seems, a second dilemma. Either Aristotle committed himself to some version of pan-psychism or he embraced the idea of a brute—at best unexplained, at worst inexplicable—connection between matter and form. Either way there is mystery at the crucial point. What is more, the latter option, even if its mystery is one to which we today have become accustomed, also calls into question the unity of the resulting substance.

Aristotle, it seems, faced major two difficulties, one concerning form, the other matter.[16] Did he develop a way to address them? How did it work in the case of living beings, whose form is their soul (*De An.* B.1, 412a10ff) and their matter, their bodies? Aristotle characterized soul as 'the essence of a natural body of a given type' (412b15–17) and as the actuality of such a body (*entelecheia*: 413a8–9) and in B.2 described it as that 'by which primarily we live and perceive and think' (414a12–13). How did he understand their form, their soul, and their matter, their body?[17]

4. Four Interpretations: The Case of Living Beings

Interpreters disagree about Aristotle's responses to these difficulties. Competing interpretations can be located along two major axes.

[1] Purism vs impurism: can the relevant form be defined in its entirety without explicit reference in its definition to matter? Purist interpreters say 'yes': impurists say 'no'.[18]

[2] Can the underlying matter present in the composite living being be defined, at some level, without explicit reference in its definition to the way that being lives or perceives. Pan-psychist interpreters say 'no', others say 'yes'.

There are, given these two distinct axes, four opposed exegetical options, each with its own advocates.

Some present Aristotle as combining *purism* about form in its entirety with the suggestion that matter (at some level) as a definitionally independent component. In their interpretation, matter and form stand to each other in an external relation of some type: the form 'supervenes' on or, in some accounts, 'emerges' from the matter. For some, the presence of the form also requires (or hypothetically

---

[16] Interpreters disagree about other major issues such as (i) are the relevant forms particular or general or both; and (ii) in what way are matter and form 'parts' of the composite? Detailed discussion of these issues, and the history of their impact on later writers, would require a further study.

[17] Several writers, Bolton (1978), Ward (1988), and Menn (2002), have suggested that the account offered in *De An.* B.2 is a more proper definition of the soul than its characterization as the essence of a natural body in *De An.* B.1. However, since both claims can equally be interpreted in both a purist and an impurist manner, this issue is not germane to our present concerns.

[18] Recent purist interpreters include Gill (1989); Frede (1995); Caston (2008/9); and Devereux (2010). Recent impurist interpreters include Balme (1987); Charles (2008, 2021); and Peramatzis (2011).

necessitates) the presence of matter. The composite object is, for all in this group, made up of its matter and its form, understood as two definitionally independent components.

This *two component* interpretation (so defined) is currently fashionable. Indeed, many modern hylomorphists presuppose a similar view in constructing their own theories. Thus, when thinking of the psychological and the physical, they understand the former (whether this be a substance or a property or a set of properties) as defined without explicit reference to anything material and the latter (at some level) as a purely material component defined without any reference to anything psychological. At this point they confront a hard question: how is the psychological (so understood) connected with the physical (so understood)?

Aristotle, for these interpreters, faced a mind-body problem similar to the one we have inherited from Descartes. Indeed, this is why many of them present Aristotle's hylomorphism as a fore-runner of a version of the non-reductionist materialist accounts of the psychological which have become fashionable in late-20th-century philosophy of mind.[19] However, this line of interpretation, despite its many attractions, faces several exegetical problems. Is there any evidence that Aristotle saw, let alone addressed, the issues it raises? Did he attempt, for example, to render intelligible the way in which the form supervenes on the matter? Did he show how, within a two component account, to preserve the unity of the resulting composite object? How did he maintain the definitional priority of form over matter if he saw form as supervening on (or 'emerging from') matter? How did he address the problems caused by the presence of multiple independent causes of the same material change?

A second school of interpreters agrees that Aristotle embraced purism about the form of living beings but, in contrast with the first group, suggests that he thought of matter as at all levels defined in terms of form at the highest level. In their view, the composite object is not made up at any level from two definitionally independent components because the relevant matter is at all levels definitionally dependent on the form of the living animal. This style of account has a long tradition and continues to find its advocates today.[20]

Both groups of purist interpreters share a common problem: they need to explain—if Aristotle is to be credited with a consistent theory—how pure forms are capable of being basic efficient causes of material changes while pure mathematical forms are not.

Impurism offers an alternative. For the impurist interpreter, the forms of natural substances can only be efficient causes of material change in virtue of their being essentially enmattered. They cannot, that is, be defined without explicit

---

[19] See, for example, Charles (1984: 197–250); Shields (1990: 19–33); Putnam and Nussbaum (1995: 27–76); Caston (2005: 245–320).

[20] See, for example, Marmodoro's discussion of this style of account (2013: 5–22).

reference in their definition to their matter. Perhaps they are essentially material capacities or material structures. As such, they may, it is claimed, be parts of a unified material object.

There are two groups of impurist interpreter, corresponding to the two types of purist commentators described above.

One group presents Aristotle as combining impurism about form with a view of matter at some level as a definitionally independent component. For some, the impure form is defined as a property of matter or as a relation between bits of matter.[21] This is the type of 'structure' form is: one dependent on bits of matter. Impure forms, like pure forms, emerge (in some unexplained way) from matter defined independently of such forms. This group, like the first group of purists, needs to show how, in Aristotle's theory, forms of their favoured type (such as souls) supervene on matter, defined independently of such forms. What, we might ask, makes the relevant supervenience conditionals true and intelligible?

A second group of impurist interpreters, by contrast, suggests that Aristotle combined impurism about form with a view of matter as definitionally dependent at every level on form at the highest level. These impurists, like the second group of purists, need to show how, if at all, Aristotle avoided pan-psychism.

Both groups of impurist interpreters face a further difficulty with regard to form and matter (that immediately underlies the relevant form): can impure forms be definitionally prior to that matter if they cannot be defined independently of it? Matter, it seems, must—in their account—be prior to the form in question if the latter is to be taken as property of some matter or in some other way dependent on it. Nor is this problem avoided by taking both form and the relevant matter to be defined in terms of each other (a position I shall call 'two-way inextricabilism'). How then can the form be definitionally prior to this type of matter?

There are, of course, other exegetical options. Perhaps Aristotle was a purist about the forms of some natural substances, such as humans, and impurist about others, such as some non-human animals or plants? Or maybe he was a purist about some aspects of human souls (such as our capacity to think) but an impurist about others (such as our capacities to perceive or digest). Even if the human soul in its entirety cannot be defined without explicit reference to matter, perhaps some parts of it can. Did Aristotle reject 'a one size fits all' approach to all aspects of all living beings?

Interpreters adopting a 'mix and match' approach confront, when thinking of pure souls (or pure aspects of a mixed soul), some of the problems purist interpreters do elsewhere. And when thinking of impure souls (or impure aspects of a mixed soul), they face the same problems as impurists. But they also have to address some further difficulties. Is the capacity to perceive pure in humans but

---

[21] See, for example, Jaworski (2016).

impure in other animals? Or is the capacity to digest pure in humans but impure in plants? Or, alternatively, if the human soul has distinct pure and impure aspects, how does it constitute a properly unified object? What makes it one thing rather than a collection of different entities? How do its distinct pure and impure aspects interact? Do different types of matter underlie our capacities to think and to digest? How do these types of matter cohere to make one unified living being?

Which of these exegetical strategies best capture Aristotle's own version of hylomorphism? Did he, in one of the ways just sketched, succeed in developing a coherent theory that successfully addresses the two difficulties, one about form, the other about matter isolated above? Or is his attempt, in the final analysis, an interesting, indeed brilliant, failure? In any event, he was, as we can see, attracted to a number of claims which it is difficult to combine in a properly unified and plausible theory.

These remain controversial exegetical questions. I have argued elsewhere that Aristotle was an impurist who successfully defended the definitional priority of the form of living animals and the unity of the resulting composite without committing himself either to pan-psychism or to brute emergentism.[22] But many, including some contributors to this volume, take radically different views. These differences will, of course, influence one's assessment of the extent to which Aristotle's views were modified in the period to be studied. I shall return to this issue in the final section after offering a sketch of parts of what happened in the centuries after his death.

5. Two Challenges: Aristotle and His Successors: a Preliminary Sketch

The two sets of difficulties just isolated played a major role in shaping the first two millennia of Aristotelian hylomorphism. Throughout that period, Aristotle's own views were discussed in great detail, fully tested and modified. Some philosophers saw serious difficulties or major gaps in his theory. Others developed their own accounts, or reformulated his, in an attempt to address them.

While there were several major challenges to his theory, two were particularly important. The first came from philosophers who envisaged—and sought to develop—a fuller and more robust upwards story, which took as its starting point a determinate material level defined independently of form (at least at the top level) and aimed to explain all the features of higher levels on its basis. They may well have found Aristotle's own account of matter inadequate or obscure

---

[22] Charles (2021: 1–17).

(perhaps as mysterious as pan-psychism is for many today). The Epicureans were the first to undertake this project. But many followed their lead, some presenting Aristotle's forms of natural substances as emergent properties of matter, so defined, others giving up talk of form altogether. None took form to be prior in being or in definition to matter. In terms of Aristotle's own commitments, as sketched above, they rejected or modified PRIORITY [A], because they sought a better version of an upwards story and applied it generally (including to the case of human beings). Several of these philosophers developed their approach in tandem with an understanding of causation in which only bodies could be efficient causes. In their view, Aristotle's capacities could not be causes because they were not bodies. However, whatever their differences about efficient causation, most agreed on the need for, and importance of, a richer and more satisfactory 'bottom up' material story than they found in Aristotle.

The major second challenge, perhaps most clearly articulated by Plotinus, came from those who insisted that the forms of human beings are to be treated as definitionally prior to matter and to composite bodies. As a result, they took a purist account of the human soul, and forms more generally: they cannot be defined as material features or as properties of matter. To do so would be, in their view, to reverse the proper order of priority: matter would now be metaphysically prior to form. Some maintained that the entire human soul is prior to, and defined independently of, matter; others that only some part of it is, such as our capacity for thought.

The philosophers who developed the second challenge had independent motivations for offering a purist account of the relevant forms, or parts of them. Some were committed to making room for the existence of an immortal soul which could survive the destruction of the body, others to constructing a composite and authoritative ancient sage (one might call the product of their labours 'Plat-otle') who successfully combined the views of Plato and Aristotle. Still others, as we shall see, aimed to find a place for genuine human freedom in a determinist material world. But whatever their motivations, all defined the human soul, or at least some part of it, as pure, independent of, and prior to matter. Further, many agreed that there is a metaphysically important gap between the form (or at least its pure parts) and the most that matter by itself can explain. Some were keenly aware of the resulting difficulties in accommodating the unity of the resulting composite object.

When these two challenges were combined, a highly compelling picture gripped the philosophical imagination, one with which we all are now thoroughly familiar. There is a robust 'bottom up' story, beginning with matter defined independently of life or consciousness, which explains many features of the world but not the nature and continued existence of (at least) some parts of the human soul or its distinctive psychological features. There are, it appears, two radically different kinds of entity, whether these be substances or properties: one purely material, defined independently of the psychological, the other purely psychological, defined independently of matter. In some accounts, the latter can exist independently of the material body. However, in all there are, in the human case, two definitionally independent components: a purely psychological component, defined independently of body or matter, and a purely material component, defined independently of the psychological. If both components are understood as substances, we have a version of Descartes' substance dualism. There is a pure subject, the thinking substance, which thinks and perceives; and another distinct entity, the body, a material substance fully explicable in terms of a matter-based upwards story. If the two components are understood as properties, we are led to property dualism. Either way, there is, as a consequence, a major, and so far unsolved, problem: the mind-body problem, which has been central in western philosophy of mind since Descartes. How are these two fundamentally different types of component, whether substances or properties, connected? What type of entity are we?

Later Aristotelians responded to these challenges in differing ways. Some understood Aristotelian hylomorphism in terms of two definitionally independent components, the soul (or later, mind) and body so understood, which are both somehow present in us. In doing so, they played a major role in setting up the two component version of hylomorphism with which we are now familiar. They helped secure the foundations for Descartes' mind-body problem.

In the next sections, I shall add some more detail to this preliminary sketch. Neither challenge, I shall suggest, had to be addressed by later Aristotelians in the way just indicated. There were other possibilities open to them as Aristotelians. (My present aim, I should note, is a limited one: merely to indicate what these other possibilities might have been, not to develop or assess them in detail.)

5.1 The First Challenge: The Beginnings of a Robust Upwards Story—Basic Bodies and Causation (Epicurus and the Stoics)

Epicurus, following Democritus, took atoms to be the explanatorily basic bodies from which all other bodies, with their distinctive natures, are in some way composed. Aristotle's forms played no official role in his account. An upwards story is all that is required. The basic ingredients of his theory are atoms, their shapes and interactions defined without reference to higher level bodies. All else is composed from, and apparently explained in terms of, a fully determinate base of minimal material bodies of this type.

Epicurus faced his own difficulties. He accepted that there are distinct unified objects, some of which Aristotle would have regarded as natural substances. These persist through time with their own natures and properties, including modal ones. Epicurus did not, it seems, take our talk about natural substances as merely a *façon de parler*, our way of looking at a world made up of atoms and the void. However, he did not—at least on the evidence available to us—develop the resources to underwrite the genuine existence of these natural substances and their distinctive properties on the basis of atoms and their interactions alone. There was, it seems, a major gap in his theory. Nor is there, as Alex Bown notes (Chapter 1), evidence that Epicurus or his followers articulated an account in which substances and their properties 'emerge' in some way from atoms and the void.[23]

Epicurus' problem was acute. It was not, he thought, by chance that we perceive natural substances, such as apples, which exist in their own right (*per se*). As a result, he had to explain, as Bown points out, why apples, and not red apples or slices of red apples, are natural substances. Why, in his terminology, are the former, not the latter, *per se* existents? However, he did not, as far as we are aware, find a way to answer this question on the basis of his claims about atoms and their interactions alone. Indeed, despite his wish to free himself completely from talk of forms, Epicurus, at this point, may have needed to appeal to them to address this issue. Material and efficient causes were not adequate for the task. Aristotelians would, no doubt, have concluded that he, and his followers, had failed to develop an upwards story that matched their philosophical ambitions. Nor, as the subsequent history of that project reveals, were they the last to fall short in this way.

The Stoics, like Epicurus, took as their starting point a set of bodies and their interactions defined without reference to composite bodies. They too aimed to account for the latter on the basis of the former. In their view, souls were a distinct type of body, with their own identity conditions and certain characteristic capacities. They developed an account of souls as a type of material body made of *pneuma*, a blend of air and fire, which moves in a distinctive way. Souls are not, it seems, to be understood, in the Aristotelian manner, as capacities or states of a natural body (or the way a body is). They have to be a type of body to stand in causal relations to other bodies and to be causally responsible for bodily actions, given the Stoic view that only bodies can be causes. The soul-body is a pneumatic body which by its constant pattern of movement brings about these effects.

Both Stoics and Epicureans took what is compositionally basic, some material bodies—and their interactions with other bodies—defined without essential reference to any composite entities as the basis of their account of composite entities. Both schools built their account of composite living substances on the foundation of a fully determinate base of material bodies and their interactions, even though they had different theories of what these were.

---

[23] However, given the limited nature of the surviving sources, it is hard to tell, as Bown notes in his essay, whether these are issues that Epicurus (i) overlooked or didn't care about; (ii) tried and failed to get to grips with; or (iii) succeeded in addressing in, for example, some lost part of the *On Nature*.

Nonetheless there remained, as Brad Inwood notes (Chapter 2), structural parallels between certain aspects of Stoic theory and Aristotle's own hylomorphic account. Even though the Stoics did not themselves talk of 'form',

(a) their soul-body plays the role of Aristotle's form and is present in the composite animal;
(b) there is, in addition, an ordinary (non-soul) body present in the composite; and
(c) when the soul-body and ordinary body combine to form a composite, the presence of the soul-body makes the ordinary body part of the composite.

In these respects, Stoic theories mirror central features of Aristotle's hylomorphism. But the Stoics also faced major problems of their own. How far did they succeed in resolving them?

Here is one: while the soul is a body, so too, in their account, is the composite made up of the soul (the soul-body) and the non-soul, ordinary body with which the soul interacts. They were, it seems, committed to the presence of three different bodies in the same place at the same time. The unity of the composite animal is, it seems, to be based on a distinctive type of two-way causal interaction between its two more basic components (the soul-body and the ordinary body). The Stoics now needed to show that the composite which resulted was itself a genuinely unified object, not a collection of distinct, interacting entities: a team of distinct objects. And it was one point at which, as Reier Helle points out (Chapter 4), Alexander, a staunch Aristotelian, questioned the success of their project.

Nor was this their only problem. In their account, when the controlling soul-body causes the extremities of the body to move, it does so by interacting with a distributed soul-body which is located between the controlling soul-body and the periphery. There is, as Christof Rapp highlights (Chapter 3), a causal chain made up of distinct bodies each with its own causal role. Given their views on causation, the Stoics could not take as basic a unified process of moving one's body, understood as extending from its starting point in the centre of the agent to their periphery. There is not one exercise of an agent's capacity to move. What happens has to be broken down into a series of interactions between distinct bodies, each acting on the one next to it. What was for Aristotle a unified bodily process of controlling the body is replaced, in their account, with a number of distinct phenomena involving different bodies, one occurring after another. Did this, an Aristotelian might ask, really capture the unity of the process at issue?

The Stoic view of causation was influential. Their causes were bodies which determined their outcome, necessitating the result they produced.[24] They applied

---

[24] For discussion of Stoic views on causation and their importance, see Frede (1987: 125ff).

this model in thinking about the soul-body, holding that it too was determined by antecedent bodies of varying types. This perspective, they maintained, was fully consistent with our being free agents. We are free in that we act on the desires and natures we have as a result of antecedent causes of this type. Indeed, our being free consists, in their view, in our choices being determined by our own natures alone.

5.2 The First Aristotelian Response

Stoic theory generated, as Inwood notes, several responses from Aristotelians who wished to retain his forms as part of their theory. Critolaus, it seems, took the soul, the form in question, to be a body, albeit one composed of *aither*, a distinctive type of matter. Dicaearchus, by contrast, talked of properties as well as bodies, describing the soul as a property of body. In doing so, he may have been reviving a version of the harmony theory, in which bodies were basic (as in Stoic theory) and souls understood as dependent properties. However, if this was his goal, he could not take the soul to be the definitionally basic entity which makes the body the one it is. He was, from an Aristotelian viewpoint, making a crucial concession to the Stoic viewpoint. Andronicus, perhaps more attentive to Aristotle's own formulations, described the soul 'either as a mixture or as a power that follows from mixture'.[25] Maybe he did not wish to take a view on whether the soul is a mixed body (as the Stoics thought) or a power or capacity present in such a body. However, from Aristotle's perspective, Andronicus' second formulation was fraught with danger. If the soul is defined as a capacity of a body, it will not, it seems, be definitionally prior to the body. It will not make the body the one it is. What is more: Andronicus appears to be giving up on the idea of form as something more than a capacity. It was not in his account an actuality, if that is understood as the way something is when it is capable of certain activities. At the very least he did not, on the basis of the evidence we possess, give prominence to this idea.

Alexander of Aphrodisias developed the most sustained Aristotelian response. He claimed (as Helle argues) that the Stoic project failed at a crucial point: they could not underwrite the distinctive unity of the composite in terms of two-way causal interaction between two distinct components. Since there are two bodies involved in these interactions, they could not, by Aristotelian lights, constitute a properly unified object, such as a composite human being.

There was, in Alexander's view, a further explanatory gap in Stoic theory: it could not, he claimed, account for the distinctive nature of the soul, with its causal role, in terms of its favoured material explanatory resources: the tensile motion of *pneuma* and its constituents: air and fire. How could, he asked, tensile motion of

---

[25] According to Galen, *QAM* 44.12–45.3.

this type act on an ordinary, non-pneumatic, bodies in the ways required of the soul? The Stoics did not have the resources, he maintained, to explain how tensile motion could make an ordinary body the body of a human being or play the required role of sustaining a unified composite capable of human actions. How was tensile motion able to cause this type of phenomenon? One senses in his remarks some of Aristotle's impatience with his own predecessors when he wrote that 'none of them penetrated below the surface...or made any definite statements about growth except such as any amateur might have made'.[26]

Alexander did not confine himself to pointing to these two gaps in Stoic theory. In his Commentary on Aristotle's *De Anima*, he constructed his own upwards story although rejecting the Stoic claim that the soul itself is a body. It did not, in his view, need to be a body to be a cause of bodily movements. In developing the second of the two possibilities canvassed by Andronicus, he regularly spoke of the soul as a distinctive type of capacity, or set of capacities, which emerged from bodies and their interactions, both defined without reference to the soul. These emergent capacities, which define the soul, have a causal explanatory role in accounting for bodily movements.[27]

Alexander's aim, it seems, was to tell as good an upwards story as the Stoics while retaining Aristotle's view that the soul is the form of a body, not itself a body. If this was his goal, when he described the soul as a type of 'perfection or completion' that arises from bodily states (a supervenient end), the relevant bodies should not themselves be defined as matter for the soul. Similarly, when he called certain capacities 'completions', he would not be defining the relevant bodies and their interactions in terms of the perfection (viz: the soul) which results from them. Indeed, it will remain open, given his general strategy, whether the soul itself is to be defined as a completion of the relevant bodies (and so an essentially embodied form) or a type of completion defined independently of these bodies which comes to be present when they are mixed. His cautious reflections and hesitations on the latter issue, central to the discussion between purism and impurism, are examined in Frans de Haas' essay (Chapter 7).

Although Alexander's strategy is of great interest, it faces a number of difficulties. Some of its strengths and problems are discussed in the essays by Victor Caston, Frans de Haas, Reier Helle, and Richard Sorabji. Here are four of the issues at stake.

(1) Did Alexander fare better than the Stoics in accounting for the existence of the soul as a distinctive type of entity? It might seem, as Helle suggests, that he had to posit as brute fact the emergence of the relevant capacities from

---

[26] GC 314b1–3.
[27] Alexander generally refers to the soul in terms of its capacities (*dunameis*), occasionally in terms of its states (*hexeis*).

the underlying bodies and their interactions, their patterns of blending. If this was his final position (as suggested by Caston; Chapter 6), Alexander appears vulnerable to criticisms somewhat similar to those he levelled against the Stoics. There would also be, it seems, a significant gap, a failure of intelligibility, at the centre of his account. He was, it may seem, unable to explain how the soul with its distinctive causal role results from a blending of the bodies that underlie it. If he was himself an emergentist, he may have been a conflicted one. Perhaps he was an emergentist *malgré soi*.

(2) Did Alexander have a better account than the Stoics of the unity of the resultant composite, assuming—that is—that he maintains the idea of basic bodies and their interactions defined independently of the soul that emerges from them? What makes the resulting composite a properly unified object with its distinctive formal capacities?

(3) If Alexander regarded forms as capacities of bodies, how can they be definitionally prior to the bodies whose capacities they are? Even if forms have a distinctive causal role, what makes them definitionally prior to matter and the bodies whose forms they are? This problem appears as acute for him as for Andronicus: if forms are capacities, can they be defined without explicit reference to the composite bodies whose capacities they are (perhaps together with their material input and output conditions)? In wrestling with this issue, Alexander entertained the idea that although forms are necessarily, perhaps even essentially, enmattered, they are not wholly defined by the matter to which they are related. However, he did not spell out the additional aspect (or aspects) of their definition. Nor is it clear, given his emphasis on forms as capacities, that he had the resources to do so, or to show how any additional elements of this type were to be integrated with other enmattered aspects of their definition.

(4) In what way are the various capacities of the human soul themselves unified? It cannot be enough to offer merely a list of the relevant capacities. There needs to be a higher degree of unity than this if there is to be a properly unified human soul.

Alexander's picture is subtle and complex. Did he succeed in finding a way to make significant concessions to the Stoic viewpoint while maintaining the basic ingredients of Aristotelian hylomorphism? Was he himself aiming at a unified picture? How did his role as an interpreter intersect with his work as an independent philosopher? There is clearly scope for further discussion of Alexander's overall contribution.

Alexander made one further influential, and highly relevant, anti-Stoic move. He rejected their idea of freedom because, in his view, it presented us, and our actions, as determined by our distinctive nature, including (one assumes) their bodily conditions. Freedom of action, Alexander thought, required us to be able to act otherwise, even given our distinctive natures and the material conditions in which we find themselves. His approach immediately prompts the question: what is the self, the free agent, which is unbound by these factors? How are we, with our distinctive material natures, capable of free action of this type?

To address these questions, Alexander invoked a type of intellect possessed of the ability to think of everything, a 'dispositional intellect' (as he called it), understood as a type of 'completion' of a basic intellect we all share. The dispositional intellect, described as 'a form of forms', is, it appears, a purely psychological phenomenon. Its definition does not refer explicitly to any bodily capacity. Even though, in Alexander's view, it is mortal, it is not defined by explicit reference to a body or its matter. Nor, it seems, given its ability here and now to think of everything and prompt action accordingly, can it be governed by the necessities that govern bodily states and their interactions. While the dispositional intellect is, in Alexander's account, to be distinguished from the external active intellect, which he identified with the intelligible order of the universe, it is not itself to be defined as an essentially embodied capacity (as perhaps desire and perception are). Human agents, to be capable of free action, must, in his view, possess a pure capacity to think and decide in addition to any essentially bodily ones. However, if we possess capacities of the latter type, we will have two definitionally distinct types of capacity, one bodily, the other purely psychological. In any event, the demands of freedom, as he understood it, seemed to require a pure part of the human form. The aspect of the human soul which is the repository of human freedom has to be defined without reference to matter. Purism is a precondition of freedom. But how then is the pure aspect of our soul to be integrated with its other aspects? (For some discussion of these issues see, in particular, de Haas' essay.)

Alexanders' response to the challenges of Stoicism was, in one respect, concessive. He aimed, as we have seen, to tell as good an upward story as theirs while insisting on a role for Aristotelian forms as causally efficacious capacities. However, in another respect, it was far from concessive. He developed an account of freedom, something akin to freedom of indifference, which not only rejected the Stoic view but went considerably beyond Aristotle's own cautious remarks on what is required for voluntary action or for the presence of states for which we are, in some way, responsible.[28] At this point, Alexander was, it seems, drawn to a conception of the self (or part of the self) as pure, not defined in terms of matter or material capacities, both of which might (as the Stoics suggested) be subject to determinist laws.

Galen offered a different response to Stoic ideas. Like Alexander, he sought to integrate them with some (admittedly fewer) Aristotelian concepts. As Patricia

---

[28] For further discussion of this issue, see Barnes (2010: 26–45).

Marechal shows (Chapter 5), he accepted the Stoic view of bodies as the only causes of material changes and shared their confidence in the possibility of a robust upwards story beginning with basic matter and its interactions, defined independently of form, and ending with the soul. Unlike Alexander, he did not think that capacities could be genuine causes. In his view, souls are unified and mixed bodies which, as bodies, cause material changes in the world. When there is a body of this type, it will have causal capacities; but the capacities themselves are not causes. Indeed, to talk of capacities was, in his view, simply a way of describing the presence of the unified mixed bodies which are the real causes of bodily changes. In effect, Galen took the second of the options suggested by Andronicus (the soul is a mixed body) rather than the first (the soul is a capacity) because he, like the Stoics, held that it was only if the soul is a body that it could be an efficient cause of the material changes involved in bodily action.

Galen, like the Stoics, seems committed to the possibility of an upwards story beginning with matter defined independently of form (at the highest level). However, at a crucial point, he appeals to the idea of a Divine Craftsman (reminiscent of the maker-god of the Timaeus) to play the central role of combining the basic material ingredients in just the way required to generate souls. Further, as Marechal notes, while our souls are, in his theory, best thought of as mixed bodies of a given type, the idea of form had a further independent role in his account: that of the principle or 'programme' followed by the Divine Craftsman in producing the appropriate type of mixture and unity in composite objects with a soul of this type. The form, so understood, is not a body or a capacity of a body. Nor is it, in Galen's view, a cause. Instead, it is the *recipé* used by the divine agent who produces such objects.

Both Alexander and Galen, in responding to Stoicism, aimed to make room for an upwards story of the general type the Stoics envisaged and, it seems, took that story as the basis (or part of the basis) of their preferred metaphysical perspective. What is compositionally basic, apparently defined independently of souls or high level forms, was an important starting point in their account of composite living substances. Did they concede too much to the Stoic viewpoint? Did they, for example, in responding in the way they did, give up Aristotle's commitment to the priority of the form of the composite object? Did they succeed in maintaining his conception of its unity?

There was, it should be noted, an alternative: an Aristotelian could have taken form to be metaphysically prior while maintaining a distinction between what is metaphysically and what is compositionally (or materially) prior. The standpoint from which the world is metaphysically intelligible need not be one which takes as a starting point the smallest or most basic of its material constituents. Indeed, Aristotle, it seems, began his own metaphysical account with natural substances (and their forms) as we encounter them in our lived experience of the world and took materially basic components as, in some way, derivative. The latter are, it appears, secondary in the metaphysical order of the world, even if they are the materially basic elements from which all else is composed.

Some of Aristotle's remarks suggest an approach of this type, as when he speaks of basic or prime matter as something akin to a determinable: something made determinate in varying ways, some of them psycho-physical. From that perspective, as we descend below the level of natural substances and their forms, we abstract away from those features which define them as the determinate entities they are. In particular, we give up our grip on their distinctively teleological natures. In this respect, matter becomes progressively more indeterminate as we lose the type of determinacy which these substances and their forms possess. Living substances are not seen, in this picture, as emerging, or as derived, from a basic, purely material level. On the contrary, the latter level is best understood as something abstracted from the natural, teleologically defined, substances which we encounter. It is, in effect, the product of a distinctive and partial way of looking at natural substances including humans, animals, and plants. The compositionally basic ingredients of the universe are not, from this viewpoint, the preferred starting points for an intelligible metaphysical account of a unified world. Indeed, we can best achieve an account of this type if we take as its primary ingredients natural substances and living organisms with their distinctive forms.[29]

It was open to Aristotle's successors to take a different, thoroughly Aristotelian, response to the challenges posed by Epicurean and Stoic theories. They could have questioned their opponents' assumption that what is compositionally basic in the best scientific theory is metaphysically basic, the starting point of a properly unified and fully intelligible account of the world. Had they done so, they would not have needed to doubt any true theory proposed by their opponents about compositionally basic matter. Nor need they have been tempted to postulate apparently mysterious, pan-psychic matter. They would only have had to question the claim, promoted by physicalist metaphysicians (or of physicists speaking as metaphysicians), that the best metaphysical picture of all aspects of the world must begin with its compositionally basic material components, as presented in a comprehensive and complete physical theory. This assumption, although commonly shared, is non-trivial. The constraints on the best metaphysical and compositional theories need not be the same.[30]

However, whatever the merits and problems of this alternative line of response, it was not, it seems, the one which Andronicus, Alexander, or Galen preferred. The concessions they made to the first challenge proved, as we shall see, important ones with major consequences.

---

[29] For a 20th-century version of this viewpoint, see Husserl (1970: 60ff).
[30] For further discussion of the approach in the last two paragraphs, see Charles (2021: 81ff, 272–9, 282–6).

5.3 The Second Challenge: Plotinus, Priority, and the Call of Freedom

Plotinus spearheaded the second challenge. If the forms of natural bodies were to be defined as the formal or essential features or capacities of such bodies, they would, he thought, be essentially embodied or enmattered forms. But how, he then asked, could they be prior to bodies or to matter? If they are to be prior in this way, they must, in his view, be non-bodily, defined without essential reference in their definitions to bodies or matter. Aristotle was, in Plotinus' understanding, an impurist about form. But this was precisely why, for Plotinus, his project was doomed. There is no way to maintain a commitment to impurism while insisting on the priority of form over matter. Forms, Plotinus concluded, must be pure, as Riccardo Chiaradonna sets out in his contribution to this volume (Chapter 8).

Plotinus made one further, highly influential, move: priority in definition, or in being, had to be underwritten, in his view, by priority in existence: the soul, taken as a form, has to be capable of existing as an independent entity prior to, and independently of, the body. The relevant form, in his view, has to be pure, defined independently of the body, and—what is more—capable of existing without it, to be prior to the body and its matter. The soul, as he understood it, must be an independent entity of this type, defined without essential reference to the body if it is to be prior in definition to it.

Aristotle, as understood by impurist interpreters, was not attracted to either of these moves. On the contrary, he was, in their view, concerned to maintain that form, at least in the case of human beings, is prior in being (and in definition) to matter without requiring the form to be capable of independent existence. After all, some mathematical or geometrical entities can be prior in being (and definition) to others even though both sets of entities necessarily exist. Priority in being does not require independence in existence.[31] Further, Aristotle's forms, some suggest, can be prior in being (and in definition) to matter in a composite object because they are the teleological cause of the latter's presence and arrangement. If priority in being (and definition) tracks priority in this form of explanation, forms can be prior in being and in definition to the relevant matter even if neither can be defined without reference to the other. More generally, if forms are understood, in Aristotle's terms, as the activities (or actualities), and as such the teleological goals, of given material capacities, they will be prior in definition to those capacities, even if they are defined as activities which result from such capacities. Further, they will be prior in definition to matter defined as what is capable of such activity. The form, it is

---

[31] As Peramatzis (2011: part 2, chs. 8–13) has argued.

claimed, can retain its status as a principle, or cause, even if it is defined as a principle of matter.[32]

Plotinus was not motivated solely by considerations of definitional priority. He had further reasons for regarding our intellectual soul, and its operations, as pure. He held that we have a genuine experience of its pure thought-activity (at least if we are philosophers). Indeed, when we have direct knowledge of its distinctive activity, we have knowledge of (at least some part of) what we really are. Further, he (like Alexander) focused on the question of what is required of subjects if they are to be free agents. To be agents of this type, we need, in his view, to engage in a distinctive activity of self-making and self-understanding. When we do so, our intellects are in complete control of a distinctive type of activity in which we create ourselves, or at least the best version of ourselves. Self-making of this kind is, Plotinus thought, not the type of activity which anything bodily can do. No bodies can, in his view, engage in self-reflective and self-creative activity. The type of intellect required, he concluded, cannot be essentially bodily or enmattered if it is to be capable of reflecting on and controlling our activities in this way. The requirements of freedom, as he understood them, led him to regard the controlling aspects of our souls as possessed of features inconsistent with their being essentially enmattered forms. These have to be definitionally pure, defined independently of bodies or matter, to make space for human freedom. On this point there was a measure of agreement between Plotinus and Alexander. For both, human freedom required our souls, or some parts of them, to be pure, defined without explicit reference to anything bodily. If we are to be free, at least parts of our souls must be essentially non-bodily.

Plotinus' account of the intellect gave rise to its own problems: how to account for the rest of our nature and, in particular, the influence our intellect has on our bodily states, emotions, and actions? This question was pressing because he was attracted, and with good reason, to the Aristotelian idea that human beings are composite and that intellect alone does not suffice to account for all our states and activities. Something must be added. But what? And how, given any such addition, to make sense of the idea of the soul as a properly unified entity? Pauliina Remes (Chapter 9) and Riccardo Chiaradonna address these issues in their contributions.

Remes considers two possible Plotinian answers. In one, what is added is not a body with distinctively material states but an intelligible principle (or *logos*) which accounts for the body's features. The principle in question is, on this view, itself an activity of the soul (6.7.5.3–4). So understood, our bodies and bodily features are, in some way, the 'images' of, or approximations to, a completely formal, non-bodily reality (see 6.7.5.14–15). If this was Plotinus' view, he transformed

---

[32] Priority in definition (so understood) is a different notion from that of independence in definition. A and B can be interdependent in definition even if A is definitionally prior to B. For further discussion of these and other options, see Charles (2021: 81–6, 246ff).

Aristotle's hylomorphic account by taking our bodies to be, in some way, a reflection of our essentially non-bodily intellects. Apparently embodied states, like anger or perception, are best defined as lower level intellects at differing levels of reality. Our bodies are reflections of such intellects (as some say our faces are reflections of our souls). The soul-body relation is, as Chiaradonna suggests, replaced by a soul-soul relation between differing types of intellect and their reflections or images at differing levels of reality. However, if this was Plotinus' picture, it comes at a high cost: it requires him to define our emotional states and actions without explicit reference to the body. Anger, fear, perception, desire, and action will have to be defined in the purist way. What, an Aristotelian might ask, is the distinctive type of state required and how does it play the causal role demanded of it? How to make sense of the idea of purely bodily aspects as 'images' of our lower level intellects?

There was, as Pauliina Remes notes, a less radical alternative. Perhaps, for Plotinus, the features of the human soul involved in perception and action are essentially embodied and the subject of such states is a composite of body and soul. Even if the soul provides the powers of judgement, it must have something else—the relevant bodily sense-affection—to judge: to serve as the content of its perceptual judgements. Even if our perceptions essentially involve the critical abilities of the rational intellect, they may also require, as part of their natures, the existence of a body of a certain kind and the sense-affections that only such a body can deliver. Perception may now be defined as the judging of bodily affections of this type: an essentially embodied type of activity. In place of a compound defined by varying types of intellect, we have a recognizably hylomorphic compound defined with essential reference to some genuinely material states. The question then is: how does the intellect itself interact with material parts of the compound in perceiving and acting? How does something which is essentially non-bodily causally interact with the essentially embodied features of the soul? What makes the resulting soul a unity? Plotinus, even on this second alternative, still needs to reconcile his views about the intellect with a more orthodox Aristotelian understanding of humans as essentially hylomorphic compounds.

Plotinus' own viewpoint, as we have seen, created its own difficulties and internal tensions. His challenge exercised later Aristotelians who were sympathetic to his views about the intellect but, nonetheless, wished to retain central aspects of Aristotle's hylomorphism.

5.4 Aristotelian Responses to Plotinus' Challenge: Philoponus, Pseudo-Simplicius, Avicenna, and Averroes

Plotinus' insistence on the purity of form sprang in part (as we have seen) from his commitment to his account of freedom as self-creation. It remains, of course, a matter of debate whether he himself succeeded in describing, without incoherence, a self which creates itself in this way. (Mustn't the intellect itself be the subject of such thinking as well as its product?) However, even if he did devise a coherent story in which the intellect is simultaneously both agent and patient, why think that the possibility he imagined is a real one? If the human intellect is causally responsible for bodily movements, can it really be essentially non-bodily? How can this part of the human soul be something non-bodily and the cause and controller of essentially bodily processes?

Plotinus, for his part, responded to these questions by challenging Aristotle's account of movement and its causes. In his view, only a pure form, or incorporeal principle, could be a genuine first cause of bodily actions. A proper account of human activity required the initiating power of an incorporeal soul, something which acts in virtue of what is (see VI.3.22–3). Aristotle's essentially enmattered forms were incapable of playing this fundamental role (even if they could be moved movers of certain types of movement). To defend his account, Plotinus needed to explain how incorporeal and unextended principles can act on extended and material bodies. Did he, one might wonder, develop—or could he have developed—an account of causation and activity adequate to this task?

For impurist interpreters of Aristotle, by contrast, Plotinus was misled by an ambitious thought experiment. He confused the idea of a pure soul, postulated to underpin his abstracted account of intellectual activity and self-creation, with what is genuinely possible, given the other roles the human soul has to play. His contention that a pure, essentially non-bodily self could play these roles could have been resisted by Aristotelians committed to the view of the human soul as essentially embodied. (Perhaps, for all we know, it was!)

Aristotle had, pre-emptively, offered the resources to address some aspects of Plotinus' challenge. He could accept that we entertain the view of the soul that Plotinus suggested but still claim that we can only do so if we abstract it from those bodily features which are essential to its nature and existence. Like the Platonists he criticized in *Physics*, one could say that Plotinus had engaged in a failed thought experiment. From this perspective, to think that our souls could exist, or be defined without essential reference to the body, is to imagine something that cannot really occur, given the essentially bodily nature of our soul, its essential dependence on perception, and its ability to cause bodily actions. Error results when we try to abstract in the way Plotinus or Platonists did (as Aristotle suggested in *Physics* 193b35). From this perspective, his challengers would have conflated, Aristotle might say, something abstracted—the Plotinian or Platonist *soul* defined without reference to the body—with the human soul which is essentially an enmattered cause of bodily movement and rest. The challenge for Plotinus, and for those who followed his lead, was to show that what they envisaged, and believed they experienced, was a real possibility, one that can be entertained without error about the nature of the human soul and its distinctive activities. The challenge for Aristotelians, by contrast, if they are to be consistent impurists, is to give an account of our intellectual activity, self-knowledge, and self-reflection consistent with a commitment to impurism. And that, clearly, is no small undertaking!

Philoponus and the philosopher we call 'pseudo-Simplicius' (whom I shall label 'Pseudo') adopted a more concessive line. They were attracted by Plotinus' idea that to be free we have to be self-aware, capable of rational attention. We have, in virtue of possessing our intellects, the ability to reflect on our actions and characters and change them through rational reflection alone. The intellect is, in their view, essentially non-bodily. No material body could, they agreed with Plotinus, have the powers it possesses.

Philoponus, as Sorabji shows (Chapter 10), viewed our other psychological capacities, such as perception and desire, as 'supervening' on a distinctive type of material blend suitable for the presence of such psychological capacities. However, he did not take this material blend to be sufficient to account for their presence. Nor were they the results of, or grounded in, those blends (as they were, in some way, for Alexander). In Philoponus' account of visual perception, by contrast:

[A] activities in the medium imprint colours on the relevant sense organ as a solid body; and
[B] the eye as the sense organ contracts and expands because of the activity of colours. When it is affected in this way, we discern colours.

[A] and [B] refer to distinct activities: there is the material impact on the sense organ as a solid body and another impact on the sense organ as an organ of sense. The former may be 'suitable' for the latter but it is not sufficient to account for it. In Philoponus' view, 'motions of [perceptual] soul are disposed together with mixtures of body... but are not generated by these mixtures', even though the soul 'comes to be present on [supervenes on] certain composition and proportionality of matter'.

There is a lively debate as to how he understood the perceptual discernment of colours and shapes. Sorabji has suggested that, for Philoponus, perception is a purely psychological activity, defined without explicit reference to matter or material change. He proposed what he calls a 'de-materialized', or pure, account of perception, even if perceptions always occur together with bodily mixtures.[33] Miira Tuominen, in Chapter 11 of the present volume, argues that the expansions and contractions in the sense organ required to discern colours and shapes are best defined as types of inextricably psycho-physical cognitive processes. There

[33] Sorabji (1991).

will be no definition of that type of cognition, for Philoponus, which does not refer to expansion and contraction of the *pneuma*, and no definition of those expansions and contractions which does not refer to perceptual discernment. Philoponus, in her view, retained a distinctively inextricabilist hylomorphic account of these processes while at the same time maintaining that the intellect is essentially non-bodily. That is: he held on to one aspect of Aristotelian hylomorphism (as understood by impurists) in his discussion of perception while embracing the Neoplatonist view of the intellect as essentially non-bodily.

Philoponus' account, on either interpretation, faces substantial challenges. Is the soul, in his view, a proper unity or a collection of different, definitionally independent parts? Has he, through his concessions to Plotinus, given up on the Aristotelian requirement that the soul be a genuine unity? Further, how does the intellect, as he understood it, causally interact with perception or desire, if the latter are essentially psycho-physical? Other Aristotelians unhappy with Philoponus' concessions could have pressed these concerns when considering Philoponus' compromises with Plotinus. Again, perhaps, for all we know, they did!

Philoponus made a further move. Psychological capacities, such as those for perceiving and desiring, are, in his view, inseparable from what he called a '*pneumatic* body', even if they are separable from a solid body. In the case of anger, he distinguished one type of desire for revenge defined without reference to the type of material bodies humans possess from human embodied anger which cannot be defined in this way. The former was, in his theory, anger in the *pneuma*: the type of anger which we might experience even after our material bodies have been destroyed and we await divine judgement and, perhaps, punishment.[34] If perceiving and desiring are inextricably psycho-physical, they belong to a special type of physical entity, the *pneumatic* body. Philoponus, in effect, introduced a new type of matter, *pneumatic* or spiritual matter, as the matter essentially involved in anger, desire, or perception. This was his way to combine impurism about perception with distinctive ideas about the type of matter involved. While he was, no doubt, partly motivated by his wish to underwrite his beliefs, as a Christian, in the possibility of divine judgement after the death of the body, he may also have taken the presence of this type of *pneumatic* body to be required to explain, in some way, how the intellect can affect and modify desire[35] Perhaps, in his view, the unity of the soul rested on the presence of this type of causal interaction between the intellect and the emotions or perception. While it is hard to track the exact trajectory of Philoponus' thought, he was clearly willing, in thinking about the self, to modify parts of the Aristotelian heritage, if necessary, to accommodate ideas drawn from Plotinus and other Neoplatonists.

---

[34] Philoponus *in De an.* 64.6-17.   [35] Philoponus *in De an.* 64.6-17.

Pseudo took a different tack. Perhaps influenced by the later Neoplatonist, Iamblichus, he thought of the operation of the intellect as at work, in some modified form, at all levels of soul. While he took the intellect itself to be separable from the body, he developed a complex and layered view of the other activities of the soul. In perception, Tuominen argues, there is an essentially psycho-physical change in the sense organs, a 'joint affection' or 'passive activity' in a living ensouled body that cannot be defined in purely material terms. The organ's sensitivity is due to the sensitive soul that gives the body a distinct kind of life that differs from that of plants, which are devoid of perception, and a purely intellectual being, living the life of the intellect alone. This psycho-physical change in the sense organ stimulates perceivers to project concepts such as that of whiteness onto objects in the world. In doing so, we are aware, as Ursula Coope has emphasized, of the activity of perceiving itself and of what we are doing when, stimulated in this way, we project concepts onto the world around us.[36] This is how we are aware of ourselves as perceivers of an objective world. This distinctive form of self-awareness, an activity which occurs in us as embodied perceivers, is not the same type of activity as that of the intellect acting by itself. Nonetheless, they are sufficiently similar for both to be species of intellectual activity, albeit with different features. This degree of similarity permitted Pseudo to underwrite the unity of the human soul more securely than in Philoponus' account, since it was not based only on two-way causal interaction between fundamentally distinct parts. Pseudo offered a possible ground for the unity of the self in terms of one type of intellectual activity found in varying ways in perception and in thought. He was looking for a distinctive response to the problem of the unity of the human soul which troubled Philoponus and Plotinus.

There is one further important aspect of Pseudo's account. In his view, perceiving is not a combination of a purely material activity in the sense organ and some pure thinking, understood as a second definitionally independent component. He retains, Tuominen suggests, the hylomorphic conception of perceiving as an inextricably psycho-physical activity to which he added a further ingredient: a type of intellectual awareness of the act of perceiving itself. He did not, she argues, analyse perception itself, as Descartes later did, in terms of a purely material act (or component) to which is added a second purely psychological act of pure thinking.

Avicenna's approach to the problems raised by Plotinus was radical and independent. In his view, the soul has immediate access to itself without any need for bodily experience—as he suggested in his famous 'flying man' thought experiment.[37] Indeed, on occasion he went so far as to suggest, as Peter Adamson notes (Chapter 12), that the soul is to be understood as the subject of self-awareness,

---

[36] Coope (2020).   [37] See also Adamson and Benevich (2018: 147–64).

the self, whose identity over time constitutes the diachronic identity of the person. The soul, so understood, can be defined by a single power: that of being aware of itself and what it is doing. We are, in this view, tacitly aware of all our cognitive activities and can through focused attention become actively aware of them. Thus, for example, when thinking about something, I can also become aware that I am thinking, simply by attending to my own thought process. The same goes for perception and imagination, action and nutrition. The presence of one potentially self-aware subject can serve to underwrite the unity of these differing powers. Our identity will consist in our being non-bodily subjects of awareness, souls capable of thinking of these capacities and their operations in this way.[38] However, as Adamson notes, this aspect of Avicenna's thought was in tension with his suggestion elsewhere that the human soul is to be defined in terms of powers or capacities to act, not as a subject aware of these capacities and activities.[39] For now the human soul is to be defined as a separately subsistent substance that projects powers onto the body, which it uses as an instrument, not as a set of essentially bodily powers or as a bodily activity (or way of being) as in standard hylomorphic accounts. Further, the capacities to perceive or take in food are treated as accidental to the human soul, defined as a subject of awareness, even though these capacities are essential to animal and plant souls. In these ways, Avicenna was going beyond the limits of hylomorphic analysis as he, and his interlocutors such as Abūl-Barakāt, saw.

Avicenna combined this account with a distinctive view of the matter of composite objects. There is in many plants and animals and in artefacts, he thought, matter suitable for the reception of a form as well as the form itself. However, the organic forms of plants and animals, unlike those of artefacts, do not arise solely from the causal interaction of their material constituents. They are produced when a form is imposed 'from outside' on parcels of suitable matter by the Active Intellect, which directs different types of form onto different types of matter.[40] Further, once the form is present, the Active Intellect is responsible for maintaining the matter's suitability to continue to receive it. For similar reasons, our existence as subjects of awareness is understood as dependent on the Active Intellect's (i) initially imposing a subject of this type on appropriate matter; and (ii) subsequently maintaining the relevant matter in a suitable condition. Neither our initial creation nor subsequent survival can be accounted for in terms of the emergence of subjects of awareness from matter. Both our souls and the organic forms of other animals and plants are to be explained 'from outside' on the basis of

---

[38] Avicenna's account of the self may be compared with that offered by Augustine in *On Free Choice of the Will*, book 2.
[39] For detailed discussion of Avicenna's account of the relation between our intellect and form, see Wisnovsky (2003).
[40] Avicenna, *Healing: Metaphysics* 9.5.4.

the activity of the Active Intellect which initially imposes them on suitable matter and subsequently sustains their presence.

Avicenna was able, using these resources, to combine a view of humans understood as simple, unified, non-bodily subjects of awareness with a view of matter as a dependent entity, defined as what is suitable for the imposition of subjects of awareness. However, his route to this conclusion had its own problems. When he attempted to spell out his account in appropriate detail, he revealed its radicalism and the extent to which it departed from Aristotle's. He required, as we have seen, the Active Intellect to be constantly at work, 'emanating' subjects of awareness and forms in the direction of suitable matter and sustaining them once imposed. It is, as it was for al-Fārābī, the 'giver of forms'. In rejecting the idea that such forms 'emerge from' matter, he was led to postulate an Intellect ceaselessly at work creating each individual living creature by transmitting individual pure entities through space in the direction of appropriately sized parcels of suitable matter (happily present, waiting to receive them) and subsequently maintaining each of them after they have been imposed on matter of this type. In these respects, his approach marked a major development, partially inspired by Plotinus' suggestions, of Aristotle's account of the role of the Active Intellect. In Avicenna's hands, Aristotle's claims were transformed in a way which captured the imagination of Islamic and Christian thinkers alike.

Averroes took a different view of human thinking, perhaps motivated by his desire to stay as close as he could to views he found in Aristotle. He was referred to as 'the Commentator', because of his deep knowledge of, and sympathy for, the views expressed in relevant Aristotelian texts.

Averroes, it has been recently argued, offered an 'impurist' account of perception and similar parts of the human soul as essentially involving enmattered forms.[41] If so, he—like Plotinus—understood Aristotle to take (at least these aspects of) the human form, that is the human soul, as essentially enmattered. Further, Averroes was aware of the need to maintain the unity of the human form, not to divide the soul into two definitionally independent parts, one essentially enmattered, the other—the part required for thinking of a type we share with the gods—essentially non-enmattered.

Averroes' response to this challenge was distinctive. As Stephen Ogden (Chapter 13) shows, instead of seeking a place for thought in his account of perception (as Philoponus and Pseudo had done) or relying on two-way causal interaction between pure thought and impure perception, Averroes, strictly speaking, denied that humans engage in the type of thinking enjoyed by the Active Intellect or, most importantly, the 'Material/Potential' Intellect (sometimes called the Passive Intellect), which, in Averroes' view, no longer belongs as an

---

[41] See di Giovanni (2011: 175–94 and 2019).

individual capacity of each human being but rather shares the same, singular, eternal, and existentially separate existence enjoyed by the Active Intellect. The Material Intellect, like the Active Intellect, is one and the same for all human beings. While we are causally connected to an intelligible world permeated by the Material and Active Intellects, we are not ourselves capable of their type of thinking. No part of the human soul is immortal or essentially non-material. At most, humans receive (in some distinctive and fallible way) the causal impact of a more powerful, and fundamentally different, type of intellect, which does not belong specifically to any of them as individuals. Human thinking is a kind of approximation to that of the Material Intellect, the best mortal, embodied creatures such as we can achieve. Averroes sees the human soul as a unity, unencumbered with an essentially immaterial part which we share with the Active Intellect. Our thinking is a distinctive type of intellectual activity (*thinking*) available to us as essentially embodied organisms.

Averroes' views about the Active and Material Intellect attracted, as Ogden emphasizes, a storm of criticism, mainly because he denied that there is a distinct material intellect in each of us as a distinct power of our human souls. However, his basic suggestion about the distinctive nature of human thinking has its roots in Aristotle's own writings. Aristotle, on occasion wrote of our thinking as being like, but not the same as or as good as, that of the gods or of the Active Intellect.[42] Human thinking, in Aristotle's view, is necessarily based on perception and imagination, while divine thinking is not. While the Active Intellect can think without stopping, we cannot. Even if we are capable, as Aristotle suggests in an optimistic mode, of thinking of everything, we may not do so in the same way as the Active Intellect. Human thinking is always the realization of a capacity which, in our case, cannot operate without embodied capacities for perception and imagination. As such, it will necessarily be an embodied form of cognition: it has to be such if it is to be sensitive to input from perception or result in bodily action. All human cognitive capacities are, at very least, necessarily embodied even if only some are defined as essentially such. In this respect our thinking differs from that of the Active Intellect. But, perhaps Aristotle went further, regarding human thinking (unlike its divine counterpart) as an essentially embodied form of cognition, the realization of an embodied capacity. Aristotle's own remarks about human thinking are cautious and telegrammatic, admitting of at least the two interpretations just sketched. Either way, even if thinking itself is neither necessarily nor essentially embodied, *human* thinking, unlike that of the gods, may be necessarily or even essentially a type of embodied cognition.

Averroes did, however, make two radical additional moves. The first was, as Ogden suggests, to claim that humans do not, strictly speaking, think at all. He

---

[42] See, for example, *NE* X.1178b25ff; *De An.* Γ.5, 430a22f; *Meta.* Λ.9, 1074b17ff.

could, had he been more cautious, have confined himself to the weaker, and perhaps more easily defended, claim that we think in a way different from the Active Intellect. (Indeed, this may be what he intended in his talk of a type of 'cogitation' which individual humans as such possess. Maybe, at this point, he was suggesting only that these two kinds of thinking are analogous but not identical, even if—as he held—we share in both.) Second, while he had further arguments for externalizing the Material Intellect, treating it as part of the external intelligible world, it could—consistently with Aristotle's circumspect (and, it must be ceded, somewhat elusive remarks in De Anima 3.5 and elsewhere)—have been treated as a feature of human minds, capturing the way in which our intellects are impacted by the presence of an intelligible world. In any event, Averroes was clearly willing, for a variety of reasons, to sail in waters far beyond those Aristotle had charted.

6. The Next Moves: Aquinas and Suárez—Some of the Christian Medievals

Aquinas, like Philoponus, Avicenna, and possibly Averroes, held that thinking, whether human or divine, is to be defined without essential reference in its definition to bodily states or composites, made up of body and soul. Further, he rejected Averroes' suggestion that humans were not capable of thinking of this type. Indeed, he took thinking, so specified, to be a defining operation of our rational soul which, in his view, constituted a central aspect of our human form. On this basis, he concluded that our form, or at least our intellectual soul, has to be defined purely, without essential reference to any bodily states.

Aquinas' account, at first approximation, resembles Philoponus' and faces similar challenges. What is the connection between our intellect, so understood, and our capacity to perceive or desire? In Aquinas' account, the latter seem to be essentially embodied capacities.[43] What then makes the soul of a living, functioning human, if it contains the intellect, a unity rather than a collection of definitionally distinct parts? Further, how does the intellect, defined without essential reference to bodily states, causally interact with perception and desire, if they are essentially bodily states? Or again: how does the rational soul, as Aquinas conceived it, come to be present in material bodies?

Did Aquinas fare better than Philoponus in answering these questions? Or did he simply accept as a basic datum, as Philoponus may have done, that different parts of a unified human soul, some essential, some non-essential, somehow come to be present in the same body and causally interact in just the way required to

---

[43] For further discussion of this issue, see Haldane (1983: 233–9); and Lisska (2016).

account for characteristic human functioning? And, if so, what view of efficient causation did he presuppose?[44]

Whatever Aquinas' answers to these questions may have been, he made two further moves which proved influential. He rejected the idea, suggested by some of Alexander's formulations, that the human soul is best defined in terms of capacities (or states). Our rational soul, in Aquinas' view, is an activity not a capacity or state. (Aquinas took over Albertus Magnus' translation of 'energeia' and 'entelecheia' as activity (*actus*).) Further, he, like Philoponus and Avicenna, believed that each of us has a particular intellect which will survive the death of our body and persist as the individual it is (until, at least, the final resurrection of the body at the Day of Judgement). In his view, we each have a particular intellect which is not the actuality of any bodily capacity—even though the rational soul of a human being is, in some way, essentially tied to the body. In any event, our souls, as individual forms, are distinct from one another. And each of us is always distinct in at least this way too.

Particular forms played a prominent role in Aquinas' thought. Forms, in his view as in Avicenna's, should account not only for the unity of each of us but also for our distinctness: what makes one of us different from any other. While the existence of souls of this type may have been required to underwrite Aquinas' religious convictions, he made great efforts to develop an independent philosophical account of their nature and ontological status. If our souls are subjects which think and can persist and journey when free of the body, what type of entity are they? Are they, for example, substances? And, if so, of what kind?

Aquinas developed his answers to these questions in Aristotelian terms, describing particular forms as *thises* (*hoc aliquid*) and thinking of them, to use Christopher Shields' helpful terminology (Chapter 14), as determinate individuals. In his view, they were a distinctive type of determinate individual, not to be identified with composite particular substances which are essentially members of species. Particular forms, by contrast, can be identified without reference to any species or genus. Each of us can refer to our individual rational souls without describing them as members of a species. This is how I refer to myself as 'I'. If particular forms and composites are both substances, they fall (as Shields puts it) under different types of 'substantial sortal concepts'. Metaphysically speaking, the identity of individual souls will be prior to the species to which the composites they inform belong. Aquinas displayed (as Shields notes) great caution in developing his account, emphasizing differences between these types of substance while offering less by way of a positive theory of the type of determinate individuals' particular forms (or individual souls) are. In finding a place for the individual

---

[44] For further discussion of these and related issues, see Rapp (2003).

souls his theory required, he presented them as determinate individual forms, which, if they were substances, were so in a distinctive way.

Aquinas' thinking resembles that of earlier writers who defined matter as what is suitable for the imposition of forms: as what is potentially informed. It was, in Aquinas' view, to be defined in terms of potentiality for form. In this way, like Philoponus and Avicenna, he combined purism about the intellectual basis of the soul with a view of matter as what is essentially apt to receive the relevant forms.

Aquinas' views about forms as determinate individuals brought a further problem into sharp focus. Assume that a statue is a completed object made from one piece of bronze. This piece of bronze is also something which can, it seems, be identified (and referred to) prior to the formation of the statue. Indeed, it seems to have as much claim to be a determinate individual object as do particular forms themselves. It is an object, not simply a quantity of stuff. Further, if the bronze in question is something which persists through time and is present when the statue is made, there will be three distinct determinate objects present in this case: the completed statue, its particular form, and the piece of bronze. However, this result raises a pressing question: how many determinate particulars can be present in the same place at the same time? Can there be more than one at any place at the same time? How are these different objects connected? Or did this piece of bronze somehow go out of existence once the statue was formed? What type of unity is the statue itself?

These difficulties were acute given Aquinas' willingness to accept particular forms as determinate individual objects. Nor could he deny that this piece of bronze is a determinate object. After all, like particular forms, it can be picked out and referred to as an individual. In relaxing his conditions for being a determinate object, Aquinas opened up the possibility of there being (at least) two determinate objects present as distinct components of the completed statue: the particular form and a particular piece of matter. Is this an acceptable result? How are the two components of the statue related? Does this problem generalize to natural substances? Or did the matter in their case fail, for some reason, to be a determinate individual object? (Aristotle expressed severe doubts about the possibility of an actual substance being made up of actual substances: *Meta.* Z.13, 1039a3–5). These problems continue to trouble those who think of individual forms as determinate particulars present in the composite object. (For a recent discussion of this problem, see Kathrin Koslicki's illuminating remarks.)[45]

Suárez, who engaged in depth with Aquinas' thought, embraced certain aspects of his approach and developed others with great clarity. In his view, particular forms, including our individual souls, are determinate objects which cause our matter to be the way it is. Forms must be objects capable of being causes of this

---

[45] Koslicki (2018).

kind. Our souls are not just objects of reference but, as Dominik Perler emphasizes (Chapter 15), makers and doers. Nor are they to be identified with capacities or even states (such as being capable). Instead, they are themselves subjects which use and can modify these capacities and come to possess the relevant states. They are, in his view, aware of the presence and activity of our capacities and can direct them. Further, since they can exist without our bodies, they must be definable without essential reference to matter, even though they are robust, causally active objects capable of bringing about changes in the material world. This is, in Suárez' view, the type of determinate individual objects our souls are. He also applied this line of thinking not just to human forms but also to those of animals, tables, statues, natural substances, and artefacts. There are particular forms in all these cases.

Suárez differed from Aquinas with regard to matter. He thought that the matter present in all composite objects, like that of the statue, was also a distinct object, capable of being defined without essential reference to the relevant form. God could have created this matter without at the same time creating our forms. He required two separate acts to make our matter and to inform it in the way it is informed. In Suárez' view, matter can actually exist by itself, without needing anything else to exist. For him, as for Ockham, it is an entity on its own. It is not defined, as it was for Thomas, in terms solely of its potential for form.

Our matter and our form are, for Suárez, two distinct, particular objects, separate components (or parts) of a completed whole substance, each capable of playing its own causal role. As he put it: 'matter and form are distinguished from each other as a thing from a thing [*tamquam res a re*]' (*DM* 13.4.5). Suárez, as Dominik Perler notes, interpreted these parts of the composite substance as really distinct. The problem which arose for Aquinas with regard to the statue and its bronze has been generalized. It now applies to any composite substance made up of particular form and matter. How many objects (*res*) are present and how are they combined? In what way are form and matter parts of a composite whole?

Suárez looked hard for answers. The two components are 'tied together' in some distinctive way to form a composite whole. As in the Stoic account, they causally interact in complex ways, even though (for him, unlike for the Stoics) the soul itself was not a body. He further developed a complex account, as Dominik Perler shows, of the causal interactions between our souls and their capacities, both natural and acquired. Composite substances are made up of a number of distinct components (forms, matter, capacities, and habits) which stand in complex and distinctive causal relations. Substances are wholes composed in these ways out of many distinct entities. In his view, as Perler notes, the task of a comprehensive metaphysical theory is to spell out what these entities are and how they are interconnected. And, as for the Stoics, one of his major problems was to define the required type of causal connections between the form and its matter in properly unified substances in an informative, non-circular, way.

7. Two Challenges Combined: The Emergence of Dualism

Descartes was a critic of substantial forms. He wrote:

> To prevent any ambiguity of expression, it must be observed that when we deny substantial forms, we mean by the expression a certain substance joined to matter, making up with it a merely corporeal whole, and which, no less than matter and even more than matter—since it is called an actuality and matter only a potentiality—is a true substance, or self-subsistent thing.[46]

In this passage, as Perler points out, Descartes embraces two theses. The first, an independence thesis, stresses that a substantial form, though present in matter, is not dependent on matter and can exist apart from it. The second, which might be called the composition thesis, emphasizes that the form-matter relation is a relation between two distinct parts or components. While these two parts have different characteristic features, one of them being actual and the other potential, they are nevertheless distinct parts that make together a whole.

Descartes opposed the view that there are substantial forms present in all natural substances. Nor did he accept that matter was in some way secondary. He believed (or at least envisaged the possibility) that matter was in the case of rocks, trees, and even non-human animals best defined independently of substantial form. It was in principle possible to define rocks, trees, and animals in terms of their material components and their purely material arrangement. Although he did not complete *Principles* V and VI, his goal seems clear. Either there are no Aristotelian natural kinds of metal or animal or, alternatively, these are derived kinds, based on differences in kinds of matter (marked out using differences in shape, move-ability, and extension). Similarly, for their substantial forms: either there is no such thing or they are derived phenomena, based on differences in kinds of matter and material interaction (defined without reference to substantial form). In neither way can they be metaphysically primary or basic. Descartes, in effect, seems committed to there being a complete upwards story for material or bodily components in terms of their material components and interactions. This perspective was one he shared with some of earlier writers such as the Epicureans and (perhaps) Galen.

The science of matter extended, in his view, as far as our bodies and the matter that makes them up. These too can be defined, Descartes held, in terms of their matter and material interactions. Our bodies are material entities defined without reference to our substantial forms as thinking, perceiving creatures. They can even be present when we are no longer capable of these activities. They are, in Suárez'

---

[46] Descartes, 'Letter to Regius', January 1642 (AT III, 502; CSMK III, 207).

terminology objects (*res*) in their own right. Descartes took our bodies to be substances whose existence and definition are independent of our souls and combined this commitment with a view of human souls which emphasized features which earlier writers had also discussed.

(1) Like Suárez, he thought of the soul as an object not as a capacity or an activity. It is the subject of thought or awareness not the capacity for these activities nor the activities themselves. Nor is it the way we are when we are capable of awareness or thought. It, as well as our body, is a thing in its own right. Perhaps, as for Suárez, the soul needed to be a thing to be a cause of changes in the world.

(2) Like Avicenna, Descartes took human souls to be primarily defined as thinking subjects—where being such a subject can be defined without essential reference to our bodies or matter more generally. Further, being such a thinker requires the relevant subject to be, and to be defined, in ways in which no body or material object could be. Our souls are capable for example of self-clarification and self-understanding. As such they are to be defined in terms of our possession of powers which no body, as he understood bodies, could have. This is why they are essentially distinct from bodies and can survive the destruction of the relevant body.

(3) Like Pseudo, Descartes took thinking to be present in many of our characteristic activities such as perception. Our perception of bodies, in his view, is due 'neither to our senses nor to our imagination but solely to the understanding' (*Meditations* 2). Seeing a body, he writes, is not to be distinguished from thinking one sees it. Thinking is not confined to one aspect of our psychological lives but permeates perception and desire.

Against this background, Descartes defined the human soul as an independent thing (*res*) with essential features that cannot be grounded in bodies or matter. It is essentially a separate thinking substance.

Descartes, so understood, combined a commitment to, and optimism about, an independent upwards material story resulting in a definition of our bodies as distinct substances with the conviction that our souls are separate substances, defined without reference to bodies and possessed of features which no material object could possess. While he shared this optimism with several earlier writers, including Suárez, who were also sceptical about Aristotle's account of matter, his second claim combined the ideas of those who, again like Suárez, thought of the soul as an object of some kind, with that of those who defined it in terms of features (such as self-reflection or self-awareness) that no material body could possess. Body and soul are definitionally and existentially independent substances, neither metaphysically more basic than the other. We have arrived at substance dualism.

Descartes' approach to Aristotle's hylomorphism was, in large measure, foreshadowed by writers who had sought to modify Aristotle's picture to meet the major challenges it faced. Alexander and later Suárez attempted to show that Aristotelianism could accommodate the richer and more detailed upwards, matter-based, explanatory story which had been developed by Aristotle's early critics, such as the Stoics and Epicureans. Later commentators, Neoplatonist, Islamic, and Christian alike, attempted, in their differing ways, to find space within a recognizably Aristotelian framework for the presence of aspects of thought, such as self-reflection, which they—like Plotinus—thought could not be attributed to essentially embodied subjects. In responding to these challenges, Aristotelians had, in effect, made moves which threatened the stability and coherence of Aristotle's original theory. Suárez made concessions to both challenges, seeing humans as made up of two independent entities, one definable in material terms, the other as an essentially non-embodied subject of awareness. In the case of human beings, Descartes saw no reason to refrain from calling either of these two distinct components 'substances'. Nor did he think that either component was definitionally dependent on the other. Substance dualism represented a small step, in the case of ensouled bodies, beyond Suárez' own version of hylomorphism. Given the earlier development of two component thinking within the hylomorphic tradition, Descartes had only to make two comparatively minor moves to generate his version of substance dualism. In his account, as in Suárez', human souls are to be defined without essential reference to our bodies, and our bodies are to be defined without essential reference to our souls. Both can be accredited with the title 'substance'. Neither is definitionally prior to the other.

Descartes, however, was acutely aware, as Lilli Alanen points out (Chapter 16), of the problems posed by his account. In thinking of us as a combination of two definitionally independent components, he had, from an Aristotelian viewpoint, endangered the unity of the composite they make up.[47] Descartes himself accepted that we are experientially aware of a 'union' between mind and body, which he described as 'substantial union', a thing in itself (as opposed to an accidental aggregate of parts). Even if he did not accord the resulting union the status of a substance, it was, in his view, possessed of its own 'real and immutable nature', even though, as he conceded, we are not 'capable of conceiving very distinctly and at the same time both the distinction between the soul and the body and their union, for to do this one would have to conceive it as one single thing and at the same time as two which is self-contradictory' (as he wrote to Elisabeth in June 1643).

---

[47] In addition, he was required to think of body and soul as causally interacting with one another, even though they are fundamentally different types of entity. Further, he had to account for the co-presence of souls, which are essentially non-bodily, with bodies with which they interact. Given that souls, with their distinctive natures, cannot emerge from, or be grounded in, material bodies, who, or what, is responsible for their presence at just the right time and place to interact with such bodies?

Descartes' aim, Alanen shows, was to retain from the traditional hylomorphic doctrine the prephilosophical experience of unified mind-body subjects, while rejecting the Aristotelian metaphysical structure that grounds it. What is perceived and thought of as one subject is, in Descartes' view, not a fictive unity but a real being, whose complex nature cannot be reduced to that of its parts. Thus, for example, the passions of the mind were, in his view, to be identified with actions in the body of whose identity we were clearly aware. However, elsewhere, when he described these very passions as states caused by the body but controlled by the mind, he appears to presuppose his own dualist metaphysics. His own position may constitute, as Alanen concludes, an unstable compromise between ultimately incompatible claims. He wished to retain the idea of a real union of mind and body in a unified composite substance while at the same time adopting a substance dualist ontology which threatens to undermine the possibility of a union of this type.

What was Descartes' own attitude to this problem? It is not sufficient to say, as he did, that we have a clear but not distinct idea of the mind-body union. After all, what justifies his confidence that there is a real union at all? And, if there is one, how is its existence compatible with his dualist metaphysics? Perhaps, as Lilli Alanen suggests, he was serious in his advice to Elisabeth: we should worry less about the metaphysics of human nature and pay more attention to our actions and passions, to what we learn from daily experience and serious conversation with fellow human beings. Was he inclined to take the unity of the soul and body as basic, as a more fundamental feature of reality than the results of his own metaphysical arguments? In any event, as Lilli Alanen concludes, it is hard to see that Descartes himself achieved a stable position in reflecting on these issues.

Descartes paved the way for many of his successors. Spinoza, as Alanen points out, combined a rigorous form of substance monism, in which any action in the mind is at the same time an action in the body, and any passion in the body is also a passion in the mind, with a form of attribute dualism.[48] Although there were not two distinct substances present in the human composite, there were nonetheless distinct types of property, some mental, some physical, defined without reference to each other. The two definitionally distinct components were properties which belonged to a distinctive type of substance, itself neither mental nor physical.

Hume, by contrast, less concerned with the underlying metaphysics, talked freely of 'mind or body, whatever you want to call it'.[49] However, he retained a strict methodological dualism in his 'anatomy' of the ideas of the human mind, leaving the physiology to the scientists of nature. Both Hume's and Spinoza's modified forms of dualism were, as Alanen notes, anticipated by elements in Descartes' own doctrine. Further, both needed to account for the way in which

---

[48] *Ethics*, part 3, scholium to proposition 2. [49] *Treatise on Human Nature*.

physical properties give rise to mental ones. In their differing ways, they engaged with the problems set by Descartes while remaining in the grip of two component thinking about the issues at stake.

8. How Far Have We Travelled? Some General Remarks and a Personal Overview

Aristotle's version of hylomorphism was, as we have seen, interpreted and reinterpreted by critics and defenders alike. This process took centuries, as subsequent writers, from the Stoics to Aquinas and Suárez, considered problems within hylomorphism itself and raised, or attempted to respond to, objections to its central claims. Some were led, as we have seen, to define some or all psychological phenomena without explicit reference to specific material components and to define the latter without reference to their psychological role. In doing so, they formulated the two component account of material substances which paved the way for Descartes to raise his mind-body problem in the form which still perplexes us. In effect, they set up the version of hylomorphism with which we are now most familiar.

To what extent was Aristotle's hylomorphism transformed in this process?

The answer will, as I have already noted, depend on one's assessment of Aristotle's own position. For some he was himself a two component theorist as just defined. From this perspective, the major changes were those that led Descartes and Suárez to understand the two components as distinct things (*res*) or substances which causally interact with each other. These later philosophers were motivated, it seems, by the thought that only things of this type can be causes, a view earlier developed by the Stoics. The soul, as they understood it, could not be a capacity or a state (such as being capable of various activities) if it was to be the efficient cause of actions or bodily changes. It had to be *reified* as an object (or substance). The body too, they thought, had to be a distinct thing if it was to be a cause. Both definitionally independent components were distinct substances, each with its own causal role. They stood in external causal relations with each other.

There was a further change. The soul, as a substance, was not merely defined independently of the material body: it could continue to exist without it. Both Suárez and Descartes had theological reasons for thinking of the soul as capable of surviving the death of the body. It was existentially as well as definitionally independent of the body. Further, in their view, the soul had essential features, such self-consciousness, which no material body could possess. It was not simply that the soul was defined without explicit reference to the body. It had to be defined, as it had been for Plotinus, by reference to features which could not belong to any material body.

There were, in addition, changes with regard to the material component. The body was not simply defined in terms which did not refer to the soul. It was defined in terms, such as being extended, which (in their view) no soul could possess. It was not just definitionally independent of the other component. It was defined as a distinct object possessed of essential features inconsistent with its being a soul. Nothing could be both a soul and a body.

For others, myself included, the changes at issue were far more radical. Aristotle, in this view, thought that neither matter nor form could be defined independently of each other. His project was to hold fast to an 'inextricabilist viewpoint' while maintaining the definitional priority of form and a defensible view of matter. From this perspective, his theory was fundamentally reshaped in the period we have studied. His original account did not contain either of the two definitionally distinct components which many later thinkers, in their differing ways, came to accept. Instead, he was committed to the following claims:

[1] Emotions, desire, perception, and human thinking are defined as inextricably psycho-physical activities, not definable by decomposition into two separately defined types of phenomena, one purely psychological, the other purely physical; [Psycho-Physical Inextricability]

[2] The preferred ontology takes as basic activities, processes, natural substances, and capacities;

[3] There are general or determinable types of material or physical phenomena that can be made determinate in psycho-physical ways; and

[4] Metaphysical explanation is not reducible to explanation in terms of basic purely physical components.

From this perspective, the development of the two component version of hylomorphism transformed Aristotle's own view. By the end of its second millennium, it was no longer an account devised to counteract two component features in Platonic thinking. In response to the two challenges we have isolated, it had been remoulded to constitute a version of the two component picture it was initially constructed to oppose. In seeking to address these challenges, defenders of Aristotelian hylomorphism reformulated his view in terms with which we are now most familiar: one in which form (or structure) is defined without explicit reference to specific material components and the relevant matter is defined without reference to that form (or structure).

The challenges which Aristotelians faced were, of course, real and difficult ones. However, as I have suggested, they might have been addressed without surrendering the central inextricabilist claim [1]. Further, in making the concessions they did, later Aristotelians played a major role in setting up a series of problems, of which Descartes' mind-body problem is the star example, which have proved to be, as formulated, insoluble. Had they held fast to [1] and invoked the other resources that Aristotle himself developed (set out as [2]–[4] above), they could, and indeed should, have rejected the conception of matter and form as independently defined phenomena (in the best metaphysical theory) that generates these intractable issues. From that perspective, Descartes' mind-body problem is not properly set up, a pseudo-problem. It rests on two component assumptions about the nature of the psychological and the physical which they could with good reason have regarded as unwarranted, indeed mistaken.[50]

Modern Aristotelian hylomorphists, however, have generally adopted the two component way of thinking about individual material substances as composed of form (or structure) and material components, defined independently of each other. Form, in their view, can be understood as an irreducible feature or object which supervenes on or emerges from a set of material components, defined independently of the form (or structure) in question. There are, in this account, two definitionally distinct components, one material, one formal or structural, which together (in some way) compose material substances. In recent years, this style of account has been revived and articulated in different ways by several philosophers, including David Wiggins, Kit Fine, Kathrin Koslicki, and Mark Johnston. Indeed, many recent writers, from Hilary Putnam and Bernard Williams onwards, have examined how far this two component account offers a way to address, and perhaps even resolve, Descartes' mind-body problem.

At this point, the reader faces two major questions, one primarily historical, the second straightforwardly philosophical:

(1) Is the prevailing two component account of hylomorphism an accurate representation of Aristotle's own view or a major distortion of it? Are we, in fact, closer to Aristotle's own viewpoint when we seek to undermine, or 'deconstruct', Descartes' mind-body problem by challenging the assumptions about matter and form that generated it? Or should we search in Aristotle's writings for a constructive solution to that problem?
(2) Does the inextricabilist version of hylomorphism, independently of questions about its historical credentials, offer a better way to think of natural substances, humans included, than the now standard two component account? Can we now, in good philosophical conscience, take the inextricabilist claims, as set out in [A]–[D] above, as the basis of a distinct and defensible account of these phenomena?

While this collection of essays focuses on the first question, an examination of the early development of the hylomorphic tradition from Aristotle onwards may also help to raise the second question in a tractable form.

---

[50] For further discussion of this approach, see Charles (2021: 254–86).

It is now your task, as readers, to think through for yourselves the best answers to these questions.[51]

Bibliography

Adamson, Peter and Benevich, Fedor (2018), 'The Thought Experimental Method: Avicenna's Flying Man Argument', *Journal of the American Philosophical Association* 4 (2): 147–64

Balme, David (1987), 'The Snub' in A. Gotthelf and J. Lennox, eds., *Philosophical Issues in Aristotle's Biology*, Cambridge, 306–12

Barnes, Jonathan (2010), 'The Opinion of Aristotle Concerning Destiny and What is Up to Us' in J. Cottingham and P. Hacker, eds., *Mind, Method and Morality: Essays in Honour of Anthony Kenny*, Oxford, 26–45

Beere, Jonathan (2009), *Doing and Being: An Interpretation of Aristotle's Metaphysics Theta*, Oxford

Bolton, Robert (1978), 'Aristotle's Definitions of the Soul: *De Anima* II, 1–3', *Phronesis* 23 (3): 258–78

Burnyeat, Myles (1992), 'Is an Aristotelian Philosophy of Mind Still Credible?' in M. Nussbaum and A. Rorty, eds., *Essays on De Anima*, Oxford, 422–34

Caston, Victor (2005), 'The Spirit and the Letter: Aristotle on Perception', in R. Salles, ed., *Metaphysics, Soul and Ethics in Ancient Thought*, Oxford, 245–320

Caston, Victor (2008), 'Commentary on Charles', *Proceedings of the Boston Area Colloquium* 24 (1): 30–49

Charles, David (1984), *Aristotle's Philosophy of Action*, London

Charles, David (1988), 'Aristotle on Hypothetical Necessity and Irreducibility', *Pacific Philosophical Quarterly* 69: 1–53

Charles, David (2008), 'Aristotle's Psychological Theory', *Proceedings of the Boston Area Colloquium* 24 (1): 1–29

Charles, David (2021), *The Undivided Self: Aristotle and the 'Mind-Body Problem'*, Oxford

Coope, Ursula (2020), *Freedom and Responsibility in Neoplatonist Thought*, Oxford

Devereux, Daniel (2010), 'Aristotle on the Form and Definition of a Human Being in *Metaphysics* Z.10 and 11', *Proceedings of the Boston Area Colloquium* 26 (1): 167–96

Di Giovanni, Matteo (2011), 'Substantial Form in Averroes's Long Commentary on the *Metaphysics*', in P. Adamson, ed., *In the Age of Averroes: Arabic Philosophy in the Sixth/Twelfth Century*, London, 175–94

---

[51] I should like to thank the contributors to this volume for their comments and advice on many of the topics discussed in this essay. I have also gained considerably from written comments by Michail Peramatzis, Bryan Reece, and two anonymous OUP readers.

Di Giovanni, Matteo (2019), *Averroes, Philosopher of Islam*, Cambridge

Frede, Michael (1987), 'The Original Notion of Cause', *Essays in Ancient Philosophy*, Minneapolis, 125-50

Frede, Michael (1995), 'Aristotle's Conception of the Soul', in M. Nussbaum and A. Rorty, eds., *Essays on De Anima*, Oxford, 93-107

Furth, Montgomery (1988), *Substance, Form and Psyche: An Aristotelian Metaphysics*, Cambridge

Gill, M.L. (1989), *Aristotle on Substance*, Princeton

Haldane, John (1983), 'Aquinas on Sense Perception', *Philosophical Review* 92 (2): 233-9

Husserl, Edward (1970), *The Crisis of European Sciences and Transcendental Phenomenology*, Evanston

Huxley T.H. (1886), *Lessons in Elementary Physiology*, London

Jaworski, William (2016), *Structure and the Metaphysics of Mind*, Oxford

Koslicki, Kathrin (2018), *Form, Matter, Substance*, Oxford

Lisska, Anthony J. (2016), *Aquinas's Theory of Perception: An Analytic Reconstruction*, Oxford

Marmodoro, Anna (2013), 'Aristotelian Hylomorphism without Reconditioning', *Philosophical Inquiry* 36: 5-22

Menn, Stephen (2002), 'Aristotle's Definition of the Soul and the Programme of *De Anima*', *Oxford Studies in Ancient Philosophy* 22: 83-109

Peramatzis, Michail (2011), *Priority in Aristotle's Metaphysics*, Oxford

Putnam, Hilary and Nussbaum, Martha (1995), 'Changing Aristotle's Mind', in M. Nussbaum and A. Rorty, eds., *Essays on De Anima*, Oxford, 27-76

Rapp, Christof (2003), 'Thomas von Aquin zum Verhältnis von Leib, Seele und Intellekt', U. Meixner and A. Newen, eds., *Seele, Denken und Bewusstsein*, Berlin, 124-52

Shields, Christopher (1990), 'The First Functionalist', *Historical Foundations of Cognitive Science*, Dordrecht, 19-33

Sorabji, Richard (1991), 'From Aristotle to Brentano: The Development of the Concept of Intentionality', in H.J. Blumenthal and H. Robinson, eds., *Aristotle and the Later Tradition: Oxford Studies in Ancient Philosophy* (suppl. vol.), Oxford, 227-59

Ward, Julie (1988), 'Perception and *logos* in *De Anima* ii 12', *Ancient Philosophy* 8: 217-33

Whiting, Jennifer (1995), 'Living Bodies', in M. Nussbaum and A. Rorty, ed., *Essays on De Anima*, Oxford, 175-92

Wisnovsky, Robert (2003), *Avicenna's Metaphysics in Context*, Ithaca

1
Epicurean Materialism

Alexander Bown

Aristotle regarded atomism as a real competitor to his own views on physics and metaphysics. In *On Generation and Corruption* 1.2, he claims that none of his predecessors except the atomist Democritus had thought about the problems of coming-to-be and passing-away in 'more than a superficial way'; in 1.8, he presents Democritus' and Leucippus' theory of action and passion as the 'most systematic and general' of those proposed by earlier thinkers.[1] Accordingly, he devoted quite some energies to attacking their views. In the post-Aristotelian Hellenistic period, Epicurus adopted a form of atomism that was modified in certain respects from the earlier account; at least some of these modifications may have been intended to address Aristotle's criticisms.[2]

My aim in this chapter is to present the fundamentals of Epicurus' views on physics and ontology and to raise some questions that a competitor to Aristotelian hylomorphism ought to be able to handle. In section 1, I present the basic ontological framework; in section 2, I introduce atoms, which most closely correspond in Epicurus' system to Aristotelian matter, and show how he attempted to account for some phenomenal and psychological properties of compound bodies by appealing just to the characteristics and arrangement of their atomic parts. But it turns out that not all macroscopic properties are regarded as explicable in this way. In section 3, I introduce an alternative Epicurean analysis of bodies that treats them not as aggregates of material parts but rather as complexes of attributes that have so-called 'permanent natures' at their core. I argue that this analysis must play an ineliminable explanatory role in

---

[1] See *GC* 1.2.315a34–5 and 1.8.324b35–325a1. In *PA* 1.1.642a24–8, Aristotle describes Democritus as the first to have come close to grasping essence ('*to ti ēn einai*') and the definition of substance ('*to orisasthai tēn ousian*')—although he immediately adds that the attempt was not yet successful.

[2] For example, there are reasons to think that Epicurus' introduction of theoretical *minima* might have been partly motivated by Aristotle's objections: see Furley (1967: 111–30). Similarly, Brad Inwood has argued that some features of Epicurus' concept of void show that he was aware of Aristotle's criticisms in *Physics* 4 (Inwood 1981: 282–4). There may also be signs of Aristotelian influence on his views on the weight of atoms and their ability to swerve (cf. O'Keefe 1996: 313–16), and his position on the laws of bivalence and the excluded middle (cf. Bown 2016b). See Gigante (1999: 33–50) for an overview. But it is unclear how well Epicurus knew Aristotle's works. The only explicit reference to Aristotle occurs in a fragment of Philodemus' *Adversus Sophistas* (fr. 127 Arrighetti), where Epicurus mentions the *Physics* and perhaps also the *Analytics*. See Sedley (1977: 126–7) and, for some cautionary remarks, Sandbach (1985: 4–6).

some contexts, in order to account for the unity of compound bodies and their persistence over time; and to ground modal claims about what belongs to them necessarily or non-necessarily. In section 4, I briefly discuss a semi-technical formulation that some Epicurean philosophers use when making such claims.

1. Bodies, Void, and Their Attributes

What kinds of thing exist, according to Epicurus? A straightforward answer is found early in the *Letter to Herodotus*: 'The all [*to pān*] is bodies and void [*kenon*]' (*Ep. Hdt.* 39).[3] This simple statement does not give the full story, however. After briefly justifying the claim that both bodies and void exist, he writes the following:

T1   And beside these [sc. bodies and void] nothing can even be thought of, either by comprehension or by analogy with things that are comprehended, as things that are grasped according to complete natures rather than as what are called the accidents [*sumptōmata*] or attributes [*sumbebēkota*] of these.

Ep. Hdt. 40

Besides bodies and void, then, further things do play a role in the Epicurean universe, namely items referred to as 'accidents' and 'attributes'. The same contrast is drawn in slightly different terms in the following report from Sextus Empiricus, who cites Demetrius Lacon, an Epicurean philosopher of the 2nd century BCE, as his source:

T2   ... of beings [*tōn ontōn*], some exist [*huphestēken*] per se [*kath' heauta*], and others are regarded as attached to [*peri*] the things that exist *per se*. And existing per se are such things as the substances, i.e. body and void, whereas they call the things that are regarded as attached to those that exist *per se* 'attributes' [*sumbebēkota*]. And of these attributes, some are inseparable from the items of which they are attributes, whereas others are by nature separable from them.

M 10.220–1

In Sextus' discussion following T2 (*M* 10.221–7), it emerges that the inseparable attributes of some body are those that it must have at any time at which it exists, whereas the separable attributes are those that it can gain or lose without being destroyed; the latter are those referred to as 'accidents' in T1. No one-word expression is used for the former; Epicurus tends to use compound expressions

---

[3] I use the text of Dorandi (2013). Translations are mine, but often influenced by Long and Sedley (1987) and Inwood and Gerson (1994).

such as 'permanent attributes' or 'eternal accompaniments' (*'ta aei sumbebēkota'* or *'ta aidion parakolouthounta'*) when discussing them.[4]

It is clear from these accounts that Epicurus operates with a multi-level ontology: he recognizes two ways in which something can count as existent. First, there are the items that exist *per se* (T2) and are 'grasped according to complete natures' (T1), namely bodies and void. (I will attempt to say something about the notion of a 'complete nature' in section 3.) Second, there are items that exist without doing so *per se* and (presumably) without being 'grasped according to complete natures', namely attributes (of which some are accidents and some permanent). It is fair to assume that these items, which are described as 'attached to' *per se* existents, are somehow ontologically parasitic: an attribute counts as existent only in virtue of being appropriately related to something that exists in its own right, i.e. some body or void.[5]

So is Epicurus a materialist? This depends, of course, on what one understands by 'materialism'—the label is vague enough to cover a large range of views. One might, for example, take materialism to be the view that everything that exists is corporeal. Clearly, Epicurus does not take this position: he must regard existence as compatible with being incorporeal, since he classes void as an existent. Void (*to kenon*) is otherwise referred to as 'place' (*'topos'*) or 'room' (*'khōra'*); it is described as that in which bodies are found and through which they move (*Ep. Hdt.* 40). It is also referred to as 'intangible nature' (*'anaphēs phusis'*), and is thus the complement of body, which is regarded as necessarily or essentially tangible.[6] Void appears to be something like empty space; any part of the universe that is not body consists of void.[7] And yet, in Epicurus' view, it has just as much claim to existence as a body—indeed, it belongs to the privileged ontological category of the *per se* existents, and is sufficiently robust that attributes (e.g. intangibility) can count as existent in virtue of belonging to it.

---

[4] See *Ep. Hdt.* 68 and 71 (in T3 and T4 below). Lucretius does have a one-word label for permanent attributes: he calls them *'coniuncta'* (and uses *'eventa'* for accidents), at *DRN* 1.449–63. It follows that the phrase 'accidents and attributes' in T1 is slightly misleading—it does not, as one might have expected, introduce two disjoint classes. See Sedley (1988: 304–11). Sedley argues against the previous orthodoxy according to which attributes are exclusively non-accidental properties. Most scholars now accept Sedley's position; one exception is Purinton (1999: 272–3).

[5] Typically, an attribute will count as existent simply in virtue of belonging to a *per se* existent: it is because of the apple that the apple's redness exists. But not all attributes belong to *per se* existents—for instance, time is described as an 'accident of accidents', i.e. an accident of such things as days and nights, movement and rest (SE *M* 10.219–27). The Epicureans presumably thought that any such chain of attributes belonging to attributes ultimately terminates in some *per se* existent, which grounds the existence of the attributes that belong to it, the attributes that belong to those attributes, and so on.

[6] Cf. Lucr. *DRN* 1.430–9 and Phld. *Sign.* 18.5–8.

[7] Here I touch on an area of controversy: scholars disagree as to whether void, on Epicurus' conception, is merely empty space or vacuum, located wherever body is not, or instead space in general, some of which is occupied and some of which is not. For discussion of these issues, see Inwood (1981); Sedley (1982b); Algra (1995: 52–8); and Konstan (2014).

But this is the only case of something incorporeal that Epicurus recognizes as a *per se* existent.[8] Moreover, its role in the Epicurean universe seems merely to be to make it possible for various things to happen (such as for bodies to be able to move—cf. *Ep. Hdt.* 40). There are few signs of Epicurean philosophers having provided any detailed treatment of causation, but they seem mainly to think in terms of efficient or material causes;[9] at any rate, they claim cases of something acting or being acted upon occur only when one body comes into physical contact (*tactus*) with another (cf. *DRN* 3.161–7), and hence are restricted to corporeal items. Indeed, it is on this basis that Epicurus argues that the soul must itself be corporeal, since it acts on the body and is affected by it (*Ep. Hdt.* 67). So it is fair to consider him a materialist in a restricted way: although not all existents are corporeal, nothing incorporeal plays any independently active role in the universe; any Epicurean account of how the beings around us are generated or destroyed, undergo change or interact with one another will ultimately rest on facts about bodies and their attributes.

2. Atoms and Their Role in Explanation

Something strikingly absent from the framework as I have presented it so far is any mention of atoms. From an ontological point of view, in fact, Epicurus does not grant them any special status. It is bodies in general rather than atomic bodies in particular that belong to the fundamental ontological category, that of the *per se* existents.[10] This may mark a point of departure from Democritus, whom some Epicureans took to deny the genuine existence of anything except atoms and void, and hence to claim that compound bodies do not really exist.[11] Whether or not

---

[8] When it comes to things that exist but not *per se*, the picture is less clear-cut: are attributes corporeal or incorporeal? They can hardly count as bodies, but Epicurus seems reluctant to call them incorporeal either. He may think that the question involves some kind of category mistake: at *Ep. Hdt.* 67, he explains that he uses the expression 'incorporeal' ('*asōmaton*'), following what he takes to be common usage, so that it applies only to *per se* existents. Accordingly, when he denies at *Ep. Hdt.* 69 (T3 below) that permanent attributes are *separate* incorporeal items, he is likely only to be denying that they are incorporeal items that exist in their own right (like void), rather than to be asserting that they count as bodies. The claim that accidents are not incorporeal at *Ep. Hdt.* 71 (T4) might be understood in the same way.

[9] Lucretius argues against some kinds of teleological causation at *DRN* 4.822–76.

[10] As David Sedley has pointed out, Epicurus' justification for the claim that bodies exist *per se* at *Ep. Hdt.* 40 shows that he has macroscopic compound bodies primarily in mind, since he simply appeals to sense perception, which has no access to the atomic level. From an epistemological point of view, the existence of compound bodies is even prior to that of atoms. See Sedley (1988: 303–4).

[11] According to Plutarch, the Epicurean philosopher Colotes took Democritus to claim that compounds exist merely by convention ('*nomōi sunkrisin*'), whereas atoms and void alone are 'real' ('*eteē*'): see *Adv. Col.* 1110E. Similarly, the Epicurean Diogenes of Oinoanda reports that Democritus claimed that *only* atoms truly exist, and everything else is merely conventional (fr. 7, II.2–13). But most accounts of Democritus' views are silent about compound bodies, and there is debate about the extent of his eliminativism. For a range of views, see Barnes (1982: 443–7); Wardy (1988); O'Keefe (1997: 122); Taylor (1999: 152, n. 141); Pasnau (2007: 115–20); and Castagnoli (2013: sect. 6).

this is Democritus' view, it is clear that Epicurus has no such position: he takes ordinary macroscopic objects to be no less real than the atoms that are their parts.

So what is the role of atoms? At *Ep. Hdt.* 41, they are introduced as the principles (*arkhai*) of compound bodies. As principles, they seem to have at least three functions. First, they are the ultimate constituents of compound bodies: at *Ep. Hdt.* 43–4, Epicurus describes a compound body as composed of atoms which are always moving but colliding with each other in such a way as to form a relatively stable system.[12] Second, atoms are taken to be necessary for generation, destruction, and change. They themselves do not go into or out of existence, or undergo any change in their intrinsic qualities, but compound bodies do;[13] and when some compound body is generated, destroyed, or undergoes some intrinsic change, this is due to the addition, subtraction, or rearrangement of the atoms that are its parts (*Ep. Hdt.* 54).[14] In this respect, Epicurean atoms have one of the important roles of Aristotelian matter: they act as an underlying substrate that persists through change. Third, there are many cases in which the fact that some compound body enjoys some attribute may be explained in terms of the characteristics of and relations between its atomic parts. For example, Lucretius reports that hard substances such as diamond, iron, bronze, and stone are tough and difficult to cut because their atoms are hooked and held closely together as if by branches, whereas water is fluid because its atoms are smooth and round, and flow around each other like poppy seeds (*DRN* 2.444–55).

In short, although atoms are not ontologically fundamental, except insofar as they are bodies, they have basic roles in certain causal-explanatory contexts.[15] In his description of the natural world, his accounts of the characteristics of compound bodies and their interactions, his meteorology and cosmology, and so on, Epicurus typically regards the microscopic as explanatorily prior to the macroscopic; a full account of a given phenomenon consists in giving an 'upwards story' that shows how it is the result of the nature and arrangement of the atoms that are involved. Sextus summarizes this as the view that atoms are 'responsible' ('*aition*') for the existence of compound bodies, and that the attributes of atoms are 'responsible' ('*aition*') for the attributes of those compounds (*M* 9.212).

Epicurus' physical theory places important constraints on what these explanatory accounts can appeal to. Atoms are simply bodies that are physically

---

[12] On Lucretius' account, an atom cannot be part of a compound body unless it is able to 'harmonize [its] motions' ('*consociare... motus*'; *DRN* 2.111) with the other atoms in that body.

[13] In fact, Epicurus claims that atoms undergo no change at all (*Ep. Hdt.* 41 and 54). But this is hard to square with the fact that they are described as moving from one place to another, as being part of one compound at one time and another at another, and so on. He probably has in mind, therefore, only change with respect to intrinsic properties; change with respect to extrinsic or relational properties (or so-called 'mere Cambridge change') must be permitted. Cf. Betegh (2006: 279).

[14] See Betegh (2006) for further discussion.

[15] As Sedley (1988: 303–4) puts it: 'Epicurus certainly holds that atoms and vacuum are in many scientific contexts... *aetiologically* primary.'

indivisible.[16] This is because they are 'full by nature', containing no empty space (*Ep. Hdt.* 41)—Epicurus seems to think that physical division can only take place by splitting a body along void gaps.[17] They have a very great number of possible shapes and sizes, although not unlimited (*Ep. Hdt.* 55–6). Furthermore, they have weight, in virtue of which they are disposed to move downwards. But this is more or less the full story: Epicurus claims that besides attributes related to shape, weight, and size, atoms have no 'quality' ('*poiotēta*') whatsoever in common with perceptible objects (*Ep. Hdt.* 54).[18] These are the resources to which he is limited, then, in giving an account of the characteristics of a compound body on the basis of its atomic composition: he can appeal to the sizes, shapes, and weights of the relevant atoms, and to facts concerning their relative positions and directions of travel, but not to anything else.

Epicurus seems to be concerned to give this kind of explanatory account above all in the case of the perceptual attributes of compound bodies. Perceptual attributes are themselves regarded as real—the talk of the redness of some apple or the sweetness of some honey is not an arbitrary convention.[19] But although perceptual attributes are real, and distinct from any properties possessed by atoms (no atom has a colour; no atom is sweet), facts about them seem to be regarded as in some way reducible to facts about the attributes of and relations between atoms. The sweetness of honey is due to the fact that it contains a relatively large proportion of smooth and round rather than rough and hooked atoms.[20] Similarly, colour properties are principally the result of the patterns in which the atoms that make up the surface of a given body are arranged.[21] The kinds of story given by Epicurus suggest that if one were able to specify in perfect detail all

---

[16] However, they are theoretically divisible into *minima*, which are the smallest possible magnitudes. See *Ep. Hdt.* 56–9 and *DRN* 1.599–634. This aspect of Epicurus' theory seems to have been an innovation with respect to Democritus' atomism, one that may have been motivated by Aristotle's arguments to the effect that motion would be impossible for a partless body. See Furley (1967: 111–30); Sedley (1976); and—for a general study of Epicurean *minima*—Verde (2013).

[17] Accordingly, Lucretius explains that the fragility of a compound body depends on the amount of empty space it contains proportionate to its constituent atoms (*DRN* 1.532–9).

[18] 'Quality' must be intended to apply only to some restricted class of attributes—perhaps only intrinsic or non-relational attributes. If not, motion would be a straightforward counter-example to the claim that atoms have no other qualities in common with perceptible objects.

[19] In this respect, Epicurus' atomism is clearly distinct from that of Democritus, who seems to have denied the genuine existence of any phenomenal properties: 'By convention [*nomōi*] sweet and by convention bitter, by convention hot, by convention cold, by convention colour; but in reality atoms and void' (SE *M* 7.135). See Furley (1993); O'Keefe (1997); and Castagnoli (2013).

[20] Cf. SE *M* 9.355, Lucr. *DRN* 2.398–407. Some complications are introduced by the Epicurean claim that honey contains *both* smooth and round *and* rough and hooked atoms, and that this is why it tastes sweet to people in healthy conditions but bitter to some who are ill (cf. *DRN* 4.642–72). Should one say that honey is sweet *tout court*, since it tastes sweet to healthy people? Or are sweetness and bitterness relational attributes, always possessed by a substance relative to some taster? It is not clear what Epicurus' answer would be; see Castagnoli (2013: sect. 5).

[21] See *DRN* 2.730–864. I simplify the account to some degree: Plutarch reports that on Epicurus' view, 'colours are not innate to bodies but rather generated according to certain arrangements and positions in relation to sight' (*Adv. Col.* 1110C). This suggests that the colour of a body partly depends

the characteristics of and relations between the relevant atoms, one would then be able to 'read off' all the facts about the perceptual attributes of a given compound body.

Epicurean philosophers seem also to have been concerned to give this kind of explanatory account in the context of psychology. In their view, the soul is straightforwardly material: it is a blend of several kinds of particle that pervade the body and is destroyed at death.[22] At least some characteristics of the soul as a whole are taken to be straightforwardly explicable by reference to the attributes of or relations between these particles. For instance, someone's having an irascible disposition is to be explained by their soul containing an unusually large proportion of a specific kind of particle that is described as 'hot'; someone's currently being asleep is to be explained by the temporary disorder of the particles that make up the non-rational part of their soul.[23]

It is not clear, however, how far this kind of explanatory account is supposed to extend: how would Epicurus account for beliefs, desires, and other kinds of mental state or disposition? Several scholars have thought that in his view, at least some of these kinds of psychological attribute are strongly emergent, in the sense that they are not explicable in terms of or reducible to the behaviour of soul atoms, and may even exhibit some independent causal powers.[24] But this question has been hotly contested.[25] The principal piece of evidence that has been brought to bear consists in some fragmentary and highly technical passages from *On Nature*, book 25, where Epicurus discusses certain psychological states that he calls '*ta apogegennēmena*' (usually rendered as 'products' or 'developments'), which are often taken to be dispositions that we come to have as the result of changes in our initial characters or sets of beliefs, and describes them as having certain kinds of effect on what he calls 'first natures'.[26] On the assumption that the first natures in question are specifically atoms, David Sedley has argued that this is an example of what he calls 'downward causation': higher level mental states are able to have a direct effect on atoms in a way that could not be predicted or explained by the principles of physical interaction that normally govern them.[27] My impression,

---

on external factors, such as the position of the observer; accordingly, the Epicurean scholarch Polystratus' defence of the reality of relative properties at *De Contemptu* 23–6 may apply to more attributes than one might ordinarily assume.

[22] See *Ep. Hdt.* 63–7 and Lucr. *DRN* 3.94–416.

[23] Both these examples are discussed by Lucretius: see *DRN* 3.288–306 and 4.907–61.

[24] Sedley (1988), Annas (1992), and Németh (2017) all ascribe roughly this kind of view to Epicurus, although their accounts differ in important ways.

[25] See Purinton (1999) and O'Keefe (2002, 2005) for some straightforwardly reductionist readings of Epicurus.

[26] For the relevant passages, see Laursen (1997: 18–24). Some have been more recently edited in Hammerstaedt (2003). The summary that I have given is already controversial: Purinton (1999) takes the *apogegennēma* to be agents, rather than any kind of mental state or disposition. See Masi (2005) for a study of the question.

[27] See Sedley (1988: 318–24).

however, is that these passages are not yet decisive evidence for this view; if higher level mental states were regarded as explicable in terms of complex atomic states, then one could speak of them as having an effect on the behaviour of atoms without thereby committing oneself to any exceptions to the usual principles of physical interaction.[28]

I do not propose to try to solve these difficulties here, since there are other, more straightforward kinds of example that will serve for the purposes of my discussion. In fact, the basic list of accidents given as examples by Lucretius early in his exposition of Epicurean ontology may already be problematic: he mentions slavery, poverty, wealth, freedom, war, and peace (*DRN* 1.455–6). It is not obvious how these kinds of social property could be explained by reference to atomic states, and Lucretius makes no attempt to do this.[29]

But the cases that Lucretius immediately goes on to discuss, namely those of various temporal attributes, are certainly problematic. The first mentioned is an entity that he refers to as 'the abducted daughter of Tyndareus' ('Tyndaridem raptam'; *DRN* 1.464); I shall use the shorter phrase 'abducted Helen'. This seems to be a kind of entity for which philosophers have used such labels as 'accidental unity', 'kooky object', and 'predicative complex': it is something that exists when and only when it is true to assert that Helen was abducted.[30] Lucretius takes abducted Helen to pose an apparent challenge to the claim that nothing besides bodies and void exists *per se*. His basic position appears to be that abducted Helen is an entity that currently exists, but is neither a body nor void; instead, it is classed among accidents as something that depends on the item to which it belongs (*DRN* 1.466, 478–82).[31] But if it is an accident of some body, then one would naturally expect it to be an accident that belongs to Helen, and she is long dead—so it would seem that abducted Helen cannot, after all, depend on the item to which it belongs, and might therefore have to count as existing *per se*. Lucretius'

---

[28] Cf. Annas (1993: 56–62).

[29] How might one try? One strategy could involve (i) explaining these social properties in terms of the mental states of relevant humans; and (ii) explaining their mental states in terms of the atomic constituents of their souls. There are some hints of an attempt to do something like (i) in similar contexts: Epicurus claims that justice does not exist *per se* but rather depends on specific agreements between individuals concerning harming and being harmed (*KD* 33). But these hints are never expanded into a complete explanatory account that reaches the atomic level, at least in our surviving sources.

[30] In Bown (2016a), I argue that entities like these play an important role in the Epicureans' truth theory: they would claim that it is in virtue of the existence of beautiful Helen at some time, for instance, that the belief that Helen is beautiful is true at that time. See Matthen (1983) for a general discussion of predicative complexes. Matthews (1982) and Cohen (2008) consider the roles these kinds of entity may have for Aristotle.

[31] It is not obvious why he thinks that abducted Helen must currently exist; it might have been easier to say that abducted Helen used to exist but no longer does, and that the past existence of abducted Helen is what makes the claim that Helen was abducted true now. Perhaps he thinks that something that is true *now* must be so in virtue of some fact about the *present* state of the world—at any rate, a similar view seems to have played a role in the Epicurean treatment of future contingents. See Bown (2016b: 260–5).

solution to this puzzle is to claim that abducted Helen is not, after all, an accident of Helen herself; rather, it is an accident of the whole world or of the specific region in which the abduction took place (*DRN* 1.469-70). He further specifies that this account holds of 'whatever is done' ('*quodcumque erit actum*')—this seems to be his way of fitting events in general into the Epicurean ontological schema.

This treatment of historical events is not too far-fetched: the gradual building up of history would be modelled as the world itself accruing these temporal attributes.[32] But Lucretius cannot have thought that these attributes are explicable in terms of the atomic make-up of the world as it presently is: he cannot have thought that the current existence of abducted Helen could be accounted for by some detailed description of the sizes, shapes, weights, and positions that atomic bodies *presently* have. For the current distribution of atoms in our world is compatible with a wide range of different past states—and, in particular, it seems quite possible that atoms should have ended up in their present positions (albeit by different causal routes) even if Helen had not been abducted.[33] But this does not seem to worry Lucretius. Rather, he is content simply to propose a macroscopic compound body as the bearer of attributes like these—what he is at pains to avoid is the view that the attribute could exist without belonging to some body, not the view that it could exist without being explicable by reference to the atomic constituents of the body to which it belongs.

It is fair to conclude, then, that the Epicurean project of providing an upwards story that explains the attributes of compound bodies in terms of the characteristics of their atomic constituents is limited in its intended scope. Although they clearly think that it is important to do this in some central cases—above all in those of phenomenal accidents—there are reasons to doubt whether they thought that it could or should be extended to all attributes.

3. Compounds: Assemblages and Complexes

So far, I have discussed how some of the attributes of compound bodies are related to those of their atomic constituents. I now turn to more fundamental questions concerning the nature of a compound itself. As I have mentioned, the basic account provided in the *Letter to Herodotus* is that compounds (*sunkriseis*) are

---

[32] One consequence of Lucretius' proposal that might be hard to swallow, however, is that when our world comes to an end (as it inevitably will, on the Epicurean account), all its temporal attributes—such as abducted Helen—will go out of existence as well.

[33] This would be the case even for a determinist. The fact that the Epicureans allow a small amount of indeterminism in their theory makes the range of possibilities even greater: the position and direction of an atom at a given time may be determined not just by its weight and past collisions, but also by so-called 'swerves', i.e. causeless changes of direction. The fullest extant account of the atomic swerve is Lucretius': see *DRN* 2.216-93.

made up of atoms that have the role of principles (*arkhai*); these atoms are in constant motion but somehow form a relatively stable system. This account raises several pressing questions. Why should a compound body count as something that exists *per se*, rather than being classed along with attributes as something that exists merely in a dependent way (i.e. as dependent on its atomic constituents)?[34] On what basis can Epicurus distinguish between accidental and non-accidental unities—why should Helen count as a *per se* existent, but beautiful Helen, an item that exists when and only when it is true to say that Helen is beautiful, not? Is a compound simply identical to the sum or aggregate of the atoms that constitute it, or something over and above them? Under what conditions does a compound body persist over time, and in what circumstances does it perish? In an Aristotelian context, one could attempt to answer some of these questions about identity, unity, and persistence by appealing to matter and form; I now consider how Epicurus might address them.

It is easy to see how Epicurus could run into difficulties if he attempted to answer these questions merely by talking about atoms. First, he can hardly say that an individual compound body is simply identical to the sum of the atoms that constitute it, since there are many cases in which the collection of atoms that constitutes some body would fail to do so if arranged in a different way. For example, a piece of sandstone counts as an individual compound body—a rock— but a heap of sand does not; and yet one and the same collection of atoms could (presumably) constitute either. Moreover, for any individual body that exists at two different times, t_1 and t_2, the collection of atoms that constitutes that body at t_1 is likely to be distinct from that which constitutes it at t_2. Organic bodies provide obvious examples: a horse takes in food, yet remains one and the same horse; a tree loses its branch, but remains one and the same tree. But according to Epicurean physics, the same is true even of bodies that one would normally assume to be undergoing no material change. In Epicurus' view, any visible object is constantly losing atoms from its surface; these form thin films or images (*eidōla*) that travel through the air and, by striking some observer's visual organs, enable the object in question to be seen. At the same time, the object in question is gaining atoms, since it absorbs some of those that are constantly striking it from outside.[35] (Presumably, the rate at which atoms are lost is typically the same as that at which they are gained, so that the size of the object remains roughly the

---

[34] This is one respect in which the Epicurean position may be disanalogous to Democritus'. If Democritus denies the existence of compounds (which is uncertain—see n. 11), then he treats sensible properties and compounds in the same way: they are both merely conventional. Epicurus does not think that either sensible properties or compounds are merely conventional, but nor does he think that they belong to the same level of reality: the latter exist *per se* and the former do not.

[35] See *Ep. Hdt.* 46–9. This kind of story does not apply to vision alone: all the senses except touch involve some exchange of particles (*Ep. Hdt.* 52–3; *DRN* 4.1–721).

same.) Hence, even an apparently static object—a diamond, a statue—is constantly undergoing change with respect to its atomic constituents.[36]

It is unclear whether the Epicureans were much exercised by questions about unity, identity and persistence—there are few signs of them in our surviving sources, aside from Lucretius' well-known remarks about diachronic personal identity in his discussion of death.[37] But a difficult passage from the *Letter to Herodotus* gives some hints about the resources that Epicurus could have drawn on if he had tried to address these problems. This passage shows that he did not only conceive of macroscopic physical objects as having material constituents, but also had at his disposal a second kind of account, according to which bodies are regarded as being made up of or analysable into their attributes.

I print the first half of the passage as T3 below. Epicurus' intention here seems simply to be to give a more detailed account of the nature of permanent attributes (having introduced attributes and accidents without much explanation at *Ep. Hdt.* 40; my T1).

T3   Moreover, as for the shapes and the colours and the sizes and the weights and all other things that are predicated of a body as permanent attributes (either all bodies or those that are visible, and themselves knowable by perception), one should not consider these to be *per se* natures (for it is not even possible to think this). Nor [should one think] that they do not exist at all; nor that they are certain separate, incorporeal items that attach to it; nor that they are parts of it. Rather, [one should think] that the whole body cannot *completely* [*katholou*] have its own permanent nature out of [*ek*] all of them, as when a larger assemblage [*athroisma*] is composed of the masses themselves, either of primary ones or of magnitudes that are less than this particular whole in size; instead, it is just in the way that I say that it has its own permanent nature out of [*ek*] all of them. And although all these things have their specific ways of being focused on [*epibolas*] and distinguished [*dialēpseis*], the complex [*tou athroou*] accompanies and is never detached; but the body receives its predicate according to the complex conception [*kata tēn athroan ennoian*].

Ep. Hdt. 68–9

---

[36] See Barnes (1988a) for more on Hellenistic treatments of the relations between physical objects and their parts.

[37] At *DRN* 4.843–61, Lucretius argues that even if (i) some time after our death, our matter were put back together exactly as it is now, and (ii) we were thereby brought back to life, still our death would not matter to us, since we would not remember it. At face value, this could be taken to suggest that he does not view the continuity of memory as required for personal identity, since he seems to entertain the possibility that we should be numerically identical to our future, reconstituted selves. But the discussion is phrased in counterfactual terms; he may not commit himself to any specific criterion of personal identity. Cf. Warren (2001).

It looks as if Epicurus' primary concern in T3 is to stake out a position that avoids committing him either, at one extreme, to the view that permanent attributes are incorporeal entities wholly distinct from and independent of bodies, or, at the other extreme, to the view that they do not exist at all. Unfortunately, although he is quite clear about what permanent attributes are not, he does not spend much time explaining what they are. The most important hints are found in the second half of the passage, where it emerges that a body has a 'permanent nature' ('*phusin... aïdion*') that is somehow composed of ('out of', '*ek*') its permanent attributes. We are told that the relevant kind of composition is not material constitution—the relation between a permanent nature and the permanent attributes is not the same as that between an 'assemblage' ('*athroisma*') and its material parts. Instead, it is such that while any given attribute has its own way of being picked out (its 'specific ways of being focused on and distinguished'),[38] the 'complex' ('*athroön*') somehow comes along with it (it 'accompanies and is never detached').

The thought is hard to follow. Perhaps the idea is that attributes are in some way incomplete: although one can focus on the hardness of a particular rock, say, and talk about it as something real, distinct from other attributes of that body (its weight; its shape) and from other hardnesses of other bodies (the hardness of that diamond; the hardness of that iceberg), one could never grasp it in isolation, but must always think of it as the hardness *of* that particular rock. It might be better regarded as an aspect of the rock than as a part of it (indeed, Epicurus explicitly denies in T3 that attributes are parts). Conversely, the atoms which make up the top half of the rock, say, can be grasped perfectly well in isolation: one could describe them adequately without any mention of the rock. If this is along the right lines, then it might explain why Epicurus distinguishes *per se* existents from attributes in T1 by saying that the former, and not the latter, are 'grasped according to complete natures'—for something to exist *per se* is for it to be complete in the way just sketched, rather than (say) for it not to depend for its existence on anything else (since the existence of a compound body *does* depend on that of its atomic constituents). One consequence of the view would be that Epicurean attributes are not universal or repeatable items: the hardness of this particular piece of rock depends on this specific object, and hence is numerically distinct from the hardness of any other rock (even one that is qualitatively indistinguishable from it). In today's philosophical jargon, they might perhaps be described as tropes; in Aristotelian terms, they might be something like the non-substantial particulars that feature prominently in the *Categories*.[39]

---

[38] The technical Epicurean expression '*epibolē*' is generally used of acts of focusing on or attending to something, acts which may be performed by means of the mind or the sensory organs (cf. *Ep. Hdt.* 37–8). See Asmis (1984: 122–6) and Tsouna (2016: 186–93).

[39] Examples of such items are a 'particular white' ('*to ti leukon*') and a 'particular grammatical knowledge' ('*hē tis grammatikē*'): see *Cat.* 2, 1a24–8. The comparison to Aristotelian non-substantial

Permanent attributes are only one kind of attribute; Epicurus continues his account by addressing the remaining kind.

T4 Moreover, there are often things that accidentally belong [*sumpiptei*] to bodies and accompany them non-perpetually, things which will neither be found among the invisibles nor be incorporeal. So, using the word in its most common sense, we make it clear that these 'accidents' [*sumptōmata*] have neither the nature of the whole which, when grasping it as a complex [*kata to athroön*], we call a body, nor that of the perpetual accompaniments, without which it is not possible to think of a body. And they each get their names according to certain ways of being focused on [*epibolas*], with the complex accompanying, but just when each is seen to be belonging [*sumbainonta*] to it, since accidents are not perpetual accompaniments. And we should not expel this evidence from being on the grounds that it does not have the nature of the whole to which it accidentally belongs, which we call a body, and does not have that of the perpetual accompaniments. Nor in turn should we consider them as *per se* entities (for this is not even thinkable, neither in their case nor in that of the permanent attributes). Rather, we should consider them all, just as they seem to be, as accidents in relation to bodies, and not as perpetual accompaniments or as things that have the status of a *per se* nature. But they are seen in the way in which perception itself marks them out.

Ep. Hdt. 70–1

As in T3, Epicurus is much concerned with rejecting views that he regards as mistaken: he denies that accidents are *per se* existents (either bodies or incorporeals), that they are permanent attributes, and that they are non-existent ('we should not expel this evidence from being'). The most helpful part of the positive characterization is the remark that accidents 'get their names according to certain ways of being focused on, with the complex accompanying', which mirrors what is said about permanent attributes and the accompanying complex in T3.[40] Accordingly, it looks as if the 'complex' mentioned in this extended discussion is a complex not just of permanent attributes, but also of accidents—indeed, of all the attributes that belong to some body.[41] Just like permanent attributes, we talk and think of accidents by focusing on aspects of this complex;

---

particulars is only apt if the latter are themselves non-repeatable. This is the traditional interpretation, but it is now controversial. For some of the relevant debate, see Ackrill (1963: 74–5); Owen (1965); Frede (1987); Matthews (2009); and Corkum (2009).

[40] The relevant part is the following: 'although all these things [sc. permanent attributes] have their specific ways of being focused on and distinguished, the complex accompanies and is never detached'.

[41] Here, I side with Betegh (2006: 280) over Long and Sedley (1987: 36). The latter take the complex to be made up only of permanent attributes.

at the end of T4, Epicurus mentions perception as a way in which we succeed in picking them out.[42]

What is the relation between the complex, on the one hand, and the individual body to which its component attributes belong, on the other? Epicurus does not directly address this question, but some of his remarks here suggest that he may just think of them as one and the same thing. Early in T4 he claims that it is 'when grasping it as a complex' that we call some whole a body; in the following two sentences, he seems to switch between talking of accidents as belonging to the complex and of talking them as belonging to the 'whole...which we call a body'. These ways of talking seem to presuppose that the complex just is the body, and vice versa.[43] Accordingly, Epicurus may well endorse some kind of bundle theory: he seems to regard an individual body as somehow composed of its properties, i.e. its permanent attributes and its accidents.[44]

So Epicurus has two modes of analysis when it comes to individual compound bodies: a material mode of analysis, whereby they are regarded as constituted by smaller (and ultimately atomic) bodies and can be called 'assemblages' (*athroismata*), and a property-based mode of analysis, whereby they are regarded as analysable into their attributes and can be called 'complexes' (*athroa*).[45] These are two parallel accounts that can be given of one and the same thing; a compound body just is an assemblage and just is a complex. In T3, Epicurus insists that the two modes of analysis involve different relations of composition: the way in which permanent natures and complexes are composed of attributes is *not* the way in which an assemblage is made up of smaller masses or of atoms. One important difference between the two relations of composition must be that whereas the atomic parts of some assemblage are prior to it in various respects (as I discussed in section 2), the attributes instead depend on the complex which they jointly compose.[46] They should not be understood as building blocks with independent claims to existence, but rather as the various aspects of a complete nature, which

---

[42] Epicurus seems to be thinking primarily of perceptual attributes in T4, but can hardly be committed to the view that all accidents are of this kind. Lucretius gives non-perceptual examples when introducing the distinction at *DRN* 1.455–8: slavery, poverty, freedom, war, and peace.

[43] I put it in these cautious terms because T3 and T4 might be read in a way which does not commit Epicurus to this view. But I can see few signs of the alternative, which would presumably be to think of the body as some kind of material substrate, and the complex as a distinct item that belongs to it.

[44] Cf. Betegh (2006: 280–1). Long and Sedley (1987: 36) have a similar view but do not use the expression 'bundle theory'.

[45] Betegh (2006: 280–1) refers to the two kinds as 'physical analysis' and 'metaphysical analysis', respectively.

[46] Epicurus seems to reserve the expression 'part' for material constituents—he denies in T3 that attributes are parts of bodies. He might be trying to avoid an obvious objection, namely that something that is made up of things that do not exist *per se* can hardly do so itself, so that compound bodies, when regarded as made up of attributes, would turn out not to be *per se* existents. See SE *M* 10.240 for a similar objection with the even more alarming conclusion that bodies turn out to be non-existent. Presumably, Epicurus' response would involve claiming that the principle that a *per se* existent must be made up exclusively of *per se* existents holds with respect to material constitution, but not with respect to the composition relation that attributes bear towards complexes.

when taken together would yield a full account of the relevant object, and are only comprehensible in relation to it.

The two kinds of analysis are useful in different contexts. Material analysis is important in the kinds of broadly scientific context discussed in section 2: the phenomenal attributes of compound bodies are typically to be explained by appeal to facts about atoms. But there are other contexts in which property-based analysis is more useful. At the fundamental level, this is the only kind of analysis available: atoms have no parts and thus cannot count as 'assemblages', whereas they can straightforwardly be regarded as complexes, composed of their permanent attributes (weight, size, shape) and their accidents (location, direction, etc.).[47] Moreover, Epicurus' remarks in the passages above make it clear that it has an important role in our access to objects, and in our everyday ways of talking and thinking about them. As I mentioned in the previous paragraph, in T4 he states that it is 'when grasping it as a complex' that we call some whole a body: it seems to be property-based rather than material analysis that is immediately relevant to applying a term like 'body' to some object.[48] This seems plausible: one is normally taken to have a good understanding of some object—to be competent at recognizing it and at describing it to others—on the basis of a grasp of its attributes, rather than on the basis of one's knowledge of its atomic parts.

More importantly for present purposes, this kind of property-based analysis might give Epicurus the resources to address some of the questions concerning the unity, identity, and persistence of compound bodies that I raised at the beginning of this section. T3 shows that he distinguishes between the complex and what he calls the 'permanent nature' of a body: the latter is composed only of permanent attributes, and is presumably used to specify the conditions under which the whole complex may be regarded as remaining numerically one and the same.[49] A complex is not simply a bundle of attributes, then, since it can persist while some of the attributes that compose it—namely the accidents—go in and out of existence.[50] One might think of the permanent nature as playing the role of some kind of inner bundle: the whole complex is destroyed just when at least one of the

---

[47] Note that Epicurus never raises the question of what, if any, material stuff a given atom might be made out of. He may think that the question would be idle: all that can be said about an atom at a given moment is that it is a complex of a specific size, weight, shape, location, direction, etc. Similarly, void might be regarded as a complex (with intangibility as a permanent attribute).

[48] Similarly, in T3 we are told that 'the body receives its predicate according to the complex conception'. I take it that 'the complex conception' refers to our conception *of* the complex: the idea would be that for a predicate to belong to some object is for the object in question to possess the relevant attributes (rather than for it to have a specific kind of atomic constitution). What makes 'human' true of some object is the fact that it is animate, rational, mortal, etc.; what makes 'fire' true of some object is that it is hot, bright, etc.

[49] Lucretius even defines a permanent attribute (*coniunctum*) as 'that which cannot be parted and separated [sc. from a body] without the division being fatal [sc. to that body]' (*DRN* 1.451–2).

[50] Cf. Betegh (2006: 281).

attributes that compose that inner bundle is lost. A body can change, therefore, with respect to its atomic constituents—undergoing rearrangements, additions, and subtractions—without being destroyed, as long as those changes do not result in the loss of any of its permanent attributes. It persists so long as the complex survives, rather than so long as its atomic parts remain numerically the same.[51]

What determines which attributes are permanent for a given *per se* existent? At face value, it looks as if there may be something arbitrary in the picture. Take an apple, say; suppose that it is red. This is surely not a permanent attribute of the apple, since the apple was once green and will be brown. But why take the *per se* existent here to be the complex that does not have redness as a permanent attribute rather than the one that does? The two complexes—which we might pick out with the expressions 'this apple' and 'this red apple' respectively—are very similar: they are made up of much the same attributes, and each persists precisely so long as certain kinds of atom are arranged in certain kinds of ways. The latter, however, will presumably be regarded as an accidental unity (like abducted Helen) and be classed among attributes; the former will be regarded as a *per se* existent, something with a 'complete nature'.

Certain features of the presentation in T3 and T4 might lead one to think that all that explains the choice of the apple over the red apple as something that exists in its own right is the fact that that is the way we happen to think of the world. After all, Epicurus repeatedly describes permanent attributes and accidents as identified by acts of mental or perceptual focusing (*epibolai*), and places great weight on the role of the complex in determining how we think about bodies and what is predicated on it. If this is Epicurus' view, it might be hard to defend against a Democritean-style objection to the effect that this is no basis to make claims about the nature of reality—it is merely a matter of convention that we favour the apple over the red apple when identifying items that exist in their own right. But there is probably more to Epicurus' position than this, since he seems to think that there are objectively right and wrong ways of carving up the universe.[52] His epistemology is optimistic: he insists that both sense perception and preconception are wholly reliable in what they tell us, and justifies this claim by giving

---

[51] One sign of the central role played by a 'permanent nature' in the Epicurean account of the identity, unity, and persistence of bodies is that Epicurus has a tendency sometimes to talk of the relevant entities *as* natures—such as at the end of T4 above, where the expression '*per se* nature' seems to be equivalent to '*per se* existent'. Plutarch comments on the flexibility of Epicurus' use of the expression 'nature' at *Adv. Col.* 1112E–F, where he ascribes to Epicurus the view that 'the nature of Colotes' and 'Colotes' just pick out one and the same thing.

[52] One sign of this is the fact that disputes between Epicurean philosophers and their opponents sometimes turn on questions about what the correct conception (or preconception) of a given kind of thing includes. One prominent example concerns gods: Epicurus insists at *Ep. Men.* 123–4 that blessedness and immortality are part of the preconception of gods, whereas people who conceive of them as punishing the wicked and rewarding the good do so on the basis of 'false suppositions' ('*hupolēpseis pseudeis*'). More than one conception of gods is available; Epicurus claims to identify the one that matches reality.

accounts of how they are more or less passively and mechanically produced in response to the external world.[53] Accordingly, he would claim that it is not a matter of chance that we think and perceive in the way we do: our faculties are such as to allow us to grasp things the way they really are. That being said, it is unclear what alternative story he might give about why reality is structured in the way it is; perhaps he could do nothing more than assert that it is a brute fact that the apple rather than the red apple counts as existing *per se*.

If the sketch that I have proposed in this section is along the right lines, then property-based analysis has an important role to play in Epicurus' overall theory of nature. This analysis of compound bodies seems to be independent of and complementary to material analysis in terms of their atomic constituents. Facts about which items count as *per se* existents and which of their attributes belong to their permanent natures seem in general to be additional to and not settled by facts about atoms. This does not yet amount to the kind of 'downward causation' that David Sedley ascribes to Epicurus in the context of his psychology; rather, it simply shows that there is more to the Epicurean universe than can be settled by a complete account of the nature and behaviour of atoms.

4. The Explanatory Grounds of Permanent Attributes

In the light of the property-based analysis of bodies that I discussed in the previous section, it is worth revisiting some of the explanations of the attributes of macroscopic bodies that I discussed in section 2. Specifically, how ought one to explain the fact that some macroscopic body has one of its permanent attributes—that some diamond, say, is hard? (I assume, for the sake of argument, that the Epicureans would regard some determinate level of hardness as a permanent attribute of diamonds.) It is clear how one could try to do this with some kind of upwards story on the basis of its atomic constituents: one might say, for example, that the atoms have shapes that allow them to interlock, and are arranged so closely that it is exceedingly difficult for any external force to break them apart.[54] Indeed, this seems a reasonably good explanation of why this collection of atoms exhibits this higher-order property. But there would be something missing if one tried to use this as an explanation of why *this diamond* is hard, since it is merely a contingent feature of the atoms that they are arranged

---

[53] These claims have struck many as over-optimistic. The Epicurean *dictum* 'All sense-perceptions are true' has attracted much attention: for some discussion of what this means, how Epicurus defends it, and whether perception can play the foundational role in his epistemology that he takes it to, see, *inter alia*, Striker (1974); Taylor (1980); Everson (1990); and Furley (1993). The account of the formation of preconceptions may partly depend on that of sense perception, since in some central cases it seems to involve having repeated perceptions of a relevant kind (as suggested at DL 10.33). For some studies of Epicurean preconception, see Glidden (1985); Morel (2007); Fine (2014: ch. 7); and Tsouna (2016).

[54] This is roughly the account that Lucretius gives when discussing this example at *DRN* 2.444–50.

in this way, whereas hardness is not merely a contingent feature of the diamond. The collection of atoms might have been arranged differently, in which case it would have failed to exhibit this property, but the diamond could not have failed to be hard.

There are some signs that the Epicureans recognized that different modal claims and different kinds of explanation are appropriate in relation to one and the same thing depending on whether one is talking about it as a collection of atoms, an 'assemblage', a complex, or something else. Epicurus himself may be dealing with this kind of issue in the following passage from book 25 of his *On Nature*, preserved only on a fragmentary papyrus roll found in Herculaneum.

T5 [*lac.*] we would call this particular thing [*lac.*] not only *qua* assemblage [*athroisma*] but also *qua* atoms and *qua* moving atoms, insofar as they are spoken of as an assemblage and not only the downwards movement itself...
PHerc. 1056, corn. 2 z. 2, lines 1–7 (= Arrighetti 34.11)[55]

The syntax of T5 is difficult, and there is no context to help make sense of it. But it seems reasonable to guess that Epicurus is using the expression 'qua' ('*hēi*') to distinguish between different things one might say of one and the same thing depending on whether one is talking about it as an assemblage, as a collection of atoms, or as a collection of moving atoms. The mention of downwards movement suggests that it may be specifically attributes related to motion that he has in mind. In this context, it would indeed make good sense to say different things depending on how the item in question is picked out: *qua* assemblage it might well be stationary, but *qua* atoms it will be in movement, since atoms are always moving.[56] But although atoms are always moving, Epicurus may not think that motion belongs to them necessarily;[57] on the other hand, motion surely does belong to *moving atoms* necessarily. So there is also a difference between what one should say of them *qua*

---

[55] The most recent edition of the text is Laursen (1995: 102), although line 4 is omitted. In Arrighetti (1973), the relevant line runs '*hēi kinoumenas atomous*'. I assume that the omission is accidental, since the line does feature in Laursen's translation. What I translate, therefore, is Laursen's text with the addition of line 4 as printed by Arrighetti.

[56] Cf. *Ep. Hdt.* 43.

[57] At SE *M* 10.222–3, Demetrius Lacon (as reported by Sextus) first introduces motion as an example of an accident *tout court*, before talking of it only as an accident of compound bodies and conceding that atoms always move. But one might doubt whether Epicurus would regard motion as an attribute without which it would be impossible for something to be an atom. The Epicureans often employ a kind of thought experiment in which they hypothesize the non-existence of void and conclude this would rule out the possibility of motion. (They then argue that since there evidently is motion, there must be void too: see *Ep. Hdt.* 40 and *DRN* 1.329–45.) But there is never any suggestion that without motion there could not be any atoms either; the thought experiment seems to involve imagining the universe as consisting of nothing but closely packed and stationary atoms. So I am inclined to think that Epicurus would not take motion to be part of the permanent nature of atoms. Rather, it is one that, given the way the universe is, atoms enjoy at all times.

atoms and what one should say of them *qua* moving atoms: *qua* atoms, they are always in motion; *qua* moving atoms, they are necessarily in motion.[58]

If this is on the right lines, then *qua*-locutions are used in T5 in order to qualify or restrict the applications of predicates to subjects: something is described as enjoying some attribute *qua* so-and-so, but not *qua* such-and-such or *tout court*. It is unclear to what extent Epicurus himself employed these formulations—there are few other uses of them in the surviving fragments of his *On Nature*. But there is evidence that some later Epicureans made substantial use of similar locutions, albeit in a different way: they feature prominently in the *De Signis* of Philodemus of Gadara, an Epicurean philosopher of the 1st century BCE. The main topic of the treatise is a certain kind of broadly scientific inference known as 'sign-inference' ('*sēmeiōsis*'), central cases of which involve making generalizing inferences such as 'Since humans familiar to us are mortal, humans everywhere are mortal'. In the surviving sections, Philodemus reports how various other Epicureans defended their account of these inferences against the objections of certain opponents.[59] Sentences containing expressions that can be translated as 'qua' or 'insofar as' ('*hēi*' and '*katho*' are most common) are used throughout the treatise as the standard way of expressing certain kinds of modal claim.

A few examples of such sentences are the following:

(A) Humans in our reach *qua* humans are mortal. (*Sign*. 33.29–31)
(B) Smooth and round things insofar as they are smooth and round are productive of pleasure. (*Sign*. 29.7–9)
(C) Bodies in our reach are destructible not insofar as they are bodies but insofar as they partake in a nature that is opposed to the bodily, one that is yielding. (*Sign*. 17.37–18.3)

In these sentences, the expression preceded by 'qua' or 'insofar as'—call this the '*qua*-term'—is not used to qualify or restrict the application of the main predicate to the subject, as in T5. Rather, the *qua*-term is better regarded as providing the grounds for the application of the predicate—that *in virtue of which* the attribute belongs to the objects in question. The Epicureans provide a couple of paraphrases of these sentences that make this clear: 'Humans in our reach *qua* humans are mortal' is to be understood as claiming that mortality 'necessarily follows' ('*ex anankēs sunepetai*', *Sign*. 33.35–6) being human, or, equivalently, that 'the latter includes the former' ('*sun toutōi tode einai*', *Sign*. 33.37).[60] Roughly speaking, the idea is that to be human is to enjoy a package of attributes that must

---

[58] See Annas (1993: 59) and O'Keefe (2005: 97) for further discussion of T5.

[59] A large proportion of one book of the treatise is preserved in a papyrus roll recovered from Herculaneum, *PHerc*. 1065. The most recent edition is De Lacy and De Lacy (1978).

[60] Strictly speaking, the text to which I refer discusses *qua*-sentences in general rather than just this example. Further paraphrases are found at *Sign*. 17.3–8 and 35.24–9.

include mortality; nobody could be human without also being mortal. In the light of T3 and T4, one might take this to amount to or to imply the claim that mortality is part of the 'permanent nature' of a human.

Sentences (B) and (C) can be understood along the same lines. According to (B), nothing could be smooth and round without being responsible for pleasure. According to (C), it is the package of attributes associated with 'partaking in a yielding nature', rather than that which is associated with being bodily, that includes destructibility: so bodies which do partake in a yielding nature must be destructible. (Conversely, atoms, being indestructible, must be counted as bodies that do not partake in a yielding nature.)

The Epicureans whose views are presented in the *De Signis* seem to have had fairly sophisticated things to say about *qua*-sentences. Philodemus goes on to report a classification of *qua*-sentences into three or four kinds based on different relations that may obtain between the *qua*-term and the predicate.[61] In particular, he distinguishes between cases in which the predicate is necessarily consequent on the *qua*-term because it is part of the preconception or definition of that *qua*-term, on the one hand, and those in which it is necessarily consequent for derivative reasons, on the other. An example of the former is 'A human *qua* human is a rational animal' (*Sign.* 34.10–11); one of the latter is 'Atoms insofar as they are solid are indestructible' (*Sign.* 34.21–3). This might be a trace of an Epicurean version of a distinction between essential and merely necessary attributes—a distinction that would be a helpful refinement of the notion of a 'permanent nature' as described in the *Letter to Herodotus*—although an explicit account is not provided in the surviving fragments of the treatise.

At any rate, it seems clear that the aim of these formulations is to make claims about the real natures of objects and the relations that obtain between the attributes that are parts of those natures, rather than to reflect more or less arbitrary facts about our linguistic usage. One of the purposes of the theories of sign-inference that are debated and defended in the *De Signis* is precisely to give an account of the conditions under which we can establish facts like these with respect to the objects of our experience—the conditions under which we can establish, for instance, that mortality is part of the nature of a human.[62] That being said, it is hard to tell in the light of our surviving sources whether these later

---

[61] The full discussion runs from *Sign.* 33.21 to 36.7. It is not straightforward, due to Philodemus' tortuous syntax and some unhelpful *lacunae*. See Sedley (1982a: 258–9) and Barnes (1988b: 120–3) for some attempts to reconstruct the classification.

[62] The details of this account are too controversial for me to be able to settle them here. One basic difficulty concerns the relation of the sign-inference 'Since the humans in our reach our mortal, also humans everywhere are mortal' to the corresponding *qua*-sentence, namely 'Humans in our reach *qua* human are mortal'. Some passages of the *De Signis* could be taken to suggest that the truth of the *qua*-sentence is a precondition for someone to be warranted in making the sign-inference (e.g. *Sign.* 17.37–18.8, 33.24–32); others might suggest rather that the truth of the *qua*-sentence is somehow or other established *by* the sign-inference (e.g. *Sign.* 17.3–8). For some of the relevant controversy, see Barnes (1988b: 120–3) and Long (1988: 140–3).

Epicurean philosophers were successful in their aims. Perhaps their use of these *qua*-sentences was underwritten by a well-worked-out account of complexes, natures, attributes, and the relations between these items; perhaps, alternatively, it was merely something they drew on in a dialectical context, to allow them to engage in modal discourse while apparently not committing themselves to the existence of further items (e.g. forms or universals) that they would have regarded as metaphysically suspect.

Regardless of these concerns, the basic moral that I would like to draw from the above is that some Epicurean philosophers did try to draw on an alternative kind of explanatory account besides those that appeal to facts about atoms. Suppose that one is asked 'Why are these hard?' by someone who is pointing at a sack of diamonds. One acceptable Epicurean answer would be the kind that emerged from section 2, namely 'Because each is constituted by atoms that have interlocking shapes and are closely packed'. But a second acceptable answer would be something like 'It is insofar as they are diamonds that they are hard': this kind of answer would account for the attribute of hardness by appealing to the nature of the body in question. In Aristotelian terms, the Epicureans turn out to have not just material or efficient explanation but also something more like formal explanation at their disposal.[63]

References

Ackrill, J.L. (1963), *Aristotle: Categories and De Interpretatione* (Clarendon Press).

Algra, K. (1995), *Concepts of Space in Greek Thought* (Brill).

Annas, J. (1992), *Hellenistic Philosophy of Mind* (University of California Press).

Annas, J. (1993), 'Epicurus on Agency', in J. Brunschwig and M.C. Nussbaum (eds.), *Passions and Perceptions: Studies in Hellenistic Philosophy of Mind* (Cambridge University Press), 53–71.

Arrighetti, G. (1973), *Epicuro: Opere*, 2nd edition (Einaudi).

Asmis, E. (1984), *Epicurus' Scientific Method* (Cornell University Press).

Barnes, J. (1982), *The Presocratic Philosophers*, 2nd edition (Routledge and Kegan Paul).

Barnes, J. (1988a), 'Bits and Pieces', in J. Barnes and M. Mignucci (eds.), *Matter and Metaphysics* (Bibliopolis), 223–94.

Barnes, J. (1988b), 'Epicurean Signs', *Oxford Studies in Ancient Philosophy* Suppl. Vol.: 91–134.

---

[63] I should like to thank David Charles, Reier Helle, Brad Inwood, and Simon Shogry for reading previous drafts of this chapter and providing extensive comments. I have been able to make substantial improvements in the light of their suggestions, but am of course responsible for any remaining deficiencies myself.

References

Betegh, G. (2006), 'Epicurus' Argument for Atomism', *Oxford Studies in Ancient Philosophy* 30: 261-83.

Bown, A. (2016a), 'Epicurus on Truth and Falsehood', *Phronesis* 61: 463-503.

Bown, A. (2016b), 'Epicurus on Bivalence and the Excluded Middle', *Archiv für Geschichte der Philosophie* 98: 239-71.

Castagnoli, L. (2013), 'Democritus and Epicurus on Sensible Qualities in Plutarch's against Colotes 3-9', *Aitia* 3.

Cohen, S. M. (2008), 'Kooky Objects Revisited: Aristotle's Ontology', *Metaphilosophy* 39: 3-19.

Corkum, P. (2009), 'Aristotle on Nonsubstantial Individuals', *Ancient Philosophy* 29: 289-310.

De Lacy, P. and De Lacy, E. (eds.) (1978), *Philodemus: On Methods of Inference*, 2nd edition (Bibliopolis).

Dorandi, T. (ed.) (2013), *Diogenes Laertius: Lives of Eminent Philosophers* (Cambridge University Press).

Everson, S. (1990), 'Epicurus on the Truth of the Senses', in S. Everson (ed.), *Companions to Ancient Thought*, Vol. 1: *Epistemology* (Cambridge University Press), 161-83.

Fine, G. (2014), *The Possibility of Inquiry* (Oxford University Press).

Frede, M. ed. (1987), 'Individuals in Aristotle', *Essays in Ancient Philosophy* (Clarendon Press), 49-71.

Furley, D.J. (1967), *Two Studies in the Greek Atomists* (Princeton University Press).

Furley, D.J. (1993), 'Democritus and Epicurus on Sensible Qualities', in J. Brunschwig and M. C. Nussbaum (eds.), *Passions and Perceptions: Studies in Hellenistic Philosophy of Mind* (Cambridge University Press), 72-94.

Gigante, M. (1999), *Kepos e Peripatos. Contributo alla storia dell'aristotelismo antico* (Bibliopolis).

Glidden, D. (1985), 'Epicurean *Prolēpsis*', *Oxford Studies in Ancient Philosophy* 3: 175-217.

Hammerstaedt, J. (2003), 'Atomismo e libertà nel XXV Libro περὶ φύσεως di Epicuro', *Cronache Ercolanesi* 33: 151-8.

Inwood, B. (1981), 'The Origin of Epicurus' Concept of Void', *Classical Philology* 76 (4): 273-85.

Inwood, B. and Gerson, L.P. (1994), *The Epicurus Reader* (Hackett).

Konstan, D. (2014), 'Epicurus on the Void', in G. Ranocchia, C. Helmig, and C. Horn (eds.), *Space in Hellenistic Philosophy* (De Gruyter), 83-100.

Laursen, S. (1995), 'The Early Parts of Epicurus, On Nature, 25th book', *Cronache Ercolanesi* 25: 5-109.

Laursen, S. (1997), 'The later parts of Epicurus, On Nature, 25th book', *Cronache Ercolanesi* 27: 5-82.

Long, A.A. (1988), 'Reply to Jonathan Barnes, "Epicurean Signs"', *Oxford Studies in Ancient Philosophy* Suppl. Vol.: 135–44.

Long, A.A., and Sedley, D. (1987), *The Hellenistic Philosophers*, vol. 1 (Cambridge University Press).

Masi, F.G. (2005), 'La nozione epicurea di ἀπογεγεννημένα', *Cronache Erconalesi* 35: 27–52.

Matthen, M. (1983), 'Greek Ontology and the "Is" of Truth', *Phronesis* 28: 113–35.

Matthews, G.B. (1982), 'Accidental Unities', in M. Schofield and M.C. Nussbaum (eds.), *Language and Logos* (Cambridge University Press), 223–40.

Matthews, G.B. (2009), 'Aristotelian Categories', in G. Anagnostopoulos (ed.), *A Companion to Aristotle* (Wiley-Blackwell), 144–61.

Morel, P.-M. (2007), 'Method and Evidence: On Epicurean Preconception', *Proceedings of the Boston Area Colloquium in Ancient Philosophy* 23: 25–48.

Németh, A. (2017), *Epicurus on the Self* (Routledge).

O'Keefe, T. (1996), 'Does Epicurus need the Swerve as an *Archê* of Collisions?', *Phronesis* 41: 305–17.

O'Keefe, T. (1997), 'The Ontological Status of Sensible Qualities for Democritus and Epicurus', *Ancient Philosophy* 17: 119–34.

O'Keefe, T. (2002), 'The Reductionist and Compatibilist Argument of Epicurus' *On Nature*, Book 25', *Phronesis* 47: 153–86.

O'Keefe, T. (2005), *Epicurus on Freedom* (Cambridge University Press).

Owen, G.E.L. (1965), 'Inherence', *Phronesis* 10: 97–105.

Pasnau, R. (2007), 'Democritus and Secondary Qualities', *Archiv für Geschichte der Philosophie* 89: 99–121.

Purinton, J.S. (1999), 'Epicurus on "Free Volition" and the Atomic Swerve', *Phronesis* 44: 253–99.

Sandbach, F.H. (1985), *Aristotle and the Stoics: Proceedings of the Cambridge Philological Society*, Suppl. Vol. 10 (Cambridge University Press).

Sedley, D. (1976), 'Epicurus and the Mathematicians of Cyzicus', *Cronache Ercolanesi* 6: 23–54.

Sedley, D. (1977), 'Epicurus and His Professional Rivals', in J. Bollack and A. Laks (eds.), *Cahiers de philologie 1. Études sur l'Épicurisme antique* (Publications de l'Université de Lille), 119–59.

Sedley, D. (1982a), 'On Signs', in J. Barnes, J. Brunschwig, M.F. Burnyeat, and M. Schofield (eds.), *Science and Speculation* (Cambridge University Press), 239–72.

Sedley, D. (1982b), 'Two Conceptions of Vacuum', *Phronesis* 27: 175–93.

Sedley, D. (1983), 'Epicurus' Refutation of Determinism', *ΣΥΖΗΤΗΣΙΣ. Studi sull'Epicureismo greco e latino offerti a Marcello Gigante*, Vol. 1 (Bibliopolis), 11–51.

Sedley, D. (1988), 'Epicurean Anti-Reductionism', in J. Barnes and M. Mignucci (eds.), *Matter and Metaphysics* (Bibliopolis), 295–328.

Striker, G. ed. (1974), 'Epicurus on the Truth of Sense Impressions', *Essays on Hellenistic Epistemology and Ethics* (Cambridge University Press), 77–91.

Taylor, C.C.W. (1980), '"All Perceptions are True"', in M. Schofield, M. Burnyeat, and J. Barnes (eds.), *Doubt and Dogmatism* (Clarendon Press), 105–24.

Taylor, C.C.W. (1999), *The Atomists: Leucippus and Democritus* (University of Toronto Press).

Tsouna, V. (2016), 'Epicurean Preconceptions', *Phronesis* 61: 160–221.

Verde, F. (2013), *Elachista. La dottrina dei minimi nell'Epicureismo* (Leuven University Press).

Wardy, R. (1988), 'Eleatic Pluralism', *Archiv für Geschichte der Philosophie* 70: 125–46.

Warren, J. (2001), 'Lucretian *Palingenesis* Recycled', *Classical Quarterly* 51: 499–508.

2
Stoics and Hylomorphism

Brad Inwood

In this chapter[1] my goal is to make a small contribution to understanding what Stoic (meta)physics[2] has to offer the study of hylomorphism in antiquity. Stoicism was a follower in its development of doctrines that bear meaningful comparison with Aristotelian hylomorphism; its physics and cosmology were also subject to great influence from Platonic theory and drew inspiration from what they took to be Heraclitean doctrine as well. However, once Stoic theory came to prominence in the Hellenistic and early imperial periods their approach to physics and cosmology exercised a certain influence on the views of thinkers from other schools, especially Peripatetics and Platonists. Parts of that story are told elsewhere in this volume. In this chapter, I will start with a general comparison of Aristotelian hylomorphism with its Stoic counterpart[3] and conclude with a brief examination of one Platonist's assessment of the relationships between Aristotle, his followers in later antiquity, and the Stoics with regard to a key application of hylomorphic theory—the relationship between body and soul.

If hylomorphism is a metaphysical theory built on the view that two principles, form and matter, are fundamental to giving a satisfactory explanatory account of the natural world and the objects in it, then Stoics cannot be said to be hylomorphists. 'Form' is not part of their theory of the natural world.[4] The terms *morphē*, *idea*, and *eidos* (in this sense[5]) are not part of their theoretical apparatus.

---

[1] I am grateful to several people for comments on an earlier draft of this chapter, including Richard Sorabji and Miira Tuominen, but most especially to Reier Helle, with whom I have also enjoyed many profitable (to me, at least) conversations on this and related material.

[2] As is well known, metaphysics is not a recognized part of philosophy for the Stoics. Nevertheless, many of the traditional problems of metaphysics are dealt with by them in their physics, which includes cosmology and theology, in their logic, and even in parts of their ethics. For present purposes it is physics that matters most.

[3] See Sorabji (1988: chs. 5 and 6) for Aristotle's and the Stoic theories of blending. His ch. 6 is especially relevant to the topic of this chapter. More recent work on the Stoic theory of blending can be found in Helle (2020).

[4] *Platonic* forms are dismissed as being mere concepts, *ennoēmata* (SVF 1.65). To the extent that Plato's focus on forms as causes encouraged his student Aristotle to adopt the terminology of form (albeit in an importantly different sense) in his physics, we might expect that the rejection of Platonic form was a factor in discouraging Stoics from adopting Aristotle's very similar terminology.

[5] Though, see Diogenes Laërtius 7.61 and Simplicius, *In Cat.* p. 165–6, where the term is used in a purely classificatory sense. Alexander (SVF 2.785) says of the Stoic corporeal soul that they refer to its *tonos* rather than using Peripatetic terms like *eidos* or *logos* or *dunamis*. Alexander's discussion at *Mantissa*, pp. 115–16, is very important for this issue when applied to the soul; see pp. 117–20 in this volume.

Nevertheless, their account of the natural world, which is for them the only domain to be explained,[6] rests fundamentally on a pair of principles, one of which is described by the terms 'matter' (*hulē*) and 'substance' (*ousia*).[7] The other basic principle in Stoicism is labelled in a variety of ways. It is most often termed 'reason' (*logos*) and 'god', though other designations can be found in our scattered sources. The most important feature of Stoic explanations of the natural world, though, is the more abstract characterization of these two principles, as 'the active' and 'the passive' (*to poioun*; *to paschon*). God or reason as opposed to matter: the active as opposed to the passive; this structural duality is built into the Stoic explanatory apparatus as pervasively as the duality of form and matter is built into Aristotelianism.

Aristotle's form and matter play an important role in his schematization of causes in the natural world. There are, he holds, four kinds of cause or explanation:[8] the form, the matter, the source of change or motion, and 'that for the sake of which' (routinely translated as 'final cause'). For the Stoics, talk of causation is notably different.[9] Although their physical theory, especially in its Chrysippean version, featured a sophisticated classification of kinds of causes,[10] they held that at the most fundamental level there is only one cause: god, reason, the active principle, or however it might be described in a given context. So the basic duality of Stoic physical theory can also be described as cause vs matter. This way of approaching physical theory is particularly prominent in Seneca's Letter 65 and (perhaps under his influence) in the work of Marcus Aurelius.[11] If the active principle is the only genuine cause, it follows that the passive principle should not be expected to contribute anything substantially informative to an explanation. And so it is not surprising that at the most abstract level matter is characterized as being completely without qualities or characteristics: *apoios hulē*.[12]

The exhaustive pairing of form and matter in explanations is not, of course, sufficient for hylomorphism.[13] Platonism, too, deploys both forms and material

---

[6] Stoicism does not countenance a distinct realm of superlunary entities made of a stuff distinct from the four elements that characterize the world of our experience; nor do they think that there are changeless entities without matter, like Aristotle's unmoved mover.

[7] The Stoic use of the term *ousia* is quite distinct from the characteristically Aristotelian use of the term, which we routinely translate as 'substance'.

[8] Whether an *aition* or *aitia* should be thought of as a cause in any of our modern senses or as an explanation is an issue that does not need to be addressed in this chapter.

[9] See Frede (1980).

[10] See, for example, Clement *Strom.* 8.9 (see LS 55I and SVF 2.346, 348, 351); also Galen at SVF 2.354. For a view of Chrysippus' theory of causes arguing that developing a fixed taxonomy of causes was not his aim, see Bobzien (2021: ch. 9, esp. p. 253).

[11] See Inwood (2020). This feature of later Stoicism may also reflect significant influence from Platonist ideas: see Sedley (2002).

[12] Diogenes Laërtius 7.134, 137.

[13] Is the pairing of form and matter *exhaustive* in Aristotle's theory? In light of the doctrine of four causes, obviously not. But his readiness to hold that three of the causes converge in contrast to the material cause (*Physics* 2.7, 198a24–9) brings him closer to this stance.

elements in its explanations of the natural world, as is evident in both the *Phaedo* and *Timaeus*. When applying the label 'hylomorphism' to Aristotle's theory we normally also have in mind the additional claim that the formal element is immanent in the changeable material phenomena for which it accounts. Plato's demiurgic god imposes forms on a material substrate, but those forms remain metaphysically distinct from the objects so generated. In hylomorphism as normally understood there is no set of separate forms that exist independently of what happens to the objects in which they are instantiated. It is, to put it very approximately, as though the immanent forms of the *Phaedo* are the only forms there are.[14]

Though the Stoics' duality of god and matter is strongly reminiscent of the *Timaeus*[15] and not of Aristotle's theology, the role of immanence points to another feature of Stoic physics which makes the comparison with Aristotelian hylomorphism attractive. If immanence is a key requirement of hylomorphic explanation, then Stoicism meets that requirement perfectly. For in Stoicism both principles, the active (which corresponds roughly to form) and the passive (matter) are bodily. Both are corporeal and extended.[16] Though the corporeality of the active principle creates challenges for the Stoic theory, it also confirms in the strongest form its immanence. With both the material principle and the counterpart of the formal principle being immanent in a world of change, Stoic physical theory shares a key feature with Aristotle's theory that Platonist theories do not.

The primacy of the causal or formal factor in the Stoic account of any entity is well illustrated by a thought experiment developed by an under-appreciated Stoic from the second century BCE, Mnesarchus of Athens. We do not know the context for his imagined scenario, but it is reported as part of a general discussion of generation and destruction (a philosophical *topos* that lends itself readily to comparison with Aristotelian theory):[17]

> Mnesarchus says it is clear that the peculiarly qualified and the substance are not the same. For things that are the same must have the same attributes. If someone were to mould a horse, for example, and then mash it, and then make a dog, it would be reasonable for us, upon seeing this, to say that the latter did not exist previously but now does. So what we say about the qualified and what we say

---

[14] Later Platonism could, then, accept a roughly Aristotelian hylomorphism as an incomplete or provisional account of the material world, to be augmented by what they regarded as an essential account of the dependence of immanent forms on higher, transcendent forms.

[15] See Sedley (2002); also Reydams-Schils (1999).

[16] See Diogenes Laërtius 7.134; the manuscript variant *asōmata* is now generally and rightly rejected in favour of the better attested *sōmata*. The philosophical motivations for the Stoics' commitment to this form of corporealism lie in their theory of causation (see esp. SVF 1.90 = *Acad.* 1.39, where Cicero notes that this distinguishes the Stoic theory of causation from that of the Peripatetics and Academics); but we do not need to discuss that issue here.

[17] Arius Didymus, Epitome *Dox.Gr.* fr. 27, p. 463 = Stobaeus *Ecl.* 1.17; it is part of LS 28D, discussion on vol. 1, p. 173.

about the matter are not the same. And in general it seems implausible to think that we are the same as our substance since it often turns out that the substance (say, of Socrates) exists before he is born, while Socrates doesn't yet exist, and that the substance persists after Socrates is destroyed, when he no longer exists.

The terminology here requires some explanation. The 'peculiarly qualified' (*idiōs poion*) is what makes something into the thing that it is; this is a distinctively Stoic technical term. 'Substance' (*ousia*), though, is more complex; it is a term with a very definite technical meaning in Aristotle but a very different technical meaning in Stoicism. For the Stoics, *ousia* is a synonym for matter (*hulē*). As Mnesarchus observes here, Socrates' substance (his matter) exists before he is born and after he passes away; at bottom it is without qualities, the rawest of raw materials. As we have seen, the Stoics sometimes refer to the passive principle in nature as 'unqualified matter', something which, if it ever existed on its own, in reality, would be the most malleable form of stuff—the prime matter, in fact, about which there is still a debate with regard to Aristotle's theory. In Stoicism, though, whether or not unqualified matter ever exists on its own, there is at least a clear concept for it.[18]

In this account of Mnesarchus' theory it is clear that the identity of any particular thing is to be located in its peculiar quality. The account of what a given individual thing, such as a horse, is depends on the peculiar quality rather than the matter; the matter cannot account for the being of the horse since the matter is common to, in this example, dogs. The peculiar quality is what comes into being when Socrates is born and passes away when he dies, though his matter both pre-exists and survives. The thought experiment summarized here calls to mind other attempts to isolate the qualityless aspect of things in pursuit of a basic stuff for the world.[19] The present thought experiment is probably not sufficiently thorough-going to get down to the level of qualityless matter, since presumably there is a level of material organization common to (say) mammals such as horses and dogs, but still specifically qualified to an extent that it could not be the substance for radically different peculiar qualities, such as trees or granite boulders. Not that one couldn't go 'all the way down', as it were, to completely qualityless matter, the Stoic version of prime matter—as of course we would

---

[18] At Diogenes Laërtius 7.137 we are told that 'the four elements taken together are qualityless substance, matter'. Long (1996: 228) points out that even at the moment of conflagration matter is qualified by fieriness. It is possible that other Stoics, such as Seneca at Letter 9.16, thought that there was a moment when the causal principle, god, was *completely* separate from all matter; but this interpretation is uncertain and controversial.

[19] For example, Descartes, in *Meditation* 2, sects. 11–12, imagines stripping a piece of wax of all its properties and discovering that its basic reality is mere extension. In *Meta*. Z.3, 1029a7–27, Aristotle considers and ultimately rejects the thought that matter stripped of all qualifications might be the basic form of being.

have to do in giving a full account of the most radical material transformations recognized by the Stoics, those which occur at the universal conflagration.

It is worth noting here that in the Stoic theory we do not have, as far as I know, evidence of a clearly articulated concept of proximate matter, matter which is determinately *matter for* a particular form, such as we see in Aristotle. At the same time, there is no reason to doubt that Stoicism could in fact accommodate such a notion.[20] Every parcel of matter available for analysis has some level of qualification; presumably the stuff common to all mammals consists of a mixture of properties (either earth, air, fire, and water; or hot, cold, wet, and dry) within a certain range. When spelled out, such matter would in effect be *matter for* mammals. But it is noteworthy that Stoics did not, as far as we know, trouble to specify a concept or technical term to pick out this feature of their theory. This absence is no doubt related to the equally striking fact that Stoics did not adopt Aristotle's crucial distinction between potential and actual as an overt feature of their theory, even though Chrysippean modal theory would readily accommodate the distinction and there are clear correlates for potential and actual being in Stoic physical theory.

It seems clear that the Stoics, while not being hylomorphists in any strong sense, had all the resources they needed to account for the *explananda* to which Aristotelians applied their hylomorphic theory as *explanans*. And those resources exhibit a number of striking similarities to hylomorphism proper, not least the dualism and immanence of the major factors in the explanation. To be sure, there are also significant differences. For instance, Stoics applied their two-factor explanation at the level of the cosmos as a whole. Their god (also referred to as nature) is regarded as a cause for the whole world, its passive counterpart being the aggregate mass of unqualified matter.[21] For Aristotle there is no one cosmic form explaining the structure and operation of the world; the unmoved mover may be a cause for the whole world (as both a moving and a final cause), but it is not the formal cause of the world.

There is, however, one domain within physics where this tempting parallel between Aristotelian theory and Stoic theory is particularly apt. The relationship between body and soul in Aristotle's theory is in some respects the clearest and most interesting application of his hylomorphism, and we routinely look to the beginning of *De Anima* book 2 for a clear statement of that theory. Soul is identified as the form and actuality of a certain kind of body, and the body in question must be specifically apt for being ensouled in the hylomorphic way: it is a

---

[20] See Long (1996: 234): 'This makes it clear that an animal's body is *matter which has a form suitable for life.*'

[21] One characterization of 'cosmos' is as that peculiarly qualified for the *ousia* of the universe (Diogenes Laërtius 7.138). In this respect the Stoic theory is importantly similar to Platonist theories of the world soul, derived from the *Timaeus*. See LS, vol. 1, p. 319. For the Stoic conception of a world soul, see Diogenes Laërtius 7.156 (= SVF 2.774); and Ademollo (2020).

potentially living body, one that has the *organa* appropriate for life.²² Form, actuality, and soul are here set in opposition to matter, potential, and body. The dualist structure of Aristotle's analysis of a living thing is clear, but equally clear is the radical interdependence and unity of these two factors. The immanence of form in matter is particularly clear in Aristotle's psychology,²³ and in this respect the contrast with Plato's view of soul could not be clearer, at least in our eyes. In Stoicism we find strong similarities with Aristotle's views on the soul-body relationship: soul and body are ontologically interdependent, at least during life; souls do not pre-exist the person; reincarnation and recollection are ruled out; the soul is not immortal.²⁴ However, as we shall see towards the end of this essay there was at least one important philosopher in later antiquity who looked at the relationship between Plato, Aristotle, and the Stoics quite differently.

First, though, we should focus on the body-soul relationship in Stoicism as an enlightening point of comparison with Aristotelian hylomorphism. In so doing, I will not be breaking new ground, since our understanding of the Stoic theory and a sketch of its similarity to Aristotle's theory has been well understood for a long time, owing mostly to the work of A.A. Long.²⁵

It might be helpful to begin with *pneuma*, the warm, breathy stuff to which Aristotle assigned an important role in his account of biology and especially in his account of animal movements in the De Motu Animalium.²⁶ Here Aristotle treats *pneuma* as a key factor in the causal chain connecting mental events best attributed to the formal aspect of the body-soul compound with the physical expansions and contractions that move the limbs. *Pneuma* has an elasticity and a susceptibility to being altered qualitatively by thoughts and feelings; hence it can supply an otherwise missing link in a chain of cause and effect beginning with events in the soul and ending with bodily movements. But as Annas rightly emphasizes,²⁷ this

---

²² *De An.* B.1, 412a27–b1.

²³ For present purposes, I set aside the difficult question of whether the so-called active intellect of *De An.* 3.5 constitutes an exception to Aristotle's general commitment to immanence and the unity of soul in body.

²⁴ Though each leaves room for a possible complication. At least some Stoics think that a suitably disposed soul, though not immortal, might be able to remain in existence for some time after death, i.e. after separation from the body; and Aristotle notoriously leaves open the question of a special status for one aspect of the intellect. This would mean that soul and body for the Stoics, though interdependent during life, are independent over the time between conflagrations; the complication for Aristotle of having one of its capacities, the active intellect, possibly immortal in some sense introduces an ambiguity into his theory which, as we will see, Iamblichus exploits.

²⁵ The fundamental account was worked out in Long (1996 and 1999). See also Annas (1992).

²⁶ See *De Motu* ch. 10. *Sumphuton pneuma* is the body corresponding to *orexis* as a *meson* in the generation of movements. It is well suited to be the *organon* of the soul in this regard (703a20); the notion that *pneuma* is a natural tool recurs at *De Generatione Animalium* 789b8–12. Throughout the *Parva Naturalia*, *pneuma* plays an important role in the operation of the hylomorphic animal.

²⁷ Annas (1992: 17–20) outlines Aristotle's inconsistent but important uses of *pneuma* in his account of living animals. She points out (p. 19, n. 8) that 'Aristotle does make the astounding claim at *GA* 789b8–12 that nature uses *pneuma* like a tool in most things; but this is not borne out by his writings'.

recourse to *pneuma* in the context of explanation in a hylomorphic context is unsystematic in Aristotle's corpus. However, when combined with the developments in medical theory in the generations after Aristotle,[28] this set the scene for Stoics to simplify Aristotle's theory by actually identifying soul with the relevant *pneuma* in an animal body. In so doing, of course, they abandoned the equation of soul with form which is at the heart of Aristotle's hylomorphic project; but they also accommodated it in their own innovative causal theory, according to which only a body can be a cause.[29] To the extent that soul was regarded as the cause of animal functioning—a view shared by Plato, Aristotle, the Stoics, and even Epicurus—the constraints of Stoic causal theory compelled them to corporealize soul. And in the context of Aristotle's incipient exploration of *pneuma*'s role in animal life and Hellenistic physiological theory, it is unsurprising that Stoics as early as Zeno chose simply to equate soul with *pneuma*.[30]

In doing so they retained some of the key features of the hylomorphic framework inherited from Aristotle, including the integration of the analysis of the soul-body relation with the more general metaphysical analysis of objects into formal and material factors. Aristotle analyses all objects into form, which determines the identity of the thing, and the corresponding matter; the Stoics analyse all objects into *pneuma* and the corresponding matter. As we have seen, 'peculiar quality' plays the role of the individuating locus of identity for an object, and so it is no surprise that such qualities, *poia*, are in fact parcels of *pneuma*. As Long explains with exemplary clarity and economy, each kind of object has its own kind of *pneuma* playing this causal and definitory role. In inanimate objects the *pneuma* is a *hexis*; in plants it is a *phusis*; in animals it is *psuchē*, soul.[31] Hence just as Aristotle's form-matter analysis is fully general across the natural world and so includes the account of soul smoothly within his general theory,[32] so the Stoic analysis of objects into *pneuma* and matter is fully general and encompasses the account of soul within their general theory.[33]

---

[28] See Annas (1992: 20–6); and the essays by Berryman (2020) and Leith (2020).
[29] See Aëtius 1.11.5 = SVF 2.340.
[30] There was, of course, abundant precedent for associating or even identifying soul with 'breath' as early as Homer.
[31] Though the relevant kind of *pneuma* is the active cause of the way each kind of thing is, the characteristics it brings to each are of course quite different. Soul *pneuma* causes a wider range of more complex and dynamic characteristics than those with which plants are endowed, and even more so for inanimate objects whose *pneuma* gives their matter shape, qualities, and cohesion, and very little else.
[32] With, of course, the exception of the active intellect in *De An.* Γ.5.
[33] The Stoic doctrine that souls can survive at least temporarily after death (see SVF 2.809-22 and, e.g., Seneca, *Consolation to Marcia* 24.5–25.2, 26.7) is perhaps a relic of Platonic theory that they chose not to abandon, but in doing so they applied a physical theory to account for it. Souls cohere owing to a high degree of physical tension (*tonos*) and not because they are encased in a body (the Epicurean theory). An Aristotelian soul-form cannot, of course, persist after death and in this respect his theory is more naturalistic than the Stoics'. However, Aristotle does leave room for a deathless active intellect which, in some respects, is an even more puzzling deviation from his basic theory.

For both Aristotle and the Stoics, then, all objects are analysed into two factors: form and matter for Aristotle; quality or the qualified (in the form of a suitably tensioned bit of *pneuma*) and matter for the Stoics. This applies even to animals, including humans, with 'soul' being the name for the first factor in the pair. Since in both cases there is a clear recognition of the unity of objects, especially animals, there is a need for an account of how these two factors are unified. The Aristotelian account of the unity of form and matter is rich, complex, and to some extent controversial—but no matter how it is understood it is one of the most philosophically rewarding aspects of his thought. I say no more about it here (except that it depends crucially on the use of the distinction between potentiality and actuality).

Things are more difficult for the Stoics in that both components of the body-soul compound are understood as definite bodies: there is no room for the body to be merely potential to the actuality of the whole living animal. Hence, in place of the challenging metaphysical story Aristotle must tell about the unity of matter and form, body and soul, the Stoics must tell a physical story about the corresponding unity.

That physical story is the theory of total blending. It is a story that deserves to be told at length, and indeed it has been.[34] The central claim is that it is possible for two bodies to be completely co-extensive with each other in what the Stoics called a 'total blend' (*krasis di' holou*); in such a mixture the ingredients are meant to retain their identity in such a way that they can in principle be separated out again. Two of the most common examples of such blending were the mixture of fire and iron seen when the metal is glowing hot at the blacksmith's forge and the mixture of wine and water so common in ancient drinking practice. In my view, these examples were originally intended as illustrations, familiar cases serving as analogues or, in a sense, proofs of conceptual feasibility for the notion of total blending. Having established that such blending is conceptually possible, the Stoics then posit it as the explanatory factor to be used in accounting for the unity of peculiar quality and matter in other cases. To the extent that the unity of quality and matter is the counterpart of the unity of form and matter in Aristotelian hylomorphism we again find a revealing parallel.

In Aristotelian theory the key role in this bit of theorizing is played by the relationship between potentiality and actuality. The body is potentially alive; soul is the actuality of that potential. Stoics do not have access to that metaphysical move to solve their problem, but as with Aristotle we can get the clearest idea of how their solution is meant to work by looking at the relationship between soul and body. And here we are extraordinarily fortunate to have particularly good evidence for such an important part of Stoic theory. The later Stoic, Hierocles,

---

[34] See Helle (2018 and 2020: ch. 3).

wrote a work on 'The Principles of Ethics', parts of which have been preserved on a papyrus.[35] Long has outlined the way body and soul operate in such a mixture, by pressure and counter-pressure on each other at every level of aggregation. This technically challenging theory has been analysed in much greater detail in the definitive discussion offered by Reier Helle (see Chapter 4, n. 34). There is no need to repeat the reconstruction here; for present purposes it suffices to point out the theoretical pressures which required the Stoics to develop such a theory. The mechanism of total blending plays a role in the Stoic counterpart of Aristotelian hylomorphism analogous to Aristotle's account of the unity of form and matter in a primary substance. Without such an account neither theory would be complete. That both theories remained controversial is unsurprising.

As indicated above, there are important differences between the Stoic and Aristotelian versions of these theories. And it is worth noting that each of them is subject to significant comparisons with Platonist theory, which clearly continued to exercise a powerful influence on both Stoicism and later Aristotelianism, a result not just of the enormous influence of the Platonic corpus throughout antiquity but also of the debates and criticisms among all three schools that carried on at least until the 3rd century CE. I would like to conclude this part of my discussion, though, by focusing briefly on another common feature of Stoic and Aristotelian theories, and that is the role of capacities or capabilities (*dunameis*) as manifested in Aristotle's substances and the Stoics' unified bodies. In both theories, what a thing is is determined by the formal constituent (the form for Aristotle and the peculiar quality or pneumatic *hexis* for the Stoics). Once a bit of relatively unformed matter becomes shaped and defined by the formal constituent, in both theories there results an object which has *dunameis*, capacities or powers which enable it to interact with other objects in the world in its characteristic way.[36] As far as I can see, the capacities attributed to various kinds of object and so the properties they manifest are not particularly problematic nor are they the subject of debate. In fact, for the most part such capacities and properties should be regarded as relatively uncontroversial *explananda*. Iron is hard, fire is hot, plants grow and reproduce, animals perceive and move, people think. These capacities and their corresponding actions (if they have any) are accounted for by the form, as opposed to the matter, and by the quality (*pneuma*) as opposed to the relatively unqualified matter.[37]

---

[35] Hierocles, *Elements of Ethics*; see Bastianini and Long (1992).

[36] At *M* 7.359 (= SVF 2.849), Sextus notes that in Stoic theory the unified soul possesses different, even opposite powers in the same body. The soul's possession of both rationality and irrationality in one body is compared to the way honey possesses both liquidity and sweetness in its entire body. If this is an accurate summary of the Stoic view, as I think it is, it must follow that the Stoics did not regard *to logikon* and *to alogon* as contradictory powers but only as different and distinct powers.

[37] I am here glossing over the distinction between the commonly qualified (*koinōs poion*) and the peculiarly qualified (*idiōs poion*). Hardness in general is no doubt commonly qualified for iron (as humanity is for Socrates), but a particular piece of iron has the hardness it has because of its peculiar qualification.

The relationship of Stoic to Aristotelian theory can be understood on its own, but in fact it played out against a philosophical background heavily influenced by Platonism. The works of Plato himself had significant influence on both Aristotle and the Stoics. In later antiquity, the framework of Platonist theory became dominant, even as it absorbed important aspects of Aristotle's physics. It will help us to get a sense of what happened to Aristotle's hylomorphism in this context if we consider a particular example of Platonist analysis in the 3rd century CE. Iamblichus, the student of Porphyry who was himself Plotinus' student, was particularly influential in this regard. We have been considering Stoic and Aristotelian hylomorphism with particular attention to the body-soul relationship, and this fits well with what can be learned from the extensive remains of Iamblichus' treatise *On the Soul*.[38] This book, now known primarily through substantial extracts preserved by Stobaeus, was primarily 'a polemical work aimed against a host of writers (Peripatetics, Stoics, Epicureans, Middle Platonists, and in particular his own immediate predecessors Plotinus, Amelius, and Porphyry), but one that aims to place in clear light Iamblichus' doctrine of the soul'.[39] Consequently its reports on the Stoic theory of the soul and its powers are set alongside those of Aristotle, Plato, and a host of others, including later Platonists and Peripatetics.[40]

For modern readers of Aristotle what is most striking about Iamblichus' work *On the Soul* is the degree to which he assimilates Aristotle's views to what he takes to be Plato's, especially the incorporeality and incomposite nature of the soul.[41] And yet in doing so Iamblichus sharply distinguishes the views of later Peripatetics from the Platonized Aristotle he has constructed. Setting aside other figures he reports on, we may look particularly at what he says about the Stoics and these later Peripatetics. We see this alleged discrepancy between Aristotle and the later Peripatetics in several fragments.

Fragment 3

As some of the Aristotelians teach, the soul is form associated with bodies, or a simple incorporeal quality, or a perfect essential quality. Closely allied to this opinion there is a view, not handed down by tradition but plausibly derivable from it, which makes the soul the combination of all the qualities and the simple summation of them, whether arising as a result of them or existing prior to them.

trans. Finamore and Dillon

---

[38] I rely on the edition with translation and commentary in Finamore and Dillon (2002).
[39] Finamore and Dillon (2002: 10).
[40] This work is the source of SVF 1.142, 379, 420 and SVF 2.720, 801, 825, 826, 830, 831, 835, 1128.
[41] Finamore and Dillon (2002: 93, 101). See frr. 7 and 10. Iamblichus' claim at the end of fr. 7 that he is relying throughout on what he takes to be the common views of Plato, Aristotle, and the Pythagoreans is striking illustration of his determination to assimilate Aristotle to Platonism.

Fragment 7

The doctrine opposed to this, however, separates the soul off, inasmuch as it has come about as following upon intellect, representing a distinct level of being, and that aspect of it which is endowed with intellect is explained as being connected with the intellect certainly, but also as subsisting independently on its own, and it separates the soul also from all the superior classes of being, and assigns to it as the particular definition of its essence, either the middle term of divisible and indivisible beings <and of corporeal and in>corporeal being, or the totality of the universal reason-principles, or that which, after the ideas, is at the service of the work of creation, or that life which has life of itself, which proceeds from the intelligible realm, or again the procession of the classes of real being as a whole to an inferior substance. It is these doctrines to which Plato himself and Pythagoras, and Aristotle, and all the ancients who have gained great and honorable names for wisdom, are completely committed, as one will find if he investigates their opinions with scientific rigor; as for myself, I will try to base this whole treatise, concerned as it is with truth, on these opinions.

trans. Finamore and Dillon

Fragment 9

Certain of the Aristotelians make the soul a body composed of *aithēr*. Others define it as the essential perfection of the divine body, which Aristotle calls 'perpetual motion' [*endelecheia*], as indeed does Theophrastus in some places; or that which is produced from all the more divine classes of being, if one may suggest an innovation on this doctrine; or that which is intermixed with bodies, as the Stoics would have it; or that which is intermingled with the principle of growth or that which belongs to the body as a 'being ensouled'—not present to the soul itself as belonging to it—which is said about the soul by Dicaearchus of Messene.

trans. Finamore and Dillon

Fragment 10

Now Plato does not think that the powers exist in the soul as separate from it, but says that they are naturally conjoined with the soul and coexist with it in a single form because of the incomposite essence of the soul. And Aristotle similarly, since he posits that the essence of the soul is simple, incorporeal, and productive of form, does not regard the powers as present in any kind of composite soul. On the other hand the followers of Chrysippus and Zeno, and all those who consider the soul a body, join the powers together as though they were qualities in a substrate and consider the soul a substance that underlies the powers, and from both of these they construct a composite nature made up of dissimilar elements. In the following way, then, the powers belong to the soul in itself or to the common living being that possesses the soul and is conceived as existing along with the body.

According to those who think that the soul lives a double life, one in itself and one in conjunction with the body, they [the powers] are present in the soul in one way but in the common animal in another, as Plato and Pythagoras think. According to those, on the other hand, who think that there is a single life of the soul, that of the composite—because the soul is commingled with the body, as the Stoics say, or because the soul gives its whole life to the common living being, as the Peripatetics confidently assert—according to them there is a single way in which the powers are present: by being shared in or by being mingled with the whole living being.

trans. Finamore and Dillon

In fragment 3, which reports not Aristotle but some Aristotelians, we begin with a view that could plausibly be elicited from Aristotle's *De Anima*, that soul is a form associated with a body. Its identification with a quality, however, suggests a recasting of Aristotle's views on the soul as the seat of *dunameis* into terminology more familiar from Stoic theory (that formal features are *poiotētes*). The recasting of Aristotelian powers as Stoic qualities is perhaps unsurprising in a work where their theories are being compared so closely and confirms what we have seen above, that Stoic peculiar qualities are meant to do the explanatory work of Aristotelian forms, and perhaps Iamblichus is merely presenting Aristotelian theory in general terms influenced by Stoic theory. But it is also possible that later Aristotelians, who were in dialogue with Stoics, themselves adopted Stoic terminology in the course of the debate.

The corporealization of soul by some Peripatetics seen in fragment 9 is not a mere figment of Iamblichus' Platonizing imagination. Critolaus is the Peripatetic who took exactly this view.[42] Similarly for Dicaearchus' adoption of the harmony theory: we have clear independent evidence of this.[43] So Iamblichus is here giving us confirmation that Peripatetic hylomorphism was subject to considerable development in a materialist direction during the Hellenistic period, no doubt partly under pressure from Stoics. The Stoic views are, interestingly, reported between these two later Peripatetic doctrines[44]—perhaps a further indication of the influence their corporealism exerted on Aristotle's school.

We see something similar in fragment 10. Following up on the alignment of Aristotle with Plato and Pythagoras announced at the end of fragment 7, Aristotle himself is converted to a Platonist view according to which the soul is simple and pure, an entity whose powers are *not* associated with its conjunction with the

---

[42] Tertullian *De An.* 5.1 (fr. 17 Wehrli); Macrobius, *In Somnum Scipionis* 1.14.20 (fr. 18 Wehrli).
[43] See frr. 5–12 Wehrli; also frr. 13–32 in Fortenbaugh and Schütrumpf (2001). The crude view that Dicaearchus denied the existence of soul is explained easily as a polemical interpretation of his adoption of the harmony theory which is clearly attested by Nemesius (fr. 11) and Aëtius (fr. 12).
[44] I am assuming that Stobaeus has preserved the approximate ordering of material quoted from Iamblichus' text.

body. By contrast, it is the Stoics and later Peripatetics who hold that the distinctive powers or capacities of the soul are inextricably linked with embodiment. The issue is cast in terms which may seem peculiar, whether the soul in a given theory has a single or double life. Since all agree that soul is the cause of life to the body, every soul has at least a single life, the life of the embodied soul in a living animal. If, however, a theory holds that the soul is *in its essence* pure and separate (embodiment being a contingent accident), then it has a second life as well, the life it leads when it is free of the body. In fragment 10 Iamblichus correctly reports that the Stoics and the later Peripatetics are committed to the one-life view of the soul, holding that its powers and capacities belong essentially to its union with the body. For the Stoics this follows from their corporealism (Iamblichus takes no notice of the Stoic view that a material soul might survive without the body for a time); for the Peripatetics the powers belong solely to the compound 'because the soul gives its whole life to the common living being'. The soul, in this view, has only one life, the life it shares with the body.

According to Iamblichus, Aristotle is exempt from this claim about the Peripatetics, which makes it so easy to assimilate them to the Stoic position (though not to Stoic corporealism—only *some* Peripatetics went down that path). Aristotle is explicitly said to hold that the capacities or powers of the soul do not belong to 'a composite soul' connected with the body but only to the simple and incorporeal soul which is not itself the form of the body but brings about form in the body without being essentially bound to it.[45] He is, then, still being grouped with Plato and Pythagoras and contrasted with the Peripatetics who hold that the soul has only one life, the one common to body and soul. Though we do not have direct evidence of this in Iamblichus' surviving text, it is not hard to imagine what features of Aristotle's *De Anima* he would have invoked to justify this Platonization of Aristotle. His repeated musing about whether some activity of the soul might *not* require a bodily organ, especially when combined with certain plausible interpretations of the active intellect in 3.5, would be all the licence needed for this polemical Platonist to co-opt Aristotle.

If this is the right way to interpret Iamblichus' strategy here—and I am closely following the line taken by Finamore and Dillon[46]—then we have a new and interesting perspective on the history of Aristotelian hylomorphism. If hylomorphism entails the claim that the soul is essentially the actuality of bodily potentials, then Iamblichus has pried Aristotle's theory of soul away from hylomorphism. In so doing he has left hylomorphic accounts of animal life, including human life, to the

---

[45] This is the interpretation of the difficult phrase *eidous telesiourgon* offered by Finamore and Dillon (2002: 101). I think it must be right.

[46] Miira Tuominen (Chapter 11, this volume), *per litteras*, suggests that Iamblichus is identifying the soul on Aristotle's view with the Platonic unembodied soul, leaving it open to identify a fully hylomorphic Aristotelian soul with Plato's embodied tripartite soul. This more nuanced view is attractive, but fragment 10 seems to me to take a less subtle position on the issue.

later Peripatetics—the materialist Critolaus, the harmony theorist Dicaearchus, and those who retained a more conventional interpretation of the soul as a formal actuality of bodily potentials. What all of these Peripatetic theories have in common is the limitation of the soul's essential nature to the life it shares with the body. These later Peripatetic theories maintain in their different ways a close similarity with Stoic corporealist theory. What most modern interpreters would see as parallels between Stoicism and Aristotle appear to the Platonist of late antiquity as only parallels between Stoicism and Aristotle's misguided followers.

There is an irony in this state of affairs. It is true that Aristotle leaves open the possibility that some aspects of the soul's activity are independent of a bodily organ and that perhaps some aspect of our soul is in some respect immortal. This is precisely what Iamblichus exploits by interpreting him as holding an essentially Platonist view of the soul. But as the long history of philosophical scholarship on the *De Anima* shows, that is not the only way to interpret Aristotle's complex and nuanced (possibly contradictory) views; and it is not an interpretation which takes as central the explicit definition of soul as essentially related to the body that we have seen in *De Anima* 2.1. At the same time Iamblichus' account highlights for us the structural similarities between Stoic accounts of the body-soul relation and the various Peripatetic versions of hylomorphism he reports. But at the same time Iamblichus has ignored one important similarity between Platonist and Stoic theories—both are explicit about the ability of the soul to survive the death of the body, whereas Aristotle is manifestly conflicted on that issue. Iamblichus has selected those aspects of Aristotle's theory which are most apt for assimilation to Platonism and ignored aspects of Stoic theory that might be presented as similar to it. This is quite likely because for Iamblichus the most important error of Stoic theory is their corporealism. Stoics, like certain later Peripatetics perhaps influenced by them, denied the kind of incorporeal reality which is at the core of Platonist metaphysics. Aristotle's text, it turns out, had enough ambiguity that it could be saved from this fate by aggressive interpretation. Aristotelian hylomorphism, like its Stoic corporealist parallel, could not.

Bibliography

Ademollo, F. (2020), 'Cosmic and Individual Soul in Early Stoicism', in B. Inwood and J. Warren, edd., *Body and Soul* (Cambridge University Press), 113–44.

Annas, J. (1992), *Hellenistic Philosophy of Mind* (University of California Press).

Bastianini, G. and A.A. Long (1992), 'Hierocles', *Corpus dei papyri filosofici Greci e Latini* Part I vol. 1 (Olschki), 296–451.

Berryman, S. (2020), 'Hellenistic Medicine, Strato of Lampsacus, and Aristotle's Theory of Soul', in B. Inwood and J. Warren, edd., *Body and Soul* (Cambridge University Press), 9–29.

Bobzien, S. (2021), *Determinism, Freedom, and Moral Responsibility: Essays in Ancient Philosophy* (Oxford University Press).

Finamore, J. and J. Dillon (2002), *Iamblichus: De Anima. Text, translation and commentary* (Brill).

Fortenbaugh, W. and E. Schütrumpf (2001), *Dicaearchus of Messana* (Transaction).

Frede, M. (1980), 'The Original Notion of Cause', in M. Schofield et al., edd., *Doubt and Dogmatism* (Oxford University Press), ch. 9.

Helle, R. (2018), 'Hierocles and the Stoic Theory of Blending, *Phronesis* 63/1: 87–116.

Helle, R. (2020), *Corporeal Unity in Stoic Philosophy* (dissertation Yale University).

Inwood, B. (2020), 'What Kind of Stoic Are You? The Case of Marcus Aurelius', in Barry David, ed., *Passionate Mind: Essays in Honor of John M. Rist* (Academia Verlag), 155–80.

Leith, D. (2020), 'Herophilus and Erasistratus on the *Hēgemonikon*', in B. Inwood and J. Warren, edd., *Body and Soul* (Cambridge University Press), 30–61.

Long, A.A. ed. (1996), 'Soul and Body in Stoicism', *Stoic Studies* (Cambridge University Press), ch. 10.

Long, A.A. (1999), 'Stoic Psychology', in K. Algra et al., edd., *The Cambridge History of Hellenistic Philosophy* (Cambridge University Press), ch. 17.

Reydams-Schils, G. (1999), *Demiurge and Providence: Stoic and Platonist Readings of Plato's Timaeus* (Turnhout).

Sedley, D. (2002), 'The Origins of Stoic god', in D. Frede and A. Laks, edd., *Traditions of Theology* (Brill), 41–83.

Sorabji, R. (1988), *Matter, Space and Motion: Theories in Antiquity and Their Sequel* (Cornell University Press).

3
The Octopoid Soul
Stoic Responses to Aristotle's Soul-Body Hylomorphism

Christof Rapp

Stoic philosophy of mind is usually not considered to belong to the history or aftermath of Aristotelian hylomorphism—for plausible reasons.[1] As is commonly known, Stoic philosophers developed a peculiar physical theory, which also provided the background for their account of the soul. It is owing to this peculiar physics and owing to Stoic ontology that the soul cannot be incorporeal. In this respect the Stoic account of the soul is markedly different from both Platonic and Aristotelian psychology and similar to the Epicurean anti-dualist and materialist position. Still, in spite of these fundamental differences, not only to Platonic dualism but also to Aristotelian hylomorphism, it turns out on closer examination that there are remarkable similarities to Aristotle—especially to the Aristotle of the *Parva Naturalia*, De Motu Animalium, and De Generatione Animalium. With regard to some of these similarities the Stoics even seem to be indebted to the Aristotelian legacy. More than that, in some respects the similarities to the Platonic and Aristotelian tradition seem to be more profound than the ties to the similarly anti-dualist and materialist theorems of the Epicureans—for example, because Epicurean materialism immediately implies the mortality of the soul, while the Stoics are not inclined to draw this conclusion[2] and sometimes describe the relation between the ruling part of rational beings to the animal's body in terms that are rather reminiscent of Platonic dualism than of material reductionism. In particular, or so I am going to suggest, the idea of a centralized soul[3] that stretches out to the animal's peripheral sense organs like the tentacles of an octopus[4] bears a significant resemblance to Aristotle's cardiocentric model of the soul, according to which the whole animal body is alive in virtue of the agency of the soul residing in the animal's heart or in its analogous part. This resemblance

---

[1] I would like to thank Francesco Ademollo, David Charles, Reier Helle, Brad Inwood, Tony Long, and Francesca Masi for very helpful oral and written comments on the first draft of this chapter.

[2] See Eusebius, *Praep. Evang.* 15.20.6 = SVF 2.809 = LS 53W.

[3] I owe this notion to Corcilius and Gregoric (2013), who outlined what they called the 'centralized incoming and outgoing motions' (CIOM) model.

[4] See Aetius 4.21.2 = SVF 2.836 = LS 53H.

includes, among other things, several anatomic and embryological details, the processing of incoming and outgoing impulses,[5] the reference to some version of the connate *pneuma* with its peculiar motions, certain arguments for cardiocentrism, the role of the rational soul and its identification with a rational animal's true self, and, on a more abstract level, the philosophical challenge to reconcile a centralized and unified, centrally located soul with the soul's responsibility for the cohesion and animation of the animal's body as a whole.

In other words, the idea that significant aspects of Stoic philosophy of mind might deserve to be mentioned as part of the history of Aristotelian hylomorphism is only surprising if we associate Aristotle's soul-body hylomorphism exclusively with the claims that the soul is the form or the *entelecheia* of a living body; for in these respects, it is easy to see that the Stoics deviate from the Aristotelian theory by emphasizing that the soul is corporeal or even a localizable body. However, there are strong reasons for assuming that there is more to Aristotelian soul-body hylomorphism than just the claim that the soul is the form or *entelecheia* of the animal's body. Above all, Aristotle's soul-body hylomorphism commits him to explaining how exactly the soul is able to perform its various functions within the animal's body. And in conformity with key theorems of hylomorphism, it is clear that the soul (with the notable exception of the intellectual soul) could perform none of its functions—nutritive, generative/reproductive, sentient/perceptual, locomotive—without an appropriate body or bodily part. All these functions are said to require something like a central hub within the animal's body where the incoming impulses are collected and from where the outgoing impulses are initiated. For these reasons, Aristotle postulates a primary and central organ where the soul resides and that is connected with each of the peripheral instruments or organs.[6] Once it is acknowledged that this requirement, which provides the grounds for Aristotle's defence of cardiocentrism, is not repugnant to hylomorphism but rather an integral element of it, it is no longer outlandish to think of the octopoid soul model in the Stoic philosophy of mind as offshoot of Aristotelian soul-body hylomorphism.

---

[5] Corcilius and Gregoric (2013) quote *De Anima* I 4, 408b15–18, for the incoming and outgoing motions: 'This does not imply that motion is in the soul, but rather that sometimes it proceeds to the soul and sometimes from it; e.g. perception proceeds from these peripheral sense organs to the soul, whereas recollection proceeds from the soul to the motions or traces in the sense organs'. Here, Aristotle mentions recollection as an example for outgoing motions. It is tempting to think, as Corcilius and Gregoric do too, that there are also outgoing motions, when the soul moves the body (even though, admittedly, the entire passage in I 4 is not yet part of the hylomorphic account of the soul).

[6] In *Metaphysics* Z (VII) 10, 1035b25–7—a passage that is clearly committed to soul-body hylomorphism—Aristotle speaks of a part that is 'dominant and in which the formula and the *ousia* are primarily lodged—be it the heart or the brain'. In Rapp (2022) I defend and elaborate on the (nowadays not unusual) view that in the *Parva Naturalia* and his biological writings Aristotle makes sense of just this claim by showing how all essential life functions originate from the heart, which is the seat of the soul.

In what follows, I will first sketch and discuss some core tenets of the Stoic theory of the soul.[7] In doing so I will refer to several minor differences and similarities between Aristotle and the Stoics as we go along, but will primarily focus on unfolding the Stoic account, while postponing the conclusions about possible relations to Aristotle to the end of the chapter. In highlighting here the relation between Aristotle and the Stoics, I do not want to dispute or diminish other influences on the Stoics, such as the influence of Plato or of Hippocratic medicine. However, these non-Aristotelian influences are simply not the topic of this chapter.[8]

Of course, I am aware of the problem that not all Stoic philosophers agreed on all aspects of the soul; especially Posidonius was considered an apostate when he tried to revive the Platonic tripartition of the soul against the Stoic orthodoxy. When I speak of a 'Stoic theory' I will mostly refer to the reports about and quotations ascribed to Zeno, Cleanthes, and, most notably, Chrysippus. When referring to the texts of Hierocles, I follow the widespread assumption that his views are compatible with or even represent the doctrine of the early Stoa, even though he lived as late as in the 2nd century CE. I will also refer to Epictetus, who seems to be less faithful to Stoic orthodoxy but still need not be treated as an apostate.

1

All discussions of this kind have to start by recalling that according to standard Stoic doctrine, nothing incorporeal can act on something else or be acted upon by something else. This is clear from Sextus Empiricus:

T1 According to them, the incorporeal can neither do anything nor have anything done to it.[9]

According to Nemesius, this is exactly what Cleanthes teaches and what he makes the basis for the claim that the soul cannot be incorporeal:

---

[7] For that purpose, I will rely heavily on the seminal paper 'Soul and Body in Stoicism' by Tony Long (= Long 1982) and the excellent discussions in Inwood (1985 and 2014).

[8] Already in 1937 a German-Jewish classicist by the name of Robert Philippson (1858–1942) published a remarkable article in response to Max Pohlenz that commented on several striking parallels between Aristotle and at least Chrysippus. In his above-mentioned paper 'Soul and Body in Stoicism', Tony Long gave similar hints to Aristotelian parallels and emphasized the peculiarity of the Stoic position compared to the Epicureans. Julia Annas' monograph on Hellenistic philosophy of mind (Annas 1992), includes an instructive discussion of the Stoics' indebtedness to Aristotle. Obviously, I disagree with Sandbach (1985) who disputes such an influence. However, my aim is not to refute Sandbach by proving an actual Peripatetic influence; the philosophical point I am interested in is rather that, on an abstract level, Peripatetics and Stoics defend a similar model—with or without causal dependence.

[9] Sextus Empiricus, *Adv. Math.* 8.263 = SVF 2.363 = LS 45B.

T2 Also he (Cleanthes) says: Nothing incorporeal suffers together with [*sumpaschei*] a body and no body with something incorporeal; but a body with a body. But the soul suffers with the body (e.g., when it is ill or cut) and also the body with the soul (when we are ashamed the body goes red, pale when afraid). Therefore the soul is a body.[10]

It is generally agreed that these passages are about causal interaction, so that the word *sumpaschei* is often rendered as 'interacting'; however more verbally, the word means 'suffering together with' or 'suffering simultaneously with'. Hierocles explicates what it means to be *sumpathes* in just this sense. He says: 'For each shares the affects of the other', and he continues with a view to body and soul: 'and neither is the soul heedless of bodily affects, nor is the body completely deaf to the torments of the soul'.[11] This would render a complete argument only if we supply an additional premise to the effect that whatever can be acted upon (*paschein*) is a body, or whatever suffers as a result of the same stimulus, must be of the same sort, i.e. bodily. However, the examples seem to suggest that body and soul not only suffer together or simultaneously, but that one suffers as a result of what the other suffers, i.e. the soul is in a way affected by bodily sickness (being, e.g., restrained through the bodily condition) and the body is affected through the affections that are commonly ascribed to the soul, such as, e.g., the emotions. We will get back to this problem in a while.

One might question Cleanthes' conclusion that the soul is *a body*, for what the argument actually seems to warrant is rather the weaker conclusion that the soul needs to be something *corporeal* or *bodily*. Calling the soul 'a body' might presuppose that, in addition to being corporeal or bodily, the soul has a certain location or perhaps even limits by which it is demarcated from its surroundings. It seems that the Stoics actually wish to defend both claims, that the soul is corporeal and that it is a body. If one wants to make sense of the stronger second claim, things quickly get complicated, for it needs to be explained how two bodies—the ordinary body and the soul-body—could possibly be co-present. This provides a challenge for the Stoic account of mixture and blending, since if the blending is total and the two bodies are fused, it would become pointless to speak of the interaction of two bodies, while if elements of the two bodies are only juxtaposed, the blending of body and soul might seem to be incomplete, i.e. without mutually pervading each other 'through and through'.[12]

---

[10] Nemesius, *De Natura Hominis* 78,7–79,2 = SVF 1.518 part = LS 45 C.

[11] Hierocles, *Elements of Ethics*, IV 10–13.

[12] According to Hierocles (*Elements of Ethics*, III 65–IV 10), the soul is enclosed in the body not as in a bucket, but is 'wondrously blended and wholly intermingled', so that not even the least part of the mixture fails to have a share (*metochē*) in either of them. This poses a challenge for the underlying theory of mixture. According to our main source on this kind of question, Alexander's *De Mixtione*, the relevant sort of mixture is the one of total blending (*krasis*) such that there is a mutual co-extension of

Hierocles, just like Nemesius/Cleanthes, assumes that in the case of emotions the body is affected through the soul, while in the case of sickness the soul is affected through the body:

T3 That is why, just as there follow upon inflammations of the vital spots of the body delirium and strange driftings of thought and even the obstruction of the entire imaginative faculty, so too the body is affected by the griefs, fears, rages, and in sum all the passions of the soul, to the point of changes of colour, trembling of the legs, emission of urine, knocking of the teeth, and right up to the blocking of the voice and a shocking transformation of the body as a whole.[13]

Before we go on, this might be the right time to note that this passage seems to echo the wording of the famous passage on the *pathê* in Aristotle's *De Anima* A 1—though of course with a divergent result. Aristotle wants to show there that the so-called *pathê tês psuchês*—'so-called' because the common habit to assign these affections to the soul is not meant to be indicative of their metaphysical status—are always together with the body (*einai meta sômatos*) and do not exclusively belong to the soul.[14] To show this, he also uses the example of emotions, but while the Nemesius and Hierocles passages mention emotions just in the soul-to-body direction, Aristotle uses emotions bidirectionally, for certain bodily states can facilitate the arousal of emotions even if there are only feeble impressions apt to excite such a state, and even more tellingly, certain bodily conditions can bring about psychic states even in the absence of any pertinent stimulus in the external world such that people find themselves in the *pathê* of someone who actually feels, say, fear (*en tois pathesi ginontai tois tou phoboumenou*). In this context Aristotle does not use the word *sumpaschein*, but he seems to paraphrase the idea behind *sumpaschein* by saying that 'the body suffers something simultaneously with them [*hama toutois paschei ti to sôma*]'.[15]

Getting back to the Stoic position, there is a second famous argument against the incorporeality of the soul that is worth mentioning. It says that death is the separation of body and soul, and that nothing incorporeal can be separated from a body, for nothing incorporeal touches the body. The soul does touch the body and

---

the whole through the whole and the ingredients retain their nature and qualities. In this respect *krasis* is opposed to both fusion (*sunchusis*) and juxtaposition (*parathesis*); for in the case of fusion, the ingredients do not retain their natures, while the case of juxtaposition is like the mixture of beans and grains of wheat; the latter do retain their natures and characteristic qualities and powers, but are not really blended in the sense 'that not even the least part of the mixture fails to have a share in either of them'. For an intriguing discussion of this challenge, see Helle (2019).

[13] Hierocles, *Elements of Ethics*, IV 13–20.
[14] For a fuller discussion of this argument, see Rapp (2006).
[15] In *De Anima*, by the way, Aristotle uses *sumpaschein* once, namely in III 3, 427b22; also, as it were, in an emotional context, when he says that we immediately suffer-with (*sumpaschomen*) when we judge (*doxazomen*) that something terrible or frightening is happening.

thus can be separated from it (in the course of dying), so the soul is body.[16] At first glance, this seems to be a flawed argument, for why should the folkloric conception of death as a separation of body and soul imply the precise sense of a spatial separation of contiguous parts? On the other hand, the argument might be taken as referring to the not-implausible assumption that life processes derive from the sort of interaction between body and soul that requires touch or contiguity in the literal sense and that touch or contiguity in the literal sense can only apply to bodies.[17]

2

Being a body or bodily, the soul must be of a certain material (or, to be sure, of certain materials) and the relation between body and soul, i.e. between the body in the ordinary sense and the soul-body, so to speak, must be subject to the general laws of physics, including its theory of matter, its theory of a unified body, its theory of motion, and its notorious theory of blending and mixing. According to Zeno there are two principles, god and matter, of which the former is responsible for acting and the latter for being acted upon.[18] The two principles do not differ by being corporeal and incorporeal respectively, but only in their mode of being corporeal or active/inactive. For god is said to be a creative principle, and matter a passive principle. Corresponding to these two principles there are two pairs of elements—water and earth are the passive and inert elements and thus side with matter, while fire and air are productive and thus side with god.[19] Indeed, god is said to be a technical (*technikon*) and intelligent fire and to be the airy element, more specifically breath, *pneuma*.[20] Air and fire can sustain themselves as well as other things, while earth and water can sustain neither themselves nor anything else.[21] Each and every thing in the universe will have traits of both principles; god is always in matter and even the inert elements are always pervaded by portions of god or *pneuma*. All things in the universe are a blend or mixture of *pneuma* and matter; on this basic level all things in the Stoic universe are created equal. Still, the *scala naturae*, i.e. the differences between lifeless and living beings, between non-rational and rational beings, is accounted for in terms of different degrees of cohesion and motion.

---

[16] Nemesius, *De Natura Hominis* 81,6–10 = SVF 2.790 part = LS 45D.

[17] The third argument, i.e. the argument from heredity, might be passed over. According to this argument, children resemble their parents not only in body, but also in soul (here: emotion and character) while likeness and unlikeness are always the properties of bodies (SFV 1.518).

[18] Diogenes Laërtius 7.134 = SVF 2.300 part = LS 44B.

[19] Nemesius, *De Natura Hominis* 164,15–18 = SVF 2.418 = LS 47D.

[20] Aetius, 1.7.33 = SVF 2.1027 = LS 46A. [21] Galen, *PHP* 5.3.8 = SVF 2.841 = LS 47H.

In general, things can be composed of separate parts (what we would call a collection or aggregate), or they can be composed of contiguous parts (as in the case of many artefacts), or they can be really unified bodies; of the unified bodies (*hênomena*) again some, probably the living ones, are *sumphua*, grown together. Lifeless things and living beings can both be unified, but the cause of their unity is different. In accounting for the cause of unification and coherence, the Stoics refer to what they call *hexis*, a condition. It is most important that the corporeal *hexis* comes in different modes. Sticks and stones, for example, are held together by what is sometimes called 'mere *hexis*' or '*hexis* alone'; this is the most basic form of cohesion. In plants the place of *hexis* is taken by *phusis*, nature/growth. Note that plants according to the Stoics have no soul, nor do embryos prior to their birth, so that the latter are also held together by *phusis*. We encounter a third kind of *hexis* in animals or living beings, for the cause of their cohesion is said to be *psuchê*. With regard to a body's cohesion we get a scale, hence, of *hexis* or mere *hexis*, *phusis*, and *psuchê*.

More or less the same scale can be derived from the consideration of the movement of bodies, as reported by Origen.[22] Some things have the cause of motion in themselves, whereas others are moved from the outside. This latter class of beings, exemplified by sticks and stones, seems to be co-extensive with things that are held together by *hexis* alone or by mere *hexis*. By contrast, plants and animals, which are held together by nature or soul, have the cause of motion in themselves, even though they are sometimes also moved from the outside. They move themselves whenever a representation (*phantasia*) occurs that stimulates the impulse (*hormê*). In animals that have *logos* the *phantasia* can be assessed and sometimes rejected and sometimes accepted.[23] Thus these animals bring about movement not only 'from themselves', but also 'through themselves [*di' hautou*]'[24]—obviously by exercising their rational faculty to assess representations.

The cause of a material body's unity and cohesion is itself corporeal. It is reported that

T4 ...the conditions [*hexeis*] are nothing but parcels of air. For bodies are held together by these, and it is air which holds together and is responsible for the quality of each of the things held together by a condition. They call this air hardness in iron, denseness in stone, whiteness in silver.[25]

It is not entirely clear whether this is meant to be an account of all three types of *hexeis* or only of the most basic one. In both cases the passage is unhelpful for the

---

[22] See Origen, *De Principiis* 3.1.2–3.
[23] See also chapter 3 in Inwood (1985), together with appendix 3 on *hormê* in Plato and Aristotle.
[24] See Origen, *De Oratione* 6.1.
[25] Plutarch, *De Stoic. Repugn.* 43, 1053F–1054B = SVF 2.449 = LS 47M.

task of distinguishing the three levels of *hexis*. The most straightforward account seems to be given by Pseudo-Galen. There are two kinds of *pneuma*, he says, the natural and the psychic one, while the Stoics introduced a third one, which they called '*hektikon*', i.e. *hexis*/condition-forming. With respect to their proper material, all three levels of cohesion are brought about by different sorts of *pneuma*:

T5   The *pneuma* which holds things together is what makes stones cohere, whereas that of nature is what nourished animals and plants and that of the soul is that which, in animate objects, bestows on animals the capacity of sense-perception and of every kind of movement.[26]

The information supplied here about the cohesion of animals, namely that there is a psychic sort of *pneuma*, accords with the ample evidence we have on the Stoic soul stuff,[27] where soul is said to be *pneuma*, inborn *pneuma*, hot and fiery *pneuma*, intelligent *pneuma*, a proportionate blend of the fiery and the aery substance, etc. All these attributes are obviously meant to bring out the peculiarity of the psychic *pneuma*. Functionally speaking, the soul *pneuma* is peculiar, as we just heard, because it bestows animals with the capacity of sense perception and self-movement. Physiologically speaking, the psychic *pneuma* seems to enhance these functions through being, according to one source, drier and hotter than the more fluid and cooler *pneuma* of nature[28] or, according to another source, a rather thinned out substance compared to the rather dense *pneuma* of nature/*phusis*.[29] According to the embryology provided by Hierocles,[30] the embryo's nature gradually becomes thinner and at the moment of birth it is immediately transformed into soul (or soul *pneuma* respectively) under the influence of the surrounding environment—just as certain stones, owing to their disposition burst into flame as a result of a blow.

The soul emerges from or comes into a fully developed body; the growth and nourishment of the embryo does not need the soul. Nutrition, growth, and metabolism are governed by nature or the natural *pneuma*, not by the soul or the psychic *pneuma*. Also, the natural *pneuma* seems to provide the form or structure of the embryo's body and its organs without any help from the soul. So we do get a structuring principle, but it is not the soul. On the other hand, the soul and the psychic *pneuma* are characterized (solely) by perception and self-motion; as opposed to Aristotle, the Stoics quoted do not introduce a nutritive soul (though reproduction, which Aristotle ascribes to the vegetative soul, also belongs to the Stoic soul). If this is so, we are facing the following problem: When after the

[26] Pseudo-Galen, *Introductio Sive Medicus* 14.726, 9–11 = SVF 2.716 part = LS 47 N part; trans. Inwood/Gerson.
[27] SVF 2.773–89.
[28] See Galen, *Habits of the Soul* 4 = SVF 2.787 = Inwood and Gerson (2008: 78).
[29] Hierocles, *Elements of Ethics*, I 14–20.   [30] Hierocles, *Elements of Ethics*, I 5–34.

birth of an animal the soul *pneuma* takes over, as it were, does it also inherit the physical *pneuma*'s responsibility for the vegetative-nutritive processes? This would be inconsistent with the view that soul is connected with an animal's sentient and self-moving functions. If, on the other hand, the soul becomes the animal's cohesive and moving principle in addition to *phusis* and *hexis* and on the top of them, wouldn't it be unfortunate to have several such unifying principles? Indeed, this would contradict the idea that there should be only one such unifying-cohesive *hexis* for every unified body.[31] And Hierocles' claim that the *phusis* of an embryo is transformed into *psuchê* only makes things worse, if we understand him as suggesting that the whole amount of natural *pneuma* is turned into *psychic* one, without leaving any residue, as it were, of the previous, natural *pneuma*. This conclusion is also in tension with testimonies that attribute the vegetative functions to the natural *pneuma* and the cohesion of parts like bones and sinews to mere *hexis*.[32] If we accept this latter scenario without qualification, there would be no point in saying that the soul must pervade the body through and through, for the body as a living metabolic system would not strictly speaking require the soul's cohesive powers. Both ancient authors and modern commentators used to emphasize in this context that, after all, the three sorts of cohesive power are all provided by *pneuma*, which only differs in tension. This is fine as far as it goes. However, if we go down that road, we are no longer referring to the specific soul *pneuma*. And it was the very point of the hierarchical scale of *hexeis* and also of Hierocles' embryology that there is such a specific soul stuff (in other words, there is the risk here of shifting between the generic and the specific sense of *pneuma*). One way out of these problems is to refer to a passage in Sextus Empiricus where he straightforwardly states an ambiguity in the Stoic notion of soul, pointing out that the Stoics use the soul in two ways, namely for what holds together the whole compound and, more specifically, for the controlling part, the *hêgemonikon*.[33]

It seems then that the Stoic approach faces a challenge similar to one that Aristotelians face when accounting for the unity of the nutritive, perceptive, and thinking soul. And there are, at least, hints that point in the same direction as the Aristotelian solution, namely in the direction of a non-accumulative ordered series or hierarchy in which the inferior items are controlled or transformed by the superior ones or included in them. One might see hints to this idea in texts stating that the soul is the highest *hexis*[34] or referring to the 'best' *hexis*.[35] For example, the purpose of Hierocles' treatise is to show that animals have self-perception of their bodily parts. Looking from this perspective, the unity and

---

[31] Sextus Empiricus, *Adv. Math.* 9.78.18–19.
[32] See e.g. Philo, *Leg. Alleg.* II 22–23 = SVF 2.458 part = LS 47P and Diogenes Laërtius 7.138–9.
[33] Sextus Empiricus, *Adv. Math.* 7.234.   [34] SVF 2.802.
[35] Sextus Empiricus, *Adv. Math.* 9.78.

cohesion of an animal's body differs before and after the birth owing to the presence of soul, since only *after* the birth does this unity become a perceptive one. It would also explain why the soul has to pervade the body through and through. And saying in this sense that the soul or the psychic *pneuma* provides the highest form of *hexis* would be compatible with the operation of subordinate sorts of *pneuma* for non-sentient functions or (relying on Philo[36]) with the idea that the same *pneuma* can have different capacities or can operate *as* reason or soul or *phusis* or *hexis*.

3

Although the soul *pneuma* pervades the whole of a living being's body, there is a difference in degree—some parts have more of it, some less.[37] And it is the controlling part, the *hêgemonikon*, that has more of it. We have already come across the observation of Sextus that Stoics used the word *psuchê* in two senses: for the soul that is present in the entire living being and, more narrowly, for the animal's controlling part. That soul is not just indifferently spread throughout the body; it is noted in all the reports and quotations referring to what the Stoics call the parts of the soul that this soul has a certain structure. Galen preserved an interesting passage from Chryssipus:

> T6 The *psuchê* is *pneuma* integral to our nature, extending continuously throughout the entire body as long as the regular breath of life is present in the body. Of the parts of the *psuchê* which are assigned to each segment of the body, the one that extends to the throat is voice; that to the eyes, sight; that to the ears, hearing; that to the nostrils, smell; that to the tongue, taste; that to the entire flesh, touch; and that which extends to the genital organs, since it has a different principle, is seminal. The heart is the location of the part where all these meet, which is the governing part of the *psuchê*. That is our doctrine.[38]

Chrysippus clearly distinguishes the connate *pneuma* from ordinary breath, but implies that the presence of the soul *pneuma* is dependent on breath and breathing. The main chunk of the text presents the distinction between a centralized part of the soul (that it is said to be in the heart need not bother us now) and several other parts of the soul that are assigned to several particular regions of the body. The text does not say that for each part of the body there is a corresponding part of the soul or vice versa; it just says that these non-centralized parts correspond to

---

[36] Philo, *Leg. Alleg.* II.22–3 =SVF 2.458 = LS 47P.
[37] See Diogenes Laërtius 7.138 = SVF 2634 part = LS 47O part.
[38] Galen, *PHP* III.1.10–12, trans. Long.

individual, definable parts of the body. They are described like vectors that originate from the centralized part of the soul within the body to the several, mostly peripheral, bodily parts that are responsible for the several soul functions. It seems there are seven such parts, five of which extend to the sense organs, one to the place where voice is generated and one to the genitals. All in all, we get eight parts of the soul, then, but the main distinction is clearly between the central part and the parts that stretch out from the centre to the periphery. As for the heart as location of the centralized part, Chrysippus offers a battery of arguments elsewhere against the brain-centred model, which are reported and criticized by Galen.[39] He argues, for example, that people, when forming the word 'egô', point to themselves by touching the breast, not the head,[40] and he refers to the speculative etymology that the heart got its name *kardia* by virtue of a certain power and strength (*kratia*).[41] More notably, he argues that we feel the arousal of anger in our heart and not in our head—the rest of the argument is first a generalization for all other affections and second a further extension beyond the realm of affections to deliberation and the like.

T7   Since anger arises here, it is reasonable that the other desires are here too, and indeed the remaining affections, and deliberations, and whatever resembles these things.[42]

That we feel anger most notably in the chest or in the heart might also be the origin for the theorem that is well known from Aristotle, namely that anger is a boiling of blood in the region of the heart—although Aristotle is not the first to introduce this idea.[43] It also seems that both Aristotle and Chrysippus derive an argument in favour of cardiocentrism from their embryology, for both argue that the heart is generated first and that it generates the remaining parts.[44]

Since the passage quoted in T6 started off with an identification of soul with (a sort of) *pneuma*, we should keep in mind that what stretches out from the centre is strictly speaking *pneuma* or its tensile movements. And these movements go in two directions. The Greek word for the outgoing motion here is *diêkein*—to extend, to reach from one place to the other—while the word for the incoming motions is *sumbainein eis*—to come together, to meet.[45] That sexual reproduction

---

[39] On this discussion in Galen, see Tieleman (1992).   [40] See Galen, *PHP* II.2.9–11, III.5.25.
[41] See Galen, *PHP* III.5.27–8.   [42] Galen, *PHP* III.2.5–6.
[43] For a fuller discussion of this kind of argument as a common thread in Aristotelian, Epicurean, and Stoic philosophy, see again Rapp (2006).
[44] For Chrysippus, see Galen, *De Foetuum Formatio*, Kühn 4, 698 = LS 53D; for Aristotle, see his *De Generatione Animalium* II 5.
[45] As for the incoming motions that come from the sense organs, I take it that they are transmitted to the centre either because this is the place where animals become aware of the perception (as in the Aristotelian common sense) or where they are synthetized and processed to other parts, e.g. in order to initiate movement that responds to certain incoming perceptions.

is assigned to the soul, which was defined mostly in terms of sentient functions, needs an explication. Maybe the ejection or emission of male seed is thought to be accomplished by the kinetic capacity of the soul. Panaitius at any rate assigned it to *phusis* rather than to *psuchê*. According to Aëtius 4.2.14, the corresponding part of *pneuma* is stretched out between the leading part and the testicles, but in Diogenes Laërtius there are indications of an internal debate about whether the soul of female animals also has a reproductive part, such that the soul in the centre would have to be connected with the ovaries.[46] Either way, it is at least clear that the postulation of parts of the soul that are responsible for voice and reproduction complies with the principle that the parts of the soul are individuated in accordance with spatially distinct parts of the body.

Since most of the parts of the soul are assigned to perceptions, one might indeed wonder why there is no part of the soul corresponding to the *kinetic* rather than to the *sentient* nature of the soul. In this context, the awkward-sounding debate between Cleanthes and Chrysippus reported by Seneca[47] about whether there is another *pneuma* called 'walking' or 'strolling around' that stretches between the controlling part and the feet does make perfect sense. According to Seneca's testimony Cleanthes required a *pneuma* extending from the leading part of the soul all the way to the feet, while for Chrysippus it is the leading part of the soul itself that causes the movement of the limbs.[48] It would be interesting to know more about the presuppositions of Chrysippus' point of view; various possible reasons for his thesis have been considered.[49] Is the difference between the initiation of locomotion and other functions of the soul a question of whether these functions are rather permanent or rather episodic? These would be a reasonable criterion; however, it is not clear that walking is less permanent than talking or reproduction. Or is it a question of whether particular functions are essential to the rational soul, while others are not? This may work for talking, because talking is more peculiar to the rational soul than walking; but apparently it does not work for sexual reproduction. Maybe if walking is seen as essential to the execution of voluntary actions, Chrysippus wanted the leading part itself to be responsible for this function, which might be plausible, especially if one considers the anatomic apparatus that is responsible for walking not as a regional and spatially clearly distinctive part of the body, such as the larynx for talking or the testicles/ovaries for reproduction, but as involving the entire body or, after all, major parts of it.

Anyhow, the general picture given in the previous quotation is confirmed and consolidated by a report we find in Pseudo-Plutarch:

---

[46] See Inwood (2014: fn. 15).   [47] Seneca, *Epist.* 113.23.
[48] This seems to resemble the picture proposed in Aristotle's *De Motu Animalium*, where however the *peuma* is not said to be soul but the movable instrument of the soul.
[49] See Inwood (2014: 69–70).

T8 The Stoics say that the leading part (of the soul), i.e., that which produces presentations and assents and sense-perceptions and impulses, is the highest part of the soul. And they call this 'reason'. Seven parts grow out of the leading part and extend to the body, just like the tentacles from the octopus. Of the seven parts of the soul, five are the senses—sight, smell, hearing, taste, and touch. Of these sight is a *pneuma* extending from the leading part to the eyes, hearing a *pneuma* extending from the leading part to the ears, smell a *pneuma* extending from the leading part to the nostrils, taste a *pneuma* extending form the leading part to the tongue, and touch a *pneuma* extending from the leading part to the surface (of the skin) for the sensible contact with objects. Of the remaining parts, one is called 'seed', which is itself a *pneuma* extending from the leading part to the testicles and the other, which was called 'vocal' by Zeno (which they also call 'voice'), is a *pneuma* extending from the leading part to the throat and tongue and the related organs. The leading part itself, like (the sun) in the cosmos, dwells in our head, which is round.[50]

The alternative location of the soul in the head (on the irresistible grounds that the head is as round as the sun[51]) is not surprising at all, because Chrysippus himself mentions in the lines following T6 quoted above that there is a controversy about whether the soul is in the chest or in the head. That the controlling part, according to this latter text, is called 'reason' is slightly incorrect, for it is only in the case of rational beings that one might refer to this part as 'reason'. With regard to the voice, our author is obviously cautious with the choice of his words, which might be an echo of ongoing debates about this particular part and its anatomic location. This aside, T8 finally presents the instructive picture of the octopus and its tentacles, from which the title of this chapter is derived. This picture convincingly captures the attempt to reconcile the idea of a centre of perception and consciousness within the animal with the requirements (first) that the soul must be present in the entire body, (second) that incoming impulses from the periphery must be processed to the centre, and (third) that the central part of the soul might wish to send impulses to the periphery or the limbs, for example in order to impart locomotion. This general picture or model—let us call it the 'octopus model' (with its incoming and outgoing movements)—is corroborated by several reports saying that for the Stoics the feelings and perceptions take place at the suffering parts, but are finally registered in the centre.[52] Compare also:

T9 When a human is said to be in pain with respect to his finger, the pain is surely in the finger, whereas surely the (the Stoics) will admit that the

---

[50] Aetius (Pseudo-Plutarch) 4.21.1–4, trans. Inwood/Gerson.
[51] Probably inspired by Plato, *Timaeus* 44D.   [52] See Aetius 4.23.1 = SVF 2.854.

perception of pain is in the leading part of the soul. Though the distressed part is different from the *pneuma*, it is the leading part which perceives and the whole soul suffers the same experience. How then does this happen? They will say, by a transmission of the *pneuma* of the soul in the finger which is suffered first and passed it on to the next *pneuma* and this one to another, until it arrives at the leading part.[53]

T10 No one, at least no one in his senses, would say that the eyes see but rather that the mind (sees) through the eyes, nor that the ears hear, but that the mind (hears) through the ears, nor that the nostrils smell but that the leading part of the soul (smells) through the nostrils.[54]

One might regard this model (for which Stoic philosophers have also coined alternative pictures, as, e.g., the spider in the middle of her web, or streams pouring from the fountainhead) as a major progress, because it presents a unified centre of psychological functions that registers, unifies, and makes sense of information of all kinds. Additionally, one might think that even though Chrysippus failed to take the insights of Herophilus of Chalcedon and Erasistratus of Ceos into the vascular and the nervous system on board and instead stuck to the heart- rather than the brain-centred approach, his octopus model did, in a sense, anticipate the functioning of a brain-centred nervous system—in quite abstract philosophical terms, of course.

4

Besides its parts, the Stoic soul in the strict sense also has capacities. The above-mentioned Philippson[55] suggests that the 'capacity' vocabulary is taken from Aristotle. For the Stoics the soul in the strict sense is at any rate characterized by the *aisthêtikon* and the *kinêtikon*,[56] the former of which includes *phantasia*. Other texts add *sunkatathesis* as a third capacity of the soul. The texts that describe assent, *sunkatathesis*, in detail seem to refer to the specific human kind of assent, but in principle non-rational animals are also said to have this capacity. In human beings there is a fourth capacity, namely *logos*. It has been argued[57] that *logos* should not be seen as a capacity alongside the three other capacities or not on an equal footing with the other capacities, but rather as a mode of the whole soul's operation, which transforms the soul's imagining, assenting, and impulse.[58] As

---

[53] Plotinus, *Enneads* 4.7.7.2–5, trans. Inwood/Gerson.
[54] Philo, *On the Posteriority of Cain* 126, trans. Inwood/Gerson.   [55] See Philippson (1937).
[56] SVF 2.844.   [57] See Long (1982).
[58] It is unclear what exactly this transformation amounts to. Is this a categorical transformation or does it allow, as it were, of degrees of integration? In Aristotle the non-rational parts of a human soul are transformed by the presence of the rational part only in that they are able to 'listen' to reason.

evidence for this interpretation one could mention that in the case of human beings *phantasia* and *hormê* are qualified as *logikê*—as rational or as belonging to reason. In addition, it seems that it is the early Stoics' psychological monism that requires an integration of all capacities of the rational soul along the lines just mentioned; for example, it is crucial that the presence of *hormê* in the *hêgemonikon* is not construed as something that is alien, or intrinsically repugnant, to the rational soul; and indeed Diogenes Laërtius mentions that for the Stoics reason supervenes[59] as a demiurge (*technitês*) of impulse.[60]

The ruling part of the soul is that which is most truly soul proper.[61] For rational beings the ruling part is rational. In some passages there is the tendency to say that, although a human being consists of body and soul, its true self is the soul or its rational soul.[62] This could be derived from the passage about the use of the word '*egô*' mentioned above in section 3; for when referring to ourselves we point to the seat of the *hêgemonikon* in the chest, as though the *hêgemonikon* was our real self. It has also been argued[63] that the animal's true self should be identified with its *systasis*, i.e. with the principle of its constitution; for this is, according to Alexander,[64] what a new-born animal becomes aware of first. The principle of constitution is an animal's *hêgemonikon* and in the case of rational beings this is the rational soul.

Epictetus seems to be even more explicit on this point. For example he is quoted as saying:

T11 You are a little soul, dragging around a corpse.[65]

He keeps contrasting the 'insignificant' body (using diminutive word endings for the body as he does for all other external possessions), to which we should be indifferent, with *prohairesis*, which belongs to the soul. The body is impeded, constrained; what belongs to our soul, the use of *phantasiai* and *prohairesis*, is not.

T12 You ought to treat your whole body like a poor loaded-down donkey, as long as it is possible, as long as it is allowed; and if it be commandeered and a soldier lay hold of it, let it go, do not resist nor grumble. If you do, you will get a beating and lose your little donkey just the same.[66]

---

[59] The Greek word is *epiginetai*, for which one might also choose a weaker translation, such as to follow or ensue.
[60] Diogenes Laërtius VII.86.   [61] Diogenes Laërtius VII.158.
[62] In a similar vein, Aristotle argues in *Nicomachean Ethics* IX 8, that the thinking element seems to be what the being of each human mostly consists in; in this sense, self-love (well understood) involves that we wish and act for the sake of the thinking element in us.
[63] See Brennan (2009).   [64] Alexander of Aphrodisias, *De An. Mant.* 150.25.
[65] Epictetus, *Disc.* 4.41.1.   [66] Epictetus, *Disc.* 4.1.79.

Epictetus, to be sure, subscribes to the standard Stoic doctrine that the soul is a body. However, being mostly driven by concerns of moral philosophy, he is rather interested in the peculiarity of the rational soul, which is a human being's true self and which should be at the centre of an agent's attention and care. Rather than equating the soul, which has turned out to be corporeal, to the body, as in some respects the Epicureans would do, Epictetus describes the relation of the rational soul to the body in terms that are even reminiscent of Platonic dualism. In this respect, again, Epictetus and the Stoics in general seem to be closer to Aristotle, who is always willing to reserve a privileged and exceptional status to the rational soul, than to the Epicurean materialists.

As we saw, it was a major difference between the Aristotelian and the Stoic map of the psychic capacities that the Stoics did not acknowledge a nutritive part of the soul. It seems that for the Stoics nutrition falls into the responsibility of *phusis*, not of the soul, even though nutrition seems to be conducted by the heart—just as in Aristotle and by similar means. One reason for the Stoics' attitude to nutrition might have been that they put more emphasis on the soul's sentient character as opposed to its merely vital functions. This is a difference to the Aristotelian theory—but a remote echo of a similar move can also be found in Aristotle's ethical treatment of the soul, in which he excludes the vegetative functions from the parts of the soul that are connected with reason and thus become insignificant, at least for ethical purposes. It is contested in Aristotle scholarship whether for Aristotle the advent of the rational soul brings about a transformation even of those capacities that can also be found in non-rational animals (as it arguably does in the Stoic account). Still, at least in the moral-psychological context he claims that the non-rational parts of the soul, i.e. the parts and capacities that are common to rational and non-rational animals, are capable of listening to *logos* when it comes to rational animals. Here Aristotle shows a similar privileged interest in those parts of the soul that are, in principle, sentient and responsive to reason.

5

This is not the place to go further into the exegetical problems posed by the reports on Stoic philosophy of mind. To some extent, the picture given remains sketchy, but the main tenets might be clear enough by now to return to the project announced in the beginning, namely to relate this Stoic picture of the soul to the hylomorphic tradition. To be sure, Stoic philosophy of mind does not, of course, sympathize in any way with the core thesis of soul-body hylomorphism, namely that the soul of living beings, since it cannot be a body, must be the form and actuality of such a body, a condition of the living body that distinguishes it from lifeless bodies. According to the position expressed in T1 and T2 above, this rejection of the hylomorphic framework might be motivated not least by worries about how such an incorporeal soul could ever interact with the body. Now, Aristotle himself, who repeatedly criticized Plato for what he took to be the causal inefficacy of Platonic forms and who touted the ability of his own forms to be causally involved in the physical world, would certainly have agreed that the interactive phenomena the Stoics refer to need to be addressed and explained in detail; in this sense he seems to be thoroughly open to the challenge of accounting for supposedly interactive phenomena. However, in the hylomorphic framework, the soul acts on the body (only) by using instruments that are 'already bodily'[67] and the various soul functions require quite specific bodily parts and organs. Accordingly, Aristotle's explanation of phenomena in the course of which the soul and the body are affected simultaneously, the soul acts on the body, or impulses are forwarded to the soul[68] usually refers to interconnected bodily parts acting on one another or sending and receiving impulses to and from one another—namely, bodily parts that are said to be ensouled or to possess the psychic capacities or in which the soul is said to reside.

Ultimately, all impulses coming from the peripheral sense organs arrive at a primary and ruling (*kurion*) part and all outgoing impulses originate from the same primary ruling part. As is well known, Aristotle identifies this part with the heart, even though some of the arguments for the need of such a primary ruling part would similarly work for any other (more or less) central region of the body. This primary part, the heart, is said to possess the soul in a peculiar way; it is the part where the soul is 'primarily lodged', presumably in the sense that it is in virtue of the heart that the whole animal is alive and performs the functions of the nutritive, the sentient, and the locomotive soul. Due to this peculiar framework, Aristotelian explanations of interactive phenomena primarily refer to alterations originating from, or arriving at, the heart and, instead of accounting in detail for the supposed interaction of body and soul, are content to point out how the part that primarily possesses soul interacts with other regions of the body that are alive, but are at least not said to primarily house the soul.

---

[67] *De Anima* III 10, 433b20; that there is such a bodily instrument is also the main message of *De Motu Animalium* 10. All this is, of course, contested territory (as is true of most of the interpretation of soul-body hylomorphism in general). For some background for my claims, see Rapp (2020: in particular sects. 5, 12, 13). For a more recent and thorough discussion, see also Charles (2021: in particular chs. 3 and 6).

[68] By this cumbersome formulation that either 'the soul acts on the body, or...impulses are forwarded to the soul' I want to capture a certain asymmetry: while the soul in Aristotle can be said to act on the body (even though it might be controversial whether this requires a mitigated sense of 'act upon'—perhaps because it is, strictly speaking, a soul-possessing bodily part that acts on the rest of the body) or to make it move, the soul is not (as I understand *De Anima* I 4; see footnote 5 above) moved in a non-accidental sense, not even by perception; still, since perception ultimately takes place in the common and central sense, the perceptual alterations coming from the sense organs need to be forwarded *to* or *towards* the soul—and this somehow leads to the activation of the corresponding sense (which itself is not an alteration).

Still, one would like to know more about how the soul, which is located in, but not identified with, the heart, is able to interact with its bodily environment. The best available account is given for the case of intentional, self-propelled locomotion, i.e. when the soul is said to move the body. Here Aristotle makes use of the connate *pneuma*. Even though this peculiar stuff is used in the connection with various vital functions (sometimes with reference to the vital heat it is supposed to carry), there is, unfortunately enough, no passage in the Aristotelian *oeuvre* that systematically explains the nature and functioning of this connate *pneuma*; Aristotle either refers to other (not clearly identifiable) places where he has purportedly dealt with it or seems to assume that his readers are broadly familiar with its features. It is clear, though, that this connate *pneuma* is meant to be responsive to perceptual alterations and, in particular, to thermic alterations that are brought about by the perception of, e.g., desired or frightening objects. It is also clear that the connate *pneuma* is supposed to serve as an amplifier and transformer of these feeble alterations. It transforms thermic alterations into extension and contraction, and transmits the transformed and amplified alterations to other regions of the body (most notably by using the vascular system), where they cause pushing and pulling. Obviously, the connate *pneuma* is specially tailored for mediating and forwarding psychic impulses or functions, and it is in this respect significantly different from the other elements; however it is nowhere depicted as being ontologically intermediate between body and soul, but is corporeal through and through. Despite the questions that it raises, the account of connate *pneuma* is at least a serious attempt to give a full, scientifically based account of one direction of the interaction of soul and body; it outlines an interlinked series of impulses and alterations starting from the perceptions that take place in the soul and leading to the movement of the extremities through which the animal progresses.

Now, let us imagine Hellenistic philosophers who were acquainted with this discussion, treating it, so to speak, as one of the loose ends of Aristotelian soul-body hylomorphism. Note also that there might have been no generally agreed upon understanding of what exactly the definition of the soul as form and *entelecheia* in De Anima II 1, another loose end in this debate, is meant to imply (especially since Aristotle himself hastens to mitigate the status of this definition). This would be rather unsurprising given that not even the early Peripatetic philosophers of this period had reached agreement on the legacy of Aristotle's *De Anima*.[69] In this context, Hellenistic philosophers might have thought about Aristotle's account along the following lines. If all or most of the explanatory work (at least in a certain domain of phenomena—and the big rise of the *pneuma* was still to come in post-Aristotelian physiology[70]) is done by the

---

[69] As impressively demonstrated by, e.g., Bob Sharples (see Sharples 2009).
[70] See the contributions in Coughlin, Leith, and Lewis (2020).

peculiar functioning of this soul stuff called 'connate *pneuma*' that is most concentrated in the heart and if, as one might object, the precise relation between the soul that is unmoved, incorporeal, and unextended and the connate *pneuma* that is corporeal and movable remains somewhat obscure, would it not be more straightforward to identify the *pneuma* or a certain mixture or concentration of it (maybe concentrated in a particular part of the body) with the soul? Seen along these lines, there is a plausible path leading from Aristotelian soul-body hylomorphism to the Stoic account of the corporeal soul—in spite of the contrary starting points of Aristotelian hylomorphism and Stoic monism. Such a path is inevitably connected, though, with the model of a centralized soul that emerges from Aristotle's attempt to give a detailed scientific account of functions that are 'common to body and soul' insofar as they are common to body and soul (which is the task of the *Parva Naturalia* and is corroborated by his biological research); this attempt again commits him to showing how exactly and where exactly in the body the soul performs its various functions.

This picture of a centralized soul, or more specifically, the cardiocentric thesis, is above all unfolded in the treatises belonging to the *Parva Naturalia* (to which the *De Motu Animalium* should be attached, as it is referred to in *De Anima* III 10 as dealing with functions that are common to body and soul—according to *De Sensu* 1, the general purpose of the *Parva Naturalia*) and is supported by many anatomic details in the biological writings. According to this picture, the Aristotelian soul resides in the heart as an *archê*, steers ontogenetic development through the heart and its nutritive functions, and is the origin of movements, i.e. movements from the centre through the body and in particular to the limbs. Aristotle argues that it is for good reason that the origin of movements is adjacent to the area where perceptual changes takes places. This is a reference to the unified perceiving part of the soul that is ultimately responsible for the perception of all kinds of objects,[71] which is first,[72] common,[73] and authoritative.[74] Just as in the Stoic octopoid picture, the *prôton aisthêtêrion* plays a role in the explanation of sleep, memory, and the unification of perceptual experience.[75] *De Iuventute* (*On Youth*) and *De Respiratione* (*On Breath*) discuss in addition the capacity for nourishment, the nutritive soul, and its *archē* that is assigned to the heart.[76] Accordingly, these treatises also point out that the heart is the *archē* of the vascular system, that it is generated first in the coming into being of an embryo, that it is the centre for the production of vital heat, and that it is the vessel for the blood and thus ultimately responsible for nourishment. In *De Iuventute* Aristotle also argues that the soul must exist in some bodily part, in particular one which enjoys control

---

[71] Aristotle, *De Sensu* 7, 449a7: *hen . . . ti to aisthêtikon esti meros*.
[72] Aristotle, *Mem.* 1, 451a16.   [73] Aristotle, *Som.* 2, 455a19.
[74] Aristotle, *Som.* 2, 455a21: *kurion*.
[75] For the Stoic explanation of sleep, see Diogenes Laërtius VII. 158.
[76] See e.g. Aristotle, *De Iuventute* 1, 467b34–468a4; *De Respiratione* 8, 474a31.

of the members.[77] Also, this treatise argues for the unity of the bodily part in virtue of which all animals live,[78] and in virtue of which all of them are called living beings. *De Motu Animalium* finally argues that in order to initiate locomotion the soul must be unextended and must reside in the same central area of the body where the perceptual alterations take place. The idea of a centralized soul is thus supported by considerations regarding all essential types of soul functions: (i) the nutritive and reproductive, (ii) the sentient/perceptual, and (iii) the locomotive functions.

This centralized account of the soul that emerges from Aristotle's general hylomorphism has a significant similarity to the octopoid soul of the Stoics and might well have been a model for the latter theory. Above all, there is the idea that the soul occupies a central place in the body and is at the same time connected with other places in the body, above all with the peripheral sense organs. Importantly, both accounts require channels between the central soul and the more peripheral regions that are used for incoming and outgoing impulses.[79] In Chrysippus' version, the centralized model of the soul is strongly connected with cardiocentrism—just as in Aristotle—and his cardiocentrism is justified by some of the arguments that can already be found in Aristotle's *Parva Naturalia* and in his biological writings. Even the terminology of a controlling part (*hêgemonikon*) is partly reminiscent of the way Aristotle refers both to the common central sense (which is said to be common, primary, and authoritative) and to the heart (which is also primary, authoritative, and controlling). It is easy to imagine that the very notion of the *hêgemonikon* was originally derived from similar ideas.

It is a concomitant phenomenon of the centralization of the soul that the notion of the soul takes on a certain ambiguity. In the course of the previous discussions we referred several times to the analysis of Sextus Empiricus, who came to the conclusion that the Stoics use 'soul' in a broader sense (for what is spread throughout a living body) and in a narrow sense (the *hêgemonikon* that holds a central position within the body). Similarly, in the Epicurean account of the soul, Lucretius used the terminological distinction between *animus/mens* for the narrow and *anima* for the more general sense. In Aristotle, this kind of ambiguity is perhaps not as obvious; it is, however, looming in the background of the scholarly debates, when it is discussed whether and how Aristotle's claim that the soul is the form and *entelecheia* of the (entire) body is compatible with the cardiocentric picture, according to which the soul resides (*tout court* or primarily) in a specific part of the body. However, even the most plausible attempts to reconcile these two claims—e.g. by saying that it is in virtue of the soul that resides in a particular primary part of the animals that the entire animal is alive and the soul becomes the

---

[77] Aristotle, *De Iuventute* 1, 467b13–16.   [78] Aristotle, *De Iuventute* 1, 467a20–2.
[79] For the parlance of 'incoming and outgoing impulses' applied to Aristotle (see footnote 5 above); for the Stoics, see the discussion in section 5 above.

form and the *entelecheia* of this animal—have to distinguish between soul in the sense of being alive and the soul that is localizable at a particular place of the living body. In a similar vein, Aristotle's famous simile of the well-governed city indirectly admits the same sort of ambiguity:

T13   ...there is no need for the soul to be in each and every part; rather it resides in some bodily origin, whereas the other parts live through being naturally attached to it.[80]

The entire animal is alive and, in this sense is 'ensouled' or 'possesses a soul'; but clearly this is not the sense in which the soul is said to be in the heart, for the quoted text explicitly denies that in the latter sense the soul is present in all parts of the body. Of course, this is no accidental ambiguity originating from the contingencies of linguistic conventions, since the phenomenon that the entire animal can be said to be alive or 'ensouled' is grounded in the fact that the animal possesses the soul in a particular place and origin.

Finally, it might be worth mentioning that there is a direct analogue of the Stoic octopod in an illustration attached to the final chapter of *De Motu Animalium*. What takes the place of the octopod in Aristotle is a diagram that looks like this:[81]

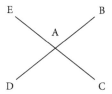

In the text that is illustrated by this diagram (703b26 sqq.) Aristotle speaks of movements caused by the parts that occur in the origin and those caused by the origin that occur in the parts. Clearly, the origin (*archê*) is illustrated by A and the various parts are illustrated by B, C, D, and E. Judging from the immediate context, the letters may stand for sense organs, for the movable extremities, and even for the genitals. Aristotle further points out that according to this model the various parts can also reach each other, namely by going through the origin

---

[80] *De Motu Animalium* 10, 703a36–b1; my trans.
[81] It is not original, to be sure, to use this diagram as an illustration for the centralized model of the soul. Corcilius and Gregoric (2013) (see footnote 3 above), used the same passage (*De Motu Animalium* 11, 703b26–35) and the diagram that is attached to this text in some manuscripts to illustrate their CIOM model. However, they were still referring to the text that has traditionally been printed in the editions of *De Motu Animalium*, which includes only three letters and thus refers to a diagram that does not look like an octopod at all, but like a Λ, very much like the diagram that is regularly printed in chapter 9 of most editions of that treatise. The x-like diagram and the corresponding textual transmission that involved five letters has been brought to light by Primavesi's new edition of the Greek text, printed in Primavesi and Corcilius (2018) and Rapp and Primavesi (2020).

A. With reference to each of the letters, the movements can come to the origin or can proceed from the origin. It is also suggested that within A, the incoming movements are changed and altered before proceeding to one of the peripheral parts.[82] Without entering into a new discussion about the upshot of this diagram within its immediate context, it seems clear that it is meant to capture the idea of the soul as the unified centre of a system that registers and unifies several perceptual impressions; that is the origin of outgoing and the vanishing point of incoming motions; and that, most notably, connects the perceptual capacity with the desiring one—by turning perceptions or representations into kinetic impulses; and this is arguably the same general scheme that the Stoics illustrate by the octopod or the spider.

Bibliography

Annas, J.E. (1992), *Hellenistic Philosophy of Mind*, Berkeley/Los Angeles/London, University of California Press.

Bailey, D.T.J. (2014), 'The Structure of Stoic Metaphysics', *Oxford Studies in Ancient Philosophy* 46: 253–309.

Brennan, T. (2009), 'Stoic Souls in Stoic Corpses', in D. Frede and B. Reis (eds.), *Body and Soul in Ancient Philosophy*, Berlin/New York, De Gruyter, 389–408.

Charles, D. (2021), *The Undivided Self. Aristotle and the 'Mind-Body Problem'*, Oxford, Oxford University Press.

Corcilius, K. and Gregoric, P. (2013), 'Aristotle's Model of Animal Motion', *Phronesis* 58: 52–97.

Coughlin, S., Leith, D., and Lewis, O. (eds.) (2020), *The Concept of Pneuma after Aristotle*, Berlin, Edition Topoi.

Galen (2005), *On the Doctrines of Hippocrates and Plato*, ed., trans., and comm. Phillip De Lacy, 3rd edition, Berlin, De Gruyter.

Gill, Ch. (2009), 'Galen and the Stoics: What Each Could Learn from the Other about Embodied Psychology', in D. Frede and B. Reis (eds.), *Body and Soul in Ancient Philosophy*, Berlin/New York, De Gruyter, 409–24.

Hankinson, R.J. (2003), 'Stoicism and Medicine', in B. Inwood (ed.), *The Cambridge Companion to the Stoics*, Cambridge, Cambridge University Press, 295–309.

Helle, R. (2019), 'Hierocles and the Stoic Theory of Blending', *Phronesis* 63: 87–116.

Inwood, B. (1984), 'Hierocles: Theory and Argument in the Second Century AD', *Oxford Studies in Ancient Philosophy* 2: 151–84.

---

[82] One might wonder though whether this x-like diagram is actually meant as a general model of the soul (or the location of the soul) or whether it just serves to address a local problem, e.g. a problem that is connected only with the locomotive soul. The compliance with *De Anima* I 4, 408b15–18 (quoted above in footnote 5) might suggest that it is meant as a more general model.

Inwood, B. (1985), *Ethics and Human Action in Early Stoicism*, Oxford, Oxford University Press.

Inwood, B. (2003), *The Cambridge Companion to the Stoics*, Cambridge, Cambridge University Press.

Inwood, B. (2014), 'Walking and Talking: Reflections on Divisions of the Soul in Stoicism', in Klaus Corcilius and Dominik Perler (eds.), *Partitioning the Soul. Debates from Plato to Leibniz*, Berlin/Boston, De Gruyter, 63–84.

Inwood, B. and Gerson, L. (2008), *The Stoics Reader*, Indianapolis/Cambridge, Hackett.

Long, A.A. (1982), 'Soul and Body in Stoicism', *Phronesis* 28: 34–57.

Long, A.A. (1999), 'Stoic Psychology', in K. Algra, J. Barnes, J. Mansfeld, and M. Schofield (eds.), *The Cambridge History of Stoic Philosophy*, Cambridge, Cambridge University Press, 560–84.

Long, A.A. and Sedley, D.N. (1987), *The Hellenistic Philosophers*, 2 vols., Cambridge, Cambridge University Press.

Philippson, R. (1937), 'Zur Psychologie der Stoa', *Rheinisches Museum* NS 86: 140–79.

Primavesi, O. and Corcilius, K. (eds.) (2018), Aristoteles, *De motu animalium. Über die Bewegung der Lebewesen. Historisch-kritische Edition des griechischen Textes und philologische Einleitung von Oliver Primavesi. Deutsche Übersetzung, philosophische Einleitung und erklärende Anmerkungen von Klaus Corcilius*, Hamburg, Meiner.

Ramelli, I. (2009), *Hierocles the Stoic: Elements of Ethics, Fragments, and Excerpts*, trans. David Konstan, Atlanta, GA, Society of Biblical Literature.

Rapp, Ch. (2006), 'Interaction of Body and Soul: What the Hellenistic Philosophers Saw and Aristotle Avoided', in R. King (ed.), *Common to Body and Soul*, Berlin/New York, De Gruyter, 187–208.

Rapp, Ch. (2020), 'Introduction: The Argument of De Motu Animalium', in Ch. Rapp and O. Primavesi (eds.), *Aristotle's De Motu Animalium: Proceedings of the XIX. Symposium Aristotelicum*, Oxford, Oxford University Press, 1–66.

Rapp, Ch. (2022), 'Heart and Soul in Aristotle's De Generatione II', in Sabine Föllinger (ed.), *Proceedings of On Aristotle's Generation of Animals—A Comprehensive Approach*, Berlin/Boston, De Gruyter, 269–317.

Rapp, Ch. and Primavesi, O. (eds.) (2020), *Aristotle's De Motu Animalium: Proceedings of the XIX. Symposium Aristotelicum*, Oxford, Oxford University Press.

Sakezles, P. (2011), 'Aristotle and Chrysippus on the Physiology of Human Action', *Apeiron* 31: 127–66.

Sandbach, F.H. (1985), *Aristotle and the Stoics*, Cambridge Philological Society Supp. Vol. 10, Cambridge, Cambridge University Press.

Sharples, R.W. (2009), 'The Hellenistic Period: What Happened to Hylomorphism?', in Gerd van Riel and Pierre Destrée (eds.), *Ancient Perspectives on Aristotle's De Anima*, Leuven, Leuven University Press, 155–66.

Tieleman, T. (1992), *Galen and Chrysippus: Argument and Refutation in the De Placitis Books II–III*, Utrecht, Utrecht University.

4
Alexander of Aphrodisias and the Stoics

Blending, Forms, and the Upwards Story

Reier Helle

0. Introduction

The Stoics hold that animals, plants, and inanimate natural bodies are composites of *pneuma* ('breath') and matter.[1] The composition relation in question is 'blending' (*krasis*). And by blending with the relevant matter, *pneuma* causes the animal, plant, or inanimate natural body to be what it is.[2]

In his work on material composition, *De Mixtione*, Alexander of Aphrodisias discusses the Stoic theory of blending and the specific case of *pneuma* and matter at length. His aim is to refute the Stoic view, and in so doing to clear the ground for his own Aristotelian theory of blending, for the development and defence of which he relies on Stoicism as a foil.[3]

Alexander remarks (certainly correctly) that the Stoic view of how matter and *pneuma* blend to form a composite whole bears a clear resemblance to hylomorphic theories, such as Alexander's own, with *pneuma* appearing to take up (certain parts of) the causal role of form. However, to Alexander's mind, the Stoic view suffers from certain explanatory deficiencies, compared to his own hylomorphism. In particular,

(1) *pneuma* cannot satisfactorily do the causal work of form; and
(2) the blending of *pneuma* and matter, as the Stoics understand it, cannot yield a unified whole.

Understanding these charges, and how Alexander himself seeks to avoid similar kinds of difficulty, is the central task of this chapter. This serves two main goals:

---

[1] I am grateful to Brad Inwood, Alexander Bown, Victor Caston, and especially to David Charles for helpful discussions, comments, and questions.
[2] For references and details, see section 1 below.
[3] Alexander, *De Mix.* is our most important source of evidence for Stoic thinking about blending. Remarkably, out of the forty-seven total pages of Groisard's edition of the text, Alexander's discussion of the Stoic position takes up twenty-one; by comparison, the presentation and defence of his own theory of blending is ten pages long.

Reier Helle, *Alexander of Aphrodisias and the Stoics: Blending, Forms, and the Upwards Story* In: *The History of Hylomorphism: From Aristotle to Descartes*. Edited by: David Charles, Oxford University Press.
© Reier Helle 2023. DOI: 10.1093/oso/9780192897664.003.0005

first, it sheds light on an interesting point in the history of hylomorphism: the clash between the Stoic view of *pneuma*-matter blending and Alexander's theory of form and matter. And second, it will be valuable for a precise understanding of Alexander's version of hylomorphism.

A central feature of the Stoic view is that *pneuma* and matter are bodies with their own independent existence, capable of existing separately from one another, which straightforwardly persists when they blend, each as what it is independently. Thus, an animal for instance is a composite of soul (the kind of *pneuma* in question) and body (the matter in question), each of which is an independently existing body that persists as what it is in the blending. And we are, it seems, in each case meant to be able to understand why the composite is what it is, solely by reference to the relevant *pneuma* and matter as they blend, each conceived of in this way; we should be able to grasp why the animal is what it is, for example, solely by reference to its soul and body as they blend, each understood as having and retaining its own independent existence.

Alexander is sharply critical of this aspect of the Stoic view (for reasons connected to his charges of explanatory deficiency). Yet, he also places significant emphasis on the material basis for natural composite bodies, that is, specifically, on how simpler bodies (beginning with the elements) blend so that more complex bodies come to be.[4] In general, the difference among the forms of the composite bodies is to be explained (at least in part) by the number and kinds of the underlying bodies, as well as their manner of blending (*De An.* 8.13–25); and so, on Alexander's view, plants for instance 'differ very much from one another with respect to form because the matter [i.e. the underlying bodies that are blended] and the mixing and blending of the matter underlying them differ' (*De An.* 9.4–5).[5] Such explanations are possible because the underlying bodies and their manner of blending are a 'principle' (*archē*) of the composite body (*De An.* 10.14–26). And similarly to the Stoics, Alexander holds that the underlying bodies subject to blending are of a nature to exist separately and in their own right (though on Alexander's view they do not straightforwardly persist in blending) (Alexander, *De Mix.* Groisard 27.12–28.2, cf. 33.13–34.7).

This 'upward story' as we may call it, which accounts for the form and coming to be of more complex composites on the basis of independently existing bodies blending with one another, is a striking feature of Alexander's hylomorphism. But it is not the whole story. For Alexander insists that the composite is

---

[4] Natural composite bodies are distinguished from simple natural bodies by the fact that the latter do not have further bodies with their own form and matter as their underlying material basis, but rather prime matter, which is not a body or a form-matter composite. See Alexander, *De An.* Bruns 3.22ff; Caston (Chapter 6, this volume). I will in this chapter be concerned with Alexander's natural composite bodies.

[5] Unless otherwise noted, all translations are my own.

what it is in virtue of its own form, and *not* the underlying blending of bodies (e.g. *De An.* 6.19–7.8).[6] The form is a further item, which 'comes to be / is produced on top of' (*epigignesthai/epigennasthai* + dative) the underlying blending, and it has its own, independent explanatory role.[7] In what follows, we shall see that Alexander's criticisms of the Stoic position helps explain precisely what need there is for forms on his view, which is not served by the blending of the underlying bodies; further, I will argue that the way in which Alexander satisfies this need while maintaining his upward story appears to leave unanswered a certain question about the connection between the form of a composite and its material basis, namely *why* a given blending of bodies should be such that a composite with a certain form comes to be.

I will proceed as follows: I begin in section 1, by presenting certain key features of the Stoic account of *pneuma*-matter blending. In section 2, I turn to Alexander's objections: that on the Stoic theory of blending, the blending of *pneuma* and matter will not yield a properly unified whole, and that *pneuma* is unable to do the causal work required of it. Then in section 3, I consider how Alexander's own view is meant to avoid such problems; and I argue that Alexander leaves himself without an explanation of precisely how the blending of underlying bodies is connected to the form of the composite. Finally, in section 4, I conclude that although the objections raise difficult problems for the Stoics, Alexander's hylomorphism suffers from similar problems and is not, therefore, a clear improvement.

1. The Stoic Theory of *Pneuma*-Matter Blending

The Stoic theory of *pneuma*-matter blending is meant to explain certain facts about animals, plants, and inanimate natural bodies.[8] Centrally, it is meant to explain the fact that the composite body in question is what it is and that it persists in so being. To see how the theory is supposed to do that, it will be helpful to distinguish two Stoic claims:

---

[6] I have more to say about the independence of form from the blending of underlying bodies in section 3 below. On the roles of form and the underlying matter (and its blending) in Alexander's hylomorphism, see also Caston (Chapter 6, this volume).

[7] Alexander expresses his position most clearly in discussing the soul, at *De An.* 24.18–25.4, 26.22–30. But the soul is not special; on the contrary, the soul is a form and it is related to the blending of the underlying bodies as any other form. On this, see for instance *De An.* 5.5–6 with 10.26–11.13; cf. Caston (2012: 11–12).

[8] These are the paradigm cases of what the Stoics call 'unified bodies' (*hēnōmena*). Unified bodies are contrasted with two other general kinds of body: bodies composed of conjoined parts (*ek sunaptomenōn*), such as houses; and bodies composed of disjoined parts (*ek diestōtōn*), such as choirs. See e.g. SE *M* IX 78–9; Simplicius, *In Cat.* 214.24–37; Seneca, *Epist.* 102.6–7 (cf. *Nat. Quest.* 2.2.2–4); Plutarch, *Prae. Conj.* 142E, *Def. Orac.* 426A.

(i) Each animal, plant, and inanimate natural body is a blend of *pneuma* and matter.[9]

(ii) The *pneuma* in each such body causes it to be what it is, by blending with its matter.[10]

According to (i), animals, plants, and inanimate natural bodies are composites of two parts, that is, they are *blends* of *pneuma* and matter. *Pneuma* and matter are both bodies.[11] *Pneuma* is a composite of air and fire with a certain sort of motion—what the Stoics call *tensile motion* (*tonikē kinēsis*) (on which, more below).[12] And in each of the three cases, a different kind of *pneuma* is at issue: in an animal, the *pneuma* is soul; in a plant, it is nature; and in an inanimate natural body, it is 'a mere holding' (*psilē hexis*).[13] The matter is in each case a body whose composition involves earth and water, i.e. the two passive elements on the Stoic view.[14] In the case of plants and inanimate natural bodies, our surviving sources do not further specify which body plays the role of matter or what that body is like; in the case of the animal, it is clear that the matter is the structured animal body in which the soul inheres (so long as the animal lives).[15] However, as we shall see shortly, the relevant body will in all cases be seen as capable of existing and being what it is apart from the *pneuma* with which it is blended.

---

[9] Our most detailed evidence concerns the specific case of the animal, which is a blend of soul (the *pneuma* in question) and body (the matter in question): Hierocles, *Elements of Ethics* IV 39–40 (with 4–10); SE *M* XI 46–7 (cf. VII 234); Seneca, *Epist.* 113.5 (cf. SE *M* XI 24); Stobaeus, *Ecl.* I.178.21–179.17 (LS 28D9–12). However, it is clear that plants and inanimate bodies are likewise (*mutatis mutandis*) blends of *pneuma* and matter: see e.g. Alexander, *De Mix.* 8.25–9; DL VII 138–9; Plutarch, *St. Rep.* 1053E–1054A; SE *M* IX 80.

[10] This claim can be gleaned from several sources, notably: Alexander, *De Mix.* 8.24–9, 19.9–11, 19.15–20, 20.17–21.5; Plutarch, *St. Rep.* 1054A, *Comm. Not.* 1085C–D; Hierocles, *Elements of Ethics* IV 3–10, 38–53; DL VII 138–9.

[11] The general Stoic definition of body appears to have stated that a body is an item extended in three dimensions with resistance: Galen, *Qual. Inc.* 19.483.13–16 (LS 45F, SVF II 381, part); Hierocles, *Elements of Ethics* III 56–IV 3 Bastianini and Long; cf. DL VII 135. Further, only bodies are held to be able to act or to be acted on: Cicero, *Acad.* I.39 (LS 45A, SVF I 90); Nemesius, *Nat. Hom.* 2.21.6–9 Morani (LS 45C), 22.3–6 (LS 45D); cf. SE *M* IX 258. See also Brunschwig 1994, 2003; Vogt 2009.

[12] *Pneuma* is in fact also a blend (of air and fire). I discuss this and some of the special difficulties attaching to *pneuma* in detail elsewhere (Helle 2021).

[13] See SE *M* IX 78–9, 81; Alexander, *De Mix.* 8.23–9; Galen, *Intr.* 14.726.7–11 (LS 47N); Philo, *Quod deus sit immutabilis* 35–6, *Leg. Alleg.* 2.22–3 (LS 47 P,Q); DL VII 138–9.

[14] At issue in this context is not unqualified prime matter but the proximate matter of a given body—i.e. the body which plays the role of underlying subject in each case, such as the animal body to which the soul is joined. On Stoic matter, see DL VII 134, 150; Calcidius, *In Tim.* 292–3 (LS 44D,E); Plutarch, *St. Rep.* 1054A–C, *Comm. Not.* 1085C; Alexander, *De Mix.* 21.16–24, 22.14–27, 23.22–24.1; cf. Long 1982: 39–40; Gourinat 2009: 48, 58. On the matter at issue in this context, see the discussion of T1 below (w. notes 21–2); cf. the texts cited in note 15. On matter and the passive elements, earth and water, see for instance: Galen, *Plen.* vii.525.9–14; Plutarch, *Comm. Not.* 1085C–D; Alexander, *De Mix.* 9.3–8.

[15] Alexander, *De Mix.* 23.22–24.1, with 8.23–9; Plutarch, *St. Rep.* 1052B–C (I thank Ian Hensley for calling my attention to this passage); cf. Hierocles, *Elements of Ethics* IV 38–53; see also notes 14, 21, 22. For an account of Stoic soul-body blending, see Helle (2018).

Claim (ii) connects this composition of animals, plants, and inanimate natural bodies to a causal function of *pneuma*: *pneuma* causes the composite to be what it is and does it *by blending* with the matter of the composite.[16] Thus, the soul of an animal (the relevant kind of *pneuma*), for instance, causes the animal to be what it is by blending with the animal's body (the matter in question). Further, the animal persists in being what it is as long as its soul does this (and no longer); and the same is true for plants and inanimate natural bodies with respect to their *pneuma* and matter.

In this way, the Stoics mean to explain the existence and persistence of the animal, plant, and inanimate natural body (as what it is), by specifying its cause—*pneuma*—and the manner in which the cause acts, i.e. through blending with the matter of the relevant body, which is accordingly seen as a blend of *pneuma* and matter.

Causation, on the Stoic way of thinking, is an active bringing about (*poiein/ facere*) by means of contact among bodies, with the primary case appearing to have been body striking or pushing body.[17] This also seems to be the kind of mechanism assumed in the case of *pneuma* and matter. When *pneuma* acts on (is a cause for) the animal, plant, or inanimate natural body by blending with its matter, *pneuma* is apparently thought to do this by striking and pushing matter in a certain way, and thereby act on the composite.[18]

This gives us a general outline of the kind of explanation the Stoic theory is supposed to provide. To illustrate the structure of this story, we may consider the example of the human being. The human being is a composite (blend) of body (matter) and soul (*pneuma*), specifically *rational* soul. What it is to be a human being, according to the Stoics, is to be 'a mortal rational animal' (*zōon logikon thnēton*; SE *M* XI 8). Now, if we ask why or on account of what, the human being (or any given human being) is a mortal rational animal, the form of the Stoic answer will be this: the human being is a mortal, rational animal (and persists in so being) because its rational soul is blending with its body, thus *causing* it to be so, by acting on the body by (a certain kind of) contact and impact.

From this outline, the ambition of the Stoics is clear. They seek to explain why animals, plants, and inanimate natural bodies are what they are, by adverting to certain bodies which compose them and a certain manner of corporeal interaction

---

[16] The relevant *pneuma* is specifically said to sustain (*sunechein*) the composite insofar as it plays this role, which is generally determined by the Stoics as *hexis*. So an animal for instance is sustained and caused to be what it is by its soul, which in so doing acts as the *hexis* of the animal. A key text here is Plutarch, *St. Rep.* 1053F–1054B; Hierocles describes this in some detail for the case of soul and body at *Elements of Ethics* IV 38–53. I give a more detailed account of the Stoic view in Helle (2021).

[17] Seneca, *Epist.* 65.4, 11ff (SVF II 346a), 13; Aetius, *Plac.* IV 20.2 Diels (SVF II 387); Proclus, *In Plat. Parm.* 841.1–6 (SVF II 343); Simplicius, *In Cat.* 302.28–32 (SVF II 342); Hierocles, *Elements of Ethics* III 56–IV 3, IV 45–47; cf. Clement, *Strom.* 8.9.27.3–4 (SVF II 347). On Stoic causes, see also Frede (1987); Bobzien (1999); Gourinat (2018).

[18] On this, see especially Hierocles, *Elements of Ethics* IV 38–53; I discuss the text in Helle (2018: 103–8).

among these bodies. Due to our lack of detailed evidence, it is difficult to determine whether and to what extent the Stoics precisely articulated their explanation. There are also important general questions whose answers do not (at least not expressly) survive, such as how the Stoics viewed the connection between basic bodily interaction by contact and impact, and the obtaining of attributes, that is, for instance, how the rational soul by acting on the body through contact and impact may cause the attribute of *being a mortal rational animal* to obtain.[19] However, thanks to Alexander's discussion in *De Mix.* we are in a position to say a bit more about blending (*krasis*), and in particular, about *pneuma*-matter blending. There are two points I want to emphasize in this context: first, that *pneuma* and matter are conceived as independently existing bodies, which persist straightforwardly while they blend, each as the body it is independently of the other; second, that when *pneuma* and matter blend so that a certain whole is composed (animal, plant, or inanimate), the blending of *pneuma* and matter is understood without reference to the resultant whole, but rather by reference to certain standing conditions of *pneuma* and matter, each seen as the body it is on its own. These points will be important for grasping Alexander's objections to the Stoic view in the next section.

We may consider two passages from *De Mix.*, 7.1–8 (T1) and 7.18–23 (T2).[20] Here is *De Mix.* 7.1–8:

T1   For he [Chrysippus] says that the mutual coextension whole through whole of two or more bodies through one another in such a way that each of them preserves in this kind of mixing its own substance [*oikeian ousian*] and the qualities in it, alone among the kinds of mixing is blending; for it is a peculiar characteristic of the [bodies] that have been blended [*tōn kekramenōn*] to be able to separate again from one another, which only happens by the blended [bodies] [*ta kekramena*] preserving their own natures in the mixing.

In this passage blending is specified as 'mutual coextension' (*antiparektasis*) of two or more bodies 'whole through whole' (*holōn di' holōn*), in which each body preserves its own substance (*oikeia ousia*) and qualities. That blending is preservative in this way secures the ability of blended bodies to separate from one another. On Chrysippus' view, this is a peculiar characteristic (*idion*) which helps distinguish blending from two other kinds of mixing (*mixis*), by juxtaposition (*parathesis*) and by fusion (*sunchusis*). In particular, it distinguishes blending from mixing by fusion. When bodies fuse, they are not preserved; on the contrary, the fusing bodies are destroyed into one another such that a new body comes to be

---

[19] For more on this connection, see section 2 below. 'Attribute' (*sumbebēkos*) is a general term used by the Stoics for a (non-linguistic) predicate which belongs to a body (see e.g. Stobaeus, *Ecl.* I.106.5–23).
[20] I also discuss these passages in Helle (2018: 89–96).

(*De Mix.* 6.20-5). By contrast, mixing by juxtaposition occurs by means of (mere) surface contact among bodies in a single location, such as when beans and wheat grains are mixed in a bowl (*De Mix.* 6.13-20). What distinguishes blending from mixing by juxtaposition is not preservation and the possibility of separation (which in fact belongs to both), but rather what it is to be mutually co-extended whole through whole; I will return to this shortly (T2).

On the Stoic view, the substance (*ousia*) of a body is its matter (*hulē*).[21] So, for Chrysippus to say here that in blending each body preserves its 'own substance' (*oikeia ousia*) will mean that each body preserves *its own individual matter* (i.e. the body playing the role of underlying subject).[22] In addition, blending bodies must preserve their qualities, but not, it seems, any and all qualities; rather the Stoics appear to have in mind the qualities that each blending body has by being what it is. For Alexander later refers to the qualities in question as 'the proper qualities' (*hai oikeiai poiotētes*; *De Mix.* 13.27-14.1); and we have a report from Stobaeus, according to which the blending bodies preserve 'the qualities natural to them' (*hai sumphueis peri auta poiotētes*; *Ecl.* I.154.14-16). This is presumably also why we are told in T1 that the blending bodies preserve 'their own natures' (*tas autōn phuseis*).

Thus, the Stoic view seems to be that bodies while they blend retain their own matter and qualities so understood, and as a result are able to separate from one another, i.e. *with these intact*. In this way, the blending bodies appear to be conceived as straightforwardly persisting, each as the particular body it is independently of the other(s). More generally we may say that blending on the Stoic view then seems to be a relation among bodies with their own individual matter and proper/natural qualities, which are capable of existing separately from one another, and which straightforwardly persist as they blend. It is clear that this is also how Alexander understands the theory. And as we shall see below, he does not share the Stoic notion that each body in blending persists as the particular it originally was; on the contrary, the particular bodies that go into the blending are on his view irretrievably destroyed (though something of the same kind can be recovered).

Now, the next point we should notice is that on the Stoic theory, blending is defined by reference to certain standing conditions of the blending bodies, and not to any further result, such as a composite whole. For this, it will be helpful to look at another passage, *De Mix.* 7.18-23:

---

[21] DL VII 134, 150; Stobaeus, *Ecl.* I.179.6-12 (LS 28D10-12); cf. Simplicius, *In Cat.* 48.11-16 (LS 28E); Stobaeus, *Ecl.* I.367.17-22 (LS 28F); for other relevant references, see note 14 above.

[22] That this is the correct interpretation of T1 is strongly suggested by Alexander, *De Mix.* 14.3-7; other sources indicate that this was indeed Chrysippus' view: see Galen, *In Hipp. De Nat. Hom.* I 32.8-11 Kühn (SVF II 463), *De Elem. Ex. Hipp.* 489.6-10 Kühn (SVF II 464); Plotinus, *Enn.* 2.7.2-22.

T2 And he [Chrysippus] supposes that such a mutual coextension of [bodies] blending occurs by the blending bodies passing through one another so that no part in them is not participating in all the [ingredients] in such a blended mix; for if this were not the case, what is occurring would no longer be blending, but juxtaposition.

In this passage, Alexander is specifying what it is, on Chrysippus' view, for blending bodies to be mutually co-extended whole through whole.[23] When bodies are so co-extended, a certain relation holds between the parts of each of them and all the ingredients in the blend: each part of each blending body 'participates' (*metechein*) in all the ingredients in the blend in question. Thus, when for example water and wine are blending, each part of the water and each part of the wine participates in both water and wine. Accordingly, each part of the wine will be watery in addition to being wine, and vice versa for the parts of the water. On the interpretation I have defended elsewhere, the participation relation obtains here in virtue of a certain kind of corporeal interaction whole through whole among the blending bodies, such that each part of the wine is watery (in addition to being wine) because it is being continuously struck and affected by (parts of) the water in the blending, and vice versa for the parts of the water (see Helle 2018 and 2021: 204–8). For present purposes, the details are not crucial. What is important, rather, is that blending appears to be defined in terms of standing conditions of the blending bodies, without reference to any kind of further result.[24] This is in contrast to the Stoics' own notion of mixing by fusion as well as Alexander's understanding of blending, which are both defined as processes by which another body comes to be, as the original fusing/blending bodies are destroyed (in Alexander's case albeit not utterly).

When we now again look at the case of *pneuma* and matter, the impression we get from the theory of blending is that the Stoics mean to explain how an animal, a plant, or an inanimate natural body is composed and caused to be what it is, in terms of *pneuma* and matter and certain of their standing conditions, without reference to the relevant composite. This impression is reinforced by our best surviving evidence of how the Stoics attempted to explain the composition and being of the animal, namely by appealing to how soul and body and their parts interrelate in blending (Hierocles, *Elements of Ethics* IV 38–53, with 3–10; cf. also Helle 2018: 103–8).

---

[23] Notably, T2 is the only report we have which describes in detail how Chrysippus understands the relation of mutual co-extension whole through whole which obtains in blending. In Helle (2022), I argue that Alexander preserves Chrysippus' definition of blending in Alexander, *De Mix.* III, and that the definition can be reconstructed from T1 and T2.

[24] In T2, the function of the phrase 'all the [ingredients] in such a blended mix' is not to define blending by reference to a further result, but to specify the ingredients in which the parts participate in each case—i.e. all the ingredients involved in each case of blending (whatever they may be).

On the interpretation I have sketched in this section, then, it appears that the theory of *pneuma*-matter blending was part of a certain explanatory project, i.e. accounting for why the animal, plant, and inanimate natural body is what it is, on the basis of certain parts of which it is composed, where the parts in question are conceived of as independently existing bodies with their own individual matter and proper/natural qualities, and the relevant composition relation is defined without reference to a resultant composite. In the next section, we shall see that according to Alexander the Stoic theory will not in fact deliver the required kind of explanation.

2. Alexander's Objections

Alexander criticizes the Stoics frequently in his extant writings. *De Mix.*, in particular, is a veritable tour de force of objections directed at the theory of blending in general as well as the specific case of *pneuma*-matter blending. We are going to focus on two objections in particular: the first, which we may call *the unity objection*, alleges that Stoic blending yields no more than a juxtaposition of bodies and thus never a composite whole with the kind of unity found in animals, plants, and inanimate natural bodies. The second objection concerns the Stoic story of *how pneuma* by blending with matter is supposed to cause the composite to be what it is. The Stoics hold that *pneuma* is able to do this on account of its material composition as a blend of air and fire and the attributes attendant upon it, including fineness of parts, flexibility of size and shape, and, most notably, *pneuma*'s continuous 'tensile motion' (*tonikē kinēsis*). To Alexander's mind, this material account falls well short of the target; what is needed is the notion of form (*eidos*), and specifically, the form *of* the composite animal, plant, etc. Now, let us begin with the unity objection.

According to Alexander, the Stoics are caught on the horns of a dilemma. Either bodies are not straightforwardly preserved when they blend (i.e. as the original particulars, with their own matter and qualities) or, if they are so preserved, blending turns out to be no more than juxtaposition. Here is *De Mix.* 14.13–27:[25]

T3 For if the blended bodies have been mixed whole through whole and neither of them has a part in the blend unmixed with the other, it is impossible that either of them is surrounded by its particular surface; for every part of them that is surrounded by its own surface will be unmixed with the other (for the surface of wine cannot be the surface of water, or that of water the surface of wine), so that blending will in this way not be mixing whole through whole,

[25] On this passage, see also Helle (2018: 96–8).

but they would be saying that blending is juxtaposition of parts with parts, being on guard against which they say that mixing is one thing and blending another. But if there should be no part of the mixed [bodies] with its own circumscription and surface, but instead the body that has come to be is a complete homoiomer, there would no longer be juxtaposition, but blending whole through whole; but the original bodies of the mixed [ingredients] would no longer be preserved, instead they would have been fused and destroyed.

De Mix. 14.13–27

Glossing over some of the details, the argument appears to proceed as follows: Alexander assumes that if bodies are preserved in the Stoic way, then they remain surrounded by their own surface/circumscription (*idia / oikeia epiphaneia / perigraphē*) while blended. But if so, they will not be blended whole through whole, but only juxtaposed, that is, they will simply be in contact at their surfaces and part with part. If, on the other hand, the bodies are not preserved in this way, they will be fused and destroyed, not blended.

That preservation involves retention of one's own surface is likely a genuine Stoic claim. It seems the Stoics thought about bodies as continuously interacting by means of contact (and impact) at their (own) surfaces (and the surfaces of their parts) while they are blending; indeed, we even have a Stoic text which describes blending in terms of juxtaposition (see Hierocles, *Elements of Ethics* IV 3–10, 38–53; Helle 2018: 97–108).[26] Nevertheless, the Stoics maintained a distinction between blending and the kind of mixing illustrated by beans and grains juxtaposed in a bowl (see section 1 above). It is this distinction that Alexander is calling into question; to distinguish blending from *mere* juxtaposition, the Stoics must abandon their notion of preservation. But to do this will be to admit that the bodies in question are not blended after all, but rather destroyed and fused together. Thus, there can be no blending, as the Stoics understand it.

Why did Alexander suppose that the Stoic notion of preservation is incompatible with blending whole through whole? The answer suggested by T3 is this: if bodies are so preserved, there will be no further body of the right sort as a result of the blending, that is, 'a complete homoiomer' (*pan homoiomeres*).[27] Alexander

---

[26] Notably, at the end of the account of Chrysippus' theory of blending in *De Mix.*, Alexander also reports that Chrysippus and his followers think that noxious gases and vapors 'blend with those who are affected by them, being juxtaposed whole through whole' (*kirnasthai tois hup' autōn paschousin, hola di' holōn paratithemena*; Alexander, *De Mix.* 9.9–10). See also Plutarch, *Comm. Not.* 1080E–F; DL VII 135; Alexander, *De Mix.* 6.16–20, 28.7–9; Stobaeus, *Ecl.* I 154.10–14 (in SVF II 471); Simplicius, *In Cat.* 302.28–36 (contains SVF II 342).

[27] A homoiomerous ('like-parted') item—a homoiomer—is composed of qualitatively identical parts. For instance, according to Aristotle, blood is homoiomerous, since it is composed of parts that are also blood; by contrast, an arm is *anhomoiomerous*, since it is composed *inter alia* of blood, flesh, and bone.

makes this point explicitly again later on in *De Mix.*, when he says concerning his own theory that the bodies going into the blending 'were not preserved in their original state in the mix; for that would be juxtaposition, not blending; for in the case of [bodies] blending, that which has come to be from the blending is one and a complete homoiomer (*hen te kai homoiomeres pan*)' (*De Mix.* 34.4–7). And the same point recurs in *De An.* 11.15–12.7. Here, Alexander argues that soul and body do not compose the animal as parts 'which are preserved in the whole', because 'that would then be a juxtaposition of soul and body' (trans. Caston 2012). It appears that Alexander thinks that Stoic blending must be rejected because it cannot produce a properly unified whole.

In *De Mix.*, Alexander does not explain precisely why a properly unified whole will not be composed through Stoic blending. It is likely that the Stoics did not share Alexander's assumption that blending ought to produce a homoiomer, a requirement derived from Aristotle's discussion in *GC* I.10 (328b21–2, 328a4).[28] But I do not think Alexander is simply pointing out that the Stoics failed to agree with Aristotle. The issue, it seems to me, is rather one of explanation. Since blending bodies, on the Stoic theory, are preserved with their own matter and natural qualities and blending is defined as a relation among bodies so preserved (see T1 above), it is not obvious how blending bodies would be joined together in such a way that a unified whole results or how their being blended would explain this. But in the case of *pneuma* and matter, at least, the Stoics do think that a unified whole results (i.e. that an animal, plant, or inanimate natural body is composed by *pneuma* and matter). It may thus seem they owe us an explanation of what the unity of the animal, plant, or inanimate natural body consists in, such that it obtains as the result of *pneuma* and matter blending.

Alexander's general line of argument is made more explicit in *De An.* 21.16–21. Alexander is here concerned with the view that the soul is the form of the body and a substance in its own right, capable of separate existence, to which he objects as follows:

> One might reasonably ask those who say that the soul is the form of the body in this way, what it is that joins them and what it is that holds them together given that they are separate [*kechōrismena*] from one another and differ in their natures, in such a way that what is composed from them turns out to be a single thing [*hen ti*] and remains together; for it is difficult to find the cause [*to aition*] of the unity of such things, both at the inception of their coming together and after their coming together.

---

[28] For an argument that Stoic blends are not homoiomerous, see Helle (2018).

Though the target in this passage is different, Alexander is raising the same general problem he raised for the Stoics in T3: it is difficult to see how a unity might be composed, given that the items that are to do the composing are conceived as independent of one another.

There is one explanation in particular that Alexander has in mind and which the Stoics reject: to say that blending is defined as a process in which the ingredient bodies *become one body*. This would be fusion, not blending, according to the Stoics. As we saw above, blending is, in contrast to fusion, defined without reference to a further result. The question, then, is this: what is it about *pneuma* and matter blending which explains that a unified body such as an animal is composed, if there is nothing in the definition of blending that tells us that this should be so?

Now, the Stoics do not hold that the theory of blending alone explains how supposedly unified items such as animals, plants, and inanimate natural bodies are composed by *pneuma* and matter. Rather, they think that *pneuma* in particular, by blending with matter, plays a certain causal role, in virtue of which there will be a composite and unified animal, plant, or inanimate natural body. Crucially, as we saw in the last section, *pneuma* is thus meant to cause the composite to be *what it is*, and this includes causing it to have the unity characteristic of animals, plants, and inanimate natural bodies.[29] The objection we have considered so far targets the Stoic theory of blending, alleging that it will not serve to explain how a unity is composed. The second objection I want to focus on is concerned specifically with *pneuma*'s role in the Stoic story.

According to Alexander, the Stoics 'refer the being of each thing and being preserved and remaining together to *pneuma*, as it passes through all things', because they are 'unable to distinguish form from matter in their theory' (*De Mix.* 21.8–15); and since they have been taken in by certain doctrines, they trace unity to 'certain bonds and material causes and to a certain *pneuma* as it passes through the substance [i.e. the matter]' (*De Mix.* 18.22–7).[30] What the Stoics need but did not see for themselves (*De Mix.* 18.22–3) is form (*eidos*), and indeed specifically the form of the composite. This will do the job to which the Stoics' own material causal story is inadequate. That at any rate, is Alexander's view.

---

[29] From the surviving sources, it seems that animals, plants, and inanimate natural bodies were considered to be unified, on the Stoic view, in each being a single subject (of the relevant kind, i.e. animal, plant, inanimate natural body, and their subkinds as appropriate) in its own right (*kath' hauto*). (See especially Seneca, *Nat. Quest.* II.2.4; SE, *M* IX 78–9, cf. Plutarch, *Def. Orac.* 425F–426A; Plutarch, *St. Rep.* 1054E-F.) If that is right, we are supposed to be able to understand how in each case there should be a composite that is a single subject (of a given kind) in its own right—and not merely a juxtaposition—from *pneuma*'s activity as it blends with the matter.

[30] In Alexander, *De Mix.* 18.12–27, Alexander is discussing the Stoic account of the unity of the cosmos; but as he well knows, this account is not specific to the cosmos, which is unified in the same way as other bodies, and the criticism is evidently not specific to the cosmos either.

Alexander is right to think that *pneuma* is meant to take up duties assigned by him (and Aristotle) to form (*eidos*), e.g. causing the composite body to be and remain what it is. It is true moreover that there are difficulties in seeing exactly how *pneuma* is to do that. The Stoics held that *pneuma* acts through a distinctive kind of motion, so-called tensile motion (*tonikē kinēsis*), which they characterized as motion moving at once inward and outward.[31] And *pneuma* was thought to have tensile motion because it is a composite of air, which moves inward, and fire, which moves outward.

Our sources do not articulate in detail how tensile motion is supposed to explain the causal efficacy of *pneuma*. But we are told that the outward tensile motion is responsible for being qualified as a certain kind of thing, and the inward for being a single determinate something (Simplicius, *In Cat.* 269.14–16; cf. Nemesius, *Nat. Hom.* 2.18.6–8). The idea is thus apparently that by moving at once inward and outward, *pneuma* may cause a body to be at once a single determinate something of a certain kind, for instance a single animal, plant, or inanimate natural body.[32]

Alexander registers several difficulties that in one way or another pertain to *pneuma* and its causal role. Here are three of them: (1) It is not clear that *pneuma* is the right sort of thing for the job; being a kind of air, *pneuma* would seem to be more passive than active, and what motive power it might possess would appear borrowed and not its own (*De Mix.* 19.21–20.5). (2) It is hard to see how tensile motion could be moving at once inward and outward; on the face of it, this seems paradoxical (*De Mix.* 21.2–7). And (3), even if such motion can be explained, it is still unclear how it is linked to *pneuma* causing the composite to be and remain what it is (*De Mix.* 21.2–5, 19.12–23).

For us, it is (3) that is of particular interest. What we want here is an account that tells us how *pneuma*'s inward and outward motion when it blends with the matter of an animal, plant, or inanimate natural body is connected to that composite being (caused to be) what it is.

It seems clear enough that the Stoics were committed to there being such a connection. For they appear to have held that whenever a body is caused to have an attribute, there is an underlying pattern of locomotion among the parts that the body is caused to have throughout itself, *by the having of which* the attribute belongs to it. So for instance, when a human being is caused to be rational by its soul (see section 1 above), there is an underlying pattern of locomotion that it is caused to have throughout itself and by which this attribute belongs to it. Likewise, when a body is caused to be hot, it is caused to have a certain pattern of

---

[31] Alexander, *De Mix.* 21.2–7; Simplicius, *In Cat.* 269.14–16; Nemesius, *Nat. Hom.* 2.18.6–8; cf. Stobaeus, *Ecl.* 153.24–154.2.

[32] For a more detailed account of what tensile motion is and how it belongs to *pneuma*, see Helle (2021).

locomotion.[33] It is hard to determine exactly how the Stoics conceived of the connection between attributes and patterns of internal locomotion among the parts of the body. There is no reason to think they believed that for a body to have an attribute F, whatever it might be, just is for it to have a pattern a locomotion throughout it, where the pattern in question can be specified without reference to being F. Nor need we think that the pattern is to be specified in purely locomotive terms. There are cases where it is so specified: for instance, when a body is caused to be hot by fire, it is caused to have expansive (loco)motion throughout it, that is, a pattern of motion in which the parts are moving outward from the centre of the body. And this is so because the attribute of being hot is understood in terms of expansive (loco)motion.[34] But there is no good reason to think this generalizes.[35]

To understand and assess the Stoic position properly, we would need an account of the general sense in which being caused to have a pattern of locomotion underlies being caused to have an attribute. We do not know to what extent such an account was developed or how precise it might have been, and I will not try to reconstruct what it could look like here. For us, it is enough to note that given the general connection, we can reasonably expect there to be a specific connection between *pneuma*'s acting through tensile motion as it blends with matter on the one hand, and the composite (animal, plant, or inanimate natural body) being caused to be (and remain) what it is on the other hand. Moreover, even when we understand the general connection, the difficulty indicated by Alexander remains. For we would still need a specific explanation linking the activity of *pneuma* in blending to the effect on the composite.

Giving a satisfying explanation of this is no simple matter. To see why, let us suppose for the sake of argument that what it is to be an animal just is for a certain kind of body to have a certain pattern of locomotion F. Having specified the pattern of locomotion that must be caused, it is not now enough for the Stoics to say that the relevant *pneuma* (the soul) by blending with the matter of the animal (the body) causes this pattern to prevail throughout the animal they compose. In addition, we want to know how and why that is—we want to know what it is that links the effect to that blending of pneuma and matter.[36]

---

[33] Simplicius, *In Phys.* 1320.19–21 Diels (SVF II 496); Simplicius, *In Cat.* 237.30–238.32; Hierocles, *Elements of Ethics* IV 38–53; Simplicius, *In Cat.* 269.14–16; Nemesius, *Nat. Hom.* 2.18.2–10; cf. Plotinus, *Enn.* 4.7.4.7–16, 16–18; SVF II 780; SE *M* IX 81–5; Menn (1999: 243–7); cf. Sambursky (1959: 27); Long (1974: 158); Bobzien (1998: 18–58).

[34] Galen, *De Caus. Cont.* 1.1–24 (LS 55F), *Nat. Fac.* 106.13–17 (LS 47E, SVF II 406); Plutarch, *De Frigido* 946B–C, 948D–E, 949B (LS 47T, SVF II 430 part), 952C–E; cf. Galen, *De Trem.* 616.4–618 (SVF II 446).

[35] The Stoics appear to have considered soul and the attributes in terms of which it is defined as fundamental, not to be specified in terms of some non-psychic pattern of locomotion. On this, note: Cicero, *ND* II 18, 21–2, 29–30; SE *M* IX 101–2; SVF III 306; Alexander, *De Mix.* 21.16–24; DL VII 134; cf. Menn (1999: 222–3).

[36] This objection to the Stoic account bears a certain resemblance to Aristotle's complaint against the predecessors at *De An.* 407b13ff, that they fail to explain how body and soul are connected and how it is that these two items in particular are such as to be connected in precisely the right ways; cf. also for instance *PA* 641b26–30; *GA* 765b4–6.

From our sources, it is not clear whether the Stoics addressed this issue; it may well be that they never spelled out their view to the degree needed for an answer, or even for an *answer schema*. However, for Alexander, the point is presumably not merely that the Stoics failed to provide an answer, but that their approach is not suited to give a good answer at all. It is not yet obvious why this stronger conclusion should be accepted. But one reason may be derived from the unity objection to the Stoic theory of blending: since blending bodies are straightforwardly preserved each as what it is independently and blending is not defined by reference to a further result, it is hard to see how and why *the right effect* should result from *pneuma* blending with matter, for instance, what it is to be an animal, which is a single determinate subject in its own right—something unified—and not a juxtaposition of soul and body.

It would be precipitate at this point to conclude that all is lost for the Stoics. The task they face is a difficult one to be sure: to explain how and why the animal, plant, or inanimate natural body is caused to be what it is by *pneuma* acting through tensile motion as it blends with matter, and to do so in a way that shows that the composite in question is unified as a single determinate subject (in its own right, *kath' hauto*; see note 29), all the while maintaining that *pneuma* and matter are preserved as each is independently, with their own matter and qualities (see section 1 above), and that their blending is understood without reference to the resultant composite. However, the task has not, it seems to me, been shown to be impossible. Toward the end of this chapter, in section 4 below, I shall indicate how the Stoics could begin to approach it. In outline, I will suggest that the unity of the composite may be explained in terms of a certain distinctive way in which *pneuma* interacts with matter in blending.

Nevertheless, it is clear that Alexander's objections raise serious difficulties for the Stoics, difficulties which demand a response if the theory of *pneuma*-matter blending is to succeed. Further, whether or not Alexander decisively refutes the Stoics, his objections give reason to adopt a different position that avoids such difficulties. In the next section we shall see how Alexander sought to do that.

3. Alexander's Account of Blending, Hylomorphism, and the Upward Story

Following his criticism of the Stoic view, Alexander proceeds to give his own theory of blending and mixing, in *De Mix*. XIII-XV. The discussion in these chapters is modelled on *GC* I.10, but Alexander expands on Aristotle's remarks and adds a significant level of detail, including several illuminating examples.[37]

---

[37] Alexander, *De Mix*. XIII-XV is Alexander's most detailed account of blending; still, he does not give us much more than a general outline of his view. We are obliged therefore to accept a degree of uncertainty on some points.

I shall begin in this section, by introducing certain key features of Alexander's account of blending, which will allow us to see how he intends to avoid the kinds of explanatory difficulty raised by the two objections considered above. Next, I am going to argue that Alexander remains open to a complaint similar to the second of these objections: that there is no explanation of the connection between a given blending of bodies and the form of the composite produced by that blending. We will see that despite the explanatory significance of blending, the form of the composite is an *emergent* phenomenon according to Alexander. In section 4 below, I examine what this means for the dialectic between Alexander and the Stoics.

In *De Mix.*, Alexander's account of blending proceeds in two stages: he first specifies the kind of items capable of blending (the relevant *mikta*); then he determines what blending is and what it is for these items to be subject to blending.

The items capable of blending are assumed to be items 'that have a nature to exist in virtue of themselves' (*ta kath' hauta huphestanai phusin echonta*; *De Mix.* 27.12–13), or equivalently, items which are separate (*chorista*) in the sense of being capable of existing by themselves (27.15–16, 18–19, 22–3). Since only substances (*ousiai*) are of this kind, only substances will be capable of blending (27.15–16). But not all substances are able to blend. Alexander takes care to specify that even though forms (*eidē*) are substances, they cannot blend, because they cannot exist apart from matter (27.21–3). Matter for its part is not a suitable subject for blending, since it cannot exist in actuality without form (27.23–4). This leaves bodies (*sōmata*) as the kind of items capable of blending (27.24–28.2).

As for what blending is, Alexander gives the following summary statement:

T4   And blending is this: the unification by means of acting and being acted on of bodies juxtaposed with one another, through change without destruction of any of them.

De Mix. 33.1–3

Blending is here said to be a certain kind of process of unification (*henōsis*). The process occurs through reciprocal action and affection among bodies that are juxtaposed. But it is not itself a process *of juxtaposition*. Rather, the juxtaposition is a precondition of the interaction required for the right kind of unification (*De Mix.* 32.15–19, 33.5–13); I return to this interaction below (T5).[38]

---

[38] In standard Aristotelian fashion, interaction is understood in terms of contrarieties, such as hot-cold, dry-moist. In order for reciprocal action and affection to occur, the bodies must be contrarily related, with respect to one or more contrarieties, e.g. as hot to cold (or hotter to colder), dry to moist (or drier to more moist), etc.; and when they interact, the bodies will act on and be affected by one another in respect of their various contrary qualities (Alexander, *De Mix.* 28.22–30.9, 31.17–19; cf. 32.15–24).

T4 brings out two important points for present purposes: (a) that Alexander defines blending as a process of unification;[39] and (b) that the blending bodies change without being destroyed.

In what sense is blending a process of unification? Alexander explains that the blending bodies are unified with respect to both their matter and their qualities, such that a single new matter and a single new quality (or: capacity/form, on which more below) are produced while the blending bodies lose their own original matter and qualities (or: powers/forms) (*De Mix.* 31.20–32.10, 32.15–24, 33.5–9). Further, the matter and quality produced are the matter and quality of a single body which the ingredients become and which thus comes to be in the blending (*De Mix.* 33.5–9). So, in contrast to the Stoics (see section 1 above), Alexander is defining blending in part by reference to a further result, i.e. a single body coming to be in the blending along with its matter and quality (form/capacity). How the matter and the quality in question are to be specified and how we should understand their being produced through blending are crucial questions, to which I will turn shortly. For now it is enough to note that they are the matter and quality of a single body by reference to the producing of which blending is defined.

Despite the fact that the bodies going into the blending (the ingredients), on Alexander's view, lose their own matter and qualities (forms/powers), he insists that they are not destroyed in the process. Like the Stoics, Alexander thinks that the ingredients in blending are *preserved*: it is a datum of our common notion of blending (a so-called 'common preconception'; *koinē prolēpsis*) that it is possible to separate the ingredients out again after blending, and for this preservation is required (*De Mix.* 36.12–17, with 33.5–34.7ff, 35.16–36.11); further, the preservation of the ingredients distinguishes blending from processes of generation and destruction (*De Mix.* 31.8–15).[40] However, Alexander understands preservation differently from the Stoics. On his view, the particular bodies that go into the blending do not straightforwardly persist, nor can they be recovered; rather, they are merely preserved in potentiality (*dunamei*), in the sense that bodies of the same kind can be produced from the single body which came to be through the blending (*De Mix.* 33.5–34.7, 34.11–35.16, 36.5–11). Thus, in a blend of water and wine (the composite) for instance, there is both wine and water in potentiality, and from the blend it is possible to produce both water and wine. And to that extent the particular water and wine that originally went into the blending will be preserved, even though they themselves no longer exist in actuality and

---

[39] Besides T4, we see this in Alexander, *De Mix.* 32.15–19, 31.20–32.10.

[40] On the preservation of the ingredients, as what distinguishes blending from generation and destruction, as well as the possibility of separation after blending, Alexander follows Aristotle in *GC* I.10, 327b6–10, 327b22–9.

never will again (34.11–35.10).[41] So understood, preservation and the possibility of recovery are taken to be consequences of the way in which the ingredients interact in blending (on which, more below).

Let us now return to Alexander's objections against the Stoics. The first objection we discussed—*the unity objection*—states that since the blending bodies, according to the Stoics, are straightforwardly preserved with their own individual matter and natural qualities (see section 1 above), there will be no proper unity existing as the result of blending, but rather merely a juxtaposition of the blending bodies. On our interpretation, the problem is to see how we might explain there being a unity on the basis of some bodies blending, when those bodies are seen as preserved in the Stoic way. As Alexander points out (*De Mix*. 34.4–7), there is no such problem on his view. For the blending bodies are not preserved in the Stoic way; and there is no need to ask how blending results in unity, since blending is now defined as a unification of the ingredients producing a single body with a single matter and quality.

The second objection states that Stoic *pneuma* is unsuited for the causal function assigned to it, i.e. causing the composite to be what it is by blending with its matter. For it is difficult to see what it is that connects *pneuma*'s doing this and the effect on the composite. If we ask Alexander in the same vein how the composite is caused to be what it is, we encounter no such difficulty. For Alexander holds that the cause in question is the form (*eidos*) of the composite; and part of being the form of something is to cause that thing to be what it is. Hence, there will be no further question of *how* the form of the composite does this; doing it is (part of) what it is for the form to be. When Alexander in *De Mix*. says that form does the work for which Stoic *pneuma* is inadequate (see section 2 above), this is plausibly what he has in mind—that the form of the composite is precisely that which causes the composite to be what it is; and no other cause will do.

However, there is another, closely related question that ought to be considered as well. For the Stoics, *pneuma* is both a cause for the composite and one of the two bodies of which it is a blend (matter being the other). Here, blending is the relation *by which pneuma* is supposed to be able to cause the composite to be and remain what it is; and in order to do that, *pneuma* must persist in the blending. For Alexander, blending plays a different role: it is the process by which the composite *comes to be*; but what causes the composite *to be* what it is, that is the form which obtains at the end of the process, when the composite *has* come to be and the blending bodies have ceased to be (in actuality). The question we should

---

[41] Alexander is concerned to show that his Aristotelian account vindicates the preconception that the ingredients in blending may be separated out again (Alexander, *De Mix*. 33.5–36.19); still, as Alexander is clearly aware (36.12–19), the worry remains that this will at best be in an extended sense of separation. And a Stoic might not unreasonably complain that the bodies that go into blending in Alexander's sense are neither really preserved nor ever separated out.

ask is this: what connects the form of the composite—the cause of its being what it is—and the blending of bodies by which the composite comes to be? If we consider for instance a blend of water and wine (the composite), we need not ask how its form causes it to be what it is. But we should ask what connects the blending of water and wine to the form of the wine-water blend.

Alexander does not explicitly address this issue. Still, the following initial form of answer suggests itself: the blending of water and wine is precisely the process of unification such that the form (and the matter) of the wine-water blend results; that the right form results is thus part of the definition of what the process in question is.[42] This feature of Alexander's account is somewhat obscured by the fact that he does not consistently use the term 'form' (*eidos*) in De Mix.; he also speaks of 'qualities' (*poiotētes*) and 'capacities' (*dunameis*): thus, the blending bodies are said to be unified 'with respect to their capacities and qualities' (32.18–19) and 'with respect to the form and the qualities' (36.21–2); further, they are said to become one body, 'both with respect to the substrate and the quality' (33.8–9) and to produce 'a single quality, when the underlying matter for both or all of them has become unified and one' (32.8–10, on which more below). However, there are clear indications that Alexander here has in mind the qualities and capacities (or the quality and the capacity) that make up and are specified by the form of the item in question.[43]

In this way, then, it seems clear what is meant to connect the form of the composite and the blending of bodies on Alexander's view, namely that the process of blending in question *is* the one from which the form arises.

If the interpretation I have proposed is correct, it appears that Alexander's account is supposed to avoid the kinds of explanatory difficulty facing the Stoics, centrally in virtue of the fact that it defines blending as a process of unification by reference to a single body with a single form (and matter), which comes to be as the ingredients cease to be (in actuality). This is an important part of the dialectic between the Stoics and Alexander in De Mix.

However, it is still unclear exactly how and why blending and the form of the composite are connected on Alexander's view. In the remainder of the section, I shall examine this in further detail. I will argue that in the final analysis there is *no* explanation of why the form of the composite should result from a given blending of underlying bodies. So, despite the fact that blending is defined by reference to the form of the composite, it turns out that Alexander is vulnerable to an objection similar in kind to the second objection directed as the Stoics.

To begin, we may consider De Mix. 31.20–32.10:

---

[42] This can be seen from Alexander, De Mix. 31.20–32.10, 32.15–19 (with 33.5–13, 34.4–7).
[43] Alexander, De Mix. 30.3–5, 30.10–13, 31.3, 36.4–11, 36.20–2; compare also Alexander, De An. 7.23–8.25, on which more below.

T5 but it is peculiar to blending in relation to generation and destruction that in the case of the latter the one completely turns into the other and takes on the contraries in accordance with which it is affected and completely loses the contraries it had before this, while in the case of blending it does not occur in this way; rather, when multiple bodies that have the capacity to act on and to be acted on by one another come together with one another, and are disposed in such a way that one is not able to exceed the other in respect of their contraries so that, destroying it, the one changes the other into its own nature, then these [bodies], because of the equality of the capacities in virtue of which they act and are acted on, proceed by reciprocally being acted on by one another in the same way to the point where losing the excesses in respect of the contraries, on account of which they were different from and contrary to one another, <u>they will produce a single quality from all the capacities, when the underlying matter belonging to both or all of them has been unified and become one.</u>

In this passage, Alexander is specifying the interaction by reference to which blending is defined (cf. T4 above). In order for blending to take place (rather than destruction), there must a certain equality (*isotēs*) among the capacities by which the bodies in question interact. Because the capacities are of equal strength, no one will overpower another; instead, a point is reached, where the blending bodies lose the contraries that originally distinguished them and in respect of which they were interacting. For us, the key part of the passage (underlined above) is Alexander's description of this point, i.e. the end of the process, when unification is complete: the blending bodies 'will produce a single quality (*mia poiotēs*) from all the capacities', when their matter 'has been unified and become one'. A few lines later, unification so described is said to be 'precisely what blending is' (*hoper esti hē krasis*; De Mix. 32.19); and at De Mix. 33.5–9 we learn that the matter and quality in question are the matter and quality of the single body that the ingredient bodies become.

Since we can legitimately talk about forms in this context as well as qualities and capacities (see above), T5 may help us understand the link between blending and the coming to be of a single body with a certain form (and matter). The idea, it seems, is that the form of the composite (cf. *its quality*; T5) is the equilibrium reached on account of the equality among the capacities (forms/qualities) of the blending bodies; because of this equality, the form of the composite is not one of the forms of the ingredients, but rather the form of a single distinct body that comes to be when the ingredients cease to be.

First, we should note that this is why, as Alexander sees it, the ingredients are preserved and can be separated out again. Because the form (capacity/quality) of the blend is an equilibrium of the forms (capacities/qualities) of the ingredients, it is possible, if the right changes are applied to the blend, for bodies of the same kinds as the original ingredients to be separated out (cf. *De Mix.* 33.13–35.16).

Second, if we now ask why a composite with a certain form, *F* (e.g. the form of a plant), comes to be in the blending of some bodies—call them *a*, *b*, and *c*—T5 suggests the following answer: the blending of *a*, *b*, and *c* is defined as the process of unification which produces a single body with a single form, specifically the equilibrium of the forms of *a*, *b*, and *c*; and *F* is that (equilibrium) form. As expected, this gives us a sense in which the process of blending is linked to the form of the composite. However, it also raises a further question: what is the relation between being the form *F* and being the equilibrium produced in the blending of *a*, *b*, and *c*? On the one hand, we could suppose that there is a definitional connection between the equilibrium of the forms of *a*, *b*, and *c* and the form *F*: the equilibrium could be defined as the one it is by reference to form *F* or the form *F* could be defined by reference to being the equilibrium of the forms of *a*, *b*, and *c*. On the other hand, there might be no connection of this kind: form *F* will then be defined without reference to being the equilibrium in question and the equilibrium produced in the blending of *a*, *b*, and *c* is not defined by reference to being form *F*.

T5 leaves this question unanswered, and Alexander does not expressly address it elsewhere in *De Mix*. However, as I will show presently, when we also take into account the *De. An.*, it seems clear there is no such definitional connection between the equilibrium produced in blending and the form of the composite.

If this is right, it means that Alexander's theory of blending is open to an objection similar in spirit to his own second objection against the Stoics. Alexander complained that there is an explanatory gap between the story about *pneuma* and matter blending and the composite (the animal, the plant, or the inanimate natural body) being caused to be what it is. But now it looks like there may be a similar gap on Alexander's view, between the account of some bodies blending on the one hand, and the fact that the process results in the form of a certain composite, on the other. For if there is no definitional connection between the form of the composite and the equilibrium produced in blending, and blending is defined by reference to the equilibrium of the forms of the blending bodies only, it shall mean that the blending of some bodies is not enough to explain why the form of a certain composite results; it will tell us why the relevant equilibrium results, but not also why the form of the composite does so, say the form of a plant (even though that form is the equilibrium produced from the blending of bodies in question).

In the most detailed account of his hylomorphism (*De An.* 1–27), Alexander places significant causal and explanatory emphasis on blending as the process by which composite natural bodies come to be. He says that the form of the composite is 'in a way a form of forms' (*eidos pōs eidōn*), insofar as the form of each of the bodies of which the composite is blended 'contributes something' (*suntelein ti*) to the form of the composite (see *De An.* 7.23–8.13). And because of this, the difference among the forms of the composite bodies is to be explained (at least in part) by the number and kinds of the underlying bodies, as well as their manner of blending (*De An.* 8.13–25); and so plants for instance 'differ very much from one another with respect to form because the matter [i.e. the ingredient bodies] and the mixing and blending of the matter underlying them differ' (*De An.* 9.4–5).[44] Generally, the underlying bodies and their manner of blending are according to Alexander a 'principle' (*archē*) of each composite body (*De An.* 10.14–26).[45] Further, as we have seen, the ingredients in blending are independent existents and the process of blending is understood and defined by reference to the equilibrium form of the ingredients, rather than by (overt and specific) reference to the form of the resultant composite.

These claims illustrate what I initially called Alexander's *upward story*: in order to explain why composite natural bodies are as they are, and why they are different from one another in their various specific ways, we must attend to the bodies of which they are blended, the forms these have, and the manner of blending; and in doing so, it seems we grasp the underlying bodies and their manner of blending without reference to the exact forms of the composites.

Despite this, it is clear that the form of the composite itself is not defined in terms of the underlying blending. Alexander is emphatic that the form of the composite is a further item which 'comes to be on top' (*epigignesthai*), when the blending is complete.[46] We are not told exactly what this means. But in his discussion of the soul, Alexander explains that the soul is *not* what it is in virtue of the way in which the underlying bodies are blended, as it is rather produced on top of the blending in question (*De An.* 26.22–30). Though a specific form, the soul is not special in this regard; on the contrary, it comes to be on top of the underlying blending in the same way as the form of any composite body (see note 7). We may conclude therefore that for Alexander, the form of a composite is not merely the equilibrium form of the bodies which blend to produce it, and it is not defined in terms of the underlying bodies and their manner of blending. Instead, it seems the forms of animals, plants, and other composites will be defined independently.

A result of this is that the form of the composite, on Alexander's view, plays an independent causal and explanatory role (i.e. independently of the underlying blending of bodies). And so, it is in some sense strictly and precisely in virtue of its own form that each composite is what it is, and not in virtue of the underlying blending of bodies.[47]

---

[44] To say that the form of the composite is in a way a form of forms is presumably a reference to the fact that the form of the composite is the equilibrium produced from the blending of the underlying bodies (see T5 above). Together with the definition of blending (as the process productive of the equilibrium) this fact then appears to play an important explanatory role in Alexander's hylomorphism; centrally, it helps explain why the form of the composite differs from other forms and so also (to some extent) why it is the form that it is.

[45] For a broader account of what the underlying bodies and their manner of blending are supposed to explain and what they are not supposed to explain, see Caston (Chapter 6, this volume).

[46] For references, see note 7 above.

[47] See for instance *De An.* 6.19–7.8. For discussion and further argument for this claim, see Caston (2012: 11–12, and Chapter 6, this volume).

We can see now that there will indeed be an explanatory gap between the blending of underlying bodies and the form of the resultant composite. Consider again the following two ways of explaining their connection: (1) we could say that the form of the composite is defined in terms of the forms of the underlying bodies and their manner of blending, that is, in terms of being their *equilibrium form*. Alternatively, (2) we might define the equililbrium of the forms of the underlying blending bodies in terms of the form of the composite, and so define blending by reference to the exact form of the composite. When some bodies blend so that a plant comes to be, for instance, we might then say that they blend *in the plant way*, i.e. in precisely the way in which something with the form of a plant comes to be.

However, it seems clear that Alexander rejects both ways: (1) straightforwardly conflicts with his insistence that the form of the composite is not defined in terms of the underlying blending. As for (2), we have seen that Alexander's account of blending, in De Mix., does not define blending by reference to the form of the composite as such; rather, blending is defined by reference to an otherwise unspecified equilibrium form of the ingredient bodies, which are seen as independent existents. The discussion in De An. does not correct this account or call its accuracy into doubt, quite the opposite. The remarks that the form of the composite is a further item that 'comes to be on top' (*epigignesthai*) when the blending is complete may reasonably be taken to suggest that the process of blending is *not* defined by reference to that form (precisely and as such). In short, (2) appears to run contrary to Alexander's upward story.

Hence, there will be no explanation, on Alexander's view, of why a given blending of bodies produces a composite with a certain form. Blending is defined as a process producing a composite whose form is an equilibrium of the forms of the blending bodies; but the equilibrium produced in blending and the form of the composite produced, taken as precisely what it is, are not defined by reference to one another. And so, there will be no explanation of why something with the form of a plant, say, should come to be from precisely that blending of bodies from which it in fact comes to be.

This rather striking conclusion is in line with Victor Caston's more general emergentist interpretation of Alexander's hylomorphism (2012: 11–12, and Chapter 6, this volume): the form of the composite, taken in its own right, turns out to be an emergent phenomenon, because there is no explanation of why it results from the underlying blending.

If I am right, then, Alexander is not vulnerable to exactly the same kind of objection as he directs at the Stoics. For the Stoics, the challenge is to explain how *pneuma* is able to cause the composite (animal, plant, or inanimate natural body) to be what it is; there is no such challenge for Alexander, since the relevant causal role on his view is played by form, which is defined as the right kind of cause for the task. But Alexander is vulnerable to a related objection, concerning the connection between a given blending of bodies and the form of the resultant composite (taken as what it itself is), which in each case shall remain unexplained—or so I have argued.

I shall now conclude this chapter with a few remarks on the dialectic between Alexander and the Stoics, including a brief outline of how the Stoics might respond to Alexander's objections.

4. Concluding Remarks

We have considered two objections raised by Alexander against the Stoics (see section 2 above). According to the first, the Stoic theory of blending is unsuited to explain how a properly unified whole is composed, since the blending bodies are straightforwardly preserved each as what it is independently of the other(s); according to the second objection, there is an explanatory gap in the Stoic story of *pneuma*-matter blending, between *pneuma* acting on matter and the composite being caused to be what it is. In the previous section, we saw that Alexander seeks to avoid objections of this sort by defining blending as a process of unification and by positing form as the cause of the composite being what it is.

Alexander doubtless thinks that his hylomorphism is preferable to the Stoic theory as a result; this is especially clear concerning the causal role assigned to *pneuma*, which to his mind can only adequately be played by form (*eidos*) (*De Mix.* 18.21ff; see section 2 above). However, the fact that Alexander's hylomorphism leaves its own explanatory gap, as I have argued, gives us reason to doubt this assessment.

Indeed, since there will be no explanation of the connection between the underlying blending and the form of the resultant composite, it may look like a stroke of good fortune that exactly the right form is produced for Alexander.[48,49] And a Stoic might not unreasonably say, therefore, that Alexander's upward story hardly does better than the theory of *pneuma*-matter blending; in fact, the two would seem to give out at more or less the same point.

---

[48] Here I am not fully convinced by Caston's assurances that the form of the composite does not adventitiously appear on top of the blending of underlying bodies. Caston (Chapter 6, this volume) may be right to say that a given composite has its own distinctive form (in some sense) as a function of the blending of underlying bodies and the forms of these bodies; the problem is that there is apparently no explanation of why that should be so—no explanation of why the form of a given composite (taken as what itself is) should obtain as a function of a given blending of bodies.

[49] Notably, we can turn this into a worry about the unity of the composite substance, as follows. The form of the composite substance comes to be on top of the blending of underlying bodies (see section 3 above); the blending is also supposed to supply the material basis for the form, that is to say, it is supposed to yield, when it is complete, precisely the matter of which the form of the composite is the form. For instance, in the case of an animal, there is a certain blending of underlying bodies, which, when it is complete, yields the body to which the soul is joined as its form; and the animal is the composite of soul and body so produced. The issue now is that since there is no explanation of why the form in question, e.g. the soul, comes to be on top of precisely that blending of underlying bodies, there will also be no explanation of why that blending yields precisely the matter of which that form is the form, e.g. the body of the animal (i.e. the organic body). For if there were such an explanation, it would also tell us why the form results from the relevant blending. But then there is a genuine question of why the form is joined to the matter produced from the underlying blending of bodies. And it could look like another stroke of good fortune that the matter produced from a given blending is just right for the form to which it is joined.

What should we make of this result? First, it is worth noting that to my knowledge there is no indication that the Stoics are emergentists. Accordingly, even if Alexander's upward story and the Stoic theory of *pneuma*-matter blending leave similar explanatory gaps, their goals seem to be different. Alexander, apparently, does not mean to provide a full account of the composite and its form in terms of the underlying blending of bodies; the Stoics by contrast, want to explain why animals, plants, and inanimate natural bodies are what they are, entirely in terms of *pneuma* and matter blending (see section 1 above). So, for the Stoics the gap means that their theory has failed, whereas for Alexander it does not.

Second, it would be dialectically suspect all the same for Alexander to complain that the Stoics leave the same sort of explanatory gap that is built into Alexander's own hylomorphism—provided all else is equal. However, I do not think Alexander would agree that it is. It would not, as far as he is concerned, be sufficient for the Stoics to adopt a form of emergentism and say that when *pneuma* and matter blend, a properly unified whole is composed and caused to be what it is by *pneuma*, but there is no explanation of how and why this is so. And the reason, I should think, is that the Stoic account would still, to Alexander's mind, be lacking the only appropriate and adequate cause, namely form. That is to say: the explanatory gap would be unacceptably large because the Stoics refuse to invoke the form of the composite.

Of course, a Stoic would presumably not be impressed with this, and not without reason. For even if Alexander is right that the Stoic theory of *pneuma*-matter blending provides a poor basis for emergence, it is not clear that Alexander's upward story fares much better.

Irrespective of Alexander's dialectical standing to complain, his two objections point to real difficulties for the Stoic theory. I have so far not said much about the Stoic prospects for meeting Alexander's objections; the last thing I want to do in this chapter is to give a very brief outline of how the Stoics could begin to respond.

On the Stoic view, we remember, animals, plants, and inanimate natural bodies are blends of *pneuma* and matter; each is caused to be what it is by the *pneuma* blended with its matter; and *pneuma* plays this causal role by acting on the matter by means of tensile motion (see sections 1 and 2 above). Now, to begin to explain the connection between *pneuma* doing this and the composite being caused to be what it is, and so answer Alexander's second objection, we should first note that there is a correspondence in each case between what the *pneuma* is and what the composite is: the animal is defined as what it is by having certain attributes which also define its *pneuma*, i.e. soul, and likewise for the plant and the inanimate natural body with respect to their *pneuma*; the animal and its soul, for instance, are both defined by having perception and impulse.[50] Second, the specific tensile

---

[50] On the correspondence, see Hierocles, *Elements of Ethics* VI 10–21; Simplicius, *In Cat.* 276.30–3; Helle (2021: 187–90). For the case of soul and the animal, the following should also be noted: Hierocles, *Elements of Ethics* I 32–5, IV 24–7, 42–3; Philo, *Leg. Alleg.* 1.30 (LS 53P, SVF II 844); Ramelli (2009: 53–4).

motion of each *pneuma* is the pattern of motion by which these attributes belong to it.[51] It will not be surprising therefore that the *pneuma* causes the composite to have the relevant attributes by acting on its matter with tensile motion; for by doing this, the *pneuma* can be thought to cause the composite to have the internal pattern of motion by which *pneuma* itself has these attributes.

It is important to note what this explains and what it does not. It helps explain how *pneuma* through tensile motion may cause the composite to be what it is, because there is an assumed connection between the tensile motion and having the relevant attributes. But we have no explanation of this connection, and so also no account of why *pneuma* has the attributes in question, for instance why soul has perception and impulse.

Further, even if all this is granted to the Stoics, we have not explained why the composite is a single subject in its own right, a single animal in its own right for instance (and so a unified body; see note 29). This is where the theory of blending comes in and so also a potential response to Alexander's unity objection. The Stoics could argue that when *pneuma* blends with matter, they interact in a certain way, which accordingly modifies *pneuma*'s pattern of (tensile) motion; and further that the interaction and modification in question cannot be specified independently of the relevant *pneuma* and matter blending. The result would be a pattern of motion specific to the relevant blending, for instance to soul and body blending, which could not be grasped independently of it. And this would be the pattern of motion in virtue of having which the composite is what it is; since each composite *is* a blend of the relevant *pneuma* and matter, one might further say that the pattern in question would be specific to and not to be grasped independently *of the composite*. Corresponding to that pattern, then, there would finally be a way for the composite to have the attributes by which it is defined, i.e. its own way. And in virtue of having the relevant attributes in this way, the composite would be a single subject in its own right: the animal for instance, would be a single subject in its own right in virtue of having its defining attributes, perception, and impulse, in its own way, i.e. the soul-body-blending way, as it were.

I am not going to try to show that the theory of blending provides the resources necessary for this argument here; suffice it to say that there are reasons to think it at least goes some way toward doing so.[52] For present purposes, the important point is that we seem to have an outline of a strategy the Stoics could pursue to begin to answer the challenges raised by Alexander. Much is left out; among other things, we still do not know how bodies being caused to have internal patterns of locomotion is connected to their having attributes, or how *pneuma* is thought to

---

[51] On the connection between patterns of motion and attributes, see section 2 above. For the specific case of pneumatic tensile motion, see Helle (2021: esp. 196–8).

[52] See Helle (2018, 2021).

have its attributes and tensile motion. But the outline nevertheless indicates that the Stoics may not be so bereft as Alexander would have us think.

Bibliography

Bobzien, S. (1998), *Determinism and Freedom in Stoic Philosophy* (OUP).

Bobzien, S. (1999), 'Chrysippus' Theory of Causes', in K. Ierodiakonou (ed.), *Topics in Stoic Philosophy* (Clarendon), 196–242.

Bruns, I. (1887), *Supplementum Aristotelicum*. Vol. 2.1: *De anima liber cum mantissa* (Berlin).

Brunschwig, J. (1994), 'The Stoic Theory of the Supreme Genus and Platonic Ontology', *Papers in Hellenistic Philosophy* (CUP), 92–157.

Brunschwig, J. (2003), 'Stoic Metaphysics', in B. Inwood (ed.), *Cambridge Companion to the Stoics* (CUP), 206–32.

Caston, V. (2012), *Alexander of Aphrodisias: On the Soul, Part I: Soul as Form of the Body, Parts of the Soul, Nourishment, and Perception* (Bloomsbury).

Frede, M. (1987), 'The Original Notion of Cause', *Essays in Ancient Philosophy* (University of Minnesota Press), 125–50.

Gourinat, J.-B. (2009), 'The Stoics on Matter and Prime Matter: "Corporealism" and the Imprint of Plato's *Timaeus*', in R. Salles, (ed.), *God and Cosmos in Stoicism* (OUP), 46–70.

Gourinat, J.-B. (2018), 'The Ontology and Syntax of Stoic Causes and Effects', *Rhizomata* 6/1: 87–108.

Groisard, J. (2013), *Alexandre D'Aphrodise: Sur La Mixtion et La Croissance (De Mixtione)* (Les Belles Lettres).

Helle, R. (2018), 'Hierocles and the Stoic Theory of Blending', *Phronesis* 63/1: 87–116.

Helle, R. (2021), 'Self-Causation and Unity in Stoicism', *Phronesis* 66/2: 178–213.

Helle, R. (2022), 'Colocation and the Stoic Definition of Blending', *Phronesis* 67/4: 462–97.

Joachim, H.H. (1922), *Aristotle: On Coming-to-Be and Passing-Away* (OUP).

Long, A.A. (1974), *Hellenistic Philosophy* (Charles Scribner's Sons).

Long, A.A. (1982), 'Soul and Body in Stoicism', *Phronesis* 27: 34–57.

Long, A.A., and Sedley, D.N. (1987), *The Hellenistic Philosophers*, vols. 1–2 (CUP).

Menn, S. (1999), 'The Stoic Theory of Categories', *Oxford Studies in Ancient Philosophy* XVII: 215–47.

Ramelli, I. (2009), *Hierocles the Stoic: Elements of Ethics, Fragments, and Excerpts* (Brill).

Sambursky, S. (1959), *The Physics of the Stoics* (Routledge).

Vogt, K. (2009), 'Sons of the Earth: Are the Stoics Metaphysical Brutes?', *Phronesis* 54: 136–54.

von Arnim, H. (1903–5), *Stoicorum Veterum Fragmenta* (Teubner).

5
Galen on the Form and Substance of the Soul

Patricia Marechal

In *On My Own Opinions*, Galen claims to agree with Aristotle that the soul is the form of the body.[1] But should we take this statement at face value? After all, as we will see in detail below, Galen says that the substance of the soul is a bodily mixture, and that the soul is the form of the body in the sense that it is the principle of mixing of the elements. As is well known, Aristotle explicitly rejects this sort of materialist account of the soul. In *De Anima*, he tells us that the soul cannot be an 'attunement' (*harmonia*) of bodily elements, understood either as the proportion according to which the elements are mixed or as the mixtures themselves (I.4, 407b32–408a2). In fact, Aristotle introduces the view that the soul is the form of the body as an alternative to these materialist positions. Some of Aristotle's followers concur, including Alexander of Aphrodisias, Galen's contemporary.[2]

This raises the following question: despite tipping his hat to the Aristotelians by claiming that the soul is the form of the body, does Galen endorse a substantive version of hylomorphism? In order to answer this question, I focus on two specific worries that Aristotelians raised against the kind of materialism defended by Galen. First, the mixtures themselves cannot account for the powers of the soul. Second, mixtures cannot explain what unifies a body as a living organism of a certain kind. We will see that Galen was aware of these worries and explicitly addressed them. According to Galen, we do not need anything other than mixtures to account for the powers of a living body or to unify it as such. Galen, thus, rejects a substantive version of hylomorphism, in favour of a view according

---

[1] *De Propriis Placitis* 7.34–5.
[2] See Temkin (1973: esp. 60–75), Nutton (1984), and Lloyd (2008) for evidence of Galen's knowledge of contemporary Peripatetics. Galen is familiar with the work of the 1st century BCE Aristotelian, Andronicus of Rhodes, whom he mentions in *Quod Animi Mores Corporis Temperamenta Sequantur* (henceforth *QAM*). We have no direct evidence that Galen read Alexander of Aphrodisias' works, although Islamic historians say the two met one another (Ibn Yūsuf al-Qiftī, *Taʾrīkh al-Ḥukamā* 54: 2–5); most likely, they confused this Alexander with another Peripatetic philosopher, Alexander of Damascus (Temkin 1973: 74, n. 75), whom Galen met, along with Eudemus, during his first stay in Rome. Nutton claims that 'almost certainly' this Alexander was the father of Alexander of Aphrodisias (2020: 32). Alexander of Aphrodisias was familiar with the works of Galen and wrote texts against Galen's criticisms of Aristotelian doctrines. See Bürgel (1968: 283, n. 1) for a list of the writings in which Alexander targets Galen.

to which the soul's substance is nothing other than bodily mixtures. Galen's position, I will argue, contains a veiled objection to the Aristotelian notion of form as a genuine metaphysical and explanatory category, and to Aristotelian hylomorphism as a psychological theory.

1. The Soul's Substance

Galen often refers to material, efficient, and final causes, but he does not typically mention forms or formal causes.[3] Forms are absent from Galen's treatises on the causes of health and disease, as well as from his texts on anatomy, natural faculties, drugs, foodstuffs, and mixtures. Yet, both in *Quod Animi Mores* (*QAM*), his treatise on the relationship between soul and body, and in *De Propriis Placitis* (*PP*), where he states his own opinions on the nature of the soul, the notion of form seems to play an important role. In *QAM*, for example, Galen says:[4]

> If all bodies are composed of matter and form, and Aristotle himself thinks that the physical body results from the four qualities arising in the matter, it is necessary to posit that its 'form' is the mixture of these qualities. Thus, somehow, *the substance [ousia] of the soul will also be some mixture of either the four qualities*, if you wish to call them that—hotness, coldness, dryness and wetness— or simple bodies—the hot, the cold, the wet, and the dry.
>
> *QAM* IV 774.9-17 K = SM 3, 37; emphasis added[5]

---

[3] Material, efficient, and final causes are mentioned in *De Causis Procatarcticis* VI 67 = 92, 17–21, together with the Middle Platonist 'instrumental' cause. Formal causes are entirely absent. Galen also omits formal causes in *De Symptomatum Differentiis* VII 47 K. For a discussion of these omissions, see Hankinson (1998: esp. 12–14); and Chiaradonna (2021). Galen possibly refers to formal causes in *De Usu Partium*, where he mentions causes that pick out 'that in accordance with which' (III 465 K = I 339, 12–18 H). In his lost *Commentarii in Aristotelis Physica*, Porphyry uses this same prepositional phrase to refer to formal causes, albeit in a Neo-Platonist context (fr. 120 Smith = Simplicius, *Comm. Phys.* 10.35–11.4 Diels). Thus, it is possible (although not certain) that Galen uses this phrase in *De Usu Partium* to refer to formal causes. Yet, Galen introduces this type of cause with a caveat ('if you wish'), thereby suggesting that he is not entirely convinced about this type of cause. For a discussion of this passage in *De Usu Partium*, see Hankinson (1998: 379–85). There is an extensive secondary literature on Galen's causal framework. See Hankinson (1998 and 2003) and Johnston (2009) for detailed treatments of Galen on causes, as well as specific references.

[4] *QAM*. References to *QAM* are by volume and page of C.G. Kühn's edition (1821–33), abbreviated 'K', and I. Müller's edition (1891), abbreviated 'SM'. I also consulted Bazou (2011). For translations, see, e.g., Ballester (1972); Vegetti and Menghi (1984); and Singer (2013). References to all other works by Galen are, where possible, indicated by volume and page number of Kühn's edition. In cases where a more modern edition exists, I refer to it.

[5] Some interpreters have argued that Galen is not presenting his own views in these lines. Instead, he is only saying that the view held by the followers of Aristotle is consistent with the dependence of soul on body. If this is correct, he would not commit himself to the view that the soul is the form of the body, and to what he takes to be entailed by this Aristotelian thesis, namely, that the soul is the mixture of the qualities or elements. See, for example, Singer (2013: 381 n. 37) who reads 'auton' for 'autou' in the crucial lines. If Singer is correct, Galen has only stated that it is necessary that *he* (i.e. Aristotle) consider that 'eidos' is the 'krasis' of the four elements. I follow Müller (1891) and Bazou (2011) in

According to Galen, if one holds (as Aristotle did) that bodies are compounds of matter and form *and* that these bodies are ultimately made up of mixtures of the elements (air, water, fire, and earth), then one is committed to the view that the form of the body is the elements thus mixed.[6] Therefore, when Aristotelians say that the soul is the form of the living body, they are (in Galen's eyes) committed to the view that the substance of the soul is simply a mixture of bodily elements.[7]

Now, the claim that the soul's substance is nothing other than mixtures of elements takes place in a polemical context. In *QAM*, Galen is engaging with different philosophical schools and examining their views on soul-body relations. Therefore, we cannot assume that he endorses this position as his own.[8] Instead, Galen could merely be saying that those who endorse the view that the soul is the form of a body made up of mixtures are committed to the identity of soul and mixtures. After all, Galen frequently says that the powers of the soul 'follow' or 'depend on' (*hepesthai*) the bodily mixtures, and he offers empirical evidence to that effect.[9] We might think, then, that Galen is only committed to the weaker view that the soul *depends* on mixtures, not that it is itself a mixture. Indeed, Galen says that 'the soul *is slave* to the mixtures of the body' (*QAM* IV 779.13-20 K = SM 2, 41), a claim that suggests dependence rather than identity.[10]

However, in *PP*, Galen presents as his own opinion the view that the soul is the form of the body:[11]

---

understanding Galen to be asserting his own views. Not only does this position allow for an interpretation of *QAM* that renders Galen's claims coherent, but also his commitment to this view is repeated in *De Propriis Placitis* (henceforth *PP*), where he endorses this position as his own.

[6] In *Generation of Animals* 1.10.327b1-20, Aristotle endorses the view that the material substrate can be reduced ultimately to mixtures of the four elements.

[7] Mixture is a translation of the Greek '*krasis*', which is also commonly translated as 'temperament' or 'blend'. It refers to blends of basic qualities or elements that compose natural bodies. Mixtures are a combination of the basic qualities (hot, cold, wet, and dry), which Galen connects with the humours (blood, phlegm, yellow bile, and black bile). See Singer (2013: 338) for a discussion of the Greek term '*krasis*' in Galen's works. For a translation and rich discussion of Galen's *De Temperamentis*, see Singer and van der Eijk (2019).

[8] See, for example, Lloyd (1988: 33-9); Hankinson (1993: 222); Singer (1997: 536, n. 46); Vegetti (2012: 279); and Chiaradonna (2021).

[9] Aside from *QAM*, see also *Foet. Form.* IV 674 K and *De Loc. Aff.* VIII 191 K. See also *In Hipp. De Nat. Hom.* 1.40, 51.9-18 Mewaldt, XV 97 K, where Galen refers not to capacities, but to character traits.

[10] Galen does not always say that the soul's capacities depend on the bodily mixtures. In *De Usu Partium*, he talks about the body as an *organon* (instrument) used by the soul and offers an account of the bodily organs in light of their psychic capacities, thus suggesting that the parts of the body depend in some way on the soul. This top-down approach seems to conflict with the views in *QAM*. Some interpreters have seen this as evidence that Galen's position on the matter changed over time. (See, e.g., Moraux 1984: 778-9 and Tieleman 1996: 9-10.) I agree with Donini (2008: 184-5) that the views in *QAM* and *De Usu Partium* are not necessarily in tension and can be made consistent. It is reasonable to claim both that the capacities of the soul correspond to the mixtures (as I will argue in detail) and that these same capacities—which are constituted by the mixtures—carry out psychic functions *by means of* bodily organs. Galen himself seems to have thought that the views are compatible (e.g. *Sem.* 2.2.5-7, 162.9-12 De Lacy, IV 611 K). See also van der Eijk (2020: esp. 65-7).

[11] A Greek manuscript of *PP* was discovered in 2005. I rely on Boudon-Millot and Pietrobelli's 2005 edition of the Greek text. Their edition borrows from Nutton (1999), itself based on a 15th-century medieval Arabo-Latin translation of *PP* and a 14th-century translation into Latin of the last two

> There isn't, I suppose, a substance of the soul in itself; [but] the soul is some form [*eidos*] of the body [*soma*]. PP 7.34–5

Galen, then, endorses the thesis that the soul is the form of the body *in propria persona*. Famously, he also agrees with the view that natural bodies are made up of mixtures of elements.[12] But if this is the case, he is himself committed to what, as he has told us, follows from holding these two theses together (QAM IV.774.9–17 K). That is, he is committed to the view that the substance of the soul is a mixture of elements.[13] A further point deserves special attention. Galen claims in these lines that there is no substance of the soul *in itself*. We can understand this claim in light of the passage from QAM quoted above: the soul does not have a substance distinct from the substance of the body. The substance of the soul just is the bodily mixtures. Soul and mixtures are numerically one.[14]

Indeed, in QAM, Galen says that he does not favour views that regard the soul as depending on the mixtures instead of itself being a mixture of elements. First, Galen says that 'it is necessary *for those who posit that the soul has its own specific substance*' to concede that the soul 'is slave to the mixtures of the body' (QAM IV 779.13–20 K = SM 2, 41). But, as we saw in the passage from PP discussed above, Galen does not think the soul has its own specific substance. The point, then, is that even those who (unlike himself) think that the soul is a substance distinct from the body must grant that the soul depends on the body in some way or another, given the empirical evidence for this. Second, Galen argues that it is preferable to say, 'not that [the soul] is slave to [the body]', as he had previously claimed, 'but that the mortal part of the soul indeed *is* this: the mixture of the body' (782.9–11 K = SM 4, 44). And he extends this claim to the intellectual soul, since 'if the reasoning capacity is a form of the soul, it must be mortal: *for it too will be a mixture*, namely a mixture within the brain' (774.19–775.2 K = SM 3, 36–8; emphasis added).

---

chapters of this text, attributed to Niccolò da Reggio, which circulated independently as *De Substantia Virtutum Naturalium*. I have also consulted Lami and Garofalo's 2012 edition and Italian translation. The Greek text is lacunose.

[12] See, e.g., *De Temperamentis*. Translation and commentary in van der Eijk and Singer (2019).

[13] I articulated and defended this argument—i.e. that we should read Galen's claims regarding the implications of holding the view that the soul is the form of the body in QAM in light of his commitments in PP—in Marechal (2019; accepted for publication in 2017).

[14] Materialist readings of QAM have been offered before. For example, Donini (2008: 196) claims that, '[a]fter having said, in the preface to [QAM], that he [i.e. Galen] has always been convinced that the capacities of the soul "follow upon" the temperaments [*kraseis*] of the body, a little later on Galen goes so far as to affirm that soul and its parts actually are the temperaments of organs in which they reside'. See also Ballester (1971 and 1972); Donini (1974); Hankinson (1991a, 1993: esp. 218–22, and 2006: 250, 'at least in regard to the two lower parts of the soul, [Galen] seems unequivocally to adopt an identity theory'); and Wolfe and van Esveld (2014). Gill (2007: esp. 92) attributes a 'physicalist' psychological theory to Galen. I defended the claim that Galen endorses a form of constitutive materialism in Marechal (2019). For a materialist reading of QAM in antiquity, see Philoponus, *On Aristotle on the Soul* 1.1.35, 25–6; 9.23–6; 26.22–3; and 33.1–6. See van der Eijk's (2005a) edition and translation of this text, esp. n. 115 and 262.

Galen makes his position clear a few lines later in a discussion of the views of the Peripatetic Andronicus of Rhodes. Galen praises Andronicus on the grounds that, 'as a free man' and 'without complicating the issue', he argued that the soul is 'a mixture or a power that follows from that mixture' (782.15–783.2 K = SM 4, 44). But he immediately adds that Andronicus should *not* have said that the substance of the soul could be a power (*dunamis*) that 'follows' (*hepesthai*) the mixture; instead, he should simply have said that it *is* a mixture (783.1–2 K).[15] For Galen, then, the substance of the soul is not merely dependent on bodily mixtures, it *is* a mixture.

But why does Galen think this is the case? Why should Andronicus not have said that the substance of the soul could be a 'power' (*dunamis*) that 'follows' (*hepesthai*) the mixtures? Here is Galen's answer:

> *If* soul, insofar as it is some substance, has many powers (and this has been correctly stated by Aristotle, who rightly distinguished an ambiguity, for substance picks out matter and form and the composite of both, and he [i.e. Aristotle] declared that soul is substance in the sense of form), *then* it is impossible [to say that the soul] is *anything other than* the mixture, as it was shown a bit earlier.[16]   QAM IV 783.1–9 K = SM 4, 44; emphasis added

Galen says in these lines that when we consider the soul as a substance (as, he thinks, Aristotle did), then the soul must be nothing other than the mixture of bodily elements. The reason for this is that only if the soul is a mixture will it be able to perform activities. Galen is expressing the view that causal efficacy requires materiality. This reveals why he thinks Aristotelians must grant that the soul's substance is a mixture. For the soul to be causally efficacious—that is, for it to be capable of actively bringing about effects—it cannot merely depend on bodily mixtures, rather it should be a mixture.

We find a similar idea in *PP*, where Galen argues that the soul and the relevant bodily mixture are in fact one in origin and being:

> I consider it reasonable [*eulogon*] that the body that receives the soul and holds it—as long as it is such as to be befitting—is perfectly sensitive, as the eye is 'perceptive', the ear is 'auditory', and the tongue is 'discursive'. The generation of the body is produced by the mixture of the four elements and, if the soul has its generation at the same time that it is fashioned with the body, *since this one*

---

[15] The view that the soul depends ontologically on the mixtures but has a distinct existence is also held by the most prominent Aristotelian during Galen's time, Alexander of Aphrodisias. I discuss this further below. See, also, Caston, Chapter 6 in this volume.

[16] Following the translation in Singer (2013).

comes to be through the mixing of the four elements, it is not possible that there be one genesis for the soul, and another one for the sensitive body.

PP 7.26–33; the text is lacunose

A few points are worth mentioning in this passage. First, Galen is cautious when making metaphysical assertions, and so he prefaces these lines with a disclaimer: 'I confess I am ignorant about the substance [*ousia*] of the soul' (*PP* 7.25).[17] We should not, however, take this as an indication that Galen has no opinions on these metaphysical issues. His point, rather, is that no one can attain demonstrative certainty on such matters. After this cautionary remark, Galen presents what in his opinion is the most 'reasonable' (*eulogon*) view on the nature of the soul's substance. According to Galen, when the four elements are mixed, the resulting mixtures are able to perform psychic activities. The mixtures of cold, hot, wet, and dry share a common origin with the powers of the soul. The soul's powers and the bodily mixtures have one and the same origin, namely, the blending of the elements. Only mixed bodily elements can be 'perceptive', 'auditory', and 'discursive'. That is, only mixtures can bring about effects. Galen's position, then, comes close to the views of Peripatetics like Dicaearchus and Aristoxenus, both recorded sometimes as denying the existence of the soul and holding that there is only body, and sometimes as subscribing to the view that the soul is the mixture of the elements.[18] Dicaearchus seems to have held the view that the soul is, as Cicero recounts, 'nothing else than simple body' configured in such a fashion as to be endowed with certain powers.[19] And Sextus Empiricus attributes to Dicaearchus the view that thinking is 'nothing apart from the body disposed in a certain way'.[20]

But if the soul's substance is a bodily mixture, in what sense is the soul the *form* of the body? Galen answers this question in *QAM*:

[W]hen this very man, Aristotle, says that the soul is the form of the body, one must ask him—or his followers—whether we should understand 'form' here to have been used by him in the sense of shape, as in the organic bodies, or in the

---

[17] In this and other passages, Galen seems to use the term 'ousia' to refer to 'essence'. Yet, he does not always use the term in this way. Galen often uses the term 'ousia' to refer to the material stuff something is made of, such as blood, *pneuma*, other homoeomerous bodily structures, and mixtures (see, for example, *Sem*. 2.2.7 = 162.17–19 De Lacy). Thus, when Galen refers to the *ousia* of the soul, we cannot readily assume that he means essence. He could be just referring to the soul's material composition. This will turn out to be relevant for my interpretation. See, van der Eijk and Singer (2019: nn. 119 and 132) for a discussion of senses of 'ousia' in Galen. See also Havrda (2017: 75, n. 24). Galen may be following the Stoics on this use of the term 'ousia'; see Helle, Chapter 4 in this volume.

[18] Cicero, *Tusculan Disputations*, book I, XXII.51; Nemesius, *De Natura Homini* 2 (= Dicaearchus fr. 11 Wehrli). See Cicero's *Tusculan Disputations*, book I, X.19 for Aristoxenus' commitment to the harmony theory of the soul, and Pseudo-Plutarchus' *Placita Philosophorum*, IV 898 c8–9 (= Dicaearchus fr. 12$_A$ Wehrli) for Dicaearchus' commitment to this claim. See Caston (2001) for more references.

[19] Cicero, *Tusculan Disputations*, book I, X.21 (= Dicaearchus fr. 7 Wehrli).

[20] Sextus Empiricus, *Adversus Mathematicos* 7.349 (= Dicaearchus fr. 8$_A$ Wehrli). As quoted in Ganeri (2011: 676).

sense of *the other principle* of natural bodies, *that by which a body is crafted*—a body which is homoeomerous and simple in terms of our perception of it not having an organic composition. They must necessarily answer that it is this other principle of natural [i.e. homoeomerous] bodies—since, indeed, it is to these, primarily, that activities belong... QAM IV 773.16–774.7 K

Galen says here that 'form' can be shape, as in the shape of a statue, but dismisses this sense as irrelevant for the discussion at hand.[21] For Galen, the soul is form in the sense of being the principle of mixing of the elements, i.e. 'that by which they are crafted' into the mixtures that compose homoeomerous bodies, such as flesh, bone, blood, or the crystalline humour in the eye. We can, then, think of the soul as the proportion according to which the elements are blended into a mixture. But the soul's *substance* is nothing above and beyond these mixtures. Indeed, according to Galen, homoeomerous bodies are constituted by mixtures (*QAM* IV 773 K = 37 SM, 1–5). Homoeomerous bodies, he tells us, are the primary cause of vital activities—a thesis that Galen repeats elsewhere and attributes to Aristotle (*De Loc. Aff.* VIII 161 K). We see, once again, Galen's preoccupation with the soul's causal efficacy. If the soul is causally efficacious, then it must be constituted by mixtures.

Indeed, when summarizing his position, Galen says that he 'showed that the substance of the soul is *composed* [*sunistemi*] of the mixture of the body' (IV 785.13 K = SM 5, 46). The term 'sunistemi' evokes the idea of constitution. To say that the substance of the soul is constituted by bodily mixtures means that the soul has its properties—including its causal properties—in virtue of being constituted by these mixtures. Thus, the mixtures explain the capacities of the soul. This explanatory asymmetry offers a different way of understanding the claim that the soul's capacities 'follow' (*hepesthai*) the bodily mixtures. The capacities of the soul are explained by the mixtures that constitute them. Thus, they 'follow' the mixtures in an explanatory sense.[22] Now, for Galen, '*x* constitutes *y*' presupposes that *x* and *y* are *numerically* the same, since *x* and *y* are intrinsically exactly alike and occupy the same space and time. This is why, as

---

[21] Aristotle, *Metaphysics* 1023a11–13. Galen mentions the sense of form as physical shape at *QAM* IV 774.1 K = SM 2, 37.9. And he explicitly states that soul is not form in the sense of physical shape in *PHP* V 202–3 K = De Lacy 92.23–94.10.

[22] 'Hepesthai' can be understood in different ways. Hankinson (2008a), for example, briefly comments that 'hepesthai' is 'artfully indeterminate: it might, but need not, indicate causal consequence; the connection may be one of mere conjunction' (243). See also Lloyd (1988: 33ff). The term can indicate logical consequence. Galen uses 'hepesthai' in this logical sense in *Institutio Logica* II 2.4, IV 7.2, XI 3.8 Kalbfleisch, and *In Hippocratis Prognosticum Commentaria* XVIIIb 306.10–307.6 K = SM 373, 1–14. I have argued elsewhere (Marechal 2019) that in *QAM* this term can be understood in an explanatory sense: the capacities of the soul 'follow' (*hepesthai*) the mixtures in the sense that the mixtures *explain* the capacities. The capacities are constituted by the mixtures, but constitutive relations ground explanations.

seen, Galen insists that the soul's substance is nothing other than the relevant mixtures.[23]

2. The Soul as Form

Galen's proposal, then, is that the soul's substance is constituted by bodily mixtures, and the soul and mixtures are numerically one. Now, this is not Aristotle's view.[24] For Aristotle, the soul is something other than mixtures of elements. The idea that the soul is a mixture of elements is at the heart of the *harmonia* theory of the soul, which Aristotle explicitly rejects:

> Attunement [*harmonia*], however, is a certain proportion or composition of the constituents blended, and soul can be neither the one nor the other of these. Further, the power of originating movement cannot belong to an attunement, while all concur in regarding this pretty well as a principal attribute of soul. It is more appropriate to call health (or generally one of the good states of the body) an attunement than to predicate it of the soul.[25]   *De An* I.4, 407b32–408a2

In this passage, Aristotle tells us that an attunement (*harmonia*) is either (1) a proportion according to which the four elements have been mixed (*logos... ton mixthenton*; 407b32–3), or (2) a composition of mixed elements (*sunthesis*; 407b33). It seems clear that Aristotle takes hylomorphism to be an alternative to the view that the soul is an 'attunement' of the elements. To be sure, Aristotle appreciates some features of this theory. In particular, he thinks that the soul is inseparable from the body, something that the *harmonia* theory also holds. But he explicitly rejects views that identify the soul's substance with mixtures. For Aristotle and many of his followers, the soul is something other than a structure or mixture of material elements. In fact, Peripatetics like Themistius and

---

[23] Philosophers have defended the view that the 'is' of constitution presupposes numerical identity against pluralism, i.e. the view that constitution does *not* presuppose numerical identity. For a particular argument defending this view and against pluralism, see Lewis (1971). The view that constitution does *not* presuppose numerical identity is typically defended with the example of a clay statue: there is the statue, and there also is the piece of clay that constitutes the statue. We can destroy the statue, but the piece of clay can survive. Furthermore, the statue can survive certain (material) changes that the lump of clay cannot. Since the properties, in particular the modal properties, of the statue and the lump of clay seem to be different, they are not one thing but two: both things are in the same place, yet they are not numerically the same. Those who, like Galen, think that the 'is' of constitution presupposes numerical identity argue, on the contrary, that we cannot distinguish between the statue and the lump of clay on the basis of mere modal, counterfactual, or dispositional differences; after all, the statue and the lump of clay are intrinsically exactly alike, so how could they fail to be one thing?

[24] Yet, some interpreters have argued that Aristotle holds (or should have held) a constitutive view of the soul along the lines of Galen's preferred view. See, e.g., Wiggins (1967) and Ackrill (1972–3).

[25] Translation slightly modified from Shields (2015).

Simplicius argued that Aristotle rejected the *harmonia* theory because, for him, the soul is itself a substance (*ousia*; *DA* 412a9), but no arrangement or composition of bodily elements qualifies as a substance in its own right. Therefore, the soul cannot be a structured arrangement or mixture of elements.[26] In *De Anima* I.4 and 5, Aristotle offers a series of arguments against the *harmonia* theory of the soul. Two concerns are of special interest for philosophers at Galen's time. First, the mixtures cannot explain the powers of the soul. Second, the mixtures cannot account for what unifies the living body as a being of a certain kind.

As to the first concern, the idea is that what something can do *qua* that thing is not just an effect of its material composition. The soul itself, for Aristotle, is responsible for the characteristic activities of a living body, even if the soul can only act in virtue of being enmattered. As Aristotle says, a wholly materialist conception of the soul is unable to explain 'the affections and actions of the soul, for example, reasoning, perception, pleasure, pain and others like these' (409b15–17). During Galen's time, some Peripatetics seem to have been especially persuaded by this view. Alexander of Aphrodisias, for example, argues that new powers result from or 'follow' (*hepesthai*) the mixtures, which are different in kind from the powers of the material basis:

> But for someone who thinks that the soul is *not* the things composed, taken simply as such, but instead a power that emerges above a certain sort of blend and mixture of the primary bodies, the blend of matter will have a proportion, but *the soul will have its being, not in virtue of the tuning and blend (as they are committed to saying), but in virtue of the power that emerges above it* [sc. the blend]. *De Anima* 26.26–30; emphasis added[27]

For Alexander, the soul is not a mixture. The soul is instead a power that *depends* on the mixtures but is ontologically distinct from them. As seen in the previous section, Galen was aware of these sorts of views on soul-body relations. He discusses them when he describes Andronicus' position. The view that the soul depends on, but is ontologically distinct from, the mixtures was favoured by these Peripatetic philosophers, in part because they thought that body and soul have different powers. If body and soul have distinct attributes (including their powers), they cannot be identical.[28]

---

[26] Fragments from *Eudemus*, Aristotle's lost dialogue on the soul, suggest that he endorsed this argument. (For collections of these fragments, see Rose (1863 and 1886); Waltzer 1934; and Ross 1955.) Themistius, *In Libros Aristotelis De Anima Paraphrasis* 24.30.26, Simplicius, *In Libros Aristotelis De Anima Commentaria* 53.15–18, and Aquinas, *In Aristotelis Librum De Anima Commentarium* 1.9.135.27, all argue that this is a central reason why Aristotle rejects the *harmonia* theory of the soul.

[27] I am following Caston's (1997) translation. For a thorough and illuminating presentation and interpretation of Alexander's position on the powers of the soul, see Caston's Chapter 6 in this volume.

[28] See *DA* 412a10, 412a19–28.

Regarding the second concern, Aristotle suggests that the view that the soul is a composition of bodily elements is problematic because it cannot adequately explain what unifies a body as a living body of a certain kind:

> Someone might also raise the problem: (if the soul is composed of different elements), what is it that makes them one? For the elements, at any rate, look like matter, while the *synechon*—whatever it is—is most powerful.
>
> *De An.* I.5, 410b10–14

Why can't mixtures of elements explain the unity and being of a living body as such? In *Metaphysics* Z.17 1041b11–28, Aristotle offers a famous argument for the view that material elements cannot unify a compound; rather, the form accounts for the unity of the compound as a certain kind of thing. Syllables like 'ba' are not identical to their constituent elements, 'b' and 'a', since these constituents continue to exist even when the syllable does not: 'when elements break up, something ceases to be, for example, flesh or a syllable; but the elements, fire and air, exist' (1041b14–16). An aggregate of elements, even when arranged or structured in a particular way, cannot explain the unity of the compound as a certain kind of being. The case of a living body and the corresponding corpse make this patently clear. But whatever unifies the compound cannot be some further material element. If it were another element, we would need something else to explain why 'b', 'a', and this other ingredient form a whole. This, of course, would result in an infinite regress. Aristotle concludes that there must be 'some other kind of thing' (*heteron ti*) that makes a whole a whole (*De An.* I.5 411b7–8). That other kind of thing is the form. Substantial forms make material composites be *something*. As Aristotle says, the soul unifies the body, not the other way around. The worry that material constituents cannot account for the unity and identity of a living body seems to have been salient for Peripatetics at Galen's time, like Alexander.[29]

But if Galen was aware that Aristotle rejected his preferred view about the soul—namely, that the substance of the soul is a mixture of elements—and, further, that hylomorphism was introduced as an alternative to it, why does he claim to agree with the view that the soul is the form of the body? Perhaps when he says that the soul is the form of the body, he is not expressing a real commitment to hylomorphism. After all, as mentioned, he does not usually resort to forms and formal causes in other texts outside *QAM* and *PP*. To put the question differently: does Galen think we gain anything by invoking forms, which we miss by referring to efficient, material, and teleological explanations? For the Aristotelians, as seen,

---

[29] *De Mixtione*. For a Greek edition with English translation, preliminary essays, and commentary, see Todd (1976). See Helle's Chapter 4 in this volume for details of Alexander's concerns about unity, and his objections to the Stoic account of mixtures based on these worries.

the answer to this question is 'yes'. First, the form is that in virtue of which a substance has the properties it has, including its *causal* properties. What something can do *qua* that thing is an effect, not just of its material composition, but of its form. Second, the form explains the existence of something as a *unified* thing of a certain kind. It is that in virtue of which a heap of structured ingredients or elements are something.

In the remainder of this chapter, I will argue that Galen addressed the 'causal' and 'unity' concerns sketched above and defended the view that the mixtures can account for the powers and unity of living beings. With this, I hope to show that Galen was aware of the philosophical debates on soul-body relations of his time, and that he consciously adopted his brand of materialism against rival positions, including Aristotelian hylomorphism. Galen is aware that prominent Aristotelians, like Andronicus and Alexander, put forward their theories in opposition to the kind of materialism he favoured, and he makes explicit efforts to answer their objections.

3. Galenic Powers

As discussed, Aristotle and some of his followers argued that the soul could not be constituted by mixtures because the mixtures by themselves cannot account for the soul's powers. There is good reason to think that Galen is mindful of this concern. For Galen, this worry is based on a mistaken account of powers (*dunameis*). In QAM, Galen explicitly says that philosophers are 'confused' about powers and have an 'unarticulated' conception of them.[30] In particular, philosophers think of powers 'as if they were something inhabiting substances, in the same way we inhabit houses' (IV 769.11-12 K = SM 2).[31] According to Galen:

> Of everything that is generated there is a productive cause, conceived in relation to something; and there is some category of this cause as a thing in and of itself. Now, the power to generate is *this* state [i.e. the thing in and of itself] in relation to what is generated from it; and so we say that the substance has as many powers as activities.   QAM IV 769.13–19K

We say that something is a productive cause or power when we consider it not in itself but in relation to something else. Something can be considered either in itself

---

[30] '*Adiarthroton*' was a term used in philosophical parlance of the time to refer to someone's lack of rigorous distinctions or concepts. It was a polemical concept used to discredit an opponent's view. For a discussion of this term in Galen, who employed it frequently, see van der Eijk (2005b: esp. ch. 10, 280–1, n. 7).

[31] For a general discussion of '*dunamis*' as capacities, powers, or faculties of the soul in Galen, see Hankinson (2006: 243–5); (2008a: esp. 223–5); and Debru (2008: 266–71).

or in relation to the effects that arise when it interacts with other bodies. A bodily state can be described by referring to its constituent elements and the proportion according to which these elements are mixed. But these same mixtures can be described as powers when they are considered in relation to the bodies with which they interact. The bodily state in question is one and the same, but when conceived relative to the activities that it is able to generate, we call it 'power'.[32] As Hankinson, helpfully puts it, Galen thinks 'we should resist the temptation to reify or hypostasize powers, even if we may speak of them as though they were things'.[33]

Immediately after this quote, Galen discusses the powers of aloe to cleanse and tone the throat, bind open wounds, and dry eyelids, which the aloe is able to do 'without there being any other thing that performs each of these actions other than the aloe itself' (IV 770.5–10 K = SM 2):

> For it is the aloe that does these things; and it is because it is able to do them that it has been said of it that it possesses these powers, as many as the actions. And so we say that the aloe is capable of cleansing and fortifying the mouth of the stomach, of agglutinating wounds and making ulcers heal over, and of drying wet eyes, as there is no difference between the statement that aloe is 'able to cleanse' and the statement that it *has* a 'cleansing power'.

We say the aloe has as many powers as activities it can generate when it interacts with other bodies. When we say that something *has* a power, we are just (confusedly) expressing the idea that something *is able to* produce certain effects. Yet, as Galen says, 'there is nothing other than the aloe performing all these actions' (IV 770.4–5 K = SM 2). The powers of the aloe, then, are nothing other than the mixtures that constitute the aloe.[34] Thus, if we want to explain the powers that characterize aloe, we must study its composition, for there is nothing over and above it.

For Galen, then, powers are nothing other than mixtures that are considered in relation to their effects on other bodies.[35] In *De Simplicium Medicamentorum Facultatibus* (XII 2–4 K) and *De Alimentorum Facultatibus* (VI 460 K), Galen says that the powers of drugs and foodstuffs can be reduced to the mixed elements. These powers are constituted by mixtures.[36] The same view is found in *De*

---

[32] Galen does not say that he has identified the specific principles of mixing and interaction that constitute and explain the soul's substance. Yet, he thinks they exist and could be discovered. Perhaps this is another reason why he says that he is ignorant about the soul's substance (*ousia*) in, e.g., PP 7.25.

[33] Hankinson (2014: 965).

[34] I thus agree with the reading of this passage defended in Hankinson (2014: esp. 965).

[35] Thus, I disagree with the interpretation defended in Havrda (2017: esp. 72–7), according to which Galenic powers are emergent properties of bodily parts.

[36] English translation by Powell (2003). See Vogt (2008) for a detailed explanation of Galen's treatment of the powers of drugs. Galen reduces these powers to mixtures of qualities which, at the same time, are invoked to explain these very same powers. I am indebted to David Charles for pointing this out.

Elementis Secundum Hippocratem, where Galen says that 'the bodies of animals and indeed of everything else come to be from the hot, the cold, the wet, and the dry; and we assert that these are the substances [*ousiai*] of the active powers both in drugs and indeed in everything else' (I 381 K). In *De Praesagitione Ex Pulsibus*, he tells us that 'the substance [*ousia*] of a power is nothing other than a certain mixture' (II 9.305–6K). In his *Commentary on Hippocrates' Epidemics VI*, Galen says that something's nature (*phusis*) 'is the power [*dunamis*] of the elements that have been arranged' and that this nature is 'the substance [*ousia*], i.e., the mixture from the primary elements: hot, cold, dry and wet' (V 10.2.2 K = 253.19–21 W).

In *QAM*, immediately after his discussion of the powers of aloe, Galen extends this view to the powers of the soul:

> In the same way, whenever we say that the rational soul grounded in the brain is able to perceive through the organs of perception, is able to remember the objects of perception on its own, to see consequence and conflict in things, and their analysis and synthesis, we are not expressing anything different than if we instead say, in short, that the rational soul possesses a number of powers: perception, memory, understanding, and each of the others.   IV 770.13–771.3 K = SM 2

Galen does not regard the mixtures of elements as inert. Mixtures are all one needs to account for psychological powers such as perception or understanding. Notably, Galen thinks that psychological activities such as perceiving and walking are not activities of the whole organ, i.e. of the eye or the leg, but of the homoeomerous bodies, for example, the crystalline humour or the muscles (*Meth. Med.* VII 2, X 459–60 K). For Galen, as we saw in the first section, the powers of a living organism are the powers of homoeomerous bodies which are constituted by mixtures. This commitment is expressed in Galen's claim that the number of activities corresponds to the number of the mixtures of homoeomerous parts (*San. Tu.* I 5, 9.4–6 Koch = VI 15 K).

The idea, then, is that philosophers who think of powers as something other than bodily mixtures are mistaken. This is, Galen thinks, a natural mistake to make, given our way of talking about powers. We say a substance has or possesses powers, but this should not mislead us into thinking that the powers have an existence distinct from the mixtures themselves. The mixtures that constitute homoeomerous bodies are able to perform activities when they interact with patients in the right conditions. Galen's point, I take it, is that the mixtures of bodily elements are causally efficacious.

Galen's discussion of powers in *QAM* suggests that he is aware that Aristotelians think that the soul is a power that depends on, but is ontologically distinct from, the bodily mixtures. His insistence that the mixtures themselves are causally efficacious targets these concerns. We do not need to posit a soul as a substance distinct from the bodily mixtures in order to account for psychological powers. In fact, for Galen, the view that the soul is nothing other than bodily mixtures able to perform psychic activities makes the causal efficacy of the soul less mysterious.

4. Unified Natural Bodies

Galen, then, is not moved by causal worries about the mixtures. Neither is he moved by the idea that the soul must be something other than a mixture to unify a living body. He does not tackle this issue in his psychological writings, but in a discussion of the so-called 'synectic' causes.[37] According to Galen, the Stoics argued that *synectic* causes are necessary and sufficient for the continued existence of something as a unified thing of a certain kind.[38] Interpreters have pointed out that *synectic* causes are the Stoic analogue to the Aristotelian formal cause: *synectic* causes unify something and explain what it is, why it acts the way it does, and why it persists as that thing.[39] Although, as said, Galen does not mention forms or formal causes often, he does discuss *synectic* causes in some detail. And, relevant for our purposes, he says that we do *not* need them or anything else beyond the mixtures to explain how homoeomerous bodies are unified. As Hankinson says, '[i]n Galen's view, no cause of existence (or persistence) on the Stoic (or Neoplatonist, or Cartesian for that matter) model is required, and every genuine cause, on examination, will turn out to be one of generation and not one of being' (2003: 38).

Now, Galen does not reject *synectic* causes altogether. According to him, *synectic* causes are 'causes of something's coming to be, not of existence' (*Syn. Puls.* IX 458.8–14 K; *CC* 7.30–1). Yet, he rejects the view that bodies need an immanent cause for their unity and being.[40] Natural bodies are what they are in virtue of the mixtures that constitute them. No further, immanent or internal, cause is needed for their unity and being. Galen offers an argument against positing *synectic* causes as causes of being:

---

[37] This term has been translated variously as 'cohesive', 'containing', and 'sustaining'. Galen characterizes *synectic* causes by contrasting them with two other types of causes: *proegoumenic* (antecedent, internal causes) and *prokatarktic* (antecedent, external causes).

[38] See Bobzien (1999: esp. 228).

[39] Frede (1980: 243). See also Long and Sedley (1987: 340–1); Hankinson (1998: 240–1); Bobzien (1999: 229); and Coughlin (2020: 242). On *synectic* causes as causes of generation, see Hankinson (1987: 81–8).

[40] Galen distinguishes things that exist as substances (primary existence) and things that exist as processes, changes, activities, and affections. While substances do not need *synectic* causes for their existence, activities do need *synectic* causes for their continuous generation. Galen illustrates the distinction between absolute existence and coming to be with one of his favourite examples, the pulse. The pulse does not exist as a substance, but as a coming to be.

We hear a number of people say that amongst the propositions that are intrinsically acceptable without established proof is that *no body* in any state whatsoever can exist without having a cohesive cause... But *this remark of theirs is inconsistent* in that, if every single extant thing needs a cohesive cause without which it cannot exist, *that cause, as it is one of the existing things* must inevitably have another *synectic* cause itself which, in turn, must have yet another and that will go on *ad infinitum*. CC 6.2.26–4.37[41]

A regress follows from assuming that bodies are held together by a *synectic* cause, if one thinks (as the Stoics did) that the *synectic* cause is some further body, e.g. *pneuma*. Galen's purpose here is to show 'that the various sayings of the Stoics are inconsistent' (*CC* 5.4.9–10).[42] The argument bears a striking similarity with the Syllable argument in Aristotle's *Metaphysics* Z.17 mentioned above. It is likely that Galen was familiar with it. For Galen, like for Aristotle, a regress follows if one assumes that the *synectic* cause (i.e. that which unifies the compound as such) is some further element or ingredient. Thus, he rejects the view that the *synectic* cause is some material body like *pneuma*. Notice, however, that Galen says the regress follows if we posit *any* 'existing thing' as a cause. In fact, Galen goes on to say that 'no extant thing is found in need of *another substance* [*ousia*] to hold it' (*CC* 7.1.27–8). For Galen, any attempt to explain the unity and being of the compound by positing 'something else' will run into the same problem. And so, positing 'forms' (as distinct from the mixtures) to unify bodies also leads to a regress. For, if a whole is not merely a heap of arranged elements because it contains 'something else' (*heteron ti*), i.e. the form, it may seem that the form is a proper part of the whole.[43] But if the soul is a proper part, then the regress follows. We might disagree with Galen here, but the point is that he may have interpreted Aristotle's position in this way. If I am right, Galen is anticipating a concern that philosophers such as Ockham, as well as contemporary commentators, have raised for Aristotelian hylomorphism. If forms are substances, then they seem to be proper parts of the compound, alongside the material parts. But if this is the case, forms cannot explain the unity of the compound, for now we need to say what unifies the form and the material components.[44]

---

[41] *De Causis Contentivis* (*Containing Causes*), translation from the Arabic by M. Lyons (1969). The text does not survive in Greek.

[42] In *De Plenitudine Liber* 3, he makes this Stoic commitment clear: '[M]ost of those who propose the cohesive capacity, like the Stoics, make what holds together one thing and what is held together another. For the pneumatic substance is what holds together, while the material (substance) is what is held together, which is why they say air and fire hold together, but earth and water are held together' (VII 525 K).

[43] Yet, one can resist the view that the form is a proper part of the whole and so defend a hylomorphic account of unity against Galen's objection. See Rotkale (2018).

[44] See Ockham, *Summula Philosophiae Naturalis*, ch. 19, 3rd objection. For this concern in contemporary literature, see Johnston (2006); Koslicki (2018: part II, ch. 7); and Fine (2010). Johnston says: 'One disputed question in the tradition is whether a whole construed hylomorphically

For Galen, then, the mixtures explain the unity and being of homoeomerous bodies, which, as we saw, are responsible for vital activities. As Galen tells us: 'I maintain that natural (i.e. homoeomerous) bodies are produced simply from fire, earth, water and air' (CC 3.1.8–9). The unity and being of natural bodies is explained by the mixtures, which Galen does not understand as a mere juxtaposition of elements but as a real mixture, in which the elements are thoroughly blended and do not maintain their individual identities.[45] In turn, secondary bodies such as organs and the entire organism, says Galen, 'resemble those constructed by craftsmen', since, just as the 'composition of chairs, bedsteads, ladders, ships, and houses is guarded and preserved by clay, gypsum, lime, nails, pegs, wedges and other similar things, in the same way the composition of the body is preserved by ligaments, tendons, flesh and cartilages' (CC 9.2.14–3.19).

Galen, then, is aware of the Aristotelian worry that bodily elements cannot account for the unity and identity of something as such. He agrees with Aristotelians that appealing to some further constituent or referring to the arrangement of elements, understood as mere juxtaposition, will not do the trick. We see him rehashing Aristotelian arguments to show this. But Galen resists positing forms (or any other immanent cause beyond the mixtures) to account for the unity and identity of natural bodies. We may still ask why the elements are mixed into *these* homoeomeous bodies, which serve these particular functions. We can also ask why these primary bodies are arranged through connective bodies into complex organs, and, ultimately, into living organisms of different species. For Galen, we cannot answer these types of questions by referring to some immanent cause beyond the mixtures themselves, but by referring to the efforts of a divine Craftsman who, as he tells us in *De Usu Partium*, exerts foresight on behalf of living things and has crafted them so that their complex organs carry out coordinated activities that promote self-maintenance, reproduction, and well-being.[46] The Demiurge is ultimately responsible for the unity and being of living organisms. Indeed, Galen's Platonism comes to the fore at this point, for he thinks that the purposiveness of the parts and subparts of living creatures reveals

---

is a composite of matter and form, with the form itself understood as another part, along with the more familiar "material" parts of the composite. The form cannot be a mere part alongside the other parts; it must also play a unifying role. Could it play that unifying role, and be a part as well?' (659).

[45] 'If, after they had been mixed, these ingredients were all to remain in their original state, that would imply that their minute parts had simply been juxtaposed and not that they had been totally mixed' (CC 5.2.36–3.1). Galen thus has an Aristotelian conception of the mixtures, and he criticizes Stoics and Epicureans for holding that the mere juxtaposition of elements can account for the unity and identity of natural bodies. Alexander launched a similar objection against the Stoics (see Helle, Chapter 4 in this volume). Doctors, says Galen, can get what they need without committing themselves to further, unifying causes because for them the mixtures are not mere a juxtaposition but a total blend. See also *In Hippocratis Librum De Natura Hominis Commentarii* XV 17.16–18.7 K = 11.22–12.2 M and *De Temperamentis*.

[46] See *De Usu Partium*, especially 17.1, 2.447.16–448.3 H, IV 360–1 K. See also Schiefsky (2007) for a helpful analysis of teleology in Galen. For an English translation of this work, see May (1968).

providential design, and that the Demiurge has fashioned bodies by crafting suitable mixtures from pre-existing matter. Nevertheless, this is compatible with the view that the natural bodies that compose complex organisms are what they are in virtue of the mixtures that constitute them, and that there is nothing other than these mixtures (i.e. elements blended according to a certain proportion) in the living organisms themselves that explains their being, powers, functions, and activities.[47]

5. Conclusion

For Galen, the soul's substance is nothing other than bodily mixtures. Saying that the soul is the form of the body makes sense, says Galen, only if we understand 'form' as the proportion according to which the elements are blended. This materialist position, and this deflated notion of form, goes against Aristotle's views. And it is likely that Galen knows this, as is suggested by the time he spends arguing against the causal and unity desiderata invoked by Aristotelians to posit forms as beings in their own right. We might wonder, then, to what extent Galen's endorsement of the thesis that the soul is the form of the body in *PP* is a sincere endorsement of Aristotelian hylomorphism. Again, it is relevant here that Galen rarely refers to forms and formal causes in his works. These omissions suggest that he did not think we need to posit forms to account for the being and the powers of living bodies. And this, in turn, suggests that, for Galen, the explanatory work done by forms can be suitably done by the mixtures themselves and the providential, purposeful design of the divine Craftsman. Perhaps Galen thought, as others before and after him did, that the best sense one can make of Aristotle's hylomorphism when it comes to soul-body relations is to read it, *pace* Aristotle, as a version of the *harmonia* theory of the soul. See, e.g., Barnes (1982, 491–492).[48]

Bibliography

Ackrill, J.L. (1972–3), 'Aristotle's Definitions of Psyche', *Proceedings of the Aristotelian Society* 73: 119–33.

Ballester, L.G. (1971). 'La utilización de Platón y Aristóteles en los escritos tardíos de Galeno', *Episteme* 5: 112–20.

---

[47] A point emphasized in Havrda (2017: esp. 80–1).
[48] I am grateful to David Charles, Brad Inwood, Mark Schiefsky, Philip van der Eijk, Jonathan Beere, Victor Caston, Riccardo Chiaradonna, and Matyáš Havrda, members of the Ancient Philosophy Colloquium at Humboldt-Universität zu Berlin for helpful comments and suggestions.

Ballester, L.G. (1972). *Alma y enfermedad en la obra de Galeno*, Cuadernos Valencianos de Historia de la Medicina y de la Ciencia 12 (Granada: Secretariado de Publicaciones de la Universidad).

Barnes, J. (1982). *The Presocratic Philosophers* (New York: Routledge).

Bazou, A. ed. (2011), Γαληνοῦ Ὅτι ταῖς τοῦ σώματος κράσεσιν αἱ τῆς ψυχῆς δυνάμεις ἕπονται (Athens: Academy of Athens).

Bobzien, S. (1999), 'Chrysippus' Theory of Causes', in K. Ierodiakonou (ed.), *Topics in Stoic Philosophy* (Oxford: Oxford University Press), 196–242.

Boudon-Millot, V. and Pietrobelli, A. (2005), 'Galien ressuscité. Édition princeps du texte grec du De Propriis Placitis', *Revue des Études Grecques* 118: 168–71.

Bürgel, J.C. (1968), *Averroes contra Galenum*, Nachrichten der Akademie der Wissenschaften in Gottingen, I. Philologisch-historische Klasse 9 (Gottingen: Vandenhoeck & Ruprecht), 265–340.

Caston, V. (1997), 'Epiphenomenalisms, Ancient and Modern', *Philosophical Review* 106/3: 309–63.

Caston, V. (2001), 'Dicaearchus' Philosophy of Mind', in W.W. Fortenbaugh and E. Schütrumpf (eds.), *Dicaearchus of Messana: Text, Translation, and Discussion* (New Brunswick, NJ: Transaction Publishers), 175–93.

Caston, V. (2012). (trans.) *Alexander of Aphrodisias: On the Soul. Part I: Soul as Form of the Body, Parts of the Soul, Nourishment, and Perception* (London: Bristol Classical Press).

Charlton, W. (2006) [1977], *Aristotle, Physics: Books I and II. Translation and Commentary* (Oxford: Clarendon Press).

Chiaradonna, R. (2021), 'Galen and the Formal Cause', *Elenchos Elenchos*, 42/1: 95–116.

Coughlin, S. (2020), 'Cohesive Causes in Ancient Greek Philosophy and Medicine', in C. Thumiger (ed.), *Holism in Ancient Medicine and Its Reception* (Leiden: Brill), 237–67.

De Lacy, P.H. ed., trans., and comm. (1978–84), *Galen: On the Doctrines of Hippocrates and Plato (PHP)*. CMG V 4.1.2 (Berlin: Akademie Verlag).

Debru, A. (2008), 'Physiology', in R. Hankinson (ed.), *The Cambridge Companion to Galen* (Cambridge: Cambridge University Press), 263–82.

Dillon, J.M. (1996) [1977], *The Middle Platonists 80 B.C. to A.D. 220* (Ithaca: Cornell University Press).

Donini, P. (1974), *Tre studi sull'Aristotelismo nel II secolo D.C.* (Turin: Paravia).

Donini, P. (2008), 'Psychology', in R. Hankinson (ed.), *The Cambridge Companion to Galen* (Cambridge: Cambridge University Press), 184–209.

Fine, K. (2010), 'Towards a Theory of Part', *Journal of Philosophy* 107/11: 559–89.

Ganeri, J. (2011), 'Emergentisms, Ancient and Modern', *Mind* 120/479: 671–703.

Gärtner, F. ed., trans., and comm. (2015), *Galeni De locis affectis III. Galen. Über das Erkennen erkrankter Körperteile III*, Corpus Medicorum Graecorum V 6.1.1 (Berlin: De Gruyter).

Gill, C. (2007), 'Galen and the Stoics: Mortal Enemies or Blood Brothers?', *Phronesis* 52/1: 88–120.

Grant, M. (2000), *Galen on Food and Diet* (London: Routledge).

Hankinson, R. (1991a), 'Galen's Anatomy of the Soul', *Phronesis* 36/3: 197–233.

Hankinson, R. (1991b), *On the Therapeutic Method, Books I and II* (Oxford: Clarendon Press).

Hankinson, R. (1993), 'Actions and Passions: Affection, Emotion, and Moral Self-Management in Galen's Philosophical Psychology', in J. Brunschwig and M. Nussbaum (eds.), *Passions and Perceptions: Studies in Hellenistic Philosophy of Mind* (Cambridge: Cambridge University Press), 184–222.

Hankinson, R. (1998), *Galen: On Antecedent Causes* (Cambridge: Cambridge University Press).

Hankinson, R. (2003), 'Causation in Galen', in J. Barnes (ed.), *Galien et la philosophie. Huit exposés suivis de discussions* (Genève: Fondation Hardt), 31–62.

Hankinson, R. (2006), 'Body and Soul in Galen', in R.A.H. King (ed.), *Common to Body and Soul* (Berlin: De Gruyter), 231–57.

Hankinson, R. (2008a), 'Philosophy of Nature', in R. Hankinson (ed.), *The Cambridge Companion to Galen*. (Cambridge: Cambridge University Press), 210–64.

Hankinson, R. (2008b), 'Epistemology', in R. Hankinson (ed.) *The Cambridge Companion to Galen*. (Cambridge: Cambridge University Press), 157–83.

Hankinson, R. (2014), 'Galen on the Ontology of Powers', *Causing Health and Disease in Classical and Late Antiquity, British Journal of the History of Philosophy* 22/5: 951–73.

Havrda, M. (2017), 'Body and Cosmos in Galen's Account of the Soul', *Phronesis* 62/1: 69–89.

Johnston, I. (2009), *Galen: On Diseases and Symptoms*. (Cambridge: Cambridge University Press).

Johnston, M. (2006), 'Hylomorphism', *Journal of Philosophy* 103/12: 652–98.

King, J.E. (1945), *Cicero. Tusculan Disputations*, Loeb Classical Library 141 (Cambridge, MA, London: Harvard University Press).

Koslicki, K. (2018), *Form, Matter, Substance* (Oxford, New York: Oxford University Press).

Kühn, C.G. (1819–33), *Galeni Opera Omnia*.(Leipzig: Knobloch, Hildesheim; re-issued in 1965).

Lami, A. and Garofalo, I. (2012), *Galeno. L'anima e il dolore. De indolentia. De propriis placitis* (Milan: Biblioteca Universale Rizzoli).

Lewis, D. (1971), 'Counterparts of Persons and Their Bodies', *Journal of Philosophy* 68/7: 203–11 (Reprinted in D. Lewis (1983), *Philosophical Papers*, Volume I (Oxford: Oxford University Press).)

Lippert, J. ed. (1903), *Ibn al-Qifṭī. Ta'rikh al-Ḥukama* (Leipzig: Dietrich).

Lloyd, G.E.R. (1988), 'Scholarship, Authority and Argument in Galen's *Quod Animi Mores*', in P. Manuli and M. Vegetti (eds.), *Le Opere Psicologiche di Galeno* (Naples: Bibliopolis), 11–42.

Lloyd, G.E.R. (2008), 'Galen and His Contemporaries', in R. Hankinson (ed.), *The Cambridge Companion to Galen* (Cambridge: Cambridge University Press), 34–48.

Lyons, M. ed. and trans. (1969), *On the Parts of Medicine, On Cohesive Causes, On Regimen in Acute Diseases in Accordance with the Theories of Hippocrates*. Latin version of *On Cohesive Causes*, in K. Kalbfleisch (ed.), re-edited by J. Kollesch, D. Nickel, and G. Strohmaier, CMG Supplementum Orientale II (Berlin: Akademie Verlag).

Marechal, P. (2019), 'Galen's Constitutive Materialism', *Ancient Philosophy* 39/1: 191–209.

May, M.T. (1968), *Galen on the Usefulness of the Parts of the Body. Peri chreias mori* (Ithaca: Cornell University Press).

Müller, J. (1891), *Galeni Pergameni Scripta Minora* (Leipzig: Teubner).

Nutton, V. ed., trans., and comm. (1979), *Galen: On Prognosis*. CMG V 8.1 (Berlin: Akademie Verlag).

Nutton, V. (1984), 'Galen in the Eyes of His Contemporaries', *Bulletin of the History of Medicine* 58/3: 315–24.

Nutton, V. ed., trans., and comm. (1999), *Galen: On My Own Opinions*. CMG V 3.2 (Berlin: Akademie Verlag).

Nutton, V. (2020), *Galen: A Thinking Doctor in Imperial Rome* (London: Routledge).

Powell, O. (2003), *Galen: On the Properties of Foodstuffs (De Alimentorum Facultatibus)* (Cambridge: Cambridge University Press).

Rothschild, C.K. and Thompson, T.W. (2014), *Galen's De Indolentia: Essays on a Newly Discovered Letter* (Tübingen: Mohr Siebeck).

Schiefsky, M.J. (2007), 'Galen's Teleology and Functional Explanation', *Oxford Studies in Ancient Philosophy* 33: 369–400.

Shields, C. (1988), 'Soul and Body in Aristotle', *Oxford Studies in Ancient Philosophy* 6: 103–37.

Shields, C. trans. (2015), *Aristotle's De Anima: Translated with Introduction and Notes* (Oxford: Oxford University Press).

Singer, P.N. (1997), *Galen: Selected Works* (Oxford: Oxford University Press).

Singer, P.N. (2013), *Galen: Psychological Writings* (Cambridge: Cambridge University Press).

Singer, P.N. (2016), 'Galen', *The Stanford Encyclopedia of Philosophy*, Winter 2016 edition, ed. E.N. Zalta. https://plato.stanford.edu/archives/win2016/entries/galen/

Smith, A. (1993), *Porphyrii Philosophi Fragmenta*, Bibliotheca Scriptorum Graecorum et Romanorum Teubneriana (Leipzig: Teubner).

Studtmann, P. (2008), 'On the Several Senses of Form in Aristotle', *Apeiron* 41/3: 1–26.

Temkin, O. (1973), *Galenism: Rise and Decline of a Medical Philosophy* (Ithaca: Cornell University Press).

Tieleman, T. (1996), *Galen and Chrysippus on the Soul: Argument and Refutation in the De Placitis II–III* (Leiden: Brill).

Tieleman, T. (2003), 'Galen's Psychology', in J. Barnes and J. Jouanna (eds.), *Galien et la Philosophie*, Volume 49 (Genève: Entretiens sur l'Antiquité classique de la Fondation Hardt) 131–69.

Tieleman, T. (2008), 'Methodology', in R. Hankinson (ed.), *The Cambridge Companion to Galen* (Cambridge: Cambridge University Press), 49–65.

Todd, R.B. (1976), *Alexander of Aphrodisias' 'De Mixtione' and the Stoic Theory of Mixture* (Leiden: Brill).

van der Eijk, P.J. (2005a), *Philoponus on Aristotle On the Soul 1.1–2: Edition and Translation* (London: Duckworth).

van der Eijk, P.J. (2005b), *Medicine and Philosophy in Classical Antiquity: Doctors and Philosophers on Nature, Soul, Health and Disease.* (Cambridge: Cambridge University Press).

van der Eijk, P.J. (2020), 'Galen on Soul, Mixture and Pneuma', in B. Inwood and J. Warren (eds.), *Body and Soul in Hellenistic Philosophy* (Cambridge: Cambridge University Press), 62–88.

van der Eijk, P. and Singer, P.N. (2019), *Galen: Works on Human Nature. Mixtures (De Temperamentis)* (Cambridge: Cambridge University Press).

Vegetti, M. (2012), 'Galen on Bodies, Temperaments and Personalities', in P. Olmos (ed.), *Greek Science in the Long Run: Essays on the Greek Scientific Tradition (4th c. BCE–17th c. CE)* (Newcastle upon Tyne: Cambridge Scholars Publishing), 265–80.

Vegetti, M. and Menghi, M. (1984), *Galeno. Le Passioni e gli errori dell'anima* (Venice: Marsilio).

Vogt, S. (2008), 'Drugs and Pharmacology', in R. Hankinson (ed.), *The Cambridge Companion to Galen* (Cambridge: Cambridge University Press), 304–22.

von Staden, H. (2000), 'Body, Soul, and Nerves: Epicurus, Herophilus, Erasistratus, the Stoics, and Galen', in J. Wright and P. Potter (eds.), *Psyche and Soma: Physicians and Metaphysicians on the Mind-Body Problem from Antiquity to Enlightenment* (Oxford: Oxford University Press), 79–116.

Wehrli, F. (1967), *Dikaiarchos. Die Schule des Aristoteles. Texte und Kommentar*, Volume 1, 2nd edition (Basel: Schwabe).

Wenkebach, E. ed. (1956), *Galeni in Hip Epidemiarum Librum VI Commentaria I–VIII*. CMG V 10.2.2 (Berlin: Akademie Verlag).

Wiggins, D. (1967), *Identity and Spatio-Temporal Continuity* (Oxford: Oxford University Press).

Wolfe, C.T., and van Esveld, M. (2014), 'The Material Soul: Strategies for Naturalizing the Mind in an Early Modern Epicurean Context', in D. Kambasković (ed.), *Conjunctions of Mind, Soul and Body from Plato to the Enlightenment: Studies in the History of Philosophy of Mind*, Volume 15 (Dordrecht: Springer Netherlands), 371–421.

6
Alexander of Aphrodisias' Emergentism
Hylomorphism Perfected

Victor Caston

There can be little doubt that Alexander of Aphrodisias (*fl.* late 2nd century CE) is one of the great Aristotelians in the tradition, alongside Ibn Rushd, Maimonides, and Thomas Aquinas. Like them, he is not a mere a commentator or interpreter, but a philosopher for whom Aristotelianism is still a living philosophy, whose commitments he is trying to work out in the most powerful way. Of the four, moreover, Alexander is the one who develops an Aristotelianism that most closely approximates that of our own contemporaries. Unburdened by the need to reconcile his views with any of the Abrahamic religions, Alexander is free to pursue the implications of Aristotle's views in a more systematic fashion, often with penetrating and illuminating insights.[1] His treatment of hylomorphism constitutes a paradigmatic instance of this approach. What drives it, I shall argue, is his emergentist metaphysics, something that Aristotle himself is arguably committed to, but does not spell out in any detail. Alexander does, and makes this central to his metaphysics.

Emergentism, to our ears, has obvious ramifications for concerns about reductionism and mental causation. But for Alexander it is primarily a way of understanding and spelling out what is involved in hylomorphism. It allows him to make precise the relation a form has to the matter that underlies it, and to see how this relation is recursively iterated at various levels, resulting in a layered conception of reality. Since the matter of a hylomorphic compound might itself be a hylomorphic compound, it may have a form and matter of its own, which in turn may again be a hylomorphic compound, until we finally hit bottom with prime matter. Therefore, there are forms all the way down, so to speak, in matter at every

---

[1] By this, I do not mean to suggest that Alexander operates free of any historical context or that all his concerns are the same as our own (as an anonymous referee worried), but only that we share many concerns in common, more so than with the medieval Aristotelians, in no small measure because of the latter's substantial theological commitments. To the extent Alexander seeks to contrast his views with those of the Stoics, moreover, and show the superiority of his own, it is a dispute between materialists, and so it involves some of the more fine-grained distinctions at issue in today's debates.

In what follows, I try to understand Alexander's mature position systematically, focusing primarily on his *De Anima*. For a more comprehensive survey of Alexander's writings on hylomorphism, within their historical and polemical context, see Frans de Haas' authoritative discussion in this volume.

level except the lowest, a feature which is significant for Alexander because of the distinctive efficient causal role he assigns to form. As a consequence, even material explanations will make essential reference to form, insofar as distinctive types of matter possess forms of their own, which makes any given matter the kind that it is and explains why it is suitable for the functions required for the form above it. And it is the form at each of these levels that figures in causal explanations. Alexander does not, then, merely gesture at a rough and ready distinction between form and matter, or the fact that it 'stacks' and iterates hierarchically. His emergentism allows him to offer a highly specific version of hylomorphism, making clear exactly what the distinctive contributions of form and matter are, as well as their relation to one another.

1. Dynamic Materialism

One of the most striking features of Alexander's treatise on the nature of the soul, that is, his own *De Anima*, is the prominence of the term *dunamis* or 'power', as I shall translate it. It is far more prevalent than *energeia*, the term for 'activity', something which might surprise us, given the priority of activities to powers in Aristotelian metaphysics. Its prevalence is significant for two reasons. The first is the close connection in Aristotelian metaphysics between powers and matter: only material compounds possess powers. Alexander's emphasis on powers is thus integral to his materialism. The second is the way Alexander uses his conception of a power to develop his notion of form. For him forms are efficient causal powers (among other things), the explanatory grounds for why substances behave in the ways they characteristically do: they are that *in virtue of which* a substance is able to do such things, and so such forms are essentially a kind of power (*De An.* 7.9–14, 9.14–26, cf. 31.10–13).[2] But he further takes it to be something that *belongs* to a material compound and so is an *attribute*, rather than something bodily or material itself (17.15–18; quoted and discussed in the next section). This stands in strong contrast with the Stoics, who regard each of the principles constituting a body as itself a body. In rejecting Stoic corporealism, Alexander is one of the first philosophers to develop explicitly and systematically the precise commitments of a substance-attribute ontology like Aristotle's. We ourselves take this framework for granted, but it was some time in the making. A crucial consequence of this view, which Alexander makes explicit, is that forms themselves are inherently immaterial, even if they belong to a material body

---

[2] I exclude from consideration here significantly different senses of *dunamis*, much as Aristotle does with regard to talk of "powers" at *Meta.* Θ.1, 1046a6–9. (I am grateful to David Charles for raising the point.)

Unless otherwise noted, all references to Alexander's own *De Anima* and the so-called *Mantissa* are to Ivo Bruns' edition in the Berlin Academy series (1887). All translations are my own.

essentially. Not being bodies themselves or constituted from bodies, they can be called 'material' only by metonymy, insofar as they are the attributes *of* a body.

One might think that an explicit commitment to immaterial entities like forms (not to mention his commitment to an immaterial God) severely compromises any claim that Alexander is a materialist or, worse, that it makes him a kind of crypto-dualist. But in fact his emphasis on causal powers allows us to ascribe materialism to him in a substantive sense while situating it properly. Materialism is not universal for Alexander but restricted to the realm of nature, where substances can undergo transitions in state or position. Being capable of such transitions, they must have the powers to undergo them and matter that can realize them: the capacity to be otherwise entails having powers, and having powers entails having matter. The same will be true of those things with active powers that can trigger changes in other things at one time and not another, since the exercise of these powers depends on changes the agents themselves undergo, even if just to make contact. So although these causal powers are not material in the sense of being bodies themselves, they must belong to things that are. Though restricted, such a materialism is still pervasive and the restriction is well motivated. Using the term 'dynamic' both for its etymological connection with *dunamis* and for its connection with change, we might demarcate the scope of Alexander's materialism as follows:

DYNAMIC MATERIALISM: Any substance whose essence is not activity [*energeia*], but which instead has the power [*dunamis*] to engage in activities, is a compound of matter and form; the only form(s) that can exist apart from matter are those that belong to or constitute a substance whose essence is activity and so does not undergo any transition itself.

Alexander can then characterize the forms of material substances—call them 'dynamic forms'—in terms of powers:

DYNAMIC FORMS: The form of any material substance is its first actuality [*entelecheia prōtē*], that is, a *power* the substance *actually* possesses to perform in the appropriate conditions its functions [*erga*]—the activities [*energeiai*] characteristic of that type of substance in so far as it is that sort of substance—and the form is that *in virtue of which* the substance performs these activities.[3]

---

[3] Aristotle introduces the term 'first actuality' at *De Anima* 2.1, 412a27 and b5, while defining the soul. But it presupposes a more general distinction: he gives the example of knowledge already acquired, but not presently in use (a22–7), and a similar distinction underlies his discussion of perception in *De Anima* 2.5 (see esp. 417a21–b2). The exercise of a power already acquired is naturally meant to contrast with the initial acquisition of a power (e.g. *De An.* 2.5, 427b16–19; *GA* 2.3, 736b21–26; 4.1, 766a5–10). Alexander calls the power to acquire a power a 'first potentiality' (*prōtē dunamis*; *Quaest.* 3.2, 81.9 and 3.3, 84.34 Bruns). Although these powers are essentially connected— they are what Barbara Vetter calls 'iterated potentialities' (2015: §4.6)—they do not collapse, but remain

These principles capture the motivation underlying the limits on Alexander's materialism. The only things that can undergo transitions are material things and they do so in virtue of their forms, the powers they actually possess to effect such transitions.

2. Levels Ontology and Ontological Irreducibility

In taking each body to be a compound of form and matter, Alexander is recognizing two fundamentally different types of component, with distinct ontological roles. It is not surprising, then, that he would insist that form, as such, is not matter and that matter, as such, is not form. But he seems to think even more strongly that nothing that is a form can be the matter of anything or vice versa, and therefore that no form is *identical* with any matter.

He argues at length against the possibility that a form might *be* or be *constituted from* form and matter (Alexander, *De An.* 17.15–19.20). He does so in part for polemical reasons, as he himself makes explicit:

> So a form is not a body [*oude sōma*] either, along the lines of those, like the Stoics, who claim that each body is either matter or composed from matter. For form is not matter [*oute hulē*], since the latter is qualityless, while the former is a kind of quality, nor is it composed from matter [*oute ex hulēs*]...
>
> 17.15–18[4]

The polemic against the Stoics may not be much more than a pretext here; at any rate, it isn't enough to justify the elaborate twists and turns of argument that Alexander pursues for two Berlin Academy pages to show that no form is a compound. But there are systematic reasons for why he might want to demonstrate this thesis, independent of any polemical aims. It is a central part of the hylomorphic view he develops at the outset of the treatise that *matter*, unlike form, *can* be constituted from form and matter. Indeed, apart from prime matter—that is, the qualityless matter that underlies the simple elemental bodies at the most fundamental level of the world—*all other* matter is a body and so is constituted from form and matter (3.21–4.4, esp. 3.23–7).[5] Such matter inherently possesses form already, *prior* to being the matter of something else: it has at

---

distinct, because Aristotle rejects the transitivity of the relation *F is potentially G* (*Meta.* Θ.7, 1049a2–5, a19–24), prioritizing (in Vetter's terms again) the immediate manifestation of a power over its ultimate ones.

[4] For the claim that form is not a body, see also Alexander, *De An.* 5.22; 7.9–13; 15.11–13; 17.8–11.

[5] For more on the distinction between simple and compound bodies, see Alexander, *De An.* 4.4–9; 5.9, 18–19; 7.14–18.13; 9.14–26; 10.26–11.13. On prime matter: 3.28–4.20; 5.20–2; 7.15–17; 8.17–18; 17.17–18. That all bodies are composed of matter and form: 2.26–3.2; 10.2–8; 11.20–1; 17.11.

the very least a form of its own and, if it is a compound higher than the elements, it indirectly contains the forms of the matter that makes it up as well. The polar opposite is true of forms. Even if one accepts the view that some forms have an account that includes (or implies) reference to matter, on Alexander's view the form itself will still not be identical with or constituted from matter. And this holds true of forms at every level.

This difference between form and matter has two important consquences, one on the material side, the other on the formal. First, form-matter compounding can be *iterated*: material compounds can serve as the matter for still more complex compounds, successively and perhaps indefinitely. This produces a hierarchical organization of natural materials into 'layers' of complexity, built from those beneath it—what Jaegwon Kim called a *layered world* or *levels ontology*.[6] Each hylomorphic compound, at each level, will be distinguished by a form of its own, as will any compound bodies that serve as its matter and, indeed, the matter of their matter, and so on, until we ultimately reach prime matter:

LEVELS ONTOLOGY: The matter of virtually all hylomorphic compounds is itself a hylomorphic compound, whose matter may in turn also be a hylomorphic compound; only the matter of simple bodies (the elements) is not a form-matter compound and so not a body, but prime matter. Every compound has a distinctive form of its own, in addition to the forms of any bodies (if any) that constitute it.

This iterated hylomorphic structure is what makes possible Alexander's distinctive take on the *scala naturae* and the original way he articulates the relation between levels (8.17–11.13), as we will see in the next section. For the moment, it is enough to note how often Alexander appeals to the *scala naturae* in order to bring out the analogous structure of all hylomorphic compounds, allowing him to show that many of his claims about the souls of living things have analogues even in elemental cases, such as the lightness of fire or the heaviness of earth.[7] There are obviously differences between compounds at different levels, often great ones. But they are due to the specific difference between their forms, not their structure as compounds, which is all that he is insisting on with his analogies.

The distinction Alexander draws between matter and form, as to whether they can themselves be compounds, has a second important consequence, this time for form. For if form is not matter or a compound of form and matter, then it follows that all forms are non-bodily (*asōmata*) and immaterial, even though he also thinks that forms—dynamic forms, at any rate—are even *less separable* than

---

[6] See Kim 1993 and 2010, respectively.
[7] Alexander, *De An.* 9.14–25; 11.5–13; 20.19–22; 22.4–12, 15–23; 23.24–24.4; cf. 5.4–18; 13.22–14.3.

matter is: most matter can exist on its own as compound bodies, but no dynamic form can (4.20–5.1; cf. 5.22–6.2).[8] We might formulate this as follows:

> IMMATERIAL FORMS: All forms are immaterial in themselves: they are not matter or constituted from matter (as bodies are), even if they are essentially the forms *of* a material compound and so *inseparable* from them. They are non-bodily [*asōmata*] in the sense that they are not themselves bodies.

But this in turn shows that forms cannot be ontologically reduced to matter. For while one might have different conceptions of what ontological reduction consists in, the following schema seems like a necessary condition that should hold for all cases:

> Ψs are ontologically reducible to Φs only if Ψs are either identical with or exhaustively constituted by Φs.

But as we have seen, this condition is violated in the case of forms, and so *a fortiori* in the case of dynamic forms as well. Therefore, Alexander is also committed to the following:

> IRREDUCIBILITY OF DYNAMIC FORMS: No dynamic form, i.e. no power, is ontologically reducible to matter, since it is neither identical with any matter nor constituted from it, even in part.

So while Alexander is committed to dynamic materialism and holds that dynamic forms are essentially the forms of material compounds and so inseparable from them and from bodies, he also maintains that they are irreducible to them.

3. Supervenience

This nuanced position raises obvious questions about the relation between forms and the matter that underlies them. If forms 'float freely' over the matter they are forms of, then Alexander's commitment to immaterial forms might seem to undercut any serious claim to materialism. For in that case, even though dynamic forms cannot exist apart from material compounds, *which* form a material compound has would not depend on the underlying composition and structure of matter—it could be

---

[8] The inseparability of dynamic forms—the fact that they cannot exist apart from matter—entails that they will, in this sense, be ontologically dependent on there being some underlying matter. But that does not entail, either for Alexander or for Aristotle, that matter is prior in any of the more substantive senses they standardly assign to form.

entirely adventitious. But that would be enormously consequential. Given the important causal role forms play as powers, it would mean that the key factor in a substance's identity and behaviour was due to an additional item, not determined by its underlying material makeup, which would constitute a merely necessary condition at best. In the case of soul, this would amount to something like vitalism, along the lines of Bergson's *élan vital* or Driesch's conception of *entelecheia* (a term he appropriates from Aristotle, but completely transforms).

In any event, this is not Alexander's view: forms do not float freely on top of matter. Which form a compound substance has is a *function* of the material bodies underlying it and how they are combined; and since the character and powers of these bodies is due in turn to their forms, the form of the original substance will be ultimately a function of the lower forms belonging to these underlying material compounds, which Alexander says 'contribute' (*suntelein*; 7.24, 8.11) to the nature of the higher compound as whole:

> The [body], then, which has many differing forms conjoined with matter as its underlying subjects, has a nature and form that is of necessity more complex and more advanced, since each nature [*hekastēs phuseōs*] in the bodies underlying it makes a contribution [*suntelousēs ti*] to the form that stands over them all and is shared by them. For this sort of form is in a way a "form of forms" [*eidos eidōn*][9] and a kind of culmination of culminations.   8.8–13

Nor is it just any sort of contribution. Differences in the forms of the underlying bodies are in some sense the *ground responsible* for differences in the forms of compounds:

> For this reason, we should also not be surprised by the difference among forms in natural bodies, since we plainly find the grounds [*tas aitias*] for their diversity in the underlying subjects. For it makes sense that the number of forms in the bodies underlying them, together with their distinctive mixture, would contain the grounds [*tas aitias pheroito*] for such great diversity.   8.13–17

Alexander makes a similar remark somewhat later. Having mentioned the vast differences in the abilities of animals, or again the even greater differences between animals and plants, he comments:

---

[9] The phrase 'form of forms' derives from Aristotle (*De An.* 3.8, 432a2), though he uses it for the relation of the understanding (*nous*) to its objects, rather than the hylomorphic relation of higher to lower forms, as here. The latter extends quite widely to all 'blends', the subject of Alexander's *De Mixtione*, not just homoeomerous materials, but anhomoeomerous bodies like organs and the living body constituted from them as well. (I would like to thank Orna Harari for emphasizing this point.) On Alexander's theory of mixture and his critique of Stoicism, see Reier Helle's excellent and illuminating Chapter 4 in this volume.

The ground responsible [*aitia*] for the proportional difference between them is the difference in the bodies underlying them, as regards their number and the particular kind of blend [*krasin*], mixture [*mixin*], and formation [*sustasin*].

10.17–19

The differences between living things thus correlates with the complexity and differences in the underlying matter and is in some sense due to them. They provide the basis for the distinctive powers and behaviour of complex beings.

In translating *aitia* here as 'ground', I do not intend anything stronger than this functional relationship. In particular it should not be taken to conflict with Alexander's commitment to the distinctive causal efficacy of the higher form.[10] To say that the differences in the underlying matter ground the differences between forms is to say that differences at the higher level are a *consequence* of differences at the lower level—they are not caused by them, in our sense of the word, but they *follow from them by necessity*:

But the proximate matter of each thing that comes to be is also an origin. So it makes sense that the difference in forms that supervene on [*ginomenōn ep' autais*] differences in the proximate matter follows [*hepesthai*] from them. For not all matter can receive the same culmination. 10.24–6[11]

The last sentence suggests, at least by litotes, that Alexander might allow *some* differences in the underlying matter in compounds that share the same highest form, that is, that some forms could be *multiply realizable*. But the converse doesn't hold. Any difference at the higher level necessarily requires some difference at the lower level—otherwise the higher level differences couldn't be said to *follow* from the lower ones. We thus have co-variation at least in one direction, from the bottom up. In short, the higher level forms *supervene* on the underlying material bodies, specifically on 'their number and the particular kind of blend, mixture, and formation' (10.18–19; quoted above).

In his *Mantissa*, Alexander explicitly applies the notion of consequence to different types of soul, arguing that this too depends on differences in the underlying body, where the difference between types of soul is a matter of the distinctive psychological powers those souls possess. Having explicitly distinguished the soul

---

[10] As I shall argue in the next section. For detailed discussion of Alexander's use of the words, *aitia* and *archē* of matter in this context, defending his overall consistency on this point, see my discussion of 10.24–6 in my (2012: 87–8 n. 92).

[11] In contrast, at 77.17–18 Alexander does describe a causal consequence, as Richard Sorabji notes (Chapter 10, this volume), namely, the heating or cooling of the musculature produced by thinking about and representing various objects of desire. Sorabji thinks there is a terminological difference here as well, though I am not sure whether Alexander's usage is so hard and fast on this point. But we agree that causation is not at issue in the passages discussed above.

from the structure and arrangement of the body, its dispositions and states, and the underlying blend of materials (104.22–5), Alexander continues:

> While these certainly come about in the body (since it is on account of these that there are organs, which the soul utilizes), the soul itself is a certain kind of power and substance that supervenes on these [*epi toutois ginomenē*]; that is, the body and its blend are the ground of the soul's initial coming into being. This is clear from the differences of animals with respect to their parts. For souls do not fashion [*ou diaplassousi*] the shapes of animals. Rather, the different souls are a consequence [*epēkolouthēsan*] of animals' structure [*sustasei*] being of a certain sort and they covary with [*summetaballousin*] one another ... Because the difference in soul follows from [*hepetai*] the body's blend being of a certain sort, it is clear that beasts possess a distinctive soul due to the body's blend being of a certain sort. *Mant.* 104.26–34[12]

The notion of following (*hepesthai*) and consequence (*epakolouthein*) in these contexts is modal: the soul and its distinctive powers follow from the constitution and arrangement of the body much as a conclusion necessarily follows from its premises, though in the case of the soul and its powers only natural or nomological necessity is involved, rather than logical or metaphysical necessity.[13] If this is right, then for Alexander the following schema will always be satisfied (where 'Ψ' and 'Φ' need not be restricted to predicates, but can be replaced by expressions for either properties or entities of various kinds):

Ψ follows from Φ $=_{df}$ necessarily, whenever Φ is instantiated, Ψ is instantiated as well.[14]

Alexander links these notions explicitly in his commentary on Aristotle's *Topics*, when he explains how the whiteness of snow supervenes on the condition of the underlying matter (*tōi sumptōmati tēs hulēs epiginomenon*; *Top.* 50.9–51.3 at 51.2–3), a property he repeatedly describes as following of necessity (50.10, 20–1, 23, 30), just as Aristotle does.[15] If so, then when Alexander speaks of supervenience

---

[12] Richard Sorabji (Chapter 10, this volume) questions the authenticity of this section and cites Sharples (2004) in support. But I find no indication, either in Sharples or in the text, that brings its authenticity into serious question.

[13] I am grateful to Jonathan Schaffer for pressing the distinction.

[14] I take the relation to be neither symmetric nor asymmetric, but non-symmetric, that is, as not requiring the converse direction, but not precluding it either.

[15] Aristotle holds that snow is white 'by nature' (*phusei*) and could not possibly be black: *Categ.* 10, 12b35–41; *APr* 1.15, 35a23–4; and *Top.* 4.1, 120b21–9. For detailed discussion of the passage from Alexander in *Top.* 50–1, see my (2012: 80–1 n. 40), which considers it in connection with *De An.* 5.5–6 and his use of the terms *gennasthai epi* and *epigignesthai* more broadly. For Richard Sorabji's alternative reading of the passage from the *Topics* commentary, see Chapter 10, n. 24, below. On the Aristotle passages, see now Ademollo (2021).

(*epigignesthai*) he does not have the loose, ordinary notion of one thing's merely happening after or along with another thing, but rather cases where there is a necessary *systematic co-variation* between types, of the sort involved in the technical philosophical sense of 'supervenience':

> SUPERVENIENCE: there can be no difference in a type of compound without differences in the type of blend and arrangement of underlying matter—in short, the former necessarily *covaries* with the latter. That is, whenever there is a certain type of compound, there must be some underlying matter such that necessarily, whenever that type of matter is arranged in that way, it constitutes that type of compound.

In my view, whenever Alexander speaks of supervenience he has this sort of following or consequence in mind.[16] Richard Sorabji (Chapter 10, this volume) questions whether Alexander is committed to this kind of exceptionless, much less necessary, co-variation, pointing out that in several cases Alexander speaks of what often happens or certain propensities.[17] Sorabji agrees that talk of 'following' implies necessitation, but he maintains that supervenience needn't be as strong and in fact normally falls short of it. In this, he is in agreement with John Philoponus, who explicitly distinguishes supervenience from following and denies that the former involves strict co-variation (*In De An.* 51.13-29).[18] In my view, though, this is precisely a point where Philoponus departs from Alexander and is innovating. Alexander never describes something as supervenient but not a consequence of the underlying condition;[19] and he nowhere draws an explicit distinction between supervenience and following in the way suggested. On the contrary, in the passage from his commentary on the *Topics* mentioned above, he expressly links the two notions.[20]

---

[16] He would not accept the converse, though: a conclusion follows from its premises and an effect from its efficient cause, but he does not (to my knowledge) ever speak of these as 'supervenient'. (I am grateful to David Charles for raising the question.)

[17] E.g. 'often' at 10.23 (comparison with branching roads); 'easier' at 13.7 (irascibility).

[18] See Sorabji's excellent detailed discussion of Philoponus in the second half of his Chapter 10 in this volume.

[19] Sorabji argues that there is one case where what supervenes cannot follow necessarily, namely when the higher powers are said to 'rest upon' lower ones (*De An.* 66.6-8). But the text does not explicitly state that these powers supervene, but merely uses the preposition *epi* (with *einai* understood), which is vaguer than passages where he describes how certain powers supervene or emerge. For consistency, I think the preposition in this passage is merely expressing the hierarchical relation between the powers and not ontological dependence.

[20] Sorabji offers a different interpretation of the passage (*Top.* 50.9-51.3): he suggests that Alexander's reference to necessity there only indicates an additional condition that doesn't hold of supervenience generally. The passage never frames it in these terms, though, but proceeds mainly by describing the necessary relation of consequence (50.10, 20-1, 23, 30) and then concludes by declaring whiteness to be something supervenient (51.3). Although this is logically compatible with Sorabji's reading, the progress of the argument more naturally suggests that Alexander views necessary co-

It is worth emphasizing that so far we have only been considering the supervenience of dynamic forms like souls and their powers, and not the states or activities such a compound can undergo by exercising these powers, for example, by perceiving, thinking, or being angry. I believe Alexander would accept supervenience in these cases too, even though it is not something he emphasizes. In a long passage from Alexander's *De Anima* a little after those quoted above, he elaborates on a key *aporia* from the opening chapter of Aristotle's *De Anima*, as to

> whether all the states of the soul [*ta pathē tēs psuchēs... panta*] are also shared by that which has it, or whether some belong exclusively to the soul.
> Arist., *De An.* 1.1, 403a3–5

Aristotle goes on to discuss the issue at some length in a passage that is rightly regarded as pivotal for his whole approach to the relation between the soul and the body (403a3–25). In his own treatment of the issues, Alexander repeatedly emphasizes that changes in the body are a necessary condition of a broad range of psychological activities, from nourishing oneself and reproduction all the way up to thought. But he also seems to think such bodily changes are *sufficient conditions* as well. He is explicit that desires and passions occur whenever the body undergoes the relevant changes, and he arguably affirms the same of perception, representation, and thought:

> One might also learn that the soul is a form of the body, and not a substance itself just on its own, from its activities. For no soul activity can occur apart from a bodily change, just as there couldn't be motion due to natural tendencies [apart from a bodily change] either, since the body engages in these activities in virtue of the power within it. For being nourished, growing, and generating another like oneself occur in virtue of a soul power, but the changes belong to the body. Moreover, an animal perceives by means of the perceptual organs [*dia tōn aisthētēriōn*], which are bodies, and desires themselves plainly occur when a certain body undergoes change [*kinoumenou tinos ginontai sōmatos*]: for appetites, passions, and rage occur in animals in this way [*toutōn ginontai ton tropon*]; both alteration and contraction of the body [*tou sōmatos hē alloiōsis te kai sustolē*] occur in fears too. Representation also occurs by means of a body [*dia sōmatos*], if at any rate it depends [*ērtētai*] on perception in activity, as will be shown. No one would deny that in striving, too, what undergoes change [*to kinoumenon*] is a body. Even thinking would itself be something that occurs by means of a body [*dia sōmatos*] too, if it does not occur without representation. If

---

variation as a distinctive characteristic of supervenience. Elsewhere Alexander treats cases where the supervenient property does not occur as a reason to restrict the supervenience base more narrowly, rather than allow supervenience with exceptions (*Top.* 303.28–9).

it is not possible to conceive of any activity of soul apart from a bodily change, then clearly [the soul] is something that belongs to the body and is inseparable from it. For if it were separate, it would be ineffectual, since it would not be able to engage in any of its own activities on its own.   Alexander, *De An.* 12.7–24[21]

When Alexander claims that an animal engages in psychological activities 'by means of' a body (*dia* + gen.), he clearly means that this psychological activity occurs *by the body's undergoing the relevant changes*; it is not something that merely transpires in the body, but through the body itself undergoing change, something the passage repeatedly refers to. If so, then it is not only necessary that there be some bodily changes in order for the psychological activity to occur.[22] They must be the sorts of changes that are *sufficient* for these psychological conditions to occur, in the same way that I sign a cheque *by* producing the relevant sort of scrawl on the appropriate line: signing supervenes on making that distinctive scrawl. But if so, then all of these psychological activities, including thinking, will supervene on bodily changes for Alexander as well. Though the passages is not as explicit as one might like, it strongly suggests that he would be comfortable with the extension of supervenience to psychological activities.

None of this need conflict, finally, with Alexander's libertarian conception of freedom, since the kind of determination involved here is at a given moment and not over time. Supervenience requires that there be a base state—here the total state of an organ or of the body as a whole—which is a sufficient condition for the psychological state that *at that moment* supervenes on it. But it in no way follows that *antecedent* bodily states necessitate bodily outcomes and thereby the psychological states that supervene on them. If Alexander is an indeterminist, as he seems to be, he can hold that even in the exact same world states, each of two alternative outcomes is still possible.[23] He can further hold that what determines the outcome in such cases will be a psychological state, the exercise of what Aristotle calls a

---

[21] For detailed discussion of the passage and its implications, see my (2012: 91–3 nn. 107–15).

[22] *Pace* Sorabji (Chapter 10, this volume), who claims that the bodily conditions are 'merely prerequisite' for the mental activity. I agree with him that the case described later at 13.6–8 only concerns a propensity towards anger, when in certain states of bodily agitation, a point that would hold even if there are sufficient conditions. But I don't take that to be evidence that Alexander holds that in general bodily states are merely necessary conditions of mental activities.

[23] Although his commitment to indeterminism is fairly clear, some of the textual evidence is the subject of dispute. In the *Mantissa*, Alexander (or perhaps a member of his school) explicitly affirms that the choices that are said to 'depend on us' (*eph' hēmin*) are those which are 'ungrounded, that is, where there is not a pre-existing ground' (*anaitiōs kai mē prohuparchousēs aitias*, 22, 171.22–3, 27; cf. 170.14); but elsewhere he denies that actions are without a cause or ground, since they depend upon our deliberation and assent (*Mant.* 23, 174.7–9; *Fat.* 15, 185.15–21, 186.2–3, 10–12). What is at stake in the latter passages, though, need not be the denial that such cases are completely ungrounded, but only the denial that there are any prior triggering causes or grounds that necessitate these outcomes. In that case, these passages would be consistent with the first one above: for discussion, see Salles (1998: 71–3); also Sorabji (Chapter 10, this volume). In any case, Alexander clearly maintains that in the exact same circumstances one could choose otherwise, if only to demonstrate that one's choice was not necessitated (*Mant.* 174.30–5; *Fat.* 29, 200.2–7; cf. 32, 204.21–8). Salles (1998) also discusses whether the

rational power (*dunamis meta logou*), through our choosing one of the outcomes.[24] That state will also supervene on an underlying bodily state, of course. But what is responsible for the outcome and explains the subsequent result is the supervenient psychological state. For that, Alexander must accept *downward causation* and thus emergentism, which we should now turn to. But it does not conflict with his indeterminism.[25]

4. Emergentism and Explanatory Irreducibility

To appreciate Alexander's emergentism properly, it is critical to see that supervenience on its own does not entail any kind of reductionism. *Which* dynamic form a compound has will be a function of the blend and arrangement of underlying matter. But the form itself is not reducible, either ontologically or explanatorily.[26] As we have seen above, Alexander is committed to the ontological irreducibility of dynamic forms (p. 159). But given the way he conceives of their causal role, they will be explanatorily irreducible as well.

According to Alexander, the only things that can act or be acted upon are bodies (21.22–22.23). But bodies are what they are and interact in the distinctive ways they do *in virtue of* their dynamic forms:

> What each thing is comes from its form, as do its differences from other beings. But the differences between bodies with respect to acting and being modified also come about in virtue of forms. For when bodies act or are modified in so far as they are bodies, they act or are modified in a particular way due to their form, since each of these is in virtue of the difference in forms.　7.9–13

The distinctive characteristics and behaviour of new, higher level compounds is thus to be explained in terms of their own proper forms, that is, their own top-level form, and *not* the forms of the matter underlying it, even if these lower forms determine which higher level form supervenes. These lower forms might figure in

---

limited concessions to behavioural determinism in *Fat.* 27 and 28—namely, that in some cases one's character may determine one's choices, though crucially without undermining responsibility for the initial formation of our character—reflect any real modification in Alexander's position (75–9).

[24] Arist., *Meta.* Θ.5, 1048a2–11; Alexander, *Fat.* 5, 169.6–10, 13–15; 11, 178.17–28; 12, 180.4–12, 20–3, 25–8, 181.5–7; 14, 183.33–184.20; 38, 211.31–3; 39, 212.15–16; cf. 2, 166.12–13; 28, 199.7–13; 36, 206.19–25.

[25] For a contemporary position that combines emergentism with freedom of the will, understood indeterministically, see O'Connor (2014, esp. 2.1), a position he regards as neo-Aristotelian (32–3); cf. also O'Connor (2000: §6.4). Elsewhere O'Connor maintains that on an emergentist view mental states are not physically realized or constituted by the underlying physical states, but only causally dependent (2018: 397). But this is decidedly not a part of the view I present here as Alexander's.

[26] The question of reduction is distinct from the question of whether dynamic forms are inseparable from, and so ontologically dependent on, their underlying matter. On this point, see p. 159 above.

the explanation of more general characteristics and behaviour that the compound shares in common with other types of compound; they also help explain what transpires when a higher level compound behaves in uncharacteristic or irregular ways, and so not as that type of thing should in the relevant circumstances, or likewise when it fails to perform at all. But what distinguishes the higher level compound as the higher compound that it is will be accounted for by its own proper form, even though that form supervenes on the matter underlying it.

That such distinctive behaviour is produced *from the top-down*—what some have called 'downward causation'[27]—despite the distribution of powers itself being a function of the underlying matter is what makes Alexander an emergentist:

EMERGENTISM: Some of the behavior of higher-level compounds—that which is characteristic and distinctive of that sort of compound, as such—is to be explained by their own higher-level form, even though which form they have is a function of the blend and arrangement of the underlying matter.

This emphasis on downward causation in cases of paradigmatic behaviour and characteristics is precisely what leads Alexander to insist, against Galen, that it is *not* the underlying blend or arrangment that explains the behaviour of a living being, but rather the power or dynamic form that emerges from them; and therefore the soul is to be identified with the latter, not the former.[28] To think otherwise is to infer, fallaciously, that the higher powers can be *reduced* to the underlying base and its powers:

For suppose that the soul cannot be separate from this sort of blend and mixture; it does not thereby follow that they are the same as the soul. For the soul is not a particular kind of blend of bodies—which is just what a 'tuning' [*harmonia*] is—but rather a power that emerges above [*epi...gennōmenē*] a particular kind of blend, analogous to the powers of medicinal drugs, [powers] that coalesce from a blend of many [ingredients]. For in their case too, the mixture, composition, and proportion of drugs—such that one of them, it might turn out, is two to one, another one to two, and another three to two—bear some analogy to a tuning.

---

[27] The term can be found at least as early as Campbell (1974), but for the classic account, see Kim (1992 and 1993: 348–53), on which I rely here.

[28] Alexander is siding with Andronicus of Rhodes here, against Galen's criticism of him (*QAM* 44.12–20). In this, I am disagreeing slightly with Richard Sorabji (Chapter 10, this volume), who takes Andronicus to hold that the soul is a tuning or *harmonia* of the body, the view Galen himself favours. What Galen says, though, is that Andronicus held that it is *either* (i) a tuning *or* (ii) a power arising from it; and he faults Andronicus for adding (ii), instead of just sticking with (i). Alexander's position is the diametric opposite: he champions (ii) and argues at length against (i). For discussion of the passage, see my (1997: 351–2) and now, in greater detail and placed within the context of Galen's views more generally, see Patricia Marechal's spirited defense in Chapter 5, this volume.

> However, the power that emerges from [*ek...gennōmenē*] the blend of drugs, in virtue of this tuning and proportion, is not a tuning as well. For while the tuning is the proportion and composition of the mixed ingredients, the ointment's power is not the proportion by which the ingredients are mixed. The soul is also like this. For soul is the power and form that supervenes [*epiginomenon*] on the blend of bodies in a particular proportion, not the proportion or composition of the blend.   24.20–25.4; cf. 24.19–20

Alexander begins by drawing a distinction between the soul, which is a dynamic form or power of a certain kind of living thing, and the blend and composition of bodies in that living thing. The latter constitute a compound and thus a body, not a power, and so cannot be identified with the soul:

> But for someone who thinks that the soul is *not* the things composed, taken simply as such, but instead a power that emerges above [*epi...gennōmenē*] a certain sort of blend and mixture of the primary bodies, the blend of matter will have a proportion, but the soul will have its being, *not* in virtue of the tuning and blend (as they are committed to saying), but in virtue of the power that emerges above it [*sc.* the blend, *ep' autēi...gennōmenē*].   26.26–30

On an Aristotelian view of blending, whenever these ingredients have been brought together in the appropriate way, the substance they form will have new, distinctive powers, powers that are not simply the sum of the powers the ingredients in the underlying mixture already have; and it is these new powers that explain the behaviour of living things as such. As Alexander clarifies in the last sentence, these occur *solely* in virtue of the power that supervenes, from the top, and *not* the proportion or the proportionate blend from which it emerges. Alexander is thus committed to downward causation.

This pattern of explanation is not peculiar to living things, though, much less to beings endowed with conscious awareness or reason for Alexander. It is something that can be found at each level of the *scala naturae*, including the lowest level, with the elements:

> In the case of fire, which is a simple, natural body, heat and dryness, along with the lightness that emerges from them and above them [*ek toutōn te kai epi toutois gennōmenē*], are its form, while what underlies these is its matter, which by its nature is not any of these, but is receptive of them and their contraries equally.
> 5.4–8

The lightness of fire—that is, its disposition to move upwards—is a power distinct from the elemental qualities of heat and dryness, and emerges from them. The only thing that sets this case apart is that at an elemental level there is no underlying blend of bodies on which lightness or the form of fire supervenes. The power of lightness emerges from the elemental qualities instead. All three qualities, though, are essential to fire in Alexander's view and so part of what it is to be fire and thus its form.

With compound bodies, such as living beings, there is the added complexity of the underlying matter, which does contain bodies and thus hylomorphic compounds; so their respective forms and matter contribute to the blend as well. But otherwise the basic relation is analogous: the top-level form supervenes on this composition, but can also possess distinctive, new causal powers that emerge from it. Alexander insists that this should not be seen as puzzling, though, but recognized as something commensurate with the complexity of the phenomena:

> If it should seem incredible to someone on first hearing that the soul is this sort of body's form and nature, just as lightness is fire's [form and nature], but then they were to look at the distinction between the bodies that have these forms and see how unspeakably greater the construction of animate bodies is than that of simple bodies, they would no longer think that those who speak this way are saying anything incredible, since it is not incredible, but makes the greatest sense of all, to say that the proportion that the bodies underlying the forms have to one another is the same as the one that their forms preserve to each other.   11.5–13

It is in this same spirit that we should understand Alexander's protreptic remarks at the very beginning of the treatise:

> Anyone who is going to examine in detail what is said about the soul and reach agreement on characterisations of its essence must first appreciate the extraordinary magnificence of nature, before all else. For once we have learned just what sort of thing nature is and have been persuaded that its workings are more incredible than any marvel produced by art, we will more easily be convinced by what is going to be said about the soul. For the view that its powers and activities cannot easily be harmonized with what is said about it, because they are 'more divine and greater than any bodily power', is no reason to get mired in puzzles about the soul. Hence, those who do not wish to go against sensible claims about the soul ought to look first at the construction of the body that has the soul and to investigate the regulation of its inner parts and then afterwards the graceful agreement of the external parts with them. For after studying these, it will no longer seem so incredible that the soul, which has within it so many origins and principles of change, is something that also belongs to this body, which is constructed so incredibly and magnificently.   2.10–25

To use a favourite phrase of a different Alexander, the 20th-century emergentist Samuel Alexander, the emergent phenomena that arise with new levels of increasing complexity should be accepted 'with natural piety'.[29] This position is not mysterian like Thomas H. Huxley's, who famously compared our understanding of consciousness to the unaccountable appearance of the Djin from Aladdin's lamp,[30] since in Alexander of Aphrodisias' view this sort of emergence is a pervasive fact of nature. We can be amazed by the wonders of nature at each new level of complexity, even once we see how the construction and materials contribute to the overall form. But we will no longer find it hard to believe, precisely because of our knowledge of how they contribute. Which higher level forms arise are not random, but systematic: these new powers necessarily correlate with specific underlying conditions, in the composition and arrangement of matter, even though the powers that emerge are not mere sums of the powers already present in that matter. To object that there is still an 'gap' presupposes that we have only fully understood the higher level phenomena if they are explained by the powers of matter itself, as reductionism holds, or by some wholly dualistic ingredient. It is here that Alexander would stand his ground. Emergentism is a form of materialism, but a non-reductive one. Which powers a compound has will be a function of the composition and construction of its matter. But a compound may nonetheless have distinctive new powers, different from those of its ingredients.[31]

5. Conclusion

Alexander's commitments, then, are to a kind of materialism whenever change is involved, since only bodies can undergo change and a body's capacity to take on

---

[29] Samuel Alexander is quoting, and putting a positive spin on, Wordsworth, who in a section of the third book of *The Excursion*, entitled 'Despondency', remarks: 'Such acquiescence neither doth imply/ In me, a meekly bending spirit soothed/By natural piety; nor a lofty mind,/By philosophic discipline prepared/For calm subjection to acknowledged law' (3.264–8). On Alexander's use of this phrase (and its subsequent acceptance by C. Lloyd Morgan and C. D. Broad), see McLaughlin (1992: esp. 55 and 66 on Alexander, but also 68 (Morgan), and 81 (Broad, who describes it as 'philosophic jam')).

[30] 'But it very frequently happens that we learn that something is going on, when a stimulus affects our afferent nerves, by having what we call a feeling or sensation. We class sensations along with emotions, and volitions, and thoughts, under the common head of consciousness. But what consciousness is, we know not; and how it is that any thing so remarkable as a state of consciousness comes about as the result of irritating nervous tissue, is just as unaccountable as the appearance of the Djin when Aladdin rubbed his lamp in the story, or as any other ultimate fact of nature' (Huxley and Youmans 1868: 178). I am grateful to David Charles for pressing me on this point.

[31] A distinction of Jaegwon Kim's is useful here (I thank Alyssa Ney for suggesting this and for the reference). Because of their exceptionless regularity, emergent phenomena can be *inductively predictable* and captured in well-confirmed laws; what emergentists deny is that they are *theoretically predictable*—the knowledge of lower level laws and conditions alone is not sufficient to know which higher level phenomena or properties will emerge from them (Kim 1999: 13–14, 27, cf. 2006: 71–2; see also McLaughlin 1992: 51, 55, cf. 81–6). This is not a bug, but a feature of emergentism: to claim that emergent phenomena are *novel* is precisely to claim they do not fall under the lower level laws; that's why they require the new laws of a higher science. But that hardly constitutes an unacceptable 'gap'. Emergent phenomena are not random occurrences, nor are they inexplicable *tout court*: their regular occurrence can be predicted by configurations of lower level phenomena and explained by the higher science.

different characteristics, to become otherwise than it is, is due to its matter. Nevertheless, bodies act and are acted upon in the specific ways that they do in virtue of their forms. The behaviour characteristic of a given kind of substance is due to what that substance is, and what makes it the kind of substance that it is is its form. Alexander thus identifies the distinctive causal powers a material substance has with its form, that in virtue of which it behaves as it does. A crucial question, then, for his hylomorphism is how exactly he conceives the relation between matter and form, along with their specific roles.

In the case of the simplest bodies, the elements, which forms they have is primitive, since the matter underlying the elements is not itself a compound of form and matter, and so it is not a body, but 'prime matter', which lacks any inherent quality or feature of its own beyond the ability to take on such elemental forms. Compound bodies differ in that their matter is itself a body and hence also a compound of matter and form. Bodies can be constituted from other bodies. In principle, it seems that this compounding could be iterated indefinitely; there is at any rate only a bottom-most limit, when the matter of a given compound is not itself compound, but consists only of simple bodies or elements, whose matter is not compound, but simple and pure.

In Alexander's view, which form a compound substance has is not adventitious, but a function of the underlying types of matter and their arrangement. The forms of compound bodies co-vary necessarily with their bases and so supervene upon them; and since the types of bodies that serve as the underlying matter of a compound body are themselves compounds and so distinguished by their own forms, the higher level forms will be a function of the forms of their underlying matter; and this relationship will be iterated as often as the underlying matter at each successive lower level is itself compound. Bodies are thus not merely constituted from matter. Their character and form is determined by the kind of matter that makes them up and the way in which they are combined and arranged, its 'tuning' or *harmonia*, all the way down to the elements. There is therefore a very specific relation between the form of a body and its matter, beyond the fact that the matter constitutes the compound to which the form belongs or that the matter must be of a suitable type if it is to implement the activities characteristic of that form, through conditional necessity.[32] There is more to hylomorphism than just material constitution and the constraints imposed on matter by functional role. Form also co-varies with the characteristics and arrangement of the underlying matter.

At the same time, Alexander regards these higher powers as irreducible to the underlying matter and its powers: at each level there are genuinely new causal

---

[32] The label 'conditional necessity' is Aristotle's (*Phys.* 2.9, esp. 200a7–15; *PA* 1.1, 642a32–34; cf. *GC* 2.11, 337b14–25): *if* a substance is to perform the functions characteristic of its form, then it *must necessarily* have matter with characteristics suitable for carrying them out. In this way, form constrains which types of matter can realize it, something Alexander explains in terms of the matter's own form.

powers that emerge. So while we can track which powers will be produced from matter of a certain type and its arrangment, the powers themselves will be something new and distinctive, beyond the sum of the underlying matter's powers. This elevates form to its proper role within Aristotelian hylomorphism and explains its explanatory prominence. A substance in one natural kind is distinguished from substances in others in large part by its efficient causal powers and the characteristic behaviour, both possible and actual, which these underwrite; and in Alexander's mind this is due to what the substance is, something it has in virtue of its form. Matter subserves these characteristic activities, insofar as it is of a type suitable for implementing the functions specified by the form, although how well it executes this will depend upon the specific types of matter and their actual condition in an individual substance. But it doesn't follow from this that the form is something independent, added in on top, like the vitalist's *élan vital*. It is something that emerges necessarily, whenever that sort of matter is brought into that sort of arrangement. Yet it rises above it, as being what distinguishes and characterizes the new kind, rather than just being a collection or sum of its parts. Form is as important for efficient causation as it is for final causation, and neither can be reduced to material causation, even though tightly integrated with it.

This emergentist framework allows Alexander to spell out, with great specificity, the distinctive roles of form and matter, as well as the relations between them, along lines familiar to us from recent debates about the irreducibility of the mental and mental causation, but extending well beyond it to the whole of nature and the way we understand natural kinds in general. In this way, Alexander completes the hylomorphic project and so, as we might also say, perfects it. Emergentism is the natural culmination of Aristotle's hylomorphism.[33]

References

Ademollo, F. (2021), 'The Anatomy of Primary Substance in Aristotle's *Categories*', *Oxford Studies in Ancient Philosophy* 60: 145–202.

Bruns, I. (ed.) (1887), *Supplementum Aristotelicum*. Vol. 2.1: *De anima liber cum mantissa* (Berlin: Georg Reimer).

---

[33] I would like to thank audiences at the original conference at Yale in 2019 (especially the insightful remarks of the two commentators, Daniel Ferguson and Lea Schroeder), Peking University, and Tel Aviv University, all of whose comments were excellent and constructive. I have also benefited greatly from generous, detailed comments from the editor, David Charles, and from Richard Sorabji, who was the other participant in my session.

Finally, I would like to dedicate this essay to the memory of my former colleague, Jaegwon Kim, who died about a half year after the original conference at Yale. I learned so much from his writings and our conversations, as well as his from sage advice, that he remains a model for me even now. He will be greatly missed.

Campbell, D.T. (1974), '"Downward Causation" in Hierarchically Organised Biological Systems', in F.J. Ayala and T. Dobzhansky (eds.), *Studies in the Philosophy of Biology* (Berkeley: University of California Press), 179–86.

Caston, V. (1997), 'Epiphenomenalisms, Ancient and Modern', *The Philosophical Review* 106: 309–63.

Caston, V. (2012), *Alexander of Aphrodisias, On the Soul, Part I: Soul as Form of the Body, Parts of the Soul, Nourishment, and Perception*, trans. with intro. and comm. (London: Bristol Classical Press).

Huxley, T.H. and W.J. Youmans (1868), *The Elements of Physiology and Hygiene: A Textbook for Educational Institutions* (New York: D. Appleton and Company).

Kim, J. (1992), '"Downward Causation" in Emergentism and Nonreductive Physicalism', in A. Beckermann, H. Flohr, and J. Kim (eds.), *Emergence or Reduction? Essays on the Prospects of Nonreductive Physicalism* (Berlin: Walter de Gruyter), 119–38.

Kim, J. (1993), 'The Nonreductivist's Troubles with Mental Causation', in J. Heil and A. Mele (eds.), *Mental Causation* (Oxford: Oxford University Press, 1993), 189–210. (Reprinted in his *Supervenience and Mind: Selected Philosophical Essays* (Cambridge: Cambridge University Press, 1993), 336–57.)

Kim, J. (1999), 'Making Sense of Emergence', *Philosophical Studies* 95 (1999): 3–36. (Reprinted in his *Essays in the Metaphysics of Mind* (New York: Oxford University Press, 2010), 8–40.)

Kim, J. (2006), 'Emergence: Core Ideas and Issues', *Synthese* 151: 547–59. (Reprinted in his *Essays in the Metaphysics of Mind* (New York: Oxford University Press, 2010), 66–84.)

Kim, J. (2010), 'The Layered World: Metaphysical Considerations', in his *Essays in the Metaphysics of Mind* (Oxford: Oxford University Press, 2010), 41–64. (Originally appeared as 'The Layered Model: Metaphysical Considerations', *Philosophical Explorations* 5 (2002): 2–20.)

McLaughlin, B.P. (1992), 'The Rise and Fall of British Emergentism', in A. Beckermann, H. Flohr, and J. Kim (eds.), *Emergence or Reduction? Essays on the Prospects of Nonreductive Physicalism* (Berlin: Walter de Gruyter), 49–93.

O'Connor, T. (2000), *Persons and Causes: The Metaphysics of Free Will* (Oxford: Oxford University Press).

O'Connor, T. (2014), 'Free Will and Metaphysics', in D. Palmer (ed.), *Libertarian Free Will: Contemporary Debates* (Oxford: Oxford University Press), 27–34.

O'Connor, T. (2018), 'Consciousness, Free Will, and the Sciences of the Mind', *Frontiers of Philosophy in China* 13: 394–401.

Salles, R. (1998), 'Categorical Possibility and Incompatibilism in Alexander of Aphrodisias' Theory of Responsibility', *Méthexis* 11: 65–83.

Sharples, R.W. (2004), *Alexander of Aphrodisias*, Supplement to 'On the Soul' (Ithaca, NY: Cornell University Press).

Vetter, B. (2015), *Potentiality: From Dispositions to Modality* (Oxford: Oxford University Press).

7
Alexander of Aphrodisias on the Ancient Debate on Hylomorphism and the Development of Intellect

Frans A.J. de Haas

Hylomorphism is a balancing act. It is not easy to specify without ambiguity how form and matter are principles of change as well as principles of substances. What is the exact nature of their combination? Is form in matter, or vice versa, and what is the meaning of being 'in' something? In which ways does form have priority over matter, and vice versa? Alexander of Aphrodisias and his school have preserved traces of the debate on these issues that took place in the centuries leading up to 200 CE: especially *Mantissa* 5, and *Quaestiones* I.8, I.17, and I.26 discuss the questions to which Alexander's general account of hylomorphism in *De Anima* 1–26 seems to be his most considered answer. That is the set of texts I shall mostly be concerned with here.[1] We shall see that Alexander discussed various interpretations of Aristotle's hylomorphism of Platonic, Stoic, and Aristotelian origin. His main concern is to provide a comprehensive version of hylomorphism, and to refute the suggestion that Aristotle's texts are in any way incoherent.[2]

A large part of these texts concerns the question of the extent to which the relation between form and matter fits the framework of the *Categories*. This question makes sense against the background of the first books of the *Physics*. In the chapters in which Aristotle introduces form, privation, and matter as principles of change, he makes constant use of the categories and their

---

[1] The connection between these texts as testimonies to an ongoing debate is clear from the following observations: (a) there are considerable overlaps; (b) in *Quaest.* I.8, 17.12–22 a new objection and reply are inserted into an argument familiar from *Mantissa* 119,32–120,9; (c) *Quaest.* I.26, 42.25–43.17 adds a possible answer which *Mant.* 5 does not yet envisage; (d) *Quaest.* I.8 starts by referring to a familiar argument with 'it has been said that' (17.12) as if picking up on an earlier installment of a (school?) discussion. For more details, see below. Cf. Sharples (1990: 110 with 1992, 43n107).—I do not wish to assume that Alexander of Aphrodisias is the (sole) author of *Mant.* 5 and the *Quaest.*, or that he agreed with every view that remains unrefuted. Nevertheless, for practical reasons, I follow custom in referring to 'Alexander' as their author. It will be seen that there is a strong correspondence between Alexander's *De An.* and the texts in our set.

[2] This is the consensus view of Alexander's overall philosophical project, see e.g. Cerami (2016: 164).

Frans A.J. de Haas, *Alexander of Aphrodisias on the Ancient Debate on Hylomorphism, and the Development of Intellect*
In: *The History of Hylomorphism: From Aristotle to Descartes*. Edited by: David Charles, Oxford University Press.
© Frans A.J. de Haas 2023. DOI: 10.1093/oso/9780192897664.003.0008

properties—both in the criticism of his predecessors,[3] and in the development of his own position.[4] If so, proving a mismatch between the *Physics* and the *Categories* can be regarded as a direct attack on the general theory of hylomorphism put forward in the *Physics*.

On the whole Alexander believes Aristotle's analysis to be correct: matter, form, and privation are principles of change; in natural substances both matter and form are parts of those substances, and therefore themselves substances; neither of them can exist on their own.[5] Form is to be regarded as the perfection or culmination (*teleiôsis*) of matter.[6] Their relation can also be described in terms of potentiality and actuality, as Aristotle suggested in *Phys.* I.8, 191b27-9.[7] This connection will prove crucial to Alexander's hylomorphism because it allows him to combine hylomorphism with the refinements of the actuality-potentiality distinction in *De An.* II.5, from which his hylomorphic analysis of intellectual processes is the result.

The aim of this inquiry is to reconstruct rival approaches to hylomorphism which helped shape Alexander's version of it, and to show how Alexander's hylomorphism enabled him to expand the scope of the doctrine to the development of intellect. The reconstruction of rival approaches to hylomorphism offers us a glimpse of the long-standing concern for the general theory of hylomorphism, over and above its important application to the relation between body and soul.[8]

In section 1, I shall discuss interpretations of the relation between form and matter that Alexander considers to be mistaken as a first encounter with the ancient debate on hylomorphism. In section 2, I shall highlight Alexander's

---

[3] See e.g. *Physics* I.2, 185a20-32 (being is said in many ways, with I.3 186a23-9; 186b1-3, 11-12 etc.); I.5 (first contraries are proper starting points, involving *Categories* 10; cf. I.6, 190b33-191a3); I.6, 189a27-34 (opposites cannot constitute substance but need something underlying); II.1, 193a9-28 (materialists believe that their substance are substance, and everything else affections, states, and dispositions of them). For more detailed discussions of *Phys.* I, see Kelsey (2010); Leunissen (2015a); Quarantotto (2018); Ierodiakonou, Kalligas, and Karasmanis (2019). On the role of the *Cat.*, see Quarantotto (2018: 34-9). For Alexander's take on I.5, see *Quaest.* I.16.

[4] In *Phys.* I.7 *both* opposites (form and privation) *and* something that underlies them (matter) constitute the solution that applies to the generation of accidents as well as substances (190a31-b3, b10-13, 191a3-5). In *Phys.* II.1 Aristotle identifies nature as the internal principle of motion and rest, and claims that everything that has such a principle is a substance (192b32-4 = T3 below). Aristotle recognizes the option that the underlying matter is nature (*phusis*), as the natural philosophers did (193a9-28), but considers form to be more nature than matter (193a28-31, b3-21). Form is more nature than matter, because (among other reasons) each thing is named when it is in actuality rather than in potentiality. Cf. Kelsey (2015); Charles (2018).

[5] The tenet that parts of substances are substances finds support in, e.g., *Cat.* 3a29-32; *Metaphysics* Δ.8, 1017b10-21, and *Meta.* Θ.7, 1049a27-36. For Alexander's use of it, see below pp. 184-185.

[6] For an excellent description of Alexander's final theory of hylomorphism under the label of 'emergentism' see Victor Caston's Chapter 6, in this volume.

[7] This connection will prove crucial to Alexander's hylomorphism. Cf. Alex., *Quaest.* I.24, arguing that there is no tension between Aristotle's claim that he has solved the problems of the ancients, both in terms of accidental and *per se* being (191a33-b27), and in terms of potentiality and actuality (191b27-34). Cf. Witt (1989).

[8] Sharples (2009) speaks of a sharp decline of interest in the general theory of hylomorphism between Aristotle and Alexander. This chapter may serve to provide some evidence to the contrary.

discussion of more positive suggestions on how to conceive of the relation between form and matter. In section 3, I shall briefly discuss which Aristotelian ingredients Alexander added in order to develop his full account of hylomorphism that we find in *De An.* 1–26. Finally, in section 4, I shall show how Alexander's brand of hylomorphism allowed him to apply it to the development of human intellect.

1. Mistaken Approaches to Hylomorphism

The most prominent conception of hylomorphism that Alexander attacks is the view that form is in matter as in a subject in the sense of *Categories* 2, which would entail that form is an accident of matter. A good point of entry to this discussion is *Quaestio* I.17, which argues that form is not in *any* matter as in a subject (29.31–30.14), and that, if so, soul is not in body as in a subject either (30.14–22). Here, as in *De Anima*, a general theory of hylomorphism precedes its application to the paradigm case of soul and body.

The discussion takes a number of passages from the *Categories* for granted. The *Categories* definition of what is 'in a subject' is at the focus of attention:

T1   We call 'in a subject' [*en hupokeimenôi*] that which, while being present in something not as a part, is unable to be separately from that which it is in.
Arist., *Cat.* 1a24–5

As we shall see, the tradition focuses on two issues of interpretation: [a] what does it mean to be present in something as a part or *not* as a part? [b] what does it mean for something to be unable to exist separately from what it is in?

In *Categories* 5 Aristotle states that it is a characteristic of both primary and secondary substances *not* to be in a subject (2a13, 3a7–8). It is considered obvious that individual substances are neither *said of* nor *in* a subject; secondary substances (genera, species, and differentiae) are said of individuals but are not in them as in a subject. E.g. 'animal', 'human being', or the differentiae 'footed' and 'two-footed' are not in an individual substance: their names and definitions apply to the subject because they constitute it. Parts of substances are not in their wholes as in a subject, or we would be forced to deny them the name of substance (3a7–32).

Aristotle rules that every primary substance denotes a this-something (*tode ti*), which is an indivisible numerical unity (3b10–13).[9] Secondary substances (species and genus) denote a qualification of being (*peri ousian to poion aphorizei*), and are

---

[9] Cf. *Meta.* Θ.7, 1049a27–36.

not mere qualities (3b18–21); their subject is a plurality, not a unity (3b16–18, 21–3). This property of substances gave rise to an extensive discussion about the categorial status of the differentia.[10] It may also have inspired, e.g., Boethus of Sidon to claim that form is a quality, not substance, and therefore inheres in matter as in a subject after all.[11] For Aristotle the criterion unique to substance is the ability to receive opposites while remaining one and the same in number (4a10–21). 'Remaining one and the same in number' reinforces the this-something criterion. This implies once more that individual substances have independent existence, and continue to exist regardless of the changes between opposites to which they are subject.

Let us now turn to *Quaestio* I.17. Which kinds of matter are rejected as being the subject form is in as in a subject? We are presented with three options:

(a) prime matter (30.2–9);
(b) the body in which the form resides now (30.9–11);
(c) the body which changed into the current composite (30.11–13).

Alexander claims that form is not in prime matter because prime matter does not underlie in actuality; moreover it needs the assistance of form to be in existence (*pros to einai en huparxei*); conversely, form needs matter to be in existence (*einai en hupostasei*).[12] Prime matter on its own is neither a this-something, nor a substance, and derives whatever actuality it attains from form. It does not qualify as a subject in the required sense.

However, in terms of existence, prime matter and form are here considered to be *interdependent* (even though the argument would succeed if prime matter depends on form but not vice versa). Since the same argument would be true for any matter in relation to its form, why the focus on *prime* matter? Can we identify anyone who proposed a view of hylomorphism in which all forms are in prime matter as in a subject?

The Platonic Receptacle is the first candidate that comes to mind. The definition of being 'in a subject' would be true in a sense of the images of the Forms that enter and leave the Receptacle in Plato's *Timaeus*.[13] The Receptacle is and remains itself uncharacterized by the images it receives, and is as eternal as the Forms. Thus it qualifies as subject that remains the same whatever images it receives, while the

---

[10] See Ellis (1994); De Haas (1997: 180–250).
[11] See Chiaradonna and Rashed (2020) for a full collection of sources on Boethus. See further below for his view on form and matter.
[12] The definition of being 'in a subject', T1 speaks of 'being present in' (*enhuparchein*) which presupposes the *huparxis* of the subject. In this context, Alexander's *hupostasis* must mean the same as *huparxis*. Cf. *Quaest.* 2.10 claiming that soul is that which is present in (*enhuparchon*) the living being in virtue of which it is a living being. A form *of* something is an enmattered form that cannot exist separately on its own but needs matter in order to exist.
[13] Cf. Plato, *Tim.* 49e7–50a4, 50b7–c6.

images (but not the Forms) need the Receptacle for their existence.[14] Perhaps, then, Alexander's insistence on the *interdependence* of form and matter in existence is directed against the independent existence of prime matter in the Platonic tradition.

Later Platonists like Alcinous use Aristotle's notion of potentiality to describe the receptacle.[15] In *Quaestio* 2.7, Alexander agrees that being matter as such consists in possessing a suitability (*epitêdeiotês*) and potentiality according to which matter is able to admit qualities. This serves as an answer to the objection that matter is nothing of its own account, if it derives lack of quality and shape from privation, and being qualified and shaped from form. This objection may well testify to another attack on hylomorphism as introduced in the *Physics*: the account of matter, as opposed to form and privation, is considered insufficient.

Contrary to Alcinous, Alexander holds that to be without quality does not complete, i.e. is not part of, the being of matter. Matter as such is as it were in a boundary zone (*methorion*) between these two options, and this potentiality remains, regardless whether any quality happens to qualify matter at a given time or not, and regardless whether it is necessary for it to be somehow qualified or shaped at any given time.[16] The opponent is accused of confusing the negation 'matter is not, in its own nature, qualified' with the statement of the privation 'matter is, in its own nature, not-qualified'.[17] History repeats itself: just like Aristotle's opponents in *Physics* I, this opponent fails to properly distinguish matter from privation.

A further target of Alexander's polemics must have been Boethus of Sidon, who is well-known for his argument that on account of being a subject only the composite and matter qualify as substances. Form is not a subject of something, so it has to fall outside the category of substance. Form may be a quality, quantity or something else.[18] If so, Boethus would have to say that form is an accident—but what is the subject it is in? Boethus is reported to have made the following distinction:

T2   For matter seems to be called matter with respect to what will be, and when it receives a form, it is no longer called matter, but substratum; for it is said to be a substratum for something because the thing is already in it.

Simpl., *In Phys.* 211.16–17 = fr. 19 Rashed

---

[14] For a concise view of (prime) matter along these lines, see Alcin, *Didask.* ch. 8. It may well be that Plato's Receptacle inspired Aristotle's concept of accidental properties.

[15] Alcin, *Didask.* 8, 163.7–8 (Hermann): 'neither body, nor incorporeal, but potentially body'. On the numerous Middle Platonist parallels of Alcinous' vocabulary, see Whittaker and Louis (1990: 96–8 nn. 139–48).

[16] This statement has bearing on a substance's need for *some* qualitative and quantitative determination to exist. See further below p. 179.

[17] Alexander adds a reference to Arist., *Anal. Pr.* 1.46, 51b5–35.

[18] For the following assessment of Boethus, see Them., *In Phys.* 26.20–4, Simpl., *In Cat.* 78,4–20, Simpl., *In Phys.* 211.15–18 (= frr. 18–20; Chiaradonna and Rashed (2020: with pp. 154–66)). Cf. Chiaradonna (2020).

Strictly speaking, then, according to Boethus we should be speaking of form-*subject* composites, not form-*matter* composites. Matter on its own is shapeless and formless and is referred to as matter only with respect to what it will become. It is perfectly possible that this stage was identified as prime matter by later commentators, even though this identification is not attested for Boethus. Once matter has received form, Boethus suggests, it has turned into something else: a subject for the form and limit in it. The distinction between matter and subject also seems to surface in our set of texts when Alexander argues emphatically, in *Quaest.* I.8, 17.22-34, that in order to answer the question whether something is in a subject or not, one should investigate cases where an accident or form is already in a *subject*—for form is not yet in *matter* considered as such.

In addition, the distinction has a role to play in rejecting the third option of *Quaest.* I.17: form is in the body which changes into the composite. Alexander replies that change of natural form is a case of generation and corruption: the body that has changed into the new composite has perished. On this view of hylomorphism the form of the composite would have nothing to be in at all. This is clearly absurd: how can forms that are supposed to be enmattered, and to be *of* something, be related to a matter that no longer exists? This argument provides us with further clues about the relation between form and matter. The forms at stake in this discussion are *enmattered* forms, which he claims to be *of* something (*enhulon ti kai tinos on*). We shall see below how matter can also feature as part of the definition of enmattered forms.

Interestingly, prime matter also found its way into Simplicius' commentary on *Cat.* 1a24–b3, as part of a different distinction that is also prominent in our set of texts. Simplicius reports Porphyry's answer to Lucius' problem concerning items that complete something's being (*sumplêrôtika tês ousias*).[19] If, e.g., body depends on the presence of at least *some* qualities and quantities in order to exist, those qualities and quantities should be regarded as parts of body, and cannot be in body as in a subject.

In reply to Lucius, Simplicius reports, Porphyry distinguished between two meanings of the term 'subject':

[a] *all* qualities inhere in the first subject, which Aristotle called potential body (*GC* 329a34) or prime matter,[20] and the Stoics qualityless matter (*apoios hulê* or *apoion sôma*); the qualities are not parts of the first subject, and incapable of existing apart from it, just as the definition requires.

---

[19] Simpl., *In Cat.* 48,1–12; cf. Dex., *In Cat.* 23.25–4.18. Cf. Ellis (1994).
[20] The so-called traditional notion of prime matter ascribes it to Aristotle as an ultimate subject that plays a role in the explanation of the change of the four elements into each other, but not in all change of form. Cf. Alex., *De An.* 3.21–4.20.

[b] the second subject is what Stoics call the commonly or particularly qualified thing (*koinôs* or *idiôs poion*), which Porphyry identifies with the Aristotelian composite substance. In the second subject qualities and quantities inhere as in a subject (e.g. white in wool, heat in iron), but only if they do not complete its essence (as white in snow, heat in fire). In this way, Porphyry can save Aristotle: he is right to classify *all* qualities as being in the first subject, and also right to classify non-essential properties as being in the second subject.[21]

This source is important for two reasons: first, it suggests a further context in which Alexander, whom Porphyry used as a source for his commentaries on the *Categories*, may have come across the claim that all qualities are in prime matter— if so, this would help explain his inclusion of forms being in prime matter as option 1. Second, we find a reference to a Stoic 'prime matter' in the discussion, which may well have motivated Alexander as well. The Stoic *apoion sôma* does not exist without qualifications either, although it is not itself in any way qualified. It is different from the Platonic Receptacle and the Peripatetic prime matter in being itself corporeal (three-dimensional with resistance). It is also different from Peripatetic matter in that the qualities it receives include what the Peripatetics would call natural forms (the determination of species and genus). So the appropriation of this Stoic context would make it even easier to conceive of the idea that Peripatetic natural forms (as opposed to accidents) are in one and the same matter as in a subject.

Lucius' objection that bodies cannot exist without at least *some* qualities is also critically discussed in *Quaest*. I.8, 17.12–22, where it is inserted in an exchange from the hylomorphism debate also rehearsed in *Mant*. 5, 119.32–120.9.[22] If the existence of bodies depends on having some accidents, but accidents are still supposed to be in those bodies as in a subject, their contribution to *existence* is clearly not sufficient to rule out their being in a subject. Hence a further specification must be added: anything that contributes to existence *as a part* is not in a subject—and this applies to form.

At *Quaest*. I.8, 18.4–19.15, the question is considered again, but now a different specification is added: forms such as the soul contribute not only to something's existence (*einai en hypostasei, suntelein pros hyparxin*) but also to its being a *this- something* (*tode ti*) and *in actuality* (*energeiai*). In other words: forms constitute the determinations in respect to which a particular thing cannot change while remaining what it is. This also applies to soul as opposed to shape and colour.

---

[21] This would result in the *same* properties belonging to different categories depending on their function in composite substances. Alexander has a different solution: white in snow is an inseparable property that is not part of the essence, but a necessary concomitant of the material changes that lead up to the realization of snow. Cf. Ellis (1994: 87–8) quoting Alex., *In Top*. 50.21–51.4.

[22] See Sharples (2004: 65 n. 199).

Whereas shape and colour do not need a determinate kind of body, soul needs a particular kind of instrumental body. A human being has some shape and colour, but it has soul in a different way, as a part.[23]

From whatever angle the problem is approached, the same argument is repeated: the subject for accidents is an actual this-something that can change in respect of accidental properties while remaining what it is; form contributes actuality and being a this-something to the composite as a part of it; change of form entails that the composite cannot remain what it was. Hence, form is not an accident but a part of the composite, and so is matter that does not exist without it.

The second option of *Quaestio* I.17, viz that form is in the body it resides in as in a subject, can be ruled out by a simple appeal to the definition of being in a subject: form is part of the composite, so not in the body as in a subject.

In the final section of *Quaestio* I.17, Alexander applies the result to the relation between soul and body: soul is not in the living being as in a subject, because it is the most important (*kuriôtaton*) part of it; nor in the body that changes into the animate body, because that no longer exists; nor in prime matter, which has no independent existence. So, if soul cannot be in something that does not possess soul, it cannot be in anything as in a subject.

Mantissa 5 focuses on the special case of the soul being in a subject, but also invokes a general theory of hylomorphism. Alexander starts with the following argument:[24]

A. no substance is in a subject (*Cat.* 3a7–8);
B. the soul is substance;
C. soul is not in a subject in the sense defined in the *Categories* (1a24–5 = T1).

He then formulates an objection to this argument:[25]

O₁ the *Categories* is about composite substance (individual, species, genus), not substance as form

∴ A is irrelevant to soul

O₂ the claim that no substance has an opposite (*Cat.* 3b24–5) is not valid for natural form either, since it has privation as its opposite

---

[23] One might wonder how far the difference goes: human souls are in human, not equine, bodies, but does my soul need to be in my individual body? On behalf of Alexander one might say that from a biological perspective it does, for my body is the instrumental body that has developed under the causal influence of my individual soul since conception. For Alexander on form and matter, hence soul and body, as parts of the composite, see *In Meta.* Δ.25, 424.25–425.4.
[24] *Mant.* 119,21–2.   [25] *Mant.* 119,23–9.

∴ soul as a natural form is not the topic of the *Categories*, so the claims that a substance is not 'in a subject' (A), and has no opposite (O₂), do not apply to natural form and soul.[26]

If so, Alexander suggests, we should leave the *Categories* behind and start an independent inquiry into whether it is possible for form to be in a subject, as soul is in body.[27] Perhaps form is in matter in some other way—to which we shall turn in the next section.

We might wonder who the authors are of the argument, and the objection. Since the sequel of *Mant.* 5 and the other texts in our set end up supporting both the argument A–C and the claim that the *Categories* is about composite substance (O₁), we might think of A–C as a first argument against the claim that soul is in body as in a subject on the part of Alexander or a like-minded earlier Peripatetic. Then someone like Boethus might object to A–C by pointing out a contradiction: if the characteristics of substance apply to composite substances only, they do not apply to natural forms, including soul. Hence there is still room for natural forms to be in a subject, and be, e.g., a quality. We already saw that Boethus argued that form is not in the category of substance.

This background shows that Alexander does not just need to find some way in which form is in matter, but also to establish at the same time that form is substance.[28] This is a further motive to argue for an independent inquiry. In the sequel of *Mant.* 5,[29] Alexander further explores the definition of 'in a subject' that Aristotle provides in the *Categories*, and shows once more that being 'in a subject' cannot apply to form in matter, hence not to soul. Such a subject should be a this-something in actuality, and matter is not; to be an actual this-something is impossible without form; hence, the matter cannot exist independently of form. If so, matter as such is not a this-something, and even though form is in matter, matter as such does not meet the requirements of being a subject according to the *Categories* definition.

2. Constructive Approaches to Hylomorphism

From the discussions set out above we can already harvest a number of clear characteristics of Alexander's hylomorphism. Natural form and matter are parts of natural substances, and cannot exist without each other. Natural substances are in actuality, and a this-something, in virtue of the form. A proper assessment of the relation between form and matter should focus on actual instances of

---

[26] This is not to deny B, as long as soul is allowed to be substance in the sense of form.
[27] *Mant.* 119,29–32.   [28] Cf. e.g. Alex., *De An.* 5.1–12.   [29] *Mant.* 119.32–120.17.

form-matter composites. Natural forms are by nature enmattered and are somehow *of* matter.

Mantissa 5 offers a discussion of two passages from Aristotle's *Physics* and *De Anima*, which begins to make room for the special way in which form is in matter.

T3 Nature, then, is what has been stated. And things that have this sort of starting point have a nature. And each of them is a substance. For a substance is *a sort of subject, and a nature is always in a subject*.

Arist., *Phys.* II.1 192b32–4; trans. Reeve (2018)

Alexander only quotes the emphasized words,[30] which allow the reading that *nature* is both a subject and in a subject. But the reader will be expected to have Aristotle's text in mind, which yields the reading the sequel of the text requires: nature, which Aristotle goes on to identify with form rather than matter (193b3–21), is in a subject. This also seems to be confirmed by a quote from *De Anima*:

T4 So every natural body that participates in life would be a substance, but a substance as a composite. But since it is both a body and of such-and-such a sort, i.e. having life, the soul would not be a body. *For the body is not among the things that are of a subject [kath' hupokeimenou]*, but rather a subject and matter. It is necessary, then, for the soul to be substance as form of a natural body that has life potentially. But substance is actuality [*entelecheia*]. Therefore, it is the actuality of such a body.

Arist., *De An.* II.1, 412a15–22; trans. Reeve (2017)

Alexander first glosses 'of a subject' as 'in a subject' and spells out the implication that not body, but soul is in a subject. On the face of it, then, both texts seem straightforward support for the interpretation that form is in matter, and soul in body, as in a subject. This may indeed be a previous interpretation of the texts, which links these passages to the *Categories* so as to make form inhere in matter as in a subject. It is this interpretation we have seen Alexander rejecting all along. Therefore Alexander immediately continues to suggest a different gloss:

T5 Rather, saying that body is not like this, but soul is, is it possible that 'of a subject' does not here mean 'in a subject', but rather what needs some subject for its being?[31] And this also applies to the form in the matter.

Alex., *Mant.* 121.4–7

---

[30] *Mant.* 121.1–2.
[31] In the light of the discussions on interdependence in terms of existence (*hyparxis, hypostasis*), I take 'being' here to refer to existence rather than essence.

What if Aristotle's 'of a subject' means that soul needs a certain subject for its being (*pros to einai*)? Note that also the *Physics* passage T3 speaks of *a sort of subject* (*hypokeimenon ti*). So these passages are now made to confirm that for Aristotle, too, there is a special way in which form is 'of' or 'in' some subject which it needs for its being. Hence Alexander triumphantly states: this also applies to the form in the matter.[32] This discussion nicely illustrates that the issue of a contribution to existence does not only rest on problems surrounding the text of the *Categories*, but is at home in the larger issue of the general theory of hylomorphism.

Regrettably, in *Mantissa* 5 Alexander does not continue to explain what this new option consists in.[33] Instead, he sets out to corroborate two claims that surround the quote from *De Anima*:

[1] in the composite living being the soul cannot be body (against materialist views of the soul).[34] Alexander explains that form and matter are not parts of something *qua* body, but *qua* substance. They do not complete the body as parts of its extension, but they complete substance.[35] That is why they share in the nature of substance, not in the nature of body.

Furthermore,

[2] soul is the actuality of the natural body, because the actualities of all natural substances—elements and living beings alike—are substances and this-something (*tode ti*). This is because substances are *from* substances (*ex ousiôn*), since no substance can come to be from non-substances. In so far as soul can be considered capable of receiving contraries (virtue and vice), it may count as substance after all.[36]

---

[32] Cf. Simpl., *In Phys.* 270.26-34. Simpl., *In Cael.* 279.5-14, adds a report on Alexander discussing *Cael.* 1.9 278 b1-3 in relation to *Cat.* 3a7, with the same conclusion that Alexander reaches here. This defines a new sense of being 'in' something, which commentators on *Cat.* and *Phys.* insert into their adaptations of the list taken from Arist., *Phys.* IV.3, 210a14-24, with *Meta.* Δ.23; cf. Simpl., *In Phys.* 552,18-24 (reporting on Alexander). See Alex., *De An.* 13.9-15.29, with *Mant.* 115.28-116.1; Porph., *In Cat.* 77.13-79.34; Amm., *In Cat.* 26.25-9.23 (with an echo of our discussion at 27.30-28.7); Simpl., *In Cat.* 46.1-15.

[33] Sharples (2004: 68 n. 211) is puzzled by the fact that the text does not proceed to show how form is in matter (as 121,7-8 indeed leads the reader to expect), but that soul is not body. However, the quote that 'body is not itself among the things that are of a subject, but soul is' is itself one of Aristotle's arguments against the identity of soul and body, so it makes sense to provide it with further corroboration by means of the arguments in *Mant.* 121,8-15.

[34] 121.8-15. For such materialist views, see, e.g., Caston (1997); Sharples (2009); Helle (2018). Helle's Chapter 4 in this volume is crucial to understand that Alexander attacked Stoic mixture as also a rival theory of hylomorphism.

[35] Cf. *Mant.* 122.4-15 with Sharples (2004: 71 n. 224) who compares Alex., *De An.* 18,7-27.

[36] *Mant.* 121,4-27. Cf. Arist., *Phys.* I.6, 189a32-4. Alexander also allows application of O_2 at Alex., *De An.* 14.25-15.1.

Let us now return to the question Alexander left us with before these excursions: in what special way is form 'in', or 'of', matter? In *Quaestio* I.8 this interdependence is framed in terms of form and matter being *relata* in the technical sense of *Categories* 7, which covers various ways of being *of* something. More in particular he regards them as relata in the strict sense, viz relata that have their being in being related to something else:[37]

T6 Matter and form cannot exist in separation from each other because they are spoken of in relation to each other, and the things which are spoken of in relation to each other [go] together by nature,[38] if the things that are relative are those of which the being is the same as being in a certain relation to something. So, in this way too, form will not be in matter as in a substrate.
Alex., *Quaest.* I.8, 18.35–19.3

This passage seems to be just one salvo in the battery of arguments of *Quaest.* I.8: to my knowledge this argument is not referred to anywhere else. It may be true that the necessary interdependence of relata is incompatible with the one-way relation of form being in matter as in a subject. But if form and matter are relata, and belong in the category of relatives, they are not substances, and can still be considered as accidents of the composite. If so, we would end up with the claim that a composite substance consists of accidents, which Alexander denies.[39]

Hence it is no surprise that this solution is rejected in *Quaestio* II.9, which is entitled 'How the soul is not relative to something, if it is the actuality of a body of a certain sort'.[40] Alexander clearly emphasizes that form and actuality are not relative to anything. Not everything that is *of* something is thereby *relative* to something, as the examples of a surface, and the parts of secondary substances show. These are *of* something, but do not qualify as relatives whose being amounts to nothing more than being in a certain relation to something. The same is true of the parts of primary substances: 'soul' and 'head' signify a certain nature and substance that is not exhausted by their being *of* something, which is accidental to such nature.[41] In this sense the parts of primary substances are unlike what is spoken of as 'similar' and 'equal': the being of these entities *qua* similar or equal is indeed exhausted by their relation.[42]

---

[37] Arist., *Cat.* 7, 6a36–7, with further specification at 8a28–37 (see also below, n. 42).
[38] Arist., *Cat.* 7, 7b15–22. [39] See above p. 184. [40] *Quaest.* II.9, 54.20–31.
[41] The phrase *oikeian tina phusin kai ousian* need not be taken as identifying these parts of substances as substances even though Alexander clearly believes they are; the phrase may just serve to point to a mode of being beyond the relation (*schesis*) these parts have to something else (e.g. the whole they are a part of).
[42] Sharples (2004: 106 and nn. 344–6) suggests this *quaestio* is probably not by Alexander. This seems to be the consequence of his translation of *ousa gar ti* at 54.26–7 in a strong existential sense as 'is [already] something [in itself]'. This would indeed contradict (a) the dependence of soul's existence on

Quaestio I.26 provides us with a final piece of information from the hylomorphism debate. This *quaestio* asks: 'How form is in matter, whether *per se* (*kath' hauto*) or *per accidens* (*kata sumbebêkos*)'. Alexander lists three options for form to be in matter:

1. form belongs *per se*₁ in matter;
2. form is in matter as accidents are;
3. form belongs *per se*₂ in matter.

Option 1 and 3 employ the distinction between senses of belonging *per se* that Aristotle discussed in *Posterior Analytics* I.4, 73a34–b3.[43] A belongs *per se*₁ to B if A is part of the definition that says what B is, e.g., 'line' belongs *per se*₁ to triangle (triangle is$_{def}$ a two-dimensional extension bounded by three equal *lines*).[44] A belongs *per se*₂ to B if B is part of the definition that says what A is, e.g. straight and curved belong to line, and odd and even belong to number (for something odd is$_{def}$ *a number* divided only into unequal parts).[45]

So if form belongs *per se*₁ to matter, it will be part of the *ousia* of matter, and matter will cease to be when the form does. This option is supported by the following considerations: it is true that matter cannot exist without its proper form, but co-exists with it: if the form perishes or is separated from the matter, the matter can no longer exist. In other words: the presence of the form contributes to its being matter. This is in line with Alexander's replies to the *Categories* objections.[46]

---

the mixture of the elements in Alex., *De An.* 24.21–3, and (b) Arist., *Cat.* 7, 8a13–8b21, on the problem whether no substance is a relative if parts of substances, which are substances, are said to be *of* something (Aristotle argues that 'hand' and 'head', when taken as primary substances, are not relatives because they are substances; taken as secondary substances, they are not relatives in the strict sense); in addition (c) Aristotle denies that soul is an accident of body.

On my reading these problems do not arise: the text focuses on the issue of naming (54.28, 29; *legetai*) and signification (54.30; *sêmainousin*): the *names* 'similar' (*homoion*) and 'equal' (*ison*) indicate relative being only and cannot be understood without reference to something else; the *names* 'soul' (*psuchê*) and 'head' (*kephalos*) indicate modes of being other than the relation these parts also have to their respective wholes. This relation is accidental to these modes of being. In the terms of Arist., *Cat.* 7, 8b13–21: if one can know precisely what something is without knowing precisely what it is related to, it is a relative according to the loose definition; if not, it is a relative according to the strict definition. I conclude that Alexander may well have accepted *Quaest.* II.9, but not the argument of *Quaest.* I.8, 18.35–19.3 (T6).

[43] At 42.28 Alexander mentions Theophrastus along with Aristotle as the source of belonging *per se*₂.

[44] See, e.g., Eucl., *Elem.* 1, 20.1.

[45] For this definition, see *Quaest.* I.26, 43.1, with Sharples (2004: 89 n. 286).

[46] Alex., *Quaest.* I.26, 41.27–8. The text that follows is probably corrupt, see Sharples (2004: 87 n. 275) for several proposals to repair it; I follow Sharples in reading <καὶ> καθ'αὑτό in line 42.2. The text provides the awkward example of 'human being' belonging *per se* to 'living being', 'and to everything that is in its [*sc.* the human being's?] being <and> belongs to him *per se*'. This is in fact an example of *per se*₂. Perhaps a later reader misunderstood the passage, and inserted the inappropriate example of how the species 'human being' (form) belongs to the genus 'living being' (matter)?

However, Alexander adds further considerations which seem to go against earlier conclusions.[47] These are best understood as directed against an opponent who has forms contribute to the nature and essence of some kind of prime matter. For Alexander lists as a consequence of this view that matter will receive *the forms themselves* as part of its nature, rather than having *the capacity to receive the forms* as part of its nature.[48] The removal of potentiality from the equation creates new problems: either [a] matter will possess all the forms at the same time or [b] each matter possesses a different form in its own being. Both options are ruled out. This should suffice to destroy option 1, for without further ado Alexander moves to option 2.

Option 2, form is in matter as an accident, meets with the counter-arguments we know from, e.g., *Quaestio* I.17: forms cannot be both substances and accidents, natural substances cannot be composed of matter and accidents. Matter does not have existence (*hypostasis*) and is not already a body, before form enters it. The body that changes into the new composite ceases to be, so cannot serve as matter. Form cannot be an accident of the composite it is itself the form of.[49]

This leaves us with the most interesting option 3: form belongs *per se*$_2$ to matter. In other words: form belongs to matter because matter is part of the definition of form, in the same way as odd and even belong to number because number is part of the definition of both odd and even. In this context it is important that we have been discussing enmattered natural forms. All enmattered beings are necessarily defined by their form and their matter, e.g. flesh, bone, hand, and face. In the case of soul, which is also an enmattered form, we also mention that which it is the form *of*, viz the natural organic body.[50]

There is a further agreement with the case of number:

T7   In the case of numbers, moreover, it is not the case that every number is odd, nor yet that every number is even; but everything that is even is number, and everything odd is similarly also itself number. Just so in the case of form and matter, all matter is not accompanied by this particular form, but every enmattered form is in matter. As in that case *number* is not destroyed in the change to even or odd, but the even and odd in it perish in turn in the change into the forms, just so matter is not destroyed in the change into the forms, but the forms perish in turn in the change of matter into them.

Alex., *Quaest.* I.26, 43.8–17

---

[47] *Quaest.* I.26, 42.3–9.
[48] Insofar as later Platonists regard potentiality as characteristic of the receptacle they would have to agree with this argument; see above p. 178.
[49] *Quaest.* I.26, 42.9–25.
[50] *Quaest.* I.26, 42.25–43.8. *Quaest.* II.8 considers whether the definition of soul is not circular if it speaks of 'the actuality of a natural organic body potentially possessing life'—given that 'life' presupposes the soul. There the suggested answer is that this is not so much a definition of the soul in itself, but rather an indication of the body the soul is in.

In other words, the problems of *per se*₁ do not attach to *per se*₂ which therefore comes out as the better option. Matter retains the potentiality to receive contrary forms, which means that generation and corruption are not abolished. Thus (we might surmise) form and matter co-exist and perish together.

Is this the view that Alexander ascribes to? It is not clear from *Quaestio* I.26, because the options, and the considerations that go with them, are merely listed, without any judgement attached. It does seem clear that option 3 is most acceptable, even though the text quoted above seems to fit accidental enmattered forms better than substantial natural forms. After all, in *Quaestio* I.17 we were told that the underlying body perishes when the form changes, and therefore the form cannot be in the previous body as in a subject.[51] Nor did prime matter fare well in that *Quaestio*. Nevertheless, the notion of *per se*₂ belonging is an interesting new attempt to provide better understanding of the necessary connection between a particular enmattered form and its matter, not least in the case of soul and body.

3. Towards the *De Anima* Account of Hylomorphism

So far, the debate has provided us with a considerable number of ingredients that went into Alexander's hylomorphism as described in *De Anima* 1–26. He demonstrates that soul is form, and starts by arguing how the living being is composed of soul and body as matter and form. Neither of these are body, nor can each exist without the other, whereas both are substance (2.25–7.8; 11.14–13.8; 17.9–15; 21.22–4). He provides a list of options of being 'in' something, in order to specify the particular way form is in matter (13.9–15.29). Relying on these arguments he then quickly moves from the soul is form to soul being an enmattered form, which is a completion (*teleiotês*), which is an actuality (*entelecheia*), viz the first actuality of a natural organic body (15.29–16.18, prepared in 6.25–7.8). He argues that form is not a body, against Stoic qualityless matter (17.15–18.10; 19.21–21.21), and dispels confusions about how form and matter are parts (18.10–19.20). All of these issues have been considered in more or less detail in the *Quaestiones* and *Mantissa* 5.

Nevertheless, it is also clear that more is needed to yield the more sophisticated layered ontology of Alexander's *De Anima* 7.9–11.13, and its later applications.[52] Within the confines of this chapter, I can merely draw attention to two Aristotelian texts that most of all seem to have inspired Alexander, *Physics* VII.3 and *De Anima* II.5.[53]

Physics VII.3, esp. 245b9–246a9, provides a more detailed analysis of the kinds of change preceding the generation of substantial form, shape, and bodily and

---

[51] See above p. 177 and 179.   [52] See also Caston, Chapter 6, in this volume.

[53] More research is needed to see how exactly Alexander combined these and other texts into his brand of Aristotelianism, which I hope to publish in a forthcoming book on Alexander.

psychic states, including virtue and knowledge.[54] Aristotle argues that neither such generations nor the resulting states are themselves alterations, even though alterations of something else are needed to make the underlying matter suitable for reaching a new state.[55] The resulting states are regarded as completion (*teleiôsis*) of a natural state, or the loss (*ekstasis*) of such completion.[56] The resulting composites—for which both artefacts (house) and natural beings (human being) are given as examples—do not exist in actuality until completion. Once the completion is a fact, and the state or form is in place, it constitutes a new determination of its owner, in the sense that it determines, e.g., the ease with which someone is affected or remains unaffected.[57]

This general view of generation and corruption is part and parcel of Alexander's layered ontology. Alexander often expresses the generation of a new form in terms of reaching completion (*teleiôsis*). A new composite may serve as matter for the completion of a higher level. It often needs to go through a variety of changes itself, before it reaches a further stage of completion. Even after the arrival of the new form, shape, or state, the same kind of alterations remains possible, even if to a lesser extent, and may always lead to the loss of the state of completion. In the case of soul and body, this spells corruption for the soul—for which Alexander was to be scolded for centuries by Neoplatonists and Christians alike.[58] Alexander also applies this theory to the emergence of different kinds of soul from different kinds of body, and to the addition of the powers of the soul.[59]

We have seen that at *Phys.* I.8 191b27–9 Aristotle announced that there is a different way to analyse change, viz in terms of potentiality and actuality 'which have been dealt with in more detail elsewhere'. Although *Meta.* Θ is usually taken to be the target of this reference, for our purposes it is important to recall *De Anima* II.5, which provides a further refinement of the distinctions in the *Metaphysics* for the purpose of explaining perception and thought.[60]

---

[54] For the complex chapter, *Phys.* VII.3, see esp. Wardy (1990); Maso, Natali, and Seel (2007); Chen (2017).
[55] This section explains how the subject that changes into something new is different from the subject the new form is in, as required in option 3 of *Quaest.* I.17, above pp. 177–9.
[56] Arist., *Phys.* VII.3, 246b1–3.
[57] Arist., *Phys.* VII.3, 246b17–20; cf. Leunissen (2015b). This statement implies that the new form has the capacity to take control of the type of changes that led to its arrival, at least to some extent. This, I suppose, is as close as Aristotle comes to downward causation.
[58] See e.g. Alex., *De An.* 21.22–4 (with Caston 2012: 108 n. 200); 90.11–16. On Philoponus' criticism, see e.g. De Haas (2019: 306–11); for the paradigm Christian polemic, see e.g. Thomas Aquinas, *De Unitate Intellectus* against the Averroists, who were inspired by Alexander.
[59] E.g. Alex., *De An.* 80.16–24.
[60] The most considered treatment is still Burnyeat (2002); see also Polansky (2007 *ad loc*). Burnyeat (2002: 63–4) acknowledges the role of *Phys.* VII.3 in the interpretation of *De An.* II.5. However, he denies the role of material processes that Alexander expressly incorporates in his theory on the basis of *Phys.* VII.3. Alexander does so in a different way from Burnyeat's opponents.

In *De An.* II.5 Aristotle distinguishes the potentiality to gain knowledge from the potentiality to apply knowledge.[61] All human beings have the potentiality to gain knowledge in common (first potentiality); it is actualized each time when a piece of knowledge is acquired (first actuality).[62] This state or disposition that is the possession of knowledge constitutes at the same time a new, second, potentiality to access this knowledge at will,[63] and apply it in new episodes of thought (which will each be instances of second actuality). E.g. knowledge of grammar (first actuality) is applied by the grammarian each time when she is contemplating a particular letter alpha (second actuality).[64]

The difference between the two processes of actualization is that the first is a genuine alteration, that is to say it consists of 'repeated transitions from one state to its opposite under instruction' (417a31–2). Aristotle does not specify how and when the first potentiality is replaced by the corresponding actuality, viz the possession of knowledge as a (more or less) permanent state. This state is unlikely to result with each transition, but rather after the longer process that Aristotle elsewhere describes as 'the first universal coming to rest in the soul'.[65] The second process of actualization is not an ordinary alteration, but rather 'a preservation of what is potentially such by the actuality' (417b3–5), and 'a development towards itself and actuality' (417b6–7). The second potentiality for applying knowledge remains unaffected no matter how often we use the knowledge we possess (as long as we possess it). For our purposes it is crucial to note that in *De An.* II.5 Aristotle speaks of the potentialities and actualities of the knowing person (*epistêmôn*), and mentions matter only once by way of comparison (417a27).

4. The Development of Intellect as a Hylomorphic Process

This framework of *Phys.* VII.3 and *De An.* II.5 found full application in Alexander's discussion of the development of intellect (*nous*) in his *De An.* 80.20–91.6.[66] He distinguishes the following stages (81.13–86.6), which are easily correlated with the distinctions of *De An.* II.5:

---

[61] On the Platonic background of this distinction and of Aristotle's vocabulary, see e.g. De Haas (2018a). There is no space here to discuss the relevance of *Meta.* Θ 7 for *Phys.* VII.3, *De An.* II.5, and Alexander's hylomorphism.
[62] Arist., *De An.* II.5, 417a21–8.   [63] Arist., *De An.* II.5, 417b23–4; III.4, 429b3–9.
[64] Arist., *De An.* II.5, 417a28–b1.   [65] Arist., *APo.* II.19, 100a6–7; cf. 100a10–b3.
[66] For a paraphrase of the entire passage, see De Haas (2019: 300–6); cf. De Haas (2020) for parallel arguments in *Mant.* 2. For a general discussion of Alex., *De An.* 85.20–86.6 (T9–T10 below), see De Haas (forthcoming). For material intellect, see Tuominen (2010).

1. natural or material intellect, innate in all human beings, capable of acquiring both practical and theoretical intellect (in that order of perfection)	first potentiality
2. common intellect, which all human beings naturally develop (in different degrees) under the impact of daily sense perception	(not in Aristotle)[67]
3. dispositional intellect, the state of completion (*teleiotês*) of material intellect, which only some people acquire by habituation and instruction	first actuality/second potentiality
4. intellect-in-actuality, which is the application of the knowledge that is dispositional intellect	second actuality

The four stages describe the development of the innate human capacity for thought from first potentiality to second actuality. The common intellect is inserted to do justice to the actual distribution of knowledge among humans, but (remarkably so) it is not considered as a state of completion of the material intellect yet. This makes the completion of material intellect a rarer event, perhaps even the prerogative of professional philosophers (in line with the Platonic dialectician and the Stoic sage). Alexander clearly regards the dispositional intellect as the form (*eidos*) and state of completion (*teleiotês*) of the material intellect (*hulikos nous*), as the following quotes show:

T8 The potential intellect, which we possess when we are born, is itself twofold as well, where one is able to receive the other. The first is called and is the 'material intellect'—since anything that can receive something is that thing's matter—while the other, which arises through instruction and habits, is a form and actuality [*entelecheia*] of the first.

Alex., *De An.* 81.22–6

The intellect that is acquired and arises later, which is a form, disposition (*hexis*), and completion (*teleiotês*) of the natural intellect, is no longer to be found in all [human beings], but rather in those who practise and learn in the manner appropriate to the various branches of knowledge.

Alex., *De An.* 82.1–3

---

[67] This is Alexander's interpretation of *tou koinou* in Arist., *De An.* 1.4 408b24–9, which found its way into later discussions of intellect; see e.g. De Haas (2018b: 115–16) on Themistius. Modern commentators understand Aristotle as referring to the perishable compound of soul and body (*to koinon*), which is held responsible for emotions, desires, and memory. Alexander takes it as a reference to a common intellect (*koinos* sc. *nous*).

... the intellect that is said to be a disposition, in contrast, is a form, power,[68] and completion of the material intellect. This disposition arises in it as a result of comprehending the universal and its being able to separate the forms from the matter, which are in a way the same as each other.

Alex., *De An.* 85.11–14

These passages clearly testify to the hylomorphic analysis of the development of intellect.[69] Alexander applies Aristotle's connection between hylomorphism and potentiality/actuality as comparable, and compatible, explanations of change (*Phys.* I.8). He brings the distinctions of *De An.* II.5 to bear on the generation of the material intellect's disposition, in line with *Phys.* VII.3. The notion of completion, viz the process of *teleiôsis*, resulting in the state of *teleiotês*, bridges the two vocabularies.

The third text of T8 shows that the acquisition of universals through the familiar process of sense perception, memory, and experience,[70] plays the role of the preliminary changes that lead up to the new form and disposition of intellect, which *Phys.* VII.3 has led us to expect. In this way Alexander is able to shed some light on Aristotle's rather vague allusions to this process, which we saw earlier. A crucial text, which bristles with echoes from *APo* II.19, gives us the following explanation:

T9 This particular kind of disposition initially comes to be in the [material] intellect in virtue of a transition from the continuous activity involving perceptibles, when it acquires from them a kind of theoretical vision, as it were, of the universal. This [universal] is at first called an object of thought [*noêma*] and a concept [*ennoia*], but as it increases [*pleonasan*] and becomes complex and diversified [*poikilon kai polutropon*),[71] so that it becomes able to produce this apart from its perceptual basis, it is eventually called intellect [*nous*]. [3] For whenever through continuous activities it becomes dispositional in such a way that it is able to engage in the remaining activity on its own, at that stage the intellect comes into being which is described as a disposition.

Alex., *De An.* 85.20–86.1

---

[68] In the CAG edition, Bruns excises *kai dunamis*, but it can stand as referring to second potentiality. Cf. *De An.* 86.4–5.

[69] Alexander often calls forms powers, because they are (first) actualities that are logically prior to (second) potentialities and their (second) actualities, cf. e.g. *De An.* 9.12–26. This hylomorphic analysis should be clearly distinguished from the notorious reference to hylomorphism at *De An.* III.5, 430a10–14, with its vexed history of ancient and modern interpretations. Perhaps, though, Alexander interpreted the passage as a licence to apply hylomorphism more widely in his discussion of intellect.

[70] Cf. Alex., *De An.* 83.2–13, with Alex., *In Meta.* 2.23–6.12; cf. De Haas (2021: 74–6).

[71] Cf. Alex. *DA* 8.5–13, for similar language concerning the contribution of lower forms to more complex and completed higher forms.

The tipping point which leads to the emergence of dispositional intellect is the ability to think a fully matured universal concept at will, without having recourse to perception. While trying to reach that state, the material intellect is developing a concept which serves as object of thought, but does not yet qualify as intellect.[72] Once matured, the universal concept *is* the dispositional intellect, because it is the form of a hylomorphic compound together with material intellect. Alexander immediately proceeds to call this process analogous to the distinction of potential and actual knowers in *De An.* II.5 (*De An.* 86.1–4). After noting that the activity of this disposition yields intellect-in-activity, he adds an intriguing sentence on the nature of dispositional intellect:

T10   For the dispositional understanding is in a certain way the concepts [*noêmata*] that have been stored and accumulated and are at rest.
Alex., *De An.* 86.5–6

So far, the development of dispositional intellect has been described as the development of a single concept, which turns intellect. In T10 it becomes clear that a single dispositional intellect is in fact the sum total of stored completed concepts, all of which the individual human being that has reached this degree of *teleiôsis* can think as she wishes. This concept of knowledge as the sum total of concepts known brings to mind Chrysippus' concept of *logos* as the system, or collection of certain concepts and conceptions.[73]

What is Alexander's Aristotelian support for this thesis? Alexander regards Aristotle's remark on the (Platonic) description of the soul as 'place of forms' to be a reference to his material intellect.[74] One would expect him to have identified Aristotle's description of intellect as the 'form of forms' as a reference to his dispositional intellect, but the corresponding passage does not mention the collection of completed universals, but rather their successive reception.[75] Apparently, the identity of dispositional intellect is not limited to a single matured concept, but should be regarded as the accumulation of all stored concepts at rest in the soul. The human being that possesses this soul has the ability to think all and any of them as she wishes. In T10 however, dispositional intellect seems to act

---

[72] On the use of *ennoia* in Alexander as an unfinished concept, see De Haas (forthcoming).
[73] See, e.g., SVF 2.56; 2.841, 23–4 (= Long & Sedley 54V); cf. SVF 2.847 (= Long & Sedley 39F).
[74] Alex., *De An.* 85.5–10, referring to Arist., *De An.* III.4, 429a27–9: those who used the phrase should rather have spoken of the noetic power of the soul.
[75] Alex., *De An.* 91.7–24, corresponding to Arist., *De An.* III.8, 431b21–432a–3: soul can be regarded as in a way everything because perception is the form of perceptibles, intellect the form of forms. Alexander does not seem to have used the phrase *eidos eidôn* in this sense, only when referring to a higher level form (e.g. the soul) comprising several lower level forms that contribute to it (e.g. the corporeal substrates). Cf. *De An.* 8.5–13, esp. 12–13: 'a kind of form of forms [*eidos pôs eidôn*], and a completion of completions [*teleiotês tis teleiotêtôn*]'.

as a kind of intellectual memory, whereas ordinary memory only serves sense perception and the preceding stages of concept formation.[76]

5. Conclusion

In this chapter, I have attempted to reconstruct part of the debate on hylomorphism in which Alexander of Aphrodisias participated, insofar as it emerges from Alexander's *Quaestiones* and *Mantissa* 5. The debate addresses *Physics* I–II.1 and the distinctions in the *Categories* that Aristotle used in that context. Alexander takes away from the debate that he needs to situate his discussion of the relation between soul and body into a general theory of hylomorphism in which form and matter need each other, both for their existence and their definition. It also needs argument that soul is the form and actuality of the body so as to apply the general theory to this paradigm case, and to further apply hylomorphism to the levels and powers of soul. The story culminates in the application of hylomorphism to the development of dispositional intellect, in which Alexander combines *Phys.* VII.3, *De An.* II.5, and *APo* II.19 with the view of form as completion (*teleiotês*). The intellect of accomplished knowers comes out as the sum total of knowable things. This is the pinnacle of hylomorphism as a physical, metaphysical, and epistemological theory. As such it is also a perfect example of how Alexander innovatives by connecting Aristotelian dots in unprecedented ways.[77]

Bibliography

Burnyeat, Myles F. 2002. '*De Anima* II.5'. *Phronesis* 47, no. 1: 28–90.

Caston, Victor. 1997. 'Epiphenomenalisms, Ancient and Modern'. *Philosophical Review* 106, no. 3: 309–63.

Caston, Victor. 2012. *Alexander of Aphrodisias On the Soul, Part I: Soul as Form of the Body, Parts of the Soul, Nourishment, and Perception.* Vol. 1. 2 vols. Ancient Commentators on Aristotle, edited by R. Sorabji. London: Bristol Classical Press.

Cerami, Cristina. 2016. 'Alexander of Aphrodisias'. In *Brill's Companion to the Reception of Aristotle in Antiquity*, edited by Andrea Falcon, 160–79. Leiden: Brill.

---

[76] Exploration of possible connections between Alexander and Plotinus' twofold memory, and the medieval issue of the plurality of forms will have to wait for another occasion.

[77] Over the years I have accumulated a great debt to Richard Sorabji, David Charles, and Victor Caston for their willingness to discuss the intricate issues involved in this chapter. I have also profited much from the feedback I received from the participants in the 2019 Yale conference, in a workshop on Alexander's *Quaestiones* organized by Gweltaz Guyomarc'h (Lyon, 2019), and in a Munich-Utrecht workshop on Ancient Greek and Arabic Epistemologies (Utrecht, 2020). Of course only I am to blame for any remaining mistakes.

Charles, David. 2018. 'Physics I.7'. In *Aristotle's Physics Book I: A Systematic Exploration*, edited by Diana Quarantotto, 178–205. Cambridge: Cambridge University Press.

Chen, Fei-Ting. 2017. 'A Hylomorphic Reading of Non-Genuine Qualitative Changes in Aristotle's *Physics* VII.3'. *Apeiron* 50, no. 2: 247–75.

Chiaradonna, Riccardo. 2020. 'Boethus of Sidon on Forms and Qualities: Some Remarks'. *Documenti e Studi sulla traditione filosofica medievale* 31: 39–55.

Chiaradonna, Riccardo, and Marwan Rashed. 2020. *Boéthos de Sidon—Exégète d'Aristote et philosophe*. Commentaria in Aristotelem Graeca et Byzantina, edited by Dieter Harlfinger, Christof Rapp, Marwan Rashed, and Dieter R. Reinsch. vol. 1. Berlin-Boston: De Gruyter.

De Haas, Frans A.J. 1997. *John Philoponus' New Definition of Prime Matter: Aspects of its Background in Neoplatonism and the Ancient Commentary Tradition*. Philosophia Antiqua, edited by Jaap Mansfeld, David T. Runia, and J.C.M. Van Winden, vol. 69. Leiden–New York–Köln: E.J. Brill.

De Haas, Frans A.J. 2018a. 'Potentiality in Aristotle's Psychology and Ethics'. In *Handbook of Potentiality*, edited by Kristina Engelhard and Michael Quante, 71–91. Dordrecht: Springer.

De Haas, Frans A.J. 2018b. 'Themistius [on the Relations between Intellects, Soul, and Body]'. In *A History of Mind and Body in Late Antiquity*, edited by Anna Marmodoro and Sophie Cartwright, 111–28. Cambridge: Cambridge University Press.

De Haas, Frans A.J. 2019. 'Intellect in Alexander of Aphrodisias and John Philoponus: Divine, Human or Both?' In *Philosophy of Mind in Antiquity*, edited by John E. Sisko, *The History of the Philosophy of Mind*, edited by Rebecca Copenhaver and Christopher Shields, 299–316. London–New York: Routledge.

De Haas, Frans A.J. 2020. 'Aristotle and Alexander of Aphrodisias on Active Intellectual Cognition'. In *Active Cognition. Challenges to an Aristotelian Tradition*, edited by Véronique Decaix and Ana María Mora Márquez, *Studies in the History of Philosophy of Mind*, edited by Henrik Lagerlund and Mikko Yrjönsuuri, 13–36. Dordrecht: Springer.

De Haas, Frans A.J. 2021. 'Deduction and Common Notions in Alexander's Commentary on Aristotle Metaphysics A 1-2', *History of Philosophy & Logical Analysis* 24: 71–102.

De Haas, Frans A.J. forthcoming. 'Alexander of Aphrodisias on Concepts'. In *Conceptualising Concepts in Greek Philosophy*, edited by Voula Tsouna and Gábor Bétegh. Cambridge: Cambridge University Press.

Ellis, J. 1994. 'Alexander's Defense of Aristotle's Categories'. *Phronesis* 39: 69–89.

Helle, Reier. 2018. 'Hierocles and the Stoic Theory of Blending'. *Phronesis* 63, no. 1: 87–116.

Ierodiakonou, Katerina, Paul Kalligas, and Vassilis Karasmanis, eds. 2019. *Aristotle's Physics Alpha: Symposium Aristotelicum*. Oxford: Oxford University Press.

Kelsey, Sean. 2010. 'Hylomorphism in Aristotle's *Physics*'. *Ancient Philosophy* 30: 107–24.

Kelsey, Sean. 2015. 'Aristotle on Interpreting Nature'. In *Aristotle's Physics: A Critical Guide*, edited by Mariska Leunissen, 31–45. Cambridge: Cambridge University Press.

Leunissen, Mariska E.M.P.J. 2015a. *Aristotle's Physics: A Critical Guide*, Cambridge Critical Guides. Cambridge: Cambridge University Press.

Leunissen, Mariska E.M.P.J. 2015b. 'Perfection and the Physiology of Habituation According to Physics VII.3'. In *Aristotle's Physics: A Critical Guide*, edited by Mariska E.M.P.J. Leunissen, 225–44. Cambridge: Cambridge University Press.

Maso, S., C. Natali, and G. Seel, eds. 2007. *Reading Aristotle: Physics VII. 3. What Is Alteration?* Las Vegas: Parmenides Publishing.

Polansky, Roland. 2007. *Aristotle's De Anima*. Cambridge: Cambridge University Press.

Quarantotto, Diana, ed. 2018. *Aristotle's Physics Book I: A Systematic Exploration*. Cambridge: Cambridge University Press.

Reeve, C.D.C. 2017. *Aristotle De Anima: Translated with Introduction and Notes*. Indianapolis–Cambridge: Hacket Publishing Company.

Reeve, C.D.C. 2018. *Aristotle Physics: Translated with Introduction and Notes*. Indianapolis–Cambridge: Hacket Publishing Company.

Sharples, R.W. 1990. 'The School of Alexander?'. In *Aristotle Transformed: The Ancient Commentators and Their Influence*, edited by Richard Sorabji, 83–111. London: Duckworth.

Sharples, R.W. 1992. *Alexander of Aphrodisias Quaestiones 1.1–2.15*. Ancient Commentators on Aristotle. London: Duckworth.

Sharples, R.W. 2004. *Alexander of Aphrodisias: Supplement to On the Soul*, Ancient Commentators on Aristotle. London: Duckworth.

Sharples, R.W. 2009. 'The Hellenistic Period: What Happened to Hylomorphism?' In *Ancient Perspectives on Aristotle's De Anima*, edited by Gerd van Riel and Pierre Destrée, Ancient and Medieval Philosophy: De Wulf-Mansion Centre. Series I, 155–66. Leuven: Leuven University Press.

Tuominen, Miira. 2010. 'Receptive Reason: Alexander of Aphrodisias on Material Intellect'. *Phronesis* 55: 170–90.

Wardy, R. 1990. *The Chain of Change: A Study of Aristotle's Physics VII*. Cambridge: Cambridge University Press.

Whittaker, John, and Pierre Louis. 1990. *Alcinoos. Enseignement des doctrines de Platon*. Paris: Les Belles Lettres.

Witt, Ch. 1989. 'Hylomorphism in Aristotle'. *Apeiron* 22: 141–58.

8
Plotinus on Hylomorphic Forms

Riccardo Chiaradonna

1. Forms and Shapes: 4.7.8⁵

Engagement with Aristotle's hylomorphism is a constant feature of Plotinus' philosophical work. It starts with Plotinus' criticism of the Peripatetic account of the soul as entelechy (4.7.8⁵) and continues with frequent references and at least two extensive critical discussions within Plotinus' investigation of causes and categories (6.7, 6.3); it ends with Plotinus' account of human beings in his penultimate treatise, 1.1. Here I will focus on some salient features of Plotinus' approach and will try to set Plotinus' discussion against the wider background of his account of physical beings.[1]

In treatise 4.7, Plotinus focuses on the view that the soul is the entelechy of the living body: this is part of his critical examination of earlier doctrines which equated the status of the soul and that of the body (mistakenly so, on Plotinus' view).[2] More precisely, in two subsequent sections Plotinus focuses on the Pythagorean view that the soul is the *harmonia* of the living body (Plotinus' obvious source here is Plato's *Phaedo*) and on the Peripatetic hylomorphic account of the soul as entelechy. Plotinus actually regards these as variants of a single general position: the soul is neither an incorporeal self-subsisting substance

---

[1] I will instead leave out the discussion about the status of matter (which Plotinus regards as identical to privation and unaffectable: the distinction between prime matter and secondary matter is problematic in his account): an extensive discussion can be found in Noble (2013a). In Chapter 9 in the present collection, Pauliina Remes offers an acute and illuminating outline of Plotinus' view on the soul-body relation which may seem to be partly at odds with my own. Unlike Remes, I am inclined to think that when Plotinus appears to give a causal or quasi-causal role to the organic body *vis-à-vis* the embodied soul and so might be seen as presenting a 'moderate embodiment view' ('body has a functional role. Embodied activities structure perception and shape our understanding'), his remarks are sometimes to be explained within their immediate context as intermediate steps in his arguments. Thus, for example, his use of the helmsman analogy in 4.3.21, which clearly depends on Aristotle (or, rather, on Alexander of Aphrodisias' reading of Aristotle in his *On the Soul*: see Aristotle, *De An.* 2.1.423a9 and Alexander of Aphrodisias, *De An.* 15.9–28) is, in my view, a step towards his final (anti-hylomorphic) conclusion (4.3.22) that the soul is not in the body, but rather the body is in the soul. Remes' discussion captures some important aspects of Plotinus' philosophy on which I tend to put less emphasis than she does.

[2] This is Plotinus' second treatise according to the chronological order reported in Porphyry's *Life of Plotinus*. Chapter 8⁵ falls within a long lacuna in Plotinus' mss, so we only know this text through the quotation in Eusebius *PE*: 4.7.8⁵.1–50 = Eus., *Praep. Evang.* 15.10. For details, see D'Ancona (2017: 271–2). The literature on this chapter is abundant and I would especially refer to Tornau (2005).

(as Plato claims) nor a body (as the Stoics claim), but an attribute or an affection that belongs to the body (see 4.7.8⁴.2: *sōmatos... ti*; 4.7.8⁵.44: *pathos sōmatos*).³ This is, of course, a generic view that is compatible with what we now regard as divergent positions (using the typical vocabulary of mind-body debates, we might speak of eliminativism, epiphenomenalism, reductionism, and emergentism: all these approaches would be compatible with Plotinus' description).⁴ Plotinus' general point throughout his writings is that, whatever one might think of the soul as an enmattered form, its status is not sufficiently distinct from that of the body and its attributes. So Aristotle cannot ground his own distinction between body and soul in his hylomorphic theory, since the soul is an attribute among others and all attempts to make sense of its status and of its causal role are doomed to fail.⁵ As a consequence of this, Plotinus suggests that Plato's view of the soul (a self-subsisting substance independent of the body and endowed with motion and causal power) ultimately provides a way out of the difficulties internal to Aristotle's hylomorphic view. That said, Plotinus' approach is considerably different in his investigations, and his early critical passages in 4.7 strike the reader as inadequate. At the beginning of 4.7.8⁵ Plotinus says that

---

³ The expression *pathos sōmatos* in 4.7.8⁵.44 is vague enough to cover all features which belong to bodies (size, colour, shape, etc.; see 4.2.1.36–40 and 6.4.1.19–23 with the remarks in Tornau 1998a: 28), but it definitely does not cover causal powers: for, as Plotinus says, *praxis* and *poiēsis* belong to the soul. According to Plotinus, bodies and their features are causally inert: all powers as such belong to incorporeal substances: irreducible causal powers emergentism (according to which the causal powers of the soul emerge from the causal powers of matter) is not an option in Plotinus' philosophy.
⁴ For the application of these notions to ancient debates, see Caston (1997).
⁵ Some caution is required in speaking of a 'causal role'. According to Charles (2021), Aristotle regards forms as efficient causes, i.e. as initiators and controllers of the relevant enmattered processes: 'The human soul itself, in whole or in part, is a per se cause of bodily movements in that its specific capacities (such as the capacity to desire, perceive and imagine) are the starting points of these movements' (Charles 2021: 214). In order to be efficient causes in the required way, forms have to be enmattered. Plotinus would agree that the soul is the genuine principle of enmattered processes, but his model of causation is different, since he regards causation as consisting in the causes producing images of themselves. So enmattered processes are nothing else that the unfolding of the formal content present in the incorporeal principles (of course, as I aim to show in this chapter, Plotinus would regard his own view of causation as capable of rescuing Aristotle's account from its internal weaknesses). The background assumptions of Plotinus' position lie in the so-called theory of double activity. Plotinus holds that real causes act without undergoing any affection and in virtue of their own essence (the first *energeia*, i.e. the internal activity that constitutes their own nature). According to the first *energeia*, real causes are what they are and 'abide in themselves' (see Plato, *Timaeus*, 42e: after carrying out his creative tasks, the demiurge abides in rest in his customary state). However, an external activity (the second *energeia*) flows from them in virtue of their very nature, as a sort of by-product, without entailing any transformation or diminution on their part. The secondary activity can never be separate from its origin and is like an image of it, whereas the first activity has the role of a paradigm. Plotinus' favourite images of fire emanating heat through its environment and of light propagation are intended to convey these features of causation. Plotinus sets out this theory in a number of passages, esp. 5.1.6.28–53; 5.2.1.12–18; 5.3.7.13–34; 5.4.2.21–7; 5.9.8.11–19. The authoritative account of this theory is Emilsson (2007: 22–68). Note that the analogy of fire and heat needs qualification, since in itself it does not imply that the product has a lower status than the maker (fire tends not merely to heat but to generate more fire), a feature which is instead crucial in Plotinus' account of causation: see Emilsson (2007: 59).

T1 [a] They [Aristotle and the Peripatetics] assert that the soul in the composite being holds the rank of form in relation to the ensouled body as matter, but is not the form of every kind of body, and not of body simply as body, but of a 'natural body endowed with organs which has life potentially.' [b] If, then, insofar as it is associated with the body,[6] it is assimilated with it, as the form of the statue is to the bronze, then when the body is divided the soul will be separated into parts along with it, and when a part was cut off there would be a bit of soul with the cut-off piece of body.

4.7.8^5.2–9[7]

Section [a] is fairly unproblematic, since Plotinus outlines the view that the soul is the hylomorphic form of a natural body potentially possessing life and in doing so he merely paraphrases the relevant passages from Aristotle's *On the Soul* (2.1.412a19–22; 412a27–8; 412b4–6). Note, however, that Plotinus does not describe the hylomorphic form as an essence (*ousia*) and that the term *ousia* only appears at the end of the chapter and after the whole set of anti-Peripatetic arguments (4.7.8^5.40), i.e. when Plotinus describes the (Platonic) soul as an essence different from the body and from what belongs to it (4.7.8^5.43–50): this choice suggests that on Plotinus' view an *ousia* is, as such, different from bodies and from their attributes (among which one should list the hylomorphic form). This plainly conflicts with Aristotle's view that the soul is an essence in the sense that it is a hylomorphic form (*eidos*: see Aristotle, *De An.* 2.1.412a19–20).

Section [b] raises further problems. Plotinus starts from the statue analogy that both Aristotle and the subsequent tradition employ in order to illustrate the status of the hylomorphic form.[8] Plotinus takes this analogy literally: if the soul stands to the body in the same way as the form stands to the bronze in a statue, then the soul is nothing but the external shape of the body, so that if some part of the body is cut off, a portion of the soul will be cut off too. Insofar as the soul is associated with the body, Plotinus says, it is assimilated with it.[9] Plotinus' point is not only that if the soul were the form of the body, it would be divisible into parts (Plotinus would actually accept this point with due qualification), but that the soul would be divided into parts in exactly the same way as the body (so the parts of the soul would directly belong to the parts of the body).[10] The use of the term *morphē*

---

[6] At 4.7.8^5.5–6 *hēi* before *parabeblētai* is probably adverbial: see D'Ancona (2017: 342).

[7] All translations are taken from Armstrong (1966–88) (with changes when necessary). Also, see Gerson et al. (2018). For the Greek text, see Henry Schwyzer (1964–82) (*editio minor*).

[8] See Aristotle, *Meta.* 5.2.1013b5–9; 1014a11; Seneca, *Epist.* 65.5; Alexander, *Fat.* 167.2–12: further details and references in Caston (2012: 75n.17).

[9] 'Assimilated' should be taken in a strong sense: according to the view rejected by Plotinus, the soul is not only compared to the body, but also shares some of its basic features, such as divisibility into spatial parts. See Horn (2012: 223).

[10] For extensive discussion about parts of the soul in Plotinus, see Karfík (2014). On Aristotle's views about parts in the soul, see Caston (2020).

(4.7.8⁵.6) further suggests that here Plotinus regards the soul as being nothing else than the external configuration of the body, its shape. This conflicts with Aristotle's idea that the form is wholly present throughout the body (see *De An.* 1.5.411b19–27; also, see 1.4.409a9–10; 2.2.413b16–21); furthermore, Plotinus' approach neglects the causal status of the form. This is obviously misleading and elsewhere Plotinus shows more care in outlining Aristotle's views. His early treatment of the topic looks like a list of disparate objections (4.7.8⁵.5–39): Plotinus probably draws at least some of them from the earlier tradition and the whole discussion in 4.7.8⁵ is not among his philosophical masterpieces.[11] That said, some further remarks are in order. Aristotle too illustrates the status of the soul by comparing it to a shape (*De An.* 2.1.412a8: *morphē*; 412b7: *schēma*). This is of course not Aristotle's last word, but Aristotle's own presentation could to some extent lead to Plotinus' conclusions, if that preliminary characterization were regarded as fully elucidating the status of the soul. This is all the more plausible, since the bronze statue analogy plays a key role in Alexander of Aphrodisias' *On the Soul*, where it paradigmatically instantiates the type of composition proper to body and soul:

T2   Form and matter are not parts of the body in this way [i.e. as the material parts of the body], but in the way that bronze and its contours are parts of the statue. Dividing up the statue does not result in them, as it does into a head, trunk, and legs. But the composite is composed from them as parts, even though not in the same way. For the shape of the statue is a part, though not in a way that contributes something to its size—it contributes to its character instead—and not as something that can persist in separation from the matter.
                                   Alexander of Aphrodisias, *De An.* 18.17–23; trans.
                                                    Caston; cf. *De An.* 12.3–4, 14.6–7

We would like to know more about Alexander's distinction between physical parts which contribute something to the body's size (*eis to poson*) and parts such as the form which contribute to its 'character' (*eis to poion*).[12] However this distinction is drawn, in T2 the contours of the statue once again illustrate the status of the enmattered form: Plotinus would be happy to subscribe to this view. These remarks, however, do not exhaust Alexander's view, for elsewhere he carefully

---

[11] Michalewski (2020) elucidates the background of 4.7.8⁵ in pre-Plotinian debates about the status of the soul.

[12] Alexander's remarks in T2 suggest that the bronze as matter is a part of the statue but not a spatial part. Galluzzo (2018: 67) and Charles (2021: 55–6) offer different arguments in support of the view that two senses of matter should be distinguished in Aristotle, i.e. matter as the sum of the material parts of a substance (as Charles puts it, flesh as matter, i.e. spatially divisible objects or quantities of matter) and matter as a principle (as Charles puts it, flesh as a principle of form, a material way of being: e.g. being bodily, being enfleshed, etc.). Alexander's distinction points to similar conclusions, although the focus of his argument is form rather than matter.

separates the status of the form in artefacts and that of the form in natural beings: artefacts 'are substances in virtue of the underlying matter and qualities in virtue of their forms' (*De An.* 6.5–6) (the form is the configuration which belongs to an independent underlying material), whereas a natural being composed of matter and form is 'a substance and a single nature of some kind' (*De An.* 6.4) (the matter is no independent substrate but is essentially what it is in virtue of the form within it). As Alexander says, the soul is not in the body 'as in a subject', i.e. as an attribute belongs to its substantial subject (see *Mant.* 119.31–120.11; cf. Aristotle, *Cat.* 2).[13] So we cannot regard the organic body as a subject whose identity conditions can be specified without referring to the form, and the form as an attribute that belongs to that subject. By contrast to what happens in artefacts, natural forms are no mere arrangements of an underlying material and their status is different from that of non-substantial qualities. Indeed, the organic body is what it is in virtue of the soul. Alexander's approach actually gives full weight to the substantial and causal status of the form in natural beings and, as Caston (2012: 8) suggests, Alexander seems to conceive of substantial forms as something akin to causal powers or dispositions: this interpretation might be debatable, but what is not controversial is that Alexander carefully distinguishes the condition of substantial forms in natural beings and that of shapes in artefacts.[14] So the bronze statue analogy is a preliminary example, which illustrates some salient aspects of the relation between body and soul: in particular, it illustrates that this kind of relation (i.e. the relation existing between two aspects or features of one and the same thing, and not between separate items that have to be put together) is different from that existing between the material parts in a body (e.g. the bricks in a house), as well as from the relation between the items out of which something blended is composed (e.g. honey and water in honey water) (see *De An.* 11.14–12.7). But, of course, the statue analogy neglects other crucial aspects, such as the substantial and causal status of the hylomorphic form. For some reason, in 4.7 Plotinus overlooks this fact. Whatever the reason for this may be, Plotinus' critical approach in 4.7 does not do justice of some key aspects of Aristotle's hylomorphism.

2. Forms as Causes

This situation changes in later treatises, where Plotinus' engagement with Aristotle's hylomorphism is connected to the investigation about causation and

---

[13] For details, see Ellis (1994); Rashed (2013).
[14] As Caston (2012: 8) says, 'the forms of natural substances, and hence souls, are ultimately to be understood as causal powers or dispositions. Forms are the features of substances that enable them to do or undergo the activities characteristic of their kind.' Also, see Caston's Chapter 6, in this volume. As we shall see, Plotinus' general point is that no feature of corporeal substances (or rather quasi-substances) can actually perform this role: causal powers require extra-corporeal principles.

physical beings. In the first part of 6.7, Plotinus focuses on genuine causes, i.e. on incorporeal causes which act in virtue of what they are and not through choice or deliberation (Plotinus conceives of their causation according to the so-called theory of double activity, which accounts for the derivation of lower realities from higher principles).[15] Genuine causes are intelligible incorporeal beings separate from bodies and, according to Plotinus, they are such that the 'thing' (6.7.2.3: *to...hoti*; 6.7.2.10: *to pragma*) and the 'reason why' (6.7.2.4: *to dioti*; 6.7.2.6: *to dia ti*) are one and the same.[16] Since in the intelligible world there is no distinction between something and its essence, Plotinus' claim here seems to be that, in the intelligible world, essence and cause are identical.[17] The vocabulary is reminiscent of Aristotle (*APo.* 2.2 90a14–16; see also *Metaphysics* 8.4.1044b10–14) and, in addition to this, Plotinus considers the remark that even here below (i.e. at the level of bodies) things are sometimes one and the same with their cause: this is shown by the eclipse, whose definition makes its reason why clear (i.e. the eclipse is the privation of light from the moon because of the screening of the earth). The Peripatetic background of this remark is evident: by considering this comment, Plotinus actually considers the hypothesis that genuine causes (i.e. items such that the thing and the reason why are one and the same) are situated at the level of bodies.[18] Unlike what happens in 4.7, Plotinus does not reject this claim from the outset:

T3 [a] But often here below also the thing and the reason why are the same, as for instance 'What is an eclipse'. What then prevents each and every thing being its reason why, in the case of the others too, and this being its substance? Rather, this is necessary; and for anyone trying in this way to grasp the essential nature of a thing, it comes out right. For what each thing is is the reason why it is. [b] But I do not mean that the form is the cause of being for each thing—this is of course true—but that, if also you open each individual form itself back upon itself, you will find the reason why in it. [c] For a thing which is inert and does <not> have life[19] does not at all have the reason why, but if it is a form and belongs to Intellect, where would it get its reason why from? But if someone were to say 'from Intellect', it is not separate, supposing that it is also itself Intellect; if, then, Intellect must

---

[15] See above, n. 5.

[16] The literature on 6.7.2 is rich (also, see 6.8.14). Excellent discussions can be found in Thaler (2011) and Noble and Powers (2015). I am especially indebted to Schiaparelli (2010). Two richly annotated translations of 6.7 are Hadot (1988) and Fronterotta (2007).

[17] This point is made by Schiaparelli (2010: 472).

[18] Aristotle's views on these issues are both difficult and controversial: see Charles (2000). Here I am only interested in Plotinus' reading.

[19] *Zōēn <mē> echon* (6.7.2.20): the negation has been added by Theiler, followed by Henry and Schwyzer.

have these things in a way that is not at all deficient, they must not be deficient in the reason why.[20]

6.7.2.11–23

In [a] Plotinus expands upon the point that genuine causes are situated at the level of bodies (so that each thing is identical to its 'why'): this does not hold only for the eclipse, but also in other cases (*kai epi tōn allōn*).[21] So in other cases too sensible beings would display what Plotinus actually regards as a typical feature of intelligible items. More precisely, as Schiaparelli (2010: 479) suggests, it seems that here Plotinus is making two identity statements: (i) a sensible item is one and the same with its cause; (ii) the cause is one and the same with its essence (6.7.2.12–14). Plotinus remarks that when they (i.e. the Peripatetics) try to grasp the essence (note the Aristotelian expression *to ti ēn einai* at 6.7.2.15) in this way (*houtōs*; i.e. as I would suggest, having in view the identity of each thing and of its cause), things work out correctly for them: so this is the right approach.[22] The Peripatetics are therefore right to claim that for each thing the essence (what each thing is) and the cause (why each thing is) are one and the same (6.7.2.15–16).[23] With these words Plotinus ends [a], i.e. his outline of the Peripatetic position, in which he emphasizes what he takes to be correct in it.

As Plotinus argues in [b], however, the Peripatetics are wrong to assume that such requirements can be satisfied by sensible items (bodies and their enmattered forms). More precisely, Plotinus concedes that the form is the cause of being for each thing (the expression 'cause of being' seems an obvious reminiscence of Aristotle's *Metaphysics* 7.17), but this is not the point (see 6.7.2.16–17): the real point is that only certain forms (the form itself, *auto to eidos*; 6.7.2.16) satisfy these requirements. These forms have to be such that 'if also you open each individual form itself back upon itself, you will find the reason why in it'.[24] As [c] makes it clear, this sentence refers to forms in Intellect separate from bodies: they are such that their 'why' (i.e. the whole of the Intellect) is internal to them. In order to ground Aristotle's claim that the thing and the reason why are one and the same in genuine causes, one must therefore go beyond hylomorphism and grasp the

---

[20] In 6.7.2.22–3, I follow Armstrong in taking the Intellect as being the subject of *echein* and 'these things' (*tauta*), i.e. the forms, as being the subject of *elleipein*.

[21] See Schiaparelli (2010: 479): 'The idea is that there is a collection of things for which the thesis of the identity between essence and cause holds. This collection contains items from the Aristotelian list together with other items in the sensible world. Still, at this stage, it remains difficult to give a full-fledged description of this collection.'

[22] Hadot (1988: 89, 201) and Schiaparelli (2010: 481) convincingly argue that the generic *peirōmenois* at 6.7.2.14 refers in fact to Aristotle and the Peripatetics. This would not be an isolated case: see 6.1.1.29–30. Plotinus' outline is selective: for he does not mention Aristotle's four causes and his account of the Peripatetic position is exclusively centred on the causal role played by form. So for Plotinus the Peripatetics hold that the essence is the only (and not merely the primary) cause of a thing.

[23] For a detailed discussion of these lines, see again Schiaparelli (2010: 483–4).

[24] On this, see Thaler (2011: 165) and below, n. 26.

nature of forms in Intellect (the form itself), which Plotinus characterizes as a domain where parts are not only connected but are fully interpenetrated and, so to speak, transparent to each other (see e.g. 5.8.4.4–5; 5.3.8.15–22). Only at that level are the thing and its cause strictly identical.

The background of these statements is formed by Plotinus' distinctive view about the relation between whole and parts at the level of intelligible beings. As is explained in 6.2.20, the universal Intellect is all things at once in actuality, while at the same time being each partial Intellect (each intelligible form) potentially (6.2.20.21–2).[25] The use of the word *dunamei* at the level of Intellect has raised some debate, but Plotinus' outline makes it sufficiently clear that he does not intend to suggest that the Intellect is subject to change: what he means is rather that the universal Intellect, being all things together at once in actuality (i.e. being a whole including all of its parts), is prior to the multiple intelligible forms and pre-contains them virtually, *in nuce* (silently: see 6.2.20.27), before their unfolding (so, in this precise sense, the universal Intellect contains each form in itself 'potentially', while being all of them at once in actuality): therefore, while containing each form in itself potentially, the genus is not the potentiality of the species, but their power (*dunamis*) (see 6.2.20.25–6).[26] This explains why Plotinus makes apparently contradictory claims in the space of a few lines: (a) all partial Intellects (i.e. each single intelligible form) are in the universal Intellect potentially; (b) the universal Intellect is all things at once in actuality; (c) the universal Intellect is each partial Intellect potentially (i.e. it is potentially each partial Intellect insofar as each partial Intellect is distinct from the others) (6.2.20.20–2). Conversely, each form is in actuality what it is (insofar as it is distinct from the other forms and provided with its own peculiar content) and is potentially the universal Intellect: this means that the universal Intellect is in each form, so that each form potentially contains the whole of intelligible being (6.2.20.23–5). Note that for each form being potentially in the universal Intellect means something different from being the universal Intellect potentially. The former statement refers to the fact that the universal Intellect contains all forms in it virtually and before their unfolding; the latter statement refers to the fact that each unfolded form has the whole of the Intellect potentially (virtually) within it:

---

[25] Scholars identify the universal *Nous* with the Intellect in its fundamental structure constituted by the supreme genera (being, sameness, difference, motion, and rest); partial intellects, on the other hand, are equivalent to the forms: see Emilsson (2017: 112 and 138). The literature on 6.2.20 is abundant. Here I would refer to Strange (1989) and Tornau (1998b). I would like to thank Camille Mouflier for discussing these passages with me.

[26] See the commentary on these lines offered by Lloyd (1990: 81). Here 'power' suggests that the genus (i.e. the universal intellect) is the cause of being for the forms which it brings about through its unfolding. This statement is apparently at odds with what Plotinus says in 6.7.2 (intelligible forms are such that the thing is one and the same with its cause): as Thaler (2011: 165) notes, however, 'Any attempt to locate the cause of being for each form will ultimately point to Intellect. But since Intellect does not exist as a separate entity from the forms in it but is identical to them all, saying that the cause is in Intellect is tantamount to saying that it is possessed by the form itself (VI.7.2.21–27)'.

for the whole of the Intellect is a genus for each single form; but while being a genus, it is also all forms together at once. That is why, as Plotinus says in T3, by unfolding each form one will find within it the whole of the Intellect in which that form is contained (6.7.2.25–7).[27] By paraphrasing Leibniz, we might say that each form mirrors the entire universal Intellect from its own particular perspective.[28] So the individual Intellects are embraced by the whole and, conversely, the whole is embraced by the individuals Intellects (6.2.20.16–18). The reciprocity, however, is not complete: both in T3 and in 6.2.20 Plotinus argues that the universal Intellect is the cause (and the power) for the forms in it and not the other way round: 'if the Intellects in specific form are going to exist in actuality, the activity proceeding from universal Intellect must be the cause' (6.2.20.28–9).

Intelligible forms (i.e. genuine causes) are, therefore, parts of a fully interpenetrated immaterial whole: they are not principles which unify material extended parts, so that these parts constitute a structured whole (in the same way as the form of the house is a unifying causal principle for the bricks). Plotinus actually sees all extended things (the distinction between artefacts and organisms is not relevant in this context) as forming a plurality whose parts are external to one another, although they are certainly connected to the other parts of the same ordered whole (see 6.7.2.30–7). One can regard the essential form as the cause that explains why these parts are interconnected so as to constitute a certain thing. However, a thing and its form can never be one and the same within this context: parts are external and their cause of being is external to them (one cannot find the form of the house by analysing each brick): 'But here below, just as each of the parts is separate, so also is the reason why' (6.7.2.9–10).[29] One could of course object that in sensible beings the identity between a thing and its cause does not hold for organized bodies, but holds for what is primary, i.e. for their essences. Plotinus, however, would reply that only forms separate from matter can lend adequate support to this statement (primary things are identical to their essence, i.e. to the cause).

The reason for this is that according to Plotinus the primary status of a form cannot adequately be grounded in the framework of hylomorphism (see below, T4 and T5). Hylomorphism takes the formed body as its starting point and enquires about its formal or essential aspects or features. But this approach is doomed to fail, if one intends to grasp the form in itself: for starting from the body and enquiring

---

[27] Both in 6.2.20 and elsewhere Plotinus expresses this distinctive relation of whole and parts by comparing the perfectly unified structure of Intellect to that of a science and its theorems: see 5.9.8.3–7; 6.2.20.15–16. On the science analogy, see Tornau (1998b) (with a commentary on 6.2.20).

[28] For the parallel with Leibniz, see again Lloyd (1990: 82).

[29] I would suggest that the expression 'the reason why' in this sentence does not necessarily refer to separate forms. Plotinus' point is rather that, whatever one might think of their reason why in bodies, it is separate from the body of which it is the reason why: of course, the form of the house in not strictly speaking separate from the bricks, but it is not in the bricks in the same way as the universal Intellect is in each form.

about its essence ultimately blurs the boundaries between matter and form. Since hylomorphism regards the form as being a feature of the body, it turns out to be impossible to answer the question as to why certain features and not others are taken to be formal. How can forms be embodied forms and prior to matter? According to Plotinus, hylomorphism provides no satisfying answer to this question. Forms must therefore be incorporeal in order to be prior to bodies and the only way they can be causes (which is what they are) is as paradigms according to the double-activity doctrine.[30] In order to ground the unity between things and their causes—Plotinus suggests—one must ultimately abandon the world of bodies and focus on forms in themselves (i.e. not as the forms of certain bodies).

3. Forms, *Logoi*, and Qualities

In 2.7.3 (T4), Plotinus focuses on bodies and their qualities. Some preliminary remarks are necessary to understand this passage. According to Plotinus, matter is incorporeal, it lacks extension and magnitude, it is completely indeterminate (matter is incapable of becoming anything: it is never actualized) and cannot properly be seen as the subject of anything: strictly speaking, matter does not receive forms, but forms appear in or are projected onto matter in the same way as images appear in a mirror (see 3.6.9).[31] Accordingly, extension, magnitude, and mass (the fundamental properties of bodies according to Plotinus) belong neither to matter nor to form: such properties actually arise when forms appear in matter (see 2.4.11). Within this framework, all qualities in bodies ultimately come from intelligible principles and, more precisely, from the *logos*, i.e. the lowest formative

---

[30] According to Plotinus, the primary status of a form *vis-à-vis* matter entails priority in existence: for only priority in existence lends adequate support to the idea that the form has to be grasped in itself and without reference to the body. According to this stance, the form exists independently of the body, while the body cannot exist independently of the form—where 'form' should be understood generously, i.e. as including both forms in Intellect and lower incorporeal principles such as the soul and the *logoi*. Aristotle's concept of natural priority in the *Metaphysics* has been interpreted as involving priority in being rather than priority in existence: A is prior to B iff A can be what it is independently of B being what it is, while the converse is not the case: see Peramatzis (2008). Priority in being is the ontological correlate of priority in definition: A is prior in definition to B iff A can be defined without explicit reference in its definition to B but B cannot be defined without explicit reference in its definition to A. Plotinus tends towards the view that we cannot establish a hierarchy of this type if we remain confined within the sensible realm. That is: no sufficient criterion can be found to support the claim that A is prior in being to B, if both A and B are sensible items, i.e. bodies or features of bodies. So, for example, it is not enough to hold that the organic body is what it is in virtue of the soul, if the soul is not conceived of as a self-subsisting entity prior to the body. Aristotle's stance is based on the idea that we can select among the features of the living body those which provide its identity and are, so to speak, responsible for its nature (its basic biological functions). Yet, according to Plotinus. no selection of this sort can be adequately grounded in the sensible realm. The same problem holds with Aristotle's *differentia*, for (a) the selection of those attributes of sensible substances which can count as *differentiae* lacks any adequate ground (see 6.3.8.27-37; 10.12-28); and (b) these attributes can in no way qualify 'substance as such' i.e. intelligible substance: see 6.2.14.18-19 (on this passage, see Chiaradonna 2016).

[31] See Noble (2013a).

principle which imparts form to matter.[32] Forms are projected onto matter and appear in it as visible and perceptible forms which are actually bundles of perceptible properties (see 6.3.8). The visible and perceptible forms in bodies are 'dead' (see 2.4.5.18; 3.8.2.23–34): they are no longer causally active (according to Plotinus only intelligible and incorporeal beings are causes, whereas bodies as such are deprived of life and causal power). In addition to this, qualities in bodies indirectly share the divisibility according to extension which is typical of bodies: (4.2.1.39–40; also, see 6.4.1.20–3). All this entails that even corporality (*sōmatotēs*) is a form: it is the sum of perceptible qualities which the intelligible formative principles impart to matter.[33] It is within this framework that Plotinus opposes the status of the *logos* (the extra-physical formal principle which generates bodies by imparting form to matter) to that of Aristotle's hylomorphic form. His point is that the genuine form (the *logos*, i.e. the formative principle) is not what stands for the nature of already existing things composed of form and matter, but what produces things by giving form to matter:

T4   If, then, this is what body is, that which is composed of all the qualities with matter, this is what corporality would be. And if corporality was a formative principle which by its coming to matter makes body, obviously the formative principle includes and contains all the qualities. But this rational principle, on the assumption that it is not merely a sort of definition which declares the nature of the thing [*horismos dēlōtikos tou ti esti to pragma*] but a rational principle which makes a thing [*logos poiōn pragma*], cannot include the matter but must be a principle in relation with matter which enters matter and brings the body to perfection...

2.7.3.4–11

T4 distinguishes the body (with all of its qualities: note that Plotinus makes no distinction between essential and accidental attributes) and the *logos* which already has all of these qualities within itself. Yet, insofar as they are in the *logos* (i.e. in an incorporeal formative principle distinct from matter), these qualities are actually essences and are not qualitative (cf. 6.3.15.24–31). Indeed, Plotinus regards bodies as being composed of all of their perceptible qualities plus matter (see below T8). All of the qualities in bodies are pre-contained in the formative principles according to an essential (and as such incorporeal) mode of being. Within this framework there is no place for what Plotinus in T4 calls the 'definition which declares the nature of the thing'. This expression refers, of

---

[32] The translation of this term is famously controversial. Here I make a rather free use of expressions such as 'formative principle', 'forming principle', 'rational principle', 'rational form'. For details, see Kalligas (2011: 770).

[33] On corporality, see Kalligas (2011: 771).

course, to a linguistic item (the definition) and this can easily be explained because this item is opposed to the true *logos*. Yet, here as elsewhere (see Alexander of Aphrodisias, *Quaest.* 1.3), the term 'definition' has a wider scope and stands both for the definition in the proper sense and for its object, i.e. for Aristotle's essence (the definable nature), the hylomorphic form. Plotinus argues that such an item does not make things (an embodied form has no efficient causal role *vis-à-vis* the body, because such a role would entail that the form is prior to the body, but no adequate priority can be ascribed to embodied forms): an embodied essence, therefore, is only meant to elucidate the 'what it is' for an already existing sensible object, while being a feature of it (see T5). Yet Plotinus' point is that each body, insofar as it is a body made out of matter, has no formal features or attributes: all formal attributes are essential and belong to the immaterial formal principle; all physical attributes are outside essence.[34] As to biological functions, from this perspective one could possibly assume that their formal aspect is extra-physical (the sense of sight in itself is pre-existent on the intelligible level), while their instantiation in bodies (the physical sense of sight as belonging to the eyes) is one of the physical attributes and its status cannot be distinguished from attributes such as—say—hair colour.[35]

These views can be connected to Plotinus' remark in T3 that intelligible forms are different from anything inactive and without life (i.e. from anything which does not have the 'why' in it). This statement apparently entails that all bodies, insofar as they are bodies, are without life: elsewhere Plotinus explicitly makes this point (the composite of matter and immanent form is a corpse adorned: 2.4.5.18; cf. 3.8.2.32). Such a conclusion is implausible insofar as it seems to suggest that there are no living bodies. Indeed, Plotinus suggests that living bodies are not provided with life insofar as they are bodies. Life comes to bodies from elsewhere, as something imparted from incorporeal principles (the soul, the *logos*). In 4.4, Plotinus explains this point by comparing the status of the living body to that of air that has been warmed: the body has soul present to it and is changed by receiving a kind of trace of soul (an imparted or borrowed life) in the same way as air receives a likeness of fire's internal heat when it is warmed by the presence of fire (see 4.4.18.1–9). That of air is a borrowed heat, whereas that of fire is a connatural one.[36] Noble (2013b) suggests that Plotinus is here indebted to Aristotle's hylomorphism while introducing qualifications into it: Plotinus accepts

---

[34] This is, at least, Plotinus' position as it emerges from T4 and T8, whereas elsewhere (see 2.6.2) he tentatively retains the distinction between essential and accidental attributes at the level of bodies and suggests that essential attributes are activities deriving from the *logoi* (the status of accidental attributes instead remains obscure): see Chiaradonna (2014b).

[35] On Plotinus' view that the faculty of sense perception (*to aisthētikon*) is pre-existent on the intelligible level, see 6.7.6 with the remarks in Thaler (2011: 170–3).

[36] In 4.4.18, Plotinus clearly prefers this analogy to that of illuminated air (he mentions both analogies in 4.4.14.1–11). As Noble (2013b: 270) remarks, 'Plotinus, as it happens, does not think that the light is a state of the air, but rather that light exists independently of the air and is merely

a quasi-psychic enmattered form as an immanent cause of the body's life. In doing so, Plotinus integrates into his psychology Aristotle's hylomorphic view that organic bodies are alive in virtue of their formal component, but at the same time he adheres to the Platonist thesis that the soul proper (the cause of the trace in the body) is not a part of the subsistent bodily structure.[37] Noble's interpretation is persuasive and compellingly argued. Here, however, I would like to stress some problematic points and internal tensions in Plotinus' account, for it remains unclear what the status of the quasi-psychic enmattered form is *vis-à-vis* its intelligible causes: these tensions, I would suggest, reveal how difficult it is to make sense of life in bodies within the framework of Plotinus' approach. Unlike Noble, I am inclined to think that Plotinus' integration of Aristotle's hylomorphic vocabulary is, more often than not, a shorthand way of speaking of the body as bearing an image of intelligible causes. Therefore, in my view Plotinus' account of bodies is ultimately at odds with hylomorphic causation since, according to Plotinus, organic bodies are not alive in virtue of their formal component, but are only alive insofar as they are images of extra-physical intelligible causes. In certain passages, however, Plotinus undoubtedly remains faithful to the Aristotelian view regarding the existence of psychic features in bodies and this is at odds with what he says elsewhere about bodies not retaining anything of the soul that is present to them.

As a matter of fact, the question remains open as to whether the borrowed life of the body can really be seen as one of its attributes. The heated air analogy, of course, supports this conclusion. So Plotinus argues that the trace of the soul is something intermediate between the soul (or more precisely nature, i.e. the lowest stage of the world soul) and the enmattered shape that nature produces in bodies (see 4.4.14.10–11).[38] The sensible shape is the bundle of qualities that make up— together with matter—what is ordinarily called 'sensible substance' (see T8). The

---

present in it... on Plotinus' theory of light, light is present throughout a (translucent) body, but is not a state of the body in which it is present. Thus, light's presence to air is an apt analogy for a soul's presence to body (4.3.22; 1.1.4). But these virtues of the illuminated air analogy for illustrating the relationship between soul and body notwithstanding, Plotinus takes the heated air analogy to be superior in one key respect: it successfully communicates the idea that soul has an effect on the body to which it is present'.

[37] It is revealing that Plotinus regards Aristotle's passage on the *koinotatos logos* of the soul (*De An.* 2.1, 412a2–4; 412a19–22) as referring not to the soul in itself, but to the living being (i.e. the psychophysical compound, the body animated by the trace of the soul): see 1.1.4.26–7. In Plotinus' view the living body depends on the soul as a self-subsistent entity (and not as a feature of the body).

[38] The status of Plotinus' 'nature' is a difficult issue. It is the lowest aspect of the soul and it is sometimes assimilated to the nutritive soul. Noble (2013b: 272n.39) remarks that *phusis* in 4.4.14 'should probably be taken to refer to a type of psychic faculty that individual organisms and the cosmos have in common'. In my view such interpretations need qualification. Plotinus is often happy to adopt Aristotle's vocabulary concerning the different faculties of life and functions of the soul (nutrition, growth, generation, etc.: see e.g. 6.7.5.9–31), but he also makes it perfectly clear that all of these functions are actually nothing other than levels or degrees of thought. Every life, as Plotinus says in 3.8.8.17–21, is actually a form of Intellection: see Wildberg (2009); Horn (2012: 227). Life, according to Plotinus, includes not so much a series of hierarchically ordered functions, as a series of levels of

soul-trace instead retains something of the soul's causal power and, as the heated air analogy suggests, it is through its trace that soul has an effect on the body to which it is present. Sometimes, however, Plotinus explains that the distinction between an intelligible and an essential attribute, on the one hand, and its instantiation in matter, on the other, is stronger than the distinction between a connatural and a derivative attribute (the connatural heat in fire vs the borrowed heat in air). This happens in 1.2.1, within the framework of Plotinus' ethical discussion about assimilation to God. When explaining the sense in which something here below can become assimilated to the intelligible paradigm, Plotinus first mentions the example of connatural and derivative heat (e.g. heat in fire and in heated water): so if an object W (say, water) becomes Z_f (say, heated) in virtue of cause F (say, fire), the connatural attribute H (heat in fire) is causally responsible for the derivative property Z_f (1.2.1.31–40).[39] After this first example (which is consistent with the example of heated air), however, Plotinus makes use of another example which adds a stronger qualification to his view and is actually meant to rule out that the cause has the same attributes it brings about in what depends on it (the distinction between connatural and derivative attributes is therefore no longer relevant). Plotinus illustrates this second step by mentioning an intelligible house and the sensible house built according to that pattern (see 1.2.1.42–5). The two issues are heterogeneous: while the perceptible house participates of the arrangement and order of its corporeal parts, the same does not hold for the intelligible house: 'There, in its formative principle, there is no arrangement or order or proportion' (1.2.1.44–5).[40] One might wonder if the same situation holds with life. Indeed, certain passages seem to suggest this view: there Plotinus argues that life as such belongs to intelligible beings, while bodies simply do not have life as an attribute: no mention is made of the imparted life in bodies (5.1.2.32–8). Plotinus adopts this approach in his account of intelligible Being (6.2). As he says, the investigation of intelligible substance and its genera entails that we remove spatial extension and the perceptible attributes characteristic of bodies. In this way, our soul has access to the incorporeal reality to which it belongs (and of which genera are the basic constituents):

---

thought: lower functions are dimmer intellections; higher functions are clearer intellections (in 6.7.7.30–1, Plotinus claims that acts of sense perception are faint acts of intellection). On this, I agree with Menn (1998: 112n.27).

[39] Here I am indebted to Kalligas (2014: 136). In this paragraph, I summarize Chiaradonna (2021).

[40] Plotinus' example may appear unclear, especially as regards the status of the intelligible house. It is actually difficult to make sense of it: one could object that the design created by an architect for building a house entails a precise arrangement or proportion of parts, even if not of the material parts which actually make up the house. Of course, the intelligible formative principle of a house has a different status than the design created by an architect and Plotinus could argue that even the design of the house is nothing else than a sensible and material manifestation of the intelligible and un-extended house in the architect's mind. Yet it is difficult to understand what the status of the intelligible and un-extended house could be—all the more so, because Plotinus is inclined to reject the idea that incorporeal causes entail some kind of geometrical or mathematical order: see Chiaradonna (2014a).

T5 when the discussion is about intelligible substance and the genera and principles there, one must remove the coming into being in the sphere of bodies and the understanding through sense-perception and the magnitudes—for it is [because bodies have size in] this way that there is separation and they stand apart from each other—and grasp an intelligible reality and that which really and truly is and is more one.

6.2.4.12–17

In T5 what leads from sensible to intelligible beings is not some kind of ascent from the lower instantiations of an attribute to the higher and paradigmatic occurrence of it (e.g. the ascent from the derivative life in living bodies to its intelligible cause), but rather the removal (cf. *aphelontas* at 6.2.4.14) of those features that characterize bodies as such and are grasped through sensory experience. Such features actually make bodies separate and divided from one another: in this context Plotinus mentions the coming to be in bodies (i.e. physical processes), the understanding by means of sense perception (probably meaning perceptible qualities), and magnitudes (i.e. mass and quantitative extension).[41] After removing these features, our soul discovers something else in itself, something which cannot in any way be drawn from bodies and must belong to a different and more unified nature (i.e. to the soul's intelligible and incorporeal nature). These items are life and essence:

T6 In fact, this being of the soul has to be inside like 'a spring and principle' [Plato, *Phdr.* 245c], indeed everything that is soul has to be inside. And life, then, too. And so both together, both being and life, are one.

6.2.6.6–8

The heated air analogy would suggest a different type of argument: an argument starting from the distinction between non-living and living bodies and inferring from this fact the existence of an intelligible cause which can account for the borrowed life in bodies. Yet Plotinus adopts a different approach: life and essence emerge when our soul removes all characteristic bodily features and turns its focus inward, to its distinctive intelligible nature.

4. Forms and Living Bodies

So Plotinus regards *ousia* and *zōē* (substance/being and life) as *items* that characterize the incorporeal and intelligible realm in itself. The compatibility of this

---

[41] See the remarks in Griffin (2022: 175).

stance with passages suggesting that living bodies have derivative life as an attribute is problematic. Furthermore, it remains difficult to determine what exactly the distinction would be between the soul-trace and the qualities of bodies and, more precisely, how this distinction can be accounted for within the framework of Plotinus' causation. After all, all qualities in bodies (and not just the soul-trace) are external activities that depend on intelligible principles: according to Plotinus, corporeality itself is a formal and intelligible principle (see T4). The soul-trace and physical qualities depend on intelligible principles according to the same causal scheme (the so-called double activity), but, unlike physical qualities, the soul-trace retains something of the causal power of its cause (as Noble 2013b puts it, the soul-trace is the immanent cause of the body's life) while, at the same time, being an attribute of the body. How so?

As noted earlier, Plotinus' distinction between formal/intelligible and bodily attributes would entail that a biological function (e.g. sight) exists as something incorporeal and essential, while its instantiation in the body (the seeing power of the eye) is only an attribute among others (having this or that size, being of a certain colour, etc.). This would be consistent with Plotinus' clear-cut distinction between intelligible essences and their bodily instantiations, but it would of course be a very counter-intuitive view. When focusing on vision, Plotinus adopts a different approach (4.4.23), insofar as he regards the perceiving organ as something intermediate between the soul (being completely outside body, the soul would apprehend nothing that is sensible) and what the soul grasps in bodies: the sense organ is thus like a ruler which would connect the straightness in the soul with that in the wood, being placed between the two (4.4.23.39–42).[42] So, once again, something in living bodies is intermediate between the soul and the lifeless material bodies.

Elsewhere Plotinus suggests that different living bodies and different parts in each living body have a different capacity or disposition (*epitēdeiotēs*) vis-à-vis the soul: that is why the soul is present to the body as a whole, but different parts of the body manifest different powers of the soul (we see through the eyes and not through the mouth) in virtue of their distinctive disposition or suitability (see 6.4.11.3–9; 6.4.14.26–8; 15.6–8). This solution, however, is open to objections, since bodies are different in virtue of the forming action of the soul on matter: so the soul is present to bodies, because bodies are disposed to receive it in a certain way, and—conversely—bodies are disposed to receive the soul in a certain way, because the soul is present to bodies. This is an obviously circular argument.[43]

A possible way out of these difficulties would be to point to the distinction between two levels of formation in bodies.[44] Sometimes Plotinus suggests that

---

[42] The most authoritative discussion can be found in Emilsson (1988).
[43] On this, see Tornau (2016).
[44] This hypothesis is developed in Tornau (2016) (who also very clearly points to its problematic aspects) and Taormina (2020). Also, see Kalligas (2012: 156) on 6.7.7.6–15.

nature (the lowest aspect of the world soul) and the formal principles in it are causally responsible for the body's material organization: this organization does not entail life and the functions typical of living beings but, at the same time, it makes the body capable of, or suitable to, receiving them. The second level of formation instead depends on the individual soul, which imparts life to the already formed body: so the borrowed life, the trace of the soul, should be situated at this second level of formation and the same would hold for all biological functions (see 6.4.15.1–17 where Plotinus makes the distinction between *epitēdeiotēs* and *ichnos*). This approach would explain the different status of the borrowed life in bodies *vis-à-vis* merely perceptible qualities. Yet such a solution seems somewhat *ad hoc* and this is confirmed by the fact that in other passages Plotinus regards the soul-trace as depending on nature rather than on the individual soul (see 4.4.20.15–25). But sensible qualities too depend on nature according to the same causal scheme: so where should we situate the distinction between psychic and merely corporeal attributes in bodies? One wonders whether the soul-trace doctrine really solves the problem (what is the status of living bodies in a theory where life as such belongs to incorporeal entities?) or only identifies it.

Plotinus' critical stance *vis-à-vis* Aristotle appears again in T7, a passage where—as usual—the intelligible formative principle (*logos*) is opposed to the enmattered form. The passage is placed in the opening section of 6.7.4–7, a long and exceedingly difficult section in treatise 6.7, where Plotinus develops an account of human nature against the background of his gradualist metaphysics. We could label these chapters as 'Plotinus' metaphysical anthropology'. In [T7] Plotinus focuses on human beings here below and he argues that the forming principle of a human being must be independent of the body. Otherwise (i.e. if we try to grasp the formal principle starting from the composite of body and soul),

T7 this rational form [*logos*] will be explanatory of what is going to be, not the sort we say is human being in itself, but more like a definition, and the kind of definition which does not explain the essential nature. For it is not even a definition of the form in matter, but explains the composite, which already exists. But if this is so, the human being is not yet found; for that was going to be the one according to the rational form. But if someone were to say 'The rational form of such beings must be something composite, this in this', he does not think fit to say by what each exists; but one must, however much one must also speak of the rational forming principles of forms in matter as including matter, grasp the forming principle itself which makes, for instance, human being; this applies especially to those who claim to define the essential nature in each case, when they define strictly and properly.

6.7.4.16–28

As in T4, in T7 Plotinus considers the possibility that the *logos* may be some kind of definition that explains the nature of an already existing object (here the human being, a living being composed of body and soul): the standard example for this definition is 'rational animal' (see 6.7.4.12). A *logos* conceived of in this way, however, does not at all show what a human being really is (i.e. the essence or nature: the form), but simply describes the factual structure of concrete beings composed of body and soul. This kind of *logos* or definition, then, has no genuine explanatory power. Here Plotinus' polemical reference to Aristotle's view of definition is clear: for he argues that even if we grant that we should focus on forms in matter (i.e. even if we provisionally accept Aristotle's position: the structure of Plotinus' argument here is similar to T3), this kind of definition is nonetheless insufficient, since it accounts for beings composed of matter and form (*tod'en tōide*: 6.7.4.22–3; see Arist., *Meta.* 7.5.1030b18), whereas it is incapable of grasping form alone. Aristotle's definition focuses on the form-matter compound, which already exists; but according to the Peripatetics themselves definition should be able to grasp the essence of things (see 6.7.4.26–8). Their account of *logos* as a definition corresponding to the hylomorphic form is therefore insufficient even according to Peripatetic standards, since it is incapable of adequately grasping the essence of the human being, even if one regards enmattered forms as the proper object of definitional *logos* (6.7.4.24–5). Here, then, Plotinus points to a typical difficulty in Aristotle's theory of form and definition in *Meta.* 7, namely the issue of whether the definition of form should include material features or not. Plotinus exploits this puzzle to his own advantage, since he suggests that the only way of solving the problematic status of Peripatetic definitions points to a different meaning of *logos*, i.e. not as the definition applying to an already existing human being, but as a principle which produces human beings and accounts for their nature (see 6.7.4.25). So the essence cannot be any of the attributes of corporeal beings, and Plotinus' statement entails that this conclusion holds for both perceptible and primary properties. This approach suggests, for example, that the essence of gold is neither identical to its perceptible properties not to its atomic number. It is rather an incorporeal formal principle which produces the yellow of gold, along with all its other properties.

Given these premises, Plotinus incorporates and transforms Aristotle's hylomorphic account of human being as an ensouled living being: he adopts Aristotle's vocabulary, but he replaces the body with the formative principles that are responsible for the bodily structure of human beings. These formative principles are nothing but activities (*energeia*) of the soul and could not exist without the soul (6.7.5.4–5). The human being here below is in fact the composite not of soul plus a body of such a kind, but the composite of soul (i.e. the intelligible principle which provides human beings with life and knowledge) plus a *logos* of such a kind (i.e. the intelligible forming principle which accounts for the features of bodies) (6.7.5.2–3). Here Plotinus' allusion to *De An.* 2.1 is evident: he uses *toiōide* to refer to the *logos*, whereas Aristotle applies this expression to the body endowed with organs (*De An.* 2.1.412a16-28: the soul is the entelechy of a body 'of a certain sort', *toionde*: 412a16; *toiouto*: 412a21).[45] Indeed, Plotinus incorporates the Peripatetic idea that human beings are composite and that the soul alone does not suffice to account for their nature. Yet what must be added to the soul is not a certain body, but a certain intelligible forming principle which accounts for the features of that body, i.e. the *logos*, which is, in its turn, an activity of the soul (6.7.5.3-4): accordingly, the corporeal human being is nothing else than an image of a completely formal compound (see 6.7.5.14-15).[46] In so doing, Plotinus transfers, so to speak, Aristotle's hylomorphic account into a different framework of thought, according to which even the nature of human beings here below is completely constituted at the intelligible level (where 'intelligible' should be taken to mean not merely the world of forms, but the different degrees or levels that constitute Plotinus' intelligible realm).

5. Classifications of Bodies

The internal tensions within Plotinus' account of sensible beings further emerge if we compare the passages focusing on the trace of the soul in living bodies with some sections from the third treatise *On the Genera of Being*. These are probably the clearest examples of Plotinus' tendency to put all bodies on the same level, insofar as they are different from genuine beings. In 6.3.8-10, Plotinus argues that no criterion is sufficient to separate essential vs extrinsic attributes in bodies: for sensible substances cannot exist without their perceptible attributes (e.g. size, shape, colour, dryness, moistness); so it is actually impossible to distinguish between accidental and essential attributes. A sensible substance is, as such, a qualified substance (6.3.8.12-16). If we look for something in bodies which can act as a subject for what belongs to it, something like a nucleus for supervening qualities, then we are forced to situate this nucleus in quality-less matter:

---

[45] Note that elsewhere Plotinus is perfectly happy to adopt Aristotle's view and that the body 'of a certain sort' can be identified with the body animated by the quasi-psychic trace of the soul (see 4.4.18.9; cf. 3.6.1.3; 4.4.20.21-6). See Noble (2013b: 273). As explained in this chapter, I take these passages to reveal an internal tension in Plotinus' account of living bodies. See above, n. 1.

[46] In 6.7.5.9-31, Plotinus investigates which level of the soul is involved in the constitution of human beings through *logoi*. The hierarchy includes three divisions or levels of the soul (as far as these expressions are appropriate for Plotinus' soul: see above, n. 38): the nutritive soul (5.10), a higher soul that 'makes a living being' (5.10) by entering into matter and shaping the body (5.14), and finally a 'more divine' (5.21) soul. This is broadly consistent with what Plotinus says elsewhere, where he ascribes the task of forming bodies to a low kind of soul that depends on the world soul. Note, however, that Plotinus usually credits the vegetative soul with making and forming the body by using the *logoi* within itself (for details and discussion, see Wilberding 2006: 178-9), whereas in 6.7.5 he apparently regards the sensitive soul as the formative one. Such inconsistencies are not surprising given Plotinus' characteristically fluid and gradualist account of levels in the soul: see above, n. 38.

T8 But is there something around which occur what make being simply substance into being qualified substance? And will fire be not as a whole substance, but something belonging to it, like a part? And what could this be? Just matter. But then, is sensible substance a conglomeration of qualities and matter...?

6.3.8.16–20

The so-called sensible substance (cf. 6.3.8.26–7), therefore, is a mere conglomeration (*sumphorēsis*) of qualities and matter so that no hierarchy separates essential attributes from those belonging to an already determined corporeal substance.[47] In stating as much, Plotinus is actually suggesting that each body can be regarded as an instance of each of its attributes (so, for example, a particular cat is a white, four-footed, green-eyed being, etc.) and that its identity, insofar as it is a sensible body, is simply determined by the sum of the sensible attributes supervening on matter with no internal hierarchy between them (cf. 6.3.15.24–38): the status of kinds in the world of bodies becomes problematic to say the least. The reason for this is that the so-called sensible substance is actually no substance at all: it is a mere image of substance (for substance as such is intelligible substance) (see 6.3.8.32).

In 6.3.9, Plotinus considers several possible classifications or divisions of bodies which are mostly based on Aristotle's natural works;[48] so he distinguishes the four elements from living bodies (plants and animals) (6.3.9.4–6); bodies are classified according to their habitat (species of earth; species of other elements) (6.3.9.6–10); then, according to whether they are light or heavy, and their position in the cosmos (6.3.9.10–15); mixtures are classified according to the predominant element (6.3.9.15–18). After these classifications, Plotinus introduces the distinction between primary and secondary substances, drawn from Aristotle's *Categories* (*Cat.* 5.2a23–4), which he discusses in detail (6.3.9.18–42).[49] These divisions are further developed in 6.3.10: so bodies are classified according to their elemental properties (hot, cold, moist, dry) (6.3.10.1–3); and animals are classified according to their bodily parts and their shapes (6.3.10.5–7). The hypothesis that through these divisions Plotinus is aiming to endorse Aristotle's natural classifications seems somewhat unlikely.[50] Plotinus actually appears to be juxtaposing different classifications without ascribing any genuine foundation to them. So, as Gerson (1994: 92) remarks, those in chapters 6.3.9–10 seems to be merely pragmatic classifications. By juxtaposing them, Plotinus actually suggests that every classification of bodies is necessarily based on perceptible attributes and is therefore conventional to some extent (for example, one could regard this or that cat as a quadruped and a mammal, but also as a white and furry being). The reason is that

---

[47] As Kalligas (2011: 764) remarks, the force of this term 'is to emphasize a haphazard "heaping together" of the qualities involved, without presupposing any order or arrangement'.
[48] See De Haas (2001: 516–17). [49] See Chiaradonna (2004).
[50] *Contra* De Haas (2001: 516): 'in VI.3.9–10 Plotinus ratifies divisions of sensible reality which Aristotle actually employed in his physical works'.

T9   this sensible substance is not simply being, but is perceived by sense, being this whole [perceived by the senses]; since we maintained that its apparent existence was a congress of perceptibles [*sunodon tōn pros aisthēsin*], and the guarantee of their being comes from sense-perception.
6.3.10.14–17; cf. 5.5.1.1.12–19

Plotinus actually regards all classifications according to sensible attributes as plausible hypotheses, for at that level 'the composition has no limits' (6.3.10.17). Plotinus' focus certainly changes in 6.3 compared to other treatises. At the beginning of 6.3 Plotinus explains that he will consider bodies in themselves and will therefore leave out the soul, which belongs to intelligible being and is present to bodies while pertaining to a different domain: it is as if someone wishing to classify the citizens of a city (e.g. by their property, assessments, or skills) were leaving resident foreigners out of his account (6.3.1.28–38). This peculiar point of view may partly explain why the approach in 6.3 is so different from that in 4.4, where the soul-trace theory comes to the forefront. But the different focus does not explain everything, for Plotinus' background assumption in 6.3 is that the soul is present to bodies but bodies do not retain anything of the soul that is present to them: according to what Plotinus says in 4.4, this is what happens with illuminated air and not with heated air. Heated air, however, is Plotinus' favourite analogy to explain the soul-trace doctrine and this analogy certainly suggests that the body retains something of the soul, a view which seems to be at odds with what Plotinus argues in 6.3.[51] In sum: Plotinus' approach in 6.3 seems hardly compatible with what he states elsewhere, i.e. that bodies have quasi-psychic attributes that are intermediate between the sensible form and the soul.[52]

Bibliography

Armstrong, A.H. (1966–88), *Plotinus*, with an English trans., 7 vols, Cambridge, MA, and London.

Caluori, D. (2015), *Plotinus on the Soul*, Cambridge.

---

[51] Caluori (2015: 186–92) suggests that 'while the soul is present to the body as light is to air, life is present to the body as heat is to air'. *Contra* Noble, Caluori regards the trace of the soul as being not a soul-like embodied form, but the life of the body: life is therefore not only present to the body, but it is located within it. The trace of the soul is, accordingly, the life of the qualified body and its source is the soul. While I agree that some sections of 4.4 may suggest conclusions of this sort, it seems to me that Plotinus is generally very cautious (or rather sceptical) about the possibility of regarding life as an attribute of the body. Furthermore, I am not fully convinced by Caluori's suggestion that the status of soul *vis-à-vis* bodies is different from the status of life.

[52] I would like to thank David Charles, for his invaluable comments and suggestions. The research for this chapter has been carried out within the PRIN project 2017 'New Challenges for Applied Ethics'.

Caston, V. (1997), 'Epiphenomenalisms, Ancient and Modern', *The Philosophical Review* 106: 309–63.

Caston, V. (2012), *Alexander of Aphrodisias:* On the Soul. *Part I: Soul as Form of the Body, Parts of the Soul, Nourishment, and Perception*, trans. with an intro. and comm., London.

Caston, V. (2020), 'Aristote et l'unité de la psychologie. Comment diviser l'âme?', in F. Graziani and P. Pellegrin (eds.), *L'Héritage d'Aristote aujourd'hui. Science, nature et société*, Alessandria, 199–229.

Charles, D. (2000), *Aristotle on Meaning and Essence*, Oxford.

Charles, D. (2021), *The Undivided Self: Aristotle and the 'Mind–Body Problem'*, Oxford.

Chiaradonna, R. (2004), 'Plotino e la teoria degli universali. *Enn.* VI 3 [44], 9', in C. D'Ancona and V. Celluprica (eds.), *Aristotele e i suoi esegeti neoplatonici. Logica e ontologia nelle interpretazioni greche e arabe*, Naples, 1–35.

Chiaradonna, R. (2014a), 'Plotinus' Metaphorical Reading of the *Timaeus*: Soul, Mathematics, Providence', in P. d'Hoine and G. Van Riel (eds.), *Fate, Providence and Moral Responsibility in Ancient, Medieval and Early Modern Thought: Studies in Honour of Carlos Steel*, Leuven, 187–210.

Chiaradonna, R. (2014b), 'Plotinus on Sensible Particulars and Individual Essences', in A. Torrance and J. Zachhuber (eds.), *Individuality in Late Antiquity*, Farnham and Burlington, 47–61.

Chiaradonna, R. (2016), 'Are There Qualities in Intelligible Being? On Plotinus VI.2 [43] 14', *Documenti e studi sulla tradizione filosofica medievale* 27: 43–63.

Chiaradonna, R. (2021), 'Ethics and the Hierarchy of Virtues from Plotinus to Iamblichus', in A. Marmodoro and S. Xenofontos (eds.), *The Reception of Greek Ethics in Late Antiquity and Byzantium*, Cambridge, 36–51.

D'Ancona, C. (2017), *Plotino. L'immortalita dell'anima. IV 7[2]. Plotiniana Arabica* (*pseudo*-Teologia di Aristotele, *capitoli I, III, IX*), intro., testo greco, traduzione e commento, testo arabo, traduzione e commento, Pisa.

De Haas, F.A.J. (2001), 'Did Plotinus and Porphyry Disagree on Aristotle's *Categories*?', *Phronesis* 46: 492–526.

Ellis, J. (1994), 'Alexander's Defense of Aristotle's *Categories*', *Phronesis* 39: 69–89.

Emilsson, E.K. (1988), *Plotinus on Sense-Perception: A Philosophical Study*, Cambridge.

Emilsson, E.K. (2007), *Plotinus on Intellect*, Oxford.

Emilsson, E.K. (2017), *Plotinus*, London and New York.

Fronterotta, F. (2007), *Plotin. Traité 38 (VI, 7)*, in L. Brisson and J.-F. Pradeau (eds.), *Plotin. Traités 38–41*, Paris, 15–171.

Galluzzo, G. (2018), 'Are Matter and Form Parts? Aristotle's and Neo-Aristotelian Hylomorphism', *Discipline Filosofiche* 28: 65–87.

Gerson, L.P. (1994), *Plotinus*, London and New York.

Gerson, L.P. et al. (2018), *Plotinus:* The Enneads, Cambridge.

Griffin, M. J. (2022), 'Plotinus on Categories', in L.P. Gerson and J. Wilberding (eds.), *The New Cambridge Companion to Plotinus*, Cambridge, 163–92.

Hadot, P. (1988), *Plotin. Traité 38*, intro., traduction, commentaire et notes, Paris.

Henry, P. and Schwyzer, H.-R. (eds.) (1964–82), *Plotini opera*, 3 vols, Oxford.

Horn, Ch. (2012), 'Aspects of Biology in Plotinus', in Ch. Horn and J. Wilberding (eds.), *Neoplatonism and the Philosophy of Nature*, Oxford, 214–28.

Kalligas, P. (2011), 'The Structure of Appearances: Plotinus on the Constitution of Sensible Objects', *Philosophical Quarterly* 61: 762–82.

Kalligas, P. (2012), '*Eiskrisis*, or the Presence of Soul in the Body: A Plotinian Conundrum', *Ancient Philosophy* 32: 147–66.

Kalligas, P. (2014), *The* Enneads *of Plotinus: A Commentary*, vol. 1, Princeton.

Karfik, F. (2014), 'Parts of the Soul in Plotinus', in K. Corcilius and D. Perler (eds.), *Partitioning the Soul: Debates From Plato to Leibniz*, Berlin, 107–48.

Lloyd, A.C. (1990), *The Anatomy of Neoplatonism*, Oxford.

Menn, S. (1998), *Descartes and Augustine*, Cambridge.

Michalewski, A. (2020), 'The Causality of the Self-Moving Soul. Platonic Responses to the Objections of *De Anima* I, 3', in S. Delcomminette et al. (eds.), *The Reception of Plato's* Phaedrus *from Antiquity to the Renaissance*, Berlin and Boston, 41–60.

Noble, Ch. (2013a), 'Plotinus' Unaffectable Matter', *Oxford Studies in Ancient Philosophy* 44: 233–77.

Noble, Ch. (2013b), 'How Plotinus' Soul Animates his Body: The Argument for the Soul-Trace at *Ennead* 4.4.18.1–9', *Phronesis* 58: 249–79.

Noble, Ch. and Powers, N. (2015), 'Creation and Divine Providence in Plotinus', in A. Marmodoro and B. Prince (eds.), *Causation and Creation in Late Antiquity*, Cambridge, 51–70.

Peramatzis, M. (2008), 'Aristotle's Notion of Priority in Nature and Substance', *Oxford Studies in Ancient Philosophy* 35: 187–247.

Rashed, M. (2013), 'Boethus' Aristotelian Ontology', in M. Schofield (ed.), *Aristotle, Plato and Pythagoreanism in the First Century BC: New Directions in Philosophy*, Cambridge, 53–77.

Schiaparelli, A. (2010), 'Essence and Cause in Plotinus' *Ennead* VI.7 [38] 2: An Outline of Some Problems', in D. Charles (ed.), *Definition in Ancient Philosophy*, Oxford, 467–92.

Strange, S.K. (1989), 'Plotinus on the Articulation of Being', *The Society for Ancient Greek Philosophy Newsletter* 155. https://orb.binghamton.edu/sagp/155

Taormina, D. (2020), 'Il corpo, la luce e l'insieme dei due. Una proposta esegetica di Plotino, enn. I 1 [53], 6, 14–7, 6', in Ch. Horn et al. (eds.), *Körperlichkeit in der Philosophie der Spätantike/Corporeità nella filosofia tardoantica*, Baden-Baden, 17–42.

Thaler, N. (2011), 'Traces of Good in Plotinus's Philosophy of Nature: *Ennead* VI.7.1–14', *Journal of the History of Philosophy* 49: 161–80.

Tornau, Ch. (1998a), *Plotin. Enneaden VI 4–5 [22–23]. Ein Kommentar*, Stuttgart and Leipzig.

Tornau, Ch. (1998b), 'Wissenschaft, Seele, Geist. Zur Bedeutung einer Analogie bei Plotinus (*Enn.* IV 9, 5 und VI 2, 20)', *Göttinger Forum für Altertumswissenschaft* 1: 87–111.

Tornau, Ch. (2005), 'Plotinus' Criticism of Aristotelian Entelechism in *Enn.* IV 7 [2], 8^5.25–50', in R. Chiaradonna (ed.), *Studi sull'anima in Plotino*, Naples, 149–79.

Tornau, Ch. (2016), 'Seelenspur und Aufnahmefähigkeit: ein plotinischer Zirkel?', in T. Dangel et al. (eds.), *Seele Und Materie im Neuplatonismus / Soul and Matter in Neoplatonism*, Heidelberg, 135–60.

Wilberding, J. (2006), *Plotinus' Cosmology: A Study of Ennead II.1 (40)*, text, trans., and comm., Oxford.

Wildberg, Ch. (2009), 'A World of Thoughts: Plotinus on Nature and Contemplation (*Enn.* III.8 [30] 1–6)', in R. Chiaradonna and F. Trabattoni (eds.), *Physics and Philosophy of Nature in Greek Neoplatonism*, Leiden, 121–44.

9
Strengths of Embodiment in Neoplatonism

Pauliina Remes

There are good reasons to think that the Neoplatonists' relation to the hylomorphic tradition is one of offering a radically different, competing view. Not only did they consider the individual souls immortal and thus capable of existence without a body,[1] there are many general considerations that enforce such a view on them. First, their general vertical metaphysical order of causation systematically highlights the role of higher principles in the origination and constitution of beings and phenomena on the lower level, and the connected asymmetrical priority and dependence relations.[2] As regards the soul, Plotinus argues, by appealing to Aristotle's actuality-potentiality distinction, that since actuality is prior to potentiality, if the body is such as to become potentially ensouled, this power of ensoulment itself must be prior—and independent—and thus 'somewhere' as actuality (e.g. *Enn.* IV.7.8³.3.11–17). The same framework is most likely also at work when Plotinus goes explicitly against the view of Alexander of Aphrodisias and argues that the lower, embodied soul powers are dependent upon the higher, rather than vice versa (*Enn.* IV.3.23.29–35; Alexander of Aphrodisias, *On the Soul* 28, 22–6). Second, Platonists do not usually give the composite of soul and body a status as a proper substance—nor to matter, which they considered as lacking, without form or any definable nature. Only the soul properly qualifies as a substance. Third, as Riccardo Chiaradonna explains in Chapter 8 in this volume, Plotinus argues that for a form to fulfil its function as both the essence and the cause of the sensible item, it must be not a part of it, but separate and intelligible. Fourth, from Plotinus onwards, the specific idea that the soul, as a power, is 'impassive' to any affections from the body presents a central

---

[1] Although it might be that disembodied souls need some kind of bodies, spherical vehicles: IV.4.5.11–22.
[2] Plotinus operates with a Platonic notion of non-reciprocal priority by nature, according to which the prior is more general and exists independently of the posterior, and has a constitutive relationship to it, and the posterior owes in some way its existence to the non-composite prior. He recognizes the Aristotelian notion of 'prior—because more knowable—to us', and this priority concerns the particular. His notion of simple or natural priority, however, is a central vehicle for the so-called 'emanation': the posterior is contained potentially in the prior, and the prior always more simple or unified than the posterior. See e.g. III.8.9.1–10; VI.3.9.37–42; see O'Meara (1996).

dogma agreed by most Neoplatonic thinkers.[3] Plotinus even objects to the formulation that soul would be 'in the body'. As a form, the soul cannot be conceived as being in place, or understood through any material terms, and if anything is 'in' anything, it would be better to say that the body is in the soul.[4] Fifth, to find a more accurate metaphor for the soul-body relationship, the Neoplatonists turn to *Alcibiades* I and its idea that the soul uses the body as an instrument (*Alc.* I 129e). Given that instruments are separate from their user, something that the user can use, leave unused, and even dispose of at will, this metaphor seems to capture a radically non-hylomorphic picture of the relationship.[5]

Yet the Neoplatonists were in no way denying many bottom-up relations where it seems that something of the bodily affects reaches the soul. As regards embodied functions, Neoplatonic explanations of them do make references to the bodies in which they are actualized. Perceptions, for Plotinus, happen in the body—a disembodied soul does not perceive anything (IV.5.1). And as in *Timaeus*, these affections are both positive and negative: on the one hand perceptions do form an undeniable part in concept acquisition and at least early phases of inquiry towards knowledge; on the other, through the body alien forces have access to the composite.[6] They then face a challenge: while metaphysical priority and independence of the soul is crucial for them, it is equally true that embodiment has an effect on the activities of the soul in the body. Perhaps somewhat paradoxically, especially the main obstacles for both knowledge acquisition and moral development must be explained, and explained with the reference to the body, and not to the intelligible, perfect principles. The soul-body relationship, then, cannot be so weakly construed that it would cease to explain these universal human features.[7]

The main challenge for thinking that the Neoplatonists must provide, within the topic of the soul-body relationship, a discussion entirely unlike anything in the

---

[3] *Enn.* I 1.3.21–6; I.1.4.13–18. One of the most helpful quotes is perhaps the following: 'But it is not proper to any form to be disturbed or in any way affected, but it remains static itself, and its matter enters into the state of being affected, when it does so enter, and the form stirs up the affection by its presence. For, of course, the growth-principle does not grow when it causes growth, nor increase when it causes increase...'. *Enn.* III.6.4.35–9.

[4] E.g. V.5.9.27–34. For an analysis of this, see e.g. Caluori (2015: 180–5).

[5] One might also add that this begins to sound as if the soul in question had more of a thing-type nature. It is not a capacity to act, but, rather, a thing external to the body, capable of using it. A simple thing ontology is made problematic, however, by Plotinus' commitment to the idea that the soul, just like the intelligibles, are actualities, fully actualized powers. Powers, then, divide into actual powers and potentialities. II.5.1.21–34. For Plotinus on act and powers, see Emilsson (2009).

[6] This ambivalence to which Plotinus himself often lapses he explicitly argues is an inconsistency in the way that Plato evaluates the role of the body. IV.8.1.23–50.

[7] The vertical explanatory model also means that it becomes harder, and sometimes pointless, to differentiate between definitional and metaphysical or causal dependency. What is possible is to locate the role of different principles on different levels of the metaphysical hierarchy—say, for example, to explain unity One has to be referred to, whereas the explanation of time will involve Soul. Typically, however, explanations and definitions have to refer to the higher principles that are, at the same time, the efficient causes of the existence of the things to be explained. And as paradigms, these also act as teleological causes. For the developments that Plotinus makes to Platonic causality, see Emilsson (2017: 48–57).

Aristotelian side, lies in the end in the idea of the asymmetry between the soul and the body. Rather than being two definitionally distinct entities *à la* Descartes, there is a commitment to the view that soul and body are essentially related, yet not interdependent. A strong form of hylomorphism according to which the definition of the soul and the body would mutually require one another must be anathema for the Neoplatonists, since the soul can and should be defined and grasped without reference to anything material. Even worse, body can*not* be exhaustively defined without reference to the soul, because the soul is a link in the generation, the coming to be, of the body. All formation, definable nature and movement in the cosmos ultimately derives from intelligible principles, and can, from one perspective, be seen as thoughts or intellections actualized in matter and time.[8] In this process, the soul acts as one link, providing further differentiations in the unfolding of being. One could claim, then, that the soul-body relationship collapses to a soul-soul relationship, where we can at best differentiate between levels of soul and their role in living and cognitive functions.[9]

Rather than denying this fact of Neoplatonic metaphysics, I propose that we look at passages where Plotinus discusses the soul-body relationship at face value, as it were, and thereby see how he conceives of that relationship. The question of the origin of the body is different from that of the relationship between the soul and the body, and we can bracket, for some time, the former when studying the latter. The two issues can then be brought together again after studying each separately, to see whether claims about the origin are being brought to bear in the explanations of the relationship. Looked at this way, there are interesting Aristotelian vestiges in the theories, and the Platonic influences already contain a view of the soul-body relationship that involves proper reference to both parties. Focal framework is a combination of the fully and essentially ensouled cosmos of the *Timaeus*, the understanding of the human being as a composite of soul and body in *Alcibiades*, and Aristotelian notions about the relevance of bodily organs and alterations.

There is space here for three relevant discussions. First, I wish to make some remarks on the notion of 'separation' central for the Platonic project of keeping intelligible causes separate from what goes on at the lower levels of existence. As we shall see, sometimes separation is for Plotinus normative or conceptual rather than actual. World Soul, for example, turns out in some sense essentially embodied, and only separate from its body in thought. My second section concerns another notion that would seem to highlight the Platonic commitments at the expense of any possible Aristotelian influences, namely the Neoplatonic

---

[8] For Plotinus as the first relatively radical idealist, see e.g. III.8.8.17–21 and Wildberg (2009).
But it should be noted that this thinking is non-personal, cosmic or universal, and thus over and above human thinking, and thus what it produces is something real or existing. Thus the picture cannot be likened to any early modern forms of idealism.
[9] This line is pursued, very persuasively, by Chiaradonna in Chapter 8 of this volume.

rendering of the 'use of the body' phrasing, utilized to preserve Platonic insights about the soul-body relationship. Yet it turns out that this metaphor sometimes captures a normative rather than descriptive separation, and when it is used for the latter, it is seen as wanting. Here I also complement the discussion of Plotinus with that of Olympiodorus, both of whom make explicit certain ideas and have a slightly diverging variant to offer. The third discussion will take us to the level of the organic body and to the issue of what happens at that level when a person perceives. While Plotinus is not concerned to argue that each token mental—or spiritual—activity involves and informs an essentially related change in the body, he seems to think that explanations of those cognitive functions that do happen in the body typically involve the explication of something on the level of the organic body.

Let me postulate a rough working classification that will hopefully help in thinking about what kind of strength of the body-soul relationship Plotinus is committed to:

Weak embodiment: body is a tool that implements practical solutions arrived at by reason, which is in its essence disembodied.

Moderate embodiment: body has a causal or functional role. Embodied activities structure perceptions and shape our understanding. Practical solutions are essentially embodied, and not merely executions of abstract decisions made by a disembodied rational ability.

Strong embodiment: embodiment constitutes the understanding of the soul; it shapes the cognitive nature of mind.[10]

I will suggest that simply locating Plotinus in the first category, as often seems to be done, is problematic, and that there are reasons to place him—and perhaps even more clearly Olympiodorus—in the second category.

1. Separation and Embodiment

Often, Plotinus' use of 'separable' (*chôristos*) of the soul captures the way that especially the higher, rational, and individual soul exists separate from the body

---

[10] This division is used in contemporary discussion on enactive agency: Clark (2008: esp. 43, 203); Lo Presti (2015: 34–5). I have chosen it for a specific purpose: the guiding idea here is to what extent activities at a lower level cause changes at a higher level, from one extreme of there being no or virtually no bottom-up significance to the other extreme whereby activities at a lower level constitute cognitive abilities at a higher level.

(e.g. III.5.3.22). Sometimes this separation is even translated as 'transcendent'.[11] One solution to the dilemma of how the soul can be both separate and present in the body is to use the 'hypostatic' levels of reality for disentangling functions and features that are apparently mutually exhaustive. Plotinus, as we see elsewhere in this volume, has sophisticated ways of differentiating the soul active in the body (for example the so-called 'trace of the soul') from the impassive aspects of the soul operating at higher levels of the metaphysical hierarchy.[12] Crucially, in some manner the activity and goal-directedness involved cannot be located in bodies devoid of life: they are ensouled, animated by the soul. Through some model, as Plotinus recognizes, perceptions as well as all psychic activities that depend upon perception (appetite, pain, pleasure, discursive reason) must nonetheless be such that they convey some contents acquired in the body, dependent either on the body or on the sense affections acquired in the body, and in the sensible world (I.1.3; discussed below).[13]

But not every usage of the verb *chorizein* and its forms has this meaning. When discussing the World Soul, Plotinus makes the following, rather startling, statement:

T1 There never was a time, in fact, when the universe was not ensouled, nor when body existed in the absence of soul, nor was there a time when matter existed and was not ordered; but it is possible to conceptualize these things theoretically in separation from each other [*epinoêsai tauta chôrizontas auta ap' allêlôn*]. For it is possible to unpack any composite in theory, that is, in an act of discursive thinking [*exesti gar analuein tô logô kai tê dianoia pasan sunthesin*]. The truth is like this: if there were no body, soul would not proceed forth, since there is no other place where it is its nature to be; but if it is going to proceed, it will produce a place, might compare the situation to an intense light which sheds its illumination to the furthest limits of the fire, and that beyond there arises darkness; this the soul sees, and since the darkness is there as a substrate, gives it form. For it is not right for whatever borders on soul to be without a share in an expressed principle, if [cosmos] has, in a way, come to be like a beautiful and variegated house, which has not been cut off from its creator.

IV.3.9.16–30[14]

---

[11] E.g. *Lexicon Plotinianum* suggests this meaning, pp. 1118–20. The verb appears in many different contexts, for example when Plotinus argues that the soul is capable of abstract thinking that does not happen essentially in the body. It separates itself from the geometrical notions of a line, circle, point, and triangle, and does not need the body to make this *chorismos* (differentiation) (IV.7.8.18–24).

[12] Some scholars think that such a trace that informs the formations of the body of the living being is very close to Aristotelian enmattered forms (Noble 2013; Caluori 2015: 186–92).

[13] This is sometimes denied through appealing to the idea that recollection actually explains all the contents of thoughts. For a rebuttal of this idea, see Emilsson (2021).

[14] Translations of *Enneads* are from Gerson (2018) (in places, slightly modified).

There is no period of time in which the body of the universe would have existed without ensoulment, nor does matter, in turn, really exist separately from the soul ordering it. But note that as soon as we look at the World Soul as it is, as the soul of the Universe rather than something immersed in the hypostasis Soul (I take to be the force of the 'proceeding' or 'going forth' (*proserchesthai*); see also IV.7.2.24), it must come to be together with the body it ensouls, for this is its natural 'place'.[15] Besides Plotinus' surprisingly positive rhetoric of the body, this claim is all the more interesting given that Plotinus elsewhere uses for the World Soul the same strategies as for the soul in general: a higher part or an aspect of the World Soul, too, remains undescended, and commands the cosmos without being immersed in it (e.g. IV.8.2.22–7). Nonetheless, it seems to be the case that the World Soul is considered, in some sense, essentially embodied. It would not have come to be what it is without having had a body to realize it. The passage is not detailed enough to determine whether or not the World Soul could be defined without any reference to its body. Certainly, any normal human attempt at explicating it will have to refer to its functions or powers, and it is hard to see how this would happen without any reference to its role in the formation and command of the organically structured cosmos. Whether such a command makes any sense without any reference to what it commands is a difficult matter. Certainly, at the level of infallible knowledge, the Intellect's pure thinking, these kinds of conceptual-discursive distinctions are superfluous.

Inside the argument on the tightness of the relationship, we are introduced to a distinct way of looking at separation that may help in disentangling this issue. In this passage, Plotinus argues that the separation of the two components is conceptual or theoretical—in thought. Cosmos is a composite, or a collection (*synthesis*), the unpacking (*analysis*) of which into soul and body happens for theoretical reasons, namely to understand the role of the parts that make up the composite. The terminology here refers to Platonic dialectic that proceeds by discerning essences and primary kinds, and 'weaving together what comes out of these until it has gone through the whole of the intelligible; and then, through analyzing them back again, it comes back to the starting-point' (I.3.4.14–16). The distinctions revealed by dialectic are not conceptual in the sense that the human mind would originate any random conceptual differentiation for some purpose—they ultimately aim at revealing the true order of the intelligible. Ideally, the human ability to grasp general features will 'cut nature at the joints' (as in *Phaedrus* 265e). Nonetheless, Plotinus wants to convey that this is different from the separation of, say, a rational soul capable of existing without a body, and being in many ways unaffected by it: there never was and never will be a time when the World Soul would actually exist without its body. It also seems that this

---

[15] Elsewhere he talks about the natural fellowship with the body (IV.8.2.4).

co-existence is not random: the function of the World Soul is to structure and animate the body of the cosmos. The actualization of its proper functions, then, in a manner, necessitate the co-existence with the body, unlike the theoretical reasoning of the Intellect that does not necessarily refer to the body. The separation 'in thought' captures a metaphysically relevant distinction, but in this case as a pair of concepts that are mutually related in actuality.

The impact of this should not be overstated. Importantly, the body is still considered to be something that the unfolding of intelligible organization produces for itself, rather than as a truly independent substance (e.g. IV.7.2.20–6; 3.16–18; 13.8). The passage also leaves out hypostasis Soul and Intellect, as well as the purely theoretical or Intellectual human soul (*nous*). But I do take it that what he says can also apply, *mutatis mutandis*, to the embodied, lower soul, the part that comes to be in the body (*en ekeinô gignomenê, en hô estin*; IV.7.13.12). Some of the sources suggest that the living and vegetative functions of the human body would actually be given to it by the World Soul rather than an individual soul (II.1.5.18–24; IV.9.3.23–8), and would accordingly be explained as tightly embodied. Some of the sources do not support this picture, and it is possible that even the lower, embodied functions are due to an individual ensoulment.[16] When looking at the soul as a principle of living functions taking place in the body, such a soul always comes to be, for some period of time, together with the body in which these functions can be realized.[17] It is this question, the question of what the living thing is, that preoccupies Plotinus in I.1. As we will soon see, while he is adamant in separating, here and elsewhere, the acts of soul from the soul itself, it is equally clear that the explanation of the living thing and its functions will involve notions that the soul itself does not—the organic body.

In another context, Plotinus formulates a separation 'by philosophy':

T2   For so long as what uses the instrument is one thing and the instrument it uses is something else, each is separate. At least, anyone who posits the soul as using the body separates them. But prior to their separation by the practice of philosophy [*pro tou chorisai dia philosophias*], how were they disposed?
Enn. I 1.3.15–18

This notion of separation could be the same as the theoretical one above. In philosophizing, we use dialectic to sort out components of compounds that in appearance and at first sight look to be simple unities. By employing a distinction between the user and what it uses, the philosopher separates the two by making a

---

[16] This is discussed in detail by Emilsson (2017: 230–41); see also Wilberding (2008).
[17] See also Rich (1961: 1–2). Whether this is the lower soul or, rather, the trace of the soul, we may here leave aside.

conceptual choice aiming at grasping the essential features of their relationship, the causal direction. The text, however, seems to add to the conceptual separation a new element, a normative notion of separation. The idea that there was a time when the soul was not separated by philosophy and a time after this separation conveys Plotinus' theory of ethical self-ennobling: philosophizing aims not only to understand intelligible principles, but towards a self-realization of the self as an intellectual or rational, unaffected soul rather than as a soul-body composite. This normative call to separate oneself from the body does not mean that the body ceases to exist or to send its impulses to the soul. Rather, the aim is a therapeutic separation from the messy existence of living and a recognition of oneself as that which is invulnerable, and most intimately 'us' (I.2.5.3–15, with ll. 4–5; *to chôrisein apo sômatos epi poson dunaton*). Even though a part of the soul (the highest part) is metaphysically separate from the body (and this fact is the necessary foundation for their normative separation), as long as the soul is embodied, other parts are in complex relationship with the body and thus bodily affected. The ethical separation—one that can never be complete (but *kata to dunaton*; I.2.7.24)—happens through recognizing these as belonging to the composite rather than the true self, and through minimizing vulnerability to them.

'Separation' in Plotinus, then, can denote something real and actual, something dialectical-conceptual, or something conceptual-normative, and these meanings will yield varying levels of dependence/independence from the body. And immediately, the threefold distinction raises questions about the relationship between these different types of separation. If dialectical-conceptual separation reveals something essential about ontological structures, does it differ from the purely metaphysical or real variant only by an (epistemic) point of view? And if some part of the soul is already undescended and free from the evils of the body, why is the normative separation needed at all? The first question is trickier and would actually necessitate a full-scale study of the notion of separation in Plotinus. Preliminarily, it seems that if we look at the example of the World Soul again, the separation in the passage is needed for explanatory purposes: to understand the World Soul, the conceptual distinction between the soul and the body (and matter) is needed. The explanation that utilizes these terms captures something about the metaphysical ordering of reality, but in the case of the World Soul the separation is merely conceptual, in the sense that these aspects do not—and could not—come apart in its existence. And most likely this co-existence is not because of a random organization but because the two functionally necessitate one another. The World Soul comes out as essentially embodied and distinct in thought and explanation from its body. As a 'big sister' of the particular *embodied* human souls, the description is also revelatory of the part of the soul that comes to be present in the body.

The second question is something that Plotinus is at least partially aware of when, in discussing emotions, he asks why one ought to make the soul free from affections through philosophy if the soul does not suffer from affections in the first place (III.6.5.1–2). The answer lies in the details of becoming free from affections. The soul, rightly enough, does not in itself undergo any *pathos*, but it is involved in the affection because reason's 'seeing' of, say, an expected evil, or a perceptual judgement that there is something present and the rational assessment that this present thing is likely to cause something bad, are needed for the emotion to arise, and is one of the soul's functions.[18] The embodied soul, then, continuously receives sense affections and potential emotional disturbances, and is, unlike the soul itself or its pure intellectual-theoretical ability, involved in turning them into conscious desires and opinions. Normative separation is a call to stop giving external impulses a role as the main cause for forming opinions, making decisions, and for acting. This separation is made possible by the rational-intellectual soul's independent ability to originate opinions and evaluations freely from the body, and it aims at mirroring the rational soul's nature as independent of the body. But it involves a different notion of separation, given that for many, if not all of us, it remains an unrealizable ideal as long as we are embodied.

2. Using the Body Instrument

One of the ways in which Platonists consciously distance themselves from the Aristotelian discussions is the way they liken the body to an instrument of the soul, rather than to a proper part, and the relationship between the two is seen as one of asymmetrical 'use'. The origin of the term 'using an instrument' lies, famously, in *Alcibiades* I. Through the examples that come from human usage of tools, shoes, and garments, Plato[19] establishes a semi-technical meaning for the term of 'use', applying it to the relationship between soul and body:

T3 Socrates: But the user and the thing he uses are different, are they not?
    Alcibiades: How do you mean? ...
    Socrates: And we said that the user and what he uses are different?
    Alcibiades: Yes.
    Socrates: So human being is different from his own body?
    Alcibiades: It seems so.
    Socrates: Then whatever is a human being?
    Alcibiades: I cannot say.

---

[18] III.6.5.2–13; see Emilsson (2017: 262).
[19] Whether the dialogue is authentic or spurious makes no difference for my purposes here, but I am less convinced of its being spurious than some other scholars.

Socrates: Oh, but you can—that he is the user of the body.
Alcibiades: Yes.

Alc. I 129e

The analogy of ordinary tools and their users offers an illustration of how the soul can be independent from and unaffected by the body, much as the person is from her shoes. In using this terminology the author establishes how soul and body are really distinct, adding arguments about proper self-care with the intention of showing that its proper object is the soul, 'the thing itself' (128d).

Again, the picture turns out to be in many ways more sophisticated. First, the body is elevated to a position of a particular tool, one more immediate to the soul than other instruments, which are instruments, strictly speaking, of the ensouled body, not the soul itself (129e–130d). Second, the notion of use involves not merely a causal idea, but the idea of intentionality: instruments are used for a certain purpose. Plato's interest, then, is not only in showing the causal inefficacy of the body when considered stripped from the soul, without a principle of motion and life, but in tracking the part of the human being capable of setting aims for herself.[20] Moreover, interestingly, the passage above has given a working definition of a human being: the user of a body. So while soul and body can be defined without essential reference to one another, it seems that to define what *a human being* is, the body must be part of that definition, as that which the human being uses.

Plotinus' position as regards who we, as ourselves, essentially are is also ambivalently between the pure user and the composite in which the soul uses the body. In one sense, the rational soul, or the pure intellect, is our true self: it is the best, most independent goal of our self-realization, while the other living this is the 'beast'. In another sense, as long as we are embodied, we are the thing in between two powers, the rational and the embodied, perceiving part (I.1.10.1–12).[21] He introduced the explicit idea of the soul using a body, in passing, in an early treatise IV.7, where he leaves it open whether the soul is related to the body as form is to matter, or user to tool, and concludes that either way, the soul is the immortal part, and the true self (IV.7.1.21–5). More details are given in his discussion on what the living being and the human being are. He takes this to be a discussion on the holder or subject of certain embodied activities of the soul:

T4 Pleasures and pains, feelings of fear and boldness, appetites and aversions and feelings of distress—to what do these belong? In fact, they belong either to the soul or to a soul using a body or to some third thing that arises from a combination of these... But before that, we should ask: what is the subject of

---

[20] Remember the *Phaedo* 87; for the notion of use in *Alc.* I, see Taylor (1979).
[21] See further Remes (2016).

sense-perception? It is appropriate to begin from there, since the [above] states are either acts of sense-perception or else they do not occur without sense-perception

I.1.1–4; 11–13

The first thing to note is that following the *Timaeus*, Plotinus considers pleasure, pain, etc., as subsumed under the main category of perceptions. Given already the Platonic background, we would expect him to connect all of these with the disturbances of the body (*Tim.* 43c–d). The main moves in the treatise consist of making a differentiation between the essence of the soul, that is, the soul as a pure, impassive power, and the soul in the body. The former obviously feels no appetites, pleasures, or pains, but it also cannot be the proper subject of perception or discursive reason, for it 'will perceive nothing nor will there be discursive thinking or belief in it. For sense-perception is taking on a form and a corporeal state, and thinking and belief are based on sense-perception' (I.1.2.25–7). The soul that is in the body turns out to be more interesting for the purposes of the treatise's central question, for the living being, the composite entity, is a combination of the soul and the body (3.1–3; I.1.9.15–18).

Plotinus then asks whether this soul, the one relevant for functions in the body, is the subject of those states. Perhaps it can be the subject of perception, as the user of the relevant sense organs, like the eyes?

T5 If, then, on the one hand, it uses the body as an instrument, it does not have to be the subject of states that come through the body, just as craftsmen are not the subjects of the states of their instruments... But how will the states go from the body into the soul? For though body will transfer its own states to another body, how will body transfer anything to the soul? For this would be equivalent in a way to saying that when one thing experiences something, another thing experiences it. For so long as what uses the instrument is one thing and the instrument it uses is something else, each is separate. At least, anyone who posits the soul as using the body separates them. But prior to their separation by the practice of philosophy, how were they disposed?

Enn. I 1.3.3–6; 11–18, the last lines already quoted in T2

Here Plotinus is about to embark on a study of the soul-body relationship that he takes to be real rather than normative. The analogy of the craftsman and his tools is, in what happens in the treatise afterwards, set aside, for the reason stated here: it is not suitable for explaining the affections that clearly do reach the soul from the body. It can be a very effective conceptualization for a philosophical therapy, but it is not suitable for explaining the soul-body relationship that grounds the psychic activities of a living thing. The first half of the treatise gives what is a peripatetically influenced view of the subject of perceptions. While to be able to perceive is due to immobile powers, it is the living, composite thing (*sunampho-teron*) that has these powers and is the subject of perception (I.1.6.1–4; 7.1–6).[22] This notion of a subject, or that which 'has' the perceptions, is not yet very elaborate. And he will go on to give a more sophisticated view, and delineate, among other things, the role of the soul in full-fledged perceptions. Nonetheless, it suits Plotinus' purposes: his need to keep the soul powers themselves immobile, unaltered.

In Plotinus' scheme, the conclusion also raises a problem, however, because now the rational soul—the 'we'—is in danger of not grasping the perceptions. Plotinus continues:

T6   But then how is it that we perceive? In fact, it is because we are not released from such a living being, even if other things more honourable than us are present in the complete substantiality of the human being, which is made of many parts. But the soul's power of sense-perception should not be understood as being of sensibles, but rather of the impressions that arise from sense-perception and which are graspable by the living being. For these are already intelligible.

I.1.7.6–12

There are two reasons for why the rational soul has a role in perception. First, the rational soul, in this embodied life, is part of the 'complete substantiality' of the human being, and not separate from it. Second, the power of sense perception operates not with the external impulses themselves, but with the already internalized, psychic impressions. Elsewhere, he offers detailed views on how full-fledged perception is not a passive potentiality but an activity. A perceptual judgement is over and above the sense affection taking place in the composite, or its sense organs.[23] We shall in the next section look more carefully at what Plotinus contends regarding the role of the sense organs and the body in

---

[22] As Gerson (2018) and his translation team notes note in the translation (p. 47), this is reminiscent of Alex. Aphr., *De An.* 23.18–24. Gwenaëlle Aubry underlines the way in which the whole treatise departs not just from *Alcibiades* I but also from Aristotle's questions about substance and subject of affections. *De An.* 403a10–12. Aubry (2004: 112). See also Pavlos Kalligas' introduction to the treatise and the way in which Platonic and Aristotelian views undergo different attempts at harmonization after the Classical period. Kalligas (2004: 102–5).

[23] For the details of this distinction, see Emilsson (1998: ch. IV). Caluori (2015: 180, 181) argues that this means that the body is 'constitutive of neither the capacities of the lower soul nor of their activities' and that 'the body is not a part of the perceptual activity of the soul, though the occurrence of sensory affections (in the body) is presumably a necessary condition for perceptual activity'. While I can see the point of these formulations—the body cannot be constitutive of any power of the composite that it has because of having a soul—I think they may overstate the issue. Body seems to become redundant, or a condition at best. For some ideas about the role of the body in perceptions, see the last section of this chapter.

perception. Here it suffices to say that the importance of something underlining the role of the rational soul in perception arises from an acceptance of the idea that the living being is the subject of sense affections, and hence that the body has a crucial role in the formation of certain features of our psychic activities. It is the role of the rational soul in those embodied activities that needs to be argued for.

Elsewhere, in IV.3, Plotinus makes it explicit that to sum up the soul-body relationship as one of an agent using a material instrument leaves crucial aspects of the relationship unexplained. In this context he goes back to a passing remark of Aristotle's on the instrumental version of the relationship.[24] Right after a firm statement that the soul is inseparable from the body, Aristotle introduces a somewhat surprising metaphor of the soul as a helmsman/steersman and the body as a the ship (*De An.* II 1, 413a8–9; cf. Alex. Aphr., *De An.* 15.9–28).[25] Plotinus finds both commendable and problematic aspects in this metaphor:

T7 but it is also said that the soul is in the body as the steersman is in the ship; this is a good comparison as far as the soul's ability to separate [*pros men to chôristên dunasthai*] from the body goes, but would not supply very satisfactorily the manner of its presence, which is what we ourselves are investigating. This is because as a sailor, the helmsman would be in the ship accidentally, but how would he be in it as helmsman? Nor is he in the whole ship in the way that the soul is in the whole body.

Enn. IV.3.21.5–11

The positive statement can be understood in two ways. The steersman and ship metaphor captures well the metaphysical separation of the soul from the body, namely the idea of the ontological independence and priority of especially the higher, rational soul from the body (as in *Enn.* I1.3.21–6). The separation intended could also mean the normative notion of separation—or both. Given that the separation in question is a *dunamis* that the soul has, Plotinus seems to be after the second, normative alternative rather than to be offering a description of the impassivity of the soul powers. The claim is that the helmsman metaphor is somewhat unhelpful in describing the presence of the soul in the body, but successful in capturing of the way that the soul can be seen to use or steer the body to achieve its goals. Separation here refers to a rational ability to understand oneself as a soul rather than as a body or composite, and thereby, through philosophical-therapeutic means, learn to refuse to self-identify with any brute appetites and disturbances arising from one's body.

---

[24] Before this discussion, Plotinus argues against two metaphors also mentioned in *De An.*: that the soul is like an attunement of the strings of the lyre, and that it is an entelechy; IV.3.8. Cf. Rich (1961: 3–4).

[25] For a detailed discussion and references, see Bos (2003: ch. 6).

The second, negative, point made in T6 is thereby strengthened: the metaphor is unsatisfactory for grasping the complex way in which the soul *is* present in the body. Besides the problem of the helmsman being too physical an object to capture the way that a non-material entity can be present 'everywhere as a whole', the metaphor comes dangerously close to explicating the relationship as an accidental one, and does not bring out how the soul really steers, or gives rise to, the activities in the body, since the helmsman could, whenever he wants, stop steering, and instead act as a mere voyager, and a voyager, in turn, is not essential to a ship, nor to the activity of sailing, in the way that the soul is for embodied activities. When Plotinus continues the analysis of the tool metaphor in IV.3, he, revises it (probably in the spirit of Alexander of Aphrodisias' *On the Soul* 13–15) into the relationship of the art, *technê*, and the tool, thus trying to improve on Aristotle's idea by instead focusing on the powers or functions that the soul's presence actualizes in the body:

T8 So, should we say that it is like a craft in its tools, for example, in the helm, if the helm were something with a soul, so that the helmsmanship which moves it in accordance with its craft would be inside it? But the difference here is that the craft originates outside. If, then, in accordance with the example of the helmsman entering into the helm, we were to propose that the soul is in the body as in a natural tool—for that is how it moves it in whatever it wants to do—would we be any further along towards what we are looking for? Will we not rather have a problem again about how it is in the tool, even if this is a different way of being in something from those mentioned before? But nonetheless we still have a desire to find out and come to closer grips with the issue.

(IV.3.21.11–21)

This time, we are to think of the soul as mainly the art, here the art of steering. We are proposed a thought experiment in which the art of steering enters the helm, and co-exists in it as 'in a natural tool' (*en organô phusikô*). Plotinus continues the discussion with *De An.* 2.1, here quoting 412b12 which continues with an explanation of how the axe is an axe only as long as it has the 'being of an axe' in it, as its essence, and an eye is an eye only as long as it has the capacity of sight. Plotinus thinks that the natural tool idea improves on the helmsman metaphor by not postulating extra agents, but by locating the origin and rule of motion inside the body, and in them not accidentally but essentially, from the point of view of the body: while the soul might be separate in a different sense of the word, the organic body is that particular organic body only insofar as the movement, life, and functions given to it by the soul are in it. Yet he also objects on two accounts.

First, the claim that the 'arts', the living and cognitive functions, 'originate outside' can be taken in two different ways. On one reading, Plotinus objects to the metaphor, on the grounds that even when implanted in the helm, the soul will borrow its craft from elsewhere, and hence the metaphor renders the craft external to the soul, and thus does not capture the way that the soul is in the body. On another reading, the origin of the craft is, for a Platonist, always outside, and the metaphor tries falsely to locate it only in the body: even when the lower soul or its trace is in the body, the origin of its powers actualized in the body lies outside.[26] The first reading renders Plotinus' following of the Aristotelian discussion closer, whereas the latter, probably more likely, reading[27] underlines his Platonic point of view. On either reading, he objects, finally, to the fact that the nature of the undeniable presence of the soul to the body has been stated rather than explicated, and thus further study is called for.

What follows immediately after this discussion are metaphors that attempt to capture the omnipresence of the soul to the body (like fire is to the air or air to the light; IV.3.22). The purpose of these is to find metaphors that capture the immaterial presence that the soul has in the body. For our purposes however, more relevant are the passages immediately after that, where Plotinus tries to give a more hands-on explanation of the presence of the soul to the organic body. In a manner perhaps rather rare for him, he shows in continuing the discussion in IV.3 and in I.1.5 some real interest in both bodily organs and their features. But before looking at these passages, let us do a short detour to the way in which the later Neoplatonist Olympiodorus, commenting on *Alcibiades* I, interprets the use and instrument ideas.

Olympiodorus returns to the original question of *Alcibiades* I, in which what is being defined is a human being. In a more systematic manner, it is being made clear that the level of this discussion—the whole dialogue, as Olympiodorus sees it, is the embodied and politically active person, and not the immortal, rational soul (which is separate for the later Neoplatonists as it is for Plotinus). What Olympiodorus makes clear is that the locution 'us as an instrument' is not suited to the way in which vegetative or appetitive souls are in their bodies:

T9 That the human being, according to Plato, is a soul using a body that moves in straight lines; for this ought to be added [to the definition] to account for the souls of the heavenly [bodies]. But the vegetative and non-rational [souls] will not be captured [in the definition 'a soul that uses the body as an instrument'], as we have pointed out, because they use the body not only as an instrument, but also as a subject [*hupokeimenon*].

In Alc. 212.10–14; see also 208.10[28]

---

[26] Rich (1961: 5); Dillon and Blumenthal (2015: 269–70).

[27] It seems the first interpretation has the difficulty that the revision from the helmsman (and external agent) to a craft implanted in the oar itself seems precisely to avoid the problem of leaving the craft external to the oar, and the objection thereby unnecessary.

[28] The translations of Olympiodorus are by Michael Griffin (2016), which again I have modified in this chapter.

Olympiodorus differentiates human soul from both the souls of the stars and the non-rational aspects of the soul.[29] It is actually only the human kind of rational soul which uses the body as an instrument, when embodied.

T10 [Socrates] defines the human being as 'a rational soul using the body as an instrument': and only the civic person is like this; for the purificatory person does not use the body as an instrument, if instruments one associates with contribute to the goal of the user [*ta organa paralambomena suntelei tô chrômenô*]; rather, the body becomes more of an impediment to the purificatory person.

In Alc. 177.14–18. See *Crat.* 386d–387b;
Tim. 46c7, 46e6, 68e4–5, for *sunaitiai* or *summetraitiai*

The references to the purificatory and the civic person contain the Neoplatonic theory of the levels of virtue available to a human being, and hence they reveal that Olympiodorus is conducting a normative discussion: by 'the purificatory person' here, he refers to a rational soul that has done her fair share of philosophizing, and has separated herself through coming to realize herself as being separate from the body. If we raise, on Plotinus' behalf, the question 'What was its status before it came to be separated by philosophy', an interesting feature emerges. If the 'use of the body' captured the metaphysical order of dependency and causation, namely the soul's ontological and causal priority to the body, surely this was not something the struggle towards acquisition of higher levels of virtues sought to achieve. Here the Platonic notions of 'use' and 'instruments' become important. Before the purification, the soul not only is in the body, it uses the body in a variety of ways. The embodied, civic person can improve her situation by realizing that her role in her body is, indeed, in originating activities in the body—using the body—and not in being a passive recipient, tossed about by external circumstances. But if 'use' properly denotes this active role, why is this feature left behind in ethical development? Instruments, Olympiodorus contends, contribute to the goals of their users. This I take to mean that a certain kind of body—here a human body— enables certain intentional activities while not others. As in *Timaeus*, intelligible order and goals are both enabled and limited by physical constraints (*sunaitiai*).[30] For this reason the notion of use is not enough for purificatory purposes: even when the soul conceives of itself as a user, the causally efficient part in the union, the powers of the soul cannot be freely actualized in the body. They are constrained by what is and is not possible in the body of a certain type. Complete,

---

[29] As Thomas Johansen points out, in *Timaeus* the circular motions are rational, while the rectilinear are irrational. Johansen (2004: 143). Olympiodorus accepts these fundamental differences between the human and star embodiment, but appeals to human rationality through another Platonic source: *Alc.* I and the use metaphor.

[30] I have discussed this elsewhere more fully, see Remes (2022).

ideal purification would involve the perhaps unrealistic ideal of not using the body at all.

In his discussion of the World Soul's relationship to its body, Plotinus employs a similar idea:

T11 For there are two kinds of care of everything, that of the totality being achieved at the bidding of an agent ordering by a 'royal' supervision that calls for no exertion, while that of particular things involves a sort of 'hands on' activity, in which the contact with what is being acted upon suffuses the agent with the nature of the object of his action.

IV.8.2.26–30

By the first option, Plotinus targets the impassive, undescended care that the World Soul and every other higher reality provides for things on the lower level of reality. But as Emilsson succinctly puts it, somebody must get dirt on their hands.[31] This means that there is another kind of care, and another kind of presence in the body: the lower, immanent variant. In this kind of 'care', upward effects from the nature of the thing done to the doer are unavoidable. Plotinus' context here is the World Soul and the way in which its different aspects are related to the body and events in the cosmos. However, he generalizes the idea of the two kinds of care, thus providing us with a clear-cut model to understand the impassive basic nature of all souls on the one hand, and the activities in the body compromised by the effects from the nature of the thing cared for on the other. For the understanding of embodiment, the second kind of 'care' must be a significant part of the story. Even in a system where the former care is paradigmatic, the latter has explanatory work to accomplish, and exists of necessity.[32] This involves, centrally, the soul's relationship with the organic body.

3. Bodily Organs and Their Conditions

In his insistence that the composite entity is the entity in which certain activities are bodily, or need a body, Plotinus draws the line between the cognitive activities belonging to the composite entity in a different place than the Aristotelians. Discursive judgements, reasoning, and memory impressions can in their functioning be derivatively dependent upon the body: they can utilize contents received through perception. But for Plotinus, these activities are not directly

---

[31] Emilsson (2017: 156).
[32] Whether the coming to be in the body, in itself, is a good thing or not is again a source of ambivalence to Plotinus. While he often laments it and talks of it as an evil (V.1.1.3–4), it seems to be somewhat necessary, in terms of the 'necessity' used in the *Timaeus*.

involved in the organic body, unlike perceptions. What follows is therefore concentrated on different kinds of perceptions.

Even though the soul, as a power, is impassive and not divisible in the body, Plotinus does believe that the perceiving soul must be divisible in the body (*Enn.* IV.3.19.11–16). In trying to capture the thing that has perception, he sometimes speaks of a third thing, between the soul and the external object, which is that which receives the forms and has the affections (IV.4.23.13–25; I.1.7.1–20). This subject—or ability—is in the middle of the object grasped and the one—the soul— that will know and be able to make proper perceptual judgements of the type: 'this is a man'. But what it produces is not a mere physical imprint of the external object: Plotinus calls it an organ of *gnôsis*—apprehension or awareness—that links together the extremes, the cognitive rational power and the object perceived (IV.4.23.28–32).[33] As further evidence for the fact that soul and body here form some third thing in which both together produce a perception, he mentions elsewhere the possibility of merely entertaining a belief in something unpleasant or dangerous being present. This in itself does not seem to constitute the kind of painful experience that involves bodily feelings. What we mean by pain is something that involves an accompanying *pathos* (I.1.5.17–18). Plotinus, then, allows for the objects of sense to make an effect in the composite entity of body and soul, and especially its sense organs. Sense organs, he contends, are naturally continuous with the objects of sense, and this common nature and communion is what guarantees *gnôsis* of the objects of sense (IV.5.1.5–13). But even these effects are not passive alterations: by actualizing a power or modality of a certain sense organ the power does not alter, but comes to cognitively possess—perhaps: entertain— its object (III.6.2.34–41).

Plotinus sometimes also enters into the details of the way the soul is divided, and how these affections become differentiated. One recurring theme in Platonism since the *Timaeus* was the way in which bodily parts and organs are teleologically formed so that they support the soul's different functions. By the time of Plotinus, the developments in medicine had significantly changed the scene, and Galenic medicine provided even within Platonism improved information on the role that different bodily parts played. Plotinus does want to explain the location of different bodily parts, but in doing so he appeals to an idea that certain physical features are connected to certain part of the soul. The rational soul

---

[33] Emilsson (2017: 245; following the original (1998) *Plato on Sense-Perception*; CUP) believes that what is being so produced is a phenomenal presence of the qualities perceived, and hence, for example, the colour of an external object as visually apprehended. See also, especially for reason's role in perception and conceptual break down, Chiaradonna (2012). Because detailed studies on Plotinus on sense perception exist, I venture here only to summarize, in part, their main views, and concentrate on raising issues that are directly relevant to the question of the strength and depth of the soul's involvement in the body.

gets no mention as it does not need a physical basis, but the nutritive, appetitive, and spirited soul are located in certain bodily parts:

T12   What I mean is this: in the process of the ensouled body's being illuminated by soul, different parts of the body participate in it in different ways. In accordance with the suitability of an organ for a given function, the soul provides the power appropriate for that function. In this way, we say that the power in the eyes is the power of sight, that in the ears the power of hearing, the power of taste in the tongue, that of smell in the nose, while the power of touch is present in the whole body; for the whole body serves as sense organ to the soul for this type of apprehension... Again, since the faculty of growth of the soul, that concerned with increase in size and nutrition, is not absent from any of the body but nourishes it with the blood, and the blood that nourishes is in the veins, and the starting point of the veins and the blood is in the liver, the part of the soul that is the faculty of appetite has been assigned to live there, since this is where this power exerts its force; for what produces generation, nourishment, and increase in size must necessarily have an appetite for these things. But for the blood that is thin, light, active and pure, constituting a suitable organ for [the faculty of] spiritedness, its source, the heart—this being where this kind of blood is separated off—has been established as a fitting home for the seething of [the faculty of] spiritedness.

IV.3.23.1–9; 35–47

In tone, this passage is in line with the *Timaeus* picture, in which the material aspects are used to explain certain cognitive functions. In the *Timaeus*, sight, for example, can transmit the disturbance caused by its object to the soul because of the material qualities of the different kinds of fire of which its ray is composed, resulting in encounters of different proportions with different external objects (45c–d; 67d3ff). The central position into which blood has been raised is, however, a result of the post-Platonic developed information about blood circulation, involving an attempt at targeting the physical side of growth, being enabled by nutrition that happens with or through blood. Blood, too, comes in different variations, and the soul's powers always take place in an appropriate kind of material.

But how essential a role do these explanations give to the body? One might object that, first, we have general statements of the kind of bodily parts that are suitable for reception, as it were, of certain faculties of the soul. This is faculty psychology located in the body rather than interest in the changes of the body needed to explain changes in perceptions or thoughts. Second, the descriptions of the bodily states seem to follow the parts or faculties of the soul differentiated already by Plato without a reference to the bodily states or physical aspects. If so, then the bodily story is posterior to the purely 'spiritual' story, and thus its explanatory power meagre.

On a couple of occasions, it does seem to be the case that features of the body have more explanatory value. One idea is about types—here sense modalities—being dependent upon sense organs:

> T13 For where some things have one function and some another, for example, eyes and ears, one must not say that one part of the soul is present in sight and another in the ears—division of this sort belongs to others—but rather that the identical thing is present, even if a different power is active in each, for all the powers are in both of them. It is due to the organs being different that there are different apprehensions, but all of them are of forms, since the soul is capable of being informed by all forms.
>
> (IV.3.3.13–19)

In this model, bodily organs play a role in determining the sense modality: we can say that without the eyes, a perception would not be one of sight, it would be something else, say touch. Plotinus likens this to the way that the craftsmen use rulers: judging the object that one is crafting is done by a choice of a certain kind of ruler—say, one used to make sure that a line is straight (IV.3.23.33–41). While the faculty of sense perception exists independently and prior to the body (VI.7.6), the bodily organs are essential for the actualization of the power of perception, and, further, their physical features determine the kind of modality that the power of perception comes to actualize in the body.[34] Through determining this, one can speculate, the organs must be involved in what types of sense qualities the composite comes to grasp. Seeing, then, is partially caused by the body, namely the organ or eyes rendering the power as a seeing kind of power. Derivatively, it is possible that the organic structure plays a part in giving rise to the kind of phenomenal qualities that different sense modalities involve. In the case of seeing, for example, Plotinus seems to think that while colour perceptions capture, for the most part, real features in the sensible universe governed by intelligible logoi (II.4.9.7–11), there is a difference to be drawn in between a colour in the object and the one perceived. Black and white as we perceive them, with the phenomenal features that they have, have the intelligible principles of black and white that lack such features as their proper objects, but obviously differ from them. (III.6.17.22; V.3.8.1–8.) This residue, or perhaps

---

[34] While I am in most cases in agreement with Riccardo Chiaradonna's interpretation in Chapter 8 of this volume, I regard here his treatment of sense perception as incomplete: true enough, the power itself is immaterial and intelligible, but there is a story to be told of the conditions of its actualization, and the an the effect that the body and its organs have on its actualization.

phenomenal particularity, must arise in the organ of perception, when serving as a tool for perception by the soul.[35]

When compared with the Aristotelian picture, something crucial seems still to be missing. Here we do not have the idea that a particular perception would arise, in part, from a certain physical *condition*, or that the properly physical particularities of that condition would causally affect the kind of perception/emotion. Plotinus probably comes closest to this when employing the Aristotelian examples of the boiling of the blood to differentiate between characters. That some people—and animals—are easily irascible has to do with bodily blends, and thus its explanation needs a reference to the corporeal, to the animal's constitution (IV.4.28.28–35).[36] Indirectly, he also acknowledges that the perceptions of the embodied, irrational composite can be physically affected by, for example, drugs—presumably through affecting the constitution of the body and its sense organs—but here his interest is in maintaining that this kind of vulnerability, rather than being an exception in the otherwise well-functioning system, is a potential problem for all areas of perception, and therefore the role of independent, pure reason becomes central. And a wise man, while being as vulnerable to being bodily affected and physically harmed as any other embodied human being, does not assent to the sense affections thus produced (IV.4.43).

4. To Conclude

Remember the categorization of the strengths of the embodiment we started with. We are now in a position both to evaluate Plotinus' location in it and to amend the formulations so that they capture the features our discussion highlights as central. The material suggests the need for following emendations (in italics):

Weak embodiment: body is a tool that implements practical solutions *and provides only raw materials for judgements* arrived at by reason that is in its essence disembodied.

---

[35] This is an interesting and difficult passage that comes in the overall rebuttal of the Aristotelian and other theories of perception happening through a medium. Rather than medium, Plotinus appeals, in the case of vision, to the body of fire coming from the eyes, treating animals with night vision as his evidence for the Platonic view. The question, then, is whether there needs to be a third body apart from the object and the perceiving organ, whereas the need of the latter is taken for granted. (He also seems to think that the fact that we are interested in how touch operates, even though in its case of which direct contact is evident. He thereby seems to deny that the flesh would be a medium, and think that the medium does not have sufficient explanatory role.) For a commentary of this challenging treatise, see Gurtler (2015: esp. p. 285).

[36] For this quote and discussion, see Sorabji (2005: 6(a)39).

Moderate embodiment: body has a functional role. Embodied activities structure perception and shape our understanding. Practical solutions *and perceptions* are essentially embodied, and not mere executions of abstract decisions made by a disembodied rational *and critical* ability.

Strong embodiment: embodiment constitutes the understanding of the soul; it shapes the cognitive nature of mind.

Within the Neoplatonic framework, it seems that any features of strong embodiment must be ruled out. Besides the general considerations this essay started with, there are specific reasons. The numerous ways of avoiding the judging, rational soul becoming immanent in matter are motivated by its causal priority and impassivity. Hence Plotinus' conscious departure and inverting of the order of dependency that Alexander of Aphrodisias suggests lies between the higher and the lower faculties of the soul. But there are reasons to think that moderate embodiment best captures some of the passages we have seen. Sometimes—for an embodied human being—separation is an ethical ideal rather than an actual state of the embodied soul. Further, the World Soul seems necessarily and moderately embodied. The embodied human soul also seems moderately embodied since the owner of perceptions is in some sense the composite: the soul provides the powers of judgement, but it must have something—the bodily sense affection—to judge. Plotinus also accepts peripatetic reasons to think that understanding the soul as a captain of a body/ship does not capture its presence in the whole of the body. Perceptions, though dependent upon the critical abilities of the rational soul, necessitate the existence of a body of a certain kind and the sense affections that such a body can deliver. The organic features of the body determine the types of sense qualities available to the human soul and are therefore essential for the explanation of different sense modalities. Certain personal characteristics, too, are due to essentially bodily temperaments.

Much, if not all, of these discussions are about types rather than token experiences, showing neglect to the question of whether at every instance of a spiritual activity something at the level of the body must alter. It also remains a matter of interpretation if the soul-caused material body can be anything like the body in Aristotelian hylomorphism. The crucial qualification, however, takes us back to the principle and origin of the body put to one side earlier in this chapter. While many of the passages presented treat the soul-body relationship without reference to the vertical causal framework, some of them do appeal to the idea of a kind of *innate suitability* of the bodily features and the soul's powers located in them. If there is something inextricably psycho-physical for Plotinus, it is due to the fact that the soul partakes in creating a body suitable for it. This leaves us with a distinctively Platonic notion of the physical. The discussions on the origin of the body cannot, in the end, be left bracketed.

Bibliography

Aubry, G. (2004) Plotin. *Traité* 53 (Cerf).

Bos, P.O. (2003) *The Soul and its Instrumental Body: A Reinterpretation of Aristotle's Philosophy of Living Nature* (Brill).

Caluori, D. (2015) *Plotinus on the Soul* (Cambridge University Press).

Chiaradonna, C. (2012) 'Plotinus' Account of the Cognitive Powers of the Soul', *Topoi* 31/2: 191–207.

Clark, A. (2008) *Supersizing the Mind: Embodiment, Action, and Cognitive Extension* (Oxford University Press).

Dillon, J. and Blumenthal, H. (2015) *Plotinus: Ennead IV.3.–4.29. Problems Concerning the Soul*, trans., intro., comm. (Parmenides Press).

Emilsson, E.K. (1998) *Plato on Sense-Perception* (Cambridge University Press).

Emilsson, E.K. (2009) 'Plotinus on Act and Power', in J. Pietarinen and V. Viljanen (eds.), *World as an Active Power: Studies in the History of European Reason* (Brill), 71–88.

Emilsson, E.K. (2017) *Plotinus* (Routledge).

Emilsson, E.K. (2021) 'Sense-Perception, Reasoning, and Forms in Plotinus', *Phronesis* 67/1, 99–130.

Gerson, L.P. (2018) Plotinus, *The Enneads*, G. Boys-Stones, J.M. Dillon, L.P. Gerson, R.A.H. King, A. Smith, and J. Wilberding (trs.) (Cambridge University Press).

Griffin, M. (tr.) Olympiodorus, On Plato First Alcibiades 10–28 (Bloomsbury).

Gurtler, G.M. (2015) *Ennead IV.4.30–45 and IV.5 Problems Concerning the Soul: Translation, with an Introduction, and Commentary* (Parmenides Publishing).

Johansen, T. (2004) *Plato's Natural Philosophy: A Study of the Timaeus-Critias* (Cambridge University Press).

Kalligas, P. (2004) *The Enneads of Plotinus: A Commentary*, Volume 1 (Princeton University Press).

Lo Presti, P. (2015) *Norms in Social Interaction: Semantic, Epistemic, and Dynamic* (Lund University Press).

Noble, C.I. (2013) 'How Plotinus' Soul Animates His Body: The Argument for the Soul-Trace at *Enneads* 4.4.18.1–9', *Phronesis* 58/3: 1–31.

O'Meara, D. (1996) 'The Hierarchical Ordering of Reality in Plotinus', in L.P. Gerson (ed.), *The Cambridge Companion to Plotinus* (Cambridge University Press), 66–81.

Remes, P. (2013) 'Reason to Care: The Object and Structure of Self-Knowledge in *Alcibiades* I', *Apeiron* 46/3: 270–301.

Remes, P. (2016) 'Self-Knowledge in Plotinus: Becoming Who You Are', in U. Renz (ed.), *Self-Knowledge. A History*, Oxford Philosophical Concepts (OUP), 78–95.

Remes, P. (2022) 'Olympiodorus on the Human Being: A Case of Moderate Embodiment', in S. Slaveva-Griffin and I. Ramelli (eds.) *Lovers of the Soul, Lovers of the Body. Philosophical and Religious Perspectives in Late Antiquity* (Center for Hellenic Studies, Harvard University Press).

Remes, P. (forthcoming) 'Plotinus on Colour', in K. Ierodiakonou and V. Decaix (eds.) *Colour Theories from Empedocles to Descartes*. Global Perpectives in the History of Natural Philosophy Series (Routledge).

Rich, A.N.M. (1961) 'Body and Soul in the Philosophy of Plotinus', *The Society for Ancient Greek Philosophy Newsletter* 12: 1–12. https://orb.binghamton.edu/cgi/viewcontent.cgi?article=1063&context=sagp

Sorabji, R. (2005) *The Philosophy of the Commentators 200–600 A.D.: A Sourcebook*, Volume 1: *Psychology (with Ethics and Religion)* (Cornell University Press).

Taylor, R. (1979) 'Persons and Bodies', *American Philosophical Quarterly* 16/1: 67–72.

Wilberding, J. (2008) 'Porphyry and Plotinus on the Seed', *Phronesis* 53/4–5: 406–32.

Wildberg, Ch. (2009) 'A World of Thoughts: Plotinus on Nature and Contemplation (*Enn.* III 8. [30] 1–6)', in R. Chiaradonna and F. Trabattoni (eds.), *Physics and Philosophy of Nature in Greek Neoplatonism*, Proceedings of the European Science Foundation (Brill), 121–43.

10
Philoponus and Alexander in Historical Context on Relations between Matter and Form Inside and Outside Philosophy of Mind

Richard Sorabji

John Philoponus, the Christian commentator on Aristotle in Alexandria of the 6th century CE, elucidated several relations between matter and form, most of them, but not all, from the context of philosophy of mind. He drew several of these relations from discussions by earlier philosophers. The soul or its activities had been said to *be* a harmony or blend of bodily items, or else to *follow* such a blend or harmony, or to *supervene* on it. I think I can now explain Philoponus' contribution better than before.[1]

1. Earlier Discussions of the Blend or Harmony of Bodily Ingredients Which Are Soul, or Which Soul or Its Activities Follow

One set of reports had been about Socrates (469–399 BCE), who had already denied such physicalist accounts of the soul. Plato's *Phaedo* 92A–93A presented Socrates as denying that the soul *is* a harmony (*harmonia*) of bodily ingredients, on the ground that such a harmony would be unable to *oppose* the body, as the soul can. In another story, when Socrates was told by the physiognomist Zopyrus that the shape of his throat showed him to be a womanizer, he silenced the resulting laughter of Alcibiades and said that that had indeed been his inborn disposition, but he had overcome it by the use of reason.[2]

---

[1] My previous contributions on Philoponus were in Sorabji (2000: ch. 7, 2003: ch. 7, 2005: 199–203, 2010: 33–4).

[2] Cicero, *On Fate* 5.10–11; *Tusculan Disputations* 4.37.80; Alexander of Aphrodisias, *On Fate*, 171, 11.

Richard Sorabji, *Philoponus and Alexander in Historical Context on Relations between Matter and Form Inside and Outside Philosophy of Mind* In: *The History of Hylomorphism: From Aristotle to Descartes*. Edited by: David Charles, Oxford University Press. © Richard Sorabji 2023. DOI: 10.1093/oso/9780192897664.003.0011

Aristotle's pupil, Aristoxenus of Tarentum (born about 375 BCE), is nonetheless recorded as holding the soul to be some kind of harmony of bodily items.[3]

The Stoic Posidonius (about 135–51 BCE) of Athens and later of Rhodes, is reported in a book by the great philosopher-doctor Galen[4] as saying that the emotional movements (*pathētikai kinēseis*) of the soul *follow* (*hepesthai*) the disposition (*diathesis*) of the body, a disposition which itself is to no small extent altered by the blend of (elemental) ingredients in the surrounding (atmosphere).

Another Aristotelian, Andronicus of Rhodes, who arranged Aristotle's works about 60 BCE, suggested that the soul *was* a harmony of bodily items. But Galen gave a different view of Andronicus, commending him for calling the soul *either* a blend (*krasis*) of bodily items, *or* a capacity following the blend, while withholding agreement from the soul itself being a capacity, though no comment is recorded on 'following'. This report on Andronicus was in a different book by Galen, to which I come next.[5]

Galen himself (129 to about 210 CE), who gave the above reports on Posidonius and Andronicus, made his comment on the latter in a book which is entitled in Greek, *That the Capacities of the Soul Follow the Blends of the Body*.[6] The very title seems to endorse the idea that the capacities of the soul *follow* the blends of the body. Furthermore, in withholding support only from Andronicus' calling the soul a capacity, Galen appears to endorse Andronicus' alternatives that the soul itself actually *is* a bodily blend, or follows from one.

I shall postpone Galen's contemporary, the Aristotelian commentator Alexander of Aphrodisisas, to a separate account below, because it will be especially important to compare Philoponus with his earlier fellow commentator Alexander, and I will move on to Proclus.

Proclus (412–485 CE), head of the Neoplatonist school in Athens, and teacher of Ammonius, the teacher of Philoponus, rejected the alternative mentioned by Galen that capacities of the soul *follow* blends in the body, saying that the body cannot *be productive of* (*poiētikon*) reflective (*emphrōn*) living, but can only interfere with thinking, and even the idea of interference needs to be qualified, for the soul is unaffected (*apathēs*).[7]

Proclus reinterpreted a passage in Plato's *Timaeus* which Galen had also cited and which blamed the fluidity in the bodies of growing children due to their intake of nourishment and encounters with external elements as interfering with their thinking.[8] Galen had further objected to some unnamed Platonists who thought

---

[3] Cicero, *Tusculan Disputations* 1.18.41, Lactantius, *Divine Institutes* 7.13, and *On Creation by God* 16.
[4] Galen, *On the Doctrines of Hippocrates and Plato* (*PHP*), 5.5.23.
[5] Galen, *QAM* (the title in Latin is *Quod Animi Mores Corporis Temperamenta Sequantur*) 44, 12–20.
[6] Galen, *QAM*.   [7] Proclus, *Commentary on Plato's Timaeus*, vol. 3, pp. 330, 9 – 331, 1.
[8] Plato, *Timaeus* 43A–44C; cited by Galen, *QAM* 42, 11–43, 19.

that the bodily disturbances in children cited by Plato were diseases. To this Galen had replied that Plato referred in his *Timaeus* to something different from disease: the need for a good blend (*eukrasia*) of seasonal climates, from which Galen inferred that a bad seasonal blend would impede the capacity for thought.[9]

Proclus replied to these earlier interpretations of the disturbance of thought in children[10] that the soul cannot be disturbed in its essence by body, and any disturbance of the soul's activities is merely like disturbance from a chattering neighbour. A child's soul may not yet know itself and therefore may wrongly think it is being disturbed when it notices flux in the body, but this is like the case of someone wrongly imagining they are in flux, when they look at their shifting reflection in running water.

2. Alexander of Aphrodisias, Commentator on and Defender of Aristotle, Prefers Supervening on a Bodily Blend

Alexander of Aphrodisias was Aristotle's greatest defender and commentator in an age of rival schools, who gained the chair of Aristotelian philosophy in Athens around 200 CE. He often *avoids* talk of *following* and speaks instead either of the apparently weaker relation of *supervening* or else of what is merely *prerequisite*. Speaking of prerequisites, in his *On the Soul* he says that the soul cannot exist *without* a bodily balance, that a mental activity cannot come into being *without* a bodily change, and that you cannot get (*labein*) any soul activity *without* a bodily change.[11] He also often says that the soul is a capacity that *supervenes* (*epiginetai*) on the blend of bodily ingredients,[12] but is not the blend itself, nor a harmony of bodily items, nor a symmetry of them.[13]

Alexander paraphrases and endorses a discussion in the first chapter of Aristotle's *On the Soul*, which makes a point about the danger, but not the inevitability in all cases, of the presence or absence of emotion simply reflecting our bodily state, independently of what is called for by the current impacts one undergoes (*pathêmata*).[14] Alexander makes it clear that his paraphrase is talking about a danger, but not something that happens always or necessarily, when he says that we get angry more easily (*raion*), when our bile is in excess.[15] It seems, then, to be left to the nature of bodily states that, although some are dangerously

---

[9] Plato, *Timaeus* 24C; cited by Galen, *QAM* 64, 19–65.
[10] Proclus, *Commentary on Plato's Timaeus*, pp. 335, 24–336, 1; 338, 6–13; 340, 14–17; 349, 21–350, 8. See also Proclus, *Commentary on Plato Alcibiades I*, 226, 12–227, 2.
[11] Alexander, *On the Soul* 12.9–10; 12, 21–2; 25, 8, in *Commentaria in Aristotelem Graeca* (*CAG*), supplementary vol. 2.
[12] Alexander, *On the Soul* 24, 1–5; 24, 18–25, 9; 26, 7–30.
[13] Alexander of Aphrodisias, *On the Soul* 24, 1–5; 24, 18–23; 25, 7–8, 26, 7–30.
[14] Aristotle, *De An.* A.1, 403a19–25; Alexander, *On the Soul* (in *CAG* supplementary vol. 2) 13,1–8.
[15] Alexander, *On the Soul* 13,6–7.

strong, they are not strong enough to make inappropriate emotion follow in a stronger sense than making it *easier*.

Alexander repeatedly asserts in this part of his *On the Soul* that blends are a *cause responsible* (*aitia*) for the supervening capacities, and for analogies between capacities.[16] But causal responsibility is not obviously connected here with invariability or necessitation, and I think that Alexander's model, Aristotle, had started a tradition of viewing cause as an explanatory factor, which did not have to depend on invariable or necessitating relations.[17]

Sometimes Alexander does bring in the strong relation of *following*, but he does not normally talk about particular psychological events following bodily situations. One context in which he does speak about following is found in the last of the passages just cited about the cause (*aitia*) responsible for something. But he is talking about the cause not of a particular psychological event, but of the one responsible for certain very general analogies holding.[18] He is discussing analogies between degrees of complexity in the forms of elementary bodies on the one hand and the souls of plants and souls capable of sense perception on the other. The cause responsible for differences of complexity among forms and souls, he says at one point,[19] is the difference of underlying bodies in respect of the number of them involved and their blend, mixture, and composition. And, he says, this *makes sense* (is *eulogon*) because a small difference in origins (*arkhai*) can make a large difference in the whole, as *often* happens with the forks in roads leading to widely separated destinations. I am struck that so far Alexander is content to speak only of what makes sense and happens *often*. But he does then go on to speak of *following*, and he also combines it with the putatively weaker relation of supervening on something, perhaps as a prerequisite, when he says that it makes sense or stands to reason (is *eulogon*) that the differences in forms or capacities of animals as opposed to plants or to the four simple elements of earth, air, fire, and water not only *supervene* on, but also *follow* differences of matter.[20]

There is another case in which Alexander postulates the relation of *following* and also combines it with the weaker relation of supervening. However, the context is not one of psychology, but of the whiteness of snow. In his *Commentary on Aristotle's Topics* (50, 9-51, 3) Alexander says that the white colour of snow not only *supervenes* on underlying material conditions (perhaps as a prerequisite), but also *follows* them. Moreover, unusually, he adds that the whiteness follows *necessarily* (*ex anangkês*) from them. Does he refer to necessity because following is a relation that normally falls short of necessitation, so that in this case the necessitation needs to be pointed out? The alternative (which I doubt) would be that following is always a matter of necessitation and that here he wants

---

[16] Alexander, *On the Soul* 8, 15, 17, 20; 10, 17, 21. [17] Sorabji (1980: ch. 2).
[18] Alexander, *On the Soul* 10,14-11,13.   [19] Alexander, *On the Soul* 10,18-19.
[20] Alexander, *On the Soul* 10,24-6.

to emphasize the fact. I believe that the reason why necessitation is stressed here is that he is talking not of a psychological effect, which humans might have the resources to counteract, but of an effect in physical nature. I think that where necessity is not stressed, following may represent a relation that holds invariably, other things being equal, rather than necessarily.

There might seem to be a third passage in which Alexander speaks of following and further speaks of it as happening of necessity, and this time he would be speaking of it in a psychological context. But against this, we should notice a warning. Alexander's standard word for following in these contexts is *hepesthai*, but here at *On the Soul* 77, 17–18, the word he uses is *akolouthein*. Moreover, the relationship appears to take the opposite direction from the normal, for he is talking of a physical effect following of necessity something psychological, rather than vice versa. Heat or cold in the body is said to follow of necessity a psychological impulse at the appearance of something to be pursued or avoided. The different word *akolouthein* is used here because he means *chronological* following. And that is also why his reference to necessity has to be made explicit here, because chronological following on its own provides no reason to suppose a necessary connection.

In the discussion of snow and of comparative degrees of complexity, Alexander allows two things to stand to each other in *both* of the two relations of following and of supervening, without making explicit in what way the latter relation is weaker. It was only my conjecture that there he meant one thing to supervene on another as a prerequisite. There are some other contexts, however, in which following and supervening could not be compatibly combined. In *On the Soul* 66, 6–8, Alexander says that among living animals, the most perfect psychological capacity is rationality and that more perfect capacities rest *upon* (*epi*; the word included in 'supervene upon') those that reach their perfection first. So in those living animals that have reason (only humans), sense perception as a whole comes first. He could not possibly say here that rationality, which rests *upon* perception, and so presupposes it, also *follows* perception as an invariable accompaniment, because non-human animals have perception, but not reason.

A further passage which treats supervening as being compatible with following is, I think, probably not by Alexander. It is taken from a *Supplement* to Alexander's *On the Soul*, at 104, 27–34,[21] *Supplement* being a name given to it by its modern editor, and *Mantissa*, or light weight, being an ancient designation. It is a patchwork of discussions by different authors, and its modern translator, Robert Sharples, explains in his translation that a good many of them cannot be Alexander's, even if some are. In the present context, the text bundles together a range of relationships between body and soul. Having said that soul *supervenes* on

---

[21] Sharples (2004: 9).

bodily blends, it adds that the blend is the *cause* (*aitia*) of the soul's genesis, and that souls *follow* on the constitution (*sustasis*) of the parts of different types of animal and that souls change reciprocally with that constitution. Supervening is here treated as compatible with following, just as *On the Soul* 10, 24–6 allowed. But in this case, a number of different relationships are being bundled together so swiftly that it has something of the look of an author who, having read Alexander, is now putting several points together at speed.

I have been pointing out that Alexander only in some contexts treats the relation of *following* as a relation of *necessitation*. This fits with another fact, as I believe, that elsewhere in the distinctive context of the causation of *particular events*, Alexander goes further than most in his opposition to causal relations involving necessitation. In his *On Fate*, he opposes the Stoics, who thought that everything was material, and whatever happened was determined to happen of necessity at least by the total material state of the universe. This deterministic view would be applied by the Stoics to what Alexander describes by contrast as merely supervening. But Alexander replies to the Stoic view in chapter 15 of *On Fate* that, even if identical circumstances recurred, there would be no *necessity* for us to act the same way as before, because we might have different standing motives. The same circumstances might, equally appropriately, trigger a different one of our standing motives, in which case the resulting action would not lack a cause, because the alternative standing motive would explain it, even if nothing explained the difference in which motive was triggered.[22]

I must acknowledge that Victor Caston disagrees with one of my earlier statements of Alexander's position in his excellent translation and commentary on the first half of Alexander's *On the Soul*.[23] He thinks that Alexander does not distinguish, as I have, supervening from following but frequently treats them as equivalent, and as both standing for *necessary* co-variation in the modern technical sense. In support, he cites several of the passages which I have just discussed, but I have cited them in order to give my own different interpretation of them.[24]

3. Philoponus' Adjudication on Following, Supervening, or Resulting from a Blend

Philoponus picked up the idea of *supervening* from Alexander, his predecessor as commentator on Aristotle, but, unlike Alexander, he added a definition of it and thereby, unlike Alexander, made explicit the difference from two other relations,

---

[22] Sorabji (2017).   [23] Caston (2012: nn. 40, 90, and 92).
[24] He cites Alexander, *On the Soul* 10,14–26 and 26, 29 (the latter stressing that the soul is the *capacity* supervening on the blend); *Supplement* 104,27–34; *Commentary on Aristotle Topics* 50–1.

following and being a *result* (*apotelesma*) of something.[25] Perception, he said, is a capacity that *supervenes* on a bodily blend.[26] Repeatedly he explains that the blend is merely suited (*epitēdeios*) to, but not sufficient for, the presence of psychological capacities.[27] Mere suitability seems thereafter to be used as a defining mark of the relation of supervening. Where I had to conjecture what Alexander intended by his concepts, Philoponus brings elucidation to how he takes them.

By contrast with supervening, for the concept of *following* Philoponus cites the doctors, presumably Galen in particular, as inferring that the soul has the body as its substrate in which to inhere, on the grounds that such and such psychological impulses (*hormai*) of the soul *follow* (*hepesthai*) the blends of the body.[28] But in reply, Philoponus cites the Attic commentators from the region of Athens, who would surely include Proclus as a commentator on Plato. They say that through philosophy, even some people with bad blends have mastered impulses (*kreittones gegonai*) and have not had them following their blends. He then contrasts non-psychological attributes like being pale, sallow, or dark, which arise from such and such a blend: one cannot, even if one philosophizes 10,000 times, control (*kataskhein*) these attributes, until the blend itself changes. Alexander had similarly distinguished white as following of necessity from the underlying conditions of snow.

Philoponus in the same passage treats the doctors' conception of *resulting* in much the same way as he had just treated the doctors' conception of *following*, as involving necessitation. In his words,[29]

> thus [*houtōs*] if such and such a psychological impulse was like [*hōsper*] a result [*apotelesma*] of one's blend, it ought by all necessity to have been quite impossible for a person to refrain from anger if their blend was in the direction of anger, and similarly for the other impulses. But as it is, that does not happen, so psychological impulses do not necessarily follow blends.

Philoponus nonetheless asserts that the doctors themselves *admit* that psychological impulses do not necessarily follow blends.[30] Indeed, although Philoponus does not mention this, Galen himself, though writing about capacities of the soul following the blends of the body, himself practised Stoic cognitive therapy to counteract distress, as he recorded in his work recently discovered in 2005, *On Freedom from Distress* (*peri alupias*). Galen wrote this when he lost his own

---

[25] Philoponus, *Commentary on Aristotle On Generation and Corruption* 169,4-27.
[26] Philoponus, *Commentary on Aristotle On the Soul* 439, 35-440, 3; *Commentary on Aristotle's Physics* 191, 11-25.
[27] Philoponus, *Commentary on On the Soul* 141, 22-9; *Commentary on Physics* 191, 18-25; *Commentary on On Generation and Corruption* 169, 6-27.
[28] For this discussion, see Philoponus, *Commentary on Aristotle On the Soul* 51, 13-52, 12.
[29] Philoponus, *Commentary on Aristotle On the Soul* 51, 25-9.
[30] Philoponus, *Commentary on Aristotle On the Soul* 51, 29-32.

writings through a disastrous fire in Rome of 192 CE, after storing them with a view to making duplicate copies later in the year, in an apparently safe storehouse protected by armed guards. However, Philoponus' point is that doctors add a qualification—and this is likely to refer to or include Galen—that the capacities of the soul follow the blends of the body 'apart from the philosophical way of life'. Philoponus again adds the words 'of necessity' in concluding that 'there is then something up to us and the impulses do not follow of necessity'.[31] His objections to the doctors' claims of psychological necessitation by blends could hardly be more far reaching. It is also easier for him to describe the concepts of resulting and following clearly, because he is describing the doctors' conceptions, and not attempting the more difficult task of defining his own, which sometimes made it more difficult to be sure of what Alexander's concepts meant.

In looking to a philosophical way of life in the Platonist tradition for counteracting blends, Philoponus can be compared with Galen, who looked to Stoic cognitive therapy. But we did not find a comparable appeal in Alexander to Aristotelian philosophy for this purpose. I do not know whether this connects with the extra requirement Aristotle stresses in his *Nicomachean Ethics* (*NE*)[32] of habituation in childhood towards habits of moderating emotion as a prerequisite for being able to learn from Aristotelian philosophy about what is noble and just, and in general about the subjects of political science.

In his commentary on Aristotle's *On Generation and Corruption* (*GC*), at p. 169, lines 4–27, Philoponus raises a new problem:

> One and the same absurdity would be thought to attend[33] those such as the doctors who say that forms are the results (*apotelesmata*) of blends and those who say that forms are not the results of blends, but supervene (*epiginesthai*) from outside upon the suitability (*epitēdeiotēs*) of the blends from the Creation as a whole, as the true account has it.[34]

Philoponus' problem is that if forms were the result of different blends of hot, cold, wet, and dry, then the resulting colours, flavours, and textures which had the same ratio of blend would have to be correlated, so that e.g. what was sweet was always red. This flies in the face of the fact that honey which is sweet, yellow, and viscous can change its colour without losing any sweetness; and wine can change its flavour without changing its colour. Philoponus' solution is that we must allow for a broad range (*platos*) of ingredient ratios corresponding to different particular qualities. So a thing's sweetness may be changed to a merely negligible degree

---

[31] Philoponus, *Commentary on Aristotle On the Soul* 51, 33–4.
[32] E.g. Aristotle, *NE* 1.4,1095b4–6.   [33] *Akolouthein* here is also one of the words for following.
[34] The world is thought both by Platonists and by Christians (both of whom Philoponus represents) to be created, but the expression tends to refer to Neoplatonist belief in the creation of the intelligible forms on which God, in Plato's *Timaeus*, models the physical world.

while its colour is pushed the same distance along its range, but across a boundary to a different colour.

A further matter of interest is that both Philoponus and Galen recognize a feedback mechanism by which the mind can have a bodily effect, as well as the body acting on the mind. Galen says, 'Because of the hot blend, people become quick-tempered, and by their hot temper inflame once again the innate heat'.[35] Philoponus says that those who frequently attend lectures on the disciplines of knowledge get lean and dry bodies, which results in their *not* easily becoming annoyed.[36] Since Philoponus' name means 'lover of toil', he may long since have been able at least in this way to avoid anger. His observation qualifies the claim that the mind can counteract the body. For when devotion to lectures does so, it may act via the body. Moreover, it may act on the body in a way that in turn produces mental effects. The same passage gives an example of communication in the lecture room: but for the physical effect on the body of someone who understands the lecturer's point, we would not be able to explain the expression of understanding in their face. The text thus finishes with reference to one of the most important guides to the lecturer.

However, in Philoponus' attack on the doctors, his insistence in his *Commentary on Aristotle On Generation and Corruption*, for example at p. 51, lines 20–5, is that even those with bad blends can remove unwanted passions without removing the blends. So he would not want therapy to depend on the removal of blends by feedback.

Bibliography

Caston, V. (2012), 'Alexander of Aphrodisias', *On the Soul*, part I: *Ancient Commentators on Aristotle*, London

Lettinck, P. (1994), 'On *Physics* Book 7', *Ancient Commentators on Aristotle*, London

Sharples, R.W. (2004), *Supplement to Alexander On the Soul, Ancient Commentators on Aristotle*, London

Sorabji, R. (1980), *Necessity, Cause and Blame*, London

Sorabji, R. (1987), 'Mind-Body Relation', in R. Sorabji, ed., *Philoponus and the Rejection of Aristotelian Science*, London (see also Sorabji 2010)

Sorabji, R. (2000), *Emotion and Peace of Mind*, Oxford

Sorabji, R. (2003), 'The Mind-Body Relation in the Wake of Plato's Timaeus', in G. Reydams-Schils, ed., *Plato's Timaeus as Cultural Icon*, Notre Dame, 152–62

---

[35] Galen, *That the Capacities of the Mind Follow the Blends of the Body* 79,4–7.
[36] Philoponus, *Commentary on Aristotle's Physics*, book 5-8; translated from surviving Arabic version by Lettinck (1994: 125).

Sorabji, R. (2005), *The Philosophy of the Commentators 200–600 AD*, vol. 1: *Psychology*, Cornell (discussion on Philoponus at pp. 199–203)

Sorabji, R. ed. (2010), 'Philoponus and the Rejection of Aristotelian Science', *Bulletin of the Institute of Classical Studies*, supplementary volume 103: 33–4 (revised 2nd edition of Sorabji 1987)

Sorabji, R. (2017), 'A Neglected Strategy of the Aristotelian Alexander of Aphrodisias on Necessity and Responsibility', in Verity Harte and Raphael Woolf, eds., *Rereading Ancient Philosophy: Old Chestnuts and Sacred Cows*, Cambridge

11
Hylomorphism in Neoplatonic Commentaries on Aristotle?
Perception in Philoponus and Pseudo-Simplicius

Miira Tuominen

1. Introduction

One of the main attractions of Aristotle's philosophy today is his so-called hylomorphism, i.e. the claim that, in sublunary things, forms exist in matter. Although its exact formulation is debated, hylomorphism is considered particularly helpful in explaining the relationship between soul and body. It is taken to offer an alternative to Cartesian dualism by stating that instead of being a home of two distinct substances, mind and matter, the human being is a hylomorphic compound in which psychological and physiological aspects are intricately interconnected.[1]

As to the respective roles of the psychological and the physiological in Aristotle's theory of perception, David Charles has argued that, for Aristotle, perception is an activity which is 'the realization of an inextricably psycho-physical goal-directed material capacity'.[2] As such, it should be distinguished both from (i) the non-reductive materialist combination of a purely physical and a purely psychological component and (ii) perception defined in the spiritualist manner as a purely psychological change with necessary material conditions that are not constitutive of perception. According to Charles, whose view has also been called 'strong hylomorphism',[3] the main interpretations of Aristotle's theory of perception in today's scholarship assume a Cartesian conceptual framework in which psycho-physical processes are analysed into purely psychological and purely physical components[4] and thus cannot give an adequate account of Aristotle's view.

---

[1] Some scholars have also argued that Aristotle is objecting to a materialistic dualism in which the soul *is* a kind of body; see Menn (2002: 83–4).
[2] Charles (2021: 152).
[3] As Victor Caston calls it in his critical response to Charles (2009), arguing for a two-component view ('moderate hylomorphism').
[4] See Charles (2021: 118) for the central assumptions of Cartesian dualism; for arguments against the two-component and spiritualist readings, see Charles (2021: 118–62).

Miira Tuominen, *Hylomorphism in Neoplatonic Commentaries on Aristotle? Perception in Philoponus and Pseudo-Simplicius* In: *The History of Hylomorphism: From Aristotle to Descartes*. Edited by: David Charles, Oxford University Press. © Miira Tuominen 2023. DOI: 10.1093/oso/9780192897664.003.0012

In this essay, I shall consider the accounts of perception in two late ancient commentaries on Aristotle's *De Anima*, that by Philoponus and that by Pseudo-Simplicius, from the perspective of the following two questions:

Q1 What role, if any, do physiological changes play in their accounts of sense-perception?
Q2 If a physiological change can be detected, how is it related to the psychological change in perception?

I shall first consider Q1 in section 2 with respect to the scholarly debate between so-called literalism and spiritualism. In section 3, I shall focus on Q2 and ask (a) whether the two commentators' accounts of perception contain elements of hylomorphism; and (b) if so, whether those elements should be understood in terms of inextricably psycho-physical activities ('strong hylomorphism') or as a two-component theory ('moderate hylomorphism').[5] It needs to be noted that I am not offering a comprehensive account of perception in the two commentaries. I focus on the passages in which something is said about the sense organs and their role in perception from the perspective of the two questions just mentioned. Therefore, attention and self-awareness as well as higher forms of rational cognition fall outside the scope of this essay.

Both Philoponus and Pseudo-Simplicius are late ancient Platonists,[6] although Aristotelian elements are central especially in Philoponus and can also be found in Pseudo-Simplicius. In Platonism, the human soul or at least its rational part is assumed to be immortal and capable of existing independently of a body as well as of being incarnated in different bodies. Some Platonist commentators maintained, however, that Aristotle and Plato are on a deeper philosophical level in agreement with each other despite their apparent differences.[7] This tendency is to an extent found in Philoponus' commentary based on the seminars of his teacher Ammonius.[8] There is a scholarly debate about the authorship of the commentary

---

[5] Moderate hylomorphism or the two-component view in fact bears resemblance to Cartesian dualism discussed in Chapter 16 of this collection by Lilli Alanen.

[6] In the title, I use the customary term 'Neoplatonic'. However, many commentators would rather have seen themselves as Platonists. Plotinus and Porphyry would probably not have accepted the idea of introducing a new kind of Platonism, while Proclus was more comfortable with the designation 'newer Platonists' (*In Tim.* 2.88.12–13). Gerson (2005) also stresses that we should not assume doctrinal unity in Platonism after Plotinus. For a critical note on the criticism of 'Neoplatonism', see Barney (2009: 101 n1).

[7] For this so-called 'harmony thesis', see Sorabji (2016c: 5). Not all subscribed to it, and some, especially Iamblichus and Proclus, argued for the superiority of Plato over Aristotle. In Pseudo-Simplicius the Aristotelian elements are subordinated to a hierarchical (Neo)Platonistic framework.

[8] Sorabji (2016a) has argued that Philoponus' commentaries based on Ammonius' seminars never merely report Ammonius but always contain Philoponus' contributions. Golitsis (2016) claims, by contrast, that Philoponus only comments on Ammonius critically when the criticism is mentioned in the titles in the manuscripts.

preserved under Simplicius' name.[9] I shall not focus on the question of authorship and shall call the author 'Pseudo-Simplicius'.

As to the physiological and physical changes in sense perception, Richard Sorabji has argued that Aristotle's theory was 'dematerialized' in late ancient commentaries. According to Sorabji,[10] Aristotle took a physical or material change in the sense organ to be a constituent in perception, while his late ancient commentators developed Aristotle's account in the direction that is nowadays known as 'spiritualism'.[11] Spiritualism in this sense takes perception to be our becoming aware of a perceptible quality, while the changes in the sense organs are merely necessary conditions for perceiving, e.g. the eyes are like the medium between us and the object and allow us to see the object through them.[12]

In order to discuss the commentators' accounts, it is important to distinguish between the following psychological and physiological[13] aspects of perception.

Ph0 A purely material change such as being heated by fire.

Ph1 A physiological change in the sense organ that is necessary for and constitutive of our awareness of a perceptible quality, e.g. compression or expansion of a sense organ or its part.

Ps1 The awareness of a perceptible quality such as a colour or a sound.[14]

Ph2 A change in the sense organs that stimulates the projection of a concept such as 'red'.

Ps2 A projection of a concept on the physiological change in the sense organ.

I shall argue that the purely material change (Ph0) is neither relevant nor necessary for perception according to Philoponus. Although sense organs can be affected in a purely material way, there is perception even without such changes. The physiological change that I argue to be constitutive of perception is of the second kind (Ph1). The first psychological process (Ps1) is especially relevant to

---

[9] Bossier and Steel (1972); Hadot (2016²). Blumenthal has argued for the authorship of Simplicius (1982), although he changed his mind and later argued against the attribution to both Simplicius and to Priscian (1996: 65–71). Steel (1997) and Perkams (2005) attribute the commentary to Priscian and defend the attribution against Huby's (1999) criticism that the *Metaphrasis* is not an epitome; see Blumenthal (2000, 4). For criticism, see also Finamore and Dillon (2002: 18–24) who take there to be a common source for Priscian and Pseudo-Simplicius and argue it to be Iamblichus. I refrain from attributing the commentary to Priscian, although it is clear that the author is not Simplicius. For a difference from Priscian, see note 37 below.

[10] Sorabji (1991).

[11] Defended by Burnyeat ([1992] 1995, 1995, 2002) and Johansen (1997).

[12] See, e.g., Burnyeat (1995: 425–6).

[13] I use 'physical' and 'physiological' interchangeably. I use 'material' below of the kind of change that belongs to all bodies and even the sense organs *as bodies*. Eyes and stones are both equally heated by fire but being heated in this merely material way is not relevant for perceiving the heat.

[14] I shall only be concerned with the so-called 'proper sensibles' here, i.e. the qualities that are perceived by one sense and not by the others, e.g. sounds for hearing.

my discussion of Philoponus. Philoponus also calls such awareness 'discernment' (*krisis*) and attributes it to the sense organs. It is possible that Pseudo-Simplicius allows such awareness (as sensation) as well. However, he (assuming the author is male) does not define perception as a psycho-physical process but rather identifies it with such projection of a concept by the perceptive soul (Ps2) that is stimulated by the psycho-physical change in the sense organs (Ph2). We do not have Philoponus' commentary on book 3, and thus what we have of his account of perception focuses on discernment in the sense organs and not on judgement made by the rational soul.[15] Therefore, it is possible that Philoponus' analysis in his commentary on book 2 concerns sensation as opposed to perception as propositional. However, in his commentary on book 2, he in no way indicates that rather than a psycho-physical process perception should be identified with rational projection of forms.

As to Q1, I shall argue first on textual grounds that both Philoponus and Pseudo-Simplicius take physiological changes in the sense organs to be necessary for perception and not merely as necessary conditions. As to Philoponus, I contend that the relevant physiological change should be understood neither in terms of literalism nor as a form of spiritualism. Rather, in Philoponus, a non-literal physiological change in the sense organ is partly constitutive of perception. With respect to Pseudo-Simplicius, I shall argue that Ph2 is not a purely physical change but should rather be understood as psycho-physical.

With respect to hylomorphism (Q2), I shall argue that Philoponus' view can be analysed as a form of strong hylomorphism in which the physiological process in perception must be defined with essential reference to the psychological process and vice versa. While Pseudo-Simplicius is a dualist of some kind and takes the rational soul and/or intellect to be separable from the body, he has a layered view in which many levels of soul activities are distinguished without necessarily assuming purity, or so I will argue. What is important for this essay is that in perception the change in the sense organs is a psycho-physical process, a 'joint affection' or 'passive effect', as he calls it, in a living ensouled body that cannot be defined in purely material terms. The body's sensitivity is due to the sensitive soul that gives the body its distinct kind of life that differs both from plant life that is devoid of perception and intellectual life that is purely immaterial.

I refer to the claim that there are two distinct substances, matter as extension and mind as thinking (*cogitatio*), together with the claim that the attributes and

---

[15] Note that according to Philoponus, flesh is a contributory cause to the intellect (388.23–4). This seems to indicate that, to the extent that intellect is needed in judgements of reason, the effect in the organ does not necessitate a rational judgement about a perceptible object but only contributes to its being and activity. The evidence for Philoponus' claim that there are material conditions on which the soul's activities supervene, as Richard Sorabji discusses in Chapter 10 of this collection, is related to what is said about intelligence here (*phronêsis* in 388.24). Sensory activities are explained in a different way, as I will argue in this chapter. Golitsis (2016) argues, contrary to the majority view, that the Greek commentary on book 3 is Philoponus' own.

modifications of the two cannot be defined by reference to those of the other, as 'Cartesian dualism'. I suspend judgement about whether Descartes himself was a Cartesian dualist.[16] With respect to Cartesianism, it is important that Philoponus introduced a new concept of matter as a three-dimensional extension that means a clear departure from Aristotle and seems rather like a precursor of the Cartesian definition of matter.[17] However, this notion of prime matter as a three-dimensional extension is not sufficient to define bodily changes in the commentators' discussions of perception.

2. The Change in the Sense Organs

2.1 Philoponus

Let me now move to discuss the nature of the physiological change in the sense organ in Philoponus' commentary. Richard Sorabji's claim about dematerialization is based on evidence against Philoponus' being a literalist in the sense of claiming that the sense organ takes on the perceived quality in the same sense it exists in the object.[18] I agree that Philoponus is not a literalist in this sense. However, from this evidence together with a discussion of how the medium is changed and the attribution of a cognitive change to flesh (T2 below), Sorabji concludes to dematerialization that seems to amount to a similar view as spiritualism in the scholarship on Aristotle.[19] As other scholars have shown, however, there is logical space between the two opposing poles of the debate.[20] To argue for spiritualism in Philoponus, it would thus need to be shown not only that he is not a literalist in the above sense but that no physiological change in the organ is constitutive of perception. I shall argue that although Philoponus is not a literalist in the sense just described, he is not a spiritualist either but takes a physiological change in the sense organ to be necessary for perception, and not merely as a necessary condition but as constitutive of it.

---

[16] For Descartes' hylomorphism, see Alanen in Chapter 16 of this collection.
[17] For Philoponus' analysis of matter (and that of Simplicius, who is not Pseudo-Simplicius), see Haas (1997).
[18] This is the kind of change that Caston (2005: 249–51) classifies as a fundamentalist reading of a primitive literal change.
[19] He says: 'The organs receive the other forms only cognitively (*gnôstikôs*), just as the sense-faculty receives them' in Sorabji (1991: 232). In a spoken exchange at the closing conference of the project 'Representation and Reality' in Gothenburg (Sweden, February 2020), Sorabji did not think that my argument for the necessity of a physiological change in the sense organs in Philoponus contradicts his claim about dematerialization. His main concern seemed to be the debate with Myles Burnyeat on Aristotle; and if Philoponus can be argued to require a physiological change in the organs too, Sorabji seemed to take that as congenial to his general argument.
[20] Caston (2005).

Other scholars have also argued that Philoponus is no spiritualist,[21] and according to Peter Lautner, Philoponus should not be understood as a literalist either.[22] However, Lautner's argument concerns literalism merely in the sense that the sense organ takes on the quality (becomes sweet or red) in the same manner as it is perceived in the object.[23] In this essay, I seek to improve on previous scholarship by, first, arguing that we should leave the debate between spiritualism and literalism behind; and, second, by analysing what the physiological change is in the case of all the senses. Finally, in section 3.1 below, I also connect the analysis to the discussion of hylomorphism.

Let me first argue for the necessity of a physiological change in the organs in Philoponus' account. Lautner's discussion on the topic is especially useful for the sensory mechanism in sight, hearing, and smell. However, as opposed to Lautner, I argue that when Philoponus talks about sense organs changing materially (*hulikôs*),[24] this should *not* be taken as a reference to a distinct physiological change that is necessary for and (partly) constitutive of perception.[25] Lautner also uses the notion of 'judgment' even for the discernment Philoponus ascribes to sense organs. Although *krisis* can of course mean 'judgement', I do not think sense organs make judgements in the sense of propositional claims like 'this is red' or 'this is sweet'. Lautner recognizes this but still talks about 'judgment' even in the sense organs.[26] I shall use 'discernment' for *krisis* instead.[27]

In order to analyse the physiological changes in Philoponus' account, let us consider the following passage.

T1 The sense-organ [*to aisthêtêrion*], then, undergoes two affections, one simply as a body [*hôs haplôs sôma*], the other as a sense-organ [*hôs aisthêtêrion*]. As a body, it is affected by body, as a sense-organ on the other hand, it is affected

---

[21] Caston (2005: 290); Lautner (2013). For the suggestion that, for Philoponus, the senses of touch and taste require a physiological change, while sight, hearing, and smell do not, see Rapp (2001: 76).

[22] Lautner (2013).

[23] While many, e.g. Lautner (2013: 378–9), take Sorabji to argue for such literalism in the case of Aristotle, Caston (2005: 251) has pointed out that Sorabji's literalism for Aristotle is what he calls 'latitudinariamism'. According to 'latitudinarian' literalism, the sense organ takes on the quality but not in the way it is perceived to be in the object but in a way similar to how it adheres in the medium.

[24] See Lautner (2013: 394) where he claims that, according to Philoponus, 'colours affect the special sense-organ "materially", *hulikôs*'. However, considering T1 (quoted on this page), this does not seem possible, since the material change Philoponus refers to is the change that is not relevant for perception but, rather, an organ or a body being affected *with its matter*. Such a change is one when, e.g., my eyes are being heated when I look at a fire, as opposed to being affected by the activities of the colour of fire that partly constitutes my seeing the colour.

[25] Lautner says that, in Philoponus, physiological processes necessarily 'accompany perceptions' (2013: 385). In the light of what I am going to argue in the following, this seems too weak. Lautner himself also allows, however, that the physical changes are material causes of perceptions (2013: 385), which seems stronger than mere accompanying.

[26] Lautner (2013: 392).

[27] For a similar argument for Aristotle, see Ebert (1983). Corcilius (2014) improves on Ebert's account, among other things, by offering a reading of *krisis* as discernment without the additional claim that discernment means awareness of the *difference* between qualities.

by the activity of the sense objects. For instance, the *eye as a sense-organ*, is affected when it is *compressed or expanded* by *the activity of colours*, while as a body it is affected by fire, as it might be, heating it.

Philoponus, *In De An.* 439.15–20; trans. Charlton; emphases mine[28]

When I sit by a fire, my eyes are warmed by it and affected *simply as bodies*. This must be distinguished from how my eyes, or more specifically, their choroid membranes,[29] are affected *as sense organs* by being compressed or expanded by the *activities* of the colour. It is such a change that makes me see the colour. Assuming that the colour is light, the choroid membrane of my eyes is compressed and, if dark, expanded by the activities.

The way in which the sense organs are affected simply *as bodies* can be taken as a *purely material or physical* change (like a stone is heated by fire). However, this change is neither relevant nor necessary for perception because perception can occur without such a purely material change. This can be seen on the basis of the following passage in which Philoponus talks about the various qualities perceived by the sense of touch.

T2 But it should be known that nor is the sense-organ of touch qualified by every perception. For when it apprehends heavy or light, viscous or friable, rough or smooth, flesh does not become like that itself but receives the forms of these things only *in a cognitive way* [*gnôstikôs*]. But since, as has often been said, every body consists of a mixture together with moist and dry[30] and hot and cold, for this reason also whenever it is affected by them, *as a sense* it apprehends and gets to know them [*kai ginôskei auta*], but as a natural body it is affected in a material way by them.

432.36–433.4; my emphasis and correction

Therefore, even though sense organs are changed by perceptible qualities simply *as bodies* (e.g. being heated by fire), such a change cannot be necessary for perception, since many qualities are perceived without such a purely material change. It is also important to note that in T2 Philoponus does not contrast the

---

[28] I use Charlton's translations for Philoponus.

[29] Lautner (2013: 389) notes that Philoponus takes the *korê* in Aristotle to mean the channel through which the optic *pneuma* that is the primary organ of sight reaches the lens. The compression is said to occur in the eye (*to omma hôs aisthêtêrion paskhei synkrinomenomenon*; 439.18 in T1). According to Lautner (2013: 391), this is the liquid and the choroid membrane, although Philoponus simply talks about 'the eye'. In the *De Intellectu* (18.2–3 and 20.3–4; quoted by Lautner 2013: 392), it is the *pneuma* that is contracted and dispersed. However, Lautner (2013: 389) maintains that Philoponus talks about the sense organs 'holistically' in the sense that the organs and their parts (such as the eyes, their membranes, and so on), as well as the *pneuma* in the sense organ as well as the channels and the brain are included.

[30] Charlton has 'moist and wet' for *tou hugrou kai xêrou* (moist and dry). I have corrected the simple lapse.

purely material change with the kind of physiological change that is necessary for and partly constitutive of perception (such as compression or expansion of the eyes). Rather, he contrasts it with a *cognitive change*. I shall argue below that this can be taken as evidence of Philoponus' strong hylomorphism.

Therefore, texts T1 and T2 show that a purely material change in the sense organ as a body is neither necessary nor relevant for perception. T1 identifies the necessary physiological change in the case of sight as compression and expansion, while T2 describes the change in the case of touch as cognitive (for which, see section 3.1 below). Next, we need to ask whether distinct physiological changes are necessary for the other senses and what kind of changes they are.

Before considering the question, one specification is needed. As Lautner notes, Philoponus talks about the sensory organism holistically (see footnote 29 above), so that sense organs can mean the particular organs such as eyes or ears and their parts (membranes and cavities), the channels or nerves (*neura*) that connect the particular organs with the brain, and the brain. Inside the nerves and apparently inside the particular organs, there is *pneuma* specific for each sense, e.g. optic *pneuma* for sight, acoustic *pneuma* for hearing, and so on. *Pneuma* is also identified as the organ of the sensory power in general. The physiological changes necessary for perception are often said to belong to the particular sense organs (e.g. the eyes in T1). However, at times Philoponus attributes the same kind of physiological change to the *pneuma* specific to the sense (e.g. compression and expansion to the optic *pneuma*). Philoponus also seems to assume that the unity of perception can be explained by reference to the *pneuma* (433.34–5) that permeates the perceptual organism as a whole.[31]

Philoponus makes it clear that the organ of smell, which according to Lautner is the mastoid process, is compressed and expanded by different olfactory qualities.

> T3   It [i.e. the sense or the sense-organ] comes to be like it [i.e. the object] when it receives the activities of the smell-objects and becomes a thing smelling in act. For it does not become foul-smelling or sweet-smelling, but it is made to *expand or contract* by the sense-object.
>
> 396.14–16; italics and additions mine

Therefore, the change in the organ is not literal in the way that the organ would be changed in a purely material way *as a body* (T1). By contrast to becoming foul-smelling or fragrant, the organ is expanded or compressed. It is not clarified which kinds of smell do which, but the order indicates that foul-smelling objects expand and fragrant objects compress the olfactory organ. Philoponus underlines that the sense organs are changed as sense organs by *the activities* of the qualities.

---

[31] See Lautner (2013: 388–9). For the role of *pneuma* and the influence of Galen on Philoponus, see also Todd (1984: 105–7).

This suggests that the contraction is (Ca) a specific contraction-by-a-sense-object or its activity, as opposed to (Cb) a contraction as mere pressing that could be defined in its own terms without a reference to (the activities of) the sense objects.

When we hear a sound, Philoponus says, the air inside the cavities by the eardrum changes (364.11–15). What exactly the change is like is not articulated. The air in the cavities is 'affected by the air from the outside changed by the activities of sounds' after which '[t]he air inside the ear receives the activities of sounds and transmits them' to the acoustic *pneuma* that is the primary organ of hearing (364.13–14). A few pages earlier, Philoponus refers to air being 'divided' (*dielôn*; 361.1), which possibly means that sounds, as it were, divide a mass of air between the percipient and the object by creating movement in it and different kinds of sound do this in different ways. It can also mean that some sounds divide the air whereas others somehow gather it together. The effect in the air inside the ear's cavities is caused by the movements of air outside our ears when the air is struck and moved by the objects. It is possible that the air in the cavities is divided (or gathered together) as well, and it seems that the change in the air in the cavities must be a distinct physical change caused by an auditory object.

Although Philoponus says that the sense organ of taste is inside the flesh (433.33–4), when he discusses the way in which the organ is affected, he talks about the tongue. Probably, he again considers the sense organism as a whole. If so, the tongue corresponds to the eyes, although the primary organ for it is gustatory *pneuma* inside the tongue ultimately reaching the brain through the nerves. The relevant physiological change of the tongue is the organ being moistened or dried by gustatory objects (405.21–4).

According to Philoponus, this requires that the tongue itself is not moist in actuality. Otherwise, the degree of moisture in the object would get mixed with the moistness of the tongue, and this would affect the perception (405.3–7). Rather, the tongue has to be potentially moist (405.4) and probably neutral with respect to moisture and dryness. If it had a degree of moisture in itself, we could not taste the objects as they are but only insofar as they are mixed with the moistness or dryness of the tongue.[32] Pepper, dried meat, and bread are said to dry the organ. Philoponus does not clarify what tastes moisten the organ, but sweet liquids probably would.

Philoponus makes it clear that moistening or drying of the tongue is not a destructive affection (405.19–20), i.e. the natural moistness of the organ is not *replaced* by another degree of moistness. Rather, the moisture is taken on in a preservative (*sôstikê*) and perfective (*teleiôtikê*) way (405.20–1). These expressions indicate that the moistening or drying of the tongue is not a primitive literal

---

[32] As opposed to the transparent that is the medium for colours, Philoponus also notes that the moist, supposedly the liquid on the tongue, becomes matter for flavours (400.14–15). This means that the medium actually takes on the qualities that are perceived and is affected *as a body*. However, this is not the physiological change that is necessary for (and partly constitutive of) gustatory perception or sensation.

change but a change that leads to the perfection of the organ's capacity to discern the quality.[33]

Finally, as with the other senses, Philoponus identifies the organ of touch as a mean (*mesotês*; 435.25).

T4   He [i.e. Aristotle] now calls the sense-organ [*aisthêtêrion*] the 'sense' [*aisthêsis*]. And he says that the sense is a mean, referring either to touch... or to every sense as well. For each sense is in the middle of the contrariety which it discerns [*hês estin hekastê kritikê*] and it is in the middle in this way, that it can receive the form of either contrary. For it is not, simply by being neither of the contraries, thereby genuinely in the middle (for how can what is colourless be said to be a middle between black and white?). But as I said, [it is in the middle] inasmuch as it is capable of receiving the form of either contrary. Similarly too the soundless, the odourless, and the flavourless.
Philoponus, *In De An.* 435.25–32, *ad* 424a4–6

While other sense organs are means which lack colour, sound, smell, or taste, the organ of touch cannot be like this. There is no body that could lack all tactile qualities, since they are constitutive (*sustatikai*) of what a body is (436.21–3). The sense organ of touch is the only mean (*mesotês*), in the sense of *having a quality* in the middle of two extremes (436.3), that determines the range of tactile qualities. Therefore, while the other senses can detect a genuine lack of their proper qualities, for touch there is a blind spot at which the quality is not sensed because we cannot sense a quality that is entirely or 'closely similar' to the quality of the organ and a 'touch-object [only] to a slight extent' (436.25–6).

Philoponus does not explain how the sense organ of touch *is* affected by the objects. T1, quoted above, excludes a primitive literal change as a mere material change of a body taking on the perceived quality, and T2 specifies that such a change is not necessary for perception. However, it seems that there must be some physiological change in the organ *as an organ* because Philoponus points out that the sense organ is not affected if the object is too similar to the sense organ (436.27). This implies that if the object is not too similar, the sense organ *is affected*. We only perceive air if it is 'too chilled or too heated' (436.28), while it remains unperceived when it is 'in a state of proportionality' (*en summetria*; 436.31). Philoponus notes that when the object and the organ are in symmetry, translated by Charlton as 'in a state of proportionality', the quality is not sensed. What happens when the quality *is sensed* is left unexplained. Charlton's translation of *summetria* as 'a state of proportionality' makes one think of Aristotle's use of *logos* of proportions between two extremes that delimit the range of qualities for

---

[33] The moistening of the tongue is what David Charles calls a '[Type 2]', not '[Type 1]', change (2021: 120–1). Below, I shall return to Philoponus' point that there is discernment in the sense organs.

a sense modality. However, it is important to note that Philoponus' wording is different and he uses *summetria* to refer to the quality being similar or identical to the sense as a mean (see below, T5).[34]

Support for the claim that the sense organ of touch is affected in a physiological way can also be found in the passage in which Philoponus explains Aristotle's claim that an excess of sense objects destroys the mean.

T5 [I]f insofar as they are sense-organs they exist in a certain proportionality [*summetria*] and mean state [*mesotês*]...and if, further, it is because *the sense-organs are changed by the sense-objects* that perception of the sense-objects then occurs, it follows that it is reasonable also that change beyond measure of the sense-organs by the sense-objects should destroy their proportionality [i.e. their being a mean]. And when the proportionality is destroyed they become unsuitable for housing the power of perception.

439.9–15; my emphasis

From this Philoponus concludes his earlier claim that the sense organ can undergo two affections (cf. T1): one simply as a body (and this change is neither relevant nor necessary for perception), the other as a sense organ. The latter kind of change is caused by the *activities* of the sense objects (439.15–17), which suggests that they are a type of change *defined* by the activities of the sense objects, i.e. option (Ca) above in connection with T3. Such a change is also described as being cognitive (T2 above), which indicates that it is constitutive of perception rather than a merely necessary condition for it. It is important to note that Philoponus does not specify how the organ of touch is affected by the activities of tactile objects *as an organ*. Some physiological change seems necessary because otherwise the argument from excess would not work; an immaterial or non-physiological effect seems unable to destroy the mean state of the organ. Aristotle uses the argument to stress that the excessive change in the organs differs from encountering highly intelligible objects precisely because the perceptive power is bodily while the intellect is not (*De An.* 3.4, 429a29–b5). The latter kind of immaterial 'excess' in intellect strengthens its power rather than destroys it.

2.2 Pseudo-Simplicius

As opposed to Philoponus who talks about discernment (*krisis*) in the senses or sense organs and ascribes cognitive change to them, Pseudo-Simplicius identifies

---

[34] *Summetria* occurs together with *logos* in 439.5–6. Some lines later (in T8), however, *summetria* refers to the mean state (*mesotês*; 439.9). *Logos* is connected with form (*eidos*) thus indicating that it refers to the defining account of the sense, not the proportions between two extremes.

perception with the projection of forms stimulated by a change in the sense organ caused by the object (see, e.g., T6 below). The point that is repeatedly stressed in his commentary on De Anima 2.5-7 is that although perception requires an external object that is present and affects a sense organ, perception itself cannot be an affection or reception; it must be an activity arising from the [perceptive] soul itself (117.28-31).

Pseudo-Simplicius also formulates his central question as an *aporia*. Although perception is 'self-aroused' or stimulated by the soul itself, it cannot take place without the sense organ being changed by something external (117.30-1). Neither do the senses perceive themselves but only cognize bodies and are changed by them (118.11-14). This distinguishes perception from purely self-aroused activities such as knowledge of universal principles within the soul and imagination (165.32-166.2). Therefore, the claim that perception is an activity of the soul needs to be reconciled with the undeniable fact that external objects must be present and affect our sense organism (see, e.g., 116.29-30; 144.17-18).

According to Pseudo-Simplicius, the solution to the *aporia* is that being entirely self-stimulated only belongs to a perfect and permanently active life, i.e. intellect or reason. The life of the sensitive soul, by contrast, 'reaches out to the external objects' and is not self-sufficient but in need of 'the activity of something else either as object or as efficient cause' (118.29-33; trans. Steel).[35] However, Pseudo-Simplicius stresses throughout the discussion that even in such cases the sensitive soul is also stimulated from within (119.5-12).

I shall not try to give a detailed account of Pseudo-Simplicius' layered view but focus on the questions formulated at the beginning, i.e. (Q1) whether physiological changes in the sense organs are necessary for perception and (Q2) what the connection is between the physiological and the psychological change (section 3.2 below).

As mentioned, Pseudo-Simplicius identifies perception with projection of forms or concepts from within the sensitive soul.

T6 But clearly the perceptible object is perfected and brought to activity by the perceptive soul itself and it also projects the form of the perceptible from itself, but it has been stimulated [*egeiromenês*] to the projection by the change that occurs in the sense-organ caused by the perceptible object. This is because neither is the perceptive life entirely separate from bodies nor does it project the appropriate concept [*logos*] on the perceptible object immediately but on the vital modification or the passive effect [*pathêtikon energêma*] in the sense-organ.

   Pseudo-Simplicius, In De An. 192.12-18; trans. Steel slightly modified

---

[35] I am using Steel's translations for Pseudo-Simplicius.

Therefore, the sensitive soul projects a form or a concept (*logos*) that is appropriate (*oikeios*) probably in the sense of corresponding to the object or its quality. If, for example, the object is red, the sensitive soul projects the concept of red. Pseudo-Simplicius emphasizes that this is not a passive process in which the object and its effect on the sense organ determine the projection. Rather, the projection is from the soul itself. However, not even the effect in the sense organs is completely passive but a vital modification (*zôtikon pathos*).

The account can be illustrated by the following example. When, say, a red, hot, and sweet object (such as mulled wine) is present to my sense organs, it has an effect on those sense organs together with the sensitive soul's activity coming from within. I can perhaps be said to sense the sweetness or probably even the object's sweetness when there is appropriate passive effect in the organs because Pseudo-Simplicius stresses that it is the objects as external bodies that we cognize when our sense organism is vitally effected in the relevant way. However, whether or not I project the concept of red, hot, or sweet on the passive effect in the organs is a different question. I might be engaged, say, in a debate about hylomorphism in late antiquity and not notice the effect the mulled wine has on my sense organism. In such a case, I can probably be said to sense the qualities of the wine but not perceive in the sense of projecting the concept of, say, sweet so that I would perceive the wine as especially sweet this year. It is only such (re)cognition in terms of a concept that Pseudo-Simplicius identifies as perception (*aisthêsis*) in a proper sense.[36]

While there is change in the sense organs caused by the object, Pseudo-Simplicius notes that the soul is not changed (125.14–15). The soul or its sensitive capacity is said to stand still at the form of the object, but the object or the activity in the organs is not the efficient cause of perception.

T7 The faculty of sense-perception [*to aisthêtikon*]...stands still at the form of the sensible object, not as being affected but in activity [*energetikôs*], not acting like efficient causes[37] but in judgement [*kritikôs*] and cognition [*gnôstikôs*]. However, some sort of affection remains in the sense-organ.
Pseudo-Simplicius, *In De An.* 125.20–4; trans. Steel.

Before considering the content of the passage, it is important to note that I follow Steel in using 'in judgment' for *kritikôs* (instead of 'in discernment') to indicate the

---

[36] It has been argued by Coope (2020: 237; 242; 243 n58) that every act of perception for Pseudo-Simplicius includes a second-order act of awareness of the act. It seems to me that the second-order acts are related to perception in the sense of projection, while they might not be there for the vital effect in the sense organs.

[37] Kalderon (2017: 444) and some other scholars takes Priscian's account to be one in which the soul is the efficient cause of its likeness to the perceived object. Here Pseudo-Simplicius seems to deny such an account. This might cast some doubt on the identification between the two authors, but I shall not pursue the issue further here.

difference between Pseudo-Simplicius and *krisis* as discernment in Philoponus. The discernment Philoponus talks about is allowed to happen even in the sense *organs*, which indicates that it is not conceptual or propositional. Here, by contrast, the derivatives of *krisis* refer to the projection of concepts that is something that the soul as opposed to the sense organs do.[38] It seems that the soul's judgement as projection of a concept means (re)cognizing the object by subsuming it under the appropriate concept: 'this is sweet' or 'the wine is sweet'. This is how I understand Pseudo-Simplicius' description of perception according to which 'the sensitive soul recognizes [*gnôrizousês*] the sensible object by projection of concepts' (128.28–9).[39]

In T7, Pseudo-Simplicius stresses again that although perception is a cognitive activity of the soul, some affection in the sense organs is necessary to stimulate the projection and to distinguish it from imagination and entirely self-aroused projection of concepts. Remarkably little is said about this affection. Pseudo-Simplicius' usual phrase is that the organ must be 'affected in some way' (*pathein ti dei*)[40] or that the 'sense-organ is changed [*kinêthê*], being first affected [*pathon*] by something external' (117.30–1). Once he notes that the tongue is moistened (155.33–5), and this indicates that the change is physical probably in a similar way as in Philoponus (following Aristotle, *De An.* 422b4–6). Moreover, Pseudo-Simplicius notes that although the organ must be affected in some way, it is perfection, not one quality being destroyed or replaced by another.[41] Pseudo-Simplicius also makes it clear that the change in the organ is not a literal change in which the organ takes on the quality that is perceived.

T8 [T]he sense-organ is not affected by things external in the way that the inanimate is. It is affected as being alive. Therefore, it is not entirely an affection nor altogether from outside... Such a joint affection and effect [*pathêma kai energêma*] which comes about as caused by the sensible objects and according to the arousal towards them of the life in the sense-organ is...

---

[38] It needs to be noted, however, that Pseudo-Simplicius is not consistent with the terminology. In 161.11–14, he notes that flesh as the medium of touch must be vitally affected and, even though faintly and secondarily, must already discern or discriminate, while the sense organ for touch is the heart (164.15–16); see Lautner (1997: 227 n215) with reference to *De Sensu* 2, 439a1–2. Steel translates *kritikê* as 'judgment' even in the medium (161.12). It seems to me that the reference is rather to the idea that even the sense organism can discern qualities although perception properly speaking as projection of concepts is impossible for them.

[39] A concept (*logos*) belongs to discursive thought in the soul and derives through rational unfolding (*kata logikên... anelixin*) from the intellect (124.21). Therefore, concepts in the soul must be distinguished from intelligible forms in the intellect. On concepts in Pseudo-Simplicius, see Helmig (2020: suppl., 'The Commentaries of Simplicius', sect. 5.3).

[40] See *pathein men ti dei* (122.12); *dei ti pathein* (124.3); *pathein men gar ti dei* (163.34); see also 'the activity in the sense-organ involves affection' (*meta pathous hê energeia*; 138.12).

[41] Again, the formulation indicates that the change is of '[Type 2]' in the classification by Charles (2021: 120–1).

made similar to the forms in the sensible objects. But that is not yet
perception since that does not occur as a pure activity.
  Pseudo-Simplicius, *In De An.* 125.31–7; trans. Steel slightly modified.

The point that the sense organ is not affected in the way that an inanimate object is implies that the relevant change in the sense organ is not a literal taking on of the perceived quality. Even plants can be passively heated by fire, but such passive affection is a mere material change and does not stimulate cognitive activity (168.25–169.1). While inanimate things and plants are passively affected along their matter, the sense organs have to be vitally modified.

I shall return to the nature of the vital modification in the organ and its relation to the projection of forms below in section 3.2. For the moment, let us note the following points in Pseudo-Simplicius' analysis:

(a) There is a vital modification in the sense organ that stimulates the soul.
(b) Having been stimulated by the vital modification, the soul projects the form or concept on the vital modification in the organ.[42]

It is (b) that is identified as perception properly speaking. Perception thus means projecting a concept on the passive activity in the organs and cognizing (*gnôrizein*) or recognizing the object. I have suggested that the recognition can be understood as a propositional judgement such as 'this is red' or 'this is sweet'.

3. The Question of Hylomorphism

3.1 Philoponus on Physiological and Psychological Changes

I have argued above that Philoponus takes a physiological change in the sense organs *as sense organs* to be necessary for perception. For sight and smell, the change is described as compression and expansion in the visual or olfactory organism, while for hearing the air inside the cavities of the ears is changed, perhaps by being divided or gathered together, or by being divided in different ways. Taste is explained by the sense organ being moistened or dried by gustatory objects, while the physiological change in the organ of touch is not explicated.

Rather than taking T2 as representing an exhaustive dichotomy between literalism and spiritualism, I have argued that the literal change of the organ as a body denied in the passage is neither necessary nor relevant for perception in Philoponus. What, then, about the cognitive change? Does it imply that

---

[42] See also 124.32–125.2 that contains a very similar account as T6.

Philoponus is a spiritualist about the sense of touch, as Sorabji's reading suggests?[43]

In the light of section 2.1 above, this would require that, as opposed to all the other senses, touch alone should be explained in a spiritualist manner. That would be surprising, since normally touch is identified as the most material of the senses.[44] However, I do not think we need to draw the conclusion that Philoponus is a spiritualist about touch. To see why, let us return to the passage in which Philoponus describes the change that flesh undergoes *as the organ of touch*.

> T2 But it should be known that nor is the sense-organ of touch qualified by every perception. For when it apprehends heavy or light, viscous or friable, rough or smooth, flesh does not become like that itself but receives the forms of these things only *in a cognitive way* [gnôstikôs]. But since, as has often been said, every body consists of a mixture together with moist and dry and hot and cold, for this reason also whenever it is affected by them, *as a sense* it apprehends and gets to know them [*kai ginôskei auta*], but as a natural body it is affected in a material way by them.
>
> Philoponus, *In De An.* 432.36–433.4; tr. Charlton.

As previously noted, Philoponus makes clear that with qualities such as heavy or light, there is no merely material change of flesh as a body taking on these qualities. By contrast to qualities such as hot and cold that change the body in such a way (flesh becomes heated or cooled), other qualities such as heavy and light do not qualify (*poioutai*; 432.36) the flesh at all. Rather, they only affect it in a cognitive way (*gnôstikôs*).

Despite flesh not being changed *as a body* by some tactile qualities, all tactile qualities are perceived by flesh (or something within) *as a sense organ*. Philoponus formulates this point by saying that flesh 'receives the forms in a cognitive way' (*gnôstikôs*) and 'gets to know them' (*ginôskei auta*). As mentioned above, Sorabji operates on the assumption that Philoponus is either a spiritualist (i.e. a dematerialist) or a primitive or perhaps a latitudinarian literalist. T2 shows that he is not a literalist in this way. Therefore, he is a spiritualist.

If David Charles' argument about how hylomorphism differs from Cartesian dualism is defensible, the debate between literalism and spiritualism is in danger of missing its mark, since it disregards the possibility that we might be dealing with positions in which the physiological and psychological processes are not *purely* physiological and psychological. Therefore, on textual, historical, and

---

[43] Sorabji (1991).
[44] For the hierarchy of the senses with respect to matter, see Philoponus, *In De An.* 416.2; 417.37; 413.6–7; 416.30–5. The hierarchy is also found in Sorabji (1991: 233).

systematic grounds and in order to consider a hylomorphic reading of Philoponus on perception, we must leave the opposition between spiritualism and literalism behind.

The point of a hylomorphic reading of Philoponus is to offer an alternative to exactly the kind of dichotomy just outlined for Sorabji's argument. Let us recall the distinction that Philoponus makes in T1 quoted above. He distinguishes between (i) the changes the sense organs undergo *as bodies* and (ii) the changes they undergo *as sense organs*. When a stone is heated by fire (i), it does not perceive the heat. Similarly, when the flesh is heated or cooled, this is not the physical change that it undergoes *as a sense organ*. Rather than excluding any physiological change in the organ of touch, Philoponus points out in T1 that the change in the organ *as an organ* (ii) is not the change of flesh being qualified *as a body* (i). Rather, it is a cognitive change.

When we recognize that this is not a denial of literalism in support of spiritualism, we can see that by saying that flesh is changed in a cognitive way Philoponus refers to a physiological change in the flesh *as an organ*. By calling the change *in the organ* of touch 'cognitive', I suggest that he means that such a change is constitutive of perception as a form of cognition and that the distinct physiological change thus described can only be defined with reference to it being a change by a sense object or probably rather by its activities. This supports reading (Ca) in section 2.1 above.

Attributing cognitive change to flesh rather than the soul or the sense faculty, Philoponus therefore seems to say that the physiological change in the flesh as the organ of touch has to make essential reference to a psychological process, i.e. our cognizing the tactile quality (433.4). Philoponus also talks about the sense organ (*to haptikon aisthêtêrion*; 432.36) as a sense (*hôs aisthêsis*; 433.3).[45] It is possible to understand this similarly as referring to the cognitive change in the flesh as a psycho-physical change in which the psychological process has to be defined with essential reference to the physiological one. These two claims, as we have seen above, are exactly what is required for strong hylomorphism.

One might suggest, however, that the passage can equally well be understood in terms of a two-component view as moderate hylomorphism. In this case, Philoponus would identify in the passages quoted in section 2.2 above the purely physiological component of perception (e.g. the compression and expansion) and now considers the purely psychological component, i.e. a cognitive change.

This reading is not impossible. However, it misses the point I have emphasized in this section. When Philoponus talks about the *sense organ* receiving the forms in a merely cognitive way in T2, he does not contrast this change with the physiological change of the organ *as an organ*. In other words, his distinction is

---

[45] Cf. the case of sight when Philoponus says it is the vitreous humour (350.31–2) or the optic *pneuma* in that humour (350.25–6) that sees; see also Lautner (2013: 392 n39).

not between the purely physical and a purely psychological component of perception *as a whole*. Rather, he contrasts the change of the organ *as an organ* with a change in the organ *as a body*. The latter is not a physical component of a psychophysical change but a merely material change that is neither necessary nor relevant for perception. The physiological change that I argue to be partly constitutive of perception is that which the sense organ undergoes *as a sense organ* (such as compression or expansion) and that Philoponus in T2 calls a cognitive change. Therefore, while it is not impossible to read the passage in terms of moderate hylomorphism, it does not offer independent support for this either, since the passage is not making a distinction between physical and psychological components of perception.

In other words, when Philoponus talks about flesh receiving the forms in a cognitive way, he does not refer to a purely psychological component of perception. It is flesh after all that is cognitively changed, not the sense faculty or soul. Rather, the point of talking about a cognitive change in the organ seems to be that our becoming aware of tactile qualities must make essential reference to the sense organ. Since the change is cognitive, it is not a purely physiological process either. A similar point can be made about the following passage:

T9 The sense [*hê aisthêsis*] is affected only by the form of the hot and in a cognitive way [*peponthe gnôstikôs*], but the sense-organ the flesh is affected as matter in respect of both together becoming underlying thing to the heat and being affected as a whole by the whole thing that heats.
                    Philoponus, *In De An.* 438.12–15; tr. Charlton.

If Philoponus had wanted to underline that there are independently definable physiological and psychological components of perception, passages like T2 and T9 should probably mention the purely physiological component and distinguish it from the purely psychological one. However, in both passages the contrast is between a purely material change in the body *as a body* and the cognitive change in the sense or sense organ.

Yet there is another distinction in T9, which seems to be what is needed for moderate hylomorphism. Philoponus distinguishes between the way in which *the sense* (*hê aisthêsis*) is affected in a cognitive way and the way in which *the sense organ* is affected *as matter*. This could be taken as a distinction between purely psychological and purely physiological components of sense perception: the sense is affected in a cognitive way *as a sense* and the sense organ is affected *as matter*.

This objection seems plausible but has the following drawback. Philoponus makes clear a few pages earlier (in 435.25 of T2 above) that Aristotle talks about the sense organ *as a sense*. If he had wanted to underline the difference between the change in the *sense as a sense* and in the *organ as matter for that sense*, it would need to be clarified here. However, Philoponus is doing quite the opposite: he follows Aristotle and uses 'sense' and 'sense-organ' interchangeably and attributes discernment (*krinein*) to the sense organs (e.g. 350.31–2).[46] This indicates that the cognitive change in T2 and T9 is the change that belongs to the organ *as an organ*. Moreover, the change in the organ in T9 is not the one that is identified in T1 as the change of the organ *as an organ* but, rather, the purely material change of a body as a body—or 'as matter', as he puts it in T9, and such a change is not relevant to perception.

One could still object that the organ can be referred to as 'sense' or as 'sense-organ', and this shows that the former is the subject of a purely psychological and the latter of a purely physiological change. However, strong hylomorphism need not deny that one can *talk about* psychological and physiological processes. The point is that Philoponus describes perception as a cognitive change in the flesh, which I have argued is not—at least not necessarily—a combination of a purely physical and a purely psychological component. Rather, it looks like a psycho-physical process, while the purely material change (being heated or cooled) is neither necessary nor relevant for perception, since there is perception without such a change (T2). The psychological change cannot seem to be purely psychological either, since it is described as a cognitive change *in the sense organ*. In sum, Philoponus' formulation is not only compatible with strong hylomorphism but, on balance, suggests it.

3.2 Physiological and Psychological Changes in Pseudo-Simplicius' Account

As mentioned above, Pseudo-Simplicius' account of perception focuses on the question of how perception can be an activity of the soul but still only take place when the object is present and affects our sense organism. His solution is that there is a vital modification in the sense organs that stimulates the perceptive soul to the projection of an appropriate concept. Let us now consider what the modification in the organ is like and especially whether it can be understood as a purely physiological change.

Although Pseudo-Simplicius says little about what happens in the organ, one point becomes clear: the effect in the sense organ is not a purely physical one. As Pseudo-Simplicius repeatedly stresses, it is not a passive affection that inanimate things could undergo as well but 'joint affection and activity' (125.34 in T8 above). The activity comes from the life given to the body and its organs by the sensitive soul, and the life in the sense organs is made similar to the forms of the objects by

---

[46] Pseudo-Simplicius, by contrast, stresses the distinction between senses and sense organs (118.2–5), while claiming that Alexander interprets them as being equivalent in Aristotle; for a conjecture concerning the reference to Alexander, see Lautner (1997: 213 n10).

the soul (T8). Therefore, the physiological process in the sense organ is not one that a lifeless body defined solely in terms of extension could undergo but a change in an ensouled being involving activity of the sensitive soul.

Someone might object that although the change in the organ is not of an inanimate (merely extended) body, it is not necessarily a mental change. If this is true, the objection rather supports the point I am making. It shows that Pseudo-Simplicius' analysis cannot be identified with Cartesian dualism simply by adding the activity of a *res cogitans* to a change in a material extended body. On the one hand, it remains possible for all that Pseudo-Simplicius says that the vital modification of the sense organ can be understood as sensation[47] distinguished from perception proper as projection of concepts. The vital effect in the sense organs is one in which there is activity from the sensitive soul, a form of life that is present in human beings and animals. While plants are alive, they cannot be subject to the kind of modification that takes place in the sense organs and stimulates the sensitive soul to project the appropriate concept.

On the other hand, the joint activity of the object's effect together with the sensitive life coming from the soul in the sense organ is not a joint production of thinking and matter as mere extension. The change in the sense organs is not a purely material change in contrast with a pure mind as a thinking substance; nor is it a joint product of these two. To the extent that perception is a kind of thought for Pseudo-Simplicius, the relevant kind of thinking is *the projection of forms stimulated by the vital effect in the sense organ*, not the effect of the object in the organ. This means that if Pseudo-Simplicius is a dualist, he is not a Cartesian one. Although he grants purely psychological activities of the soul (such as knowledge of the forms), such processes must be distinguished from both (a) the active element in the vital effect of the sense organs and (b) the projection of forms stimulated by the effect of the object in the sense organs.

Therefore, there is evidence that the effect of the sense organs for Pseudo-Simplicius is not a purely material one. Although the evidence is not conclusive, it seems that the effect on the organs is an inextricably psycho-physical change rather than a combination of a purely physical and a purely psychological change. In particular, the physiological change in the organ is not purely physical or material because a purely physical change could take place in lifeless things. Rather, the change is partly defined by the activity of the soul. Moreover, the activity part is not one of a pure thinking soul but derives from the sensitive soul that gives life to the psycho-physical complex of a living human body.

What, then, about the projection of forms? Is it purely psychological? Pseudo-Simplicius (122.10–12) distinguishes perception from the soul's activity of knowing (*epistêmonikôs energêsai*) on the grounds that while the organ does not need to

---

[47] This is suggested by the extension of discernment to flesh as the medium. See note 38 above.

be changed at all for the soul to exercise knowledge, an affection is necessary for perception (*pathein men ti dei*; 122.12, 124.3–11). While I can exercise my (limited) knowledge of elephants in their absence, I cannot perceive one if no elephant is present.

The difference between perception and the transition from possessing knowledge to exercising it can be illustrated by the following example. Imagine that you see the flag of Nepal. Thanks to the effect that the redness of the flag causes in your sense organism, you can project the concept of redness to that effect in the organs and judge that the flag of Nepal is (partly) red. In Pseudo-Simplicius' analysis you now perceive that the flag of Nepal is (partly) red. After work you go to the pub where there is a pub quiz with a question about the colours of the flag of Nepal. Possessing that knowledge now, you can proceed to exercising it. While seeing a picture of the flag and judging it to be (partly) red is perception, answering correctly in the pub quiz seems like a transition from possessing knowledge to exercising it. It is important to note, however, that this does not necessarily count as knowledge in the proper sense in Pseudo-Simplicius' account because he stresses that knowledge is about universals within the soul that are not predicated on particulars (124.10–11). Knowing the answer in a pub quiz probably is an activity of such predicating and, therefore, not a pure activity of knowing in Pseudo-Simplicius' terms.

The exercise of knowledge about universals seems without a question to be a purely psychological activity, and even imagination in the soul is 'completely self-aroused' (165.32–166.2). It is another question, however, whether knowledge of particulars is purely psychological for Pseudo-Simplicius. As T6 above shows, the 'perceptive life' or the sensitive soul that probably has such knowledge is not 'entirely separate from bodies' and needs to project the appropriate concept 'on the vital modification or the passive effect in the sense-organ'. This suggests that the judgement as projection of forms is dependent on the psycho-physical effect in the sense organ and does not seem to be purely psychological, so that it could, as a component of perception, be defined without essential reference to the vital modification of the organs.

It seems plausible that the projection has to make some reference to the effect in the sense organs. When (i) perceiving that the flag of Nepal is (partly) red, the concept of redness is projected on the effect of the object in the sense organs. In the pub quiz (ii), the concept cannot be projected onto it. Therefore, at least, as a psycho-physical process *as a whole* (i) is different from (ii). However, whether the projection itself is a purely psychological component in the two, is another question.

At the moment, the evidence does not seem sufficient to decide how to answer this question. There is, however, some reason to think that the projection of forms in perception is not a purely psychological process or not as pure as a psychological process can be. On the one hand, the perception of the proper sensibles ('this is red') is characterized as a 'corporeal type of cognition' (*sômatoeidês gnôsis*) and 'more affective and more corporeal' than the perception of common sensibles like substance that are only recognized by reason (127.8-13). On the other hand, perception is described as 'not completely self-aroused' (166.1) and contrasted in this respect not only with intellect (*nous*), knowledge (*epistêmê*), and belief or opinion (*doxa*), but even with imagination (*phantasia*; 166.2). This seems to imply that the projection is at least not *as purely psychological* as intellect, knowledge, opinion, and imagination. There is no doubt that all activity is derived from the soul's side,[48] while the body as such is passive or receptive.

In any case, soul's connection with the body in Pseudo-Simplicius comes in layers. The highest layers of intellect and pure knowledge of forms are not involved in perception and the purest soul activity in perception is the projection of the forms. However, as we have seen, the projection is not on a purely material change but a joint affection or vital modification of the sense organ that is active to the extent that the sensitive soul enlivens it and makes it sensitive. Therefore, even if projection of forms is or were a pure soul activity, the physiological process in the organ remains, I have suggested above, inextricably psycho-physical.

4. Concluding Remarks

In this essay, I have argued that the opposition between spiritualism and literalism is not appropriate for analysing the accounts of perception in Philoponus and Pseudo-Simplicius. Instead of forcing Philoponus' account into the Procrustean bed of spiritualism and literalism, I have argued that his view can be articulated in terms of strong hylomorphism. While Pseudo-Simplicius has a layered view of the soul in which the highest activities are entirely independent of the body, I contend that Cartesian dualism is not required to analyse his account of perception. The most important reason for this is that the change in the sense organ necessary for perception is psycho-physical in a sense that it cannot be reduced to a material component defined in terms of extension and mind as pure thinking. In Pseudo-Simplicius' account, thinking is the projection of forms on passive activity in the sense organ. That activity is not thinking but the activity of sensitive life in a material organ. Therefore, there is no reason to assimilate Pseudo-Simplicius' position with Cartesian dualism.

The result is important because, on the one hand, a new notion of prime matter as a three-dimensional extension was introduced by Philoponus. On the other hand, the commentators could have resorted to a more dualistic account building on Plato's *Timaeus* according to which the affect in the organs has to reach the

---

[48] See also 125.37-126.1 where perception is described as pure activity.

soul (45d) or on *Philebus* (43b), in which perception is analysed as awareness of an affection. However, they did not choose such an account but, I have argued, opted for a more inseparably psycho-physical analysis.

References

Barney, R. (2009), 'Simplicius: Commentary, Harmony, and Authority', in *Antiquorum Philosophia: An International Journal* 3: 101–19.

Blumenthal, H.J. (1982), 'The Psychology of (?) Simplicius' Commentary on Aristotle's *De Anima*', in Blumenthal and Lloyd (eds.), *Soul and the Structure of Being in Neoplatonism* (Liverpool University Press), 73–93.

Blumenthal, H.J. (1996), *Aristotle and Neoplatonism in Late Antiquity: Interpretations of the De anima* (Duckworth).

Blumenthal, H.J. (2000), *'Simplicius': On Aristotle On the Soul* (trans. with intro. and notes) (Bloomsbury).

Blumenthal, H.J. and A.C. Lloyd (eds.) (1982), *Soul and the Structure of Being in Late Neoplatonism: Syrianus, Proclus, and Simplicius* (Liveripool University Press).

Blumenthal, H.J. and H. Robinson (eds.) (1991), *Aristotle and the Later Tradition. Oxford Studies in Ancient Philosophy* (suppl. vol.) (Clarendon Press).

Bossier, F. and C. Steel (1972), 'Priscianus Lydus en de *in De Anima* van Pseudo(?)-Simplicius', in Tijdschrift *voor Philosophie* 34: 761–822.

Burnyeat, M. ([1992] 1995), 'Is an Aristotelian Philosophy of Mind still Credible? A draft', in Nussbaum and Rorty (eds.), *Essays on Aristotle's* De Anima (Oxford University Press), 15–26.

Burnyeat, M. (1995), 'How Much Happens When Aristotle Sees Red and Hears Middle C? Remarks on *De Anima* 2.7–8', in Nussbaum and Rorty (eds.), *Essays on Aristotle's* De Anima (Oxford University Press), 421–34.

Burnyeat, M. (2002), '*De Anima* II 5', in *Phronesis* 47: 28–90.

Caston, V. (2005), 'The Spirit and the Letter: Aristotle on Perception', in Salles (ed.), *Metaphysics, Soul, and Ethics* (Oxford University Press), 245–320.

Caston, V. (2009), 'Commentary on Charles', in Cleary and Gurtler (eds.), *Proceedings of the Boston Area Colloquium in Ancient Philosophy* XXIV (Brill), 30–49.

Charles, D. (2009), 'Aristotle's Psychological Theory', in Cleary and Gurtler (eds.), *Proceedings of the Boston Area Colloquium in Ancient Philosophy* XXIV (Brill), 1–29.

Charles, D. (2021), *The Undivided Self: Aristotle and the Mind-Body Problem* (Oxford Aristotle Studies Series) (Oxford University Press).

Cleary, J. J. and G. M. Gurtler (eds.) (2009), *Proceedings of the Boston Area Colloquium in Ancient Philosophy* XXIV (Brill).

Coope, U. (2020), *Freedom and Responsibility in Neoplatonist Thought* (Oxford University Press).

Corcilius, K. (2014), 'Activity, Passivity and Perceptual Discrimination in Aristotle', in J. F. Silva and M. Yrjönsuuri (eds.), *Active Perception in the History of Philosophy* (Springer), 31-53.

Ebert, T. (1983), 'Aristotle on What Is Done in Perceiving', in *Zeitschrift für Philosophische Forschung* 37/2: 181-93.

Finamore, J. F. and J. Dillon (2002), *Iamblichus De Anima: Text, Translation, and Commentary* (Philosophia Antiqua 92) (Brill).

Gerson, L. P. (2005), 'What is Platonism?', in *Journal for the History of Philosophy* 43/3: 253-76.

Golitsis, P. (2016), 'John Philoponus' Commentary on the Third Book of Aristotle's De Anima Wrongly Attributed to Stephanus', in Sorabji (ed.) (2016b), *Aristotle Re-Interpreted* (Bloomsbury), 393-412.

Haas, F. A.J. de (1997), *Philoponus' New Definition of Prime Matter* (Brill).

Hadot, I. (2016²), 'The Life and Work of Simplicius in Greek and Arabic Sources', in Sorabji (ed.) (2016d), *Aristotle Transformed* (Bloomsbury), 295-326.

Helmig, C. (2020), 'Simplicius', in Zalta (ed.), *The Stanford Encyclopedia of Philosophy* (Summer 2020 edition). https://plato.stanford.edu/archives/sum2020/entries/simplicius/

Huby, P. and C. Steel (1997), *Priscian: On Theophrastus' On Sense-Perception with 'Simplicius' on Aristotle's On the Soul 2.5-12* (Cornell University Press).

Johansen, T.K. (1997), *Aristotle on the Sense Organs* (Cambridge University Press).

Kalderon, M. E. (2017), 'Priscian on Perception', in *Phronesis* 62/4: 443-67.

Lautner, P. (1997), 'Notes', in Huby and Steel (trans. with intro.), 213-29.

Lautner, P. (2013), 'Γνωστικῶς and/or ὑλικῶς: Philoponus' Account of the Material Aspects of Sense Perception', in *Phronesis* 58: 378-400.

Menn, S. (2002), 'Aristotle's Definition of the Soul and the Programme of the *De Anima*', in *Oxford Studies in Ancient Philosophy* XXII: 83-139.

Nussbaum, M.C. and A.O. Rorty (eds.) (1995), *Essays on Aristotle's De Anima* (Second Edition) (Oxford University Press).

Perkams, M. (2005), 'Priscian of Lydia. Commentator on the *De Anima* in the tradition of Iamblichus', in *Mnemosyne* 58/4: 510-30.

Perkams, M. (2008), *Selbstbewusstsein in der Spätantike. Die neuplatonischen Kommentare zu Aristoteles' De Anima* (De Gruyter).

Perler, D. (2001), *Ancient and Medieval Theories of Intentionality* (Brill).

Rapp, C. (2001), 'Intentionalität und *Phantasia* bei Aristoteles', in Perler (ed.), *Ancient and Medieval Theories of Intentionality* (Brill), 63-97.

Salles, R. (ed.) (2005), *Metaphysics, Soul, and Ethics: Themes from the Work of Richard Sorabji* (Oxford University Press).

Sorabji, R. (1991), 'From Aristotle to Brentano: The Development of the Concept of Intentionality', in Blumenthal and Robinson (eds.), *Aristotle and the Later Tradition* (Clarendon Press), 227-59.

Sorabji, R. (2016a), 'Dating of Philoponus' Commentaries on Aristotle and of His Divergence with his Teacher Ammonius', in Sorabji (ed.) (2016b), *Aristotle Re-Interpreted* (Bloomsbury), 367–92.

Sorabji, R. (ed.) (2016b), *Aristotle Re-Interpreted: New Findings on Seven Hundred Years of Commentaries* (Bloomsbury).

Sorabji, R. (2016c), 'The Ancient Commentators on Aristotle', in Sorabji (ed.) (2016d), *Aristotle Transformed* (Bloomsbury), 1–33.

Sorabji, R. (ed.) (2016d), *Aristotle Transformed: The Ancient Commentators and Their Influence* (Second Edition) (Bloomsbury).

Steel, C. (1997), 'Introduction', in Huby and Steel (trans. with intro.), 105–40.

Todd, R. (1984), 'Philosophy and Medicine in John Philoponus' Commentary on Aristotle's *De Anima*', in *Dumbarton Oaks Papers* 38: 103–10.

12
Natural, Artificial, and Organic Forms in Avicenna

Peter Adamson

Avicenna (d. 1037) was very interested in the question of how we come to know about forms. The most striking case is the human soul, which for Avicenna is in a sense difficult for us to know and in a sense easy. Knowledge of the soul is difficult because we can use sense perception only to grasp its effects in the body, not the soul in itself. Avicenna thinks that Aristotle's famous definition of soul ('form of the organic body potentially having life') and indeed the very word 'soul [*nafs*]' only apply to the former: the soul grasped through its accidental and temporary relation to body, in which it manifests some of its activities.[1] Rather advanced philosophical argumentation is required to go beyond this, to establish that the soul is indeed a self-subsisting, immaterial substance.[2] Yet knowledge of the soul is also easy, since we all have constant, albeit mostly tacit, self-awareness. The soul thus has immediate access to itself without even the need for bodily experience, as is brought to our attention by Avicenna's famous flying man thought experiment.[3] This twofold mode of access to the soul may be compared to our knowledge of God, who can be known on the one hand indirectly, through His effects, and on the other hand by direct reflection on the meaning of His necessary existence.[4]

It is the inapplicability of sense perception to the substance of the soul and to God, entities that exist (or can exist) free of attachments from matter, that makes them special cases. Usually things are much more straightforward, since Avicenna assumes that we can grasp the essences of physical substances through empirical investigation.[5] The understanding reached in this way is such as to satisfy the rigorous criteria laid down in Aristotle's *Posterior Analytics*. But substantial forms

---

[1] *Healing: Soul* sect. 1.1, 10. On this, see further Sebti (1999); Wisnovsky (2003: ch. 6); Alpina (2018a and 2021: ch. 3).

[2] I discuss this in Adamson (2020).

[3] Black (2008); Adamson and Benevich (2018); Alpina (2018b).

[4] I speak here of Avicenna's views about how we come to know God's attributes; see on this Adamson (2013). For the question of how we know that there is a Necessary Existent in the first place, and whether this can be determined only by working back to Him from His causes, see Mayer (2001); Bertolacci (2007). For the parallel between knowing God and knowing the soul, see Alpina (2021: ch. 3).

[5] On the role of empirical knowledge in Avicenna, see McGinnis (2003); Janssens (2004); Gutas (2012). On knowledge as a grasp of essences, see Benevich (2018); Janos (2020).

are not directly perceptible, of course. Rather, we come to know about them by observing how the substances causally interact with other things. We cannot, for instance, just see or feel the substantial form of fire. But we can learn about that form by seeing fire set other things aflame, or feeling the heat it radiates. This thought lies behind a passage in which Avicenna contrasts 'nature [*ṭabīʿa*]' and 'form [*ṣūra*]', two terms which at least in simple things (namely the four elements) have the same reference but different sense:

Healing: Physics 1.6.2: It is a 'nature' when considered in one way, whereas it is a 'form' when considered in another. So when it is related to the motions and actions that proceed from it, it is called 'nature', whereas, when it is related to bringing about the subsistence of the species water [for example], and if the effects and motions that proceed from it are not taken into account, it is then called 'form'.[6]

Now, in the previous chapter Avicenna has told us that natural philosophy takes from the higher science of metaphysics the idea that bodies are 'moved only as a result of powers [*quwan*] in them that are principles [*mabādiʾ*] of their motions and actions' (*Healing: Physics* 1.5.3). From this we might infer that the contrast in the quote just given, between 'nature' and 'form', correlates to the contrast between natural philosophy and metaphysics. In natural philosophy, predictably enough, we deal with 'natures', that is forms insofar as they give rise to observable effects. In metaphysics, these same principles are understood as 'forms' in the strict sense, which are responsible for the subsistence of things. That this is the properly metaphysical way to think about form is confirmed by the definition of 'formal cause' given in the *Metaphysics* of the *Healing*: 'the cause which is part of the thing's subsistence and through which the thing is what it is in actuality' (*Healing: Metaphysics* 6.1.2).[7]

Bringing all this together, we can say that in natural philosophy the inquirer works towards an understanding of forms in terms of their causal function. Though Avicenna in the passages cited above speaks only of the motions, effects, and actions produced by the form, as we'll see the inquirer is also interested in the causal relations that produce the form itself. That is, the form is understood in natural philosophy in terms of causal relations and not in terms of itself. The metaphysician, by contrast, understands what form is in itself: it is part of the thing's quiddity, and makes it subsist.[8]

---

[6] I cite from this work in McGinnis' translation and with his section numbers, with modifications.
[7] Likewise, I cite from this work in Marmura's translation and with his section numbers, with modifications.
[8] Only 'part of' the quiddity, for the usual Aristotelian reason that the definition of the quiddity must at least implicitly include reference to the matter, at least in composite things (*Healing:*

When Avicenna comes to sort forms into their different types, he uses the approach that is germane to natural philosophy. That is, he offers a *functional* classification of forms, by which I mean one that distinguishes them in terms of the sorts of effect they can produce and the sorts of cause that give rise to them. By bringing together Avicenna's rather scattered remarks on this topic, we will be able to see that he has an original and systematic basis for the traditional distinction between natural, artificial, and organic forms.[9] In particular, his functional approach enables him to show why these three types of form should be so sharply distinguished, and to address the problem of how a single form explains numerous causal powers. His account thus offers welcome clarity on issues that remained rather unclear in Aristotle, though as we shall see, this did not stop it from being subjected to fierce critique.

1. Forms as Causes

Let us begin with the contrast between natural forms and organic forms, that is, between 'natures' and 'souls'. Avicenna explains this in a systematic passage that sets up a fourfold division of types of 'power [*quwwa*]' (*Healing: Physics* 1.5.3).[10] The division is made in terms of the presence, or absence, of 'volition [*irāda*]' and 'variation in movement and action':

(1) Nature: no volition, no variation
(2) Celestial soul: volition, no variation
(3) Nutritive soul: no volition, variation
(4) Animal soul: volition, variation

Avicenna adds here that the term 'nature' may also be applied to type (3), so that the natural power is just the power that lacks volition; but in this context he prefers to maintain the narrower use of the term 'nature' to cover only type (1).

Metaphysics 5.8.5). It should be noted that Avicenna does, however, sometimes equate the form with the quiddity; my thanks to Damien Janos for making this point. In section 3 below, I return to the idea that formal cause accounts for 'subsistence'.

[9] I should say that I here use 'organic' not to translate any particular term in Avicenna, but as covering the cases of animal and vegetative forms, that is the souls of animals and plants. The human soul is not easy to place in this classification, since as already noted, Avicenna has some hesitation in thinking of the human or rational soul as a 'form'. In what follows, we will mostly be concerned with this substance *qua* source of activity in the human body (that is, soul as studied in natural philosophy: see Alpina 2021: ch. 4), not *qua* subject of human thought. The substance in question is, as Avicenna has told us, aptly called 'soul' and 'form of the body' precisely insofar as it is a source of bodily activities. Souls of animals and plants may less problematically be understood just as organic forms, which unlike human souls are essentially embodied; thus when I speak of organic forms in what follows, it will be more helpful to have in mind the non-human animal and plant cases.

[10] On this passage, see Lammer (2018: 287–9).

Natural forms in this sense are those like the form of fire, which always and without choice gives rise to the same effects, such as heating and upward locomotion towards fire's natural place, where it comes to rest. Notice that natural forms are here defined negatively, as conferring powers that involve neither volition nor variation. Conversely, organic forms are defined positively, albeit disjunctively, as involving either volition, or variation, or both. But the whole division is made within a positively characterized class, namely powers for producing action, motion, and rest. So as we anticipated, the division is set out in terms of causal efficacy.

Avicenna is accordingly happy to endorse Aristotle's definition of nature as 'a first principle and cause of motion and rest for that in which it resides, essentially and not accidentally' (*Healing: Physics* 1.5.6).[11] He thinks that Aristotle stipulated that nature belongs to the natural body 'first ($\pi\rho\acute{\omega}\tau\omega s$, *awwalan*)' in order to contrast natural forms to souls.[12] For souls 'use natures and qualities' to induce motions and actions in their bodies, with the natures retaining their independent causal powers. Were this not the case, then nature could be completely dominated by the soul's command, and 'what is demanded by the soul would never be at odds with what is demanded by nature'. When you jump off a chair, you can't decide not to fall, because the earthy constituents of your body have a natural form 'demanding' downward motion. This motion has as its causal principle the nature of the elements in your body, as does the process of aging, in which the gradual loss of moisture and heat in the body undermines the functions of life.

Prima facie this casts some doubt on the conclusions reached recently by Kara Richardson and Andreas Lammer, to the effect that Avicenna rejected form pluralism, that is, the view that substances have more than one substantial form.[13] Both scholars focus on the question of whether the form of *body* is distinct from the organic form, but this is a rather different case from the ones just mentioned, since mere corporeality never works 'at cross-purposes' to the organic form and can thus easily be thought of as a component of that form. On the other hand passages like *Healing: Physics* 1.6.3 (cited below at the beginning of section 4), also strongly suggest that bodily 'nature' is somehow part of the single form that is the human soul. Furthermore, as we will see shortly, a crucial difference between artificial and non-artificial forms is precisely that in the artificial case, the material constituents retain their own independent nature, so that the form is

---

[11] *Physics* 2.1, 192b21–3: Being a principle and cause of movement and rest in that in which it is present primarily in itself and not accidentally. On this definition, see Kelsey 2003. Avicenna goes on to criticize an alternative definition offered by Philoponus, and recommend sticking with Aristotle's. On Philoponus' account and its Arabic reception, see Lammer 2015.

[12] My translation of the definition places the word 'first' in accordance with the construction of the Arabic, which has it as an adjective modifying 'principle' (*mabda' awwal*) whereas in the Greek it is an adverb modifying *huparchei*, as noted at Lammer 2018, 227.

[13] Richardson 2011, 258 n.26, and Lammer 2018, 174 (with references to earlier discussions by Hyman and Goichon).

related to these constituents only accidentally. This too seems to require that even if material nature works at 'cross purposes' to form or soul in the organic case, it is still to be considered as being subsumed within that form, because that is a key difference between organisms and artefacts. To put it more simply: the wood in a bed is still present as a full-blown substance, whereas the earth in my body is not. This point is particularly clear with artefacts that are mere mixtures, which we will discuss further in section 2. Avicenna devotes a chapter of *Healing: On Generation and Corruption* (133–9) to showing that the natures of ingredients are retained in a mixture; he offers as proof the observation that ingredients can be made to separate using a heated alembic.

For another passage on the question of what makes organic forms distinctive, we can turn to the very beginning of the treatise on soul in the *Healing*.[14] Here he says, 'in general, everything that is a principle for the production [ṣudūr] of activities that do not happen always in the same way ['alā watīra wāḥida], in the absence of volition, is what we call "soul"' (*Healing: Psychology* 4). The wording is almost verbatim what we find in the fourfold classification from *Healing: Physics* 1.5.3, which said that nature 'produces [yaṣduru] activity always in the same manner ['alā najh wāḥid], without volition'. Even though, in the *Psychology*, Avicenna has just stressed that soul's activities are distinct from the features that belong to the organic body due to its corporeality (li-jismiyyatihā), this parallel makes it clear that his intention at the outset of discussing soul is to contrast it to natures (forms of type (1)). So his point is presumably the same, namely that organic forms are those that confer powers to perform activities involving volition, variation, or both (forms of types (2), (3), and (4) respectively). It is when we observe such activities that we should speak of 'soul'.[15]

Avicenna seems to bear in mind his fourfold division of powers as he proceeds with his treatment of soul. In the following chapter, he takes issue with the Platonist idea that soul might be characterized as essentially 'self-moving', and as passing on motion to the body by virtue of its self-motion. He rejects this, pointing out that soul is a cause of rest just as much as it is a cause of motion. Then

---

[14] I cite this part of the *Healing* from the edition of Rahman; I have consulted the translations of some chapters in Alpina (2021), and would like to thank him for making available to me a manuscript of the book prior to publication. For a complete French translation, see Bakoš (1956).

[15] The relevance of *Healing: Physics* 1.5 has also been noted by Lammer (2018) and Alpina (2020: 237). I differ somewhat from Alpina in my assumption that, given the parallel wording, here at the start of the *Psychology* Avicenna must have in mind a *disjunctive* contrast between nature and soul. Organic forms, in other words, may differ from natural forms *either* by manifesting volition *or* by acting 'not always in the same manner'. Since plants satisfy the latter criterion, they should count as having souls and being alive, even though the way Avicenna puts his point here could suggest otherwise, because he does not explicitly use disjunctive language as he did in the fourfold classification at *Healing: Physics* 1.5.3. Still, overall I am convinced by Alpina's argument, correcting Tawara (2014), that Avicenna uses the word 'life' differently in the contexts of medicine (where life presupposes the functions borne by *pneuma*, thus excluding plants) and natural philosophy (where life only presupposes a nutritive faculty, thus including plants).

he adds that, if we are talking about locomotion, 'this can be only by nature, compulsion, or soul, and if it is nature, then it inevitably moves in one given direction [*jiha*]; so the soul would give rise to motion only in one direction' (*Healing: Psychology* 20).[16] Here then, the soul's characteristic of displaying *variation* in its activities is crucial to the argument, which even alludes to the contrast between souls and mere natures. Still further on, he defines animal soul as a perfection of a natural body that gives rise to perception and motion by *volition* (*Healing: Psychology* 40).

We now have a good understanding of the functional difference between natural and organic forms. What about artificial forms? For this we need to return to Avicenna's treatment of the Aristotelian definition of nature. Avicenna explains the clause 'that in which [nature] resides [ἐν ᾧ ὑπάρχει, *mā yakūnu fī-hi*]' with the terse remark that this is 'in order to distinguish nature, art [*ṣināʿa*], and agents that act by force' (*Healing: Physics* 1.5.6). An artificial form then, unlike natural forms (and *a fortiori*, unlike organic forms), is not 'in' the thing but somehow extrinsic. This raises the question of whether the forms of artefacts are even comparable to natural and organic forms. After all, the latter are clearly substantial forms. But if the form of a bed is extrinsic to the wood of which it is made, it stands to reason that this form is only an accidental arrangement of the wood.[17] This seems to be confirmed by Avicenna's remark elsewhere that the form of a bed is *ṭāriʾ*, meaning 'incidental' or 'extraneous', like white for a white body (*Healing: Physics* 1.10.9). However, in still another passage, Avicenna says explicitly that artificial forms are essential:

Healing: Physics 1.12.5: The form that is essential [*bi-l-dhāt*] is, for instance, the shape of chair that belongs to the chair, while the form that is accidental is, for instance, white or black for [the chair].

How are we to reconcile this with his claim that form is accidental or 'incidental' to the bed? Obviously the point is not that chairs have essences, and beds don't.

Rather, we must understand Avicenna to say that an artificial form is essential *to the artefact*, but accidental *to the matter* out of which the artefact is made. This is because the form (or shape, or arrangement) of a bed or house is, as we saw, 'extrinsic' to the 'element' or matter. By contrast, the form of a natural body like fire is 'intrinsic' to the body in question. Another way to put this is that the material constituents retain their own character or essence even as they are made

---

[16] On nature as cause and 'principle' of motion through 'inclination [*mayl*]' of the natural body, see *Healing: Physics* 1.5.6. Here then the unvarying inclination to move towards a certain place is the observable expression of the natural form.

[17] For discussion of this issue in Aristotle, see, e.g., Witt (2015); Papandreou (2018).

into an artefact. This is why one and the same wood can be first a bed, and then a chair, without being destroyed. Again, Avicenna says this explicitly: 'it is said that a bed was *from* the wood and the wood *was* a bed, because the wood, as such, does not undergo corruption in the way the seed does' (*Healing: Physics* 1.2.19). But this does not stop it being the case that artefacts have essences and are substances.

This point was noticed by later thinkers. One of Avicenna's most incisive critics, Suhrawardī (d. 1191), mentions as an anomaly the fact that the production of an artefact yields a change in definition through merely accidental modification:

> In response to the well-known proof on which people rely, that when [substantial] forms change, the answer to the question 'what is it' changes, unlike [what happens when] accidents [change], the representative of the ancients says that in some cases, a change in accidents does change the answer to the question 'what is it?' If you take some iron and ask what it is, wouldn't it be a good answer to say 'iron' or to respond with the definition of iron? But then, if the configuration (*hay'a*) of a sword arises in it, and one asks what it is, what would one say other than, 'a sword'? But what has arisen in it apart from accidents, like shape, edge, and so on?[18]

For Suhrawardī, the moral of this story is that one cannot, as the 'Peripatetics' would like to do, distinguish neatly between substantial and accidental forms. But I think Avicenna would simply accept the premises, while denying the conclusion. For him, the form of sword is accidental to the *iron* out of which the sword has been fashioned, but it is essential to the *sword*. So when asked 'what is it?' one should respond, 'what do you mean by "it", the iron or the sword?'[19]

2. Forms as Effects

I said earlier that Avicenna distinguishes between types of forms not only in terms of the causal efficacy exercised by what has the form, but also in terms of how form comes to be in matter. The three kinds of form can also be distinguished in light of this question of causal origin. This is the case even though, like Aristotle, Avicenna usually mentions artificial hylomorphic compounds in order to provide analogies for natural and organic ones, not to explain how they are different. He does so even in setting out the basic contrast between matter and form:

---

[18] Corbin (1945: vol. 1, 288). My thanks to Hanif Amin Beidokhti for bringing the passage to my attention.

[19] The question whether there are actually two items here, the sword and the iron, or just one item—a sword made from iron—comes down to the issue raised at n. 13 above, as to whether Avicenna recognizes multiple substantial forms in a single thing.

Healing: Physics 1.2.3:   The natural body, as such, has principles... one of the two is like the wood of the bed, the other like the form or shape of the bed... what is like the form of the bed is called 'form'.

One analogy is that both natural and organic forms can only be realized in suitable matter. It may seem obvious that here the analogy is not perfect, since artefacts tolerate a higher degree of variation in the matter used: you can make a bed out of wood or iron, but a human only out of human seed. Avicenna does however suggest that in any given case of artistic production, there will at least be an exact answer as to why this specific matter was chosen:

Healing: Physics 1.15.4:   When it is said, 'why did so-and-so turn *this* wood into a bed?' saying 'because it was the wood he had on hand' is not enough, unless one adds, 'it was wood he had on hand that was solid and suitable for realizing a bed from it, and he did not need it for anything else'.

He also sees the natural and artificial cases as similar in that the potential in the agent (e.g. the carpenter's power to make a bed) is perfectly matched by the potentiality in the matter (e.g. the wood's power to become a bed) (*Healing: Physics* 1.12.8). And finally, he remarks that art (*ṣināʿa*) is like nature in that it is purposive but requires no deliberation, and is even inhibited by conscious thought (1.14.11).

Still he does identify at least one significant disanalogy between the making of artefacts and the making of natural and organic substances:

Healing: Metaphysics 6.4.8:   If the element has the principle of its motion within it essentially, then it is moved by nature, and what comes from it will be natural. But if the principle of motion in it is from the outside [*min khārij*], and it does not belong to it to move to this perfection by itself [*min-nafsihi*], then whatever comes to be from it is artificial [*ṣināʿī*], or works in the same way.[20]

A point worth noting about this passage is its echo of the definition of 'nature' from *Physics* (much of the same wording reappears: 'principle of motion', 'in', 'essential'). This is another example of Avicenna's habit of quoting or paraphrasing definitions and classifications given in one passage in other, far-flung passages, without alerting the reader that he is doing so.[21] When reading Avicenna, it helps

---

[20] The final caveat presumably means that a natural or organic body can be used as a tool in the way a real artefact can, like a rock being used as a hammer: then its principle of motion will be outside it in respect of the hammering.

[21] The other examples we have mentioned were the resonance between *Healing: Physics* 1.6.2 and *Healing: Metaphysics* 6.1.2, and the near quotation of *Healing: Physics* 1.5.3 in *Healing: Psychology* 1.1.

to be able to hold his entire philosophy in your head all at once, as he supposedly did (or failing that, to take notes).[22]

The point of the passage, in any case, is that the matter out of which an artefact is made has no internal principle for turning into that artefact, the way that an animal has an internal principle for growing to maturation. A corollary is that the final end of an artefact is also going to be imposed on it from the outside, by the artisan, whereas the final cause of a growing animal is intrinsic to it:

Healing: Metaphysics 6.5.33–5: The end [*ghāya*] that occurs in the activity of the agent is divided into two kinds: the end that is a form, or an accident, in that which is acted upon; and the end that is not at all a form or an accident in the recipient that is acted upon, and so must be in the agent... An example of the first is the form of humanity in the human matter. For [this form] is an end for the agent power of the formation in the matter of the human, and its activity and setting-in-motion are directed towards [this form]. An example of the second is shelter. For it is an end for someone who wants to build a house, which is the principle for the motion of its generation, but it is in no way a form in the house.

In short, it looks as though artefacts are differentiated from natural and organic substances above all by their lack of any internal principle for motion and activity. That might explain why the fourfold taxonomy to which I keep returning (from *Healing: Physics* 1.5.3) has no place for artefacts: it classifies the types of *intrinsic* power.

Now, we may be surprised to be told that artefacts are inert in this sense, and that no artefact has its own principle of motion. After all, sophisticated automata were among the ingenious inventions of medieval Islam, and one might assume that such devices are in a sense capable of self-motion (why else call them 'automata'?). Yet this claim that artefacts are moved externally is found elsewhere in the Arabic Aristotelian tradition. It is expressed with particular clarity by the Andalusian thinker Ibn Bājja (d. 1139):

The artificial forms that exist in their material substrates [*mawādd*] have no power to move that in which they reside, nor to move anything else. This is the difference between artificial and natural forms: in natural forms, there are powers through which they move bodies, and the bodies are set in motion[23] through [the

---

[22] His student al-Juzjānī tells us that *Healing* was written following the loss of some of Avicenna's writings, on the basis of, as Avicenna put it, 'whatever I have readily in mind [which I have thought] on my own'. Al-Juzjānī goes on to say that *Metaphysics* and *Physics* were written 'without having available any book to consult, but by relying solely upon his natural talents'. Translations from Gutas (2014: 32), who casts doubt on this breathtaking claim at 111.

[23] I use 'set in motion' for the fifth form verb *yataḥarraku*, and simply 'move' for the second form, *yuḥarriku*.

forms] as well, so that [the forms] are motive [*muḥarrika*]. Thus the human is set in motion through the form of the human, and through it is moved also the menstrual blood, which thus becomes the human. No such thing belongs to the power of a bed. For the bed, insofar as it is a bed, does not move at all.[24]

Ibn Bājja immediately goes on to draw a parallel between artefacts' causal inertia and the conditions of their making:

> Nor is wood set in motion by some power in it to become a bed. Nor is it set in motion to become a bed by a power that a bed gives to it. In fact, the wood is not set in motion through a power given to it by anything else, either. Rather, it is set in motion only so long as its mover exists and is appropriately disposed [*mulā'im*]. This mover is an art, not nature.

Just as a hammer cannot drive nails on its own, so a bed cannot build a bed, or develop into a more perfect bed on its own, as a human generates other humans, who then have their own principle of growth and development.

We should, however, note that the passages just surveyed from Avicenna and Ibn Bājja concern specifically *motion*. Common sense would tell us that even if beds, hammers, chairs, and the like cannot move themselves, they do at least have dispositional powers, for instance to provide shelter or support. And artefacts can have much more highly developed powers than that. Consider the example of drugs, as discussed in this passage by Avicenna:

> *Healing: Physics* 1.10.7:   Neither the mere combination of the elements, nor there being a composition from them (be it by touching, meeting, or receiving shape), is sufficient for things to be generated from them. Instead, it [requires] that some of them act upon others, while others are acted upon, so that a uniform quality settles in the whole which is called a 'mixture'.[25] At that point it is prepared for the species form. This is why, when the ingredients of theriac or the like are mixed, combined, and put into composition, it is not yet theriac, nor does it have the form of theriac until a certain period of time elapses, during which some [of the ingredients], as a result of their various qualities, act upon others and are acted upon by others, after which a single quality settles as something homogeneous in all of them. Then a single action arises from them, because they share [the mixture].

This passage comes directly after another allusion to the case of house-building, which in Avicenna's opinion does require nothing more than 'combination and

---

[24] Ibn Bājja, *Kitāb al-Ḥayawān*, sect. 14, in al-ʿImārātī (2000). My translation.
[25] Avicenna also speaks of the emergence of a 'uniform quality' from a mixture at *Healing: On Generation and Corruption* 126.

composition'. By contrast a complicated drug like theriac, which is made of dozens of (hard-to-find) ingredients, has an intrinsic power to affect the body that Avicenna dignifies with the term 'action'.[26] Here we should recall that his fourfold classification concerned powers to cause either motion *or action* (*ḥaraka, fiʿl*). Notice too that Avicenna says that theriac has a 'species form [*ṣūra nawʿiyya*]' of its own. This is not surprising, since we already found that even more rudimentary artefacts like chairs are substances with their own essences.

Yet even in this highly sophisticated case, we can observe a stark difference between artificial production and natural generation. Avicenna seems to be saying that the 'activity' of theriac is due to the mixture of the ingredients of the drug. It is not enough just to put them in a bowl and stir. You need to wait for the ingredients to 'act on one another' until the power of the drug manifests by virtue of a homogenous quality that penetrates through the whole mixture.[27] Thus theriac is caused through a 'bottom-up' process. Even more obviously would this be the case for things like houses that are made through mere combination. Natural and organic substances are not like this. As we have seen, they do have in common with artefacts that, to produce them, suitable matter needs to be prepared for the reception of form. But their substantial forms never arise solely from the causal interaction of material constituents.[28]

Instead, Avicenna believes that these substances are produced through the bestowal of form by the Active Intellect, which automatically emanates a form onto every parcel of matter that is suitably prepared for that form.[29] Since the Active Intellect is emanating all forms all the time, it must be matter that specifies the kind of form that is received at a given time and place (*Healing: Metaphysics* 9.5.4). The role of the parents in animal generation is, strictly speaking, not to give form but to prepare the matter so it is ready to receive form. A notable application of this theory is Avicenna's treatment of spontaneous generation. Notoriously, he

---

[26] A whole treatise on theriac is ascribed to Galen: see Leigh (2015). A sense of its complexity can be had from reading about the difficulty Renaissance doctors had in recreating the recipe; see Palmer (1985: 108).

[27] Cf. *Healing: Metaphysics* 6.4.2: the cause of the house is mere 'composition [*tarkīb*]' whereas in an electuary made of the plant myrobalan there needs to be 'transformation [*istiḥāla*]'. For Avicenna's account of how powers of ingredients are preserved in mixtures, see Stone (2008).

[28] An objection to my reading here is that even theriac, much like a spontaneously generated animal, would receive a form from the Active Intellect once its material temperament is appropriate. Against this I would point to the fact that Avicenna explains theriac's medicinal action in light of the 'quality' that pervades it. In his treatises on *Actions and Affections* (*Afʿāl wa-infiʿālāt*, 262 ed. Qāsim), Avicenna, in the context of discussing drugs, distinguishes between the action a drug has through its 'substance' and that it has through a mere 'quality', which it exercises 'on the basis of the elements [*min-al-ʿanāṣir*]' of which it is made 'or through its mixture [*mizāj*]'. (Here, by the way, he gives the example of scammony which unlike theriac is a plant, not an artefact; theriac should thus have even less claim to perform all its acts through a superadded, emanated form.) The parallel to our passage shows clearly, I think, that theriac is effective because of its material temperament and not an emanated species form. My thanks to Andreas Lammer and Tommaso Alpina for discussion of this point, and to Alpina for the reference.

[29] For the concept of emanation in Avicenna generally, see Lizzini (2011). For the 'giver of forms', see Janssens (2006); for the Latin reception Hasse (2011).

claims that complex non-human animals, and even humans, can generate spontaneously if the conditions are right.[30] This is precisely because the organic form comes from the Active Intellect, not the parent. The relevant form is always 'available' from the Active Intellect, so all that is needed to trigger generation is an apt material substrate. While organic substances are the most eye-catching case of generation, the generation of merely natural substances works the same way:

Healing: Metaphysics 9.5.6: When this [sc. the warming of water] becomes excessive, then [its] preparation is greater and then, it is appropriate [*min ḥaqq*] for the form of fire to emanate, and for this [form of water] to depart.

So in cosmological terms, there is no difference between natural and organic forms: both come from the Active Intellect when matter is ready.[31]

What then is the difference in the causal origin between these two kinds of form? Given what we have just seen, it can lie only in the matter that receives these two different kinds of form. Avicenna explores this contrast in a passage from the section on soul found in his *Salvation* (*Najāt*), a philosophical *summa* that is more concise than the *Healing*. He tells us here that the reception of soul requires a material substrate whose qualities are near the 'mean'.[32] Obviously a natural substance like fire is at the extreme in its heat and dryness, and so maximally distant from this mean. By contrast the best organic substance in the sublunary realm, the human, has a body whose matter is very close to having heat and cold, and dryness and moisture, in perfect balance.[33] The human soul (*qua* form of body) is thus nearer to the mean than are the souls of animals, and plant souls are even further away than animal souls. Avicenna compares the Active Intellect's bestowal of these different grades of form upon variously prepared matter to the way that the sun can provide heat to a ball, illuminate it, or set it on fire, depending on the ball's position relative to the sun. The sun does the same thing, radiating light and heat, but its effects can differ because of differences in what receives its influence.

With this, Avicenna has taken the comparison between artefacts and natural things further than Aristotle himself ever did. The 'giver of forms' is like a permanently active artisan that automatically fashions substances out of matter as soon as the matter is rendered suitable. Real artefacts, though, are unique in Avicenna's world, in that they are the only substances *not* made by the Active

---

[30] See Kruk (1990); Hasse (2007).
[31] For discussion of the passage just cited, see Lammer (2018: 171). The point that elements, just as much as more complex substances, receive form from the Active Intellect is made at McGinnis (2010: 88). For the identification of the 'giver of forms' with the Active Intellect, see his discussion at 135–6.
[32] Translated in Rahman (1952: 67); Arabic at ʿUmayra (1992: 42).
[33] The idea that the healthy human body is balanced is taken from Galen, who speaks of a 'well-tempered mixture [*eukrasia*]'. See van der Eijk (2014). Here 'perfect balance' may be understood in crudely quantitative terms, that is, the heat of the body is exactly balanced by the cold, and the same for moisture and dryness.

Intellect. Instead, of course, it is a human craftsperson who introduces the form into suitable matter to make an artefact, and as we have seen this is achieved simply by manipulating the material constituents. A carpenter has the form of a bed in her mind, but unfortunately she cannot simply 'emanate' this into the wood like the Active Intellect does when it makes substances. Rather, she rearranges, cuts, and otherwise modifies wood and the like until a chair emerges from this process.[34] This explains our findings in the previous section of this chapter: humans who make artefacts only ever change material ingredients in respect of features like relative position, place, and quantity. That is why the constituents of an artefact are only ever accidentally organized as, say, a house or bed. A substantial form does result, but as emerging from the modified and combined materials, as we saw in the case of theriac: artificial forms are caused from the bottom up.[35]

Here we may pause to note a parallel between Avicenna's account of generation and his account of human knowledge. Knowledge is, after all, another case of forms being received, albeit in this case immaterially. There is a long-running scholarly debate about why, exactly, the Active Intellect is needed to bestow a form upon the rational soul when the soul comes to have knowledge. Why wouldn't it be enough for the soul simply to abstract the form from its sensory experiences?[36] Without entering into that debate here, it may be noted that in both substantial generation and the generation of human knowledge, forms do indeed come from the Active Intellect and do not just emerge from changes in the recipient, as we find with artefacts. In natural and organic generation, the way is prepared through the modification of matter and its qualities; in the case of knowledge the way is prepared through experience, imagination, and abstractive thought. But in neither of these two cases is such preparation enough. Suitability for form means the form will automatically be received, but the form does need to be *received*: it comes from the Active Intellect above, rather than emerging from below.

3. Forms and Sustaining Causes

A counter-intuitive aspect of the account just sketched (or one of them) is that, as mentioned, animal parents are not the true efficient causes of form in their

---

[34] By speaking of 'emergence' I do not mean to imply that artificial forms are epiphenomenal. To the contrary, we just saw Avicenna saying that the power of theriac is a new quality arising in the ingredients once suitably mixed, and likewise it the *house* that provides shelter thanks to its form, not the ingredients of the house.

[35] This is in harmony with the conclusions of Stone (2008), who shows that in the specific case of mixtures we have only 'a collection of bodies united by cohesion and by common sensible qualities'. To get a non-accidental relation between the form and the matter, the 'giver of forms' needs to be involved (117, citing *Healing: On Actions and Effects* 256, edited in the same volume as *Healing: On Generation and Corruption*).

[36] See, e.g., Davidson (1992); Hasse (2001); McGinnis (2007); Black (2013); Hasse (2013); Black (2014); Alpina (2014); Gutas (2014: sect. 3.2).

offspring. Rather the parents only help to prepare matter for the reception of the relevant form in the matter that becomes an embryo:

Healing: Physics 1.10.3: The principle of motion is either what prepares or what completes. What prepares is that which makes the matter suitable, like what moves the semen during the preparatory states, whereas what completes is that which gives the form.

Healing: Metaphysics 6.2.3: The father is the cause of the motion of the seed, while the motion of the seed, when it reaches its end in the way mentioned above, is a cause for the seed's arriving in the womb, and its arriving in the womb is the cause of something [else]. But its being formed as an animal, and its remaining an animal, have another cause.

This 'other cause', which 'gives the form', is of course the Active Intellect. Avicenna's point is that the true efficient cause of a thing needs to account not just for its initial generation, but also its continued persistence. What natural and organic efficient causes produce will only be a certain motion, and this makes them 'efficient causes' of the sort studied in physics. But causes that 'complete' a thing and then preserve it in existence are, Avicenna says, efficient causes in 'a more general sense', which is studied in metaphysics.[37] Let us call such an explanatory principle a 'sustaining cause'.

The father and mother can hardly be sustaining causes for the animal, since the animal can keep on living without further causal connection to its parents, or even after their death. Likewise, as we saw Avicenna mentioning above, animal seed is actually destroyed in the process of generating the animal child. So it cannot be the sustaining cause of that child either (*Healing: Physics* 1.2.18–19, 2.7.1). In this respect, the apparent efficient causes of an animal are like the craftsperson who makes an artefact:

Healing: Metaphysics 6.2.1: Someone who thinks [that the effect can exist without its cause], on the grounds that the son persists after the father, and the building after the builder, and the warmth after the fire, has fallen into confusion because of his ignorance about what 'cause' really [*bi-l-ḥaqīqa*] is. For the builder, the father, and the fire are not really 'causes' of the subsistence [*qiwām*] of these effects. For the builder, who is mentioned as the one who makes [the building], is not the cause for the subsistence of the mentioned building, nor of its existence.

---

[37] On this contrast, see Richardson (2015: sect. 2.2.2).

Which leaves us with a problem. It's clear enough that the builder does not keep causing the structural integrity of the building for all the years it stands, any more than the parents are needed to keep the animal in existence throughout its lifetime. But in the case of an animal, that role is played by the Active Intellect. What is the sustaining cause of an artefact?

The answer, it turns out, is simply the material constituents of the artefact as they were originally arranged by the craftsperson:

Healing: Metaphysics 6.2.5: The cause of the shape [*shakl*] of the building is combination [*ijtimāʿ*], and the cause of this is the natures being combined and staying as they are, the cause of this being the separate efficient cause of the natures.

Thus for example the roof stays in place because it is made of heavy materials like stone and wood, which are joined and fastened in place. The joining and fastening, which constitute an accidental arrangement of the parts brought about by the builder, and the natural heaviness of the stone and wood, are enough to keep the house together. As for the stone and wood whose heaviness is being exploited to maintain the house, these are natural. So they do depend on the Active Intellect for their subsistence. All of this fits nicely with what we saw in the last section. In artefacts, the cause of persistence is the same as the cause of generation, namely the arrangement of material constituents. Thus in the case of theriac, the continued power of the drug would depend on the continued mixture of the ingredients. In natural substances, the cause is instead the giver of forms (the 'separate efficient cause of the natures' mentioned in the passage just cited).

From an Aristotelian point of view, this may seem strange. If we have to identify a sustaining cause for an organism, then why not its form? Avicenna would say that this is right in a sense, because forms (at least organic ones[38]) are indeed sustaining causes. It is just that they are not sustaining causes for the whole hylomorphic substance, but only for the *matter* of that substance. He says in his definitions of formal cause, in both the *Metaphysics* (6.4.9) and *Physics* (1.10.9) of the *Healing*, that the term 'form' may be used for whatever is responsible for 'causing matter to subsist [*taqwīm li-l-mādda*]'. His meaning is clarified in the treatise on soul, where we read:

---

[38] It seems to me that what follows cannot be generalized to other kinds of forms. As we just saw artificial forms depend on the arrangement of their material; they do not sustain the material or the arrangement. As for the natural forms of elements, prime matter is always the same (i.e. indeterminate) and so does not need to be kept in an apt condition. The only doubt would concern non-organic bodies that are composed from the elements, like, say, a granite boulder or a cloud. Avicenna might just say that these are 'heaps' which have no substantial forms and no robust diachronic identity.

Healing: Psychology 27–8: The proximate matter in which these souls [sc. plant and animal souls] exist is what it is only because of a specific mixture and specific configuration, and [the proximate matter] remains existing in actuality, with that specific mixture, only as long as the soul is in it. The soul is what renders it as having that mixture. For the soul is unquestionably the cause for the plant and the animal to exist according to the mixture belonging to them,[39] since the soul is the principle for reproduction and nurture [*tarbiya*].

Here we learn that the soul has an important role in ensuring the continued existence of a living substance. As we saw in section 2, an organic form is given to matter by the Active Intellect when that matter is suitably prepared, whether by the motion of seed or the chance processes that yield spontaneous generation. Once the plant or animal is alive, its soul is responsible for maintaining the matter's suitability to receive form, which it continues to get from the Active Intellect. To be more specific, this is especially the role of the nutritive power, as intimated at the end of the passage just cited and stated more explicitly later on, where Avicenna says of this power:

Healing: Psychology 56: It is by itself preservative [*ḥāfiẓa*] of this composition and mixture, relating to that which has the composition by way of compulsion, since it does not belong to the natures of the elements and opposed bodies to enter into composition on their own.

So the organic form is involved in the persistence of the whole organism: it unifies the material constituent parts as a formal cause, and ensures that those parts continue to play their part in the hylomorphic relationship despite their own natural inclinations.

4. Powers and Forms

If we now return one last time to the fourfold classification at *Healing: Physics* 1.6.2, we may notice a puzzling fact about it: that Avicenna simply equates 'powers' with 'natures' and 'souls', also known as natural and organic forms. But even natures, to say nothing of souls, actually confer more than one capacity on their possessors. Fire can burn, illuminate, and move to its natural place; the animal soul brings with it the capacity for both sense perception and self-motion. So we are faced with yet another question that will be familiar to scholars of

---

[39] I agree with Alpina (2021: 205 n.78) in retaining here *la-hā* from the manuscripts rather than *la-hu* as in Rahman, as referring back to 'the plant and the animal'.

Aristotle: how exactly do forms and souls relate to 'powers' or 'faculties'?[40] Avicenna addresses this question right after setting out the fourfold classification:

Healing: Physics 1.6.3:   It is as if those powers are a part of their form, and as if their form is a combination of a number of factors [*maʿānī*], which are then united; like humanity, since it includes the powers of nature and the powers of the vegetative, animal, and rational soul.

Here Avicenna tentatively suggests that the soul is nothing but a unified bundle of powers. Depending on what he means by 'unification [*ittiḥād*]' one might even ascribe to him a reductionist account, according to which 'humanity' or 'human soul' would be a mere *façon de parler* for an aggregate of distinct powers.

This hypothesis has a certain plausibility, when we take into account two features of Avicenna's thought. First, one I have emphasized in this chapter: that forms are known to us through the effects they manifest. If we observe a plurality of different effects, why not assume a plurality of different forms, with one form per power? 'Animal soul', for instance, would actually just be the power for motion plus the power for sensation. And, to follow the line of thought even further, the power for sensation could be nothing more than an aggregate: the power of sight, plus the power of hearing, etc. Second, there is Avicenna's famous principle that 'from one comes only one'. This rule is usually discussed in the context of God's giving rise to only a single effect. But it is just as relevant here: if the animal soul were truly a unity, how could it give rise to multiple effects or types of effect, e.g. both motion *and* sensation?

Nonetheless the reductionist interpretation does not hold up to scrutiny. Avicenna devotes a chapter of the *Psychology* section of the *Healing* to the question 'whether or not it must be the case that every type [*nawʿ*] of activity has a single power specially dedicated to it' (*Healing: Psychology* 33).[41] In a passage that may ring bells for readers of Plato's *Republic*,[42] he says that we individuate 'powers' in the following terms: 'the power, in itself and primarily, is a power over some object [*amr mā*], and it cannot be a principle for anything else' (*Healing: Psychology* 36). For instance sight is a single power because it is set over a single object, namely colour, even if it has incidental 'offshoots [*furūʿ*]' as when sight grasps other features that are connected to colour, like shape. Beyond this, a single power's effects may be diversified by several factors:

---

[40] For a recent example, see the discussion of the unity of the vegetative soul in Coates and Lennox (2020).

[41] My thanks to Tommaso Alpina for making available to me his draft translation of this chapter, which is *Healing: Psychology* sect. 1.4. In sect. 1.5, Avicenna seems to say that approaching the soul as a bundle of three faculties is merely correct only by 'convention [*waḍʿ*]'; see Alpina (2021: 118).

[42] See *Republic* 477c–d, where Plato has Socrates distinguish each *dunamis* in terms of what it is 'set over' and does.

Healing: Psychology 35:   From a diversity of activities, one cannot infer a diversity of powers. For (a) one and the same power may produce contraries; (b) in fact [*bal*], one and the same power, through diverse volitions, can perform diverse motions; (c) in fact [*bal*] one power may produce diverse activities in diverse materials.

Here Avicenna makes three claims of increasing ambition (hence the use of *bal*). (a) A single power can produce opposed effects, like both locomotion and rest. (b) A single power can produce indefinitely varying effects of the same kind, like locomotion in various directions. (c) A single power can produce varying effects of different kinds, like both motion and sensation.

Variation of type (a) could be explained by appealing to the simple power itself, as when fire's power for motion makes fire move upward but also makes fire rest upon reaching the natural place. To explain variations of type (b) we need to invoke 'volition', giving us a nice link to Avicenna's fourfold classification of powers, which made volition and varied motion the distinctive features of animal soul. Finally, variations of type (c) are explained by material diversity. We saw an example already, as it happens: the power of the sun causes light, heat, and flame depending on the disposition of what receives that power. Another illustration would be that the capacity for bodily self-motion has widely different effects thanks to the diversity of the muscles. Avicenna explicitly names this as a way to escape the apparent implications of the 'from one only one' principle, writing that 'from one and the same motive power, using one and the same organ, there can proceed only one and the same motion' (*Healing: Psychology* 37).[43] This explains how it is that we have one soul, one organic form, but several powers or faculties (distinguished by the objects these are set over), each of which can cause a diversity of activities and actions.

5. Epilogue

One of Avicenna's most trenchant and influential critics, Abū l-Barakāt al-Baghdādī (d. 1160s), argued that this psychological theory, with its multiplicity of 'powers', should be abandoned.[44] He explicitly mentions, and rejects, the Avicennan rationale for positing multiple powers, namely that, as he phrases this principle on Avicenna's behalf: 'the powers are single essences [*dhawāt*] each of which has a single true reality and essence, from which only one action

---

[43] Relatedly, Avicenna much later says that the heart is the central organ of the body, and produces many activities, but through the intermediary of *pneuma* and the subsidiary organs (*Healing: Psychology* 264).

[44] My thanks to Michael Noble for discussion and for his translations of the relevant passages. On the topic, see also Pines (1979).

[fiʿl] proceeds'.[45] Against this, he argues that our souls, or selves, are the subjects of all the activities of which we are capable. For example when I see something it is *me* who sees, not my 'power of vision'.[46]

Ironically, it was Avicenna who provided Abū l-Barakāt with the tool to undermine his own theory. At the beginning of this chapter, I mentioned Avicenna's theory of self-awareness, which is showcased by the flying man argument. This theory was based in part on Avicenna's observation that we are always tacitly aware of all our cognitive activities, and can through focused attention become actively aware of them.[47] So for example, if I am thinking about something, I can also become aware that I am thinking about it, simply by attending to my own thought process. This goes for sensation and the 'internal senses' (like imagination and memory), as well as intellection. The generality of the psychological observation suggests that there is, in each human, a subject of awareness that cuts across the distinction between powers of soul and even across the divide between animal and human soul. In some passages, Avicenna went so far as to suggest that this subject of self-awareness is the true self, whose identity over time is equivalent to the diachronic identity of the person.

Abū l-Barakāt perceptively noticed that all this was in tension with Avicenna's strategy of postulating forms, and powers, as causal principles to explain different types of 'motion and action'. After all, humans are capable of causing many types of action—for instance intellection, imagination, sensation—but Avicenna himself admits that all of these have a single subject of awareness. Abū l-Barakāt therefore suggested that we can replace talk of 'powers' with talk of the soul or self (*nafs, dhāt*) and its activities as a single essence or subject.[48] Avicenna's approach to the classification and differentiation of forms and their powers called for distinguishing them on the basis of the effects they produce. But as Abū l-Barakāt saw, this functionalist strategy could be challenged with a subjectivist account invoking our own immediate access to the self, a phenomenon Avicenna himself had highlighted. Of course, Abū l-Barakāt's proposal is applicable only to the case of humans (and other self-aware entities like God).[49] So, whatever its other merits, his position would have the consequence of removing human souls from Avicenna's general account of forms, which constantly appeals to functions that may be studied by a third-person observer. We might have supposed it is a distinctively modern question whether we should learn about the mind and

---

[45] Yaltkaya (1938–9: vol. 2, 313).

[46] See Abū l-Barakāt's discussion at Yaltkaya (1938–9: vol. 2, 318).

[47] In addition to the references given above, see Kaukua (2015) for Avicenna's account and its later reception.

[48] Anticipating the objection that the functions of the lower soul (which he calls 'the natural powers') might still seem to be independent, Abū l-Barakāt simply argued that these too have the self as their subject. If we are never actively aware of their activities it is simply because they are so gradual. See Yaltkaya (1938–9: vol. 2, 315–17).

[49] On post-Avicennan accounts of self-knowledge in both humans and God, see Adamson (2018).

consciousness through objectively available empirical evidence or through subjective phenomenology. But as it turns out, this dilemma already emerged in the Islamic world almost 1,000 years ago.[50]

Bibliography

Sections from the *Healing* of Avicenna

Healing: Metaphysics = M.E. Marmura (ed. and trans.), *Avicenna: The Metaphysics of the Healing* (Provo: 2005).

Healing: Physics = J. McGinnis (ed. and trans.), *Avicenna: The Physics of the Healing*, 2 vols (Provo: 2009).

Healing: Psychology = F. Rahman (ed.), *Avicenna's De Anima, Being the Psychological Part of Kitāb al-Shifā'* (London: 1970).

Other Literature

P. Adamson, 'From the Necessary Existent to God', in P. Adamson (ed.), Interpreting Avicenna: Critical Essays (Cambridge: 2013), 170–89.

P. Adamson, 'The Simplicity of Self-Knowledge after Avicenna', *Arabic Sciences and Philosophy* 28 (2018), 257–77.

P. Adamson, 'From Known to Knower: Affinity Arguments for the Mind's Incorporeality in the Islamic World', *Oxford Studies in the Philosophy of Mind* 1 (Oxford: 2020).

P. Adamson and F. Benevich, 'The Thought Experimental Method: Avicenna's Flying Man Argument', *Journal of the American Philosophical Association* 4 (2018), 1–18.

T. Alpina, 'Intellectual Knowledge, Active Intellect and Intellectual Memory in Avicenna's *Kitāb al-Nafs* and Its Aristotelian Background', *Documenti e studi sulla tradizione filosofica medievale* 25 (2014), 131–83.

T. Alpina, 'Knowing the Soul from Knowing Oneself: A Reading of the Prologue to Avicenna's *Kitāb al-Nafs (Book of the Soul)*', *Atti e Memorie dell'Accademia Toscana di Scienze e Lettere 'La Colombaria'* 82 (2018a), 443–58.

T. Alpina, 'Soul of, Soul in itself, and the Flying Man Experiment', *Arabic Sciences and Philosophy* 28 (2018b), 187–24.

---

[50] This research was supported by funding from the European Research Council (ERC) under the European Union's Horizon 2020 research and innovation programme (grant agreement No. 786762), and by the DFG under the aegis of the project 'Heirs of Avicenna: Philosophy in the Islamic East from the 12th to the 13th Century'. An earlier draft of this chapter received valuable comments from Tommaso Alpina, David Charles, Damien Janos, Andreas Lammer, Stephen Ogden, and Bligh Somma. I am very grateful to all of them for their feedback.

T. Alpina, 'Is Nutrition a Sufficient Condition for Life? Avicenna's Position Between Natural Philosophy and Medicine', in R. Lo Presti and G. Korobili (eds), *Nutrition and Nutritive Soul in Aristotle and Aristotelianism* (Berlin: 2020), 221-58.

T. Alpina, *Subject, Definition, Activity: Framing Avicenna's Science of the Soul* (Paris: 2021).

J. Bakoš (trans.), *Psychologie d'Ibn Sīnā (Avicenna) d'après son oeuvre as-Šifā'* (Prague: 1956).

F. Benevich, *Essentialität und Notwendigkeit: Avicenna und die aristotelische Tradition* (Leiden: 2018).

A. Bertolacci, 'Avicenna and Averroes on the Proof of God's Existence and the Subject-Matter of Metaphysics', *Medioevo* 32 (2007), 61-98.

D.L. Black, 'Avicenna on Self-Awareness and Knowing that One Knows', in S. Rahman et al. (eds), *The Unity of Science in the Arabic Tradition* (Dordrecht: 2008), 63-87.

D.L. Black, 'Rational Imagination: Avicenna on the Cogitative Power', in L.X. López-Farjeat and J.A. Tellkamp (eds), *Philosophical Psychology in Arabic Thought and the Latin Aristotelianism of the 13th Century* (Paris: 2013), 59-81.

D.L. Black, 'How Do We Acquire Concepts? Avicenna on Abstraction and Emanation', in J. Hause (ed.), *Debates in Medieval Philosophy: Essential Readings and Contemporary Responses* (London: 2014), 126-44.

C.F. Coates and J. Lennox, 'Aristotle on the Unity of the Nutritive and Reproductive Functions', *Phronesis* 65 (2020), 1-53.

H. Corbin (ed.), *Sihābaddīn Yaḥyā as-Suhrawardī. Opera metaphysica et mystica* (Istanbul: 1945).

H.A. Davidson, *Alfarabi, Avicenna, and Averroes on Intellect: Their Cosmologies, Theories of the Active Intellect, and Theories of Human Intellect* (Oxford: 1992).

D. Gutas, 'The Empiricism of Avicenna', *Oriens* 40 (2012), 391-436.

D. Gutas, *Avicenna and the Aristotelian Tradition: Introduction to Reading Avicenna's Philosophical Works*, second edition (Leiden: 2014).

D.N. Hasse, 'Avicenna on Abstraction', in R. Wisnovksy (ed.), *Aspects of Avicenna* (Princeton: 2001), 39-72.

D.N. Hasse, 'Spontaneous Generation and the Ontology of Forms in Greek, Arabic, and Medieval Latin Sources', in P. Adamson (ed.), *Classical Arabic Philosophy: Sources and Reception* (London: 2007), 150-75.

D.N. Hasse, 'Avicenna's "Giver of Forms" in Latin Philosophy, Especially in the Works of Albertus Magnus', in D.N. Hasse and A. Bertolacci (eds), *The Arabic, Hebrew, and Latin Reception of Avicenna's Metaphysics* (Berlin: 2011), 225-50.

D.N. Hasse, 'Avicenna's Epistemological Optimism', in P. Adamson (ed.), *Interpreting Avicenna: Critical Essays* (Cambridge: 2013), 109-19.

J. al-ʿImārātī (ed.), *Ibn Bājja. Kitāb al-Ḥayawān* (Beirut: 2000).

D. Janos, *Avicenna on the Ontology of Pure Quiddity* (Berlin: 2020).

J. Janssens, '"Experience (*tajriba*)" in Classical Arabic Philosophy (al-Fārābī-Avicenna)', *Quaestio* 4 (2004), 45–62.

J. Janssens, 'The Notion of *Wāhib al-ṣuwar* (Giver of Forms) and *Wāhib al-ʿaql* (Giver of Intelligence) in Ibn Sīnā', in M.C. Pacheco and J.F. Meirinhos (eds), *Intellect et imagination dans la philosophie médiévale* (Turnhout: 2006), 551–62.

J. Kaukua, *Self-Awareness in Islamic Philosophy: Avicenna and Beyond* (Cambridge: 2015).

S. Kelsey, 'Aristotle's Definition of Nature', *Oxford Studies in Ancient Philosophy* 25 (2003), 59–87.

R. Kruk, 'A Frothy Bubble: Spontaneous Generation in the Medieval Islamic Tradition', *Journal of Semitic Studies* 35 (1990), 265–82.

A. Lammer, 'Defining Nature: From Aristotle to Philoponus to Avicenna', in A. Alwishah und J. Hayes (eds), *Aristotle and the Arabic Tradition* (Cambridge: 2015), 121–42.

A. Lammer, *The Elements of Avicenna's Physics: Greek Sources and Arabic Innovations* (Berlin: 2018).

R. Leigh (ed. and trans.), *On Theriac to Piso, Attributed to Galen* (Leiden: 2015).

O. Lizzini, *Fluxus (fayḍ). Indagine sui fondamenti della metafisica e della fisica di Avicenna* (Bari: 2011).

T. Mayer, 'Avicenna's *Burhān al-Siddiqīn*', *Journal of Islamic Studies* 12 (2001), 18–39.

J. McGinnis, 'Scientific Methodologies in Medieval Islam: Induction and Experimentation in the Philosophy of Ibn Sīnā', *Journal of the History of Philosophy* 41 (2003), 307–27.

J. McGinnis, 'Making Abstraction Less Abstract: The Logical, Psychological, and Metaphysical Dimensions of Avicenna's Theory of Abstraction', *Proceedings of the American Catholic Philosophical Association* 80 (2007), 169–83.

J. McGinnis, *Great Medieval Thinkers: Avicenna* (Oxford: 2010).

R. Palmer, 'Pharmacy in the Republic of Venice in the Sixteenth Century', in A. Wear et al. (eds), *The Medical Renaissance of the Sixteenth Century* (Cambridge: 1985), 100–17.

M. Papandreou, 'Aristotle's Hylomorphism and the Contemporary Metaphysics of Artifacts', *Discipline Filosofiche* 28 (2018), 113–36.

S. Pines, 'La Conception de la conscience de soi chez Avicenna et chez Abu'l-Barakāt al-Baghdādī', in S. Pines, *Studies in Abu l-Barakāt al-Baghdādī: Physics and Metaphysics* (Jerusalem: 1979), 181–258.

F. Rahman (trans.), *Avicenna's Psychology: An English Translation of Kitāb al-Najāt, Book II, Chapter VI* (London: 1952).

K. Richardson, 'Avicenna and Aquinas on Form and Generation', in D.N. Hasse and A. Bertolacci (eds), *The Arabic, Hebrew, and Latin Reception of Avicenna's Metaphysics* (Berlin: 2011), 743–68.

K. Richardson, 'Causation in Arabic and Islamic Thought', *Stanford Enyclopedia of Philosophy* (Stanford: 2015), https://plato.stanford.edu/entries/arabic-islamic-causation/

M. Sebti, 'La Signification de la définition avicennienne de l'âme comme "perfection première d'un corps naturel organique" dans le livre I du *Traité de l'âme du Šifa*", *Bulletin d'Études Orientales* 51 (1999), 299–312.

A.D. Stone, 'Avicenna's Theory of Primary Mixture', *Arabic Sciences and Philosophy* 18 (2008), 99–119.

A. Tawara, 'Avicenna's Denial of Life in Plants', *Arabic Sciences and Philosophy* 24 (2014), 127–38.

'A. 'Umayra (ed.), *Ibn Sīnā: Najāt fī manṭiq wa-l-ilāhiyyāt* (Beirut: 1992).

P. van der Eijk, 'Galen on the Nature of Human Beings', in P. Adamson, R. Hansberger, and J. Wilberding (eds), *Philosophical Themes in Galen* (London: 2014), 89–134.

R. Wisnovsky, *Avicenna's Metaphysics in Context* (Ithaca: 2003).

C. Witt, 'In Defence of the Craft Analogy: Artifacts and Natural Teleology', in M. Leunissen (ed.), *Aristotle's Physics: A Critical Guide* (Cambridge: 2015), 107–20.

S. Yaltkaya (ed.), *Kitāb al-Muʿtabar fī l-ḥikma*, 3 vols (Hyderabad: 1938-9).

13
Averroes, Intellect, and Liberal Hylomorphism

Stephen R. Ogden

This chapter is focused on the medieval Muslim philosopher Ibn Rushd or Averroes (d. 1198), introducing some main facets of his somewhat exotic intellectual or noetic hylomorphism. I will also use this study of Averroes to make some comments on hylomorphism in general.

Averroes is the most important medieval commentator on Aristotle because of his prominence in all three Abrahamic traditions. Many will know that in the later Latin Christian tradition he was simply known as 'The Commentator', second only to Aristotle as 'The Philosopher'. Averroes had a major influence in the Latin west on figures like Albert the Great, Thomas Aquinas, et al. He was also, however, *the* Aristotelian authority within the Jewish tradition, possibly even more so than Aristotle himself.[1] Finally, within Averroes' own Islamic tradition, he towers over the rest as the chief and most strictly Aristotelian thinker. Although his influence was not as great within the Islamic world, we are learning more about his later impact there as well, e.g. on disciples and other thinkers such as (possibly) 'Abd al-Laṭīf al-Baghdādī and Ibn Taymiyya.

Yet, even in this short chapter, I plan to show that he is something far more than a mere commentator. He does not simply mimic Aristotle, but rather constructs a truly unique kind of hylomorphism, even upon an undeniably Aristotelian foundation.

In section 1, I will argue that Averroes is an instructive, even if not immediately attractive, case study. He casts into stark relief some of the more difficult points of hylomorphism and gives us a better sense of the dizzying diversity within the hylomorphist camp. Thus, 'liberal hylomorphism' names not only a specific feature within Averroes' system (which I will explain), but I also think of it as a call to not foreclose rashly the bounds of hylomorphism. I doubt, for example, that 'essential embodiment' of all types of soul or soul activity is 'the default position for any hylomorphic theory...'[2] That position was certainly not the case historically, and it is not obvious that this sort of dogmatism is beneficial for the view

---

[1] Harvey (1992: esp. 108).   [2] Jaworski (2016: 163).

Stephen R. Ogden, *Averroes, Intellect, and Liberal Hylomorphism* In: *The History of Hylomorphism: From Aristotle to Descartes*. Edited by: David Charles, Oxford University Press. © Stephen R. Ogden 2023.
DOI: 10.1093/oso/9780192897664.003.0014

even today. Thinking more liberally about hylomorphism allows us to see it in its historic dynamism and opens up potentially strong possibilities we might not otherwise consider.

In fact, in section 2, I try to motivate Averroes' infamous 'unicity thesis' by providing some basic reasons and briefly examining one of his arguments. Unlike most of the Aristotelian tradition, in which commentators often defend the idea of a single, separate, and eternal Active or Maker Intellect (*nous poiētikos*) (*De Anima* Γ.5), Averroes further argues for a single, existentially separate, and eternal Potential or (as he calls it, following Alexander) Material Intellect for all human beings.[3] This is his signature unicity thesis. I argue in section 3 that this view does, indeed, imply some radical consequences. When interpreted as a stricter form of hylomorphism, Averroes denies that we human beings have intellect or understanding. That is because even the Material-Potential Intellect is not the individual human intellect (or the so-called Passive Intellect) at all—as it is usually taken to be by other commentators.[4] So we cannot simply interpret away the initially unattractive elements of Averroes' noetic hylomorphism.

Even granting those shocking results, however, I propose in section 4 that Averroes develops his own fascinating *liberal* hylomorphism which can help explain our connection to and composition with substantially separate intellects. This also helps explain why we might be *said* to understand in some non-standard, looser sense. In section 5, I consider some important objections to this liberal hylomorphism. Ultimately, my goal is to show that Averroes' position constitutes an interesting extension of hylomorphism that

(i) builds on a liberal hylomorphism common to standard hylomorphic accounts from Aristotle forward;
(ii) plays an important historical role in bridging Aristotle and Arabic Aristotelianism to later western developments; and
(iii) uniquely preserves two important hylomorphic desiderata (viz., a more parsimonious, broadly naturalist treatment of human beings as such, albeit coupled with genuinely transcendent intellect).

There is no doubt that Averroes' position is a novel and surprising view, but it gained adherents well into the Renaissance. Even those who fulminated against his position were forced to take it surprisingly seriously. This was in part because of the strength of Averroes' various arguments, but also, I suggest, because of the attractiveness of various aspects of his liberal hylomorphism.

---

[3] Though Averroes uses the term 'Material Intellect', that intellect, on his view, is existentially *immaterial* and separate from any body, just as the Active Intellect.

[4] Given that Averroes holds the Material Intellect to be an eternal substance, he also does not identify it with the destructible *nous pathētikos* ('passive intellect') at the end of *De An.* Γ.5 (430a24–5), which he interprets, instead, as the faculty of *phantasia*.

1. Averroes and Hylomorphism

Hylomorphism is often billed as an intermediate position, for those who want to unify the mental and material as much as possible, but without reductionism. Some proclaim for it an almost salvific role. For example, Charles Kahn says:

> [I]s an Aristotelian philosophy of mind still possible? My answer is that it is not only possible but necessary, since Aristotle offers us the best alternative to the dualist and anti-dualist theories of mind that have plagued philosophy with persistent and fruitless conflict for more than three centuries... [Aristotle's] real advantage, as I see it, is to be exempt from the Cartesian curse of mind-body opposition with all the baffling paradoxes and philosophical blind alleys that this antithesis gives rise to.[5]

I am sympathetic; I find hylomorphism to be a plausible and promising alternative. But just consider an (imaginary) Descartes* (channelling Kahn):

> Is a new physics at all possible? My answer is that it is not only possible but necessary, since a new physics offers us the best alternative to the Scholastic theories of form that have plagued philosophy with persistent and fruitless conflict for more than nineteen centuries!... The real advantage, as I see it, is to be exempt from the Scholastic curse of substantial forms with all the baffling paradoxes and philosophical blind alleys that this thesis gives rise to.

Hylomorphism is, indeed, an *alternative*, as Descartes himself plainly saw, but its viability does not stem primarily from its being somehow simpler and more straightforward (or from the alternatives' relative complexity).

Indeed, in addition to its prolific historical manifestations, contemporary debate regarding hylomorphism in the nearly thirty years since Kahn's comment bear witness to all sorts of complications within the broadly hylomorphic system. As a quite persistent case in point, we must grapple with what has been dubbed Aristotle's own *nous*-body problem, i.e. the intellect-body problem.[6] In response to this difficult issue, many varying models of intellect were developed throughout ancient and medieval Aristotelianism. If hylomorphism promises a better analysis of the psychology and metaphysics of human beings, we need to understand how it incorporates the strange case of intellect, and this is no small task. (Note that even thinking of this intellect-body issue as a central problem, rather than the more familiar contemporary *mind*-body problem, requires a certain conceptual realignment, since the vast majority of phenomena lumped under *mind* by

---

[5] Kahn (1992: 359).   [6] See Modrak (1991); Charles (2021: 220).

contemporary thinkers are clearly considered essentially and existentially linked with the body for Aristotle.) Insofar as there are many importantly divergent views of Aristotelian *noetic* hylomorphism, there will, in turn, be many importantly divergent views of Aristotelian hylomorphism *tout court*.[7] Averroes is one of the most intriguing of such cases.

Aristotle in *De Anima* (*De An.*) A.1 argues that most affections or functions of the soul are common to body and soul and therefore inseparable, requiring both body and soul: 'And it would seem that all the affections of the soul involve the body—anger, gentleness, fear, [etc.] ... For at the same time as these, the body is affected in some way'.[8] Even the definitions of these kinds of activities must, like that of the substance as a whole, incorporate the matter and the form.

Averroes, in turn, is a sensible, card-carrying hylomorphist in his understanding of the form-matter composition of substances and most psychological capacities. Regarding the lower faculties of soul, Averroes propounds a genuine and somewhat standard hylomorphism marked by existential and definitional inseparability and non-reductivity in either direction of the body-soul, matter-form relations.

> Then he [Aristotle] said: For the body is affected along with these [i.e. soul activities or affections, like anger, etc.]. That is, alteration and change appear in it [the body]. For every affection made with alteration and change [*taghayyur wa-istiḥāla*][9] is necessarily in a body or in a power in a body.[10]
>
> Since he has shown that these affections are *material forms* [*forme materiales / ṣuwar hayūlāniyya*?], it is necessary that matter appear in their definitions.[11]

We can safely conjecture the Arabic of 'material forms' as *ṣuwar hayūlāniyya*, which appears elsewhere in the Arabic fragments of the *LCDA* and his other commentaries.[12] This may represent Averroes' happy acceptance of the Arabic equivalent of the Greek *logoi enuloi* (a possible reading of 403a25), which he likely

---

[7] One could argue that we can sidestep these issues because, even if certain activities of *nous* turn out to be <u>not</u> essentially enmattered, *nous* is still existentially dependent on the body, and the human soul itself is essentially enmattered—see, e.g., Charles (2021: 221-3). But these are not the only possibilities. We shall see that Averroes agrees that the human soul is essentially enmattered, but argues that *nous* is not existentially dependent on any body.

[8] *De An.* 403a16-19; Shields trans.

[9] These terms correspond to *alloiōsis/metabolē* in Greek and *alteratio/transmutatio* in Latin.

[10] Long Commentary on De Anima (*LCDA*) I, comment 14, 21, and Arabic Fragments, 31. Unless otherwise noted, all translations (and added emphases) are my own. For the complete English translation of the *LCDA*, see Taylor (2009a).

[11] *LCDA* I.15, 22; cf. Arabic Fragments, 32. See also *Long Commentary on Metaphysics* (*LCM*), E.2, 709.

[12] *LCDA*, Arabic Fragments, 32. The rest of the line is extant in Arabic and matches the Latin. Averroes uses *al-ṣuwar al-hayūlāniyya* also in I.26, Arabic Fragments, 34, and in III.4, Arabic Fragments, 44. See also *Middle Commentary on De Anima* (*MCDA*), 8, and the *Short Commentary on De Anima* (*SCDA*): 'The relation of form to matter is one in which it is impossible to conceive any

read in the Arabic Themistius, even if not in his translation of Aristotle proper.[13] Whether or not this is convincing evidence that Averroes has an 'impurist' view about natural forms, he clearly holds here (and in other passages) at least that matter and form must be mentioned by the definition and that most soul activities and powers are essentially embodied.[14] (For the rest of the chapter, I will attempt to stay neutral on Averroes' impurism or purism, which would require further study to settle.)[15]

These typical hylomorphic selling points, however, seem abandoned by Averroes once he considers intellect (*nous*, ʿ*aql*, *intellectus*). Far from a unitarian account of *nous/noēsis* as a form or account in matter, within the single human hylomorphic composite, Averroes' account veers towards substance trialism![16] BOTH active/agent/*poiētikos* intellect (hereafter, AI) (*De An.* 430a12, 15) and material/potential/*dunamei* intellect (hereafter, MPI) (*De An.* 429a15-16 and 430a10-11) are single, existentially separate substances which we (a third substance) must 'log onto' in order to explain basic acts of *noēsis*. In that sense, Averroes' position seems even worse than dualism! If this is actually where hylomorphism leads, it is hardly the panacea in philosophy of mind some have taken it to be.

Now, if this is really Averroes' position, why not simply jettison hylomorphism? Some readers of Aristotle who reach similar conclusions (at least about the AI or about *nous* in general) do just this: *nous*, especially in its highest form, is a categorical exception to hylomorphism. Some interpret Aristotle as a dualist.[17] The most prominent of Averroes' Muslim predecessors, Avicenna (Ibn Sīnā), developed his own Aristotelian psychology in a decidedly dualist direction. Commentators who think the AI is God or some other, lower divine intellect,

---

separation, given that it is a material form [*ṣūra hayūlāniyya*]' (SCDA, 9.4-5). Cf. *Short Commentaries on Metaphysics* (SCM), 61; and *Long Commentaries on Metaphysics* (LCM), α.1, 8.2-5, and Λ.37, 1603.2-3.

[13] The relevant lemma and comment in the Latin (I.14, 20-1; *forme in materia*), the MCDA (7), and one of Averroes' Arabic translations of the *De An.* (Arabic, 6) all suggest that he would have read Aristotle's words as *maʿānin fī hayūlā* ('intentions / accounts in matter'), corresponding to *logoi en hulē(i)*. For discussion of the Greek, see Shields (2016: 98-9).

[14] For a prominent impurist account of Aristotle's psychology, see Charles (2009 and 2021). See Caston (2009) for one reply and Meister (2020) for a helpful overview of the debate with other relevant literature. Di Giovanni (2011) provides an excellent explanation of Averroes on substantial form in his metaphysics. In fact, especially if Di Giovanni is correct, there does seem to be additional *prima facie* evidence that Averroes holds a kind of impurism about form. He tends to identify substantial form and essence, and even form and species. Though the latter seems based at times on faulty translations, the result is that parts of the species are, in turn, parts of form. Furthermore, various kinds of material parts (e.g. elements, flesh, and bone) may likewise be parts of form (Di Giovanni 2011: esp. 186-9).

[15] The second quote above at n. 11 is, again, evidence for impurism, not only because of the essentially material forms, but also because the matter-mentioning definition is *of those forms*—see Peramatzis (2011: ch. 2) and Charles (2021: 9). But in other metaphysical contexts, Averroes can speak just as naturally about definitions of the composite—e.g. LCM Z.34, 900.13-901.2.

[16] Cf. Cottingham (1985) on a different trialistic interpretation of Descartes. I will return to this potential objection in section 4.

[17] E.g. Robinson (1983); Sisko (2000).

naturally tend to eschew any hylomorphic analysis for the AI.[18] But Averroes does not do any of that. He insists (as we will see) on trying to preserve a hylomorphic explanation for these separate intellects and their relationship to us, even though they are entirely distinct substances. Especially if Averroes has a good case here, he not only proves that hylomorphism is not so cut and dried, in contrast to myriad supposedly unacceptable forms of materialism and dualism. He is showing us that the hylomorphism tent is bigger than we might have thought.

2. Arguments for Averroes' View

The MPI in Aristotle seems to be merely a power or capacity to think in universals. What possessed Averroes to reify the MPI (and the AI) in such a dramatic fashion, as some sort of separate substance? First, we must recall that such reification of the two kinds or capacities of *nous* was thoroughly embedded in the Aristotelian tradition long before Averroes. Alexander's identification of the AI with the prime mover already and decisively opens the door to thinking of intellect generally in more substantial terms. This basic line of thought—albeit with the AI more commonly considered some lower divine (and not the first) unmoved mover— is found also in Themistius and other more Neoplatonist Greek thinkers, which all became part and parcel of the entire Arabic reception in al-Kindī, al-Fārābī, and Avicenna. And in Avicenna, for example, human rational souls are existentially separable substances precisely in virtue of their immaterial and individuated MPI powers.

Second, there are in fact strong reasons in *De An.* itself to think that intellect is a special case and somehow separate. In key parts of *De An.*, Aristotle infamously follows some of his own most canonical statements of hylomorphism with caveats about *nous*: A.1 (403a5 ff.); B.1 (413a3–9); and B.2 (413b24–9). In *De An.* Γ.4, as he begins his explicit discussion of *nous*, he asks again 'whether it is separable/separate [*chōristou*] or is not spatially separable [*kata megethos*] but only in account [*kata logon*]' (429a11–12). The first possibility can reasonably be taken as ontological or modal-existential separation, i.e. 'separability without qualification' (*chōristos haplōs*).[19] The second possibility, in contrast, would be a qualified separability, i.e. definitionally separable or separable in account (*kata logon*).[20] In the argumentation that follows, however, nowhere does Aristotle

---

[18] Caston (1999: 206) takes the *en tē(i) psuchē(i)* at 430a13 to mean 'in the case of the soul'—i.e. not the human soul, but rather a distinct type of divine soul. Alexander, *De Anima*, conveniently says these differences are 'in the intellect' (*epi tou nou*) (88.22–3).

[19] See *Meta.* H.1, 1042a31–2, and Z.10, 1035b23–4. Cf. Fine (1984); Miller (2012: 309–10); and Shields (2016: 80). For more fine-grained types of ontological and existential separation and for why I categorize this as 'modal-existential' (i.e. that X can exist without *any* Y), see Peramatzis (2011); Corkum (2016); and Cohoe (2022).

[20] Cf. Peramatzis' (2011: ch. 8) priority in being or essence.

qualify the kind of separability that *nous* enjoys (and certainly not with the explicit qualification *kata logon*). Rather, he strikingly argues that *nous* is not mixed with the body (*oude memichthai...tō(i) sōmati*) (429a24–5), that it is without a bodily organ (a26–7), and that it is separable/separate (*chōristos*)—with no qualification given—unlike the sensitive faculty which does not exist without the body (*ouk aneu sōmatos*) (b5). Aristotle then further hypostatizes *nous* as the 'place of forms' (*topon eidōn*) at 429a27–8. This suggests the argumentation of Γ.4 is pushing towards existential separability, rather than merely definitional separability.

All of these points address the MPI specifically (or possibly *nous* generally) as discussed in Γ.4, to say nothing of the more rarefied case of the AI in Γ.5.[21] As Averroes argues, however, these two intellects are discussed by Aristotle in largely the same important terms—separable (*chōristos*), impassible (*apathēs*), and unmixed (*amigēs*).[22] Indeed, prior to the distinction between MPI and AI in Γ.4–5, Aristotle says *nous* seems to be 'some kind of substance' (*ousia tis*) and indestructible (*phtheiresthai*) (A.4, 408b19). Elsewhere in the *Generation of Animals*, Aristotle states that *nous* is divine and enters from 'outside' (*thurathen*) the body (736b21–9), which raised serious questions about its separate status even as early as Theophrastus. Of course, one can argue that there are better interpretations for many of these passages. But it is certainly not implausible to read the above combined evidence as suggesting that *nous* in general or the MPI specifically is existentially separate, perhaps even a separate substance, as many regard the AI.

Finally, Averroes launches independent philosophical arguments for his position that mirror and yet magnify what we find in Aristotle. The one argument I will touch on here is the Determinate Particular Argument (DPA) (*LCDA* III.5, 388–9).[23] Though it is based roughly on Aristotle's *De An.* Γ.4, this DPA appears to be entirely Averroes' own. It runs as follows:

(1) If something is a material determinate particular, it can only receive particular forms.
(2) The MPI does not receive particular forms.
(3) Therefore, the MPI is not a material determinate particular.
(4) If something exists that is not a material determinate particular, then it is a substance that is neither generable nor corruptible.
   ...etc.

---

[21] Most of the arguments seem to address the MPI specifically as the intellect capable of receiving all intelligible forms, presumably in its theoretical, rather than practical, capacity. This evidence puts pressure on interpretations that limit the MPI's separability to definitional.
[22] *LCDA* III.4 and III.19.   [23] For more on this argument, see Ogden (2016 and 2022: ch. 2).

Premise (1) can be supported in a variety of ways. First, Aristotle thinks it is a necessary truth, exemplified by the case of sensation.[24] Second, (1) seems like the kind of proposition that many philosophers might accept (*prima facie*), even if they are opposed to the rest of the argument—materialists, naturalists, nominalists, etc. Third, it is plausible to think that matter will always exclude in some way (consistent with an Aristotelian notion of matter as a principle of individuation), and even more so in the case of material organs.[25] Premise (2) is definitional. (4) is too quick (as stated by Averroes), but it can be partially supported by the conclusion in (3), that the MPI is something immaterial which furthermore exists and performs an activity.

It is by no means a fringe interpretation of Aristotle to think that the MPI is existentially immaterial. Many interpreters, including today's, think that is exactly what Aristotle is arguing in Γ.4. Thomas Aquinas is another famous historical example. Nevertheless, Averroes' view stands out from these interpretations because he argues that the MPI is only *one* for all human beings and that it is a separate substance altogether (premise (4)). Thus, we do not each have our own intellect (immaterial or otherwise) at all.

Averroes puts forward another argument, the Unity Argument, which I think is crucial for proving the oneness of the MPI. In order to explain how human beings can all think the same thing, Averroes argues that there must simply be one thing that is thought, in one and the same intellect.[26] My objective here is not to defend fully these arguments from Averroes, but rather to discuss their consequences and the interesting version of hylomorphism that falls out of them.

3. Do We Understand? (Strict Hylomorphism)

Once we see that Averroes holds that the MPI is not the human or 'passive' intellect but rather a single, separate, eternal substance, there are at least two main questions we might ask, which I will discuss in sections 3 and 4, respectively:

---

[24] See *Analytica Priora et Posteriora* (*APo.*) A.31, 87b28–30 and 37–9. Averroes argues in the same passage that prime matter always receives particular forms, which suggests *prima facie* that souls and substantial forms for him are particular. Indeed, I think that is his view, but that is a complicated issue which I cannot discuss at length here.

[25] Cohoe (2013) characterizes this idea as Aristotle's 'conduit condition'. More cautiously, Shields (1995) suggests that being mixed with body would give *nous* a structure limiting its plasticity with respect to all *noēta*, and thus unacceptably undermining the irreducible nature of intentionality.

[26] See Ogden (2021 and 2022: ch. 3). David Charles raises the question about other common human capacities or skills, e.g. building. Does Averroes' reasoning lead us to the (absurd) conclusion that there is only a single builder? No, because building involves practical rationality and various particularized actions involving matter. The Unity Argument only concerns theoretical, universal knowledge. But to the extent that *technē* relies on universals (*Meta.* A.1, 981a17), skill is partially subsumed under the argument.

A. Do we human beings understand?

and

B. How are we connected to the separate intellects?

On my view, Averroes responds to (A) in the negative through a stricter, complicated hylomorphic analysis, but he answers (B) by developing a more liberal hylomorphism.

To take his reply to the first question, we must understand his 'dual subject theory'. For Averroes, every cognitive act (or cognitive form in actuality) has two subjects:

(i) Subject of truth (the immediate cause of the form which at least partially fixes the form's nature or content, e.g. the brown in the table)
(ii) Subject of existence (the cognitive power affected in which the form in act is received and exists, explaining the cognitive production, e.g. the eye/sense organ where the form of brown is received, constituting sight).

The same schema holds for the intelligible form, except that (i) (the subject of truth) = images, and (ii) (the subject of existence) = the separate MPI. (The separate AI, by the way, is responsible for abstracting the intelligible form from (i) so that it can be received by (ii).)

Importantly, Deborah Black has argued that because we are highly cognitive in our own right as possessors of subject (i) (*phantasia*/imagination), we can be aware of acts of understanding that originate and are individuated by us, even though subject (ii) is the separate MPI.[27] According to Black, this defeats the famous arguments of Aquinas, which, for example, contend that Averroes has no way to affirm that human beings understand (*hic homo intelligit*).[28] My view is that Black gives us good reason to think Averroes can defuse Aquinas' argument at the phenomenological level, which is significant. But I argue that Averroes is forced to *deny* that human beings understand or have intellects strictly speaking, that is, on a strict hylomorphic analysis.

Consider one of the most important but complex texts at issue, which I call the Conditions Passage. Note that Averroes appeals here to a *strict* hylomorphic explanation.

---

[27] Black (1993). See also Taylor (2009b).
[28] See Aquinas, *In De An.* III.7, 205.275 ff. See Black (1993: 350, n. 3) for a complete list of works where Aquinas makes this same basic argument.

Conditions Passage

[1] Therefore, let us say that it is clear that a human being is not understanding in act [*non est intelligens in actu*] unless [*nisi*] on account of the conjoining of the intelligible with him in act.[29] [2] And it is also clear that matter and form are joined to each other such that the composite from them is a single thing, and maximally [so in the case of] the Material Intellect and the intelligible intention in act. For what is composed from them is not some third thing distinct from them as in the case of other things composed from matter and form. [3] Therefore, it is impossible that there be a conjunction of the intelligible with the human being unless it is through the conjunction of one of these two parts with him, namely (A) the part that is of it [the composite] as matter, and (B) the part that is related to the latter (namely, the intellect)[30] as form [i.e. the intelligible intention in act]. [4] Since it was shown from the previously mentioned doubts that it is impossible that the intelligible be joined with each human being and be multiplied by number with him through (A) the part of it [the composite] that is as matter, namely the Material Intellect, [5] it remains that the conjoining of the intelligibles with us human beings is through the conjoining of the intelligible intention with us (and they are the imagined intentions), i.e., of the part of them [*de eis*] [the intelligibles] that is in us in some way [*aliquo modo*] as form.[31]

Averroes puts forward two related conditions for the possibility that humans understand in act. The first condition, in [1], claims that a human being will not actually understand unless the intelligibles *in act* are conjoined with her. In [3], Averroes proposes that that first conjunction of the intelligible with the human being is impossible unless it is through the conjunction of (A) or (B) with her, i.e. the matter-form parts of the relevant composite. The immediately preceding lines in [2] make it clear that this hylomorphic composite is that of the MPI (A) and the intelligible in act (B) (*intellectus materialis et intentio intellecta in actu*).

A truly hylomorphic composite is always a completely unified single thing, and this is maximally true with respect to (A) the MPI and (B) the intelligible form in act since there is no literal, sensible matter here (see *De An.* 430a3–5). On these hylomorphic grounds, Averroes reasons that we can satisfy condition [1] either by conjoining directly with (B), the intelligible form in act itself, or with its intimately connected 'matter', (A). He then immediately claims in [4] that to do so through (A) the MPI is 'impossible' since it is singular and not uniquely possessed by any of us. That leaves us with (B).

What Averroes asserts in [5], however, is *not* exactly that we conjoin with (B), intelligibles in act. Rather, we join with the formal part (B) *in some way (aliquo*

---

[29] I will discuss the notion of 'conjoining' further below, esp. in section 4.
[30] Following the MSS in ll. 511–12.
[31] *LCDA* III.5, 404.501–405.520. Numbers and letters inserted for clarification.

modo), i.e. through the part of the intelligibles that is in us, namely the imagined intentions (*intentiones ymaginate*). He is clearly appealing here again to the fact that our images serve as the subject of truth. Averroes himself, however, argues explicitly for a stark distinction of imagined vs actually intelligible universal intentions.

> [I]maginable intentions are universals in potency, although not in act. Therefore, [Aristotle] said these [universals] 'are, *in a way* [*quasi*], in the soul', and he did not say, '*are*' [in the soul], because a universal intention is different from an imagined intention.[32]

Averroes' explanation of how the universal intelligibles are only *quasi* in the soul is echoed by [5] in the Conditions Passage, stating that the intelligibles are only in us *in some way* as form.

A major reason we cannot join directly with (B) is that the normal way we unite with cognitive forms is by possessing the relevant power (A). One unites with sensible forms, for example, primarily by having one's own individuated power of sense, along with its requisite organ(s). But, as Averroes explicitly argues in [4] and earlier in the text, that normal, stricter hylomorphic analysis (of a power receiving its proper form and object) is not possible when it comes to the singular intellect. If that were the case, we would all know exactly and only the same things, given the unity of the intellect.[33] But that is obviously false.[34]

At most, then, both condition [1] and condition [3] with respect to (B) are satisfied only *in some way*. Simultaneously, then, Averroes must also deny that we understand in the standard hylomorphic sense of cognition, which is demanded by conditions [1] and [3]. This upshot of the Conditions Passage is confirmed later in the *LCDA* where he offers a crucial definition of what understanding is.

> For to abstract is nothing other than to make imagined intentions intelligibles in act after they were in potency; however, *to understand is nothing other than to receive these intentions* [in act] ... Thus, the material [intellect] is the receiving [cause], and the agent [intellect] is the efficient [cause].[35]

Something is only actually understanding, by definition, if it receives intelligibles in act, and, according to Averroes, the only being that receives the intelligibles in

---

[32] *LCDA* II.60, 220.20–4. Averroes is here quoting and commenting on Aristotle, *De An.* B.5, 417b23–4 (*tauta d'en autē(i) pōs esti tē(i) psuchē(i)*); cf. *De An.* Arabic, 43 (*hādhihī wa-mithluhā lil-nafs*). Averroes has *ka-annahā fīl nafs* in the *MCDA* 63.11.

[33] *LCDA* III.5, 402.454–403.465.

[34] In contrast, our numerically distinct powers of sense allow us at times to see some of the same objects, but still only from different perspectives.

[35] *LCDA* III.18, 439. Cf. *LCM* Λ.44, 1649.4: 'the intelligible is the cause of understanding [*al-maʿqūl huwa ʿillat al-ʿāqil*]'.

act (and thus makes the relevant kind of hylomorphic union with them) is the separate MPI. Just as the sense power receives the sensible forms in act (and not the external sensible objects themselves), so too it is only the MPI that receives the intelligible forms in act (and not the potentially intelligible images). Thus, properly speaking, we cannot ascribe the activity of understanding to human beings, even though we play some indispensable part in this activity as the subject of truth, i.e. the source and individuator for these intellectual acts. It follows that Averroes must, after all, deny that this (or any) human being *noei/ʿaqala/intelligit*.

In turn, Averroes immediately adds (following the Conditions Passage) that the Aristotelian definition of soul only applies equivocally to the intellect, which he also affirms elsewhere in the *LCDA*:

> It is better to say, and seems more to be true after investigation, that this [intellect] is another kind of soul and, if it is called a soul, it will be so equivocally [*secundum equivocationem*]. If the disposition of intellect is such as this, then it must be possible for that alone of all the powers of soul to be separated from the body and not to be corrupted by [the body's] corruption, just as the eternal is separated. This will be the case since sometimes [the intellect] is not joined [*copulatur*] with [the body] and sometimes it is joined with it.[36]

The separation of the MPI (and AI) from the human body is clearly existential here, just as the other eternal unmoved movers and intellects can exist without any human bodies and despite the generation and corruption of the latter. So the intellect is not really a part of the human soul—it is 'another kind of soul' and called soul only equivocally.[37]

This is a brief case for the controversial claim that Averroes answers question (A) in the negative, denying that we have intellect and understanding.[38] But we see that it rests upon a stricter sort of hylomorphic analysis. Human beings are not hylomorphically united to the relevant intelligible forms in actuality through our own distinct psychological powers of intellect; rather we are united with them only in potentiality, in virtue of the potentially intelligible *phantasmata*. Therefore, we do not perform the activity of understanding. Intellect is not really a part of the human soul but is rather a separate substance, the eternal MPI.

---

[36] *LCDA* II.21, 160.24–161.33; Taylor trans. (2009a: 128). Similarly, he claims in a passage of *Tahafot at-Tahafot* (*TT*) 5, 295.5–9, that 'intellect' itself is an equivocal term as applied to us and the separate intellects: '[T]wo distinct things can be distinct in their substances [*fī jawharayhimā*] without agreeing in anything except in the term [*fī l-lafẓ*] alone, and that is when they do not agree in a common genus... for example, the name "intellect" [*al-ʿaql*] said of the human intellect and of separate intellects [*al-ʿuqūl al-mufāriqa*]...So the resemblances of these terms more closely falls under equivocal [*mushtaraka*] names than under univocal names...'

[37] Averroes is obviously appealing to the very similar comment in Aristotle, *De An.* B.2, 413b24–7. Cf. Caston (1999: 210).

[38] I provide a more thorough argument in Ogden (2022: ch. 4).

4. How Are We United with Separate Intellects? (Liberal Hylomorphism)

Given the stark consequences outlined in the previous section, we should ask question (B): How, then, are we united with these entirely separate intellects at all? In what way are human beings unique among animals in our ability to reason (and so on) if we do not have intellects or at least some special connection to the separate MPI and AI? So far, if my interpretation is correct, we have seen a more standard hylomorphism with respect to the MPI and the intelligible form (in which the form certainly cannot exist in actuality without its 'matter', the Material-Potential Intellect).[39] But Averroes' conclusions about intellect seem to rupture entirely any stricter Aristotelian hylomorphic relation between intellect/understanding and human beings. What room is left for a noetic hylomorphism if intellect has thus exited the realm of psychology in all but an equivocal sense? Averroes' response to these legitimate lines of inquiry appeals to a more liberal hylomorphism, which I argue is not hylomorphic in name only. His explanation also reveals how we might be said to understand and intelligize *in some way*.

Richard Taylor has argued that Averroes throughout his career describes the separate intellects (especially the AI) as 'form for us' or 'our forms'.[40] Taylor refers to this as the 'Principle of Intrinsic Formal Cause', and it is an elaboration of what Averroes and the Arabic tradition more broadly call 'conjunction' or 'contact' (*ittiṣāl*) with separate intellects—a term we have already seen Averroes use hylomorphically in the Conditions Passage above. On this point, Averroes is critical of his predecessor al-Fārābī and his view that the AI is merely an extrinsic efficient cause in relation to us.[41] But it is difficult to know what all this amounts to. In fact, Taylor says pessimistically that Averroes' idea of the separate intellects as formal cause 'strains the limits of his Aristotelian philosophical project'.[42] What could Averroes mean by his insistence that the

---

[39] Indeed, it certainly seems the intellect-intelligible composite (which constitutes understanding in act) cannot be defined without reference to both parts, and in some cases both Aristotle and Averroes suggest an even stronger form of ontological *identity* between the two, as we saw in the Conditions Passage. See Averroes, *LCDA* III.15 and *LCM* Λ.39, 1617–18; Aristotle, *De An.* Γ.4, 430a3–5 and *Meta.* Λ.7, 1072b20–5. It also seems that the intellect could not be defined without reference to the intelligible. But, conversely, can the intelligible form as such be defined without reference to the intellect? There, too, it seems plausible to say no, as the tightly linked nouns and verb attest (*nous—noēton—noei*).

[40] See esp. Taylor (2005 and 2009b).

[41] As Taylor highlights (esp. in 2005 and 2009b: 207 ff); see also Geoffroy (2007). The influence of Themistius is evident, especially the AI's not being 'outside' (*exōthen*) but rather 'entering into [*enduetai*] the whole of the potential intellect'—*De An. Paraph.* 99.13–15. The entire Arabic tradition of conjunction with the AI is also heavily based on interpretations (and misinterpretations) of Alexander and his conception of intellectual union with the AI / prime mover (e.g. *De Anima* 89.21–91.6), which he also emphasizes 'comes to be in us from outside' (91.2) as an 'immaterial form' (89.19) and object of our knowing. See Geoffroy (2007: esp. 87–9 and 92–5).

[42] Taylor (2005: 50).

separate intellects are not only efficient causes in relation to us but also formal causes?[43]

There is rich historical territory beyond Averroes regarding this issue. For example, the doctrine of multiple substantial forms was motivated for some thinkers partly because of concerns regarding intellect. On some of these views, the separate intellects / separate forms are our final (of multiple) forms. Other later Averroists develop unique anthropologies, according to which the human being is a literal composite of separate intellect plus the animated human body.[44]

But Averroes himself has something else in mind, perhaps simpler and more attractive from a hylomorphic point of view. He argues compellingly against the metaphysical possibility of substances within substances. For example:

> If the universal were a substance existing in an individual determinate particular [al-shakhṣ al-mushār ilayhi], it would be a substance added to the substance through which the individual determinate particular is an individual substance... [T]hen two substances would be in the individual determinate particular. And how can one substantial whole [mujawhar wāḥid] be two substances?[45]

He also reasons elsewhere:

> For the compound is only called one through the unity existing in the form... And if matter and form were [already] existing in act in the composite, then the composite would not be called one except as is said in things that are one according to contact and being tied together [i.e. per accidens].[46]

These metaphysical principles would be violated if Averroes held that we could be united with the separate intellects according to *strict* hylomorphism, since the intellects are distinct substances and such a joining would be a *per accidens* union of substances, like a heap.

Since a stricter, ontological reading of our union with the separate intellects is impossible, then, Averroes likely thinks of the conjunction more liberally. I mentioned the equivocation regarding intellect above. But liberal hylomorphism allows us to say something more positive on Averroes' conception. We should not conclude that the separate intellects are no more our forms than the dogfish (or a Dogfish Head beer) is a dog. Intellect is not equivocally soul in the sense that there

---

[43] Of course, some efficient causes are also formal causes, plausibly including *technē*, which, from *De An*. 430a12–14, might immediately support the idea of the AI as both.

[44] For an overview of some of these positions, see Brenet (2019); also his full study of Jean of Jandun in (2003).

[45] *LCM* Z.48, 968.7–10. On the difference between Aristotle's argument (*Meta*. Z.13, 1038b29–30) and Averroes' distinct view, see Di Giovanni (2007: 200).

[46] *LCDA* II.7, 139.36–42.

is absolutely no connection between the intellects and us. In other words, Averroes probably has *pros hen* or analogical predication in mind. In the following quote, Averroes lays out some of the key features of his liberal hylomorphism.

Liberal Hylomorphism Passage:

For every two things of which one is a subject and the other is more perfect, the relation of the more perfect to the imperfect is just as [*sicut*] the relation of form to matter [e.g. the relation of the power of imagination to the common sense]... And in this way we will be able to generate the intelligibles when we want [*voluerimus*]. For, because that through which [*per quod*] something performs its proper action [*propriam actionem*] is form, and since we also perform our proper action through the agent intellect, it is necessary that the agent intellect is a form in us.[47]

What does it mean, then, to say that the AI or the MPI is form for us?[48] The intellects are more perfect, but that is not all. Rather, the intellects stand in a *perfecting* and actualizing relation to our imaginative-cogitative powers, which contain the potential intelligible forms (just like imagination further actualizes and perfects the sensible forms in common sense).[49] Moreover, the intellects are that *through which* (*per quod*) we perform our *proper* action, i.e. any 'intellectual' acts, when we *will* to do so.[50] Let me now discuss these last three important components of the Liberal Hylomorphism Passage.

First, Averroes' liberal noetic hylomorphism appeals to the notion of will (*boulēsis*; *mashī'a*; *voluntas*). We find this idea in another significant passage from the *LCDA*:

Attribution Passage:

It was necessary to *attribute* [*attribuere*] these two actions to the soul in us, namely to receive the intelligible and to make it, although the agent and the recipient are eternal substances, because of this [fact] that these two actions, namely to abstract the intelligibles and to understand them, are traced to [*reducte*] our will.[51]

---

[47] *LCDA* III.36, 499.
[48] Averroes' longest concentrated discussion on this topic (*LCDA* III.36) focuses on conjunction with the AI, which was the norm in the Arabic tradition. But Averroes' unique account of the MPI as also a separate substance means he has to accommodate a conjunction with the MPI as well—see, e.g., *LCDA* III.5, 410–11 and III.36, 486.199–202.
[49] Averroes goes on to explain that the AI is conjoined with the theoretical intelligibles which are conjoined with us through the imaginative forms—*LCDA* III.36, 500.592 ff.
[50] On my view, Averroes does think we perform 'intellectual' acts, e.g. philosophizing or thinking about logic, which are really acts of cogitation/imagination in consort with the separate intellects. But I think he must deny that these acts attain to the high-grade level of universality which is only truly appropriate to the separate intellects.
[51] *LCDA* III.18, 439.71–6.

The MPI and AI are *in* our soul and they can be reckoned as form in us because their properly intellectual acts are brought about by our willing. This also explains why Averroes is critical of al-Fārābī, who (according to Averroes) thought of the separate AI only as an efficient cause and external mover.[52] Given that the simple acts of understanding belong, strictly speaking, only to the intellects, and not to us, it is true that the MPI and AI are more like efficient and final causes relative to us.[53] But insofar as we initiate and perform the 'intellectual' acts that we want through the separate intellects, we are *their* movers, and we should consider them as form, as that through which we accomplish our goals. If that is correct, Averroes is presenting an interesting form of compatibilism (similar to notions of *eph' hēmin* in later Greek and Stoic philosophy): Understanding is technically up to us, though not technically in us. Or 'in us' only in the sense that it is up to us.

Second, Averroes' Liberal Hylomorphism Passage underscores that our conjunction with the separate intellects as our form is not ontological or existential (at least not in the sense of strict hylomorphism) but rather operational—the MPI and AI are the things *through which* we perform our actions. Though many scholars of Averroes have utilized this 'operational' terminology, Hyman offers one preliminary and clarifying account:

> [T]he manner in which the agent intellect is the form of the speculative intellect [i.e. the conjunction between us and the separate intellects in intellectual acts][54] differs from that in which a corporeal form is the form of a corporeal substance. For in the latter case, form and matter are united as different aspects of *the same substance*, while in the former case the agent and speculative intellects are, in some fashion, ontologically distinct. From this it follows that ... [they are joined] through an *operational* rather than an ontological union.[55]

We can extend this insight about ontologically distinct things which can be joined in an operational, liberal hylomorphic union. After all, Aristotle's hylomorphism is a model for explaining not only the ontological nature of composite substances and their various accidents but also the actualization of cognitive powers through their particular objects—a very particular kind of change in the world that (typically) involves ontologically distinct substances. The same goes for Averroes. When I see the brown table, I do not become a brown table, nor is a new composite substance generated. And yet there is a new cognitive connection or union between

---

[52] Averroes ends *LCDA* III.36 with this criticism (502).

[53] Averroes sometimes emphasizes these kinds of causality rather than the formal; see *LCM* Λ.38, 1612-13.

[54] The speculative or theoretical intellect (*speculativa*) is Averroes' term, more accurately, for the generated and individuated acts of understanding formed through the conjunction of the MPI with our images; see, e.g., *LCDA* III.5, 406. In III.36, the AI is said to conjoin with the theoretical intelligibles, though not actually the theoretical intellect (499–500).

[55] Hyman (1981: 190), emphasis mine. Cf. Bazán (1981: 426).

the visible form and the 'matter' or seeing subject (the subject of existence). Black has noted Averroes' wide usage of conjunction (*ittiṣāl, continuatio*) language, including not only the items in the noetic case seen above (i.e. images, human individuals, the MPI, the AI, and intelligibles), but also between humans and sensible forms in cases of sensation.[56] Hence, some scholars argue that *ittiṣāl* is better translated as 'contact'.[57] Thus, operational conjunction generally applies in any case of cognitive activity, wherein we connect cognitively with some form. Hence Averroes posits another general liberal hylomorphic principle in III.36, very similar to the one we already saw above in the Liberal Hylomorphism Passage: 'For every *action* produced from the composition of two diverse things, it is necessary that one be as if matter and instrument and the other be as if form or agent'.[58]

In other words, Averroes' liberal hylomorphism with respect to the separate intellects is not *ad hoc*, but rather builds on a liberal hylomorphism he already finds in Aristotle's canonical formulation. For every Aristotelian, cognition qualifies as an extension of the strict ontological hylomorphic model used to explain substantial change, since, in cognitive acts, neither we nor our relevant powers become *substantially* and existentially constituted by the received form.[59] In both sensation and understanding (even the qualified kind Averroes proposes), we make contact with external forms which are in (or identical to) external substances, and, through this connection, we perform our properly human life activities. Clearly understanding is very different from sensation on Averroes' view, and I do not want to deny that. In understanding (as I argued above) we do not have the relevant power as an intrinsic and individuated part of our individual souls, as we do have in sensation. Nor do we (or any of our proper powers) receive the relevant intelligible forms in act, as occurs in sensation. However, because Averroes thinks there is still a looser kind of composition and conjunction with the separate intellects and intelligibles (insofar as they cooperate with our images and proper cogitative powers) he can legitimately extend the liberal hylomorphism already latent in the account of sensation to a still further, but related level. We provide the 'matter' through our lower, imaginative-cogitative power which is then perfected by a higher power or form (just like the common sense : imagination analogue mentioned in the Liberal Hylomorphism

---

[56] E.g. *LCDA* III.5, 402–3. Black (1999: 167–8). She also notes a generic usage in other works (167, n. 20).

[57] Gutas (2016: n. 7) at least makes this claim with respect to the philosophy of Avicenna.

[58] *LCDA* III.36, 497.509–12.

[59] For a similar expression of this extension, see Shields (2016: xvi–xvii). Another corollary distinction to which we have already alluded and which makes cognition a case of liberal, rather than strict hylomorphism is that neither the cognizing subject nor its cognitive power *are* sensible matter, as in strict hylomorphism. They are rather the subject or substrate of the perceived form and only in that sense its 'matter'. This is not necessarily to deny that the subject or power are material, nor to suggest a 'spiritualist' explanation. The cognizing subject itself is, in cases of sensation, a strict hylomorphic composite in its own right, and its powers are not matter but rather parts of form.

Passage). It is just that the higher power itself in this last step is modally-existentially separate from any body and, thus, also from us and our souls, which does not occur in cases of strict hylomorphism or even in the liberal hylomorphism in cases of sensation. Despite the differences, it is therefore best to think of the intellects as quasi-accidental, perfective forms (for us), just like our other powers, which are also accidental, perfective forms (albeit intrinsic to the soul).

Third and finally, however, the Liberal Hylomorphism Passage makes clear that our operational union with the MPI and AI is actually what allows us to perform our *proper* actions. Our operational conjunction with the separate intellects constitutes what is *proprius* (Arabic, *khāṣṣ*; Greek, *idios*) to us, an activity unique to our essence and tied to us by definition. If we compare this case to the liberal, cognitive hylomorphic union of sensory power with sensible or even intellect and intelligible, I suggested above that the latter are still cases where the relevant form and matter are both existentially and definitionally inseparable.[60] Though we have reiterated how the MPI and AI (form) are, in contrast, existentially immaterial and separate from human beings (matter), the composite (which Averroes refers to as the speculative intellect, as seen in the Hyman quote) cannot be defined without reference to both parts. Furthermore, at least we human beings cannot be defined or perform our distinctively human acts without reference (implicit or explicit) to the separate intellects! The separate intellects for their part certainly cannot perform their essential activities without human beings either—human images are the subject of truth, and intelligibles in act cannot be received by the MPI until abstracted by the AI from those images. That might suggest that they could not be defined without some explicit or implicit reference to human beings (though I am happy to leave that an open question for now). Either way, we certainly see here a tighter sense in which the separate intellects are our forms and in which liberal hylomorphism, even at this level, is not entirely severed from strict hylomorphism. Our very essence as rational animals is constituted by our connection to these separate intellects.[61]

	Form and matter are...	Form and matter...
Strict Hylomorphism	existentially and definitionally inseparable	compose a single ontological substance
Liberal Cognitive Hylomorphism (e.g. sense power and sensible form)	existentially and definitionally inseparable	do not compose a single ontological substance

---

[60] See n. 39.
[61] Rationality certainly implies intellect, for Averroes, even if he might well distinguish them. I briefly discuss Averroes' views on the separate intellects and the human essence in Ogden (2022: ch. 4, sect. 9). There I make some of the same points about Averroes' understanding of the MPI and AI as our forms, but I have expanded and clarified here the key features of his liberal hylomorphism, especially these last points related to essence and definition.

| Liberal Noetic Hylomorphism (i.e. human beings and separate intellects) | existentially separable definitionally inseparable | do not compose a single ontological substance |

The table above represents a rough sketch of some of the key distinctions and similarities we have drawn.

As a final example to motivate Averroes' view, think of another difficult case for hylomorphism from contemporary biology. How should we think of, say, bacteria in our intestines ('gut flora') which help us digest food? In similar fashion to Averroes' intellects, we are naturally and essentially constituted to unite with these *separate* organisms/substances in order to perform our basic human activity of digestion. They are operational and perfective forms for us. There are, of course, some disanalogies. In the case of human digestion (unlike that of understanding), it seems undeniable that we are still the primary agents, those doing the digesting. That follows because the main organs (stomach and intestines) belong to our body. The process as a whole is contributing to our life, only part of which is contributing to the life of the bacteria. Still, the parallels between the bacteria and the intellects help to illustrate liberal hylomorphism. Separate substances can act as our perfective forms and as integral parts of our most essential activities, even if we do not strictly perform *their* proper acts (e.g. the bacteria's proper metabolism and the intellect's proper understanding). And since both digestion and understanding are activities that we initiate (at least partly) through our willing, we can see how we might be said to understand *in some way*, thus mitigating Averroes' stark denial that we understand in section 3.

5. Objections

Let us briefly consider some objections. Isn't Averroes' liberal hylomorphism *too* liberal? Especially if we look at the features in the Liberal Hylomorphism Passage and consider the last example of gut flora, it might appear to validate too many instances of (liberal) forms. Should we count a hammer, for example, or your laptop—which are also separate instruments that we use to perform our willed actions—as one of our *forms* on the liberal view? This relates to the idea that perhaps Averroes' position is a proto-version of the 'Extended Mind Thesis' (EMT).[62] I think that is correct, so, for any fans of EMT, this objection may have less force. But in any case, Averroes can still make a principled distinction between the separate intellects (on the one hand) and other external instruments/tools (on

---

[62] I thank Peter Adamson and Deborah Black for suggesting this to me in correspondence. See also Ben Ahmed and Pasnau (2021: sect. 5).

the other)—in that way, perhaps Averroes' is a more plausible form of EMT. Averroes needn't accept the parity implied by the objection, precisely because of the third feature of liberal hylomorphism discussed in the last section. All human beings are naturally and essentially constituted to unite with the separate intellects in order to perform our proper actions, so the intellects are like essential accidents (again, like a typical power).[63] That is not the case for the hammer or even your laptop.[64]

Even more pressing, what about Cartesian substance dualism? I mentioned above that Averroes' account of understanding qualifies as substance trialism (MPI + AI + human beings) and, thus, might be even worse than dualism. If Averroes' noetic substance trialism is my chief exhibit for liberal hylomorphism, then, *a fortiori*, why can't substance dualism count? If it does, however, then many will rightly conclude that we have completely lost our grip on hylomorphism.

There are certainly affinities between Averroes' noetic liberal hylomorphism and dualism. Though Descartes rejects strict hylomorphism, it seems, *prima facie*, that there would be nothing to prevent him from accepting the liberal hylomorphic notion of the soul as an essential, perfecting (liberal) form of the body (although the two are distinct substances). After all, Descartes urges that 'I am not merely present in my body as a sailor is present in a ship, but ... I am very closely joined and, as it were, intermingled with it, so that I and the body form a unit'.[65] Though Averroes does not tend to speak of the three substances in his noetic trialism as a single metaphysical 'unit', he does call it the 'speculative intellect' (as mentioned above), and we have seen how 'conjunction' or 'uniting' underwrites his liberal hylomorphism. Of course, we might protest that the union of soul and body for Descartes is not a real and ontological substantial unity, but I have claimed the same about Averroes' liberal hylomorphic union between human beings and the separate intellects. In sum, Averroes and Descartes agree that the relevant intellects are separate substances which causally interact with human bodies, an interaction that might be understood along the lines of (even essential) accidental unions that we are apt to form by our very nature.[66]

---

[63] On essential or *per se* accidents, see, e.g., Aristotle, *APo.* A.7, 75a39–b3; *Meta.* B.1, 995b18–21 and Δ.30, 1025a30–4, cf. *Meta.* Z.5, 1030b14–28. From Porphyry, these also took on the name of *propria*, properties entailed by the essence.

[64] Though perhaps the hammer is an essential accident in the same way for the carpenter *qua* carpenter. Perhaps the craftsperson *qua* craftsperson is definitionally inseparable from the essential tools of their craft.

[65] Descartes, *Meditations* 6 (CSM II:56, AT VII:81). See also Clarke (2003: ch. 8).

[66] I compared the intellects to essential accidents above. Descartes even qualifies 'the nature of man as a combination of mind and body' (CSM II:61, AT VII:88). Still, his emphasis in the *Meditations* is obviously their distinction and separability, suggesting a kind of accidental unity. See Sixth Replies (CSM II:297–8, AT VII:441–2 and CSM II:299, AT VII:444–5)—'For it is a conceptual contradiction to suppose that two things which we clearly perceive as different should become one and the same (that is intrinsically one and the same, as opposed to by combination)...'

Nevertheless, there are crucial divergences. Most basically, liberal hylomorphism makes sense of Averroes' view precisely insofar as it constitutes an analogical extension of his otherwise unquestionably Aristotelian and strict hylomorphism. But Descartes, after all, rejects the ground of strict hylomorphism, severing any possible analogical relations. To call Cartesian substance dualism 'liberal hylomorphism' makes about as much sense as calling the Copernican revolution 'liberal Ptolemaism'. Not only would the title offend Descartes, it genuinely misrepresents the thrust of his new physics. On the other hand, it may be that other non-Cartesian substance dualisms *could* qualify as liberal hylomorphisms. Avicenna's substance dualism, for example, might reasonably be construed as liberal hylomorphism, since it retains strict hylomorphism as a base.[67]

More specifically, we must remember that Averroes only resorts to substance trialism in his account of acts of understanding; he maintains strict hylomorphism for his explanation of all natural substances, including human beings (more on the advantages of this outlook below, in section 6). Descartes' rejection of strict hylomorphism, however, is universal, and substance dualism constitutes his entire explanation of human nature. Consequently, we can list several related major disagreements. First, Descartes reifies the body (not just the intellect) as a substance in its own right. He thus discards the notion of matter as potentiality and the body as potentially enformed. Averroes, however, retains the strict view: matter is what it is solely due to form, and matter and form are both definitionally and existentially inseparable. Second, Descartes consigns the full range of human cognition, including sensation, to the mind/soul alone. But, for Averroes, only understanding belongs properly to the separate intellect while all other human activities (including our quasi-'intellectual' ones) are common to body and soul. Third, for Averroes, the substance that I essentially am is the strict hylomorphic composite of my body and soul. I am certainly not identical to the higher perfecting (liberal) form, i.e. the separate intellects.[68] For Descartes, by contrast, the substance that I essentially am just *is* the higher perfecting 'liberal form', i.e. the mind/soul.[69] Thus, the relation of the human substance to the perfecting liberal form is asymmetric in the two systems. For these reasons, it would be a mistake to classify Cartesian substance dualism as a type of liberal hylomorphism; the latter does not collapse into the former, and liberal hylomorphism remains genuinely hylomorphic.

---

[67] See Peter Adamson's Chapter 12 of this volume. For starters, according to Avicenna, bodies are *not* formless, and forms are not causally and explanatorily useless. Though Avicenna demurs about the aptness of calling the human rational soul 'form', he lands on identifying it as a 'perfection [*kamāl*]' (*Psychology* I.1, 6–7), which fits nicely with the liberal hylomorphic conception of perfecting (albeit separable) forms.

[68] Averroes does not use the language of identification, and he denies an instance of it in Themistius—*LCDA* III.5, 406.

[69] 'My essence consists solely in the fact that I am a thinking thing'—Descartes *Meditations* (AT VII:78, CSM II:54).

6. Conclusion

Averroes explodes some useful myths about hylomorphism and highlights one of its thorniest difficulties. The *nous*-body problem can lead committed hylomorphists into some seemingly wild territory, but Averroes' liberal hylomorphism offers at least one way to navigate and tame the terrain. It is, thus, historically important and allows us to see that Averroes' noetic hylomorphism enjoys greater plausibility. It expands our conception of the varieties of hylomorphism and points up the need to distinguish hylomorphism from nearby competing views.

Historically, Averroes and his 'form for us' conception is a crucial connective piece between Aristotle and later western developments. Though Averroes' own path was distinct, it inaugurated further, highly interesting forms of Latin Averroism. Moreover, by building on the liberal hylomorphism already found in Aristotle (as I argued in section 4) and, importantly, in the loose Arabic adaptation of the *Parva Naturalia* (*Kitāb al-Ḥiss wa-l-Maḥsūs*), Averroes largely drives a tradition that explains (lower kinds of) cognitive hylomorphism in terms of receiving a form in 'spiritual' or 'intentional' being (rather than ontologically as a substantial or accidental form in real being).[70] Obvious examples of this influence appear from Aquinas down to the 'spiritualist'-'literalist' debates among Aristotelian commentators today.[71]

Finally, and more specifically, I will close by arguing that Averroes presents a unique view of intellect that neatly preserves two crucial hylomorphic desiderata. Think of Averroes as giving us the best of both worlds: on the one hand, a clean, unified, broadly naturalist account of the human being as such; on the other, the god-like element of/within us as fully and properly transcendent. As Aristotle puts it in *Nicomachean Ethics* X.7, the life characterized by the 'activity of *nous*' (1177b19) would be

> too great for a human being. For it is not in so far as he is human that he will live so, but in so far as something divine is present in him; and by so much as this is superior to our composite nature [*sunthetou*] is its activity superior to that of the other kind of virtue. If *nous* is divine, then, in comparison with the human being, so also is the life according to it divine in comparison with human life.[72]

---

[70] E.g. Averroes, *SCM*, 61. See Hansberger (2019) and, on the *Kitāb al-Ḥiss wa-l-Maḥsūs* more generally, Hansberger (2010). Avicenna, by contrast, disavows this 'spiritual', cognitive hylomorphic account. See Black (2011: 159).

[71] For an overview of the debate and some of the literature, see Caston (2005). I am not suggesting Averroes (or Aquinas) was a spiritualist in the contemporary sense; only that many of the terms of this debate spring from the Arabic tradition and Averroes in particular, not to mention the inborn liberal hylomorphism within Aristotle's own system.

[72] EN X.7, 1177b26–31, Ross translation modified. See Averroes, *Middle Commentary on Ethica Nicomachea (MCEN)* 154c: '[T]he existence of any human, insofar as he is human, is through this substance which is called intellect since it is the more noble and better thing which is in him'.

Arguably, Averroes was attractive to some medieval and Renaissance philosophers for precisely this balance. While he has to develop an admittedly somewhat strange account of intellect and acts of understanding, the payoff is a far more straightforward account of human beings. We, like every other sublunar substance, are generable and corruptible, strict hylomorphic composites of matter and form. We are essentially enmattered. We have special capabilities and, indeed, a special role to play in the cosmos, since the intellects are dependent on us for abstracting and receiving intelligible forms from images.[73] But human beings as substances do not disrupt the material order of the natural world around us.

Yet neither is the view deflationary or wholly materialist. Averroes takes intellect and its existential immateriality quite seriously, but he elevates the transcendence to where it plausibly belongs in the Aristotelian system—with every other eternal, immaterial, and intellectual being, the realm of separate substances/forms.[74] Nonetheless, we have seen precisely how the separate intellects are 'in the soul' and are our operational, perfective forms, connected directly to our essence. Averroes can explain how these distinct natural and transcendent levels meet in us through his liberal hylomorphism.[75]

Bibliography

Alexander of Aphrodisias (1887), *De Anima Liber cum Mantissa*, ed. Ivo Bruns (G. Reimer), CAG Suppl. II.1.

Aquinas, Thomas (1984), **In De An.** *Sententia Libri De Anima*. In *Opera Omnia* 45, ed. R.A. Gauthier (Commissio Leonina).

Aristotle (1894), *EN. Ethica Nicomachea*, ed. I. Bywater (Oxford University Press; English trans., David Ross; rev. Lesley Brown, *The Nicomachean Ethics*, Oxford University Press, 2009).

Aristotle (1954), *De An.*, **Arabic**. *Arisṭūṭālīs Fī-l-nafs*, ed. Abdurrahman Badawi (Imprimerie Misr S.A.E.; reprint. Kuwait and Beirut: Dār al-Qalam, 1980).

Aristotle (1958), **Meta**. *Aristotle's Metaphysics*, ed. W.D. Ross, 2 vols (Oxford University Press).

---

[73] *LCDA* III.5, 406.569–408.629; Taylor (2009a: 322–5).

[74] However, by conceiving the MPI and AI as the lowest of separate intellects, distinct from and inferior to the prime mover, Averroes avoids one of the chief difficulties of Alexandrian interpretations—viz., that Aristotle, at least in his most explicit discussion of God in *Meta.* Λ, does not seem to envisage the prime mover as immanent within human beings at all. See, e.g., Ross (1995: 153).

[75] I would like to thank especially David Charles and Peter Adamson for many detailed comments and fruitful ideas on this chapter. Thanks also to many other helpful questions and comments from audiences at the Yale History of Hylomorphism workshop, the University of Chicago, and the University of Notre Dame, and particularly Therese Cory and David Cory.

Aristotle (1961), *De An. De Anima*, ed. David Ross (Oxford University Press; English trans. in Shields 2016).

Aristotle (1964), *APo. Posterior Analytics*. In *Analytica Priora et Posteriora*, ed. W.D. Ross (Oxford University Press).

Aristotle (1965), *De Generatione Animalium*, ed. H.J. Drossaart Lulofs (Oxford University Press).

Averroes (1564), MCEN. *Middle Commentary on Ethica Nicomachea*. In *Aristotelis Opera cum Averrois Commentariis*, Vol. 3 (Apud Iunctas; reprint. Frankfurt: Minerva, 1962).

Averroes (1919), *SCM. Short Commentary on Metaphysics*. In *Averroes. Compendio de Metafísica*, ed. Carlos Q. Rodríguez (Imprenta de Estanislao Maestre).

Averroes (1938–52), *LCM. Long Commentary on Metaphysics* = *Tafsīr mā baʿd aṭ-Ṭabīʿat*, ed. Maurice Bouyges, 4 vols. (Imprimerie Catholique).

Averroes (1950), *SCDA. Short Commentary on De Anima* = *Talkhīṣ* [sic] *Kitāb al-nafs*, ed. Ahmed Fouad El-Ahwani (Imprimerie Misr).

Averroes (Ibn Rushd) (1953), **LCDA**. *Long Commentary on De Anima* = *Averrois Cordubensis Commentarium Magnum in Aristotelis De Anima Libros*, ed. F. Stuart Crawford (Mediaeval Academy of America; English trans. in Taylor 2009a).

Averroes (1985), **LCDA Arabic Fragments**. In Abdelkader Ben Chehida, 'Iktishāf al-naṣṣ al-ʿarabī li-ahamm ajzāʾ al-sharh al-kabīr li-*Kitāb al-Nafs* taʾlīf Abī l-Walīd ibn Rushd'. *Al-Ḥayāt al-Thaqāfiyya* 35: 14–48.

Averroes (1987), *TT. Tahafot at-Tahafot (L'Incohérence de l'incohérence)*, ed. Maurice Bouyges. 2nd edn (Dar el-Mashreq).

Averroes (2002), *MCDA. Middle Commentary on Aristotle's De Anima: A Critical Edition of the Arabic Text with English Translation, Notes and Introduction*, ed. and trans. Alfred Ivry (Brigham Young University Press).

Avicenna (Ibn Sīnā) (1959), *Psychology. Avicenna's De Anima: Being the Psychological Part of Kitāb al-Shifāʾ*, ed. F. Rahman (Oxford University Press).

Bazán, Bernardo (1981), '*Intellectum Speculativum*: Averroes, Thomas Aquinas, and Siger of Brabant on the Intelligible Object', *Journal of the History of Philosophy* 19: 425–46.

Ben Ahmed, Fouad and Robert Pasnau (2021), 'Ibn Rushd [Averroes]', in Edward Zalta (ed.), *The Stanford Encyclopedia of Philosophy*, fall edn). https://plato.stanford.edu/archives/fall2021/entries/ibn-rushd/

Black, Deborah (1993), 'Consciousness and Self-Knowledge in Aquinas's Critique of Averroes's Psychology', *Journal of the History of Philosophy* 31: 349–85.

Black, Deborah (1999), 'Conjunction and the Identity of Knower and Known in Averroes', *American Catholic Philosophical Quarterly* 73: 159–84.

Black, Deborah (2011), 'Averroes on the Spirituality and Intentionality of Sensation', in Peter Adamson (ed.), *In the Age of Averroes: Arabic Philosophy in the Sixth/Twelfth Century* (The Warburg Institute), 159–74.

Brenet, Jean-Baptiste (2003), *Transferts du sujet* (J. Vrin).

Brenet, Jean-Baptiste (2019), 'Averroism and the Metaphysics of Intellect', in Stephan Schmid (ed.), *Philosophy of Mind in the Late Middle Ages and Renaissance: The History of the Philosophy of Mind*, Vol. 3 (Routledge), 83–100.

Caston, Victor (1999), 'Aristotle's Two Intellects: A Modest Proposal', *Phronesis* 44: 199–227.

Caston, Victor (2000), 'Aristotle's Argument for Why the Understanding is not Compounded with the Body', *Proceedings of the Boston Area Colloquium in Ancient Philosophy* 16: 135–75.

Caston, Victor (2005), 'The Spirit and the Letter: Aristotle on Perception', in Ricardo Salles (ed.), *Metaphysics, Soul, and Ethics in Ancient Thought: Themes from the Work of Richard Sorabji* (Oxford University Press), 245–320.

Caston, Victor (2009), 'Commentary on Charles', *Proceedings of the Boston Area Colloquium in Ancient Philosophy* 24: 30–47.

Charles, David (2009), 'Aristotle's Psychological Theory', *Proceedings of the Boston Area Colloquium in Ancient Philosophy* 24: 1–29.

Charles, David (2021), *The Undivided Self: Aristotle and the 'Mind-Body Problem'* (Oxford University Press).

Clarke, Desmond (2003), *Descartes's Theory of Mind* (Oxford University Press).

Cohoe, Caleb (2013), 'Why the Intellect Cannot Have a Bodily Organ: *De Anima* 3.4', *Phronesis* 58: 347–77.

Cohoe, Caleb (2022), 'The Separability of *Nous*', in Caleb Cohoe (ed.), *Aristotle's On the Soul: A Critical Guide* (Cambridge University Press), 229–46.

Corkum, Phil (2016), 'Ontological Dependence and Grounding in Aristotle', *Oxford Handbooks Online in Philosophy*. DOI: 10.1093/oxfordhb/9780199935314.013.31

Cottingham, John (1985), 'Cartesian Trialism', *Mind* 94: 218–30.

Descartes, René (1984), **CSM**. *The Philosophical Writings of Descartes*, ed. John Cottingham, Robert Stoothoff, and Dugald Murdoch. 2 vols. (Cambridge University Press).

Di Giovanni, Matteo (2007), 'Individuation by Matter in Averroes' "Metaphysics"', *Documenti e studi sulla tradizione filosofica medievale* 18: 187–210.

Di Giovanni, Matteo (2011), 'Substantial Form in Averroes's Long Commentary on the Metaphysics', in Peter Adamson (ed.), *In the Age of Averroes: Arabic Philosophy in the Sixth/Twelfth Century* (The Warburg Institute), 175–94.

Fine, Gail (1984), 'Separation', *Oxford Studies in Ancient Philosophy* 2: 31–86.

Geoffory, Marc (2007), 'Averroès sur l'intellect comme cause agente et cause formelle, et la question de la "jonction", in Jean-Baptiste Brenet (ed.), *Averroès et les averroïsmes juif et latin. Actes du colloque tenu à Paris, 16–18 juin 2005* (Brepols), 77–110.

Gutas, Dimitri (2016), 'Ibn Sina [Avicenna]', in Edward Zalta (ed.), *The Stanford Encyclopedia of Philosophy*, fall edn. https://plato.stanford.edu/archives/fall2016/entries/ibn-sina/

Hansberger, Rotraud (2010), '*Kitāb al-Ḥiss wa-l-maḥsūs*: Aristotle's *Parva naturalia* in Arabic Guise', in Christophe Grellard and Pierre-Marie Morel (eds.), *Les Parva naturalia d'Aristote. Fortune antique et médiévale* (Éditions de la Sorbonne), 143–62.

Hansberger, Rotraud (2019), 'Averroes and the "Internal Senses"', in Peter Adamson and Matteo Di Giovanni (eds.), *Interpreting Averroes* (Cambridge University Press), 138–57.

Harvey, Steven (1992), 'Did Maimonides' Letter to Samuel ibn Tibbon Determine Which Philosophers Would Be Studied by Later Jewish Thinkers?', *Jewish Quarterly Review* 83: 51–70.

Hyman, Arthur (1981), 'Averroes as Commentator on Aristotle's Theory of the Intellect', in Dominic O'Meara (ed.), *Studies in Aristotle* (Catholic University of America Press), 161–92.

Jaworski, William (2016), *Structure and the Metaphysics of Mind* (Oxford University Press).

Kahn, Charles (1992), 'Aristotle on Thinking', in Martha Nussbaum and Amélie Oksenberg Rorty (eds.), *Essays on Aristotle's De Anima* (Oxford University Press), 359–79.

Meister, Samuel (2020), 'Aristotle on the Purity of Forms in *Metaphysics* Z.10–11', in *Ergo* 7. https://doi.org/10.3998/ergo.12405314.0007.001

Miller Jr, Fred (2012), 'Aristotle on the Separability of Mind', in Christopher Shields (ed.), *The Oxford Handbook of Aristotle* (Oxford University Press), 306–39.

Modrak, Deborah (1991), 'The *Nous*-Body Problem in Aristotle', *Review of Metaphysics* 44: 755–74.

Ogden, Stephen (2016), 'On a Possible Argument for Averroes's Single Separate Intellect', *Oxford Studies in Medieval Philosophy* 4: 27–63.

Ogden, Stephen (2021), 'Averroes's Unity Argument against Multiple Intellects', *Archiv für Geschichte der Philosophie* 103: 429–54.

Ogden, Stephen (2022), *Averroes on Intellect: From Aristotelian Origins to Aquinas's Critique* (Oxford University Press).

Peramatzis, Michail (2011), *Priority in Aristotle's Metaphysics* (Oxford University Press).

Robinson, Howard (1983), 'Aristotelian Dualism', *Oxford Studies in Ancient Philosophy* 1: 123–44.

Ross, David (1995), *Aristotle*, 6th edn. [??] (Routledge).

Shields, Christopher (1995), 'Intentionality and Isomorphism in Aristotle', *Proceedings of the Boston Area Colloquium in Ancient Philosophy* 11: 307–30.

Shields, Christopher (2016), *Aristotle: De Anima* (Oxford University Press).

Sisko, John (2000), 'Aristotle's *ΝΟΥΣ* and the Modern Mind', *Proceedings of the Boston Area Colloquium in Ancient Philosophy* 16: 177–98.

Taylor, Richard (2005), 'The Agent Intellect as "Form for Us" and Averroes's Critique of al-Fārābī', *Tópicos* 29: 29–51.

Taylor, Richard (2009a), *Averroes: Long Commentary on the De Anima of Aristotle* (Yale University Press).

Taylor, Richard (2009b), 'Intellect as Intrinsic Formal Cause in the Soul According to Aquinas and Averroes', in Maha Elkaisy-Friemuth and John Dillon (eds.), *The Afterlife of the Platonic Soul: Reflections of Platonic Psychology in the Monotheistic Religions* (Brill), 187–220.

Themistius (1899), ***De An. Paraph.*** *De Anima Paraphrasis*, ed. R. Heinze (G. Reimeri), CAG V.3 (English trans., Robert Todd, *On Aristotle's On the Soul*, Cornell University Press, 1996).

Themistius (1973), ***De An. Paraph.*** **Arabic**. *An Arabic Translation of Themistius' Commentary on Aristotle's De Anima*, ed. M.C. Lyons (B. Cassirer).

14
Hoc Aliquid
Aquinas' Soul Is This Something

Christopher Shields

1. A Problem in Hylomorphism

Canonical hylomorphism teaches that the relation of soul to body is a special case of the more general relation of form to matter: the soul is the form of the body, which in turn is the matter of the soul. As matter and form combine to yield a compound substance, so soul and body come together to make up a special kind of compound substance, namely an animate substance, a living being. Living beings comprise not only humans, but other kinds of beings as well: human beings—rational animals in Aquinas' view—are ensouled, but so too are plants and non-rational animals, dogs and donkeys and the rest. Hylomorphism thus provides a broad explanatory framework for investigating the phenomena of life, including but not limited to human life. Initially, the application of Aristotle's hylomorphic framework to the domain of the living seems a natural, even attractive fit. As a metaphysical framework for explaining change, unity, and categorial fundamentality, hylomorphism seems tailor-made for explaining living beings and their activities.

Already, though, even in its easy, attractive first deployment, hylomorphism suffers a problem lurking in its most basic formulation. For it is natural to understand a form as a universal, individuated by the matter whose form it is. There is, for instance, the form *being a penny*, shared by all and only pennies; what makes a penny *this* penny is a form's being realized in this quantity of copper and what makes another penny *that* penny is the same form's being realized in a different quantity of copper. The form, unlike any quantity of copper, appears wholly present in two places at once and so counts as a universal. It is shared, or, in the parlance of Scholastic philosophy, *communicable* across more than one individual.

So far, so good. Yet the lurking problem comes into view as soon as we reflect on the fact that, at least where humans are concerned, it is equally natural to think of souls as particulars, indeed as particulars which are qualitatively distinct from one another. Already in Plato, Socrates talks easily about the care of one's soul as required for success in the afterlife, insisting over and over again that the wicked souls shall go one way and the virtuous another, each obtaining its individual due (*Phaedo* 107c1–d5; *Rep.* x 614b2–621d3). He goes further, in fact, evidently contending that he *is* his soul, such that when he is released from the prison of his body, he will carry forwards unencumbered by the dragging demands of his flesh (*Phaedo* 115c2–116a1). Aristotle's hylomorphism parts company with Plato's soul-body dualism, of course, but he does not retreat from the thought that the soul of each human being is an individual sort of thing. He calls the soul *this something* or *some this* (τόδε τι; *De An.* ii 1, 412a7–8; cf. *Meta.* Z 11, 1037a7; *GA* iv 2–3, 767a20–768b1), where the immediate implication seems to be that the soul for Aristotle, just as for Plato, is a particular. If it is a form, though, and forms are universals, then the soul is both a universal and a particular. Thus, the problem emerges.

This same problem emerges in an especially urgent way in the philosophy of the 13th-century hylomorphist Thomas Aquinas. At one basic level, the problem arises in Aquinas for the same general reason that it arises in Aristotle and every other hylomorphist: souls seem, as souls, to be particulars, but souls also seem, as forms, to be universals.[1] The problem is especially urgent in Aquinas, however, because of a theological overlay present in his system but absent in Aristotle's: Aquinas accepts as a Catholic dogma a thesis redolent of Platonic dualism, that the soul can subsist without the body whose soul it is, at least, it seems, in the period after death but before the resurrection.[2] Aquinas thus accepts the hylomorphism of Aristotle alongside a broadly Platonic commitment to the qualitative particularity of the individual soul: if a disembodied soul bears your personal identity, and your identity is distinct from your neighbour's personal identity, then your disembodied soul is a particular and is qualitatively distinct from your neighbour's disembodied soul, which is equally a particular and, of course, qualitatively distinct from your soul. Both souls are, though, forms. So, for Aquinas, as for Aristotle, if now with a new kind of urgency, the soul is both a form and a particular.

---

[1] There is a peremptory response to this problem where Aquinas is concerned, but it should be set aside as a non-starter. This is that Aquinas is, after all, a nominalist, and so does not think that forms (or anything else) are universals; for there are no universals (*In Sent.* I 19.5.1, II 17.1.1). The contention is rendered a bit unstable, however, by Aquinas' complicated attitudes towards universals. More to the point, there remains a clear sense in which he contrasts what he calls *universalia* with particulars, so that this sort of response is at best a sort of postponement strategy, since the way in which Aquinas thinks this contrast obtains sets a framework for recasting the question here engaged. For if he really is a nominalist in any appreciable sense of the term, he nonetheless recognizes a distinction between things understood universally and things understood as particulars. See Brower (2016) for a full discussion of Aquinas' attitude towards universals.

[2] Kretzmann reasonably treats this as a kind of danger to the consistency of Aquinas' hylomorphism (1993: 135): 'The subsistence thesis, however, especially as employed in support of immortality, threatens to leave the human being *identified* with the human soul, looking like an incorporeal, subsistent entity that is temporarily and rather casually associated with a body—looking like Plato's rather than Aristotle's human being.'

Much to his credit, Aquinas addresses this problem head on. In fact, the very first question of his *Quaestiones de Anima* (*QdA*) poses it directly. He wants to know, first and foremost, whether the soul can be both a form and *this something* (*utrum anima humana possit esse forma et hoc aliquid*; *QdA* 1). This is an issue Aquinas really must address and sort successfully if the remainder of his questions about the soul are to be worth pursuing. Thus, while it is a problem he shares in common with Aristotle, his version poses challenges made pressing by commitments altogether absent from Aristotle's immediate framework. Still, again, the general problem is a problem for all hylomorphists, whether theistic or pagan: if the soul is a form and the soul is a particular, then there are particular forms in addition to being universal forms.[3] What is a soul, though, such that it is both a form and a particular?

Given his particular exigencies, Aquinas rightly turns to this problem and makes some noteworthy progress in addressing it. This is not to say that he lays the problem to rest altogether. Still, he does provide a useful set of distinctions tailored to address a problem common to all proponents of hylomorphism. To this extent, at least, his discussion marks a signficant advance in the ongoing dialectic about souls understood hylomorphically.

2. Aquinas' Question: A Linguistic Preamble

In setting the first question of his *QdA*, Aquinas poses a question which captures his attention throughout his philosophical career,[4] even to his last period, during which he composed his commentaries on Aristotle.[5] His question is direct and his concern seems plain: 'First it is asked whether the human soul can be a form and this something' (*et primo quaeritur utrum anima humana possit esse forma et hoc aliquid*; *QdA* 1, 1). Or perhaps his concern is not so plain, depending upon how

---

[3] This suggests a second sort of peremptory response to the question we are pursuing: perhaps Aquinas is simply a pluralist of a sort, one who thinks that there are both particular and universals forms—souls are particular forms and species forms, like the form of human beings, are universal forms. In a way, this is in fact Aquinas' final position, but he thinks, rightly in my view, that he needs to come to terms with the thought that there are both particular and universal forms; for forms seem to be communicable, and so universal; but if they are universal, forms are not particular. Yet the soul is both a form and a particular—which is to say, then, that we are back where we began. At any rate, Aquinas thinks that a simple assertion of pluralism does not suffice, in that it mainly postpones the question. This is why, as we shall see in the next section, Aquinas thinks he needs to address this question head on, as he does in the first of his *Quaestiones de Anima*.

[4] *ST* I q.75, a.2, q.76, a.1; *SCG* II 56–9, 69–70; *De Pot.* q.3, a.9, a.11; *De Spir. Creat.* a.2; *Comm. in De An.* bk. II, lect. 4; bk. III, lect. 7.

[5] The exact date of *Quaestiones de Anima* is unknown. Since it would have been debated in a public forum, this work, like other disputed questions, would not have been put into a determinate written form until sometime after the occasion of its public disputation. Further, given that we often find several versions of disputed questions successively refined and revised (see Stegmüller 1947 on one such case), perhaps there is no one definitive date to be offered. Still, it is reasonable to suppose, as does Robb (1984: 2–7), following Glorieux (1932), that the public disputation took place in Paris, perhaps in the first half of 1269. So, its composition was no earlier than that and presumably not too very much later.

the phrase *hoc aliquid* (here 'this something') is understood. Kretzmann, for instance, frames the question in still sharper terms, translating: 'Can the human soul be both a form and a real particular [*hoc aliquid*]?'[6] Robb, by contrast, gives the question a different complexion altogether, offering as the issue to be assayed: 'Whether a human soul can be both a form and an entity.' It might be that this is house style, and, if so, then I won't make a fuss—beyond mentioning that as a boy I was taught p[unctuation] before q[uotation].[7] So far we have emphasized a worry about the particularity of form; but the translations of Kretzmann and Robb point at a different, if related problem, namely, how is it that the soul can be both an entity in its own right and also a form, which seems precisely not to be an entity in its own right: a form is always a form *of* something.

So, before delving into the motivation for Aquinas' response, a word on the phrase *hoc aliquid* is apposite. Rendered neutrally as 'this something' or 'some this', the phrase seems to capture the problem sketched initially exactly: the demonstrative 'this' (*hoc*) seems to indicate particularity, which is precisely the feature of souls seemingly at variance with their being forms, which, again, according to a traditional understanding, are universals. Some forms are essential, like the form *human being*, and are shared, or communicated across all and only human beings, serving to place their bearers into substantial kinds; other forms are accidental, for instance *being white*, which seems to be predicated indifferently across substantial kinds, and indeed across entities which are not substances at all: humans, snow swirls, champagne froth, and shards of shattered porcelain vases. Whatever is *this*, scil. this particular, is not such, *quale*, this quality or universal.

There is, though, a second contrast, the one implied by the renderings of Kretzmann and Robb. The problem put in these terms is not so stark, however, and so requires a bit more motivation. Even so, it is a problem all the same. If we take *hoc aliquid* to mean 'entity' as does Robb, and we think, in this context, that entities are, as he suggests,[8] things capable of subsisting in themselves (*per se*), then we will run into another worry, distinct from our first, as long as we think that forms are precisely not entities capable of subsisting by themselves. If on the basis of a general hylomorphism we begin by identifying forms with shapes, then

---

[6] Kretzmann (1993: 134). Notice that given this emphasis, it is natural for Kretzmann to identify a distinct if compatible concern: 'Aquinas must offer a more precise account of the soul as a form. He takes up this challenge repeatedly, sometimes explicitly addressing the issue of the compatibility of the two claims that (1) the soul is a subsistent entity and that (2) the soul is a form' (altering Kretzmann's labelling of the claims for clarity).

[7] Robb (1984: 42). He expands slightly in a note (1984: 51 n. 1): 'The Latin term *hoc aliquid*... is translated here as "entity" and denotes a particular thing which subsists of itself [*per se*]'. Robb does not explicate in this connection what it means for a particular thing to subsist *per se*, but we may note first that he is thinking of such entities as particulars and then second *per se* subsistence involves at a minimum a kind of independence, whether definitional or existential. We cannot say with any confidence which of these alternatives Robb has in mind, and so cannot say precisely how he understands Aquinas' question. Even so, in the present context, we should appreciate that different understandings of Aquinas' *hoc aliquid* yield different understandings of the question he poses himself.

[8] Robb (1984: 51 n. 1), as quoted in n. 7 above.

forms would be no more subsisting than shapes are subsisting: a shape is a shape *of* some quantity of matter, and not something capable of floating free of the matter whose shape it is. (Where would the form of a house go when the house is razed?) Indeed, even as the notion of form becomes more sophisticated and metaphysically loaded, the notion of dependence seems to carry forward with it. This is, after all, presumably why Aristotle began his own account of the soul in hylomorphic terms by declaring roundly that it is clear 'that the soul is not separable from the body' (*De An.* ii 1, 413a45–5). So, depending on how we understand *hoc aliquid*, we have two contrasts from which to choose, and so also two distinct but related problems to address: (i) universal vs particular, where the problem is that nothing is both a universal and a particular, though souls seem to be both; and (ii) subsistent entity vs form, where the problem, presuming, as is presumed here, that form is dependent rather than independent, is that souls are both dependent and self-subsisting.

We may hope for some guidance about which problem, if either, is to be foregrounded here, by noting that Aquinas' terminology, like his general problem, goes back to Aristotle, courtesy of the scrupulous translations of Aristotle by William of Moerbeke. These translations appeared in the Latin west during Aquinas' productive lifetime, and it is upon these he relies in his most mature work. The Latin phrase *hoc aliquid* is Moerbeke's rendering of Aristotle's *tode ti*,[9] a phrase which on the face of it simply seems to mean 'this something' or 'some this', that is, some particular. This impression seems initially verified by Aristotle's tendency to contrast something's being a *tode ti* with universality, or, more directly, with being a 'such' (*toionde*) or a quality (*poion*). The contrast is reinforced in the many passages where Aristotle treats suches as predicables, as species or genera, or as items predicated in non-substantial categories (*Cat.* 3b10; *APo.* 71a20, 73b7; *Soph. El.* 178b36, 179a8–10; *Phys.* 191a12; *De Caelo* 278a12; *Gen. et Corr.* 317b7–12, 21–2, 26–8, 31–3; *De An.* 402a27, 410a 14, 416b 13; *Meta.* 1003a9, 1033b9ff., 1034a6, 1038b23, 34, 1039a32, 5). Still, though widely supported, the case for restricting being a *tode ti* to particularity is not sealed, because Aristotle also at times seems willing to refer to entities he regards as universals with this same term (so, e.g., evidently, justice (*dikaiosunê*) at *Soph. El.* 166a23–4). Moreover, his tendency when contrasting universals with particulars is to use slightly different terminology. His preferred locution for being particular in contrast to being common or universal is

---

[9] See, for example, the opening of *Meta.* Z 1, 1028a10–13: Aristotle: 'To on legetai pollachôs kathaper dielometha proteron en tois peri tou posachôs·sêmainei gar to men ti esti kai **tode ti**... Moerbeke: Ens dicitur multipliciter, sicut diximus in his quae de quoties. Significat enim hoc quid est, et **hoc aliquid**...' For another example, from *APo.* i 4, 73b5–8: Aristotle: 'eti ho mê kath' hupokeimenou legetai allou tinos, hoin to badizon heteron ti on badizon esti kai to leucon <leukon>, hê d' ousia, kai hosa **tode ti** sêmainei...'; Moerbeke: 'Amplius quod non de subiecto dicitur alio quodam, ut ambulans, cum alterum quoddam sit ambulans, et album, substantia autem et quaecumque **hoc aliquid** significant...' Moerbeke has not offered translations of all the works containing the eighty-eight instances of τόδε τι in Aristotle, but his practice is consistent across those works he has translated.

not *tode ti* but rather *kath' hekasta*—'taken individually' or 'taken as individuals', a phrase often rendered simply as 'individuals'. This in turn leads some scholars to regard something's being *tode ti* as indicating not its being particular so much as its being *completely determinate*; if this is right, a *tode ti* might not be restricted to being particular in the sense of being non-repeatable, or, again in the medieval locution, to its being incommunicable.[10]

So, if we are relying simply on Moerbeke as a faithful renderer of Aristotle, we cannot assume directly that *hoc aliquid* simply means or otherwise implies particularity. That would have the welcome consequence of dissolving the question of translation, at least as a linguistic matter. Still, the metaphysical problem would remain, and then too there would be an unavoidable question concerning what Aquinas means to be asking whether the human soul can be both a form and *hoc aliquid*. For, after all, there seems to be no immediate puzzle as to whether a soul can be both a form and completely determinate. There is, for instance, no reason we should suppose a universal or a relative should not equally be completely determinate, if that is understood to mean merely that something admits of a precise or non-vague definition.[11]

When we turn to Aquinas' arguments in *Quaestiones de Anima* for guidance, we seem to find support for both translations and so for both problems. Aquinas initially seems to side directly with the problem of particularity. He states directly that being *hoc aliquid* is sufficient for being an individual. In fact, he makes two closely related but distinct points in this direction, marked with a slight difference in diction. First, in the first premise of his second argument on behalf of a negative answer to the question of whether the soul can be both *hoc aliquid* and a form, he states: 'If the soul is *hoc aliquid*, it is necessary that it be something individuated.

---

[10] Some useful discussions of this issue in Aristotle include: Kung (1981), who engages the philosophical issues pertinent to the phrase in great depth; Smith (1921), who helpfully reviews the philological issues, concluding that *tode ti* means 'anything which is both a this and a somewhat', though infers haphazardly on this basis that every *tode ti* is also a primary substance (*prôtê ousia*) (though he observes, correctly, that 'The conventional equivalents of the term current [*tode ti*] in translations were *hoc aliquid, dies etwas*, [and] *this somewhat* are mere 'transverbations'); Sharples (1999), who traces the phrase from Aristotle to Alexander and then back again to Aristotle and renders it 'this-something'; Preiswerk (1939) prefers, unadvisedly against Bonitz' '*bestimmtes Etwas*' the phrase 'das und das'. Kung (1981: 239 n. 6) rightly observes that 'Aristotle is not altogether consistent in his terminology'. It is not clear, however, that he is inconsistent in just the way she suggests. It should in any event be borne in mind that Aristotle is perfectly willing to call the form *tode ti*, on which, see Cherniss (1962: 351–2 n. 26) and Shields (1999).

[11] It is worth emphasizing where *hoc aliquid* is concerned that the two approaches to being *tode ti* deployed in the text need not be regarded as in competition with one another. In fact, in a way, one can see both particularity and determinateness in play in Aristotle's suggestion in *Meta*. Z 3 that being separate (*chôriston*) and being *tode ti* belong chiefly to substance: 'For being separate and *tode ti* seem to belong most of all to substance (*ousia*); this is why form and the compound would seem to be substance rather than matter' (*Meta*. Z 3, 1029a27–30). Here being separate and being *tode ti* tell in favour of the particularity of substance, and they equally promote the form and compound over matter, which is set aside elsewhere as introducing indeterminacy (*aoriston*) (*Meta*. Z 1037a27).

For no universal is *hoc aliquid* (*QdA* 1.2).[12] Here Aquinas seems to state directly, if only in the context of posing an objection, that no universal is *hoc aliquid*. This draws the contrast more sharply than Aristotle had ever done, even if he clearly tended in the same direction. That this contention crops up in an objection does not dampen its force; in the response to this objection (*QdA* 1 *ad* 2) Aquinas in no way qualifies this assertion.

Note, however, that in this premise, the first claim is not that the soul must be *individual* (*individuum*), but rather that it be individuated (*individuatum*). So, although we get the claim that no universal is *hoc aliquid*, which implies that nothing which is *hoc aliquid* is universal and so also—on the assumption that the universal-particular distinction is exclusive and exhaustive—that everything which is *hoc aliquid* is particular, we still do not get the direct assertion that the soul is an individual. That statement comes forward in the next objection, again as the first premise: 'If the soul is *hoc aliquid*, it follows that it is a certain individual [*individuum*]'.[13] Here again, Aquinas' response does not reject as false the claim that being *hoc aliquid* is sufficient for being an individual. Still, it does colour his commitment in a certain way, in effect calling attention to the circumspection implied in the suggestion that everything *hoc aliquid* is a 'certain' (*quoddam*) individual, perhaps to be rendered as 'an individual of a certain sort' where this might be taken to mean even 'as some kind of individual'. The question then arises as to how far, for instance, the phrase 'an individual of a certain sort' might be taken to extend.[14] Indeed, as we shall see in the next sections, that is part of Aquinas' resolution to the problem he poses.

For now, however, on the basis of these texts we can state Aquinas' worry, in Moerbeke's terms, which closely echo Aristotle's diction, as just this: can the human soul be at once *hoc aliquid*—something particular—and a form? That said, we should not take this formulation of the problem as precluding altogether the second formulation suggested by the renderings of Kretzmann and Robb. For the question of whether the soul can be both a particular and a form might yet be sharpened, by asking whether the soul can be both a particular *of a certain sort* and a form. Here it bears extending a point Geach was fond of making,[15] namely that nothing just exists, but that everything that exists does so as something or other. Same again, then, for particularity: nothing is just a

---

[12] 'Si anima est hoc aliquid, oportet quod sit aliquid individuatum. Nullum enim universalium est hoc aliquid' (*QdA* 1.2).

[13] 'Si anima est hoc aliquid, sequitur quod sit individuum quoddam' (*QdA* 1.2).

[14] Shields (2008) develops a distinction between thin and robust particulars, such that everything which is one is a thin particular, including, then, universals, while robust particulars are particulars which are not logically repeatable, with the result that no universal is a particular. In the current discussion, particularity is understood robustly. Note, however, that something might yet be a completely determinate robust particular and yet be a relative—for instance, an individual slave.

[15] See, e.g., Geach (1954 and 1968).

particular, but every particular is a particular something or other. So, one might wish to know: if the soul can be a particular, what sort of particular can it be? Posing the question that way comes close to reintroducing the question of whether the soul can be a form and yet self-subsisting. It does not, however, take us quite all the way. For after all something might be a particular, and so not a universal, but not yet self-subsisting. Such would be, to take just one sort of example, an individual accident in the category of quality, like Abelard's pallor. Still, we should remain alive to both questions, without prejudging the issue as being a mere matter of translation: (i) can the human soul be both a form and a particular (*scil.* as opposed to being a universal); and (ii) can the human soul be both a form and a self-subsisting particular (*scil.* as one sort in particular as opposed to another)?

We learn more about Aquinas' concern when we reflect upon the sorts of arguments, pro and con, he deems relevant to the adjudication of his question. That question, put neutrally rather than peremptorily, again, is simply: can the human soul be a form and *hoc aliquid*?

3. Four Reasons to Suppose Not

Quaestiones de Anima comprises fully eighteen objections, which is to say eighteen reasons for offering a negative answer to this question, together with a response to each stating Aquinas' positive answer to it, followed in turn by eighteen brief rejoinders to the objections initially advanced. Each of these arguments merits consideration, but four above all seem to move us to the core of the question. We find in two of them that Aquinas has a special interest in the sense in which the soul, as *hoc aliquid*, might fail to be a substance while yet subsisting as a kind of privileged non-substantial particular.

The four objections of special note are: QdA 1.1, concerning the relation between the soul's subsisting and having *esse per se*; QdA 1.3, which investigates directly the relation between something's being *hoc aliquid* and being an individual; QdA 1.9, which takes up the question of the soul and subsistence; and QdA 1.11, which focuses on the operations of the soul. We will consider each of these in turn, noting any obscurities of formulation, and presenting Aquinas' responses. Thereafter, we may pull back to determine what morals regarding the general question can be drawn.

It seems that the human soul cannot be [a form and *hoc aliquid*]. For if the human soul is *hoc aliquid*, it is a subsisting thing having complete being [*esse completum*] in its own right. Now whatever accrues to something beyond (its) complete being [*esse completum*], accrues to it accidentally as whiteness and clothing do to a human being. Hence, the body united to the soul adheres to it accidentally. If therefore, the soul is this something, it is not the substantial form of the body.

QdA 1.1[16]

The argument here is straightforward:

(1) If the soul is *hoc aliquid* it subsists and has complete being (*esse complete*) in its own right (*per se*).
(2) If *x* accrues (*advenit*) to *y* beyond (*post*) *y*'s being (*esse*), *x* accrues to *y* accidentally.
(3) If (1) and (2), then if the body accrues to the soul, it does so in a manner beyond the soul's being (*esse*).
(4) Hence, if the soul is *hoc aliquid*, if the body accrues to the soul, it accrues to the soul accidentally.
(5) If the body accrues to the soul accidentally, the soul is not the substantial form of the body.
(6) The soul is the substantial form of the body.
(7) Hence, the soul is not *hoc aliquid*.

Of special significance in this objection is the first premise, which ties the notion of being *hoc aliquid* to subsisting and having complete being. On the assumption that 'having complete being' is understood existentially rather than definitionally, it is then but a small step to the further conclusion that if it is *hoc aliquid*, the soul can exist in its own right and so must be something capable of independent existence.

In fact, this has been the almost unanimous understanding of Aquinas' interpreters, who suppose that if *x* is a subsisting being *x* can exist independently.[17] Aquinas does not, however accept this claim.[18] He notes that some parts of the body subsist, even though, according to the doctrine of analogy, they cannot exist independently of the body of which they form part (*ST* I 75.2 *ad* 1). So, the premise says less than at first may seem. This is a point to which we will return below, in the ninth objection, but for now we need to note that in his response, Aquinas makes primarily two points, the second of which is that 'even if the can subsist in its own right, nonetheless it [the soul] does not have a complete species,

---

[16] 'Et videtur quod non. Si enim anima humana est hoc aliquid, est subsistens et habens per se esse completum. Quod autem advenit alicui post esse completum, advenit ei accidentaliter, ut albedo homini et vestimentum. Corpus igitur unitum animae advenit ei accidentaliter. Si ergo anima est hoc aliquid, non est forma substantialis corporis' (*QdA* 1.1).

[17] See, e.g., Maritain (1959); Novak (1987); Cross (1997); Stump (2003); DeBoer (2013); Brower (2014).

[18] This is a point rightly made by Pasnau (2002). I have also been instructed on this point by Fr Raphael Mary Salzillo, whose excellent doctoral thesis on Aquinas' conception of the soul (2019) made clear to me the valuable intricacies of his approach.

for the body adheres to it to compete its species' (*'etsi possit per se subsistere, non tamen habet speciem completam, sed corpus advenit ei ad completionem speciei'*; *QdA* 1 *ad* 1). So, whatever else is true of being *hoc aliquid*, according to Aquinas, this is not by itself sufficient for being independent in the manner in which a human being, or any other member of any other species, is independent.

The next argument to be considered explores further the connection Aquinas sees between being *hoc aliquid*, being a determinate individual, and being sufficiently independent to qualify as an individual member of a species.

Further, if the soul is *hoc aliquid*, it follows that it is a determinate [*quoddam*] individual. Every individual, however, is in some species and in some genus. It remains, then, that the soul would have its own species and its own genus. It is impossible, however, that something having its own species should receive an additional supplement from another in order in order to constitute its own species, because, as the Philosopher points out *Meta.* H [*scil.* 3, 1043b36], forms or species of things are like numbers, for which something added or subtracted changes the species. Matter and form, however, are united in order to constitute a species. If, therefore, the soul is *hoc aliquid*, it is not united to the body as a form to matter.

QdA 1.3[19]

The argument here is more complicated, running several themes together; it also trades on a linguistic subtlety so far not introduced for consideration. Probably it is best to treat the passage as containing two arguments, one main and one ancillary:

(A) Main Argument:
(1) If the soul is *hoc aliquid*, then it is a determinate individual.
(2) If x is a determinate individual, then x is in some species and genus.
(3) So, if the soul is *hoc aliquid*, it is in some species and genus.
(4) If x has its own species and genus, it is impossible that it should receive any additional supplement in order to constitute that species.
(5) The soul does receive an additional supplement in coming to constitute a species, namely the body as matter.
(6) So, the soul does not have its own species and genus.
(7) So, the soul is not a determinate individual.
(8) So, the soul is not *hoc aliquid*.

[19] 'Praeterea, si anima est hoc aliquid sequitur quod sit individuum quoddam. Omne autem individuum est in aliqua specie et in aliquo genere. Relinquitur igitur quod anima habeat propriam speciem et proprium genus. Impossibile est autem quod aliquid propriam speciem habens recipiat superadditionem alterius ad speciei cuiusdam constitutionem; quia, ut philosophus dicit VIII Metaph., formae vel species rerum sunt sicut numeri; quibus quidquid subtrahitur vel additur, speciem variat. Materia autem et forma uniuntur ad speciei constitutionem. Si igitur anima est hoc aliquid, non unietur corpori ut forma materiae' (*QdA* 1.3).

One obscurity in this argument concerns (4), the claim that whatever is in some species and genus cannot receive any supplement and still constitute the species it does. Aquinas' contention relies on the thought that, as purely formal, souls are rather like numbers, at least in one respect: if one adds or subtracts anything to a given number, then one changes that number altogether. One changes, so to speak, the species the number constitutes. Of course, this is in one way an odd sort of claim to make, since, 12 does not change in any way when one adds 17 to 12, yielding 29. Aquinas seems really to be saying that numbers have all of their intrinsic properties essentially; so if, *per impossibile*, one were to alter an intrinsic property of 12, namely the property of being twelve, one would alter the number altogether. By parity of reasoning, then, one cannot add or subtract anything to a form, considered as already constituting its own species, without altering the species it constitutes. That yields the following ancillary argument.

(B) Ancillary Argument, on behalf of (4):
(1) If x fully constitutes some species, then x is (in the relevant respect) like a number.
(2) If x is (in the relevant respect) like a number, then x is such that any addition or subtraction would place x into another species.
(3) So, if x has its own species and genus, it is impossible that it should receive any additional supplement in order to constitute that species (= our original (4)).

With that ancillary argument in place, Aquinas is able to move to the final conclusion of the objection, namely that the soul is not *hoc aliquid*. It should be observed here that Aquinas is not saying that a form or a soul is in fact like a number. Rather, he is suggesting that a form, considered just as a form, on the assumption that it already, by itself, constitutes its own species, would be number-like. If so, any addition or subtraction would change its nature, and so change its species. If we think, as Aquinas does think, that a human form does not of its own accord constitute a species, then the human soul will, after all, not be like a number in that respect. Still, the counterfactual point stands.

What is striking in the dominant argument is the move across the first three premises, from being *hoc aliquid* to being a determinate individual, and thence to being a fully fledged member of some species. What is added in the middle step is its being not just an individual, but its being a determinate (*quoddam*) individual, which, again, tends to push somewhat in the direction of Kretzmann's approach, but, also again, does not yet take us all the way there. This is partly because Kretzmann does not specify what it takes to be a 'real particular'; perhaps one can now say, according to the terms of this argument, what is *hoc aliquid* is a particular sort of particular, namely the sort which suffices for being a fully fledged member of a species.

This in any event in the locus of Aquinas' response to this argument: 'To the third argument, it must be said that the human soul is not *hoc aliquid* in the manner of a substance having a complete species, but rather in the manner of a part of something having a complete species, as is clear from that has been said' (*QdA* 1 *ad* 3).[20] One might read this as denying either the first or the second premise, depending on how robustly one takes '*quoddam*': if it means 'fully determinate' in the sense of sufficing to be a member of a species, then (1) is false; if it means 'fully determinate' in the sense of something's being an individual available as a referent of a singular term, then (2) is false.[21] Probably, as we shall see, Aquinas means to reject the second premise, which, if so, shows that in his view something can be *hoc aliquid* without thereby qualifying as an individual substance. That would then, in effect, amount to his rejecting (2) in the current argument.

The next argument teases out still further the relation of something's being *hoc aliquid* and its subsisting, which turns out, too, to carry a special resonance where the nexus of being *hoc aliquid*, having complete being, and being a substance are concerned.

Further, whatever is *hoc aliquid* subsists in its own right. It is proper to a form, however, that it should be in another—which things seems to be incompatible [with its subsisting in its own right]. If, therefore, if the soul is *hoc aliquid*, it appears that it would not be a form.

QdA 1.9[22]

This argument, though short, raises a crucial question regarding the relation between being *hoc aliquid* and subsisting:

(1) If *x* is *hoc aliquid*, *x* subsists in its own right (*per se*).
(2) If *x* is a form, *x* exists in another (*in alio*).
(3) If *x* exists in another, then *x* does not subsist in its own right.
(4) Hence, if the soul is *hoc aliquid*, then it both persists in its own right (*per se*) and does not subsist in its own right (*per se*).
(5) Therefore, the soul is not *hoc aliquid*.

The crucial question raised in this argument is this: what is the relation between subsisting *per se* and existing in another? It is natural to suppose that what exists in

---

[20] 'Ad tertium dicendum quod anima humana non est hoc aliquid sicut substantia completam speciem habens; sed sicut pars habentis speciem completam, ut ex dictis patet' (*QdA* 1 *ad* 3).
[21] See Salzillo (2018) on the question of what Aquinas supposes makes something apt to be a subject of determinate reference.
[22] 'Praeterea, id quod est hoc aliquid per se subsistit. Formae autem proprium est quod sit in alio, quae videntur esse opposita. Si igitur anima est hoc aliquid, non videtur quod sit forma' (*QdA* 1.9).

another does not subsist in its own right; yet the form, it is held, if *hoc aliquid*, does subsist in its own right even while forms exist in another (*in alio*).

This argument thus brings to the fore the issue of what it means for something to 'subsist'. This is a topic of great moment throughout the first question of *Quaestiones de Anima*,[23] and it is easy to see why. The entire locus of issues pertaining to the soul's varying forms of dependence and independence revolve around the issue of subsistence.

Aquinas' immediate response is underwhelming. He responds:

> To the ninth argument it must be said that what is in something as a subject in the manner of an accident precludes an account of its being *hoc aliquid*. To be in something as a part, however—and this is the way in which the soul is in a human being—does not exclude that which is in another from being able to be called this something.   *QdA* 1 *ad* 9[24]

On the one hand, the response is clear, in that it implicitly distinguishes two ways in which one thing can be in another (*in alio*). This has the effect of treating (3) as ambiguous, and as false taken one way but true in the other. If x is in y in the manner of an accident, then x cannot subsist in its own right. So, for instance, if Benedict is pale, then an instance of pallor is in Benedict; but this gives us no reason to suppose that Benedict's pallor can subsist in its own right. For this range of cases, then, (3) comes out true. Still, insists Aquinas, taken another way, (3) is false, when, that is, it is understood to range over 'parts'—parts in the way in which, Aquinas assures his readers, the soul is a part of that in which it is, that is to

---

[23] Aquinas uses the term subsistence twenty-two times in the first question of *QdA*, out of a total of fifty-seven times in the entire *QdA*, which comprises twenty-one questions in total. It equally shows up with some frequency in parallel discussions (e.g. *ST* I 75 a.2). It is worth noting, perhaps, that Aquinas' preoccupation does not flow in any direct way from Aristotle. Moerbeke barely uses the term *subsistere* in his translations, even when one might expect him to do so. That may, though, be due to his being especially attentive to Aristotle's diction. The correlative abstract noun in Greek, *huparxis*, does not occur in Aristotle at all (it occurs only in the spurious *On Plants* i 2, 817b17), though the verb form and the nominal participle are both very common. The abstract noun shows up more regularly in the commentators, where it does tend to come into Latin as one nominalized form or another of *subsistere*. As for the substantive particle *ta huparchonta*, Moerbeke tends to fall back on the use of subordinate clauses, rendering the participle simply as *quae insunt*, or, when Aristotle seems to be indicating necessary non-essential features, as *quae secundum se insunt*. See, e.g. Moerbeke's renderings *Meta. Γ* 1 1003a22, *Γ* 2, 1005a14, and E 1, 1025b12. It should be noted in this connection, however, that in one passage Aquinas, rather curiously, several times identifies *subsistentia* with the Greek term οὐσίωσις (*QdP* 9.1 *resp.*; *ST* I 29 a2 obj. 5), which does not show up in Aristotle at all, and so is not translated by Moerbeke; it is, moreover, infrequent even in the commentators (Simp., *In Phys.* 433.17; Philop., *In De Anima* 208.9, though more common in *De Aert. Mundi*, where it has eleven occurrences). In none of these passages does it recognizably mean anything like what Aquinas means by subsistence. Aquinas himself seems to ascribe this usage to Boethius (*QdP* 9.1 *sed contra*; *ST* I 29 a2 obj. 5).

[24] 'Ad nonum dicendum quod in alio esse sicut accidens in subiecto, tollit rationem eius quod est hoc aliquid. Esse autem in alio sicut partem (quomodo anima est in homine), non omnino excludit quin id quod est in alio, possit hoc aliquid dici' (*QdA* 1 *ad* 9). On Aquinas' complex mereology, see Salzillo (2021).

say the compound of form and matter. In this sort of case, he avers, it is possible for *x* to be in another and yet subsist in its own right. So, the objection is defanged and it remains true that the soul can be *hoc aliquid* and so subsist in its own right, even while it is in something other.

That seems fair enough, though in the end it only serves to refocus our question: when is something in something else as a part (*sicut partem*) in the relevant way and when not? Aquinas cannot be thinking of the soul as a physical part, since he later in the same work denies that the soul is itself a form-matter composite.[25] So, it is a part (*pars*) in some other, extended, sense of that term. Consequently, we cannot judge his rejoinder here without first determining what is involved in something's being in something other (*in alio*) as a part in such a way as to be consistent with its subsisting in its own right. Obviously it will not suffice to say: this is the sort of part which is compatible with the part's being *hoc aliquid*.

What the relevant sense of part might be receives at least some illumination from the next objection Aquinas considers. Some parts, he implies, have operations of their own; others do not.

Further, if the human soul is *hoc aliquid* existing in its own right (*per se*), it is necessary that it have an operation of its own, because it belongs to anything existing in its own right to have an operation of its own. But the human soul does not have an operation of its own, because understanding itself, which seems above all to be its own [proper activity], does not belong to the soul, but to the human through the soul, as is said in *De anima* i [*scil.* i 4, 408a14]. Therefore, the human soul is not *hoc aliquid*.

QdA 1.11[26]

The argument here deals with the vexed question of whether the soul has its own proprietary operation. The basic argument given in this objection, somewhat streamlined, is:

(1) If *x* is this *hoc aliquid* and exists in its own right, *x* has a proprietary operation.
(2) If anything is the proprietary operation of the (human) soul, it is understanding (*intelligere*).

---

[25] 'Consequently, since the soul is a certain form which subsists of itself, it can be composed of act and potency, that is, of an act of existing and an essence, but not of form and matter' (*QdA* 1.6 *resp.*).
[26] 'Praeterea, si anima humana est hoc aliquid et per se existens, oportet quod per se habeat aliquam propriam operationem; quia uniuscuiusque rei per se existentis est aliqua propria operatio. Sed anima humana non habet aliquam propriam operationem; quia ipsum intelligere, quod maxime videtur esse eius proprium, non est animae, sed hominis per animam, ut dicitur in I de anima. Ergo anima humana non est hoc aliquid' (*QdA* 1.11).

(3) Understanding (*intelligere*) does not belong to the soul as its proprietary activity, but to the human being in virtue of the soul.

(4) Hence the soul is not *hoc aliquid* and something existing in its own right.

The argument turns on a disputed matter, namely whether it is right or wrong to regard understanding (*intelligere*) as belonging in the first instance to the soul, as its own proprietary operation, or rather to the human being, in virtue of her being ensouled.

Aquinas' response to this objection locates understanding as proprietary activity in the soul, and thus accepts (2) while rejecting (3): Aquinas' response:

> To the eleventh argument it must be said that understanding is an operation of the soul, if it is regarded as a principle from which that operation eventuates; for it does not eventuate from the soul as mediated by an organ of the body, as sight is mediated by the eye, but the body none the less shares in this operation on the side of the object, for phantasms, which are the objects of intellect, cannot exist without corporeal organ. *QdA* 1 *ad* 11[27]

There is a fair bit in this response pertinent to Aquinas' view of the soul as separable from the body. In the present context, however, we are primarily concerned with the question of how the soul is understood to be the kind of part which can subsist in its own right.

Aquinas' dominant idea is that the intellect, unlike the other faculties of soul, serves as an unmediated principle or source (*principium*) of an activity without the need or mediation of any organ. In this respect, Aquinas understands intellection to be unlike, for instance, vision, since seeing requires a functioning eye for its operation. In the current context, we may set aside the grounds for Aquinas' confidence on this point, focusing instead on the question of how this belief shapes his conviction that the soul is *hoc aliquid* in virtue of its being a part of the requisite sort. One may readily suppose that he is thinking that if *x* is present in something else (*in allo*) as a part with its own proprietary operation, then *x* can nonetheless subsist in its own right despite its being a part of some larger whole. That would, after all, differentiate souls from intrinsic accidents, like being pale. Benedict's soul, unlike Benedict's pallor, has an operation of its own, unmediated by the body, such that it is a *hoc aliquid*, even while in another (*in allo*), and is thus capable of subsisting in its own right (*per se*). The soul might then be likened to a lens in a telescope: it exists in another, the telescope, as a part, but it is capable of

---

[27] 'Ad undecimum dicendum quod intelligere est propria operatio animae, si consideretur principium a quo egreditur operatio; non enim egreditur ab anima mediante organo corporali, sicut visio mediante oculo, communicat tamen in ea corpus ex parte obiecti; nam phantasmata, quae sunt obiecta intellectus, sine corporeis organis esse non possunt' (*QdA* 1 *ad* 11).

subsisting in its own right, not in such a way as to be a member of a free-standing species in its own right, in terms of its own intrinsic composition. The thought would then be that at least where its full expression is concerned, the soul, like a lens, must be enmeshed in a larger functioning system of some sort, a lens in a functioning ocular device of some sort and a soul in a functionally suitable body. Now, the parallel is imperfect in a number of ways, not least in that a telescope is an artefact and a human being is not. Even so, one can see the difference between a telescope's lens and a telescope's being shiny white: a lens is a part whose definition does not make ineliminable reference to the whole of which it is a part.

Taking all that together, a picture of Aquinas' conception of the soul as both a form and a *hoc aliquid* begins to emerge: the soul is a part of the compound, he thinks, but even so it is a particular in its own right, and indeed a particular of a certain sort, namely the sort of particular which can subsist by itself, again in its own right. Lest that last commitment be thought a bridge too far, it bears repeating that it says less than it may at first seem. Aquinas is not contending that the soul is, by itself, an autonomous substance, capable of existing as a member of its own species and genus, as, for instance, a human being does. Rather, it is a sufficiently determinate particular that it can be identified as the particular it is without reference to the composite of which it is part. Still, when it is enmeshed in that composite, it plays a key, and, well, formative role in the composite's being the composite it is. Put another way, Aquinas is contending that among the sortals under which individuals fall, not all are substance sortals: a soul is a determinate sort of thing, but not everything falling under a determinate sortal is, in its own right, a substantial sort of thing.[28] Such a sortally determinate something may be, then, both a form and *hoc aliquid*.[29]

---

[28] The notion of being a sortal is variously used in philosophy. Sometimes it is taken to mean, effectively, *substance sortal*. It need not be, however, and here it is not. Rather, the term is used in a sense aligned with Strawson's (1959: 168) use: 'A sortal universal supplies a principle for distinguishing and counting individual particulars which it collects'. Not every individual particular is a substance, and not every kind is a substantial kind. Put in the terms here engaged: the task of indicating that a particular falls under some sortal or other is the contribution of *aliquid* to the phrase *hoc aliquid*.

[29] The notion of *being determinate* in this formulation seeks to reflect Aquinas' occasional claim that whatever is *hoc aliquid* is such that it can be on object of non-derivative demonstrative reference. So, e.g. '[Matter] therefore is one of the principles of nature, one that is not one [*unum*] as is a *hoc aliquid*, which is some demonstrated individual [*individuum demonstratum*], such that it has form and unity in actuality [*Hoc igitur est unum principium naturae: quod non sic unum est sicut hoc aliquid, hoc est sicut aliquod individuum demonstratum, ita quod habeat formam et unitatem in actu; sed dicitur ens et unum inquantum est in potentia ad formam*]; *In Phys.* I.13.118. Again, 'For this reason one ought not accept the infinite as something that exists complete all at once, as a demonstrated *hoc aliquid*, as we take a man or a house to be [*Unde non oportet accipere quod infinitum sit aliquid totum simul existens, sicut hoc aliquid demonstratum, sicut accipimus hominem vel domum*]'; *In Phys.* III.10.375. Finally and most directly, 'and it is *hoc aliquid*, i.e. a certain subsisting thing that can be demonstrated...[*et est hoc aliquid, idest quoddam demonstrabile subsistens et separatum a sensibilibus...*]'; *In Meta.* VII.14.1593.

4. Two Ways to Be *Hoc Aliquid*

One way of looking at that finding is this: Aquinas envisages a continuum of individuals, some of which are not *hoc aliquid* at all (Benedict's pallor and other individual intrinsic accidents), some of which are *hoc aliquid* but not therefore members of a substantial kind (Benedict's soul), and some of which are fully fledged members of a species (Benedict). The rational soul thus falls into a sort of half-way house, able to be designated as what it is, in its own right, without reference to anything else, but not yet fully autonomous or capable of existing in its own right. It can *subsist* in its own right says Aquinas, but this seems to mean little more than that it can be identified as what it is without reference to anything beyond itself. This is how the soul differs from intrinsic accidents and other beings definitionally dependent on the substances whose features or accidents they are.

Note that the point here is *definitional* and not existential: necessarily Benedict's surface and Benedict travel together, and necessarily, if Benedict exists, Benedict has a surface; but in order to provide an essence-specifying account of what Benedict's surface is, we will perforce make reference to Benedict, while the converse is not true. This Aquinas makes clear enough elsewhere: x subsists if and only if x 'does not require some outside foundation in which it is sustained, but is sustained in its own self' (*QdP* 9.1c).

We have, then, to make the matter crisp, two notions of being *hoc aliquid* in Aquinas, one weak and one strong:

- x is *hoc aliquid^w* iff (i) x is non-derivatively subject to demonstration in its own right; and (ii) x is not complete with respect to its species

so, e.g., the hand, the kidney, the soul.

- x is *hoc aliquid^s* iff (i) x is non-derivatively subject to demonstration in its own right; and (ii) x is complete with respect to its species

so, e.g., the human being.

This provides a way of seeing how the soul can qualify as *hoc aliquid* without enjoying all the privileges of a fully fledged, categorically delimited substance. It is something, it falls under a determinate sortal, but it is not such that it falls under a substantial sortal as members of a species do.

The matter is slightly more complicated, however, due to the fact that Aquinas shows himself willing to regard bodily parts in addition to the soul as *hoc aliquid*. So, for instance, he regards the human hand as *hoc aliquid*, though he equally denies that it can exist without the body, except by analogy, which is to say, in this case, only by reference to the state in which it is when functioning as a part of a living human body (*ST* I 75.2 *ad* 1).[30] What is more, given the point about analogy, it emerges that even definitional dependence is too coarse: a hand, even a functioning hand, depends definitionally on its role in the living body whose hand it is. That is why a severed hand is not a hand except analogically. In this sense, a human hand seems to occupy a precarious position: it is neither a fully fledged member of a substantial kind, nor the sort of particular we think an intrinsic accident is. In this respect, it seems rather more like a human soul, but, unfortunately, unlike a human soul, a hand has no operation of its own and so cannot exist apart from the whole of which it is a part. It is definitionally dependent on the operation of the living animal, but not, Aquinas implies, in the manner of either an intrinsic accident or a soul.

This complication, though, does not so much upset the picture of the soul as *hoc aliquid* as bring into sharper relief that the soul's separation is extraordinary. As we have seen, the soul, it is alleged, has an operation which belongs to it in its own right, its intellection, and in this the soul differs markedly from other parts of a living compound and indeed from the souls of non-human animals (*ST* I 75 c3; *SCG* II 60.1465; *In De An.* I 2, 94–7). One might reasonably ask, on another occasion, whether Aquinas is right about the form of functional autonomy he offers human souls but denies to the souls of other animals and plants. In the current context, however, what matters is that his doing so serves to differentiate human souls from other parts of the compound which are equally *hoc aliquid* in the weak sense. Souls are not separable because they are subsistent or *hoc aliquid*, but because they are *hoc aliquid and* capable of functioning without the composite. Given its operation, a hand is evidently definitionally dependent on the composite without remainder. Still, unlike an intrinsic accident, it has an operation of its own, albeit one derived from its role in a larger functional system. In this way a hand is indeed like a soul and not like an intrinsic accident; and it is like a soul in being a *hoc aliquid* without, though, being separable, definitionally or otherwise. If there is more texture in Aquinas' account than first meets the eye, this is because there is, similarly, more texture in the *explananda* as he understands them.

---

[30] This issue is well discussed by Pasnau (2002: 45–50, 66–70).

5. Concluding Considerations

From its inception in the texts of Aristotle, hylomorphism struggles to articulate its conception of the soul as a substance: the soul seems somehow both a substance and not a substance. It is a form, and forms seem, at least at first pass, to be universals; yet substances are meant to be particulars. Further, even supposing that some forms are particulars and that souls are just such forms, there remains a worry about autonomy: forms seem to be forms *of* quantities of matter, quantities of matter upon which they depend, it seems, for their very existence; yet substances are meant to be basic beings, capable of existing in their own rights, separately, as Aristotle says, where this evidently implies a kind of definitional or existential autonomy not readily extended to dependent forms.

Already issues of concern and the subjects of discussion in Aristotle's own writings, these issues come into sharper relief later in the Aristotelian tradition, especially in the Latin west, when Catholic philosophers sought to articulate and defend many of their theistic commitments within a hylomorphic framework. One flash point, recognized as such by Thomas Aquinas in his *Quaestiones de Anima*, centres squarely on the soul's status as a form. Aquinas maintains a commitment to the separability of the soul, which commitment, he sees, does not marry easily with the soul-body hylomorphism he full-throatedly espouses. He equally thinks of the soul as a particular of a certain sort, as *hoc aliquid*, and rightly wonders whether this is compatible with its being a form, as, in hylomorphic terms, surely it must be. He concludes that it can, once the notion of being *hoc aliquid* is sufficiently investigated and delineated.

About that much, Aquinas is on firm ground. Whether his account of the soul's character as both *hoc aliquid* and a form adequately serves his larger goal of integrating Christian theism into hylomorphism is a further, larger matter. At this juncture, however, it seems fair to say that he has cleared some otherwise cluttered ground, freeing space for hylomorphists of many different stripes. In so doing, and irrespective of his larger goals, Aquinas has answered to good effect a question any proponent of hylomorphism must in any case address. His answer: yes, the soul can be a form and this something.[31]

---

[31] A draft of this chapter was delivered to an audience at Yale University. I am grateful to the members of that audience for their alert and helpful questions, and especially to Benjamin Koons, who began the discussion on that occasion with a set of helpfully focused, perceptive comments. Still more grateful am I to David Charles, who subjected a subsequent draft to a series of incisive questions and challenges. While I cannot presume to have addressed them all adequately, I am confident that the chapter has been improved immeasurably by the trying.

Bibliography

Brower, J.E. (2014), *Aquinas's Ontology of the Material World: Change, Hylomorphism, and Material Objects* (Oxford University Press)

Brower, J.E. (2016), 'Aquinas on the Problem of Universals', *Philosophy and Phenomenological Research* XCII: 714–35

Cherniss, Harold (1962), *Aristotle's Criticism of Plato and the Academy* (Russell and Russell)

Cross, Richard (1997), 'Is Aquinas's Proof for the Indestructibility of the Soul Successful?', *British Journal of the History of Philosophy* 5: 1–20

De Boer, Sander (2013), *Science of the Soul: The Commentary Tradition on Aristotle's De anima, c. 1260-1360* (Cornell University Press)

Geach, Peter (1954), 'Form and Existence', *Proceedings of the Aristotelian Society* 55: 251–72

Geach, Peter (1968), 'What Actually Exists', *Proceedings of the Aristotelian Society* Supp. Vol. 42: 7–16

Glorieux, P. (1932), 'Les Questions disputées de saint Thomas et leur suite chronologique', in *Recherches de Théologie Ancienne et Médiévale* 4: 5–33

Kung, J. (1981), 'Aristotle on Thises, Suches and the Third Man Argument', *Phronesis* 26: 207–47

Maritain, J. (1959), *Distinguish to Unite: Or the Degrees of Knowledge*, trans. G.B. Phelan (Charles Scribner's Sons)

Pasnau, R. (2002), *Thomas Aquinas on Human Nature: A Philosophical Study of Summa Theologiae Ia 75-89* (Cambridge University Press)

Novak, Joseph A. (1987), 'Aquinas and the Incorruptibility of the Soul', *History of Philosophy Quarterly* 4: 405–21

Robb, James (1984), *St. Thomas Aquinas, Questions on the Soul*, trans. with introduction (Marquette University Press)

Salzillo Fr., Raphael Mary (2018), *The Soul as Part in Thomas Aquinas*, Ph.D. Dissertation, University of Notre Dame

Salzillo OP, Raphael Mary (2021), 'The Mereology of Thomas Aquinas', *Philosophy Compass* 16: 1–10

Sharples, Robert (1999), 'On Being a $TO\Delta E$ TI in Aristotle and Alexander', in *Méthexis: La Recepción de Aristóteles en el Pensamiento Post-Aristótelico hasta el Año 230* 12: 77–87

Shields, Christopher (1999), *Order in Multiplicity: Homonymy in the Philosophy of Aristotle* (Oxford University Press)

Shields, Christopher (2008), 'Plato and Aristotle in the Academy: An Aristotelian Criticism of Platonic Forms', in *The Oxford Handbook on Plato*, ed. G. Fine (Oxford University Press), 504–26

Smith, J.A. (1921), '*Tode ti* in Aristotle', *Classical Review* 35: 1

Stegmüller, F. (1947), *Repertorium Commentariorum in Sententias Petri Lombardi*, vols. I and II (Würzberg)

Strawson, Peter (1959), *Individuals: An Essay in Descriptive Metaphysics* (University Paperbacks)

Stump, Eleanore (2005), *Aquinas* (Routledge, Kegan and Paul)

Van Dyke, Christina (2014), 'I See Dead People: Disembodied Souls and Aquinas's "Two Person" Problem', *Oxford Studies in Medieval Philosophy* (Oxford University Press), 25–45

15
Suárez' Compositional Account of Substance

Dominik Perler

1. Introduction: Two Puzzling Theses

Aristotelian hylomorphism had a bad press in the 17th century. It was considered an outdated research programme that lacked explanatory power and empirical evidence—a programme that should be abandoned as quickly as possible and replaced with a mechanistic one. The idea that trees, dogs, human beings, and many other things in the material world consist of form and matter looked so strange or even unintelligible to many early modern philosophers and scientists that they simply dismissed it, often without making an effort to examine it in detail or to reject it with compelling arguments. On their view, one should not pay intellectual attention to what is unintelligible.

However, not all 17th-century philosophers discarded hylomorphism without examining it. Some of them realized that it was important to take it seriously because it still dominated the teaching at the universities, and they took the trouble to refute it with arguments. René Descartes is a good example.[1] When writing to Henricus Regius, who was surrounded by traditional Aristotelians at the University of Utrecht, he acknowledged that hylomorphism was still influential and that it needed to be rejected. He clearly saw that it was necessary to attack the idea that material things consist of form and matter, and introduced his critique of this idea as follows:

> To prevent any ambiguity of expression, it must be observed that when we deny substantial forms, we mean by the expression a certain substance joined to matter, making up with it a merely corporeal whole, and which, no less than matter and even more than matter—since it is called an actuality and matter only a potentiality—is a true substance, or self-subsistent thing.[2]

---

[1] For detailed analysis of his refutation, see Garber (1992: 94–116); Hattab (2009); Ariew (2011: 127–56).
[2] Letter to Regius from January 1642 (AT III: 502; CSMK III: 207).

As this passage makes clear, Descartes understands hylomorphism not just in a broad sense as a theory that explains the constitution of a corporeal thing with reference to a substantial (and not just accidental) form and matter. He rather takes it to be based on two specific theses: (i) the substantial form is itself a thing, even a self-subsistent thing, and hence something that can exist without matter, (ii) the substantial form and matter are two components that together make up a whole. The first thesis could be called the *independence thesis*, since it stresses that a substantial form, though present in matter, is not dependent on matter and can exist apart from it.[3] The second thesis could be called the *composition thesis*, since it emphasizes that the form-matter relation is a relation between two parts or components. Of course, these two parts have different characteristic features, one of them being actual and the other potential, but they are nevertheless distinct parts that together make a whole.

Any attentive reader of Aristotle will be surprised or even puzzled by these two theses. First of all, why should the substantial form be a self-subsistent thing? Isn't Aristotle's main point that the form is the principle of life and therefore something that has to be present in a living being? The independence thesis seems to flatly contradict the basic idea that there can be no principle of life without a living being, which must always have a body. Or how should there be a living being without bodily organs? Perhaps one could make sense of the independence thesis by assuming that it is not meant to be Aristotle's thesis, but a thesis defended by Christian Aristotelians who argued for the immortality of the human soul. For these authors the substantial form in a human being is a very special form that can be separated from matter and continue to exist apart from it.[4] But even these authors agreed that non-human forms are not self-subsistent things. Trees, dogs, and many other living beings do not have a form that can exist apart from matter. Why then should one think that the independence thesis is at the core of hylomorphism?

The second thesis is equally puzzling. When introducing form and matter, Aristotle did not speak about two components, even less about two things that somehow come together and make a whole.[5] He rather characterized them as two basic principles and noted that each of them could be called 'substance' in some sense—not because they are two independent things, but because they are both constitutive for a substance.[6] Later Aristotelians took this idea very seriously,

---

[3] It is because of this independence that Descartes takes a substantial form to be a substance. On his view, existential independence is the mark of a substance; see *Principles of Philosophy* I.51 (AT VIII–1: 24; CSM I: 210).

[4] Thomas Aquinas, for instance, explicitly called the human form or soul something that subsists; see *Summa Theologiae* I, q. 75, art. 6.

[5] Consequently, he considered the states of the whole to be 'inextricably psycho-physical' (Charles 2021: 6). They cannot be decomposed into two components belonging to two different things.

[6] See *De Anima* II.1 (412a6–9). In his commentary on this passage, Shields rightly emphasizes that Aristotle does not take matter to be a thing or substance in its own right. Aristotle only says that matter belongs to substance or is an aspect of substance; see Aristotle (2016: 167).

emphasizing that form and matter are constitutive principles and not things.[7] Consequently, they did not speak about a composition of two things, but about the way the form as one principle actualizes and unifies matter as the other principle. Why then should the composition thesis be the second core thesis of hylomorphism?

One might think that Descartes attacked some kind of imaginary hylomorphism when he claimed that this metaphysical theory was based on the independence thesis and the composition thesis. However, a closer look at late scholastic texts reveals that these two theses were indeed defended. In his influential *Metaphysical Disputations* (*DM*; published in 1597), Francisco Suárez did in fact claim that a form is a thing, combined with matter as another thing. He unmistakably held: 'Matter and form are therefore distinguished from each other as a thing from a thing [*tamquam res a re*]' (*DM* 13.4.5).[8] Moreover, he conceded that a form could exist apart from matter, and vice versa, because a thing that is distinct from another thing could always be separated from that second thing— perhaps not through natural processes, but certainly through divine intervention. God could separate a form from matter and thereby demonstrate that it is metaphysically possible for these two things to exist apart from each other (*DM* 15.9.5). This applies not just to human beings, but to all material things. Hence, even the form of a tree or a dog could be separated from matter. In the normal course of nature they are, of course, never separated. They rather form a unity that serves as the bearer of many accidents. But in principle, they are separable, for what is composed of two things can always be decomposed.[9]

For a traditional Aristotelian philosopher (or for a modern-day proponent of hylomorphism) these statements are hard to swallow. Is Suárez not betraying the basic idea of hylomorphism by saying that a material thing is a composition of two things (*res*), which are supposed to be two self-subsistent entities? How can he maintain the thesis that a material thing is a unity if he takes it to be made up of two things? And how can he explain other features of a material thing, such as its basic powers and its acquired capacities? Are they also things? And are they somehow attached to the two most fundamental things? If so, how are they attached? These are the questions I want to examine in what follows. I will first look at Suárez' account of form and matter, paying particular attention to his

---

[7] See, for instance, Aquinas (1950: ch. 2, 82). Principles are important for the generation of a substance, as Aquinas emphasizes, because they structure it and make it the very substance it is. But they are not things that are somehow joined together.

[8] He spells this out by saying that the entire substance is a composition of these things. In fact, 'among creatures one never finds a complete substance without a real composition' (*DM* 33.1.8). All references to the *Disputationes Metaphysicae* (*DM*) apply to the *Opera Omnia*, vols. 25–6. The first number refers to the disputation, the second to the section, the third to the paragraph. All translations from Latin are mine.

[9] Suárez even claims that they are really (and not just conceptually) distinct from each other (*DM* 7.1.1) and hence mutually separable: matter can exist without form and form without matter.

arguments for the independence thesis and the composition thesis (section 2). I will then examine the way he explains other features in relation to form and matter (section 3). Finally, I will attempt to sketch the metaphysical picture that emerges from his compositional account of substance (section 4). It is a picture that radically differs from the original Aristotelian picture and paves the way for non-Aristotelian ways of analysing material things. It even prepares the ground for a new way of doing metaphysics, namely, as a form of reverse engineering—or so I will argue.[10]

2. Matter and Form as Things

Suárez introduces the composition thesis by arguing that matter is a real entity or thing that can be combined with a form as another thing (*DM* 13.4.5). When talking about a thing (*res*), he refers to something that can be defined as such, without any reference to something else, and that exists by itself. Or to put it in technical terminology, a thing is something that has its own essence and actual existence.[11] So, when arguing that matter is a real thing, Suárez does not simply make the harmless claim that matter somehow exists. He defends the much stronger and more controversial claim that matter actually exists without needing anything else to exist. He thereby rejects the Thomistic account of matter as pure potentiality. According to this account, matter cannot have actual existence unless it is combined with a form. Of course, Suárez is not the first scholastic author to reject this account. Ockham and other late medieval authors already claimed that matter is indeed an actually existing thing—an entity on its own.[12] Suárez spells out this claim and adduces explicit arguments for defending it. Let me focus on his most important arguments and the consequences he draws from them. What is at stake in all these arguments is the status of prime matter, for it is clear that matter combined with a form (the so-called 'secondary matter') is something with actual existence.[13]

---

[10] I am not the first to observe that Suárez deeply transformed Aristotelian hylomorphism. In his comprehensive study, Pasnau (2011) already pointed out that one cannot understand theoretical innovations in the 17th century without looking at Suárez and other late scholastic authors. But most commentators have focused on a single aspect of Suárez' hylomorphism by analysing either his account of substantial form or his account of matter. For the first approach, see Hattab (2009, 2011, and 2017), Shields (2012), Richardson (2015); for the second, see Des Chene (1996), Akerlund (2015), Schmaltz (2020a). My aim is to bring together different pieces of his theory and to elucidate his general hylomorphic framework.

[11] In some passages (e.g. *DM* 3.2.4) Suárez takes a thing to be just a being (*ens*). But in other passages he points out that a thing is a certain type of being: it is a self-standing being and hence something that is really distinct from other things, having its own essence and existence (*DM* 7.2.9).

[12] On Ockham's defence of this thesis, see Adams (1987: 671–95); on later authors, see Pasnau (2011: 35–52).

[13] Prime matter as such has neither a special quantity nor a quality. It is, as it were, bare matter that needs to be combined with a form in order to acquire accidents. On its status, see Des Chene (1996: 81–121) and Schmaltz (2020a: 64–100).

Why should matter that is devoid of any form have actual existence? Suárez' first answer to this question refers to instances of change and can therefore be called *the argument from change*. It is quite obvious, he observes (*DM* 13.1.6), that material things change all the time, mostly by losing and gaining accidents. However, in all these changes there is something that persists. This can easily be illustrated. When a tree turns green in spring, it is gaining an accident and thereby changes. But the tree itself as the bearer of this accident remains the same. After all, it is the very same tree that is first brown and then green. Hence, there must be something that persists in the process of accidental change. What could that be? According to Suárez, this thing must be the form-matter compound. It is this compound that is enriched, as it were, by changing accidents.

Yet not only are there accidental changes, there are also substantial changes. This is most evident in cases of destruction. Suppose the tree is cut down and its branches are used as firewood. It then ceases to exist as a tree, because only a living tree is a real tree.[14] Nevertheless, something persists when the form is lost. What could that be? For Suárez, it must be matter, which somehow survives the loss of the form. To be sure, it does not survive as naked matter. As soon as it loses the form of a tree, it gets a new form and thereby becomes part of a new thing, for instance of a piece of firewood. Nevertheless, it does persist. Consequently, matter must be something with actual existence, namely a thing that can lose a substantial form and gain a new one (*DM* 13.1.8–9).

It is quite striking that Suárez takes the case of substantial change to be analogous to that of accidental change: in both cases there needs to be some stable basis that persists. But why should there be an analogy? Why shouldn't one say that substantial change crucially differs from accidental change as it amounts to destruction? After all, a tree that is cut down is fully destroyed and ceases to be a tree. Why then should one suppose that there is something that persists? From Suárez' point of view, there must be something that persists because in every case of destruction something new emerges, and this would be impossible without an adequate basis. Thus, no firewood could come to exist if there were no basis for that new thing; firewood is not created *ex nihilo*. Hence, there must be something in place, namely matter, in which the form of the new thing comes to exist. This is why there can never be full destruction. Or as Suárez puts it, 'there is no natural change through a total destruction and inception, but through the transformation that comes out of a common subject' (*DM* 13.1.9). Thus, when the tree is cut down a transformation occurs, the form of the living being is replaced with the form of the firewood. This process could not take place if there were no matter to serve as the basis or the 'common subject' for the old and the new form.

---

[14] Following Aristotle, Suárez holds that a dead tree can only homonymously be called a tree. He spells this out by discussing the case of the dead human being (*DM* 15.10.10–15). For details, see Perler (2020a: 150–2).

Suárez adduces still another argument to show that matter must have actual existence. With this argument, which could be called *the argument from potentiality*, he openly attacks the Thomists who claim that matter is pure potentiality. He points out that talking about potentiality can be quite misleading, because the words 'potential' and 'potentiality' can be used in two different ways (*DM* 13.5.12). On the one hand, we can use them when we speak about something that can exist but does not actually exist. For instance, when we speak about the grandchild of a young person, we can make a statement like 'The grandchild has potential existence', meaning thereby that there could be a grandchild in the future. Clearly, we are then speaking about something that does not yet have actual existence. Some years later, when the grandchild is born, we can also make a statement about it, for instance by saying 'The grandchild is a potential musician', meaning thereby that the child has the potential to become a musician. We then speak about a thing that actually exists, and we refer to one of its capacities or abilities. But it is of crucial importance to distinguish these two uses of the word 'potential', for what lacks actual existence is not the same as a thing that has the potential to become a certain type of thing.

From Suárez' point of view, the Thomists of his time mix up the two uses of the word 'potential'.[15] They first talk about matter as something that has the potential to become a certain type of thing and then claim that it has no actual existence. In making this claim, they are confused about the potentiality at stake: what has the potential to become a certain type of thing is not the same as that which has mere potential existence. Suárez makes this point by introducing a subtle terminological distinction (*DM* 13.5.12): what is in potency (*in potentia*) is not a mere potency (*potentia*). And what is in potency is an entity or a thing that really exists, namely matter, which can be combined with a wide range of forms. In fact, it is only because of its being in potency that it can take the form of a tree, or a dog, or some other form, and thereby become this or that material thing.[16]

Finally, Suárez presents a third argument to defend the thesis that matter must have actual existence. It could be called *the argument from causation*, since it refers to the way matter comes into existence and remains in existence. Everything that exists, Suárez holds, ultimately depends on God, because he constantly keeps everything in existence. And God is not just the first creator of all things; he is, rather, constantly related to all things by keeping them in existence and acting

---

[15] Whether or not Aquinas mixes them up is a controversial question. For two different evaluations, see Pasnau (2002: 131–40) and Brower (2014: 113–29).

[16] Suárez refers to an 'intrinsic directedness towards a form' (*DM* 13.4.9) when explaining how matter can be in potency. This amounts to saying that matter needs to be completed by a form and even strives for completion. Matter is therefore not a completely indeterminate thing, despite the fact that it has no special quantity or quality. It has, right from the beginning, an inner striving that is built into it, and it can be defined as such. On its definition, see Des Chene (1996: 83–97).

with them.[17] He should therefore be understood as a constantly active cause. But what exactly does he cause? Suárez emphasizes that he does not simply cause trees, dogs, and other material things. He also causes the constitutive parts of these things, namely form and matter. This requires two causal activities, one for the form and another for the matter. In fact, 'the creation of the matter of creatable things and the introduction of a form are distinct actions' (*DM* 15.8.19). Thus, it is one thing to cause or create the matter of a tree, quite another to endow it with a form. This is most evident in the case in which God uses his absolute power and stops acting according to the laws of nature. In that case he can do two things: he can destroy a form and replace it with another form (say, by miraculously turning a tree into a tulip), or he can destroy the underlying matter and thereby fully eradicate a thing. The simple fact that there are two distinct activities shows that form and matter are not merely two aspects or inner principles of a single thing. They are rather two different entities, each of them standing in a causal relation to God. Hence, both form and matter must be things that actually exist as long as they are standing in this relation.

I hope these three arguments make clear that Suárez does not simply postulate matter as something with actual existence. He thinks that there are good reasons for accepting matter as something that exists *by itself*, thus being a self-standing entity. Of course, in nature as we know it, matter never exists by itself. As long as God does not intervene, matter is always—and even necessarily—combined with forms. But this is only a physical necessity, not a metaphysical necessity. It is indeed possible for God to destroy all the forms and to keep just matter in existence. Should he do that, he would create quite an impoverished world, but nevertheless it would be a real world.[18]

But what is the form with which matter is combined? Here again, Suárez stresses that it must be a thing (*res*) with actual existence, and he hastens to add that this thing is distinct from matter (*DM* 15.2.1). On his view, the best example is the form of a human being.[19] This form is something that exists in a piece of matter and endows it with a number of capacities. When doing that, it acts as a cause. This clearly shows that it must be distinct from matter, for a cause is always distinct from the thing in or upon which it acts. The same is true for all other forms, say, for those of a tree or a dog. They are always active causes and therefore things with power that act in or on matter.

---

[17] Technically speaking, he is not just a conserving cause, but a concurring cause. On this *concursus* theory, see Freddoso (2002).

[18] Suárez explicitly refers to God's possible intervention (*DM* 13.9.5). In sketching this scenario, he does not intend to introduce God as a capricious tyrant who could destroy the natural order at any time. He rather uses it to distinguish different types of necessity and possibility. On this methodological use, which can be found in many medieval authors, see Courtenay (1985).

[19] He uses the case of the human form to explain forms in general, as Hattab (2009: 40–64) shows in detail. And he insists that forms need to be accepted as real components although they cannot be directly observed. He adduces a number of abductive arguments for their existence; see Shields (2012).

From a traditional Aristotelian point of view, this argument looks rather suspicious. No doubt, every Aristotelian would concede that a form is a cause. But is it not of crucial importance to distinguish different types of causes? After all, a formal cause should not be conflated with an efficient cause; that is, one should not think that the form of a tree acts in the same way as a woodcutter who acts upon a tree and takes it down. As an efficient cause, a woodcutter is indeed distinct from the tree he acts upon. By contrast, the formal cause is not a distinct thing. It is rather a structuring principle that is present in the tree and makes it the very thing it is. Aquinas emphasizes this point by saying that the formal cause as an internal cause needs to be clearly distinguished from the efficient cause as an external cause.[20]

In response to this objection, Suárez would certainly concede that a form is an internal cause. In fact, he explicitly calls it an 'intrinsic cause' (*DM* 15.1.6). But on his view, even such a cause must be a thing that acts upon the thing in which it is present. This becomes clear if we look at his general account of cause. Every cause, he asserts, must be 'a principle that essentially pours being [*influens esse*] into another thing' (*DM* 12.2.4). So, every cause must be an active thing that somehow brings about or makes something else. Yet it is important to note that it can do that in two different ways.[21] First, it can come, as it were, from the outside and 'pour being' into something else by producing it. This is exactly what the efficient cause as an external cause does: it literally produces something by giving existence to a new thing. But a cause can also act in another way. It can be present inside a thing and 'pour being' into it by making it a certain type of thing. In doing so, it does not give existence to a new thing; it rather endows an already existing thing with an essence. This is exactly what the formal cause as an intrinsic cause does: it gives essence, not existence. Nevertheless, it *does* something to something else. Hence, it must be an active thing that acts upon another thing. Metaphorically speaking, it must be a thing that pervades another thing and thereby shapes it.

In providing this account, Suárez radically transforms the Aristotelian notion of cause.[22] On his view, every cause is a thing (*res*) in the strict sense, that is, an entity that acts in or upon another thing. The crucial question for him is not whether a cause is in fact an active thing, but how that thing acts and what exactly it brings about when it acts. It is therefore not surprising that he has no doubts that a form, which clearly is a cause, must be a thing that acts upon matter. To be sure, it does not act by creating or producing matter; this is what God as the first efficient cause does. It rather acts by somehow pervading matter and turning it into a thing that

---

[20] See Aquinas (1950: ch. 3, 90).
[21] I confine myself to sketching the main points. For a detailed account of both ways of acting, see Richardson (2015); Schmid (2015); Tuttle (2016).
[22] In emphasizing that a cause is a thing that does something to another thing, he takes efficient causation to be the paradigmatic form of causation and thereby paves the way for later theories that give priority to efficient causation. On his impact on later discussions, see Schmaltz (2014).

possesses certain fundamental features. In a nutshell, it *does* something. It is like an inner agent that arranges matter in a certain way and thereby turns it into a tree, a dog, or some other thing.[23]

It should be obvious by now that Suárez takes both matter and form to be things with actual existence. However, he points out that they are only incomplete things. He even goes so far as to call each of them an 'incomplete substance' (*DM* 13.4.8 and 15.5.1) and claims that together they make a 'complete substance' (*DM* 15.5.2). This clearly shows that he endorses the composition thesis. At the same time, he also endorses the independence thesis, for he holds that a form is really and not just conceptually distinct from matter (*DM* 7.1.1 and 15.2.1). This amounts to saying that it differs from it in extra-mental reality, not just in our thinking about it. Given this distinction, a form can exist without matter, for real distinction entails separability.[24] It is therefore not just the human form that can exist without matter. In principle, the form of a tree or a dog can also be separated from matter. Of course, this never happens as long as God does not intervene in nature and miraculously extracts a form.[25] But separability is a metaphysical possibility, even if it is never realized. The case of the human form that is separated from the body after death only shows what is in principle possible for every form.[26] Every form is a separable thing.

Now, the composition thesis gives rise to a crucial question: how exactly do form and matter as two incomplete things together make a complete thing? At first sight, one might think that they do that simply by co-existing. Thus, as soon as the form of a tree comes to exist in a piece of matter, these two things somehow merge and together make a tree—nothing else is required. If Suárez were taking this line, he would defend a reductionist position; that is, he would claim that a complete thing is nothing over and above the two incomplete things that co-exist. However, a closer look at his texts reveals that he does not hold this position.[27] He thinks that co-existence is only a necessary, but not a sufficient condition for the

---

[23] Hattab (2009: 64) aptly remarks that 'material substantial forms are re-conceived as internal active soul-like entities' and hence as active things. To be sure, they are not always cognitive things since they do not necessarily perceive or otherwise cognize the purpose of their action. Nevertheless, they are active things. In defending this view, Suárez contributes to a redefinition of substantial forms: they are conceived as concrete, causally active things, not as abstract principles. On this redefinition, which marks a difference with 13th-century definitions, see Pasnau (2004).

[24] It even entails mutual separability: if x is really distinct from y, then x can exist without y and y without x (*DM* 7.2.9). For a discussion of this rule and some exceptions to it, see Schmaltz (2020a: 34–40). Note that the exceptions only apply to special cases like the real distinction between God and creatures, but not to the real distinction between form and matter.

[25] According to the normal course of nature, the forms of plants and non-human animals are always 'educed' from matter and remain in matter (*DM* 13.3.13–15). By contrast, human forms are directly produced by God and somehow implanted in matter. So, there is a significant difference between non-human and human forms as far as their origin is concerned. But they do not differ as far as their status as separable things is concerned.

[26] Suárez adduces additional arguments to explain why separation is not just a possibility but a real fact in the case of the human soul; see South (2012).

[27] Schmaltz (2020a: 54–5) rightly emphasizes this point.

generation of a complete thing, and illustrates this point with a telling example (*DM* 13.8.9). Suppose the form of an angel came very close to some piece of matter and were even present in it. Would an angel with a body result from this co-existence of form and matter? Would there be a real unity? No, because there is no unity as long as the form simply exists in or with matter. For a real unity, the form has to be intimately connected with matter so that it can have an impact on it and structure it. This is why something more than co-existence is required. What could that be? Suárez is not at a loss for an answer: there needs to be a relation between form and matter. He calls this relation a 'mode of union' and describes it as 'some chain [*vinculum*] between form and matter' (*DM* 15.3.11).[28] This chain is naturally forged when form and matter come together, but it is not necessarily forged, as the case of the angel shows. There is such a chain only if (i) the form has the right kind of inner disposition to be united with matter (a disposition that is missing in the case of the angel), and (ii) God does not intervene in nature. But if these two conditions are fulfilled, a chain will naturally and even inevitably be forged. Form and matter will then be united.

It is important to note that the chain uniting form and matter is not a thing in the strict sense; that is, it is not something that has its own essence and existence. Consequently, it cannot exist on its own. Suárez holds that it is anchored in the form, emphasizing that it cannot exist apart from it (*DM* 7.1.26 and 13.9.13). It is like a special feature the form acquires as soon as its inner disposition to be unified with matter is actualized. Thanks to this feature, which could be called a relational feature, the form is then in fact united with the matter that is present. But this feature is not an independent thing. This is the main reason why Suárez calls it a mode (*modus*) and not a thing (*res*), for a thing can in principle exist by itself, even if it happens to exist in or with something else. By contrast, a mode can never exist by itself.[29] Not even God can separate it from the form in which it is present and keep it in existence.[30] Nevertheless, it is something real and not something we simply ascribe to the form because we conceive of it as being related to matter. The form is *really* related to matter because it has a mode as a *real* relational feature.

---

[28] See also *DM* 36.3, where Suárez dedicates an entire section to the description of this mode. He holds that there is just one mode in a complete substance, rejecting the view that there needs to be a mode in each of the two incomplete substances. For detailed analysis, see Anfray (2019) and Schmaltz (2020b).

[29] In his general characterization of modes, Suárez emphasizes that 'they are not sufficient to constitute a being or entity in reality, but they intrinsically require an entity which they actually affect and without which they cannot exist' (*DM* 7.1.18). This means that modes have the status of dependent entities.

[30] Of course, God can destroy the mode and thereby separate a form from matter. But he cannot detach the mode from a form and preserve it as a self-standing entity or transfer it to another form. This is the main reason why Suárez insists that a form and a mode are only modally and not really distinct from each other: there is no mutual separability (*DM* 7.1.16–20). On the modal distinction, see Schmaltz (2020a: 41–7).

It is at this point that Suárez' compositional account of substance becomes fully visible. He does not only break down a substance into two really distinct things, thereby reifying form and matter, but also claims that these two things need to be united. After all, either of them is an actually existing thing that can exist on its own. There needs to be something that connects them so that a complete substance emerges. This additional element is a special relational feature, a 'mode of union'. Hence, a substance has a complex inner structure: it consists of two things and a mode. And when analysing it, we need to refer to all three items. In fact, we cannot give a satisfactory metaphysical analysis of a material substance unless we somehow zoom into it and become aware that it is far from being a simple thing, even though it might appear simple. It is quite a complex thing, which can be dissolved into two things and a mode—not in nature, of course, where form and matter always stick together (provided God does not intervene), but in our analysis. We can mentally decompose what is essentially a composed thing.

3. Thin and Thick Substances

It has become clear so far that Suárez does indeed defend the two fundamental theses that Descartes ascribed to the scholastic proponents of hylomorphism. He subscribes to the composition thesis (a substance as a complete thing is composed of two incomplete things) and the independence thesis (the form as one of the two components can exist without matter as the other component). However, what results from the composition of form and matter is not yet a full-fledged material thing. This compound is only a 'thin substance', which is the bare minimum of a material thing, and ought to be distinguished from a 'thick substance', which is a much richer thing.[31] Take Peter, an individual human being, to illustrate this distinction. When we observe him in his daily activities, we realize that he is not just a form-matter compound. In addition to the two basic components, he has a number of capacities (e.g. the capacities to speak French and to play the guitar), and he displays a number of states (e.g. the state of actually being tanned). What makes him a full-fledged human being at a given moment is exactly the presence of a large amount of individual capacities and actual states. A comprehensive description of Peter should take them into account; that is, it should focus on the thick and not just the thin substance.

But what exactly is the thick substance? What is its inner structure, and how does it relate to the thin substance? Suárez is fully aware that these problems need to be addressed; otherwise, a metaphysical analysis would be dealing just with the

---

[31] I borrow this terminological distinction from Pasnau (2011: 99–102).

bare minimum of a substance. It is therefore not surprising that he attempts to give a detailed account of the capacities and actual states that can be found in a material thing, and he aims at showing how they relate to form and matter. Since he is mostly interested in the human being as the most complex material thing, I will focus on the way he analyses this kind of thick substance.

One might expect that he would start by focusing on the acquired capacities (e.g. the capacity to play the guitar) and the way they are related to the form-matter compound. However, this is not how he proceeds. He instead opens the analysis by examining the naturally given, non-acquired capacities that can be found in every human being. These are the three fundamental capacities or faculties which all Aristotelians ascribed to human beings: the vegetative, sensory, and rational faculties.[32] It is only by understanding the status of these faculties, Suárez assumes, that we can also understand the acquired capacities. This is why he first asks what kind of entities they are and how they are related to the form-matter compound.

At first sight, this way of opening the analysis of a thick substance looks like a non-starter. Why should we examine the fundamental faculties as special entities and ask how they are related to the two basic components? In particular, why should we ask how they are related to the form? After all, when we characterize the form of a human being, we usually say that it makes activities such as breathing, perceiving, and thinking possible; that is, we refer to the three fundamental faculties. It therefore hardly makes sense to set these faculties apart from the form and to ask how they are related to it. The form is simply a set of faculties that makes a wide variety of activities possible, and we can distinguish the human form from other forms by spelling out the faculties that are at stake. Thus, unlike the form of a dog, which consists just of vegetative and sensory faculties, the human form also comprises a rational faculty—the set of faculties is simply richer in the human case.

A number of scholastic philosophers argued along this line, claiming that it is misleading to draw a line between form and faculties and to conceive of the faculties as special entities that are somehow added to the form. They took the form to be identical with the faculties.[33] However, Suárez clearly rejects this widespread view. He states that 'it is required that there be a form that presides, as it were, over all the faculties and accidents and that is the source of all actions and natural movements' (*DM* 15.1.7). In making this claim, he unmistakably defends a distinction thesis: the form is distinct from the fundamental faculties (and also from the accidents that result from their actualization) and should therefore not

---

[32] Suárez presents and endorses this traditional classification in *De Anima* (*De An.*), disp. 2, q. 5 (vol. 1: 318–30).

[33] This identity theory was fully developed by William of Auvergne in the 13th century and defended by many later authors, among them William Ockham and John Buridan. For an overview, see King (2008) and Perler (2015).

be conflated with them.[34] As the quote makes clear, he even goes so far as to posit a hierarchical order, for he says that the form 'presides' over the faculties. Thus, the form of a human being is distinct from the vegetative, sensory, and rational faculties and rules over them.[35]

Why does Suárez defend the distinction thesis? His main reason has to do with the problem of unity. Suppose the form were just a set of faculties. Why then should all of them stick together and form a unity? Why shouldn't there be just a loose assemblage of three (or perhaps even more) distinct faculties—an assemblage that could easily be dissolved? As long as it is not clear how the faculties come together and stay together, their unity remains a mystery. It is precisely to solve this problem that Suárez appeals to the form as something that 'presides' over the faculties and holds them together. On his view, the soul must be a separate entity that unifies all the faculties and guarantees that they stay together, both at a given moment and over time. Consequently, he distinguishes two types of entities when talking about the soul: the soul itself as the unifying entity and the faculties as the unified entities.

This is quite an astonishing thesis that shows to what extent Suárez is parting ways with Aristotle. It is well known that Aristotle repeatedly referred to faculties of the soul, assigning different tasks to them. But he never took them to be entities that are distinct from the soul itself and unified by it. He rather considered them to be parts of the soul and assumed that all the parts together form a whole.[36] It is at this point that Suárez transforms the original Aristotelian theory by interpreting the part-whole relationship as a relationship between really distinct entities. Moreover, he takes these entities to be hierarchically ordered: the faculties as the unified entities are subordinated to the soul as the unifying entity.

But it is not just the unity problem that motivates Suárez to posit a hierarchical order. He adduces a number of additional arguments to corroborate his claim that the soul as the 'presiding' entity needs to be distinguished from the faculties. Let me focus on two of them (*DM* 18.5.2–3).[37] First, Suárez refers to the phenomenon of attention. In a normal situation, he remarks, we receive sensory inputs from many things that are present to us. This is a well-known phenomenon that can easily be illustrated. For instance, when you are sitting in a garden, you receive visual and other inputs not just from the trees around you, but also from the grass, from the flowers, and from many other things. Why then do you look at the trees

---

[34] Suárez defends this claim both in *DM* and *De An*. For a comprehensive analysis, see Heider (2021: 51–8).

[35] Note, however, that the form must have a basic power that is *not* distinct from it, namely the power to rule over the faculties. Suárez does not intend to set apart the soul from all powers, but to distinguish between powers that belong to the essence of the soul (e.g. the ruling power) and powers or faculties that do not belong to it.

[36] See, for instance, *De Anima* I.1 (402b9–11) and II.2 (413b13–16). For detailed discussions of these crucial passages, see Corcilius and Gregoric (2010); Johansen (2014).

[37] For an analysis of all his arguments, see Rozemond (2012: 162–4) and Perler (2015: 131–3).

and not at other things? There is nothing in your sensory faculty that makes you look just at the trees, for this faculty is purely passive (it simply receives sensory inputs), and it is equally affected by all the objects that are present to you. Therefore, there must be something else that is responsible for the fact that you steer your attention to the trees and nothing else. This is exactly the soul that 'presides' over the faculties: it guides your sensory faculty so that it will be directed towards the tree and nothing else, thereby giving rise to a perception of the trees and nothing else. Hence, there must be a clear difference between the soul as the steering entity and the faculty that is being steered by it.

Second, Suárez mentions the phenomenon of coordination. It seems quite natural that we do not have a random mixture of perceptions and thoughts at a given moment. Our cognitive activities are rather well coordinated. For instance, when you first look at the trees, your perception will most likely be followed by a thought about the trees and not by any other thought; that is, when seeing their colour, you will most likely think that they look beautiful. Why does this thought and not some other thought follow your perception? There must be something that coordinates the sensory and the intellectual faculty so that their activities go along with each other. This is true not just for these two faculties. According to Suárez, there must be a perfect connection or 'harmony' (*consonantia*) among all the faculties so that all of them are well coordinated in their activities (*DM* 18.5.3).[38] Now, there must be something that coordinates them, for each faculty is only responsible for its own activities. This coordinating entity is the soul, which has a supervising function: it makes the faculties work together and produce activities that fit each other. Here again, it is important to have an entity that is distinct from the faculties and 'presides' over them, for it is only with such a supervising entity that one can have a well-coordinated unity of activities.

These two arguments in favour of the distinction thesis are, of course, far from being self-evident. One could immediately make the objection that a person can very well pay attention to an object without having a special inner entity that guides her sensory faculty. After all, the strength or intensity of the sensory input could be responsible for the fact that she focuses on a certain object and produces a perception of that object and nothing else. Moreover, it does not seem necessary for well-coordinated activities to have a supervising entity. After all, there could be something built into the structure of the faculties that makes them produce activities in a well-coordinated way.[39] But what matters here is less the cogency

---

[38] See also *De An.* disp. 2, q. 5 (vol. 1: 328) and an analysis in Knuuttila (2014). Note, however, that coordination does not require interaction. Suárez insists that faculties do not literally act upon each other. The activity of a faculty can only be an 'occasion' for the corresponding activity of another faculty. On this model of occasional causation, see Perler (2020b).

[39] Aquinas assumes that there is a teleological structure built into them so that, for instance, the sensory faculty produces activities for the sake of the functioning of the intellectual faculty. On his view, no supervising entity is required. See *Summa Theologiae* I, q. 77, art. 4.

of the arguments than their general thrust. Suárez thinks that there is a need for distinguishing the faculties from the soul itself and for positing a hierarchical order between them because he assumes that there are certain functions—guiding and coordinating—that cannot be exercised by any faculty. On his view, it is only the soul as a special entity that can exercise them, for it is only this entity that has a special regulating power. Consequently, he sets the soul as the coordinating entity apart from the faculties as the coordinated entities.

But how exactly do all the faculties come into existence? It is in his response to this question that one sees how Suárez further develops his compositional model. He claims that there is a causal relation between the soul and the faculties, for 'the soul has an efficacy with respect to its faculties, which are really distinct from it. Therefore, as the soul is God's effect, so a faculty is a new effect produced by the soul. But where there is a new effect, there is also a new action' (*De An.* disp. 3, q. 3; vol. 3: 124–5). It is quite remarkable that Suárez draws a parallel between God and the soul. Just as God produces the creatures, which are fully dependent on but nevertheless distinct from him, so the soul produces the faculties, which are fully dependent on but nevertheless distinct from it. This amounts to saying that a relation of *efficient* causation obtains between the soul and its faculties: the soul literally produces the faculties, which are then subordinated to it.[40] This production happens naturally and effortlessly, but it need not happen. God could intervene at any time and prevent the soul from producing the faculties.[41] The soul would then still have the force to produce the faculties, but nothing would come out of it. So, there is at best a physical necessity, but not a metaphysical necessity for the production of the faculties. In principle, there could be just the 'naked soul' without any faculties coming out of it. To be sure, this does not happen in the normal course of nature. But it *can* happen. Given this possibility, the faculties must be special products that are to be distinguished from the producing soul.

It is at this point that it becomes clear how Suárez understands the composition of a human being. He first posits form and matter as the two core components, which make together a thin substance, and then introduces more components. On his view, the thin substance is somehow enriched by a number of faculties, which are additional entities that are naturally (but not necessarily) caused by the form. The faculties then cause activities such as breathing, perceiving, and thinking, which are further entities. In fact, all the activities are distinct things (*res*) that are produced at a given moment and therefore need to have a cause.[42] This means that

---

[40] Suárez repeatedly says that the faculties flow out (*fluunt*) from the soul; see *De An.* disp. 3, q. 3 (vol. II: 116–26). He thereby turns the mereological relation into a causal relation; for details, see Shields (2014).
[41] Suárez explicitly mentions this possibility in *De An.* disp. 3. q. 3 (vol. III: 130).
[42] Suárez spells this out for the cognitive activities, which are literally produced by the rational faculty; see *De An.* disp. 5, q. 4 (vol. II: 350–68) and an analysis in Heider (2019).

there are two levels of causes inside a human being. At the fundamental level there is the soul, which causes all the faculties, keeps them in existence and coordinates them. At a higher level there are the faculties, which cause specific activities. When describing a human being, we need to refer to both levels.

The faculties can be found in all human beings, no matter how much they differ from each other. It is clear, however, that there are also individual capacities that cannot be found in all human beings, for instance the capacity to speak French or the capacity to play the guitar. How are these capacities related to the form-matter compound and to the fundamental faculties? Suárez clearly sees that this problem needs to be addressed, for it is only when taking individual capacities into account that one can give a detailed description of a particular human being and distinguish him or her from other human beings.

Like most of his predecessors, Suárez considers individual capacities to be habits (*habitus*) that are acquired over time through the repeated exercise of a certain type of activity.[43] Thus, a person who repeatedly plays the guitar acquires a certain habit; and a person who repeatedly speaks French acquires another habit. The most prominent habits are the virtues that are acquired through the repeated exercise of moral activities. Thus, a person who repeatedly acts in a just way acquires the virtue of justice: she gradually becomes a just person. But the crucial point is that, metaphysically speaking, it is not just a virtue that is a habit. Every acquired capacity, whether it is of moral significance or not, is a habit. And every habit is based on the repeated exercise of activities. In fact, the activities are the causes that produce a habit as a 'persistent quality' that has 'stable existence in a subject' (DM 44.1.6). This amounts to saying that a habit persists once it has been acquired—it is so deeply entrenched in a person that it will not easily be lost. And as long as it persists it gives rise to the same type of activities that caused it. Thus, the habit to speak French will give rise to acts of speaking French, and it can be strengthened over time: the more often a person speaks French, the stronger her habit will become.

Two points are significant about this characterization of a habit. First, it is quite striking that Suárez takes it to be a special entity. He even assigns it to a special category of entities by calling it a quality; this is one of the accidental entities.[44] Thus, a person who learns French acquires a certain quality, and if this person also learns to play the guitar, she acquires another quality. The more habits she acquires, the more qualities she will have. According to Suárez' overall theory of categories, qualities are real entities or things (*res*) that are distinct from other

---

[43] He discusses them at length in *DM* 44. For an analysis of their metaphysical status, see Perler (2018).

[44] He thereby follows Aristotle who mentions habits as the first type of qualities; see *Cat.* 8 (8b27–9a12).

entities.[45] This means, of course, that the thin substance of a person is not just enriched by the faculties. It is even more enriched by the acquired habits. A person will then have a rich package of things: form and matter as the two fundamental things, faculties as additional things, and habits as things on top of that. To be sure, these items belong to different categories of things. Only form and matter are incomplete substances (see section 2), whereas faculties and habits are qualities; and only faculties are naturally given qualities, whereas habits are acquired qualities. Nevertheless, all of them are real things, distinct from each other, and all of them are required for an activity such as speaking French or playing the guitar. It is therefore important to look at a network of things when analysing a person, for it is this network that distinguishes her from other persons and makes her a special person who can bring about specific activities.

The second point to be noted is that all the things that make a person the very person she is are inner causes. Or to be more precise, they are all *efficient* causes. As has become clear, the form efficiently causes faculties, which in turn efficiently cause activities. And if some activities repeatedly occur, they efficiently cause a habit, which then efficiently causes more activities. Of course, a habit cannot do that by itself but needs to cooperate with one or more faculties. Suárez remarks that it is not an autonomous cause. It is rather a cause that acts 'by supporting and facilitating' the faculties (*DM* 44.1.6). Thus, the habit to speak French does not produce the utterance of French sentences by itself. It rather cooperates with the rational faculty, which makes thinking in general possible, and with the sensory faculty, which makes speaking possible. Should these two faculties be destroyed (or miraculously removed), the habit could no longer be productive. But in the normal course of nature it is an active cause, and it remains productive as long as it cooperates with the rational and the sensory faculty.

Given this causal function, it is important to look at the place that each and every habit occupies in a complex network of causes. The better we see what kind of activities caused it, the better we will understand what kind of activities it will cause in turn. And the better we realize how it cooperates with one or more faculties, the better we will understand the way it functions. In any case, we always need to pay attention to causal relations *inside* a human being, for it is always the complex interaction of many inner causes that makes activities possible. This is important not just for an understanding of successful activities. It is equally important for an understanding of failed or missing activities. Suppose a person who was a competent French speaker has forgotten her French. Why does she then no longer speak French? If we follow Suárez, we need to say that this person

---

[45] When describing different types of qualities, Suárez explicitly holds that habits are real entities (*DM* 42.3.4), stressing that they cannot be reduced to or identified with other entities.

has lost a particular habit as one of her inner causes.[46] Since this cause is missing, the effect is also missing; and it is exactly this cause that needs to be brought back in full strength so that it can be used again in cooperation with other causes, above all the rational faculty. Only then will the activity of speaking French become possible again. In a nutshell, the inner causal mechanism needs to be repaired.

I hope this example makes clear how Suárez conceives of a full-fledged human being as a thick substance. Unlike God, who is a simple substance, a human being is a rather complex substance that consists of many things. Each of them is an efficient cause, and they all work together to produce a wide variety of activities. On Suárez' view, we cannot gain an understanding of various types of activities unless we examine their relevant causes and their connections. We always need to ask what kind of form is at stake and which faculties and habits are rooted in that form. It is only when proceeding in this way that we come to understand the full structure of a thick substance.

4. Conclusion

I opened this chapter by pointing out that Descartes interpreted hylomorphism as a metaphysical theory that takes a material substance to be composed of two things, form and matter, which can but need not be united. I hope it has become clear that Suárez did indeed conceive of hylomorphism in this way, thereby endorsing the composition thesis. He even went a step further by claiming that not only form and matter are things, but faculties and habits as well—all of them together make a particular substance the very substance it is. In fact, a substance is nothing but a composition of many things.[47] On Suárez' view, a comprehensive metaphysical theory has to spell out what these things are and how they are interconnected.

It is quite obvious that this conception of hylomorphism is far away from the original conception. To use Wittgenstein's famous expression, one could say that there is at best a family resemblance between Aristotle's and Suárez' hylomorphism—a resemblance between rather distant family members. Suárez turns Aristotle's principles into things, and he sees a complex network of really

---

[46] It is also possible that the habit is not completely lost but reduced in its power. Suárez explicitly refers to the possibility of decreasing (or increasing) a habit, thereby making clear that a habit can come in degrees (*DM* 44.10–11).

[47] He is of course not the first to present this view. Duns Scotus and Ockham already conceived of substances as complex things that are composed of other things. They took them to be 'complex functional packages' (Adams 2022: 6), thereby breaking with an earlier tradition that considered substances to be the most fundamental things. But Suárez goes beyond these earlier authors by taking all features, including matter, and all faculties and capacities, to be really (and not just conceptually) distinct things. Or for short, all features are turned into things.

distinct items where Aristotle refers just to parts of a whole.[48] How are we to understand this change when we look at the development of Aristotelianism in the late medieval period? It is tempting to speak about a distortion and to tell a story of decline.[49] This decline, one could say, started shortly after Aquinas when matter was no longer seen as something with potential existence but rather was conceived as a real thing with actual existence. The decline then continued with authors like Ockham, who took the qualities added to a form-matter compound to be real things, and culminated in Suárez, who took all the features of a substance, including natural faculties and acquired capacities, to be real things. Hylomorphism then collapsed, because it became impossible to explain the unity of all these things: a single substance was dissolved into a multitude of things.

Tempting as this story of decline is, it is hardly convincing because it neglects an important point. When discussing and defending the composition thesis, Suárez does not ignore the unity problem. On the contrary, he is fully aware that a satisfactory metaphysical theory has to explain why a substance is more than an assemblage of things. He provides this explanation by referring to special relations that obtain between the things inside a substance. As has been pointed out (see section 2), he claims that there is a special 'mode of union' between form and matter—a mode that is naturally built into them and cannot be found in other things.[50] And when introducing faculties and habits as entities, he makes clear that they are qualities that inhere in the form.[51] It is precisely the inherence relation that guarantees that they are intimately connected with the form and not just attached to it. The faculties even have to inhere in the form as long as the natural order is maintained. It would therefore be misleading to compare a substance to a flock of sheep or to some other assemblage of things. Unlike the sheep, the things that together make a substance are not complete entities that simply happen to co-exist with other complete entities. They are rather incomplete entities that exist with or in other incomplete entities. Hence, a material substance is not just an assemblage of things: it is a complex thing but nevertheless *one* thing.

---

[48] The crucial point is that Suárez takes the parts to be really distinct and hence really separable, whereas Aristotle speaks about parts that are separable in definition only. For Aristotle, parts are nothing but 'elements in the definition of the different kinds of soul', as Johansen (2014: 51) aptly remarks. It is the move from separability in definition to real separability that makes Suárez' theory quite radical.

[49] Interpreters who take Aquinas as their point of reference tend to tell this story. For an exposition and critical discussion of this view, see Heider (2008).

[50] It is because of this mode that there is an essential unity (*unio per se*) and not just an accidental unity between form and matter (*DM* 4.3.8). These two components are naturally designed to be united and to stay united as long as there is no external intervention. For an analysis of this type of unity, see Perler (2020a) and Schmaltz (2020b).

[51] In fact, all the qualities of a substance inhere either in form or in matter. Inherence is a special relation, which Suárez also characterizes as a mode (*DM* 7.1.17–18). Unlike the mode that unifies form and matter, it is only an accidental mode, since it applies to one of the accidental entities. Nevertheless, it is a relation that ties an entity to the underlying form or matter.

Given this emphasis on the unity of a material substance, it would be wrong to accuse Suárez of dissolving a substance into a multitude of things. However, it is undeniable that he deeply transforms the original Aristotelian theory by claiming that there are many things—even really distinct things—inside a material substance. What is his motivation for this transformation? Unfortunately he is not explicit, but when looking at his broader metaphysical framework one can detect at least two main motivations for his tendency to reify not just form and matter, but also other features of a substance.[52]

The first motivation has to do with the problem of functional complexity. Suárez starts with the simple observation that a substance is not just an inert piece of matter, but an active thing that can do many things: it can exercise different functions and engage in different activities. A human substance in particular can engage in many activities, ranging from breathing to perceiving and thinking. Some of these activities (e.g. breathing) can be found in all human substances, whereas others (e.g. playing the guitar) are distinctive of a particular substance. Now, all these activities need to have a cause; it would be absurd to assume that they arise *ex nihilo*. And different types of activities need to have different types of causes; it would be implausible to assume that there is one single cause that miraculously produces different activities. It is therefore important to look for the adequate cause for each type of activity. This is why one should first identify various causes and then draw a map that shows how they are interconnected. But one should not stop here. It is also important to explain why all the causes are in fact interconnected. And to provide this explanation, one needs to point to something that unifies and coordinates them in their production of activities. Or for short, one needs to indicate the cause of all the causes. It is only when proceeding in this way that it is possible not just to observe functional complexity, but also to give an account of it.

When looking at this first motivation, it becomes possible to understand why Suárez assumes that there is a network of causes inside a substance. But why does he take these causes to be things? To find an answer to this question, we need to look at his second motivation for reinterpreting hylomorphism. It is deeply rooted in his general conception of a cause. Criticizing earlier Aristotelians, he holds that it is not enough to mention four different types of causes and to describe them. It is also necessary to explain what makes each of them a cause in the first place. This is why he starts his analysis by characterizing a cause in general, and calls it something that 'pours being' into something else

---

[52] I confine myself to mentioning two philosophical motivations. There are also theological motivations (e.g. the attempt to explain theological puzzles like divine creation or transubstantiation). Schmid (2015: 118–21) rightly emphasizes that it would be inadequate to see Suárez as a thinker who separated philosophy from theology and looked at metaphysical issues from a purely philosophical point of view. Nevertheless, there are philosophical motivations for his transformation of hylomorphism—motivations that can be understood apart from his other motivations.

(see section 2). He then provides a detailed description of every cause—be it formal, material, efficient, or final—and spells out how it does in fact give being to something else. As has become clear, even a formal cause must somehow give being to something else by endowing it with an essence. Of course, this kind of acting differs from that of an efficient cause, which produces something, or from that of a final cause, which presents the goal of an action and thereby attracts an agent. But no matter how it acts, every cause acts. A cause is therefore not just an explanatory principle, and presenting a cause does not simply amount to providing an explanation. Or, to use a well-known slogan: a cause is not just 'a because'. A cause is rather an active thing—a thing that literally *does* something.[53]

Given this characterization of a cause, it is not surprising that Suárez takes not only the fundamental form, but also the faculties and the habits to be things. In fact, they must be things, for otherwise they could not function as causes and give rise to a rich variety of activities. For Suárez it would hardly make sense to just call them explanatory principles. Admittedly, they do play an explanatory role, for they make intelligible why all the activities arise. But they play this role only insofar as they are active things; that is, they explain something in virtue of really doing something. It is therefore indispensable to understand the network of inner causes as a complex combination of acting things.

I hope this way of looking at Suárez' understanding of a cause as his source of motivation for transforming hylomorphism makes clear that he does not simply misinterpret the Aristotelian theory. He deliberately reinterprets it by presenting it as a theory that aims at giving an account of the causes inside a material thing. In other words, he turns the theory of substance into a theory of inner causes. In doing that, he paves the way for new, non-Aristotelian theories. In particular, he prepares the ground for theories that look at a material thing as something complex that can be broken down into its parts. These parts are all powerful, and they all interact as efficient causes—perhaps even in a mechanical way so that one can establish a plan that indicates the role each part plays in a large mechanism.[54] Explaining a material thing then amounts to spelling out its inner mechanism. And the better one understands its mechanism, the better one can build it. In fact, one cannot really understand a thing unless one is able to build it.

---

[53] In his pioneering study, Frede (1987) pointed out that this conception of a cause was already present in antiquity. He referred to the Stoics who were motivated by the problem of responsibility. On their view, a cause must be an active thing that can be taken as responsible for what it does. As far as I can see, Suárez is not so much motivated by this problem (or influenced by the Stoic tradition). Of course, he builds his theory of responsibility on a conception of intellect and will as inner causes that produce an action and can be taken as responsible for what they do (see *DM* 19.2–9). But his account of these special causes is an application of his general theory of causation. He is mostly concerned with the core meaning of the notion of cause.

[54] To be sure, Suárez does not make the strong claim that all the causes are nothing but efficient causes. As has become clear, he makes room for all the four Aristotelian causes; for a full account, see Fink (2015). But he sketches a mechanistic idea by explaining a substance as a network of inner causes that act in the manner of efficient causes.

Reverse engineering is then the paradigmatic way of gaining understanding: one comes to know what a material thing is by decomposing it into its parts and reconstructing it. It is only when proceeding in this way that one really understands what all the parts are, how they act as inner causes, and how they contribute to the functioning of the whole. In a nutshell, knowing what a thing is amounts to knowing how to make it.

Admittedly, Suárez is still far away from this epistemic ideal, which became quite prominent in the modern period. He is also still far away from presenting a mechanistic picture of a material thing. After all, he insists that some parts of a material thing—above all the substantial form—are immaterial; hence they cannot be reduced to parts of a machine. Nevertheless, he does conceive of a material thing as a composition of smaller things, and he considers them to be efficient causes that are well coordinated. Knowing what a thing is amounts to understanding what all these things are, what they produce, and how they are interrelated. And the best way of gaining this understanding is by decomposing a material thing and recomposing it out of its parts. Of course, we cannot do that by literally taking it apart and putting all the parts together. But when doing metaphysics, we can proceed in this way at a mental level. We can then decompose a material thing in our thoughts and show what its components are, how they function, and how they must be combined. Doing metaphysics is then a way of doing reverse engineering.

To be sure, Suárez never presented his metaphysical analysis of a material thing as an exercise in reverse engineering. But in providing a compositional account and focusing on the causal role of all the components, he contributed to the emergence of a new way of doing metaphysics.[55]

Bibliography

Adams, McCord M. (1987), *William Ockham* (Notre Dame: Notre Dame University Press).

Adams McCord, M. (2022), *Housing the Powers: Medieval Debates about Dependence on God* (Oxford: Oxford University Press).

Akerlund, E. (2015), 'Material Causality—Dissolving a Paradox: The Actuality of Prime Matter in Suárez', in J.L. Fink (ed.), *Suárez on Aristotelian Causality* (Leiden: Brill), 43–64.

---

[55] Earlier versions of this chapter were presented at Yale University, Humboldt-Universität, and the Medieval Philosophy Network in London. I am grateful to the audience in all three places for inspiring questions, and I am indebted to Simona Aimar, David Charles, Reier Helle, Paolo Rubini, Stephan Schmid, and Gabriel Watts for detailed written comments.

Anfray, J.-P. (2019), 'A Jesuit Debate about the Modes of Union: Francisco Suárez vs. Pedro Hurtado de Mendoza', *American Catholic Philosophical Quarterly* 93: 309–34.

Aquinas, Thomas (1950), *De Principiis Naturae*, ed. J.J. Pauson (Fribourg and Louvain: Société philosophique and Édition Nauwelaerts).

Aquinas, Thomas (1952), *Summa Theologiae*, ed. P. Caramello (Turin and Rome: Marietti).

Ariew, Roger (2011), *Descartes among the Scholastics* (Leiden: Brill).

Aristotle (1956), *De Anima*, ed. W.D. Ross (Oxford: Clarendon).

Aristotle (2016), *De Anima*, trans., intro., and comm. Ch. Shields (Oxford: Clarendon).

Brower, J.E. (2014), *Aquinas's Ontology of the Material World: Change, Hylomorphism, & Material Objects* (Oxford: Oxford University Press).

Charles, D. (2021), *The Undivided Self: Aristotle and the 'Mind-Body' Problem* (Oxford: Oxford University Press).

Corcilius, K. and Gregoric, P. (2010), 'Separability vs. Difference: Parts and Capacities of the Soul in Aristotle', *Oxford Studies in Ancient Philosophy* 39: 81–120.

Courtenay, W. J. (1985), 'The Dialectic of Omnipotence in the High and Late Middle Ages', in T. Rudavsky (Ed.), *Divine Omniscience and Omnipotence in Medieval Philosophy* (Dordrecht: Reidel), 243–69.

Des Chene, D. (1996), *Physiologia. Natural Philosophy in Late Aristotelian and Cartesian Thought* (Ithaca and London: Cornell University Press).

Descartes, R. (1982–91), *Oeuvres*, ed. Ch. Adam and P. Tannery (= AT) (Paris: Vrin).

Descartes, R. (1984–91), *The Philosophical Writings*, ed. J. Cottingham, R. Stoothoff, D. Murdoch, and A. Kenny (= CSMK) (Cambridge: Cambridge University Press).

Fink, J.L., ed. (2015), *Suárez on Aristotelian Causality* (Leiden: Brill).

Freddoso, A.J. (2002), 'Introduction', in F. Suárez, *On Creation, Conservation, and Concurrence. Metaphysical Disputations 20–22* (South Bend: St. Augustine's Press), xi–cxxiii.

Frede, M. (1987), 'The Original Notion of Cause', *Essays in Ancient Philosophy* (Minneapolis: University of Minnesota Press), 125–50.

Garber, D. (1992), *Descartes' Metaphysical Physics* (Chicago: Chicago University Press).

Hattab, H. (2009), *Descartes on Forms and Mechanisms* (Cambridge: Cambridge University Press).

Hattab, H. (2011), 'Suárez and Descartes: *A Priori* Arguments against Substantial Forms and the Decline of the Formal Cause', *Studia Neoaristotelica* 8: 143–62.

Hattab, H. (2017), 'The Metaphysics of Substantial Forms', in B. Hill and H. Lagerlund (eds.), *The Routledge Companion to Sixteenth Century Philosophy* (London and New York: Routledge), 436–57.

Heider, D. (2008), 'Suárez on Material Substance: Reification of Intrinsic Principles and the Unity of Material Composites', *Organon F* 15: 423–38.

Heider, D. (2019), 'Suárez's Metaphysics of Cognitive Acts', in R.A. Maryks and J.A. Senent de Frutos (eds.), *Francisco Suárez (1548-1617): Jesuits and the Complexities of Modernity* (Leiden: Brill), 23-45.

Heider, D. (2021), *Aristotelian Subjectivism: Francisco Suárez's Philosophy of Perception* (New York: Springer).

Johansen, Th. K. (2014), 'Parts in Aristotle's Definition of Soul: *De Anima* Books I and II', in K. Corcilius and D. Perler (eds.), *Partitioning the Soul: Debates from Plato to Leibniz* (Berlin: De Gruyter), 39-61.

King, P. (2008), 'The Inner Cathedral: Mental Architecture in High Scholasticism', *Vivarium* 46: 253-74.

Knuuttila, S. (2014), 'The Connexions between Vital Acts in Suárez's Psychology', in L. Novák (ed.), *Suárez's Metaphysics in Its Historical and Systematic Context* (Berlin: De Gruyter), 259-74.

Pasnau, R. (2002), *Thomas Aquinas on Human Nature: A Philosophical Study of Summa Theologiae Ia 75-89* (Cambridge: Cambridge University Press).

Pasnau, R. (2004), 'Form, Substance, and Mechanism', *The Philosophical Review* 113: 31-88.

Pasnau, R. (2011), *Metaphysical Themes 1274-1671* (Oxford: Clarendon Press).

Perler, D. (2015), 'Faculties in Medieval Philosophy', in id. (ed.), *The Faculties: A History* (Oxford: Oxford University Press), 97-139.

Perler, D. (2018), 'Suárez on the Metaphysics of Habits', in N. Faucher and M. Roques (eds.), *The Ontology, Psychology and Axiology of Habits (Habitus) in Medieval Philosophy* (New York: Springer), 365-84.

Perler, D. (2020a), 'Suárez on the Unity of Material Substances', *Vivarium* 58: 143-67.

Perler, D. (2020b), 'Suárez on Intellectual Cognition and Occasional Causation', in D. Perler and S. Bender (eds.), *Causation and Cognition in Early Modern Philosophy* (London and New York: Routledge), 18-38.

Richardson, K. (2015), 'Formal Causality: Giving Being by Constituting and Completing', in J.L. Fink (ed.), *Suárez on Aristotelian Causality* (Leiden: Brill), 65-84.

Rozemond, M. (2012), 'Unity in the Multiplicity of Suárez's Soul', in B. Hill and H. Lagerlund (eds.), *The Philosophy of Francisco Suárez* (Oxford: Oxford University Press), 154-72.

Schmaltz, T.M. (2014), 'Efficient Causation: From Suárez to Descartes', in id. (ed.), *Efficient Causation: A History* (Oxford: Oxford University Press), 139-64.

Schmaltz, T.M. (2020a), *The Metaphysics of the Material World: Suárez, Descartes, Spinoza* (Oxford: Oxford University Press).

Schmaltz, T.M. (2020b), 'Suárez and Descartes on the Mode(s) of Union', *Journal of the History of Philosophy* 58: 471-92.

Schmid, S. (2015), 'Efficient Causality: The Metaphysics of Production', in J.L. Fink (ed.), *Suárez on Aristotelian Causality* (Leiden: Brill), 85-121.

Shields, Ch. (2012), 'The Reality of Substantial Form: Suárez, *Metaphysical Disputations* xv', in D. Schwartz (ed.), *Interpreting Suárez* (Cambridge: Cambridge University Press), 39–61.

Shields, Ch. (2014), 'Virtual Presence: Psychic Mereology in Francisco Suárez', in K. Corcilius and D. Perler (eds.), *Partitioning the Soul: Debates from Plato to Leibniz* (Berlin: De Gruyter), 199–218.

South, J.B. (2012), 'Suárez, Immortality, and the Soul's Dependence on the Body', in B. Hill and H. Lagerlund (eds.), *The Philosophy of Francisco Suárez* (Oxford: Oxford University Press), 121–36.

Suárez, F. (1861), *Disputationes Metaphysicae*, in C. Berton (ed.), *Opera Omnia*, vols. 25–6 (Paris: Vivès).

Suárez, F. (1978–91), *De Anima*, ed. S. Castellote (Madrid: Xavier Zubrini and Editorial Labor).

Tuttle, J. (2016), 'Suárez's Non-Reductive Theory of Efficient Causation', *Oxford Studies in Medieval Philosophy* 4: 125–58.

16
Descartes' Mind-Body Holism and the Primacy of Experience

Lilli Alanen

0. Introduction

Descartes famously rejected final causes with form and matter as general principles of explanation in philosophy of nature. He introduced a radical dualist ontology to ground his new mechanistic philosophy of nature without threatening traditional views of mind and morality. Among these was the doctrine of human being as a unity of mind and matter that captures important aspects of our experience, and was granted by Descartes in some form all along. In confronting objections to his dualism he fell back on hylomorphic language, arguing that mind and body although complete substances in themselves are incomplete with respect to the human being they compose through a real or substantial union, describing the mind (the rational soul) as a substantial form and as informing the body.

This chapter examines Descartes' use of and entitlement to hylomorphic language, and reflects on the tensions that his view of human nature creates for his dualism. Recent discussions of Descartes' relation to hylomorphism have sensibly focused on its late medieval scholastic versions. Both the concepts of soul or mind and those of matter had changed enough over centuries of discussions to adjust hylomorphism to Christian doctrine, and the concept of matter to scientific discoveries and practice, so that the step from the doctrines discussed by the later scholastics to Descartes' would seem less of a leap and more of a continuum than earlier thought.[1] I will not trace that development here but examine some crucial texts in the light of recent interpretations which take Descartes' holistic view of the mind-body union seriously while at the same time trying to save his dualist commitments.

The first section summarizes the reading of Aristotle's hylomorphism and psychology that I use as my point of reference in discussing Descartes' debt to and adoption of elements of this doctrine. The second and third section review his mind-matter distinction and mechanistic account of the human body which seem to exclude any adaptation of strong hylomorphism, leaving us with the choice

---

[1] See, e.g., Hoffman (1986, 1999, 2008); Baker and Morris (1996); Rozemond (1998); Des Chene (2000); Brown and Normore (2003, 2019); Schmaltz (2020a).

between accepting substance dualism without a coherent view of human nature, or accepting a strong form of mind-body holism with deflated notions both of substance and dualism. The reading I pursue is along the lines of the latter, but it comes with worries concerning both the nature of Descartes' dualism and the traces of hylomorphism in his doctrine. Sections 4–5 examines the most consistent recent attempt to defend the attribution of hylomorphism to Descartes without jeopardizing his dualism and its textual evidence. Descartes, I argue, has no metaphysical solution to his problem with strong mind-body unity but points instead to incontrovertible experience of it. The last sections discuss the primacy and nature of the experience Descartes appeals to as a basis for our understanding of the unity of human nature and explores its implications for Descartes' dualistic psychology.

1. Form, Matter, and the Inseparability of Soul and Body in Aristotelian Hylomorphism

A living human being, arguably, is a paradigm for an individual corruptible substance in one traditional use of this controversial term: a determinate, living thing composed of form and matter. As the highest kind of animal, humans are endowed with three kinds of vital principles, souls, or form: the *nutritive soul* or plant soul whereby we live, the *animal soul* or *sensitive soul* whereby we move and perceive, and the *rational soul* whereby we know and think. These are integrated with each other in the human animal and ordered so that the functioning of the highest principle presupposes the two lower ones. Aristotle famously characterizes the soul as the (first) actuality of a natural body having life potentially in it. The soul is the form or actuality of the animal body corresponding to sight for the eye. The visual organ with the sight constitutes the (living) eye.

(1) Suppose that the eye were an animal-sight would have been its soul, for sight is the substance of the eye which corresponds to the account, the eye being merely the matter of seeing, when seeing is removed the eye is no longer an eye, except in name—no more than the eye of a statue or of a painted figure.

De An. 412b18–21

What the sight is to the eye, the faculty of sense is to the animal, and the faculty of thought to the human animal. Likewise the soul *plus* the body constitutes the animal, so 'that the soul is inseparable from its body, or at any rate that certain parts of it are' (*De An.* 412b17–413a3).[2]

---

[2] See also *De An.* 412a25–7: '[W]hile waking is actuality in the sense corresponding to sight and the power in a tool; the body corresponds to what is in potentiality: as the pupil *plus* the power of sight constitutes the eye, so the soul plus the body constitutes the animal'.

Form is the *actuality* (or *essence*), *matter* the *potentiality*, and the complex of the two, form and matter, constitute the individual *substance*, here the living human being, and are inseparable.[3] Being the actuality of a body possessing the required capacities or powers potentially, the soul can neither be defined nor exist in separation from the body. As the actuality of the body it exists only as the body lives and acts. This view grounds Aristotle's account of virtue and the highest good, of how the exercise of reason is as it were its own reward: it is an exercise of our highest capacity, which when it is done well, is the fulfilment or completion of our function, so our highest good. It also grounds his psychology and theory of emotions, to which, as I will argue in the last section of this chapter, Descartes' account of the passions of the soul comes surprisingly close.

How to interpret Aristotle's own hylomorphism is a matter of controversy and subject to debate along two dimensions of relevance here. They have to do with whether form and matter of human beings are inseparable in definition or only in existence and whether they are mutually inseparable.[4] The hylomorphism that I will take as my point of contrast is a strong version of hylomorphism in which the form in question is inseparable in definition from matter and the matter in question is inseparable in definition from the form. The strong version of hylomorphism is an appealing doctrine in itself which holds that most affections of the soul can be described as 'inextricably psychophysical', so as to be non-decomposable into separate types of activity.[5] It also represents the clearest contrast to Descartes' doctrine where the soul or mind in general is defined in terms of thinking without reference to matter and the matter in terms of extension without reference to soul, and where both are seen as mutually separable.

2. Cartesian Dualism of Mind and Matter

Let us now look at Descartes' dualistic doctrine and its implications for his account of human nature, which according to some commentators means the end of anthropology (Voss 1994). Descartes defines matter in terms of extension

---

[3] When the human body is destroyed, so is the soul, and when its capacity to reason is gone, it is no longer a human body (*De An.* 414a12–24).

[4] I am indebted to David Charles for help in shortening this section.

[5] See Charles (2009) and the examples discussed there. Aristotle writes: 'We have said [or sought to say] that the affections of the soul are inseparable from the physical matter of living beings in the way in which anger and fear are inseparable and not in the way in which line and plane are' (*De An.* 403b17–19). The line and plane are inseparable from matter in that they are never instantiated without matter, but they are *not* dependent on any specific matter for their existence, and they can be defined independently of their matter. Fear and anger are inseparable on all three accounts: 'It is clear that the passions are enmattered formulae and so their definitions will be of the following form: to be angry is a process of this type of body or part or capacity of such a body caused in this way for the sake of such and such a goal' (*De An.* 403a24–7). Cf. Descartes' definition of passions quoted in section 7 of this chapter.

or continuous quantity (*Le Monde* AT IX 35–6; *Principles* II 8–9; *Regulae* 14), and mind in terms of thought taken in a new wide sense. These he argues are 'really distinct', i.e. not only are they definitionally and really independent of each other, but they are also mutually exclusive, so that there are no real properties that mind *qua* thinking can be said to share with matter *qua* extended or spatial. Excluding material properties, thought can be neither located in nor derived from matter. Thought and matter each are their own genera, in Descartes' preferred terminology, they are 'really' distinct natures or attributes (AT 7 7; CSM 2 54).

This mind-matter distinction is introduced as primarily epistemological: it is between the two main, general, and essential attributes of which our knowledge of things depends. All other attributes or properties of things are called modes that presuppose the principal ones (AT 8A 25; CSM 2 210–11). But Descartes' dualism is not merely a conceptual or explanatory dualism. He holds that we have no cognitive access to substances in themselves except through their main attributes. If two things differ through their main attributes, they must differ in substance (AT 7 161; CSM 2 114. Cf. *Principles* a. 51–2, AT 8A 24–5; CSM 1 210). Descartes' dualism, therefore, is also a substance dualism. Thinking and extended things are the only two essentially distinct substances there are, or can be known by finite human minds.[6]

To be physical for Descartes is just to be extended and movable, moreover, matter in itself is inert: it has no inherent force or activity, but depends for both its existence and its movement on God. Physical things or processes, including all the properties of living beings except thinking, are describable in terms of extension, motion, and related concepts, like size, shape, situation, speed, etc., which are 'modes' or ways of being of extended things that have no being in themselves apart from the substance they modify.

Mind or intellect, the highest and only kind of soul of the three interdependent Aristotelian psychological principles Descartes retains, stands traditionally for potential and actual understanding or intelligibility. It presupposes forms accounting for the nature of things and making them objects of understanding and judgement. While rejecting hylomorphism as a general principle of explanation, Descartes follows the tradition in taking mind or intellect as essentially a power to discover (true and immutable) ideas of things. But in defining mind as a thinking thing including everything of which we are 'immediately conscious', he expands it from the rational or intellectual powers of understanding and judging

---

[6] See also Reply to the Fourth Objections (AT 7, 226–7; CSM 2 159f). Note though that God alone is a substance in the strict or absolute sense of a self-subsisting thing. Created things that depend on God alone for their existence are substances in a less strict sense—secondarily (*Principles* I, a. 52). Descartes, as will be seen, is prepared to count as real things (*res* and *quid*) things that he does not count as substances in either sense. These can, like substances, be predicated and they depend on God not only for their existence but for their possibility as well. For illuminating discussions of Descartes' ontology, its scholastic terminology, background, and difficulties, see Brown and Normore (2019: ch. 1).

to cover also imagination, sense perception and passions, turning the latter into ideas or modes of thought. Differently from purely intellectual activity they depend causally also on the mind's unity with the body and the stimulation of its sensory organs by external things acting on the body.[7]

3. The Human Body as a Machine and Its Union with the Rational Mind

That the human soul or mind is really embodied is something Descartes always seems to have taken for granted, even while developing a new metaphysical framework that renders this assumption problematic. He develops his mathematico-mechanistic doctrine of physical nature and body before reflecting on the mind and its relation to the body, and there is a sense in which his account of their problematic union remains unfinished work in progress.

Thus in his early essay *On Man*, Descartes compares the human body to a machine arguing that all its vital functions including the circulation of blood can be explained by strictly mechanical principles. Its last part was supposed to describe the rational soul, and how 'unlike the other things of which I had spoken, it cannot be derived in any way from the potentiality of matter, but must be specially created'. Not only is it directly created but it is also joined by God so as to act in the body (AT 6 59; CSM 1 141). In the *Discourse on the Method*, having presented his first argument for strict dualism, he argues that the soul is not just located or lodged in its body, like a pilot in a ship, but it forms a real unity with it.[8] A machine operated by a soul or homunculus regulating its motions is not a *real* human being, and what a real human being is, is something each one of us, as Descartes explains in later writings, knows through experience or what his 'own nature teaches' him (AT 7 80–1; CSM 2 56).

There are obvious tensions between these two ways of interpreting the union of mind and body. The first is based on causal interaction between two distinct substances: between an immaterial, substantial soul standing, in Descartes' hierarchy of being, above extended nature, and the machinery of the body immersed in it.[9] The

---

[7] For Descartes' definition of thought, see AT 7 28, 160; CSM 2 19, 113. It is often equated with consciousness, but consciousness in the modern sense of the word was not yet on the table. The activities essential to the Cartesian mind, what John Carriero calls its core capacities, are reasoning, judging, understanding, seeing that something is thus and so. But thinking for Descartes also includes willing, doubting, even imagination, sense perception, and passions. See Carriero (2009), Alanen (2003a and 2016).

[8] '[I]t must be more closely joined and united with the body in order to have, besides this power of movement (of moving the limbs of the body), feelings and appetites like ours and so constitute a real man' (AT 6 59; CSM 1 141).

[9] *Qua* immaterial, the soul or mind is indivisible and indestructible, and it is also a 'self-mover', having its own inner principle of activity, so it is the paradigm of an individual unitary substance. Extension *qua* substance is indestructible too, though finite extended things are themselves corruptible. See Schmaltz (2020b).

causal interaction between the two, though inexplicable by the only kind of natural causality Descartes accepts (by motion and impact), is localized to a specific organ in the brain and according to an influential line of reading supposed to constitute and explain the union.[10] The second is a holistic notion of mind-body unity, where the mind is embodied and intermingled with the body, reacting with and acting on the whole body as it were. It is introduced in the Sixth Meditation, where Descartes, having proved that he is essentially a thinking thing, goes on to argue that he is intimately united to his body, something that his sensory experience reveals to him:

(2)   Nature also teaches me, by these sensations of pain, hunger, thirst and so on, that I am not merely present in my body as a sailor is present in a ship, but that I am very closely joined and as it were intermingled [*illi arctissime esse conjunctum et quasi permixtum*] with it so as to make up one thing [*unum quid*].

AT 7 81; CSM 2 56

It matters to distinguish the notion of nature introduced here from nature in the sense of extended physical nature, both of which are problematic but for different reasons. 'Nature' in this last quote is used in a wider sense than 'extended nature', since it comprises both 'thinking' and 'extended' nature, i.e. 'all the things God has bestowed upon me' (AT 7 80; CSM 2 56) 'as a combination of mind and body' (AT 7 82; CSM 2 57), and to which he also refers in terms of the 'Natural Institution'.[11] The holistic notion of the mind-body union represents Descartes' mature thinking on this matter. Pressed to explain it by his critics, who have problems with the idea of causal interaction between an immaterial and material substance, he describes it as a third 'primitive notion' after those of thought and extension. It is listed as one of three main objects of knowledge, or 'ultimate classes of things': thinking minds, extended bodies, and composites of these with their specific properties depending on each of them (*Principles* 1 a. 48). The first two are known through the clear and distinct evident notions of thought and extension, which are presupposed in all our cognition of the things or modes depending on them. The third, the mind-body union, is not an object of distinct or evident intellectual perception on its own, and cannot be explained through the other two notions of the natures that compose it. We are said instead to know the union and what depends on it clearly through sensory experience.

What makes the mind-body union hard to explain for Descartes is the very argument proving their distinction, where mind and body are defined not only as different but as mutually exclusive concepts. On his view, it is unintelligible how a mode of extension, shape, or motion could be attributed to thought or how a mode of thought, e.g. understanding, imagination, sensation, or will, could be

---

[10] Wilson (1978: 206–8); Rozemond (1998).
[11] I discuss Descartes' different senses of the term nature in Alanen (2008a).

attributed to matter (*Principles* I, a. 53, AT 8A 23; CSM 1 208–9). Descartes does not in fact seem entitled to posit the kind of real union between mind and matter that he also calls a 'substantial union', or a third kind of 'thing' yet nowhere describes as a third kind of substance. He is however prepared as will be seen to call it an 'ens per se'—a true being or 'thing in itself' as opposed to an 'ens per accidens'—an accidental aggregate of parts.

Descartes' idea of a clearly experienced real mind-body union is in deep tension with his metaphysical dualism. The latter excludes any form of hylomorphism where thought or mind, as a distinctive form of activity, could be seen as actualizing and perfecting a certain type of matter (living animal body organized in a determinate way). How could the two distinct substances making up our nature form a real unity? If it is known only through experience does it then lack metaphysical grounding? Is the unity that is very clearly perceived by the sense unintelligible or inconceivable to clear and distinct perception?

Many of Descartes' followers have endorsed the idea of an unproblematic, straightforward, and strict dualism. Given that he also defends this notion of the mind and body forming a real union constitutive of human nature, we are left with this challenge: To grasp the real distinction between mind and body we have to abstract from all cognition depending on sensory impressions and the body, bracketing the experience that feeds our imagination, and use instead our intellect alone and its throve of innate ideas, as argued in the Second Meditation; while to grasp our nature as embodied, we must as it seems bracket the ontological thesis of their separation and rely on sensory experience. This is precisely what Descartes does in the Sixth Meditation and explicitly asks Elisabeth and Arnauld to do when they press him to explain the union (AT 3 692–3; CSMK 227). Intellect and reason show us that we are essentially thinking, active beings and that mind and body are really distinct natures, while everyday experience testifies that we are at once active and reactive, thinking and sentient embodied beings. We confront these two sets of evidently cognized facts that we cannot quite put together—not a satisfactory starting point for Cartesian anthropology.

This leaves those of us who do not want to read Descartes as an idealist, or turn him into a materialist in disguise, with—very roughly—the following main alternatives: (1) accept the two substance dualism and let substantial union go; (2) accept both and conclude that Descartes' theory is incoherent; or (3) recognize the deeply problematic nature of substance dualism and Descartes' argument for it, while taking the notion of the mind-body union seriously, and working out ways to understand it. The first two are represented—in one form or another—in the main types of reading of Descartes' dualism offered in the literature.[12] If the first precludes the union, or treats it as fictional, the second, which has been most

---

[12] See the literature referred to in Alanen (2008b) from which part of the material in this section is taken, e.g. Wilson (2000); Clarke (2006).

influential and is better supported by the texts, provides no satisfactory way of understanding of the mind-body union. I for my part accept the third, which opposes me to the first, which takes dualism in a strong sense and downplays the union.[13] To me it has seemed less of a problem to go the other way, which has Descartes working with a deflated or weaker notion of substance as applied to finite created things, and taking the real distinction as a conceptual or explanatory rather than as a metaphysical distinction. What is important to save in this problematic doctrine is the intuition behind attribute dualism with its conceptual and methodological implications: mind cannot be explained by reduction or reference to matter as early modern physics defines it, or vice versa. Where, however, would such a third alternative leave us insofar as the metaphysics of the union is concerned? What type of *ens per se* would it be? To shed some light on this issue, I propose to look briefly at one of the most carefully argued interpretations of Descartes as endorsing hylomorphism and some of the difficulties it faces.

4. The Metaphysics of Mind-Body Unions

Let me first note that the three alternatives mentioned above are not exhaustive. Deborah Brown and Calvin Normore challenge my reading of Descartes as offering, in correspondence with Elisabeth, the irreducibility of the third primitive notion of the mind-body union in answer to her questions, instead of providing a coherent metaphysical grounding of it. They also reject the reading of Descartes as endorsing hylomorphism. There is, they argue, a way of saving Cartesian dualism without drawing the union into question and committing Descartes to inconsistency—a fourth option to be added to the three I listed.[14]

They note first that Descartes does not use the notions of substance and subject interchangeably,[15] and second that he works with a different conception of metaphysical unity, besides unity of substance (Brown 2019: 29). The mind-body union is 'one instance of a general, explanatory strategy', which is systematically at work in the new ontology of parts and wholes Descartes is developing. A whole need not be only a mereological sum of its parts, but has its own

---

[13] This, basically, is what the Rylean picture of Cartesian dualism described as 'Ghost in the Machine' (Ryle 1949) invites us to do. For classic defences of this reading, see the literature quoted in note 12 above. While this second line of reading is more likely than the first, it offers a problematic account of how the two distinct substances could interact (in terms of the 'natural institution' theory and the interaction of thoughts and animal spirits) which, in the absence of any internal connection between thought and extension, is unsatisfactory as an answer to how they are united. The union here is accidental, not real. I am grateful to John Carriero for helping me to clarify this. Cf. the distinction made by Hoffman (2008) between the different mind-body problems that are not always separated. The problem that is my main concern is that of the mind-body unity, not the interaction.

[14] See Brown (2019) and Brown and Normore (2019).   [15] Cf. Menn (1995).

persistence conditions distinct from the latter. One advantage of this line of thinking is that there need not be logical priority of the parts over the whole, which without being a substance itself can be the subject of emergent properties and have causal powers not possessed by the parts. The mind-body union for Descartes would be an instance of such a unity of composition where the whole is the subject of emergent qualities that are irreducible to those of its parts, the two distinct substances composing it. According to this ingenious new proposal Descartes can be seen as applying the idea of mereological unity across a number of domains: in explaining animals and automata, the functional integrity of the human body, and to more intangible wholes like the unity of the lover with the object loved, of families and nation states, and the mind-body union. The last is 'in many ways the paradigm of a single-yet-composite "subject" of unique forms of predication, unique forms of activity, causal powers, and forms of life' (Brown 2019: 30).

This reading avoids many of the problems of the hylomorphic reading yet makes the union intelligible in terms of a clear and distinct conception of how there can be wholes with irreducible properties of their own and yet also with properties depending on the thinking and extended substances composing them. While welcoming this, one may still worry about the unique status of the whole formed by the mind-body union. Differently from other naturally formed composite entities that it is in some sense a paradigm for, it requires for its 'substantial mode of union' a special unifying (and miraculous) act of God (Brown and Normore 2019: 187–94). The mereological reading, no less than the hylomorphic reading defended by Paul Hoffman we will now turn to, leaves us with the fact of a union we can sense but whose formation eludes clear and distinct perception and must in the end be taken as it were 'on faith'.[16]

To see Descartes as endorsing Aristotelian hylomorphism given his language and examples is tempting. According to Hoffman, Descartes' solution to the problems of the mind-body union is based on his 'retention of two fundamental Aristotelian metaphysical doctrines'. The first is that of *hylomorphism:* mind and body are related as form and matter, which means that a human being is a composite being which is itself a substance. Hoffman, like most commentators, treats substance, *ens per se* and subject as equivalent.[17] The second doctrine is that of *'the identity of action and passion:* that whenever a causal agent acts on something (referred to as the patient), what the agent does (the action) and

---

[16] Indeed Brown and Normore suggest Descartes understands the substantial union on the model of Trinity, which would explain his remark to Regius that this idea is one that 'everybody accepts but no one explains, so you need not do it either' (AT 3 493; CSMK 3 206). It could be tempting also to consider it as a useful fiction for practical purposes, but Descartes would hardly go that way.

[17] Normore (2011) points out a serious reason for questioning this, which is that Descartes, though defending its real unity, never calls the composite of mind and body a substance. This is noted in Alq. 2, p. 902n1, and 3, 19–20n1.

what the patient undergoes (the passion) are one and the same'.[18] Whether or not one agrees on the first point, the second alone—which I discuss briefly in the last section—is a serious reason for reinterpreting Descartes' dualism.

Hoffman's Descartes endorses a weak version of a position called 'trialism', according to which the human being is a substance or unitary being in itself, but one without any distinctive attribute of its own.[19] On this view there are only two ultimate classes of created substance, which together form the composite substance of a human being falling under what Descartes in his letter to Elisabeth calls a 'third primitive notion' (AT 3 665; CSMK 3 218). What classifying a composite of two substances under a primitive notion amounts to on this reading is 'saying that it is not subject to further analysis'. The weak version of trialism would not, as the strong one does, require that the third sort of substance formed by mind-body unions are known through an attribute of their own.[20] Thus, in stressing in correspondence with Elisabeth that the relation between mind and body is not subject to further analysis, Descartes, Hoffman claims, is simply echoing a remark made earlier in a letter to Regius (AT 3 493; CSMK 3 206). This letter which is also the main evidence for Brown and Normore's mereological reading is worth a closer consideration.

5. Substantial Forms and the Union that Needs No Explanation: The Correspondence with Regius

Descartes' independent-minded follower Regius, who was teaching the new philosophy at the University of Utrecht, developed his doctrine in a direction Descartes found provocative. Regius claimed that the human being is an *ens per accidens*, using language that distorted Descartes view on human nature and rendered it offensive to Catholic dogma.[21] The term 'accident', Descartes explained, means 'anything which can be present or absent without its subject

---

[18] Hoffman (2008: 391 and 2009: 4).

[19] Hoffman distinguishes two versions, noting that Descartes' hylomorphism falls under the first, weak sense, according to which 'minds, bodies, and human beings are all substances'—a position one could hold without holding strong trialism. In the strong version that Hoffman rejects Descartes 'thinks there are three ultimate classes of created substances: minds, bodies and human beings, each with their own distinctive principal attribute' (Hoffman 2008: 391). John Cottingham (1985) defends the first, Tad Schmaltz (1992) the second strong version.

[20] Hoffman rejects the strong version of trialism according to which the primary notion of mind-body union should itself be read as 'something constituting the nature or essence of a substance' (Hoffman 2008: 392).

[21] The council of Vienna 1311 had declared it false and a heresy to assert 'that the substance of the rational or intellectual soul is not of itself and essentially the form of the human body', and the Fifth Lateran council (1512) 'that the soul not only truly exists of itself and essentially as the form of the human body... but it is also immortal; and further, for the enormous number of bodies into which it is infused individually, it can and ought to be and is multiplied'. Quoted in Brown and Normore (2019: 175).

being destroyed', and in this sense, the union of soul and body is not accidental. Yet there is *some sense* in which one can say that it is accidental to the body to be united to mind, considering that they can exist (God so willing) separately. What Regius should have argued, is that body and soul in relation to human being 'are incomplete substances;' and that it follows from their being incomplete that what 'they compose is an *ens per se*' (Letter to Regius, December 1641, AT 3 460; CSMK 3 200). This may sound like an endorsement of the hylomorphic view, as does the characterization in Descartes' next letter of the soul as united 'really and substantially' to the body. They are not, as Regius incorrectly suggested, united 'by location and disposition' (*per situm aut dispositionem*) only, but '*by a true mode of union [per verum modum unionis], as everyone agrees, though nobody explains what this amounts to*, and so you need not do it either'. The term Descartes uses here however is not substance, but 'being in itself' (AT 3 493; CSMK 3 206; emphasis added).[22]

The matter is pressing, and Descartes' concern no mere paranoia: between his first and second letter, Regius had been deprived of his right to teach the new philosophy of nature. Moreover, Descartes' dualism was at stake.[23] So, though this passage might suggest that *ens per se* and substance are equivalent for Descartes,[24] there are reasons to hesitate. One can still side with Hoffman that Descartes need not be accused of insincerity here, and grant that whenever the formulations he recommends to his protégé are confirmed by views he expresses elsewhere, they must reflect his own (Hoffman 2008: 393). But what view exactly would the talk of a substantial mode of union reflect? Answering this question turns out to be tricky. Having just said that it need not be explained because nobody does, Descartes adds:

(3) You could do so [explain the union], however, as I did in my *Metaphysics*, by saying that we perceive that sensations such as pain are not pure thoughts of a

---

[22] '[A] human being is a true *ens per se*, and not an *ens per accidens*, and that the soul is united really and substantially to the body. You must say that they are united not by location or disposition, as you have written in your last, (for this too is open to objection and in my opinion, quite untrue), but *by a true mode of union (sed per verum modum unionis), as everyone agrees, though nobody explains what this amounts to, and so you need not do it either*' (to Regius, January 1642, AT 3 493; CSMK 296; emphasis added).

[23] Regius had been attacked by the rector of the university, Voetius, who did not want Descartes' unorthodox views to be spread. Because of his bold use of Descartes' doctrine, Regius' position was threatened, and Descartes—who was eager to have a supporter at the university—offered his help to defend him. Later correspondence with Regius shows that Descartes thinks he should focus on medicine and stay away from philosophy, and not to mention metaphysics, which Regius does not understand well enough: the materialist turn Regius has taken threatens the carefully worked out Cartesian compromise system. This need not have been a mere matter of politics, for there were good philosophical reasons for Descartes to be upset with Regius' use of his doctrine which had to do precisely with the delicate question of the mind's union with the body—to what extent it could be explained in terms of Cartesian thought and extension. See AT 3, 491–509, in part, 491–4.

[24] Descartes, after all, does not hesitate to call the soul a substantial form, and what substantial form does is to actualize the matter it informs into a particular substance with a particular essence.

mind distinct from a body, but confused perceptions of a mind really united to a body. For if an angel were in a human body, he would not have sensations as we do, but would simply perceive the motions which are caused by external objects, and in this way would differ from a real man.

AT 3 492–3; CSMK 4 206

An angel, as a pure intellectual being, would not register bodily affections through obscure sensations but would understand what affects the body clearly and distinctly, as it were from the outside. An angel united with a human body would form an *ens per accidens*—not a real union.

Descartes then drafts on Regius' behalf an answer to his critic Voetius, who had complained about the rejection of 'those "harmless entities" called substantial forms and real qualities... from their ancient territory', arguing that though they are not rejected 'absolutely' they are of no use for explaining 'the natural causes of things'. The Cartesian philosophy of nature does not depend 'on uncertain and obscure assumptions of this sort'. He clarifies how the term 'substantial form' should be taken in this context:

(4) [w]e mean by the expression a certain substance joined to matter, making up with it a certain merely corporeal whole [*substantiam quondam materiae adjunctam, & cum ipsa totum aliquod mere corporeum componentem*], and which, no less than matter and even more than matter *is a true substance, or self-subsistent thing*, since it is said to be the act [*actus*] and the latter merely the potency [*quia nempe dicitus esse actus, illa vero tantum potentia*]. Such a substance, or substantial form, present in purely corporeal things but different from matter [*a materia diversa*], is nowhere, we think, mentioned in Holy Scripture.

AT 3, 500; CSMK 3 207; emphasis added

The notion of substantial form that Descartes bans from his new physics is that of a true substance or self-subsistent thing consisting in corporeal properties (modes of extension) added to matter to constitute physical things. The whole constituted by the joining of the substantial form with matter is said to be no less a thing than the former and even more of a substance than the matter in which it is present because it is the act, not potency.[25] We have to tread carefully here. Act and potency for Descartes refer to activity and passivity, rather than actuality growing

---

[25] In a letter to Mersenne on 23 April 1643 Descartes explains that he does not suppose real qualities in nature attached to corporeal substances 'like so many little souls to their bodies, and which are separable by divine nature'. He does not reject qualities interpreted as modes of the substance like motion (speed, size, and shape)—*qua* ways of being of bodily substances they cannot exist without them (AT 3 648; CSMK 236). According to Garber (1983) this notion as applied in this context is of his own making, though not one that the scholastics used. But, see Menn (1995) who questions Garber's reading with good reason. See also Dominik Perler's Chapter 15 on Suarez in this volume.

out of and crowning the potentialities of matter.[26] A soul or substantial form is not the act or actuality of some potentiality in matter, but is an active (corporeal) principle adjoined to the, in itself, passive extended matter from without. Yet it is striking that Descartes here makes a point of emphasizing that it is *more* of a substance than matter, because it is supposed to be in act or active, something that explains its privileged status, to which Descartes turns in the next paragraph. It does not, thus, complete but, rather, transforms the in itself passive matter by being united to it. What one can retain from this passage though is that substantial form for Descartes is a substance, and so presumably is the matter that it informs.

The most important of Voetius' objections is that denying substantial forms in purely material things may lead to doubting 'whether there is a substantial form in man' and make it harder to silence the errors of heretics (AT 3 503; CSMK 3 207). Descartes counters that it is precisely the view affirming substantial forms in natural things that puts one on the slippery slope to taking the human soul to be corporeal and mortal. Instead one should recognize that the human soul, differing in nature from the others which are mere configurations of matter in motion, is the only true substantial form.[27] He goes on to offer another argument against the substantial forms in physics, which is that substances are created directly by God:

(5) [T]he soul [*Animae*], which is the true substantial form of man ... *is thought to be immediately created by God for no other reason than that it is a substance*. Hence, since the other 'forms' are not thought to be created in this way, but merely to emerge from the potentiality of matter, they should not be regarded as substances.

AT 3 505; CSMK 3 208; emphasis added

Having replaced the scholastic 'real qualities' with 'modes', Descartes cannot see how the latter which are ways of being of extended substances could be substances, i.e. independent from matter. The substantial forms adopted by the school are supposed to be material and yet they are misconceived on the model of rational souls—the only substantial form he recognizes. They explain no natural action but are 'occult qualities', that nobody understands (AT 3 508; CSMK 209).

---

[26] AT 7 505; CSMK 208. See, e.g., to Regius, December 1641: 'For incorporeal things, all actions and passions consist simply in local motion: we call it an "action" when the motion is considered in the body that imparts the motions, and "passion" when it is considered in the body moved'. In incorporeal things action is applied 'to whatever plays the role of a moving force, like volition in the mind, while we apply the term "passion" to what plays the role of something moved, like intellect and vision in the same mind'. Force is here to be understood as 'analogous to motion'. AT 3 454–5; CMSK 199.

[27] '[T]his privileged status above other things shows most clearly that it differs from them by its nature; and this difference in nature opens the easiest way to prove its immateriality and immortality, as may be seen in the recently published *Meditations on First Philosophy*. Thus one cannot think of any opinion on this subject that is more congenial to theology' (AT 3 503; CSMK 3 208).

To actually explain natural changes requires forms of an altogether different kind—mathematical essences as used in Descartes' philosophy of nature, of which only the *Meteorology* had been published so far. These 'essential forms' are different from substantial forms: they are not 'created *de novo*', they do not make up individual things or substantial unions, but are modes of extension subject to general and universal causal laws.

One may ask if Descartes thinks that extended things like this lump of salt, the piece of wax, or things coming into being by accident like mice or other animals are substances in the proper sense of the word. One may indeed wonder if there are any genuine particular substances apart from indivisible substantial forms like the rational soul and the bodies they inform.[28] If Descartes avoids calling the mind-body union a substance he certainly talks about it as a composite of two substances, which is an *ens per se* and is treated as subject of predication. He urges Regius to affirm that human beings 'are made up of body and soul [*ex Corpore & Anima componi*], not by the mere presence or proximity of one to the other, but by a true and substantial union'. It presupposes as 'a natural requirement' on the side of the body a proper disposition and 'arrangement' of its various parts but extends beyond the bodily dispositions to the incorporeal soul.[29] The union which joins a human body and soul to each other so that they constitute 'a single *ens per se*' is essential to human being, which as a result of this union is a genuine being in itself (AT 3 508; 3 209).

This union is the necessary and sufficient condition of being human, and the body informed by the soul is a new subject, an embodied human person, that could not subsist on its own without one of its two essential components. The prerequisite of special dispositions for the union and interaction of the two substances composing it are what makes these incomplete without their union.

So far, we have seen Descartes referring to the human being as a whole composed of 'the human body informed by a soul', as a 'substantial union', and as an 'ens per se'. Yet Normore (2011) warns us that everything that is an *ens per se* is not, as such, a substance. The category of *ens per se* was treated by some scholastics as wider than that of substance, so includes real substance as a subcategory or class. Descartes himself notes to Regius that mice which, like other animals, are devoid of souls, so not informed by a substantial form but generated accidentally from dirt, are counted as *entia per se*.[30] Animals according to Descartes are real beings on their own which are accidentally formed as natural

---

[28] Letter to Mesland, 9 February 1645. See the related discussion in Lennon (2016).

[29] AT 3 508; CSMK 3 209. The positioning and arrangement of the various parts is something very special here because it extends to or affects the incorporeal soul. The way it affects the soul is described in *L'Homme*, where certain dispositions in the body, notably in the brain, when altered by external action are said to cause different sensations in the mind, e.g. pain. See AT 11 143; CSM 1 101-6.

[30] Descartes uses this example to show in what sense something can be an *ens per accidens* on account of its origin and still be an *ens per se*. (To Regius December 1641, AT 3 460; CSMK 3 200.)

composites of substances. So are human beings, in spite of the fact that the parts composing them not only differ with respect to their origin but also through their essences which are radically distinct. If they do not count as substances they seem more substantial than mice and other animals, for they are the only *entia per se* distinguished by having as one of their components a specially created incorruptible substance.

If the correspondence with Regius is not sufficient to vindicate Hoffman, it is not his only evidence, however. The list of passages he refers to includes claims like the one made in the early *Rules* about the body being informed by the human mind (*mens*) (AT 10 411; CSM 1 140), repeated in the *Principles* 4 a. 189, where the human soul (*anima*) is said to 'inform the whole body', though it is also said to have 'its principal seat in the brain' (AT 8-A 315; CSM 1 279). In the Fifth Set of Replies, Descartes specifies what he means when taking 'soul' in the sense of the 'first actuality' or 'principal form of man': 'anima' here refers not to 'the principle by which we are nourished' but only 'to the principle in virtue of which we think', and it is in order to avoid this ambiguity that Descartes says he prefers to use the term 'mind' (*mens*) throughout (AT 7 356; CSM 2 246). Finally, in the Sixth Replies the mind is said to be 'coextensive with the body—the whole mind in the whole body and the whole mind in any one of its parts' (AT 7 442; CSM 2 298). In his last work, the *Passions of the Soul*, the soul is said to be 'truly joined to the whole body' (AT 11 351; CSM 1 339). One can add to this the correspondence with Elisabeth that will be discussed later.

If Descartes thought of a 'substantial union' as hylomorphic, this union would have to count for him as a substance. Yet in spite of evidence for this reading, Descartes' entitlement to fall back on hylomorphic language can be questioned, given his other commitments inconsistent with an explicit endorsement of these claims (2008: 393). What does Hoffman have to say about these?

Consider the claim about attributes and substance in the *Principles*, where Descartes makes his most sustained effort to define them. The term substance is there said to apply univocally to mind and to body, to things that only need God's concurrence to exist (*Principles* 1 a. 51–2, AT 8A 24–5; CSM 1 210). Each substance has one principal property which constitutes its nature or essence. This yields the following line of argument: There are only two essential attributes, extension and thinking, so there are only these two kinds of substances, extended bodies and thinking minds. The third kind of thing, referred to in a. 48 as arising from 'the close and intimate union of our mind with the body', is not known through a third kind of attribute but is directly experienced. Lacking a distinctive main attribute through which it can be known, the mind-body composite cannot properly, it seems, be a hylomorphic substance.

Hoffman's response to this type of objection is not very satisfactory. His subtle interpretations of Descartes' employment of the scholastic vocabulary, in my view, stretches the meaning of the terms. The distinction between principal attributes is transformed from opposition to mere difference and non-mutual separability (Hoffman 2002).[31] Hylomorphism itself is taken in a weak sense, and the very notion of substance deflated to the point of threatening both hylomorphism and a realist reading of Descartes' dualism.[32]

According to a line of reading by Hoffman closer to the texts the human soul is created to be united with a human body, the latter being appropriately structured to receive a soul. The soul's human nature requires that it is united to and acts in an appropriately structured moving body. The human soul and body are human only because they are united and are made for this union. It is true that the rational soul is complete on its own—it is as Descartes claims the only substance directly created by God—and can, God willing, survive or subsist without the body. Yet it is a human soul only in virtue of its union with the body. As constituents of this union the mind and the body are incomplete substances in themselves. This all seems to fit well with how Paul Hoffman reads the passages from the letters to Regius quoted above (AT 3 460; CSMK 3 200; AT 3 493; CSMK 3 206),[33] but does not, in my view, warrant the additional conclusion he draws that Descartes 'can still claim to have a hylomorphic conception of a human being so long as he maintains that it is unnatural for its parts to be separated' (Hoffman 2008: 399).

Mind and body have different essences, but they constitute, together, by nature, a whole with substantial unity though not a substance. According to their essence they are substances subsisting on their own, according to their nature as created (for each other) they should be united. Their substantial union is, one could say, essential to the human being, even when we cannot grasp its mode of union that we so clearly experience by the attributes through which we know the two things composing it. Whether, and in what sense, this is 'hylomorphic conception' is however debatable. To support that conclusion Hoffman's reading waters down all those ontological commitments that hinder Descartes from expressly endorsing strong hylomorphism, not least Descartes' own version of the real distinction arguments which have this presupposition few other scholastics may have been prepared to defend—namely that mind and body are not only really distinct and mutually independent things but that their natures are mutually exclusive.[34]

---

[31] Hoffman detects five different senses of separability and argues that the one that counts for Descartes' real distinction argument is weak (Hoffman 2002: 57–8). For a different reading, see Alanen (1986).

Hoffman argues, e.g., that Descartes' remarks in the *Principles* are 'superseded' by his discussion in a later text, 'Comments on a Certain Broadsheet', written in 1648 in response to a publication by Regius, who by this time has gained assurance enough to openly list his points of disagreement with Descartes. (Hoffman 2008: 395). For critical discussions of Hoffman's reading see Rozemond (1998 and 1999); and Brown (2006).

[32] Mind and body for Hoffman's Descartes are not substances 'in the stronger sense in which the Aristotelians considered a human being to be a substance' (Hoffman 2008: 397).

[33] See also the Fourth Set of Replies (AT 7 22–228; CSM 2 156–60).

[34] Ockham and his nominalist followers may be an exception. Suarez, as Perler argues in Chapter 15 of this volume (section 1), claims that matter and form are really distinct and mutually separable.

For Hoffman, 'Descartes' account of the unity of the composite human being is no worse than that of his Aristotelian predecessors with whom he is so often unfavorable compared' (2008: 399). Maybe so, but it is many times removed from Aristotelian hylomorphism of the strong variety considered in section 1 of this chapter—a compelling metaphysical doctrine in itself that is not easily transposed into the world of early modern mechanism. The forms of hylomorphism to which Hoffman compares Descartes' are weaker, dualist variants defended in the late scholastic tradition. One can worry whether the being that is left is indeed real and unified enough to qualify as 'hylomorphic' at all—a substance that is supposed to be the very paradigm of a real individual thing.

Relying on the Fourth and Sixth Replies, Brown and Normore also read Descartes as thinking that the mind-body composite has a nature, which is more than a mere unity of composition (like flesh and bone in an animal) but less than an 'essence'. It is instead a unity by composition that does not threaten the real distinction between mind and body, yet, they argue, there is something natural about it, in the same sense of natural that applies to the unity of flesh and bone in the animal.

(6) The whole human being is a single subject of distinct predicates—mental and physical—as the whole animal is the single subject of bones and flesh—but that is consistent with its being a composite thing.

Brown and Normore 2019: 173

They are the same not 'intrinsically' but by 'combination' because they can exist apart (AT 7 444-5; CSM 2 299). To account for the sense in which the composite of mind and body forming the human nature is natural here Brown and Normore appeal to the notion of 'true and immutable nature' (2019: 173).[35] In virtue of its true and immutable 'nature' the union 'is something irreducible to the sum of its essential parts because it is the subject of unique sensory and affective predicates'. These predicates must be understood as modes of the mind and modes of the body respectively, which are paired together through what Descartes calls 'Institution of Nature', so that they depend causally on each other (Brown and Normore 2019: 192-3).

---

[35] This is not the whole story though, which I cannot dwell on here. Bone and flesh can be naturally united in one composite since they are both composed of modes of extension. Not so mind and body, and it takes extraordinary action by God to make a composite of these. Here, as Brown and Normore show, the notion of a substantial mode of union and how it is used by, e.g., Suarez, comes in handy and could well have been exploited by Descartes. It can be understood as a special mode of the soul that accounts for the way it is united to the body that is not accidental but essential to it as a God-created human soul, yet without forming a new kind hylomorphic substance with the body. See their excellent discussion in chapter 6 of their 2019 (esp. pp. 187-93). Cf. Schmaltz (2020a) and Perler, Chapter 15 of this volume.

At this point one may ask why the being (*ens per se*) emerging from the union of mind and body is not a substance with its own nature, where this immutable nature would play the role of an essential attribute?[36] Is it perhaps because Descartes' attribute dualism has no room for more than two essential attributes for distinct cognition of things? Would not any true and immutable nature have to fall under one or the other of these?

In the letter to Regius (cited above in (3)) the difference between the hypothetical union of an angel with a human body, which is merely accidental, and the 'real' or 'substantial' union of mind and body shows up in the confused perceptions we have of the latter. The same point is made in the Sixth Meditation (cited above in (2)) where the unity and 'intermingling' of mind and body is said to be revealed through 'teachings of nature' which include (confused) perceptions caused by internal bodily senses like 'sensations of pain, hunger, thirst and so on' (AT 7 81; CSM 2 56). As Brown and Normore interpret this: 'the special mode of union that the mind has with the body produces a unique phenomenology, which no mere aggregate would possess' (Brown and Normore 2019: 177).

6. From Metaphysics to Phenomenology: Taking the Mind-Body Experience Seriously

Whether the union is taken, as Hoffman argues, to be a third kind of hylomorphic substance or, as Brown and Normore contend, a mere composite being in itself (*ens per se*) with a true and immutable nature, strict attribute dualism still gets in the way of conceiving the relation between its two components in a clear and distinct way.[37] Hence the appeal to the third primitive notion in correspondence with Elisabeth that is worth considering closely. In answer to her question of how the immaterial mind that lacks extension can act and be acted on by the extended body, Descartes offers the third primitive notion as an epistemically irreducible and in some sense self-evident notion, that cannot be fully analysed in terms of other more basic notions: those of thought or extension of which all our knowledge of things depends. That Descartes has no metaphysical account of the mind-body union is not, I argue, to say that it would not be a real object of cognition. It does, however, show the limit of attribute dualism and the mathematical science of nature—the limits of what can be explained in terms of the two distinct attributes, of which our knowledge of created things—minds and bodies—depend. That this would be the end of our science of human being may suggest itself to those who

---

[36] I am indebted to David Charles for pressing this question.

[37] Descartes confesses: 'It does not seem to me that the human mind is capable of conceiving very distinctly and at the same time both the distinction between the soul and the body and their union, for to do this one would have to conceive it as one single thing and at the same time as two which is self-contradictory'. (To Elisabeth 28 June 1643, AT 3 693; CSMK 3 227.)

reduce the experience Descartes invokes to sensory perception in the strictest sense of (blind) sensation or mere feeling, and take Descartes to be discrediting the senses as a source of knowledge altogether. But the senses, as Descartes concludes in the Sixth Meditation, always contain some truth in them, and are, when used in tandem with the intellect, in the right context, for the most part reliable.[38]

A richer notion of experience is suggested in Descartes' answers to Elisabeth's questions. He starts by confessing that of the two main things about the human soul 'of which all the knowledge we can have of it depends', the first being 'that it thinks', the other 'that being united to the body, it can act on and be acted upon by it', he has 'said almost nothing about the latter', so that the question about their interaction that Elisabeth poses is one which 'in view of my published writings, one can most rightly ask me' (AT 3 664; CSMK 3 217). He goes on to explain that what pertains to the soul considered in itself depends on the notion of thought, while what pertains to the soul as embodied depends on the third primitive notion, that of the mind-body union. The first is discovered through metaphysical meditations, the second through experience. Yet like the first, thought, the notion of the mind-body union is said to be natural to the soul or innate, which indicates that the experience Descartes here appeals to cannot be acquired by sensory perception alone, but involves the intellect.

(7) For we cannot look for these simple notions elsewhere than in our soul, which has them in itself by its nature, but which does not always distinguish one from the others well enough, or even attribute them to objects to which it ought to attribute them.

AT 3 666–7; CSMK 3 218

To say that the soul has this notion in itself by its nature is to say that every one of us has the power to form it merely by reflecting on her voluntary motions or actions. We 'experience in ourselves [*nous expérimentons, en nous-mêmes*] that we have a specific notion for conceiving this' (that the soul moves the body)—a notion that was given to us for this purpose alone and is misused when carelessly applied to other bodies like in accounting for heaviness (AT 3 667; CSMK 3 219). If this notion is natural in the sense of being innate as suggested above—one that everyone can form by reflecting attentively on her experience as a cognitive and moral agent—we also seem to have a natural tendency to confuse simple notions with one another. Not only are we constantly tempted to explain thoughts by corporeal motions that we can easily imagine, or to attribute thoughts to other things than ensouled human beings in explaining their motions. A common example of such confusion is the scholastic notion of gravity as an inner power

---

[38] Meditation 6, AT 7 80 and 89, CSM 2 56 and 61–2; the Sixth Reply §9, AT 7 437–9, CSM 2 292–4. For discussion, see, e.g., Simmons (2013 and 2017); and Brown (2006 and 2019).

directing heavy bodies towards the centre of the earth, where the natural notion we have of the power of our soul to direct our body is confused with the power one body has to act on another (AT 3 667; CSMK 3 219). It is not that we as acting subjects are aware of our soul interacting with the body, but we do have a direct or immediate awareness of our body moving according to our intention to act—one that we mistakenly generalize in explaining motions of mindless pieces of extension of which we have no similar inner experience.[39] True knowledge for Descartes is based on intuitively known, indubitable foundations and requires that the primitive notions it depends on—of which the notion of the mind-body union is one—be carefully distinguished from each other and attributed only to those things they pertain to (AT 3 665–6; CSMK 3 218).

Descartes' answer, invoking the misuse of this notion in explaining the action of gravity and other 'real qualities' in extended bodies, is not as Elisabeth notes, helpful (AT 3 684–5; S 67–8). To clarify the matter he points to the different cognitive operations through which the primitive notions are made familiar. Metaphysical insights depend on the exercise of pure intellect (the knowledge of God and the soul), or the pure intellect aided by mathematical imagination (extension, shapes, and motion), whereas 'things that pertain to the mind-body union' are known 'only obscurely by the intellect alone, or even by the intellect aided by imagination' yet 'are known very clearly by the senses' (AT 3 692; CSMK 227). Metaphysics teaches us to conceive the real distinction between mind and body but hinders us from conceiving their union. Thus, Descartes argues:

(8) [T]hose who never philosophize and who use only their senses do not doubt in the least that the soul moves the body and that the body acts on the soul. They regard them both as one single thing, that is to say, they conceive their union, for conceiving the union between two things is to conceive them as one single thing.
AT 3 692; CSMK 3 227

Metaphysical thoughts help us make the notion of the mind better known while the study of mathematics helps us form distinct notions of corporeal things, whereas:

(9) [I]t is using only life and ordinary conversations, and in abstaining from meditations and the study of those things that exercise the imagination, that we learn to conceive the union of the soul and the body.
AT 3 692; CSMK 3 227

---

[39] In the Sixth Replies Descartes refers to the idea of gravity as a quality coextensive with a heavy body while exercising its force in one point—idea which is misconceived when applied in the explanation of gravity—comparing it to 'exactly the way in which I now understand the mind to be coextensive with the body—the whole mind in the whole body and the whole mind in any of its parts'. The explanation of gravity Descartes rejects is modelled on the idea we have of our mind as knowingly directing the movements of our body and 'was taken largely' from the latter (AT 7 442; CSM 2 298).

Is Descartes serious? How can one know or conceive anything clearly through the senses, elsewhere described as a source of confusion? By restricting them to their proper context of informing us of what is useful to the well-being and survival of the mind-body union. For as Descartes defines them, clear perceptions are of 'what is present and manifest to the attentive mind'—distinct perceptions again, in addition to being always 'clear', are so precise and sharply separated from all other perceptions that they contain nothing that is not clear and evident (*Principles* I a. 45, AT 8A 21–2; CSM 1 207–8). We perceive the mind-body union very clearly but not distinctly, so cannot have the clear *and* distinct conception of it that we have of its two constituents considered separately. Yet our nature teaches us to conceive the union clearly enough for us to accept it on that basis.

As I read this text, Descartes' recommendation that Princess Elisabeth use less time on metaphysical meditations (to which one should devote at most a few hours in the year) and rest her mind instead, does not mean he tells her to put her mind or reason on holiday (or autopilot). Life and ordinary conversation are matters that require serious attention, which depends on the alertness of mind or reason, but keeping one's mind alert requires a certain amount of rest and leisure. What Descartes can be read as telling Elisabeth here is that she would have no problem with conceiving the mind-body unity, i.e. experiencing it, or herself, as one, if she gave her full attention to things other than metaphysics: not only to the study of nature or mathematics, but to affairs and circumstances of importance for her life and actions, where sensory perceptions and imagination play a crucial role, but which can fulfil their function properly only if accompanied by attentive reason and judgement. It is in coping, as cognitive and moral agents, with practical matters of life, essentially those including interaction with fellow human beings, that one experiences oneself as a wholesome, thinking, and embodied being. This experience includes passions and uncontrolled emotional reactions as well as practical deliberation and rational action. Reflecting on it one may come to consider one's thinking or mind on the one hand and one's body on the other as distinct but interdependent aspects of a single person (AT 3 694; CSMK 3 228).

There is a sense, as Henri Gouhier (1962) suggested, in which what Descartes retains from the hylomorphic doctrine is the prephilosophical experience of the human condition.[40] Translating this experience within his own dualist metaphysics Descartes comes up with this compromise, here called Descartes' 'mind-body holism'. It retains elements of the Aristotelian doctrine—better suited it would seem than his own to human experience and also truer to it—but rejects the metaphysical structure that grounds it. Instead it takes the notion of the mind-body union as a 'primitive', innate, or natural habit of thinking of ourselves and human beings generally as at once bodily and thinking subjects.[41] What is

---

[40] Alanen (2003a: 72).   [41] Cf. de Buzon and Kambouchner (2015: 290).

perceived and thought of as one here is not a fictive unity but a real being in itself, whose complex nature cannot be reduced to that of its parts.

7. Action and Passion Identity

In his last work, *The Passions of the Soul*, written at the request of Elisabeth, Descartes provides a fuller answer to her questions, the first being about the power of the soul to move the body; and the second, which we have not yet considered, its power to resist and control the passions.[42] A central role is given here to another important element of the Aristotelian theory, that of the identity of action and passion introduced in its first articles that can only be briefly considered here. Descartes argues that what 'is a "passion" with regard to one subject is always an action in some other regard', so that even though the agent and the patient might be different, 'an action and passion must always be a single thing which has these two names on account of the two different subjects to which it may be related'. Treating here the body as an agent and the mind as a patient, or vice versa depending on which of the two subjects is the cause and which suffers the effect, this is used as a general principle for the analysis of human passions, for 'we are not aware of any subject which acts more directly on our soul than the body to which it is joined'. The emotions or passions of the soul are caused by actions, i.e. motions in the body, and there is no better way to know them than 'to examine the difference between the soul and the body in order to learn to which of the two we should attribute each of the functions present in us' (AT 11 328; CSM 1 328).

Note the three subjects involved here: Descartes, the embodied person examining the passions on behalf of all of 'us' who experience them, his soul (*âme*) and body. Soul stands here for mind or thinking, and body for the mechanically working, extended body, with the organs and members structured to sustain its vital functions. Descartes' psychology is a complex affair that requires us to take account not only of the functions of the soul and the body, separately considered, but also the capacities and limitations generated by their union. If the union makes rational, cognitive, and practical agency possible, it also renders the (immaterial) mind subject to passions—these thoughts that are not under direct

---

[42] Elisabeth to Descartes, 10 June 1643: 'I admit that it would be easier for me to concede matter and extension to the soul than to concede the capacity to move a body and to be moved by it to an immaterial thing. For, if the first is achieved through *information*, it would be necessary that the spirits, which cause the movements, were intelligent, a capacity you accord to nothing corporeal. And even though, in your *Metaphysical Meditations*, you show the possibility of the second, it is altogether very difficult to understand that a soul, as you have described it, after having the faculty and the custom of reasoning well, can lose all of this by some vapours, and that, being able to subsist without the body, and having nothing in common with it, the soul is so governed by it' (AT 3 685, S 68).

control of reason but depend on the body and the contingencies of external causes acting on the body.[43] Passions in the strict sense of the word or emotions turn out to be confused thoughts caused and accompanied by motions of the animal spirits in the body, and are defined as

(10) perceptions, feelings [*sentiments*] or emotions of the soul which we refer particularly to it, and which are caused, maintained and strengthened by some movement of the spirits.

a.27 AT 11 349; CSM 1 338–9; my translation

The identity of action and passion as Descartes applies it means that the motions of the bodily animal spirits and the perceptions they cause in the mind occur simultaneously and are two sides or aspects of one phenomenon considered in different ways. The passions *qua* thoughts are modes of the mind which are in some sense identical to the physical modes (motions in the body) that cause and accompany them. Passions are psycho-physical phenomena that can neither be nor be defined *qua* mental modes without the motions in the blood, the nerves, and the muscles of the body that cause and accompany them. They are, one is tempted to say, 'inextricably united' just as is the desire for revenge with the boiling of the blood in the Aristotelean theory.[44]

Large parts of Descartes' *Passions of the Soul* are devoted to describing the physiological or bodily changes co-occurring with the various passions—their causes and effects on the soul-body union. Remarkably, their principal effect is 'to move and dispose the soul to want [*vouloir*] the things for which they prepare the body'. Fear, for example, moves the soul to want to flee, whereas courage makes it willing to fight, and both come with particular changes in the disposition of the body and its members, each preparing the body for the behavioural reaction (flight or defence as the case may be) for which it incites a desire in the soul (a. 39 AT 11 359; CSM 1 343). Again, given the action-passion identity theory, the dispositions or inclinations and desires caused in the mind must be somehow the same as the dispositions to various behavioural reactions in the body. One way of understanding this is to take the sameness as a matter of experience, where the bodily reaction is not perceived separately from but as part of the mental reaction, say, as when experiencing fear or courage as a sudden change in the disposition of the body with a desire to pursue a certain course of action.[45]

---

[43] The soul is here again said to be 'united to all the parts of the body conjointly' (a.30) although 'it exercises its functions more particularly' in that famous little gland mentioned above (a.31. AT 11 351; CSM 1 339–40).

[44] Charles (2009).

[45] See my reading of Descartes' account of passions as being 'referred to the soul' (AT 11a 345–50; CSM 1 339) in Alanen (2003b: 110 ff), which I hope to defend more fully in a separate paper on dualist theories of passions and embodiment.

How to interpret Descartes' claim about the identity of actions and passions, given the difference of the subjects to which they are related as agent and patient, is a matter of controversy.[46] As Hoffman points out, Descartes must understand causality here as different from the notion of causality by motion and impact used in his physics: cause and effect are simultaneous. Hoffman solves the challenge this poses to Cartesian dualism by introducing the notion of 'straddling mode' to account for the fact that an action in the body and a passion in the mind are here one and the same—a mode that is at once a mode of extension and a mode of thinking. But this clashes with attribute dualism and leads to problems of its own.[47] Brown and Normore argue that there are two different modes—one of thinking and one of extension that are jointly required for the phenomenon of the passion to occur. They remain distinct in the sense that they could occur one without the other, but what would so occur would not then be the passion that their co-occurrence produces—it would not be the same *thing*.[48] What that thing or state of mind is that retains some of its identity without the bodily state to turn it properly into a passion, however, is not all that clear.

As Descartes defines the passions, their bodily causes are as we saw included in their definition.[49] So this thing or phenomenon, i.e. the sensations, perceptions, or emotions that the passions consist in on the mental level, could not be identified as the passions they are without their particular bodily causes or effects, nor could the latter be identified without their particular mental effects. The trembling I cannot control, or the tears I shed, could occur, but without the sense of panic or danger in the first case, or the sadness they cause in the second—they would not be emotional states. Whatever understanding we can have of the mind-body union depends on and is given with our direct experience of it, most vividly, with our experience of the passions. They are experienced as affections of one's whole person: the pain in my fractured foot, the fear of the vicious dog, or the sadness I suffer because of a broken relationship affect me, mind and body, my thoughts, physiology, and behaviour, at once. Their mental aspect cannot be disentangled or identified separately from their bodily causes. The mind, in being affected by passions, is aware of its affections, which are mostly affections

---

[46] See Hoffman (2009: 101–4 and 1990); he is the first after Grene (1985) to devote serious attention to Descartes' use of this principle and its metaphysical implications. For an alternative reading, see Brown and Normore (2003) and Brown (2006).

[47] Hoffman illustrates this with an example from Descartes' discussion of the Eucharist in his Replies to the Sixth Objection of extended surfaces or bodies in contact with a single boundary that is common to both and is 'the same mode of each body' (AT 7 433; CSM II 292; Hoffman 2009: 109–10). This is precisely what—according to Descartes' advice to Elisabeth—we should avoid: to try to understand what pertains to the union through reduction to or analogies with one of the two other primitive notions (AT 3 691–2; CSMK 3 226–7). For a thorough discussion of Hoffman's proposal and Descartes' problem with action passion identity, see Brown (2006: ch. 5, esp. pp. 117–34).

[48] For an instructive discussion of this obscure issue, see Brown and Normore (2003: 83–106; esp. pp. 89–95).

[49] AT 11 349; CSM 1 338–9. See also a. 37, AT 11 357; CSM 1 342.

of its will, but does not separately perceive their bodily components, i.e. their causes and effects.[50]

On the one hand, Descartes' analysis of passions as states of the mind caused by the body and controlled by the mind presupposes and corroborates his dualism. On the other, the thesis of the identity of passions in the mind with actions in the body (or actions in the mind with passions in the body)—identity that is clearly experienced by the whole subject representing the mind-body unity—undermines any robust variant of dualism. Where does this leave us? We must rely on our experience, such as it is, studying our passions in a Humean way, by observing regularities (co-variances) in their occurrence and the circumstances that cause them. Heeding Descartes' advice to Elisabeth we should worry less about the metaphysics of human nature and pay more attention to our actions and passions, and what we learn from our daily experience and serious conversations with fellow human beings.

Descartes' dualist anthropology and mechanistic physiology pave the way for his more consistently naturalist followers, Spinoza and Hume, both of whom ridiculed and rejected his account of free will as providing a weapon for the control of passions, yet they developed Descartes' new approach to the passions in their own theories. Spinoza took the metaphysics seriously, and advocated a rigorous substance monism with strict attribute dualism, where any action in the mind, given identity theory, is an action in the body; and any passion in the body, also a passion in the mind.[51] Hume, worrying little about metaphysics, could write in his careless manner 'mind or body, whatever you want to call it',[52] yet like Spinoza he retained a strict methodological dualism in his 'anatomy' of the ideas of the human mind, leaving the physiology to the scientists of nature. Both developments are anticipated by elements of Descartes' doctrine, which remains an unstable compromise between what may in the end be incompatible intuitions.[53]

Bibliography and Abbreviations

Alanen, L. (1986), 'On Descartes's Argument for Dualism', in Knuuttila, S. and Hintikka, J. (eds.), *The Logic of Being: Historical Studies* (D. Reidel), 223–48.

---

[50] This is why Descartes describes the passions *qua* thoughts as irremediably confused. The passions agitate us more the less we understand them: '[T]he passions are to be numbered among the perceptions which the close alliance between the soul and the body renders confused and obscure' (a. 28, AT 11 349; CSM 1 339).
[51] *Ethics*, part 3, scholium to proposition 2.   [52] *Treatise on Human Nature*.
[53] David Charles' paper on recent interpretations of Aristotle's hylomorphism inspired by Cartesian dualism, presented at Humboldt University of Berlin in around 2005, challenged me to work on this topic again. I am deeply grateful to David for discussions over the years and for incisive questions and generous comments on an earlier draft of this chapter. My thanks are due also to Deborah Brown for discussions, encouragement, and helpful comments on earlier versions; and to John Carriero and Frans Svensson for valuable remarks on the final version.

Alanen, L. (2003a), *Descartes's Concept of Mind* (Harvard University Press).

Alanen, L. (2003b), 'The Intentionality of Cartesian Passions', in Williston, B. and Gombay, A. (eds.), *Essays on Passions and Virtue in Descartes* (Humanities Press), 107–27.

Alanen, L. (2008a), 'Cartesian Scientia and the Nature of the Soul', *Vivarium* 46/3: 418–42.

Alanen, L. (2008b), 'Descartes's Mind-Body Composites, Psychology and Naturalism', *Inquiry* 51/5: 464–84.

Alanen, L. (2016), '"Thought" and "Mind"', in Nolan, L. (ed.), *The Cambridge Descartes Lexicon* (Cambridge University Press).

Aristotle (1984), *De Anima*, in Barnes, J. (ed.) *The Complete Works of Aristotle* (Princeton University Press). [= *De An.*]

Baker, G. and Morris, K. (1996), *Descartes's Dualism* (Routledge).

Brown, D.J. (2006), *Descartes and the Passionate Mind* (Cambridge University Press).

Brown, D.J. (2019), 'The Metaphysics of Cartesian Persons', in Reuter, M. and Svensson, F. (eds.), *Mind, Body and Morality: New Perspectives on Descartes and Spinoza* (Routledge), 17–36.

Brown, D.J. and Normore, C. (2003), 'Traces of the Body: Descartes on the Passions of the Soul', in Williston, B. and Gombay, A. (eds.), *Essays on Passions and Virtue in Descartes* (Humanities Press), 83–106.

Brown, D.J. and Normore, C. (2019), *Descartes and the Ontology of Everyday Life* (Oxford University Press).

Carriero, J. (2009), *Between Two Worlds: A Reading of Descartes's Meditations* (Princeton University Press).

Charles, D. (2009), 'Aristotle's Psychological Theory', *Proceedings of the Boston Area Colloquium in Ancient Philosophy*, Colloquium I 24/1: 1–49.

Clarke, D. (2006), *Descartes: A Biography* (Cambridge University Press).

Cottingham, J. (1985), 'Cartesian Trialism', *Mind* 94: 218–30.

de Buzon, F. and Kambouchner, D. (2015), 'L'Âme avec le corps. Le sense, le movement volontaire, les passions', in de Buzon, F., Cassan, É., and Kambouchner, D. (eds.), *Lectures de Descartes* (Ellipses), 279–328.

Descartes, R. (1963–7), *Oeuvres philosophiques*, ed. Alqiuié, F., 3 vols. (Garnier). [= Alq.]

Descartes, R. (1964–76), *Oeuvres de Descartes*, ed. Adam, C. and Tannery, P., 12 vols. (Vrin). [= AT]

Descartes, R. (1985a), *The Philosophical Writings of René Descartes*, trans. Cottingham, J., Stoothoff, R., and Murdoch, D., Vols. 1–2 (Cambridge University Press). [= CSM]

Descartes, R. (1985b), *The Philosophical Writings of René Descartes*, trans. Cottingham, J., Stoothoff, R., Murdoch, D., and Kenny, A., Vol. 3: *Correspondence* (Cambridge University Press). [= CSMK]

Descartes, R. (1989), *Correspondance avec Elisabeth et autres lettres*, ed. Beyssade, J.M. and Beyssade, M. (Flammarion).

Des Chene, D. (2000), *Life's Form: Late Aristotelian Conceptions of the Soul* (Cornell University Press).

Elisabeth of Bohemia and Descartes, R. (2007), *The Correspondence Between Princess Elisabeth of Bohemia and René Descartes*, ed. Shapiro, L. (Chicago University Press). [= S]

Garber, D. (1983), 'Understanding Interaction: What Descartes Should Have Told Elisabeth', *Southern Journal of Philosophy* 21: 5–32.

Gouhier, H. (1962), *La Pensée metaphysique de Descartes* (J. Vrin).

Grene, M. (1985), *Descartes* (Harvester Press).

Hoffman, P. (1986), 'The Unity of Descartes's Man', *The Philosophical Review* 95/3: 339–70.

Hoffman, P. (1990), 'Cartesian Passions and Cartesian Dualism', *Pacific Philosophical Quarterly* 71: 310–33.

Hoffman, P. (1999), 'Cartesian Composites', *Journal of the History of Philosophy* 37: 251–70.

Hoffman, P. (2002), 'Descartes' Theory of Distinctions', *Philosophy and Phenomenological Research* 64/1: 57–78.

Hoffman, P. (2008), 'The Union and Interaction of Mind and Body', in Broughton, J. and Carriero, J. (eds.), *A Companion to Descartes* (Blackwell), 390–403.

Hoffman, P. (2009), *Essays on Descartes* (Oxford University Press).

Lennon, T. (2016), 'Individuation', in Nolan, L. (ed.), *The Cambridge Descartes Lexicon* (Cambridge University Press), 400–6.

Menn, S. (1995), 'The Greatest Stumbling Block: Descartes on Real Qualities', in Ariew, R. and Grene, M. G. (eds.), *Descartes and His Contemporaries: Meditations, Objections and Replies* (University of Chicago Press), 182–207.

Nolan, L. (ed.) (2016), *The Cambridge Descartes Lexicon* (Cambridge University Press).

Normore, C. (2011), 'Cartesian Unions', in Carriero, J., French P.A., and Wettstein, H. (eds.), *Early Modern Philosophy Reconsidered* (Midwest Studies in Philosophy 35), 223–29.

Rozemond, M. (1998), *Descartes' Dualism* (Harvard University Press).

Rozemond, M. (1999), 'Descartes on Mind-Body Interaction: What's the Problem?', *Journal of the History of Philosophy* 37/3: 435–67.

Ryle, G. (1949), *The Concept of Mind* (Hutchinson).

Schmaltz, T. (1992), 'Descartes and Malebranche on the Mind-Body Union', *The Philosophical Review* 101: 281–325.

Schmaltz, T. (2020a), 'Suarez and Descartes on the Mode(s) of the Union', *Journal of the History of Philosophy* 58/3: 471–92.

Schmaltz, T. (2020b), *The Metaphysics of the Material World: Suárez, Descartes, Spinoza* (Oxford University Press).

Simmons, A. (2013), 'Descartes on the Cognitive Structure of Experience', *Philosophy and Phenomenological Research* 67/3: 549–77.

Simmons, A. (2017), 'Mind-Body Union and the Limits of Cartesian Metaphysics', *Philosophers Imprint* 17: 1–26.

Spinoza, B. (1985), *Ethics*, in E. Curley (ed.), *The Collected Works of Spinoza* (Princeton University Press).

Voss, S. (1994), 'Descartes: The End of Anthropology', in Cottingham, J. (ed.), *Reason, Will and Sensation* (Clarendon Press).

Wilson, C. (2000), 'Descartes and the Corporeal Mind: Some Implications of the Regius Affair', in Gaukroger, S. et al. (eds.), *Descartes' Natural Philosophy* (Routledge), 659–79.

Wilson, M.D. (1978), 'Cartesian Dualism', in Hooker, M. (ed.), *Descartes: Critical and Interpretative Essays* (Johns Hopkins University Press), 197–211.

General Index

For the benefit of digital users, indexed terms that span two pages (e.g., 52-53) may, on occasion, appear on only one of those pages.

Actions 13, 15–16, 24–5, 94, 141, 144, 281, 283, 297, 317, 321–2, 362–3, 394–5, 400
   See Activities, Changes and Processes
Activities 3, 21–2, 25–6, 81, 119, 155–6, 164–5, 192–3, 205–6, 214–15, 223–4, 232–3, 266, 268, 274–6, 288, 303–4, 313–14, 344, 366, 382
Anger 22–4, 92–3, 251, 306
Artefacts 1, 3–4, 28–9, 33–4, 89, 188–9, 201–2, 282–5, 288–90, 294
Atoms 12–13, 47–54, 60–2, 64

Blends 25, 109, 118, 120, 130–1, 241, 246, 248, 251–3
Bodies 2, 14–15, 36–7, 44–63, 75–7, 86, 106–18, 126–9, 134, 143–4, 149, 160, 166, 171, 197–8, 212–17, 222, 235, 248, 261, 266, 283, 314, 390, 394–5
'Bottom-up' Story: *see* Upwards Story

Capacities 5–6, 8–9, 13, 16, 32, 76, 80, 96–8, 124–5, 139–40, 246, 249, 306, 308, 357, 366, 378
   Enmattered and pure capacities 8–9, 18, 30
Causes
   Causes, efficient 2, 8, 14, 19, 39, 47, 56–7, 64, 109, 117, 123, 134, 142–3, 155–6, 171–2, 197–8, 207–8, 222–3, 266, 292–3, 318, 358–9, 365–7, 370–2, 398
   Causes, formal 2–3, 134, 142–3, 146, 281, 291–2
   Causes, material 13, 64, 134, 142–3
   Causes, teleological/final 4, 21–2, 47, 142–3, 222, 227, 235, 241, 315–16, 358
Changes 5, 25–6, 48, 70, 156, 164–5, 174–5, 189, 252–3, 257, 262–76, 286, 306, 319–20, 355, 368–9 *See* Actions, Activities and Processes
Colour 49–50, 180–1, 212, 240–1, 248–9, 252–3, 257, 261, 296, 364
Composite entities 2, 4, 14, 19, 37–8, 77, 107–8, 114, 123–4, 128–30, 137, 178, 181, 184, 208–9, 213, 221–2, 231, 237–8, 307, 312, 323, 343, 345, 384–5, 392 *See* Compounds

Compounds 47–50, 52–4, 57–9, 73, 79–80, 147, 157–9, 166–7, 171, 191, 255, 316, 330, 342–3, 345, 355, 361–2, 368–9
   See Composite Entities

Definitions 3–4, 7, 17, 36, 63, 81, 100–1, 117, 124, 177–8, 182, 187, 201–2, 213, 283, 285, 287–8, 306–7, 313, 335, 368–9, 378, 399–400 *See* Essences, Unity and Priority
Desire 18, 25, 31, 40, 197–8, 234, 398
Determinables, determinates 10–11, 20, 33–4, 118, 120, 309, 316, 335, 339–41, 345, 377
Dualism
   Attribute 38, 393, 399–400
   Substance 11–12, 35, 72, 83–4, 258–9, 270–1, 276, 307–8, 322, 330–1, 376–80, 382–3, 386

Emergence 6, 16–17, 28–9, 130, 154–5, 166, 172, 189, 197–8, 291–2 *See* Supervenience
Emotions 22, 40, 87, 229, 241, 247–8, 378, 397
Essences 7, 77, 138, 156, 169, 180, 199, 207–8, 214, 221–2, 235, 241, 325, 346, 354, 360, 378, 388–90 *See* Definition
Eye 25, 92, 95, 137–9, 212, 234, 240–1, 261–2, 311, 344–5

Fear 22–3, 87, 230–1, 306, 378, 398–400
Forms 1–2, 4, 11, 15, 19, 34, 52–3, 68, 79, 84, 98–9, 102–3, 106, 114, 120–1, 124–8, 133–4, 139, 142–3, 154–9, 166, 174–5, 177, 182, 189, 199, 205–7, 221–4, 233, 240, 280–1, 287, 290–1, 305–7, 318–19, 330, 335–6, 338, 341, 351, 354–5, 359–61, 368, 376, 378, 387–8
   Impure (enmattered) and Pure Forms 7–9, 23–4, 29–30, 177, 179, 186, 193–4, 197–9, 204–7, 213, 359
   Particular forms 7, 32–3, 203–4, 309–10, 332
   Platonic forms 68–70, 98–9, 177, 180
   Ontology of forms 3, 17, 35, 125–6, 155–6, 159, 171, 248, 252, 266, 281, 290, 295–6, 321, 331, 333 *See* Artefacts

Forms as Efficient Causes 5, 8–9, 24, 129, 134, 160, 197–8, 205, 281–2, 323 *See* Causes
Freedom 11, 17–18, 22–3, 165–6, 400

Harmony 15, 79–81, 245–6, 364
Hearing 92, 169, 239, 260, 262, 269, 296
  See Sounds
Hylomorphism, Varieties of 1, 7–8, 23, 25–6, 39–41, 68, 77, 85, 100–1, 106–7, 130, 133–4, 147–9, 154–6, 171–2, 174–5, 194, 202–6, 223, 255–6, 272, 304–6, 310, 316–17, 322–3, 330–1, 348, 352, 368–9, 376–7, 384–5
  See Forms (Pure and Impure), Matter, Inextricability, Spiritualist and Literalist Interpretations, Two component Accounts, Upwards Story

Imagination 27–8, 30, 275, 292, 298, 311, 317, 381–2, 395–6
Impure Form Interpretation (Impurism) 7–9, 24–5, 29, 306–14 *See also* Impure Forms, Pure Forms, Pure Form Interpretation
Inextricability 25–6, 40, 79–80, 242, 255, 274, 352–3, 378, 398
Intellect 22–4, 31, 77, 191–4, 202–5, 226–7, 258, 266, 305–6, 308–9, 314, 316–17, 344–5, 379–80, 393–5
  Active intellect 18, 28–31, 72–3, 80, 290–3, 304, 307
  Dispositional Intellect 18, 191, 193–4
  Material Intellect 29–31, 191–2, 304, 312–13
Intellect-Body Problem 304, 324

Materialism, varieties of 46, 133–4, 143, 155–6, 159–60, 170–1, 307–8
Matter 1, 4, 7–10, 26, 33–6, 48, 68–9, 71–6, 88, 106–17, 119–20, 129–32, 134, 142, 154–61, 166–7, 169–72, 174–6, 178–9, 183–4, 186–8, 206–11, 213–16, 221–2, 242, 248, 255, 272–3, 280–1, 287, 291–2, 306, 312, 316, 322–3, 330, 339, 345, 352–3, 372, 377–82, 387–9
  Matter, Form-dependent, Form-Independent 4–8, 29, 37, 157–8, 199, 207–8, 320, 353–4, 360, 378
  Prime matter 10, 20, 71–2, 109, 154–5, 157–8, 171, 177–9, 197, 258–9, 276–7, 294, 296, 310, 354
  Proximate matter 72, 109, 161, 295
  See Upwards Story
Matter-form composites, *see* Composites and Compounds
Mind-body problem 8, 11–12, 40–1, 305–6, 376–7, 382–4, 389, 394–6 *See* Soul and Intellect-Body Problem

Nutrition 27–8, 84, 90–1, 98, 239, 282, 295, 377

Pain 95–6, 141, 224–5, 230–1, 381, 386–7, 393, 399–400
Pan-psychism 6
Passions 38, 87, 164–5, 253, 378, 390, 397–400
Perception 23, 25–7, 40, 90–1, 95–7, 130–1, 145, 164, 190, 211, 224–5, 230–3, 240–1, 248, 250–1, 255–77, 280, 285, 295–6, 363–4, 380, 393–5 *See* Hearing, Senses, Sight, Taste, Touch
Plants 9–10, 27, 74, 107, 109–10, 126–7, 160, 269, 274, 284, 330, 342, 359
Pleasure 62–3, 141, 224–5, 230–1
Pneuma 13, 25–6, 73–4, 88–96, 100–1, 106–11, 117–20, 128–32, 138, 147, 262–3, 284
Pneumatic body 13, 26
Priority 4–5, 10–11, 21–3, 155–6, 174, 177, 221–2, 233, 242, 383–4
  Priority in Definition 5, 10, 40
  Priority in Existence 21, 206–7
Processes (*kinēseis*), 2, 5, 23–4, 40, 87–8, 113, 121–2, 146, 190, 192, 197–8, 211, 239, 255, 257–60, 275–6, 290, 321, 355 *See* Actions, Activities and Changes
Pure Form Interpretation (Purism) 7–11, 16, 33, 306–7 *See* Impure and Pure Forms, Impure Form Interpretation, Two Component Accounts

Self 17–18, 23–4, 27, 97, 209–10, 230, 298–9, 380–1
Self-awareness 22, 27, 36, 256, 280, 298–9
Self-creation 22–4
Senses, Special and Common 256–7, 276
Separability 26–7, 45, 87–8, 111–12, 158–9, 185, 200, 211, 224–9, 233–4, 322, 348, 390–1
  Separability in Definition 7–8, 224–9, 306–7
  Separability in existence 200, 224–9, 308–9, 359 *See* Priority
Sight 25, 54, 92, 207–8, 212, 231, 240–1, 252–3, 260, 262, 296, 311, 344–5, 377
Soul
  Ontology of the Soul 2, 6, 15, 17, 24, 27–8, 36
  Unity of the Soul 22, 31–2
Spiritualist and Literalist Interpretations 256, 259–60, 270–2, 276
Sound 221–2, 257, 263
Substances 32–3, 39, 44–6, 70–1, 90, 106, 129, 136–8, 145–6, 155–6, 171–2, 176–7, 181–5, 197–8, 215–16, 227, 283–4, 291, 307, 314, 318, 330, 334–5, 345, 351, 361–2, 377, 382–3, 387–8, 390–1

Substances, immaterial 197–8, 280, 380–1
Substances, unity of 7, 34, 111–12, 129, 135, 160, 185, 221–2, 318, 353–4, 361, 369–70, 382–3, 392
Substances, separate 2, 27–8, 34, 116, 136–7, 147, 211–12, 308–9, 320, 337, 352–3, 368, 377, 383–4, 390, 400
Supervenience 6–8, 162–6, 168, 215, 247–51
See Emergence

Taste 92, 239, 260, 263, 269
Thought 22, 29–30, 189, 193, 379–82, 394
See Intellect

Touch 53–4, 87–8, 92, 95, 239, 260, 264–5, 269–71
Transparent (*diaphanes*) 263
Two-component Accounts 8, 34, 39–41, 255–7, 271, 361, 369, 393–4

Unity
  of Composites 3, 5–6, 15, 33, 37–8, 45, 51–2, 59, 75, 89, 114, 117, 123, 131, 142, 147–9, 176–7, 296, 310, 353–4, 359–60, 368–9, 376, 382, 392
  of the Soul 23, 26–7
Upwards Story 4, 10–11, 16, 36–7, 48, 52, 60–1, 107–8, 127–30, 161, 222, 290–2 *See* Matter, Materialism

Index Nominum

For the benefit of digital users, indexed terms that span two pages (e.g., 52-53) may, on occasion, appear on only one of those pages.

Abū I-Barakāt al-Baghdādī 297-9
Adamson, P 27-8, 280-1, 321-2
Alanen, L vii, 37-9, 256, 376, 378
Albertus Magnus 32
Alcinous 178
Alexander of Aphrodisias 14-19, 22, 97, 106-33, 141-3, 154-72, 174-94, 197, 199-200, 208-9, 221-2, 234, 242, 246-8, 252, 304, 332
al-Fārābī 29, 308, 315-16, 318
al-Kindī 308
Andronicus 15-17, 20, 136-7, 141, 143, 246
Aquinas, T 31-4, 154, 303, 310, 324, 330-48, 352, 356, 368-9
Aristotle vii-viii, 1-11, 14, 21-2, 24-5, 29, 39-42, 44, 68, 72-81, 83-5, 93, 98-104, 118, 120-1, 133, 137-43, 154, 159-60, 164, 172, 174-7, 179, 182, 190, 192-4, 197-201, 213-16, 221-2, 233, 248, 252, 255, 259, 264-5, 272-3, 280-1, 283, 291-2, 295-6, 303, 305-9, 318-19, 324, 330-6, 348, 352, 363, 368-9, 377-8
Aristoxenus 138, 246
Augustine 27-8
Aurelius, M 69
Averroes (Ibn Rushd) 29-31, 303-25
Avicenna (Ibn Sīnā) 27-9, 32, 36, 280-99, 307-8, 323

Boethus 176-9, 182
Bown, A 12-13, 51-2
Brown, D 383, 392-3, 399
Burnyeat, M 6, 189, 257, 274

Caston, V 8, 16-17, 107, 115-16, 127, 129, 136-7, 184, 197-8, 200-1, 250, 255, 260, 273, 306-8
Charles, D 7, 10, 20, 197-8, 200-1, 255, 263-4, 270-1, 305-7, 378
Chiaradonna, R 21-3, 134, 176-7, 207-10, 221-2, 238
Chrysippus 69, 77, 85, 92-6, 102, 111-13, 193
Colotes 47-8, 58-9

Coope, U 27, 267
Corcilius, K 83-4, 103-4
Critolaus 15, 79-81

De Haas, F 16, 18, 154, 174, 176-7, 190, 216
Democritus 12, 44-52
Descartes, R 1, 8, 12, 27, 35, 39, 71-2, 223, 258-9, 275-6, 351-3, 361, 368, 376-400
Dicaearchus 15, 77, 79-81, 138
Diogenes Laërtius 69-71, 77, 93-4, 96-7, 101-2

Elizabeth, Princess of Bohemia 37-8, 382-3, 390, 393-7, 400
Epicurus 12-13, 44-64, 73-4

Fine, K 41, 147
Frede, M 14-15, 69, 146, 370-1

Galen 18-19, 35, 88, 92-3, 119, 133-49, 246-7, 251-3, 262, 289-90
Gill, ML 7

Helle, R 14-15, 68, 75-6, 87, 109, 113, 115, 118, 138, 184
Hierocles 75-6, 85-7, 90-2, 110, 113, 115
Hoffman, P 384, 386, 390, 393-4, 399
Hume, D 3, 400
Huxley, TH 6, 169-70

Iamblichus 27, 87, 89-94, 256-7
Inwood, B 14-15, 44-5, 69, 85

Johansen, T 236-7, 368-9

Kim, J 158, 167, 169-70
Knuuttila, S vii, 364
Koslicki, K 33, 41, 147

Lautner, P 260, 262
Leucippus 44
Long, A 73
Lucius 179-80
Lucretius 46-9, 51-2, 54, 58-9, 63-4, 102-3

Maimonides 154
Marechal, P 18–19, 136, 139–40
Mnesarchus 70–2

Nemesius 85, 87, 118
Normore, C. 383, 392–3, 399
Nussbaum, M 8

Ockham, W viii, 34, 147, 354, 362–3, 368–9, 391
Ogden, S 29–31, 310, 314, 320
Origen 89
Olympiodorus 223–4, 235–7

Peramatzis, M 7, 21–2, 205–6, 306–7
Perler, D 33–4, 355, 362, 366–7, 391–2
Philodemus 62–3
Philoponus 25–7, 31–3, 163, 189, 245, 250–3, 256–65, 267–73, 276, 282–3
Plato 2, 11, 72–4, 77, 79–80, 85, 98–9, 177–8, 197–8, 211, 229, 235, 246–7, 251, 256–7, 330–1
Plotinus 11, 21–9, 37, 39, 77, 197–217, 221–2, 242, 256–7
Plutarch 47–50, 109–10, 117
Porphyry 77, 134, 179–80, 256–7, 321–2

Pseudo-Simplicius ('Pseudo') 25, 27, 29–30, 36, 256–8, 265–9, 273–6
Putnam, H 41

Rapp, C 14, 84, 93, 98–9, 260
Remes, P 22–3, 197, 230

Scotus, D viii, 368
Sedley, D 44–8, 50–1, 60
Seneca 71, 74, 94, 108, 110, 117
Sextus Empiricus 45, 85, 90–1, 102–3, 138
Shields, C 8, 32–3, 306–9, 335–6, 352–4, 357, 365
Socrates 2, 70–2, 229, 236, 245, 330–1
Sorabji, R vii–viii, 25–6, 68, 161–5, 167, 245, 250, 257–60, 270
Spinoza 38, 400
Suárez, F 33–7, 39, 351–72, 392

Tuominen, M 25–7, 80–1, 190

Whiting, J 5–6
Wiggins, D 41, 140
William of Moerbeke 334–5
Williams, B 41

Zeno 73–4, 77, 85, 88, 95